MOUS Essentials Word 97 Expert

Jane Calabria

Dorothy Burke

Suzanne Weixel

An Imprint of Macmillan Computer Publishing

MOUS Essentials: Word 97 Expert

Copyright© 1998 by Que® Education and Training

All rights reserved. Printed in the United States of America. No part of this book may be used or reproduced in any form or by any means, or stored in a database or retrieval system, without prior written permission of the publisher, except in the case of brief quotations embodied in critical articles and reviews. Making copies of any part of this book for any purpose other than your own personal use is a violation of United States copyright laws. For information, address Que Education and Training, Macmillan Computer Publishing, 201 W. 103rd Street, Indianapolis, IN 46290.

Library of Congress Catalog No: 98-066772

ISBN: 1-58076-053-8

This book is sold *as is*, without warranty of any kind, either express or implied, respecting the contents of this book, including but not limited to implied warranties for the book's quality, performance, merchantability, or fitness for any particular purpose. Neither Que Education and Training nor its dealers or distributors shall be liable to the purchaser or any other person or entity with respect to any liability, loss, or damage caused or alleged to be caused directly or indirectly by this book.

01 00 99   4 3 2

Interpretation of the printing code: the rightmost double-digit number is the year of the book's printing; the rightmost single-digit number, the number of the book's printing. For example, a printing code of 98-1 shows that the first printing of the book occurred in 1998.

Screens reproduced in this book were created using Collage Plus from Inner Media, Inc., Hollis, NH.

Composed in *Stone Serif* and *MCPdigital* by Que® Education and Training

Publisher:
Robert Linsky

Executive Editor:
Randy Haubner

Acquisitions Editor:
Jon Phillips

Director of Product Marketing:
Susan L. Kindel

Managing Editor:
Caroline Roop

Development Editor:
Nancy D. Warner

Project Editor:
Susan Hobbs

Copy Editor:
Cliff Shubs

Acquisitions Assistant:
Ken Schmidt

Technical Editor:
Ed Metzler

Cover Designer:
Nathan Clement

Book Designer:
Louisa Kluznick

Production Team:
John Etchison
Christy M. Lemasters
Eric S. Miller

About the Authors

Jane Calabria has authored 13 Macmillan Computer Publishing books. As a consultant, Jane works on a national level with large corporations and training organizations, developing user training programs and modeling help desk support structures. As a trainer, Jane teaches Microsoft desktop applications, operating systems, and Lotus Notes and Domino. She is a Certified Lotus Notes Professional (Principal level) and a Certified Microsoft User Specialist.

Jane and Dorothy Burke have teamed up successfully on several MCP books, including the *Certified Microsoft Office User Exam Guide(s) for Microsoft Word 97*, *Microsoft Excel 97* and *Microsoft PowerPoint 97*. They also co-authored *Microsoft Works 6-in-1*, *Microsoft Windows 95 6-in-1*, *Microsoft Windows 98 6-in-1*, *Using Microsoft Word 97*, and several Lotus Notes books.

Dorothy Burke traveled a few career paths before becoming a computer instructor and consultant. She has worked as an editor for an engineering trade magazine, in customer service and management in the home medical equipment industry, and in a management consulting firm as an office manager and editor of its newsletter and catalogs. Dorothy is a Certified Lotus Instructor and a Certified Lotus Professional in Lotus Notes. With a strong background in graphics and desktop publishing, Dorothy develops applications in Lotus Notes and for Domino web sites. Writing with Jane Calabria, she has contributed to the *10 Minute Guide to Lotus Notes Mail 4.5* and *Lotus Notes 4.5 and the Internet 6-in-1* published by Que Corporation. She is also a contributing author to Que's *Special Edition Using PowerPoint 97* and is the co-author of the *10 Minute Guide to Lotus Notes Mail 4.6*, *10 Minute Guide to Lotus Notes 4.6*, *Microsoft Works 4.5 6-in-1*, *Microsoft Windows 95 6-in-1*, *PowerPoint 97 Exam Guide*, *Word 97 Exam Guide*, *Excel 97 Exam Guide*, and *Using Microsoft Word 97*.

Suzanne Weixel is a self-employed writer and editor specializing in the technology industry. Her experience with computers began in 1974 when she learned to play football on the Dartmouth Time-Sharing terminal her brother installed in a spare bedroom. Suzanne has written or contributed to more books for Que Education and Training than she can keep track of, including *Microsoft Office Professional 97 Essentials*, *Word 97 Essentials Level III*, *Excel 97 Essentials Level I*, *Personal Computing Essentials*, and *Success with WordPerfect 7 for Windows 95*. She has also written, edited, and contributed to numerous Que books, including *Using Windows 3.11*, *Using DOS*, *Using PCs*, and *Easy PCs*, Second, Third, and Fourth Editions. She also likes to write about non-computer-related subjects whenever she has the chance. Suzanne graduated from Dartmouth College in 1981 with a degree in art history. She currently lives in Marlborough, MA with her husband, Rick, their sons, Nathaniel and Evan, and their dog, a Samoyed named Cirrus.

Trademark Acknowledgments

All terms mentioned in this book that are known to be trademarks or service marks have been appropriately capitalized. Que Education and Training cannot attest to the accuracy of this information. Use of a term in this book should not be regarded as affecting the validity of any trademark or service mark.

Preface

Que Education and Training is the educational publishing imprint of Macmillan Computer Publishing, the world's leading computer book publisher. Macmillan Computer Publishing books have taught more than 20 million people how to be productive with their computers.

This expertise in producing high-quality computer tutorial and reference books is evident in every Que Education and Training title we publish. The same tried-and-true writing and product-development process that makes Macmillan Computer Publishing books bestsellers is used to ensure that educational materials from Que Education and Training provide the most accurate and up-to-date information. Experienced and respected computer application instructors write and review every manuscript to provide class-tested pedagogy. Quality-assurance editors check every keystroke and command in Que Education and Training books to ensure that instructions are clear, accurate, and precise.

Above all, Macmillan Computer Publishing and, in turn, Que Education and Training have years of experience in meeting the learning demands of students across all disciplines.

The MOUS Essentials of Hands-On Learning

The *MOUS Essentials* are appropriate for use in both corporate training and college classroom settings. They can be used effectively as computer-lab applications modules to accompany any of Que Education and Training's computer concepts text or as stand-alone texts for an applications-only course. The *MOUS Essentials* workbooks enable users to become self-sufficient quickly; encourage self-learning after instruction; maximize learning through clear, complete explanations; and serve as future references.

The *MOUS Essentials* series uses the following elements to get the most out of the material:

Objectives list what students do and learn from the project.

Required Activities are the objectives as they relate to the Microsoft Office User Specialist exams.

Why Would I Do This? shows students why the material is essential.

Step-by-Step Tutorials simplify the procedures with large screen shots, captions, and annotations.

If you have problems...anticipates common pitfalls and advises students accordingly.

Inside Stuff provides tips and shortcuts for more effective applications.

Key Terms are highlighted in the text and defined in the margin when they first appear, as well as in an end-of-book glossary.

Jargon Watch offers a layperson's view of "technobabble" in easily understandable terms.

Exam Notes provide information and insight on topics that are covered on the MOUS exam and that should be reviewed carefully.

Checking Your Skills provides true/false, multiple choice, matching, and completion exercises.

Applying Your Skills contains directed, hands-on Practice exercises to check comprehension and reinforce learning, as well as self-directed Challenge exercises requiring students to use critical thinking skills.

CD-ROM contains files for the text's step-by-step tutorials and end-of-project exercises.

Annotated Instructor's Edition

If you have adopted this text for use in a college classroom, you will receive, upon request, an Annotated Instructor's Edition at no additional charge. The manual contains suggested curriculum guides for courses of varying lengths, teaching tips, answers to exercises in the "Checking Your Skills" and "Applying Your Skills" sections, test questions and answers, and data files and solutions for each tutorial and exercise. Please contact your local representative or write to us on school or business letterhead at Macmillan Computer Publishing, 201 West 103rd Street, Indianapolis, IN 46290-1097, Attention: Que Education and Training Sales Support.

Microsoft Office User Specialist Exams

In order to validate your skills using Office, Microsoft has created the Microsoft Office User Specialist program. The Specialist Program is available for many Office 95 and Office 97 applications at both Proficient and Expert User levels.

The Specialist designation distinguishes you from your peers as knowledgeable in using Office products, which can also make you more competitive in the job market.

The *Microsoft Office User Specialist* exams are for anyone who:

- Wants to expand their skills.

- Is seeking certification in a particular software.

- Wants to learn or reference tasks in short, concise lessons.

- Is an instructor or trainer preparing groups of people for the Microsoft Exams.

Que Education & Training Certification Resource Center

To keep up to date on the Microsoft Office User Specialist program exams, check the following Web sites:

```
www.queet.com/certification
www.mous.net
www.microsoft.com/office/train_cert
```

MOUS PinPoint® Training and Testing Software

MOUS PinPoint training and testing software is designed to supplement the projects in this book. It aids you in your preparation for taking and passing the *Microsoft Office User Specialist* exams. The MOUS PinPoint software consists of:

- Trainers

- Evaluations

Each **trainer** asks you to perform specific tasks that were covered in a particular project in this book. If you don't know how to perform a particular task, you can watch a demonstration (**SHOW ME**) of the task. Immediate feedback (concerning the correctness of performance) is given after each task in each trainer. Each **evaluation** consists of the same questions that were given in the trainer. However, with an evaluation, you may not view demonstrations and you do not receive feedback after trying each task. After performing a **trainer** or **evaluation**, you can view a report of your overall performance.

Preparing to Install the MOUS PinPoint Training and Testing Software

To install the MOUS PinPoint training and testing software, we recommend following these steps:

1. Check to see if your computer meets the minimum requirements (see Table I.1).

2. Perform a full installation of Office 97 on your computer, if you have not already done so (see the section "Installing Office 97").

3. Install the MOUS PinPoint testing and training software (see the section "Installing the MOUS PinPoint Training and Testing Software").

Using the MOUS PinPoint Training and Testing Software

To use the MOUS PinPoint training and testing software, we recommend following these steps:

Study the projects in this book. After reading each project:

1. Run the **trainer** for the project (see the section "Running the MOUS PinPoint Software"). Then view a report on your performance (see the section "Viewing Reports").

2. Run the **evaluation** for the project (see the section "Running the MOUS PinPoint Software"). Then view a report on your performance (see the section "Viewing Reports"). Note: Some projects may not have a corresponding MOUS PinPoint trainer and evaluation.

After you have finished reading this book, take the MOUS PinPoint Final Exam:

1. Run the **evaluation** for the Final Exam Part 1. Final Exam Part 1 covers material included in the first half of this book.

2. Run the **trainer** for the Final Exam Part 1. Only the items missed in the trainer will be set to run.

3. Run the **evaluation** for the Final Exam Part 1 (again) as a final check.

4. Repeat steps 1–3 given for the Final Exam Part 2. Final Exam Part 2 covers material from roughly the second half of this book.

5. When you are finished using the MOUS PinPoint software, you can remove it from your computer (see the section "Removing the MOUS PinPoint Training and Testing Software").

Running MOUS PinPoint Testing and Training Software Requirements

The system components in Table I.1 are required to run the MOUS PinPoint Testing and Training Software.

Table I.1 System Component Requirements		
Component	Minimum	Recommended
CPU	Pentium 90	Higher than Pentium 90
Operating System	Windows 95 or NT 4.0 Note: You must have an Administrator's or Power User's login if you are working on a Windows NT workstation.	N/A
Installed Apps	Office 97 (full installation)	N/A
RAM	16 MB	32 MB or higher

continues

Table I.1 Continued		
Component	**Minimum**	**Recommended**
Hard Drive	Adequate space for installation space for Office 97 and for MOUS PinPoint training and testing software.	N/A
CD-ROM Drive	2X speed	4X speed or faster
Pointing Device	Windows-compatible mouse or pointing device.	N/A
Video	Color VGA video display	N/A

Installing Office 97

Important: It is necessary to do a complete installation of Office 97. This means installing *all* components.

To perform a full installation of Office 97, complete the following steps:

1. Start Windows 95 or Windows NT 4.0 and close any applications that are running (other than Windows).

2. Insert the Office 97 CD and run **setup.exe**.

3. Click on the **Add/Remove** button, as shown in Figure I.1 (if a previous installation of Office 97 is already on your computer). If you do not have a previous installation of Office 97 on your computer, select **Custom** installation from a different screen.

Figure I.1
The Microsoft Office 97
Setup dialog box.

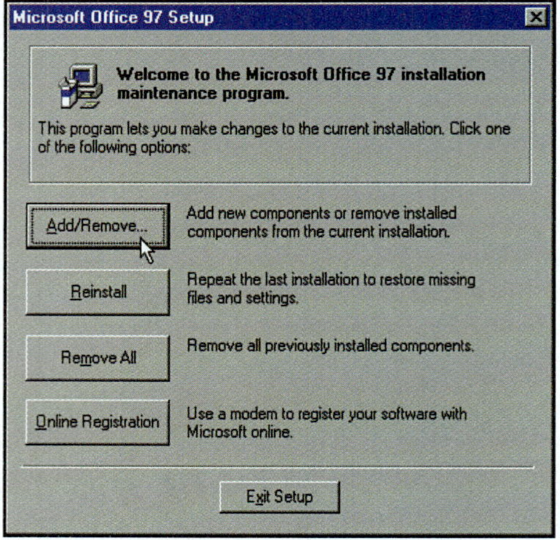

4. Click on the **Select All** button (see Figure I.2).

5. Click on the **Continue** button.

6. Continue with the installation until it is finished.

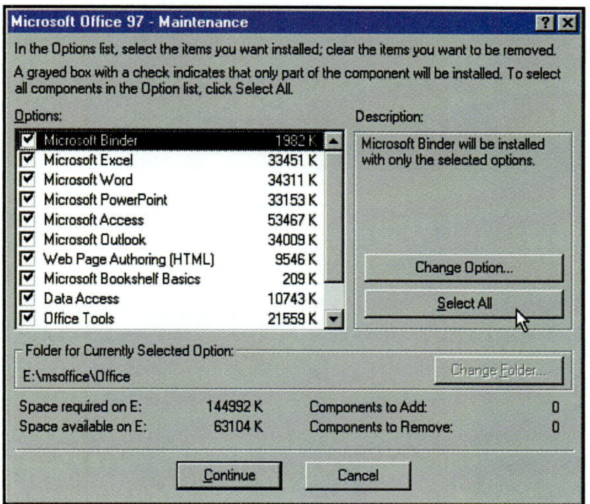

Installing the MOUS PinPoint Training and Testing Software

To install and run MOUS PinPoint trainers and evaluations on a single-user computer, you must first install the MOUS PinPoint **Launcher** by running a setup program from the MOUS PinPoint CD.

Installing the MOUS PinPoint Launcher

To run the setup program for the MOUS PinPoint Launcher:

1. Start Windows 95 or Windows NT 4.0 and insert the MOUS PinPoint CD into the CD-ROM drive.

2. Select **Start/Run** from the Windows desktop.

3. Enter (or browse to) **[Drive Letter]:\SETUP.EXE** (where **[Drive Letter]** is the assigned drive letter of the CD-ROM (see Figure I.3).

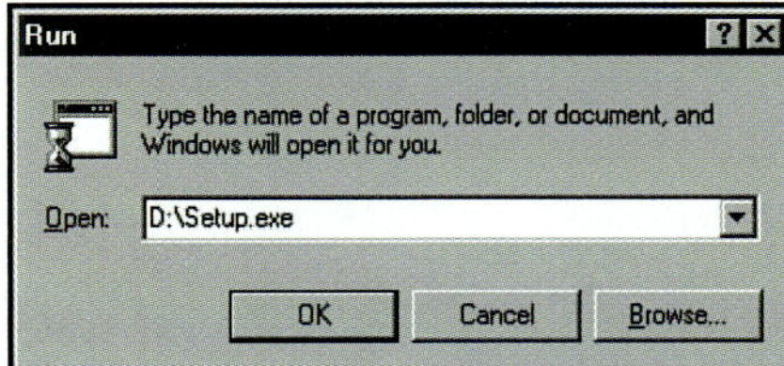

4. Click on **OK.** The setup program runs.

5. Answer the questions that appear during the installation.

6. When the dialog box in Figure I.4 displays, choose **Normal Single-User Installation**.

7. Click **Yes** when you are asked if you want to install MOUS PinPoint modules to your hard disk. The dialog box in Figure I.5 appears. The installation program is getting ready to install the **Launcher** to your computer. It needs to know the directory where you would like it installed.

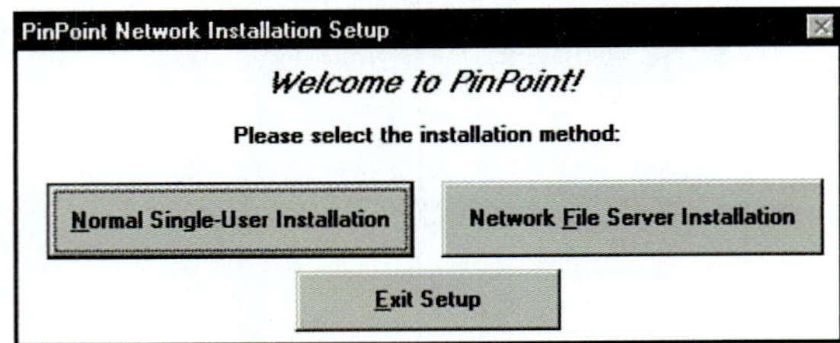

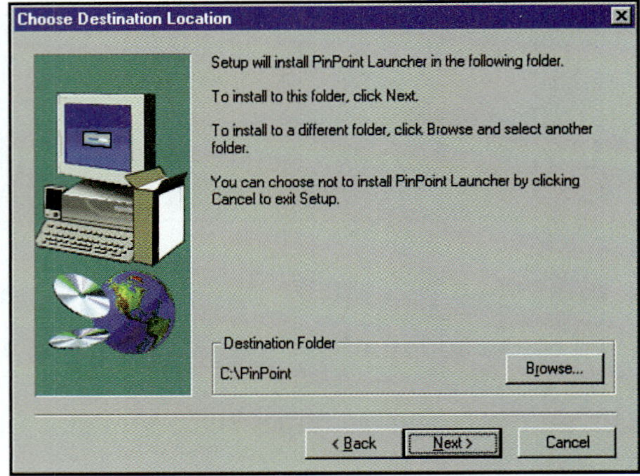

8. To install the **Launcher** to the default location, click on the **Next** button. Otherwise, enter a new path for the **Launcher** and then click on the **Next** button.

9. Confirm the installation location by clicking on **Yes** in the dialog box in Figure I.6.

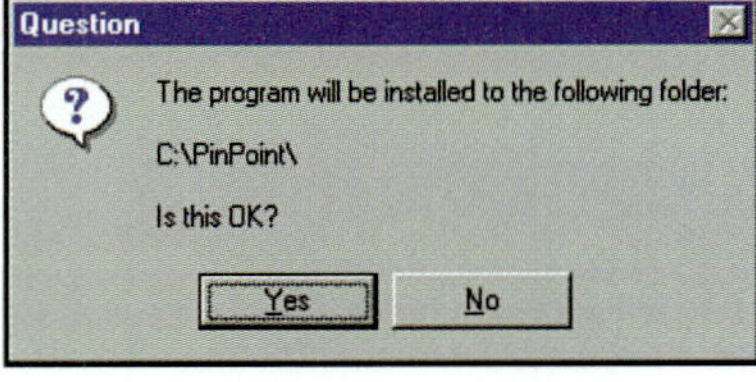

10. When Figure I.7 appears, click on Next.

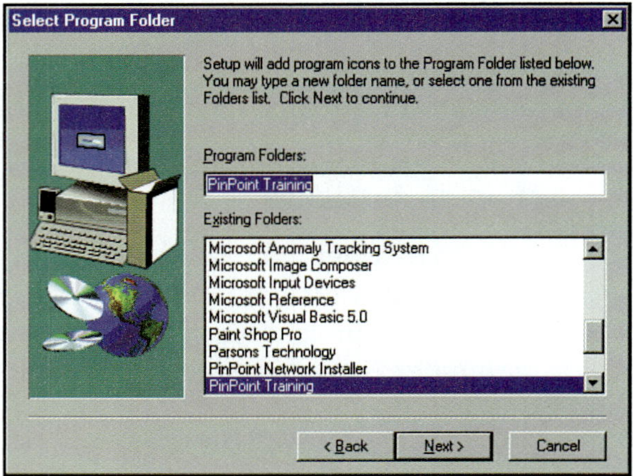

A **PinPoint Training** group window is created (see Figure I.8). You can close this window. It is not necessary to use this window to start the PinPoint Launcher in the future since you can always select Start/Programs/PinPoint Training/PinPoint Training from your desktop.

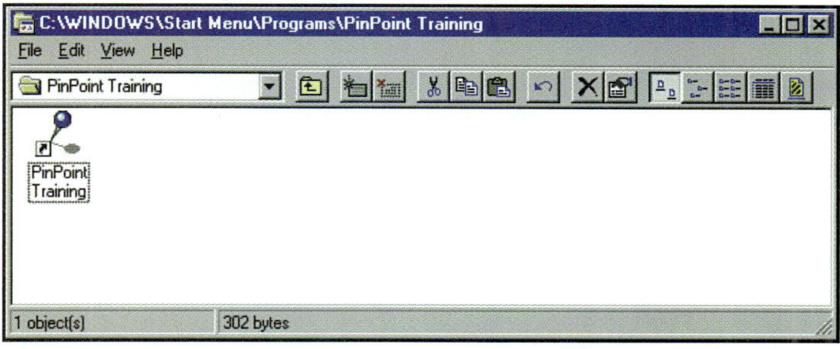

The PinPoint **Launcher** is used to:

- log on with your **UserID** and **Password**.
- install your MOUS PinPoint training and testing software for an exam.
- run your MOUS PinPoint training and testing software for an exam.
- view reports after you have run the MOUS PinPoint training and testing software.

To install the MOUS PinPoint training and testing software for an exam, continue with the next section.

Installing the MOUS PinPoint Software

To install the MOUS PinPoint training and testing software:

1. Start the Launcher by selecting Start/Programs/PinPoint Training/ PinPoint Training (see Figure I.9).

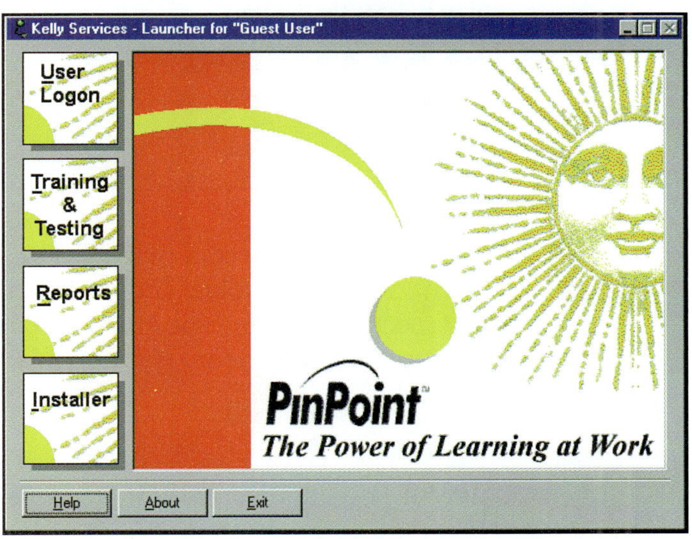

2. Click on the **Installer** button (see Figure I.10).

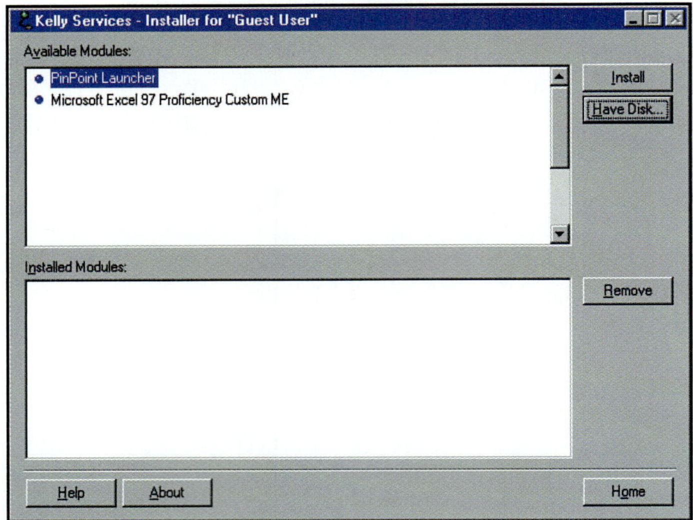

3. Install your MOUS PinPoint software by selecting the specific module (for example, **Microsoft Excel 97 Proficiency Custom ME**) from the **Available Modules** list box and clicking on the **Install** button. (Do not install the **Launcher**. It's already installed!)

4. Answer the questions that appear during installation. You are asked to verify the location where the MOUS PinPoint software will install to your hard drive (see Figure I.11)

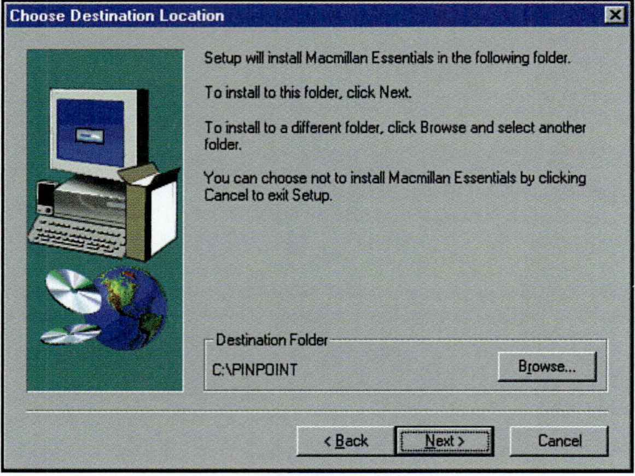

5. Make changes as necessary by clicking on **Browse** and selecting a different destination folder. Important: The MOUS PinPoint software for the specific exam and the PinPoint **Launcher** must be installed under the same main directory (for example, **C:\PinPoint**) in order to work properly.

6. Click on **Next**.

7. Accept the subdirectory (for example, **xl8prome**) where the MOUS PinPoint software will be placed. You do not have a choice concerning the name of this subdirectory.

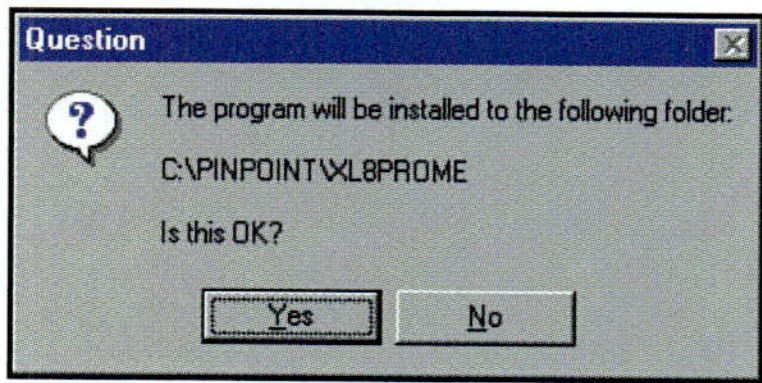

8. Click on **Yes.**

9. If you would like to view a README file concerning MOUS PinPoint software, click on **Yes** in the dialog box in Figure I.13. Otherwise, click on <u>N</u>o.

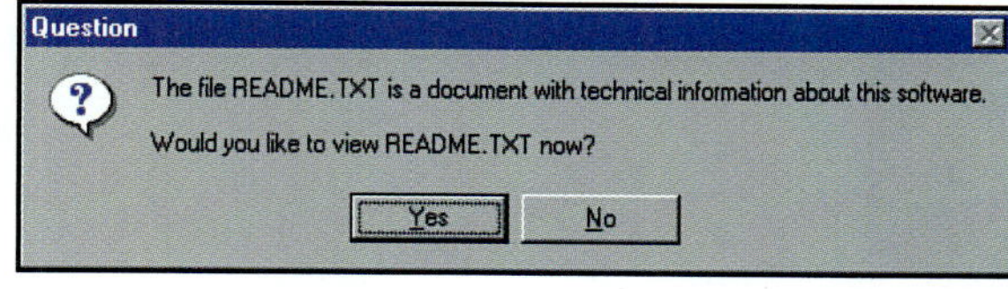

A PinPoint Training group window is created (see Figure I.14).

Close this window. It is not necessary to use this window to start the PinPoint **Launcher** in the future since you can always select **Start/ Programs/PinPoint Training/PinPoint Training** from your desktop.

If you want to run the MOUS PinPoint software that you just installed, don't exit from the **Launcher**. Continue on with step 3 in the next section.

To exit from the **Launcher** to Windows, click on the **<u>E</u>xit** button.

Running the MOUS PinPoint Software

To run the MOUS PinPoint software, it is necessary to start the PinPoint **Launcher**. Important: Shut down all applications.

To run the MOUS PinPoint software:

1. Shut down all applications (except Windows and the Launcher) that are running, including any shortcut bars (such as Microsoft Office shortcut bar). If the Office 97 exam application is running, shut it down.

2. Start the Launcher by selecting Start/Programs/PinPoint Training/ PinPoint Training from the Windows desktop.

3. Click on the User Logon button (see Figure I.15). Logging on under your name allows the **Launcher** to keep track of your personal progress. This enables the **Launcher** to reconfigure a module the next time you take it. It also enables the **Launcher** to create a report containing information about your training or evaluation sessions.

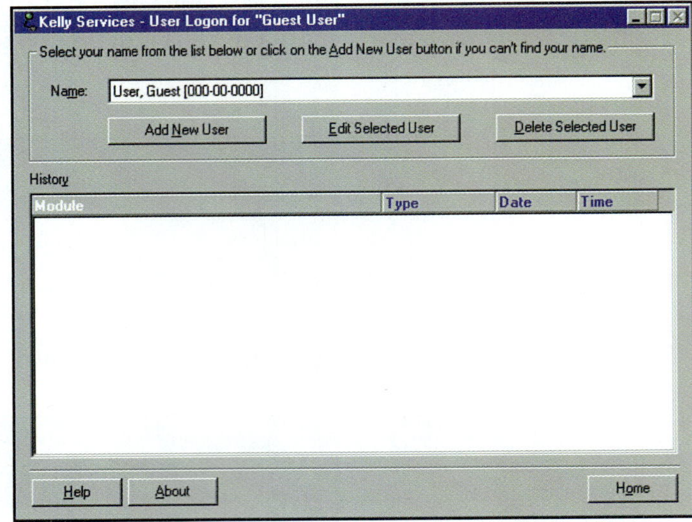

4. Select your name from the drop-down list in the **Name** combo box in Figure I.16:

   ■ You may need to use the scroll bar to find your name.

   ■ If your name is not in the list, go to step 5.

   ■ If you found your name, skip to step 8.

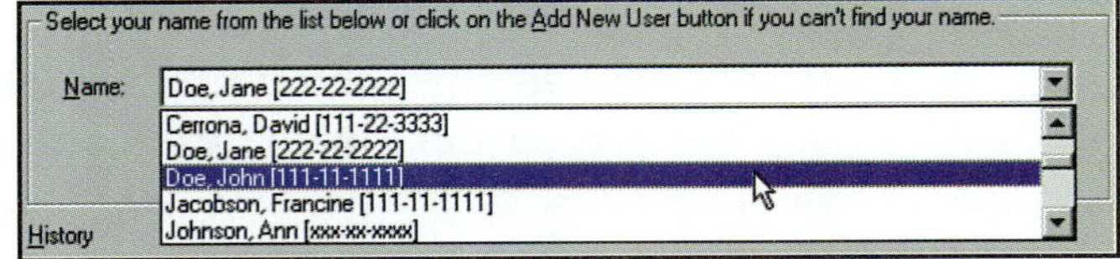

5. If this is your first time running MOUS PinPoint software, your name will not be in the list. If that is the case, create a user account for yourself by clicking on the **Add New User** button.

6. Enter your personal data, tabbing between fields in Figure I.17:

   ■ Enter all five data items. If one or more of the data items are missing, the **OK** button will remain grayed out (disabled).

   ■ Your **User ID** and **Password** may both consist of up to 14 characters and are both case sensitive.

■ After entering your **Password** in the **Password** field, you must confirm this **Password** by entering the identical **Password** again in the **Confirm Password** field.

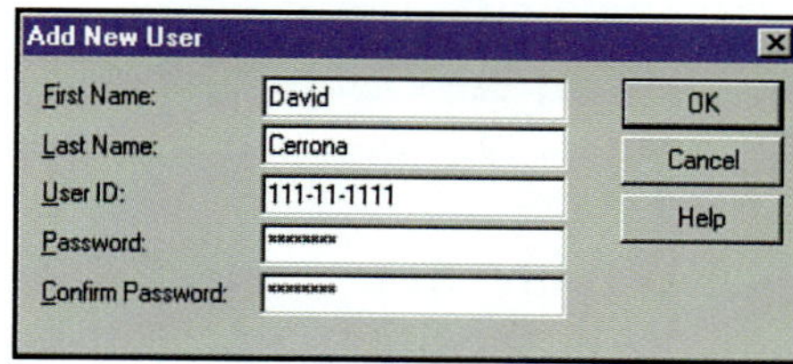

7. Click on **OK.** Your account is created and you are logged on. You are ready to move to the **Training & Testing** screen.

8. Click on the **Home** button to move to the **Home** screen.

9. Click on the **Training & Testing** button (see Figure I.18).

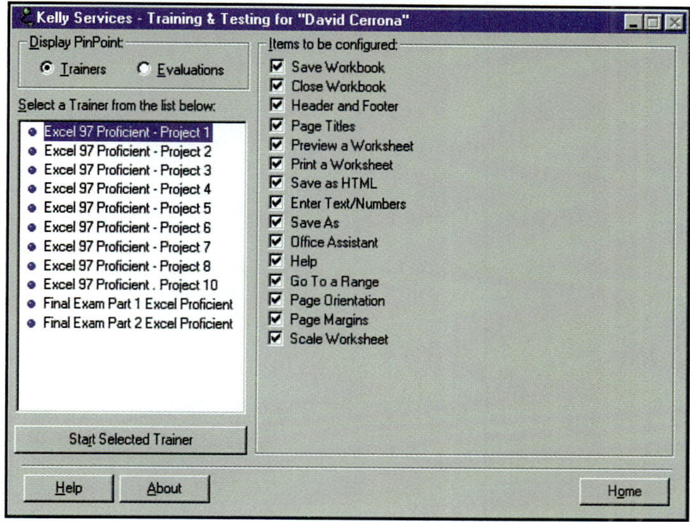

10. Select **Trainers** (or **Evaluations**), depending on which you would like to run (see Figure I.19). A list of trainers (or evaluations) displays.

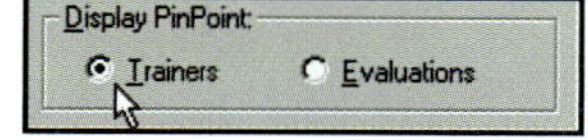

11. Select the particular trainer or evaluation that you would like to run. Each trainer and evaluation is named by the project that it covers. Trainers may be configured. That means you can select the tasks that you would like to run. The first time you run a trainer, all tasks will automatically be selected. (Note: Evaluations may not be configured.)

12. If you are running a trainer, configure it by selecting or deselecting tasks in the **Items to be configured** section:

■ A check indicates that the task will run.

■ No check indicates that the task will not run.

You are now ready to start (launch) the trainer or evaluation for the project.

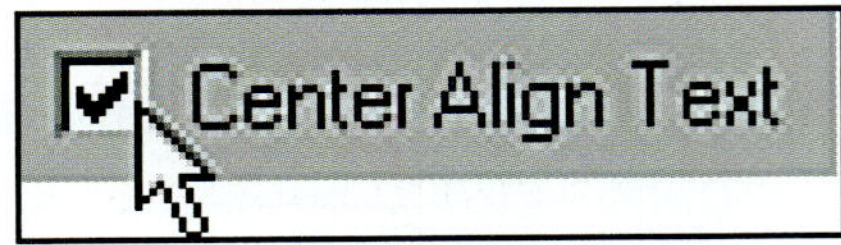

13. Click on the **Start Selected Trainer** button if you are starting a trainer or the **Start Selected Evaluation** button if you are starting an evaluation. Before the trainer or evaluation runs, you are asked to confirm (see Figure I.21).

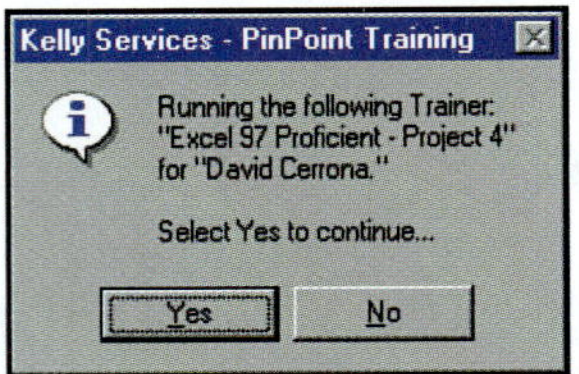

14. Click on **Yes** to confirm. While running the trainer or evaluation, you may use the controls in Figure I.22.

After running a trainer or evaluation, the **Training and Testing** screen reappears. You can continue to run other trainers or evaluations for other projects. When you are finished studying the whole book, you can also run the trainers and evaluations for the final exams.

To view reports for each trainer or evaluation that you ran, click on the **Reports** button (see the section "Running the MOUS PinPoint Software").

To exit from the **Launcher**, first move to the **Home** screen by clicking on the **Home** button. Then click on the **Exit** button.

Viewing Reports

In the **Launcher,** you can view two kinds of reports after running a MOUS PinPoint trainer or evaluation:

To display reports in the Launcher:

1. Start the **Launcher** and log on.

2. Click on the <u>**Reports**</u> button (see Figure I.23). This report displays a line (record) of data for each instance that you have run a MOUS PinPoint trainer or evaluation:

   - **Accuracy** is the number of tasks you performed correctly

   - **Maximum** is the total number of tasks that were configured to run

   - **Time** is the total elapsed time in minutes (from the moment you started running the trainer or evaluation to the moment that you exited the trainer or evaluation)

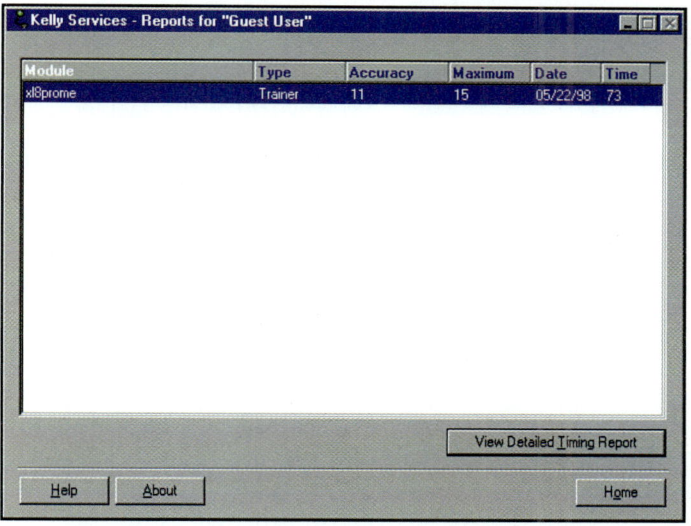

3. The second kind of report is the **Detailed Timing Report** (see Figure I.24). If you wish to view this report, select the record for which you would like the timing report and click on the **View Detailed Timing Report** button.

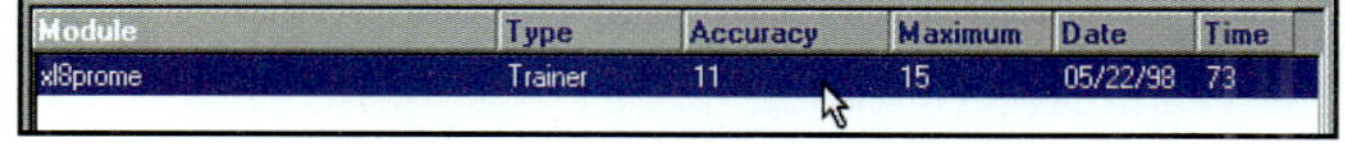

4. To print the **Detailed Timing Report**, click on the <u>**Print**</u> button:

   - **Actual** is the time, in seconds, you used to complete the task. This time is considered the "involved time," the time that was taken from the moment that you clicked with the mouse (or entered something on the keyboard) to the moment that you clicked the **Done** button. It does not count the "thinking time" before you first moved the mouse (or used the keyboard) and it does not count the time used to run and view a SHOW ME demonstration.

Timing results of xl8prome for Guest User

Item No.	Item	Actual	Optimal	Correct	Did Show Me
1	Save Workbook	2	10	No	No
1	Save Workbook	8	10	Yes	No
2	Close Workbook	2	10	Yes	No
21	Header and Footer	130	30	No	No
21	Header and Footer	1	30	No	Yes (1)
26	Page Titles	23	25	No	No
26	Page Titles	21	25	No	Yes (1)
26	Page Titles	29	25	Yes	Yes (1)
35	Preview a Worksheet	8	20	No	No
35	Preview a Worksheet	24	20	No	Yes (1)
35	Preview a Worksheet	7	20	No	Yes (1)
35	Preview a Worksheet	7	20	No	Yes (1)
35	Preview a Worksheet	1	20	No	Yes (1)
36	Print a Worksheet	26	20	No	Yes (1)
41	Save as HTML	12	45	No	Yes (1)
44	Enter Text/Numbers	58	30	No	No
44	Enter Text/Numbers	66	30	Yes	No
45	Save As	12	30	Yes	No
49	Office Assistant	24	25	Yes	No
50	Help	13	30	Yes	No
51	Go To a Range	10	10	Yes	No
53	Page Orientation	12	15	Yes	No
54	Page Margins	27	20	Yes	No
55	Scale Worksheet	36	10	Yes	No

Close   Print

- **Optimal** is a reasonable amount of time, in seconds, required to perform a task by an efficient method

- **Correct** - **Yes**, if you performed the task correctly; **No** if you did not perform the task correctly

- **Did Show Me** - **Yes**, if you viewed a SHOW ME demonstration for the task; **No**, if you did not view a SHOW ME demonstration for the task. The **Did Show Me** column appears only if the timing report contains data for a **trainer** and not for an **evaluation**. (Evaluations do not have SHOW MEs.)

5. Close the **Detailed Timing Report** window by clicking on the **Close** button. The **Reports** screen of the **Launcher** returns.

Removing the MOUS PinPoint Training and Testing Software

When you are finished using the MOUS PinPoint training and testing software, you can remove it. Be sure to follow the procedure below.

To remove your MOUS PinPoint training and testing software:

1. Start the **Launcher**.

2. Click on the **Installer** button.

3. Select the exam module from the **Installed Modules** list.

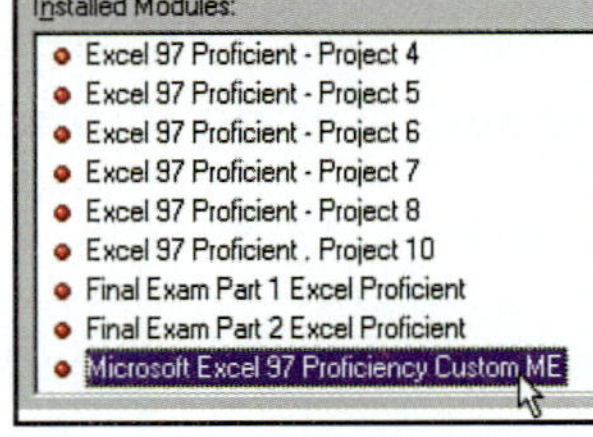

4. Click the **Remove** button.

5. When the **Confirmation** dialog box appears, click **Yes**.

6. When the **Remove** dialog box appears, click the **Yes** button.

7. An **"Uninstall complete"** message appears.

8. Find the MOUS PinPoint directory on your computer and delete it.

Troubleshooting

Table I.2 lists a few problems that can arise while running the MOUS PinPoint training and testing software. For each problem, a solution or explanation is given.

Table I.2 MOUS PinPoint Training and Testing Software Problems and Solutions	
Problem	**Explanation or Action**
A task is grayed-out and not selected on the Training and Testing screen in the Launcher program (see Figure I.27).	

Problem	Explanation or Action
An example of a grayed-out option.	A particular component has not been installed. Exit the Launcher and perform a full installation of Office 97 (see the section "Installing Office 97").
Your computer crashes (locks up or exits ungracefully) while running the MOUS PinPoint training or testing.	Start your computer again and rerun the desired MOUS PinPoint training or testing. Exit the trainer or evaluation in the normal way. It is important to do this, even if you have no desire to run a trainer or evaluation. By running any trainer or evaluation, you will insure that your computer's registry is reset to normal.
You see a message that says **"program was left in an unfinished was changed by running the registry and state"** AND you have deleted the MOUS PinPoint directory (or one of its key components).	The problem is that your Windows Registry needs to be set back to the state it was in before you started the MOUS PinPoint training and testing. Do the following: 1. Go to the **Windows** directory and find the following files: **OFC97.PIN** **OFC971.PIN** **OFC972.PIN** **OFC973.PIN** **OFC974.PIN** 2. Delete the **OFC97.PIN** file. 3. Rename the other four **.PIN** files so that they have a **.REG** extension. 4. Double-click on each of the **.REG** files to run them. This will reset your Registry.

Microsoft Word Expert Specialist User Skills

The skill areas covered in the exam and the required tasks for those skill areas are listed in Table FM.1.

Table FM.1 Expert User Skills			
Skill Set	**Required Activity**	**Project**	**Lesson**
Use advanced formatting	Use text flow options (Widows/Orphans options and keeping lines together)	5	5
	Use nonbreaking spaces	5	5
Use page numbers and footers	Create watermarks	3	6
	Format first page differently than subsequent	5	7
Use footnotes and endnotes	Create footnotes and endnotes	4	2
	Revise footnotes and endnotes	4	2
Workgroup editing	Track changes to a document	11	4
	Insert comments	11	2
	Route documents	11	4
	Highlight text in a document	11	1
	Create multiple versions of a document	11	7
	Create master documents	11	8
Use columns	Balance column length	10	6
	Keep text in columns together	10	6
Calculate tabular information	Import worksheets in a table	14	3
	Modify worksheets in a table	14	4
	Perform calculations in a table	1	4
	Create worksheets in a table	14	2
Use charts	Create and modify charts	13	1, 2
	Import data into charts	13	3, 4
Use forms	Create and modify a form	12	1
	Create catalogs and lists	12	1
Apply borders and shading	Create and modify page borders	5	3
	Apply paragraph and section shading	5	4
Insert graphics and special characters	Add graphics	1	5
	Delete and position graphics	1	5
	Change page orientation	5	2
	Insert fields	12	3, 4, 5, 6
	Insert special characters	5	8

Skill Set	Required Activity	Project	Lesson
Use macros	Record and run macros	9	5
	Edit macros	9	6
	Copy, rename, and delete macros	9	6
	Use macros to create templates	12	1
Generate a mail merge	Merge a document using variable data	8	4
Use sort	Sort lists, paragraphs, tables	2	8
	Sort records to be merged	8	3
Generate reference documents	Create and modify a table of contents	4	4
	Create and modify an index	4	4
	Create cross-reference	4	3
	Use bookmarks	8	3
Manage files	Protect documents	11	6
	Add comments to the file properties	11	2

Table of Contents at a Glance

Table of Contents

Conventions Used in This Book

The *MOUS Essentials* series uses the following conventions to make it easier for you to understand the material:

- Text that you are to type or that appears onscreen appears in a `special font and color`.

- Underlined letters in menu names, menu commands, and dialog-box options are the shortcut keys. Examples are the <u>F</u>ile menu, the <u>O</u>pen command, and the File <u>n</u>ame list box.

- Key terms appear in *italic* the first time they are discussed and are defined in the margin as soon as they are introduced.

Project 1 / One

Using Tables and Graphics

Completing a Newsletter

In this Project, you learn how to:

Objectives

Required Activities

Objectives	Required Activities
➤ Create a Table	
➤ Enter Text into a Table	
➤ Format a Table	
➤ Calculate Values in a Table	Perform Calculations in a Table
➤ Insert a Picture	Add Graphics
➤ Move and Resize a Picture	Delete and Position Graphics

Why Would I Do This?

The Tables feature is one of the most versatile and easy-to-use features in Word. A *table* allows you to organize information in a row and column format. Although you can use the Tables feature in many ways, people most often use it to display information that needs to be formatted into columns. You can use the Columns feature or tabs settings to organize information in columns, but the Tables feature is easier to use and has more options for formatting the information and for formatting the table itself. In fact, the Table AutoFormat tool enables you to assign complex formatting with just a few mouse clicks. The Tables feature also has several built-in *spreadsheet* functions that perform basic mathematical operations. A table can contain text, graphics, and just about anything that a Word document can contain. The one exception is that a table cannot contain another table.

Information is entered into table **cells**, and each cell is independent of all other cells. You can format the contents of a cell or the cell itself differently than other cells in the table and you can have almost any number of **rows** and **columns** in a table.

There are two ways to create a table. The first way is to design the table and then add the data in the table. The second way is to convert existing lists into a table format. You learn both methods in this lesson.

Word tables are designed to help organize data and to help you perform simple calculations in a table. If you need to create a complicated spreadsheet (one with advanced formula needs), it is recommended that you use Microsoft Excel.

You can also use *graphics* in your documents to illustrate a point, provide excitement, or add creative flair. You can add graphic images that you create in Word, as well as those created in other programs. Stock graphics called *clip art* are available through software stores, mail-order catalogs, and online services. In fact, Word includes a wide variety of clip art for use in both formal and informal documents.

In this project, you use tables and graphics to put the finishing touches on a company newsletter.

Lesson 1: Creating a Table

Word's tables are similar to spreadsheets, such as those in Microsoft Excel, in both operation and terminology. Spreadsheets and Word's tables are made up of a grid of columns and rows. When you create a table, you estimate how many columns and how many rows (or lines) you need.

Table

A series of rows and columns. The intersection of a row and column is called a cell, which is where you type text and numbers.

Graphic

A drawing or picture created by a graphics application or scanned and stored in a file.

Clip art

A collection of graphic images.

Spreadsheet

An accounting form that contains rows and columns. The intersection of a row and column is called a cell.

❶ Open the folder Project-01 and then the file Proj0101 and save it as `June Newsletter`.

The sample newsletter has two columns under the title as shown in Figure 1.1. Because Normal view is faster to work in, most of the figures in this book are shown in Normal view. The advantage of using Page Layout view is that it shows you what the document will look like when printed. Switch to Page Layout view now so you can see how the newsletter looks in both Page Layout and Normal view.

❷ Choose View, Page Layout.

In the sample newsletter, the columns are shown side-by-side below the masthead. Because editing is faster and easier in Normal view, however, you need to change to that now.

Figure 1.1
The sample newsletter open in the document window.

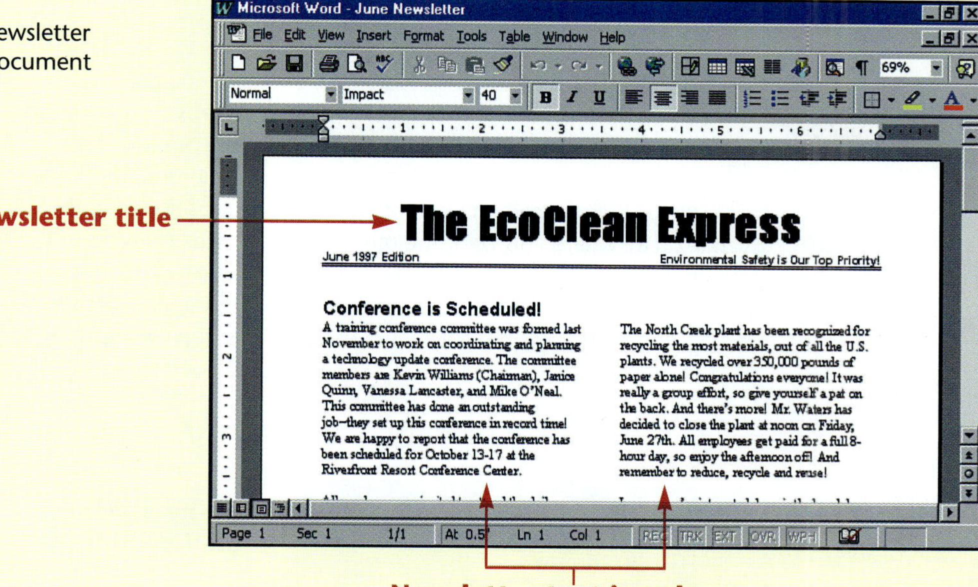

❸ Choose View, Normal.

In Normal view, the text is formatted into one single column on the left side of the screen. You can switch back and forth between the two views, so you can use the one that helps you the most, depending on which type of document you are working on.

In Normal view, you can see the **section break** that has been inserted below the masthead. Any document can have multiple sections, and each **section** can be formatted separately without affecting any of the other sections. In this case, the second section is formatted into two columns.

continues

To Create a Table   (continued)

④ Scroll through the document until you see the heading Just a Reminder..., **and position the insertion point on the blank line above this heading.**

You want to create the table that shows the training class schedule, and place it in this spot.

⑤ Click the Insert Table button.

Word displays an empty grid. You have to click and drag the mouse in the grid in order to highlight the number of rows and columns you need. Drag the mouse slowly until you get the hang of it.

⑥ Click and drag the mouse over and down until the bottom of the grid reads 6x2 Table; **then release the mouse button.**

The number 6 represents the number of rows, and the number 2 represents the number of columns. Make sure that you have two columns and six rows selected.

If you have problems...

If you have problems clicking and dragging across this grid, you can create the table by using the Table menu. Before you use this method, drag the mouse back up to the top-left corner of the grid until the bottom reads Cancel. Make certain your insertion point is positioned in the document exactly where you want the table to be inserted. Then, from the Table menu, choose Insert Table. The Insert Table dialog box is displayed (see Figure 1.2). Use the spinner arrows next to Number of Columns and Number of Rows to specify two columns and six rows. Choose OK to create the table.

Figure 1.2
You can also insert a table using the Table, Insert Table menu option.

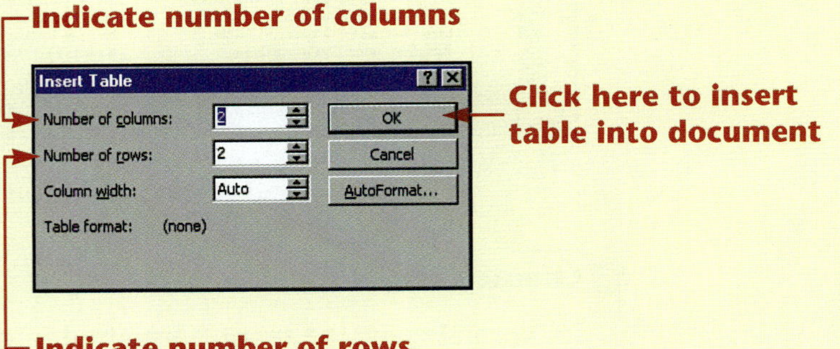

If you have already inserted the table but chose the wrong dimensions, use the Undo command to remove the table. Then try again, either by clicking the Insert Table button or by choosing Insert Table from the Table menu.

Word creates the table at the insertion point. Notice that the table is created within the margins of the newsletter column and that both columns in the table have the same width. By default, Word creates evenly spaced columns between the available margin space. You can easily change the column widths, if necessary. Your newsletter should now look like Figure 1.3.

Figure 1.3
The newly created table in the company newsletter.

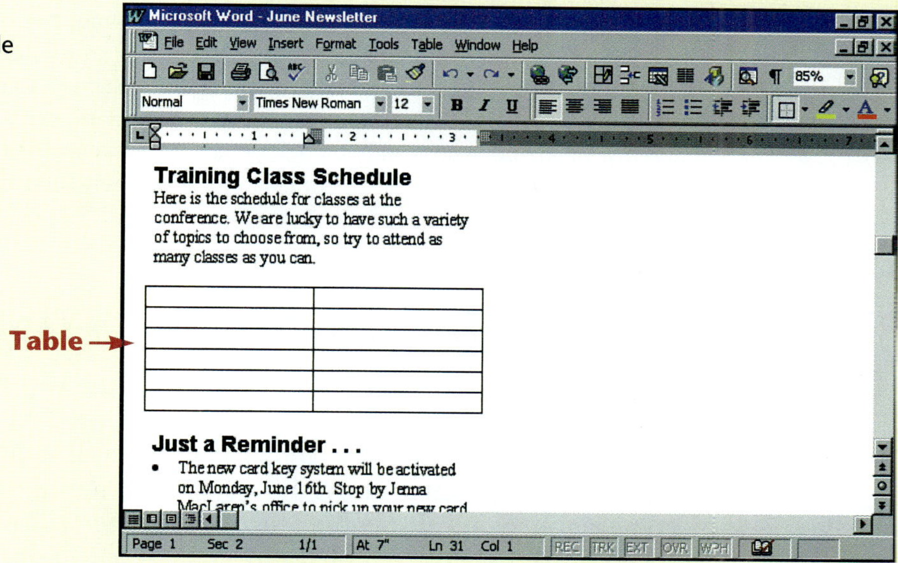

By default, tables are created with a single-line border that prints out with the rest of the table. You learn more about borders in Lesson 3, "Formatting a Table," later in this chapter and also in Project 2. If you choose a different table format or remove some of the borders in your document, table **gridlines** appear on your screen to help you see the table structure.

7 **Save your work and keep the** `June Newsletter` **file open to use in the next lesson, where you learn to enter text into a table.**

Tables are composed of **rows** and **columns**. The intersection of a row and a column is called a **cell**. Rows are numbered from top to bottom, and columns are labeled with letters from left to right. Each cell has a unique address, called a **cell address**, which is composed of the column letter followed by the row number. For example, the top-left cell is A1.

Gridlines, dotted lines in and around the table, help you see the size and position of the table cells. These lines don't print.

A **section break** divides a document into different sections, which you can format separately. For example, in the sample newsletter, a new section was created so the newsletter text could be formatted into columns. Any time you want to format a portion of a document separately, you insert a section break and format that section.

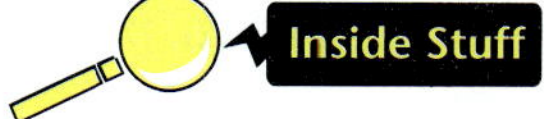

In this lesson, you learned how to create a table by clicking and dragging through the Insert Table grid to select the number of columns and rows. You also learned that you can use the Insert Table option on the Table menu to create a table. There is another option, called Draw Table, that is lots of fun to use. You use a drawing tool in the same way that you would use a pen to draw a table. You simply click and drag to draw the table itself; then you click and drag within the table to create rows and columns. You can quickly create a custom table with cells of varying widths and heights.

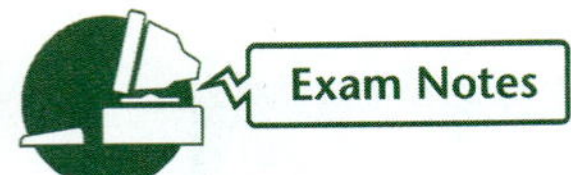

Word inserts a table at the exact position of your insertion point. Be very careful when you place a table in a new document. Press the ⏎Enter key a few times before you insert the table, or you won't be able to position the cursor outside of the top of the table to add text. If you find yourself in this position, and you need space above the table to type text in your document, place your cursor in the first row of the table and press the ⏎Enter key. This moves the table down one line on your document and places your cursor outside of and above the table.

Lesson 2: Entering Text into a Table

Typing text into a table works nearly the same way as typing text into the document window, with only a few differences. One difference is that you use Tab⇆ and ⬆Shift+Tab⇆ to move from one cell to another in a table. Tab⇆ moves you one cell to the right; ⬆Shift+Tab⇆ moves you one cell to the left. When you type information into a cell, the text wraps within the cell's margins so that you don't have to worry about the cell's size.

In the newsletter document, you need to type the column headings first; you then type the date in the first column and the class title in the second column.

The insertion point is already displayed in the first cell (Word puts it there when you create the table), so you can start typing the first entry right now.

To Enter Text into a Table

1 **In the June Newsletter file, type Date in the table's first cell (A1).**

This is the column heading for the first column, which contains the dates for the classes. Column headings act as labels for the information listed in the column.

2 **Press Tab⇆.**

Pressing Tab⇆ moves the insertion point one cell to the right (cell B1). You type the second column heading here.

3 **Type Class Title.**

Unless you change the alignment, Word aligns the text on the left side of the cell. You can also center text or right-align text in the cell.

4 **Press Tab⇆.**

When you press Tab⇆ in the last cell of a row, the insertion point moves to the first cell in the next row (cell A2).

5 **Type Monday, October 13 and press Tab⇆.**

Now type the name of the class scheduled for Monday.

Word

6 **Type** `Navigating on the Internet` **and press** `Tab↹`.

Notice how the cell expands as the text wrapped down to the second line of the cell. Your insertion point should now be positioned in the first cell of the next row (cell A3).

7 **Type the following information to complete the table:**

Tuesday, October 14	Multimedia
Wednesday, October 15	Publishing Web Pages
Thursday, October 16	Presentation Graphics
Friday, October 17	Navigating on the Internet

Don't press `Tab↹` in the last cell; if you do, Word automatically creates a new row that you don't need. Your table should now look like Figure 1.4.

Figure 1.4
The completed table with the dates and class titles.

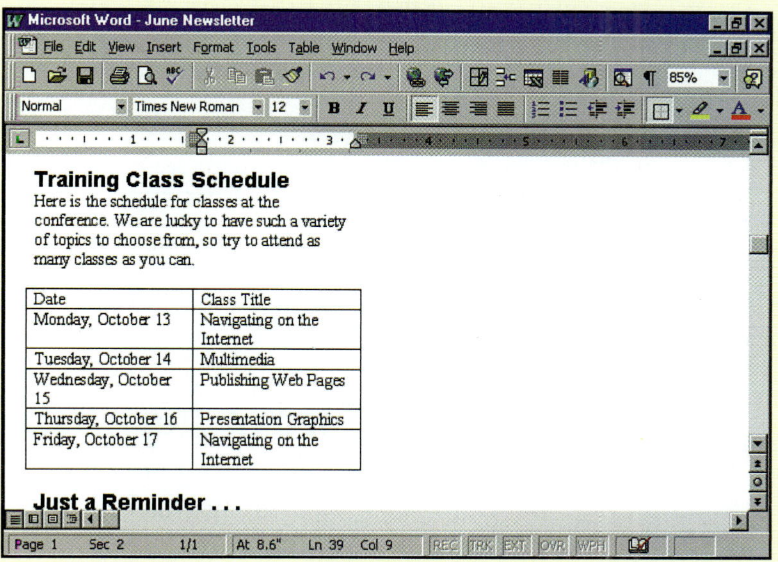

8 **Save your work and keep the** `June Newsletter` **file open to use in the next lesson, where you learn to format a table.**

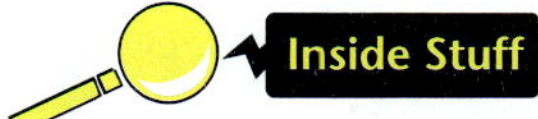

You can also use the mouse to position the insertion point within a table. To move the insertion point to a specific cell, position the mouse pointer on the cell and click the left mouse button.

As mentioned earlier, you can align text in the center, on the right side, or on the left side of a cell. For a single cell, simply place the insertion point in the cell. For multiple cells, click and drag over the cells (just like you would to select text). Now, click the Align Left button, Center button, or Align Right button. If you click the Justify button, Word justifies the text within the cell so that the left and right margins are smooth.

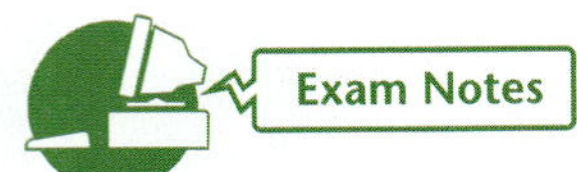

When your cursor is in a table cell, enter and edit text as you would in the rest of your document. Text entered in a cell automatically wraps to the next line in the cell within the column width. Move the cursor to any cell by clicking on that cell or by using the arrow keys ⬅ ➡ or the tab Tab key. Table 1.1 shows you some keyboard shortcuts for navigating in a table. In this table, "current" refers to the position of your insertion point at the time you press the keyboard shortcuts. For example, if your Insertion point is positioned in the third row and you press Alt+Home, your insertion point moves to the first cell in the third row.

Table 1.1 Keyboard Shortcuts to Move Around in a Table	
Press This	To Move Here
Tab	To the next cell in the row (if you press Tab when you're in the last cell of a table, Word adds another row to the table)
⬆Shift+Tab	To the previous cell (move left) in a row
Alt+Home	To the first cell in the current row
Alt+PgUp	To the top cell in the current column
Alt+End	To the last cell in the current row
Alt+PgDn	To the last cell in the current column

Because Tab navigates you through a table, you must press Ctrl+Tab to insert a tab stop within a table cell.

Lesson 3: Formatting a Table

When you create a new table, Word uses a number of default format settings. As mentioned, single-line borders appear inside the table and form the outside border; the text is aligned on the left side of the cell, and the columns have equal widths. Word's Table AutoFormat feature enables you to adjust the format of your table by using preset templates.

You can also adjust individual format settings, such as column width. Try formatting the newsletter table now.

To Format a Table

❶ In the June Newsletter file, position the mouse pointer on the vertical border between the first and second columns.

When you position the mouse pointer on this **vertical border**, the mouse pointer changes to a double vertical line with arrows on either side (see Figure 1.5). You use this **sizing pointer** to adjust the width of the columns.

You may have noticed that the row with Wednesday, October 15 has the 15 on a second line by itself. Adjust the columns so that the 15 fits on the same line as October.

Figure 1.5
You can use the mouse pointer to adjust the column widths in the table.

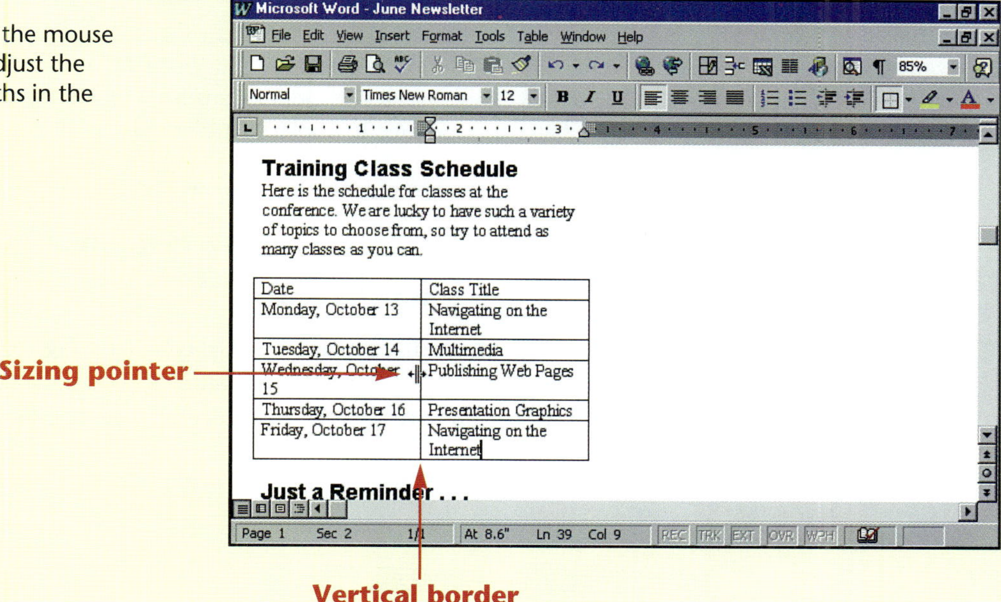

② Click and drag the border to the right, just enough to make room for the 15.

When you click the vertical border with the sizing pointer, a dotted guide line is displayed, running from the ruler down to the status line. As you drag the mouse, this line helps you see the new column width. You need to increase the size of the left column so that all the dates fit on one line.

③ Release the mouse button.

Releasing the mouse button clears the guide line and adjusts the width of the columns. Your table should now look like Figure 1.6.

Figure 1.6
You can resize the left column to allow more room for the dates.

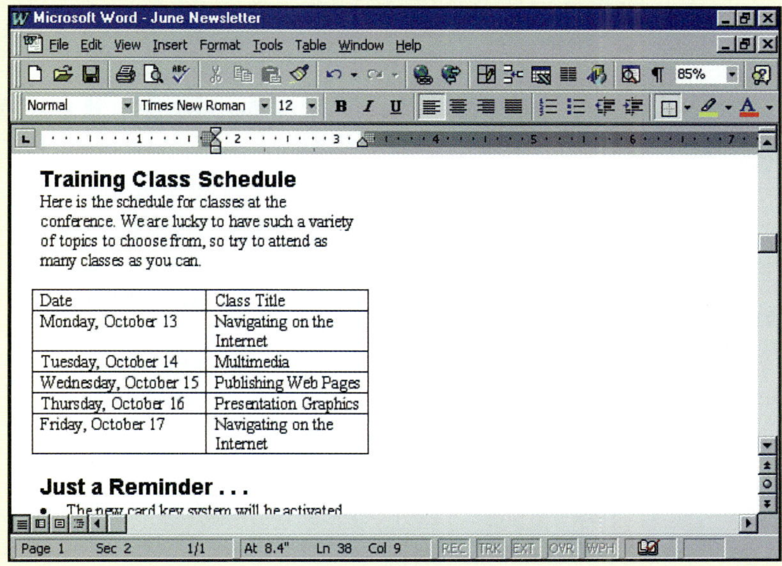

continues

To Format a Table (continued)

If you have problems...

If the date (`Wednesday, October 15`) still won't fit on one line in the table, click and drag the vertical border farther to the right. Be sure to wait until the sizing pointer is displayed before you click and drag the border.

4 **Position the insertion point inside the first cell of the table.**

5 **Choose Table, Table AutoFormat.**

The Table AutoFormat dialog box is displayed (see Figure 1.7). A list of available formats appears on the left side of the dialog box. When you choose a format, the sample table changes to show the new format.

Figure 1.7
The Table AutoFormat
dialog box.

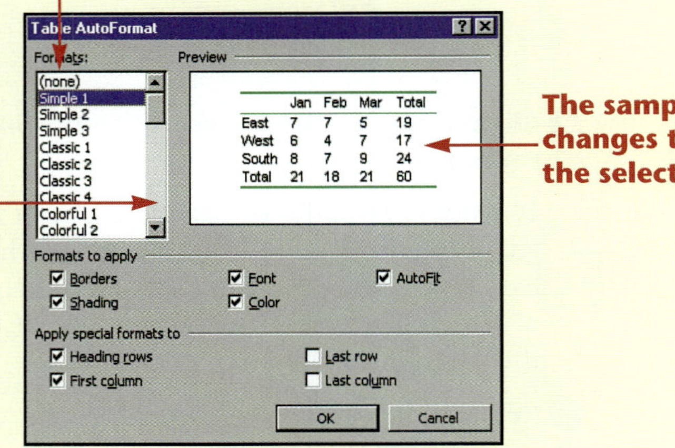

6 **Press ↓ several times.**

Take a minute and scroll through the list so that you can see the variety of styles available.

7 **Select `Colorful 2` (by clicking it once) in the list of Formats; then choose OK.**

The Colorful 2 style is applied to the table, making it look like Figure 1.8. The table has white text against red fill column headings, italicized column headings, an italicized left column, and a yellow background for the table content.

Figure 1.8
The table with the
Colorful 2 style.

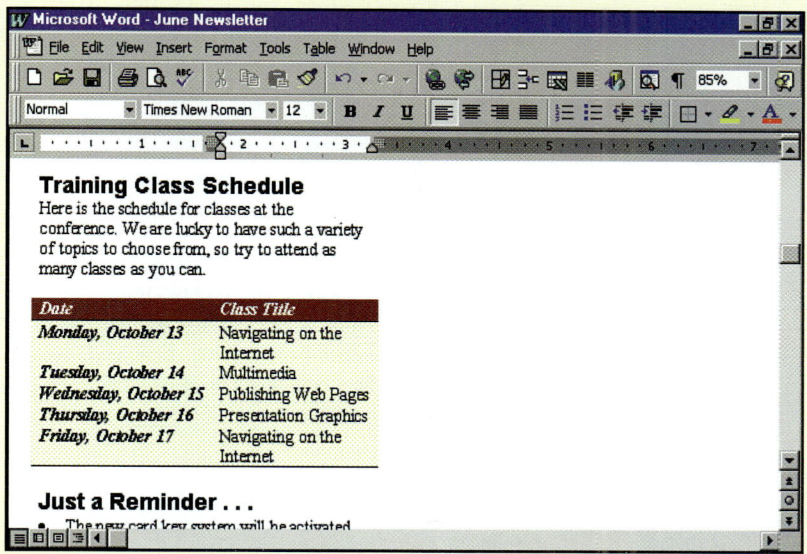

8 **Save your work and keep the** `June Newsletter` **file open to use in the next lesson, where you learn to perform calculations in a table.**

Jargon Watch

A **vertical border** separates two columns in a table. A **sizing pointer** is displayed when the mouse passes over a vertical border. When you see this pointer, you can click and drag the border to resize column widths in a table. You can also click and drag the outermost vertical borders to change the table margins.

Inside Stuff

In this lesson, you learned how to adjust the column widths by clicking and dragging the vertical border between columns. You can also adjust the height of a row by clicking and dragging the horizontal border between rows. Position the mouse pointer over a horizontal border and wait until the sizing pointer is displayed; then click and drag up or down to adjust the row height. (Clicking and dragging horizontal borders only works in Page Layout view.)

You can also use the Cell Height and Width dialog box to format rows and columns in a table. Choose Table, and then choose Cell Height and Width to open the dialog box. The Row page enables you to move to each row in the table and set the options for that row. You can align table rows at the left margin, centered between margins, or at the right margin of the page. You can set an indent amount, and you can choose to allow the row to break across pages if necessary. You can also set a specific row height on the Row page.

Click the Column tab to switch to the Column page, which enables you to move across the columns in a table and specify a particular width (in inches) for each. This page has an AutoFit option that automatically adjusts the width of the column to accommodate the contents.

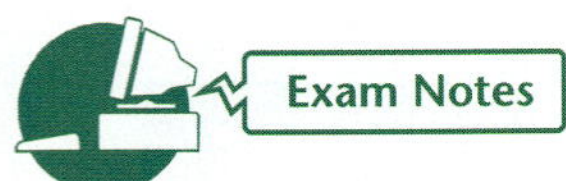

If a table's formatting has no borders, you can display nonprinting gridlines on-screen to make it easier to work with the table. If the gridlines are not already showing, choose Table, Show Gridlines to display the gridlines. Choose Table, Hide Gridlines to turn the gridlines off.

The fastest method for formatting a table is to use the automatic formatting options. However, if you want to format your table manually, apply shading and borders by using the Borders and Shading dialog box or the Borders button on the Formatting toolbar.

To apply border options quickly, select the cells you want to border (or choose Table, Select Table to select the entire table) and click the Borders button drop-down arrow on the Formatting toolbar. Select the border you wish from the drop-down menu. You learn more about borders and shading in Project 2, "Advanced Table Features."

When you do apply formatting manually, you'll find that knowing how to quickly select portions of a table is very helpful. Use these methods:

- To select a single cell, double-click within the cell.

- To select an entire row, position your cursor in the left margin of the row. When your cursor changes to a white arrow pointing toward the row (pointing right), click once with your mouse. The row is now selected and any formatting options you choose apply to the entire row (including shading, borders, and font formatting, such as bold).

- To select an entire column, position your cursor at the top of the column, just outside of the top border or gridline of the table. When your cursor changes to a black arrow pointing down toward the column, click once with your mouse. The column is now selected, and any formatting options you choose apply to the entire column.

- To select the entire table, position your insertion point anywhere within the table and choose Table, Select Table. Alternately, position your insertion point anywhere within the table and choose Table, Select Table from the menu.

Lesson 4: Calculating Values in a Table

Word's Table feature includes built-in *spreadsheet functions* that you can use to perform mathematical calculations. The most common calculation, the SUM formula, adds *values* together to produce a total.

At the bottom of the newsletter, another table lists the amount of materials that were recycled in a year. The first column lists the material; the second column shows the number of pounds for each item. Try entering values and calculating a total in the table now.

Spreadsheet functions
In spreadsheet programs, the most commonly performed numeric calculations (such as adding a column of numbers and averaging) are already set up for you to use.

Value
A numeric cell entry.

1 **At the bottom of the `June Newsletter` file, position the insertion point in the second row of the second column in the second table (in the first blank cell).**

This table has already been formatted with the Classic 2 style in the Table AutoFormat dialog box. The left column and the column headings are shaded (see Figure 1.9). In the left column, text is aligned on the left side of the cell. In the right column, the numeric cells have been formatted to align the values on the right side of the cell.

Figure 1.9
In this table, the values will align flush right.

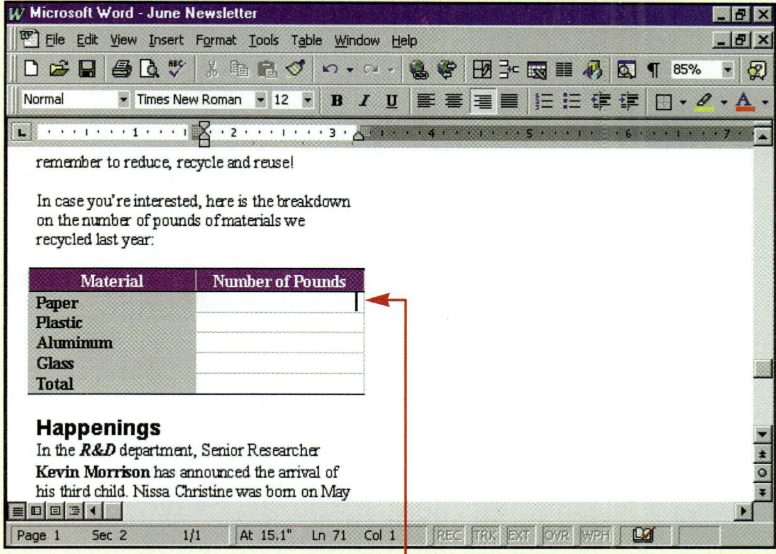

Position the insertion point here

2 **Type `355,127` and press ⬇.**

This is the number of pounds of paper recycled last year. Pressing ⬇ places the entry in the cell and moves you to the next row in the column. Make sure that you press ⬇ to move down to the next cell. If you press `⏎Enter`, Word inserts a blank line in the cell instead of moving you to the next cell.

3 **Type `111,098` and press ⬇.**

This is the number of pounds of plastic that were recycled last year.

4 **Type `75,842` and press ⬇.**

5 **Type `73,951` and press ⬇.**

This completes the typing of the amounts for the recycled materials. Your table should now look like Figure 1.10.

continues

To Calculate Values in a Table (continued)

Figure 1.10
The table with the values entered.

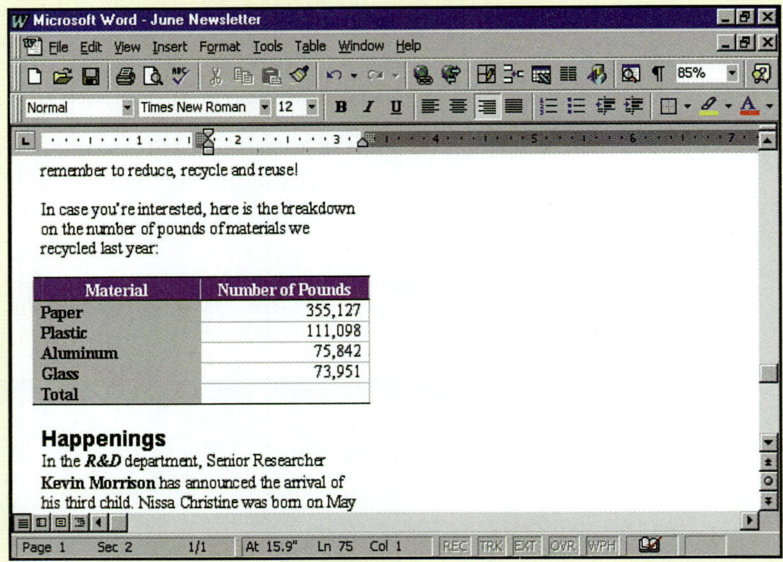

The insertion point should be displayed in the last cell in the second column (B6). If it isn't, click in this cell to move the insertion point now. You need to insert a formula to calculate the total amount here.

6 **Choose T̲able, F̲ormula.**

The Formula dialog box is displayed with the suggested formula (see Figure 1.11). Word assumes that you want to add the numbers in the column and place the total inside this cell. Because Word has assumed correctly in this case, you don't need to change the entry in the F̲ormula box. Next, you choose a format for the total amount.

Figure 1.11
The Formula dialog box with the suggested formula.

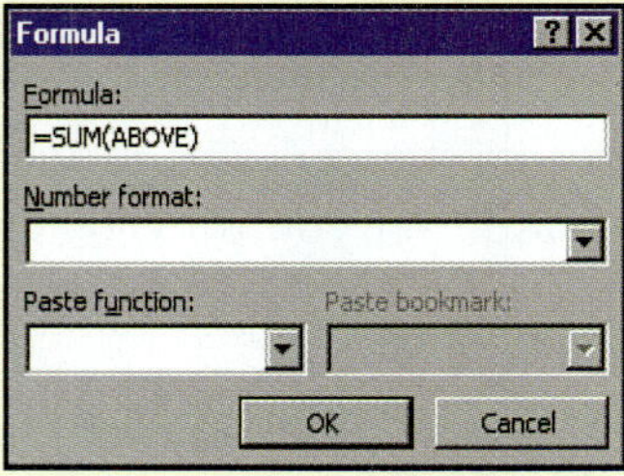

7 **Choose N̲umber Format.**

Choosing N̲umber Format opens a drop-down list of formats for the result of the calculation.

8 **Choose the first format in the list,** #,##0.

This format inserts a comma if you have a number greater than or equal to 1,000. If the amount is zero, a zero will be shown.

9 Choose OK.

Choosing OK inserts the result of the SUM formula into the cell, using the chosen format. The table should now look like Figure 1.12.

Figure 1.12
The table with the total amount calculated.

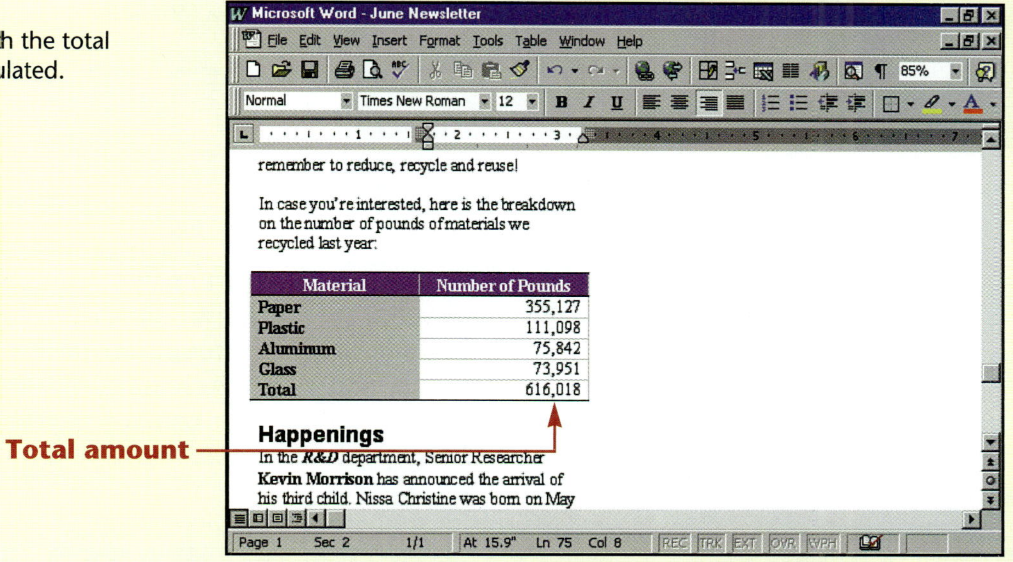

Total amount

10 Save your work and keep the June Newsletter file open to use in the next lesson, where you learn to insert a picture.

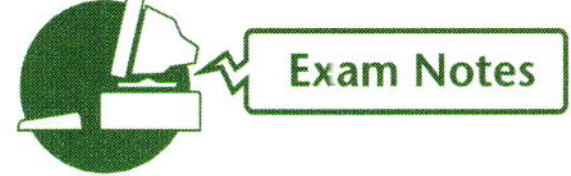

Calculations that you perform in a table resemble operations you perform in Microsoft Excel. The results of calculations in Word appear in a field. When you change data in the referenced cells of a formula, update the calculation by selecting the field and pressing F9.

As discussed previously, formulas are entered into a table using the Formula dialog box. When the dialog box appears, Word tries to anticipate your needs by entering a formula for you. If you don't want to use that formula, delete it and enter your own or choose a function from the Paste Function drop-down list (see Figure 1.13). If you click the Paste Function drop-down list with the mouse after clicking the What's this? button on dialog box, you see a button that opens a list of function definitions.

Click here, then click the Paste Function text box to get help with available functions in Word

Figure 1.13
Type formulas or use the Paste Function feature to create formulas in the Formula dialog box.

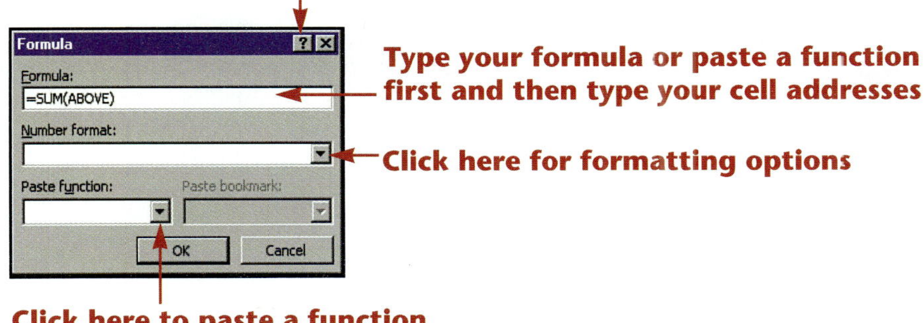

Type your formula or paste a function first and then type your cell addresses

Click here for formatting options

Click here to paste a function

continues

When building formulas, reference the contents of a table cell in the Formula: field of the Formula dialog box by typing the cell addresses in parentheses. Each cell has an address, which is a combination of its column name and it's row number. The first column on the left of the table is column A, the second is B, and so forth. The first row of a table is row 1, the second is 2, and so forth. Therefore, the address (or cell reference) of the cell in the third row down and second column across is B3.

Use the number format drop-down list to select a format for the numbers in your table (for example, currency and percentage).

Lesson 5: Inserting a Picture

Word makes it easy for you to insert a wide variety of graphic images into your documents by either creating your own images or importing graphics files from other programs. Word accepts most popular graphic file formats, including WordPerfect Graphic Files, files found on most online services (GIF, JPEG), Windows Bitmap, and Windows Metafile. The Office 97 suite includes the Microsoft 3.0 Clip Gallery that contains a variety of clip art, pictures, sounds, and video clips. Try inserting a picture into the newsletter now.

To Insert a Picture

1 **In the June Newsletter file, position the insertion point at the beginning of the paragraph under the heading Recycling Effort Pays Off.**

This is where you want to insert an illustrative picture.

2 **Choose Insert, Picture, Clip Art.**

The Microsoft Clip Gallery 3.0 dialog box is displayed (see Figure 1.14). There are four tabs in this dialog box: Clip Art, Pictures, Sounds, and Videos. The Clip Art page contains vector (or draw-type) images; the Pictures page contains scanned images, digital photographs, and other bitmaps; the Sounds page contains sound files; the Videos page contains video clips and animations.

If you have problems...

If your dialog box doesn't match the one shown in Figure 1.14, click the Clip Art tab to switch to the Clip Art page. Next, click the (All Categories) item at the top of the list of categories. If the images still don't match the ones shown in the figure, your system may have the additional images available on the MS Office 97 CD already installed in the Clip Gallery. Your system may also have images from other applications in the Clip Gallery.

Figure 1.14
You use the Microsoft Clip Gallery 3.0 dialog box to preview clip art, pictures, sounds, and video clips.

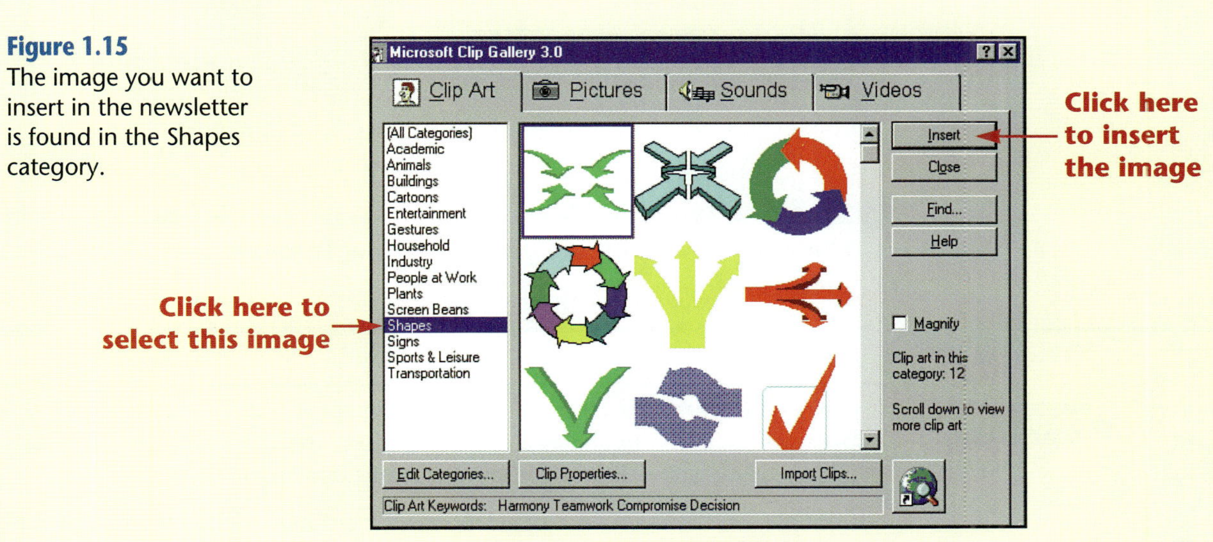

③ In the list of categories, click Shapes.

When you choose a category, only those images in the category are displayed in the preview window (refer to Figure 1.14). In this case, you want to use one of the arrow-based shapes.

④ Click the image in the left corner of the second row.

If you have additional images installed on your system, you may have to scroll down through the list to find the image shown in Figure 1.15.

Figure 1.15
The image you want to insert in the newsletter is found in the Shapes category.

continues

To Insert a Picture (continued)

5 Choose Insert.

Word inserts the picture at the insertion point (see Figure 1.16). The original size of the clip art is maintained, so you'll probably need to resize the image to fit within the available space. When you insert a picture in a document, Word automatically switches to Page Layout view. This view enables you to see how objects will be positioned on the printed page, which is helpful when you are working with graphics.

Notice that when you insert a clip art image in the document, a border with eight small squares appears around the picture. The squares—called sizing handles—enable you to increase and decrease the size of a picture.

Figure 1.16
The clip art image is inserted into the document in its original size.

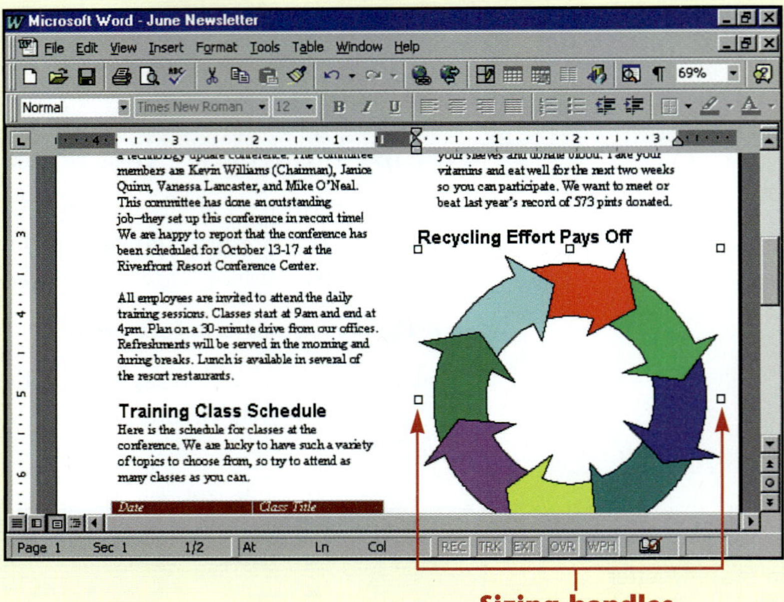

6 Save your work and keep the June Newsletter file open to use in the next lesson, where you learn how to move and resize a picture.

If you need to know the format of a selected image in the Clip Gallery, click the Clip Properties button to display a properties sheet. The Clip Properties dialog box details the name of the file, the file format, and its location on your system.

You must have the appropriate drivers installed on your computer to be able to play sound and video clips in the Clip Gallery (or in your documents). Some of the most commonly used drivers are installed automatically with Windows 95. If you still can't play a clip, check with the source of the clip for the necessary driver(s).

Lesson 6: Moving, Resizing, and Deleting a Picture

When you insert a picture into a document, Word maintains the original size of the image. You can easily resize the picture to suit your needs.

The easiest way to move and resize a picture is to use the mouse. When you click a picture, you select it. Sizing handles display on all four sides and at all four corners. The locations of the sizing handles indicate which way the graphic box will be resized. If you click and drag a sizing handle at the corner, you can resize the box in two directions at the same time. Moving a picture is easy; you just click and drag the picture to the new position.

The easiest way to delete a picture is to select it and press Del. If you want to move the picture to another page in your document, cut the picture by selecting it and pressing Ctrl+X, then position your cursor in the new desired location and paste the picture by pressing Ctrl−V.

In the company newsletter, you need to size the graphic box so that it takes up roughly one-third of the column width. In addition, you need to move the box into the paragraph so that the first two to three lines of text are above the picture and the rest of the lines wrap around it. Try moving and resizing the image now.

To Move and Resize a Picture

1 **In the June Newsletter file, position the mouse pointer on the sizing handle at the lower-right corner of the picture.**

The mouse pointer should change to a two-headed diagonal arrow (see Figure 1.17).

Figure 1.17
Click and drag a corner sizing handle to resize two sides at the same time.

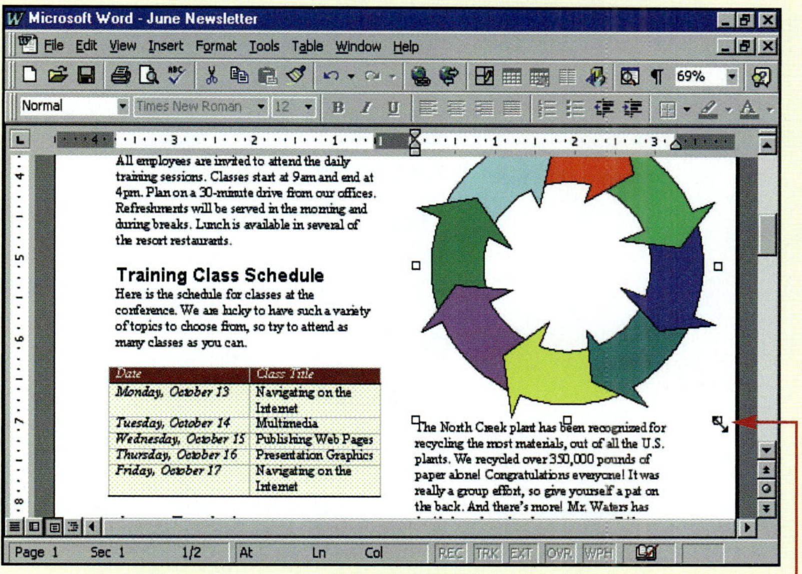

Date	Class Title
Monday, October 13	Navigating on the Internet
Tuesday, October 14	Multimedia
Wednesday, October 15	Publishing Web Pages
Thursday, October 16	Presentation Graphics
Friday, October 17	Navigating on the Internet

Two-headed diagonal arrow

continues

To Move and Resize a Picture   (continued)

2 Click and drag the sizing handle upward and to the left.

Resize the picture until it becomes roughly one-third of the width of the column. When you drag a **sizing handle**, a dotted guide line is displayed to show you how big the graphic box will be when you release the mouse button (see Figure 1.18). Dragging a corner handle causes Word to maintain the original proportions of the picture. If the height changes, the width adjusts automatically, and vice versa.

Figure 1.18
The dotted line acts as a guide while you resize the box.

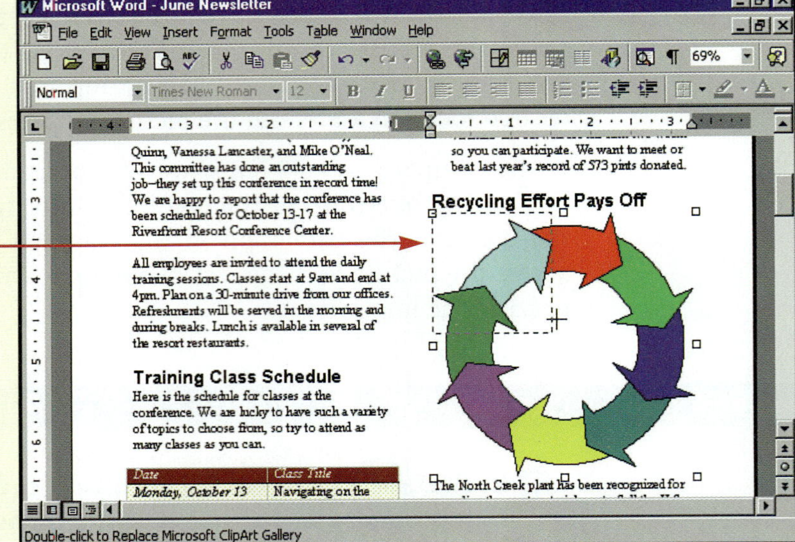

Guide line

3 Release the mouse button.

When you release the mouse button, Word resizes the picture to fit the new dimensions. Now, you want to move the picture down into the paragraph and have the text wrap around the picture. First, format the picture so the text wraps around the image.

4 Choose Format, Picture.

The Format Picture dialog box is displayed. All of the formatting options for pictures have been consolidated into this single dialog box. You need to switch to the Wrapping page.

5 Click the Wrapping tab.

The Wrapping page displays sample pages illustrating the differences in the Wrapping options (see Figure 1.19). To have the text wrap around the contours of the object itself, choose Tight. To have the text wrap around the object's bounding box (the border with the sizing handles), choose Square. In this case, you want the text to wrap around the object itself.

Figure 1.19
The Wrapping page contains all the different options for wrapping text around or through pictures.

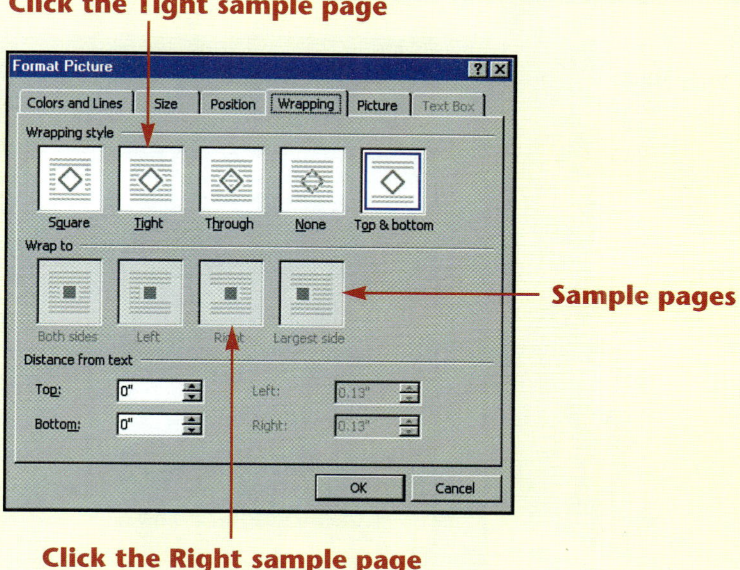

6 **Choose Tight.**

When you choose Tight, the items in the Wrap section become available. In this example, you want the text to wrap on the right side of the picture. If you want to position the picture in the middle of a paragraph and have the text wrap around both sides, you need to choose Both.

7 **Choose Right and then OK.**

Next, you want to drag the picture down into the paragraph so that the first three lines are above the picture and the other lines are below the picture.

8 **Click and drag the picture into the middle of the paragraph.**

You may have to make small adjustments to move the picture to this position. When you finish, your newsletter should look similar to Figure 1.20. Notice how the text wraps around the contour of the arrows, not around the invisible **bounding box**.

9 **Click inside the document window.**

Clicking inside the document window deselects the picture. You have now completed the newsletter.

10 **Save your work and print a copy of June Newsletter. If requested by your instructor, print two copies. Close June Newsletter after printing it.**

If you have completed your session on the computer, exit Word and shut down Windows before turning off the computer. Otherwise, continue with the sections "Checking Your Skills" and "Applying Your Skills."

continues

To Move and Resize a Picture   (continued)

Figure 1.20
The text of the paragraph wraps around the graphic box.

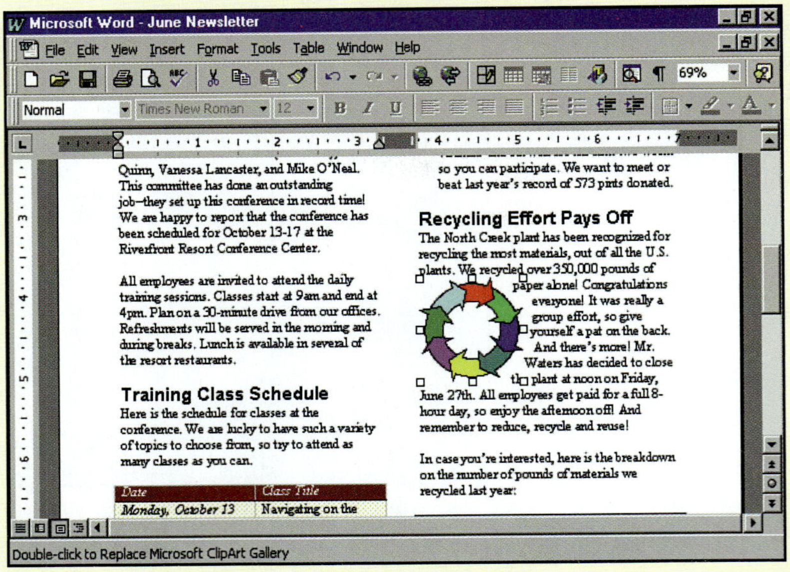

Sizing handles are small squares on a picture border that you use to size a picture. A corner sizing handle sizes in two directions at the same time. The **bounding box** is an invisible box around a graphic file. By default, text wraps around the bounding box. If you choose to wrap text around the contour of the graphic, the text is placed next to the actual contours of the image, not the bounding box.

If you prefer, you can right-click a picture and choose Format Picture from the shortcut menu to open the Format Picture dialog box.

You can choose from a color palette for the fill (or background) to be used in the picture. There is also a variety of fill patterns, and you can choose a foreground and background color for them. You can also choose a line color and pattern if you decide you want a border around the picture.

Moving and sizing a picture with the mouse is fast and easy, but it can be difficult to be precise. Use the Size and Position pages of the Format Picture dialog box to type in exact measurements.

If necessary, you can crop a picture from any side and you can change the brightness and contrast settings in the Picture page of the Format Picture dialog box. See Project 3 for more information on sizing and cropping a picture.

Project Summary

To	Do This
Change to Page Layout view	Choose View, Page Layout
Change to Normal view	Choose View, Normal.
Create a table	Click the Insert Table button. Click and drag the mouse to select the number of rows and columns you need. You can also choose Table, Insert Table, and then specify the number of rows and columns in the Insert Table dialog box. Finally, you can choose Draw Table from the Table menu and use the pencil pointer to draw the table border, columns, and rows.
Type text in a table	Position the insertion point in the cell and then type the text.
Move forward one cell	Press Tab.
Move backward one cell	Press Shift+Tab.
Move the insertion point to a cell	Click in the cell.
Select cells	Click and drag over the cells.
Select a row	Position your cursor in the left margin of the row and click.
Select a column	Position your cursor outside of the top border of the column and click.
Adjust the width of a column	Position the mouse pointer over the vertical border between the columns. When the sizing pointer is displayed, click and drag the mouse to adjust the column width. Release the mouse button to resize the column.
Adjust the height of a row	Position the mouse pointer over the horizontal border between the rows. When the sizing pointer is displayed, click and drag the mouse to adjust the row height. Release the mouse button to resize the row.
Use the Table AutoFormat feature	Position the insertion point in the table. Choose Table, Table AutoFormat. Select a style from the list of Formats and choose OK.
Add a column of numbers	Position the insertion point in the cell below the column of numbers. Choose Table, Formula. The Formula text box should contain =SUM(ABOVE). Choose Number Format and pick a format for the total figure. Choose OK.
Insert a picture	Position the insertion point where you want the picture inserted. Choose Insert, Picture, Clip Art. Click the Clip Art tab to switch to that page. Double-click a clip art image to insert it in the document.

continues

To	Do This
Resize a picture	Click the picture. When the sizing handles display, position the mouse pointer over a sizing handle. Click and drag the mouse to size the picture. Release the mouse button.
Move a picture	Click the picture. Move the mouse pointer into the picture. A four-headed arrow appears. Click and drag the mouse to move the picture. Release the mouse button to drop the picture. Alternately, select the picture and cut it, then paste it in the new desired position.
Delete a picture	Select the picture and press Del.
Format a picture	Click the picture. Choose Format, Picture.
Set the wrap options	Click the picture. Choose Format, Picture, and then click the Wrapping tab.

Checking Your Skills

True/False

For each of the following, check *T* or *F* to indicate whether the statement is true or false.

__T __F   **1.** The Table AutoFormat feature has a series of styles that you can choose from to format a table.

__T __F   **2.** Tables can be used to format text and numbers into columns.

__T __F   **3.** The spreadsheet functions in Word are similar to those seen in powerful spreadsheet programs such as Excel.

__T __F   **4.** You can wrap text around both sides of a picture.

__T __F   **5.** A table formula is inserted as a field.

__T __F   **6.** By default, tables are created with a single-line border.

__T __F   **7.** Gridlines print automatically in a table.

__T __F   **8.** Clicking and dragging horizontal borders works only in Page Layout view.

__T __F   **9.** You cannot update the results of a calculation in a table.

__T __F **10.** If you type an entry that is too long for a table cell, Word displays an error message.

Multiple Choice

Circle the letter of the correct answer for each of the following questions.

1. Which of the following items can be inserted into a document?

   a. Video clips

   b. Sound clips

   c. Clip art files

   d. All the above

2. What is the most commonly used calculation in the Table feature?

   a. AVERAGE

   b. MIN VALUE

   c. MAX VALUE

   d. SUM

3. What feature do you use to position text on all sides of a picture in a document?

   a. Borders and Lines

   b. Wrapping

   c. Text Placement

   d. Picture Positioning

4. Pressing ⬆Shift + Tab⇄ moves you where within a table?

   a. One cell to the right

   b. One cell to the left

   c. To the top cell of a table

   d. To the bottom cell of a table

5. Clicking and dragging which type of border adjusts the row height?

   a. Vertical

   b. Sizing

   c. Horizontal

   d. Bounding

6. If you choose 6 X 2 in the grid after you click the Insert Table button, what size table is created?

   a. Six columns and two rows

   b. Six inches tall by two inches wide

   c. Six centimeters tall by two centimeters wide

   d. Six rows by two columns

7. What happens if you press Tab⇄ in the last cell of a table?

   a. Word moves into the document

   b. A new row is automatically created.

   c. A new column is automatically created

   d. You receive an error message

8. How do you recalculate a selected table?

   a. Press F9

   b. Choose Table, Recalculate

   c. Click the Recalculate button on the Standard toolbar

   d. Click the Recalculate button in the Tables dialog box

9. How do you size a picture to exact measurements?

   a. By using the mouse

   b. By using the Size and Position pages of the Format Picture dialog box

c. By using the drop-down list that displays when you click the Size Picture button

d. By using the ruler to accurately measure the picture

10. What is a quick way to position the insertion point in a specific table cell?

a. Click in the cell

b. Use the Go To command

c. Use the <u>E</u>dit, <u>F</u>ind command

d. Click the Insert Cell button on the Standard toolbar

Completion

In the blank provided, write the correct answer for each of the following statements.

1. A(n) _____________ formula adds together a series of numbers.

2. The Microsoft _____________ contains clip art, pictures, sounds, and video clips that you can include in your documents.

3. A table _____________ is the intersection of a row and a column.

4. The cell address is composed of the column _____________ and the row _____________.

5. You can resize a picture by clicking and dragging the sizing _____________.

6. _____________ are non-printing borders that define table rows and columns onscreen.

7. When you insert a picture in a document, Word automatically switches to _____________ _____________ view.

8. The _____________ box is an invisible box around a graphic file.

9. When you are moving a picture, the mouse pointer displays as a _____________-_________ arrow.

10. To have text wrap around the contours of an object, choose the _____________ wrapping option.

Matching

In the blank next to each of the following terms or phrases, write the letter of the corresponding term or phrase. (Note that some letters may be used more than once.)

a. Cell Height and Width

b. Spreadsheet

c. Letters

_______ 1. Numeric cell entry

_______ 2. A view that shows how the document looks when printed

_______ 3. The view in which editing is fastest

_______ 4. Used to identify rows

d. Numbers   _______ **5.** Used to identify columns

e. Normal   _______ **6.** The dialog box that provides options for formatting rows and columns

f. Clip art

g. AutoFit   _______ **7.** Automatically adjusts the width of a column to accommodate its contents

h. Value

i. Table   _______ **8.** Graphics images

         _______ **9.** A series of rows and columns

j. Page Layout   _______ **10.** An accounting form that contains rows and columns

Applying Your Skills

Practice

The following exercises enable you to practice the skills you have learned in this project. Take a few minutes to work through these exercises now.

Adding Clip Art to an Invitation

Clip art can make any document more interesting, but it is particularly useful for fun documents such as an invitation. In this exercise, you insert a picture into an invitation document.

To add a picture to an invitation, follow these steps:

1. In Word for Windows, open Proj0102 from the Project-01 folder on the CD. Create a new folder on the disk where your instructor tells you to save your student files, and name it `Practices`. Save the Proj0102 document in the Practices folder as `Invitation`.

2. Change to Page Layout view.

3. Insert a blank line at the top of the document so that you have a place to insert the picture.

4. Open the Clip Art folder and choose an appropriate picture. For example, insert a picture of champagne popping or of balloons. If available, look in the Special Occasions category for clip art.

5. Preview the invitation to see how it fits on the page.

6. Delete the picture and insert a different one. If necessary, adjust the size and position of the picture to complement the invitation text.

7. Drag the picture to the bottom of the document, below the text.

8. Select the picture and choose Edit, Cut, then move the insertion point back up to the top of the document and choose Edit, Paste.

9. Preview the document again and make any necessary adjustments to the picture's position and size. (Hint: You can move or resize the picture in Print Preview. Click the Magnifier button to toggle it off, then click the picture to select it.)

10. Save the document and, if requested by your instructor, print it. Close the document when you are finished.

Adding Tables to a Loan Proposal

You can use tables to organize columns of numbers. You can create tables that automatically calculate totals and other functions. In this exercise, add tables to a loan proposal document.

To format the loan proposal, follow these steps:

1. Open the file Proj0103 from the Project-01 folder on the CD and save it in your Practices folder as Loan.

2. Between the second and third paragraphs of the main document, insert a table that is two columns wide by five rows high.

3. In the first cell of the first row, enter the title Anticipated Expenses.

4. In the remaining cells, enter the following data, beginning with cell A2. Remember to press Tab⇆ to move from one cell to the next:

Demolition	$10,000.00
Construction	$10,000.00
Decorating	$ 2,500.00
Total	

5. In the last cell of the second column, create a formula to calculate the total anticipated expenses. Click in the cell where you want the result to appear, then choose Table, Formula. Word automatically enters the formula for adding the column of values. Click OK.

6. Using the AutoFormat feature, format the table with the Professional Format. Make sure the AutoFit option is selected.

7. Between the fourth and fifth paragraphs, insert a table to accommodate the following data (six rows by four columns), then enter the data:

	This Year	Next Year	Increase
Quarter 1	$20,000.00	$25,000.00	
Quarter 2	$22,000.00	$26,000.00	
Quarter 3	$23,000.00	$27,000.00	
Quarter 4	$24,000.00	$28,000.00	
Totals			

8. In columns two and three of the sixth row, use the SUM function to create formulas to calculate the total for each year. Click in the cell where you want the result to appear, then choose Table, Formula. Word automatically enters the formula for adding the column of values. Click OK.

9. In rows two through five in the fourth column, enter a formula to calculate the increase from this year to next year. Remember, you reference cells using the letter of the column and the number of the row, so the top left cell in a table is cell A1. To enter the formula for calculating the increase in Quarter 1, click in cell D2 (the cell at the intersection of the fourth column (D) and the second row (2), then choose

Table, Formula. In the Formula text box, type =C2-B2. Select the number format for dollar values with decimal places from the Number format drop-down list, then click OK. The formula for Quarter 2 will be =C3-B3. For Quarter 3 it will be =C4-B4, and for Quarter 4 it will be =C5-B5.

10. Format the table to match the other table, then preview the document.

11. Check the spelling and grammar and then save the document. If requested by your instructor, print it. Then close the document.

Creating a Schedule of Activities

A table is a useful format for lining up information in a schedule. In this exercise, use a table to create a schedule of activities for a symposium.

To create a schedule, follow these steps:

1. Open the file Proj0104 from the Project-01 folder on the CD, and save it in your Practices folder as `Schedule`.

2. Insert a table to accommodate the following data:

Time	Monday	Tuesday	Wednesday	Thursday	Friday
7:30 - 8:00	Breakfast	Breakfast	Breakfast	Breakfast	Breakfast
8:00 - 9:00	Round Table	Panel	Lecture	Panel	Round Table
9:00 - 12:00	Panel	Round Table	Panel	Round Table	Panel
12:00 - 1:30	Lunch	Lunch	Lunch	Lunch	Lunch
1:30 - 3:00	Seminar	Seminar	Seminar	Seminar	Seminar
3:00 - 5:30	Free	Free	Free	Free	Free
5:30 - 7:00	Reception	Free	Free	Free	Reception
7:00	Free	Free	Free	Free	Dinner

3. Enter the data in the table.

4. Use the Grid 8 AutoFormat to format the table so that it looks good on the page and is easy to read.

5. Insert a picture at the bottom of the document (below the table) to enhance the appearance of the schedule. Use a picture that captures the spirit of the symposium, such as shaking hands.

6. Preview the document and adjust the size, spacing, and position of the picture and the table as necessary.

7. Check the spelling and grammar in the document, then save it. If requested by your instructor, print it. Close the document when you have finished.

Creating an Invoice

A table is also useful for setting up a document to use as an invoice. You can easily align information in columns and rows, and you can calculate values. In this exercise, create an invoice for music lessons. Use calculating fields to total some of the values. You can insert a picture to customize the invoice.

To create an invoice, follow these steps:

1. Open the file Proj0105 from the Project-01 folder on the CD and save it in your Practices folders as `Invoice`.

2. Insert a table to accommodate the following data:

Date	Description	Amount
5/1/99	1/2 hr. Piano	$15.00
5/8/99	1/2 hr. Trombone	$20.00
5/15/99	1/2 hr. Piano	$15.00
5/22/99	1/2 hr. Trombone	$20.00
Total		
Total Piano		
Total Trombone		

3. Create a calculating field to total the amount due. Click in the cell at the intersection of the third column and the sixth row (C6), choose Table, Formula, then click OK.

4. Use the SUM function to enter one formula for calculating the total amount due for piano lessons, and one for the amount due for trombone lessons. First, click in the cell at the intersection of the third column and the seventh row (C7) and choose Table, Formula. Delete all but the equals sign from the Formula text box. Select SUM from the Paste function drop-down list. Type C2,C4 in the Formula text box, within the parentheses. The formula should look like =SUM(C2,C4). Click OK. In cell C8, use the same process, but enter C3,C5 in the parentheses.

5. Use the Contemporary AutoFormat to format the table.

6. Select the entire table and click the Center button on the Formatting toolbar. This centers the table on the page.

7. Select the entire table and select 18 from the Font Size drop-down list. This increases the font size in the entire table.

8. Adjust the width of each column so that each row is only one line high. Remember, you can drag the column border to change the column width.

9. Insert a picture in the bottom left corner of the document to enhance the invoice. Choose a picture that has something to do with the type of business, such as musical notes, a piano, or a trombone. If necessary, adjust the size of the picture to fit the document.

10. Preview the invoice and make adjustments to the size, position, and spacing of the picture and the table, if necessary.

11. Check the spelling and grammar in the document, then save the document and, if requested by your instructor, print it. Then close the document.

Adding Art to a Letter

When you insert a picture at the top of a document, it can be part of a letterhead or logo. Insert a picture into a letter now.

To edit a letter, follow these steps:

1. Open the file named Proj0106 from the Project-01 folder on the disk, and save it in your Practices folder as CTA Letter.

2. Replace the date with the current date and replace the text (Student's Name) with your name.

3. Insert a Clip Art picture in the top left corner of the document. Choose one of the pictures in the People at Work category that depicts people at a computer.

4. Select the picture and press Del$.

5. Insert a different picture form the People at Work category.

6. Resize the picture so that it is approximately 1 1/2 inches high. Let the width adjust automatically to stay in proportion.

7. Adjust the text wrapping so that the picture is to the left of the name and address of the association, on the same lines. (Hint: Try the Square or Tight wrapping setting.)

8. Adjust the position of the picture in the document so the bottom of the picture is even with the address line of text.

9. Select the picture and click the Cut button, then move the insertion point to the right side of the text and click the Paste button.

10. Preview the document.

11. Move the picture back to the left side of the text so that the picture, association name and address look like a letterhead with logo across the top of the letter.

12. Save the document and, if requested by your instructor, print a copy. Then close the document.

Challenge

The following challenges enable you to use your problem-solving skills. Take time to work through these exercises now.

Adding a Table to a Letter

You want to use the formatting techniques you have learned to improve the appearance of a letter to be sent to those who request information from a company called Computer Training Concepts. Open the file Proj0107 from the CD. Create a new folder called `Challenges` in the location where your instructor tells you to store your student files. Save the Proj0107 document in the Challenges folder as `Cover Letter`.

Add a table at the end of the document, listing course descriptions. The following information should be included in the table:

Excel I	This course teaches you the basics of creating spreadsheets, including using functions, creating simple graphs, and using database features.
Excel II	In this advanced-level course, you learn to automate your work by using macros, linking worksheets and creating summary reports, and using the Scenario Manager.
Word for Windows I	You learn the basics of word processing, including creating, formatting, and editing documents. In this class, you also create mail merge documents.
Word for Windows II	In this course, you learn more advanced Word features including working with styles, creating tables, and using macros.

Apply the Classic 4 AutoFormat style. You need to remove the check mark from the Heading rows checkbox in the Table AutoFormat dialog box because this table does not have a heading row. Preview the document and adjust spacing as necessary. Check the spelling and grammar, then save it. If requested by your instructor, print the letter. Close the file when you have finished.

Adding a Picture to a Main Street Deli Sign

You decide to insert a picture to improve the appearance of a sign you created for the Main Street Deli. Open the Proj0108 file from the Project-01 folder on the CD and save it in your Challenges folder as `Deli`.

Insert a picture into the document. The picture you select should have something to do with eating, or with Main Street. Depending on the clip art you have available, you might find a sandwich, a cup of coffee, a restaurant building, or a traffic light. You decide how to size and locate the picture, and what type of text wrap to use. Practice deleting the picture and inserting a different picture. Practice using the Cut and Paste commands to move the picture.

Save the document and print it. Close the document when you have finished.

Adding a Table to a Business Proposal Document

You can use a table to organize and total proposed budget information in a Business Proposal Document. Open the file Proj0109 from the Project-01 folder on the CD and save it in your Challenges folder as `Proposal`.

Create a table that is two columns by five rows after the paragraph of text under the Budget heading. Title the table Proposed Budget, then enter the following two columns of data:

```
Personnel              $200,000.00

Materials              $95,000.00

Travel                 $150,000.00

Total:
```

Set up a calculating field to display the total. Change the Materials cost to $89,000.00, then update the total. Use the Simple 3 AutoFormat to format the table. Preview the document and adjust spacing as required. Check the spelling and grammar, then save your changes. If requested by your instructor, print the document and close it.

Creating a Computer Training Concepts Price List

You need to set up a simple price list for the courses Computer Training Concepts (CTC) offers. Open the file Proj0110 from the Project-01 folder on the CD and save it in your Challenges folder as `Prices`. Create a table that is three columns by eleven rows. Enter the information below:

```
Course                 Members        Discounted Price

Excel I                $90

Excel II               $90

Excel III              $95

Word I                 $90

Word II                $90

Word III               $95

Web Publishing I       $99

Internet Explorer I    $95

Microsoft Office       $95

Average Price
```

Enter a formula in each cell of the third column to calculate the discounted price (Hint: Member price minus 10% of the member price. For the Excel I course, the formula will be =B2-(B2*10%). For the Excel II course, the formula will be =B3-(B3*10%). Increase the row number for each new formula.) Select the Average function from the Paste function drop-down list to create a formula to find the average cost of a course for members, and based on the discounted price. (In cells B11 and B12, enter =AVERAGE(ABOVE).)

Use AutoFormat to format the table. Add the heading Course Prices Fall 1999 on a line above the table. Format the text `Course Prices` flush left, and the text `Fall 1999` flush right. Use 18-point Bold Arial.

Add the sentence `10% Discount is offered for three or more students from the same company.` on a line below the table. Format the sentence with 12-point Arial, underlined.

Preview the document and make any necessary adjustments to spacing, positioning and page setup. Save the document, check the spelling and grammar, then, if requested by your instructor, print a copy. Close the document when you are finished.

Adding a Table and a Picture to a Health Club Membership Renewal Document

You decide to add a table to a Membership Renewal document for a health club to explain the annual membership fees. You also insert a picture to enhance the appearance of the document. Open the Proj0111 from the Project-01 folder on the CD and save it in your Challenges folder with the name `Renewal`.

Replace the date with the current date, and the text (Student's Name) with your own name. On the last line of the document, type the sentence `The following table explains our membership rates.` Then create a table that includes the following data:

Type of Membership	Annual Dues	Annual Dues Less 10% Discount
Basic	$600	$540
Basic Plus	$800	$720
Extended	$1000	$900
Premier	$1200	$1080

Insert a formula in the third column cells to calculate the discounted price. Use the Contemporary AutoFormat style to format the table.

Insert an appropriate sports picture at the top of the document, such as a runner. Adjust the size, position, and text wrapping of the picture so that it fits in with the letter. Preview the document, check the spelling and grammar, then save your changes. If requested by your instructor, print it. Close the file when you have finished.

You have completed the project and the associated lessons, as well as the "Checking Your Skills" and "Applying Your Skills" sections. Now use the PinPoint software evaluation mode to assess your comprehension of the specific exam tasks you have just learned. You can also use the PinPoint Trainer Mode and the Show Me tutorials to practice these specific exam tasks.

Project 2

Two

Advanced Table Features

Creating an Agenda for a Conference

In this Project, you learn how to:

Objectives   **Required Activities**

➤ Insert Rows and Columns into a Table

➤ Delete and Move Rows and Columns

➤ Change a Column's Width

➤ Format Text in a Table

➤ Align a Column of Numbers on Decimal Points

➤ Merge Cells in a Table

➤ Add Borders and Shading to a Table

➤ Add Figures and Sort Rows in a Table   … … … … …   Sort Lists, Paragraphs, and Tables

Why Would I Do This?

magine that you are creating an agenda for a two-day orientation conference for new employees. You need to create a list of days, times, speakers, discussion topics, and other related information. To make this information easy to read and understand, you arrange it in rows and columns. You should already know how to create a table, so this project concentrates on formatting the table specific to this project.

Now it is time to finish the table so that you can distribute it to everyone attending the conference. This might mean adding or removing rows and columns, adjusting column widths to accommodate information better, or dressing up the table with borders and other formatting. In this project, you use Word's advanced table features to put the finishing touches on the agenda. You can apply these techniques to any tables that you create in Word.

Lesson 1: Inserting Rows and Columns into a Table

When you first start a table, you usually have a basic idea of the number of rows and columns that you want. As you work with the table, however, you might realize that you need to insert more rows or columns or delete existing rows or columns. This lesson shows how to insert a row and column into a table.

To Insert a Row and a Column into a Table

1 **Open the Project-02 folder and the file called Proj0201 from this CD and save it as** `Orientation Agenda`.

2 **If Word is not already in Normal view, choose View, Normal.**

You just learned that a new speaker, Jack Clark, is available to speak on Monday morning, so you want to add a new meeting to the agenda. To do so, you need to add a row to the table. Jack will speak before Phil Jones, so you add his row between Phil's row and the column headings.

3 **Click the cell that contains the name** `Phil Jones`.

Word inserts a new row above the row that contains the insertion point. (You can actually place the insertion point anywhere in the second row, and Word inserts the new row above it.)

4 **Choose Table, Insert Rows.**

Word adds the new, blank row to the table (see Figure 2.1). When inserting a new row, Word highlights the entire row to show that the row is selected. You can deselect the row by clicking any cell of the table. Now you can add the information about Jack Clark's speaking session.

Figure 2.1
The table with a new row inserted.

New row ⟶

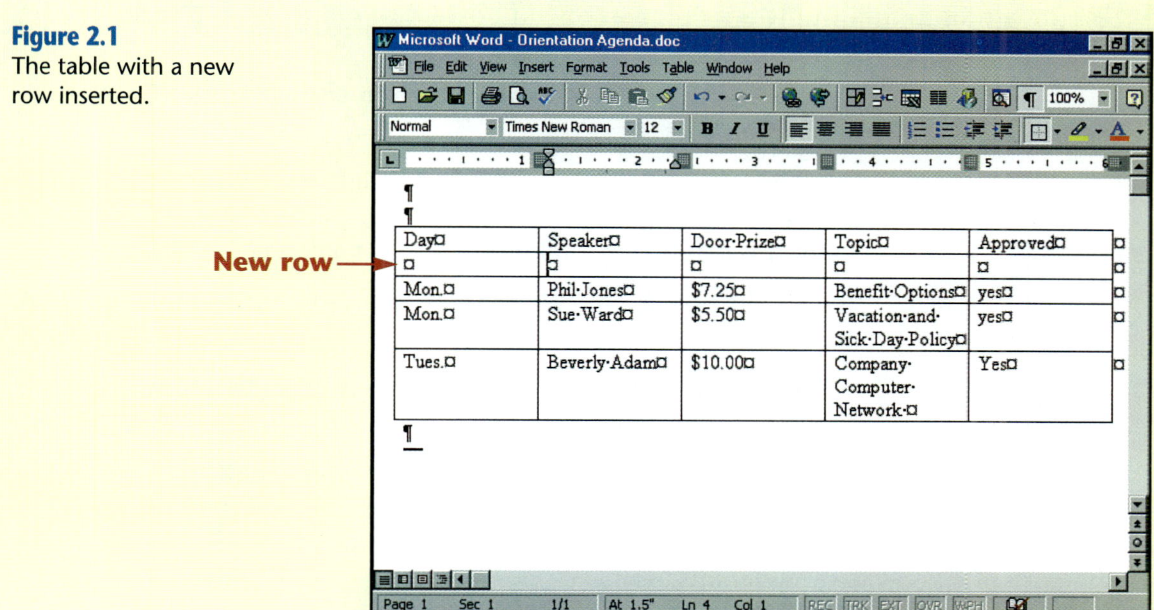

You might wonder why Figure 2.1 displays a box symbol in each cell. This is because the toolbar's Show/Hide button is selected. Some people like to see spaces, tabs, and paragraph returns represented by symbols.

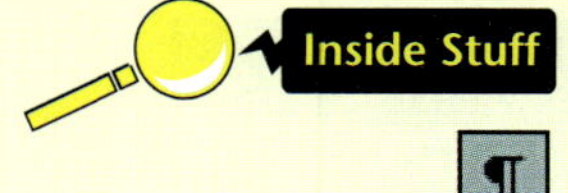
Inside Stuff

5 Click the first cell of the new row and type the following information in the appropriate cells:

Mon. Jack Clark $8.75 Corporate yes

Several people who reviewed the agenda mentioned that there is no column to indicate the times of the sessions. Add a new Time column between the Day and Speaker columns.

6 Click the cell that contains the word Speaker.

Word inserts a new column to the left of the column that contains the insertion point. You can actually place the insertion point anywhere in the second column, and Word inserts the new column to the left of it.

Inserting a column, compared to inserting a row, requires an extra step. Insert Rows is a default choice in the Table menu; Insert Columns is not. The Insert Columns choice appears only if you first select an entire column. Therefore, your next step is to select a column.

7 Choose Table, Select Column.

You have selected the second column and are ready to insert the new column. This time, use the shortcut menu.

continues

To Insert a Row and a Column into a Table   (continued)

8 **Right-click the selected column, then choose Insert Columns from the shortcut menu.**

Word inserts the new column to the left of the selected column, and the table expands to accommodate the new column. The new column is completely highlighted; click its first cell to deselect it.

You might not be able to see the entire table onscreen. To view all the table, adjust the Zoom control.

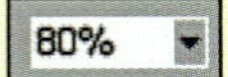

9 **If you cannot see the entire table, type 80 in the toolbar's Zoom control. Then press** Enter.

Now you can see the entire table. It should look like the one in Figure 2.2. (Note that the table extends into the right margin. In a later lesson, you delete a column so that the table fits inside the page's margins again.)

The Zoom control changed to 80 percent

Figure 2.2
A new column inserted in the table.

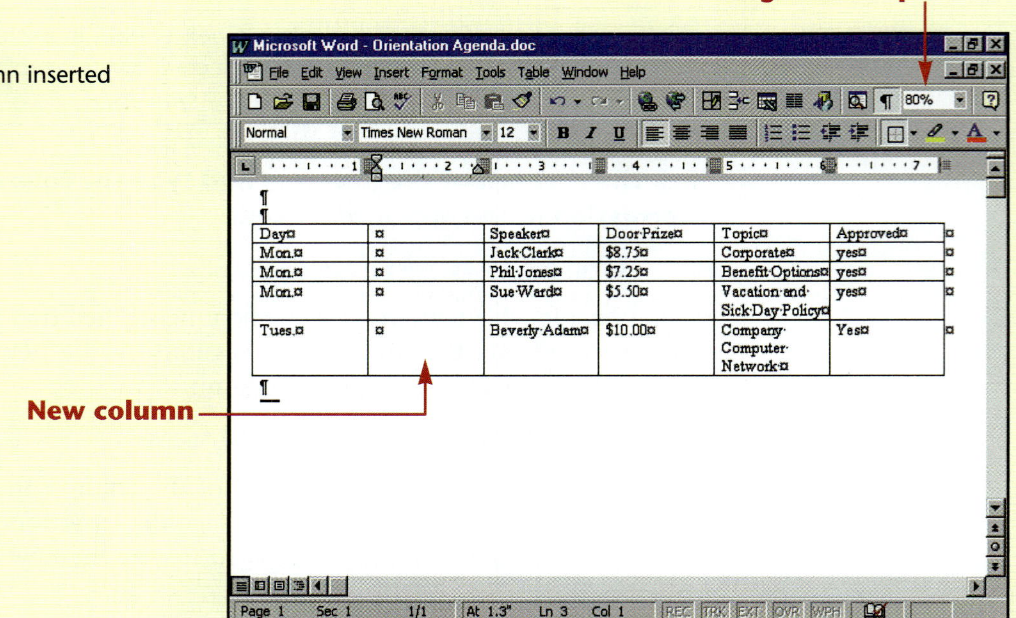

Day¤	¤	Speaker¤	Door·Prize¤	Topic¤	Approved¤	¤
Mon.¤	¤	Jack·Clark¤	$8.75¤	Corporate¤	yes¤	¤
Mon.¤	¤	Phil·Jones¤	$7.25¤	Benefit·Options¤	yes¤	¤
Mon.¤	¤	Sue·Ward¤	$5.50¤	Vacation·and·Sick·Day·Policy¤	yes¤	¤
Tues.¤	¤	Beverly·Adam¤	$10.00¤	Company·Computer·Network¤	Yes¤	¤

New column

10 **Type each of these items in the Time column, one time per cell:** Time, 8:00 AM, 10:00 AM, 1:00 PM, and 8:00 AM.

Your table should now look like the one shown in Figure 2.3.

Figure 2.3
The table with new entries.

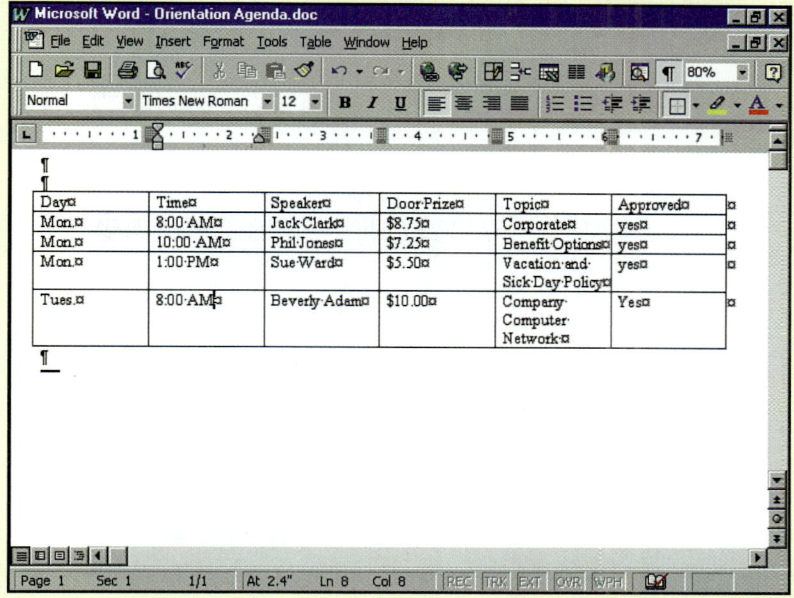

⑪ **Save the file and leave it open for the next lesson.**

Select the column to the right of where you want to insert new columns or select the row below where you want to insert new rows (to insert just one row, position your cursor in the row below where you want the new row, you don't have to select the row).

1. To insert more than one column or row, select the same number of rows or columns as you want to insert.

2. Right-click the mouse. From the pop-up menu, choose Insert Columns, or Insert Rows.

When you insert a row or column, Word places the new row above your current insertion point, and a new column to the left of your current insertion point. Inserting columns and rows in this way makes it impossible to add a new last row of a table, or a new last column of a table because, in this case, you need to add below and to the right of your cursor. Adding a new column as the last column and a new row as the last row is referred to as appending a column or row. To append columns or rows, follow these steps:

■ To append a column, position your cursor at the top of the markers just outside the current right-most column. Click once to select the column of markers (your cursor changes to a down-pointing arrow), then right-click and choose Insert Columns. Word automatically appends a new column at the right side of your table.

■ To append a row, place the insertion point in the last cell in the table and press the Tab⇥ key. Word automatically appends a new row at the bottom of your table.

You should be able to create the table in this sample document on your own. To review quickly, here's how to do so.

With the insertion point on a blank line, click the toolbar's Insert Table button, then drag to select a 4 by 5 table. When you release the mouse button, the table appears. Type the text in the cells, pressing Tab↹ or the arrow keys to move between cells.

You can also draw a table from scratch by choosing T̲able, Draw Ta̲ble. This feature enables you to draw a table in your document in much the same way that you would use a pencil to draw on paper. You can drag across the area of your document where you want the table to appear, and then use the special pointer to draw in the lines to add rows and columns. You learn more about this new border-drawing feature in Lesson 7.

Lesson 2: Deleting and Moving Rows and Columns

The Approved column is not part of the final agenda published for people attending the orientation sessions. You originally included that column to indicate whether each speaker had approved of his or her part in the sessions. Now that all speakers have approved their parts, you can delete that column. You also have just found out that Sue Ward is not available at 1:00 p.m. on Monday, so you need to delete her session from the agenda. You also move the Topic column next to the Speaker column.

To Delete a Row and a Column from a Table

❶ Click the first cell of the row for Sue Ward.

Start by deleting this row. When you delete a row, you must delete it in its entirety so you can click anywhere within the row. The Delete Rows option is available under the Table menu only when you have selected an entire row.

❷ Choose T̲able, Select R̲ow.

The entire row for Sue Ward is selected. Now you can delete the row.

❸ Choose T̲able, D̲elete Rows.

You can't simply press Del or ◄Backspace to remove a row or column from a table. Those actions delete text only within the selected row or column.

Word deletes the row for Sue Ward. Next, delete the Approved column.

❹ Click the first cell of the Approved column.

You must select the entire column. The Delete Columns option is available only when you have selected an entire column. Let's use the shortcut menu to delete a column.

5 **Choose Table, Select Column.**

6 **Right-click the selected columns, then choose Delete Columns from the shortcut menu.**

Word deletes the Approved column. You no longer need the reduced zoom onscreen because the table now fits between the page margins. You can change the zoom setting back to 100 percent.

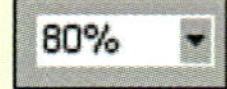

7 **Click the down arrow next to the Standard toolbar's Zoom control box. Select 100 percent from the drop-down list.**

It makes more sense for the Topic column to follow the Speaker column. To move a column, just select it and drag it to the new location.

8 **Place the insertion point in the Topic column, then choose Table, Select Column.**

9 **Click the selected column and, while holding down the mouse button, drag the pointer into the Door Prize column and release the mouse button.**

The Topic column is now next to the Speaker column. Dragging and dropping is the easiest way to move columns and rows. Your table should now look like the one in Figure 2.4.

Figure 2.4
The table after you delete a row and a column and move a column.

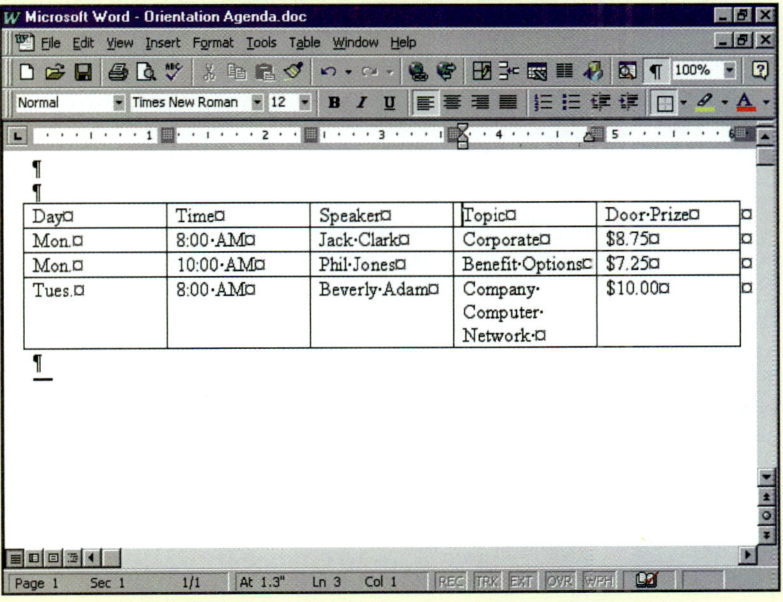

10 **Save the file and leave it open for the next lesson.**

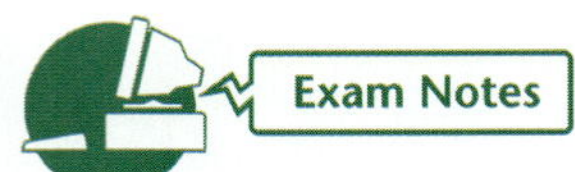

You can quickly delete rows and columns by first selecting them with your mouse and then right-clicking the mouse. From the pop-up menu, choose <u>D</u>elete Rows or <u>D</u>elete Columns.

The commands on the T<u>a</u>ble menu and the commands on the right-mouse pop-up menu change as you work in your document and table because they are context-sensitive. For example, if you select a column in a table, the <u>I</u>nsert Columns command is displayed but the <u>I</u>nsert Rows command is not.

To move a row or column:

- Select the row or column and click the Cut icon on the toolbar (alternately, right-mouse click and choose Cu<u>t</u>).

- Position your cursor below (for rows) or to the right of (for columns) where you want to paste your column or row. Click the Paste icon on the toolbar (alternately, right-mouse click and choose <u>P</u>aste Cells).

Lesson 3: Changing a Column's Width

When you first create a table, Word makes all columns the same width, and the table fits perfectly between the left and right margins of the page. However, you can adjust any column's width to fit the amount of text in its cells better. In your agenda, notice that the Topic column contains more information than the other columns do, yet that column is no wider than the others. If you made the Topic column wider, its contents would be more readable. The Day column, on the other hand, contains very little information and is wider than it needs to be, so you can make it narrower to create more room for other columns.

The table needs to fit within the six inches of typing that the margins allow, so adjust each column manually, narrowing some and widening others. (Of course, you can also change the margins to make more room for the table on the page, but you don't need to do so here. In this case, it's better to adjust the columns to fit the text that they must hold.)

To Change a Column's Width

❶ Click the first cell of the first column.

Look at the ruler, as shown in Figure 2.5. You can click anywhere in a column to change its width.

If you have problems...

If the ruler is not visible onscreen, turn it on by choosing <u>V</u>iew, <u>R</u>uler. If the ruler does not look like the one in Figure 2.5, make sure that the insertion point is located somewhere in the table.

When the insertion point is inside a table, the ruler changes to display the boundary markers for each column.

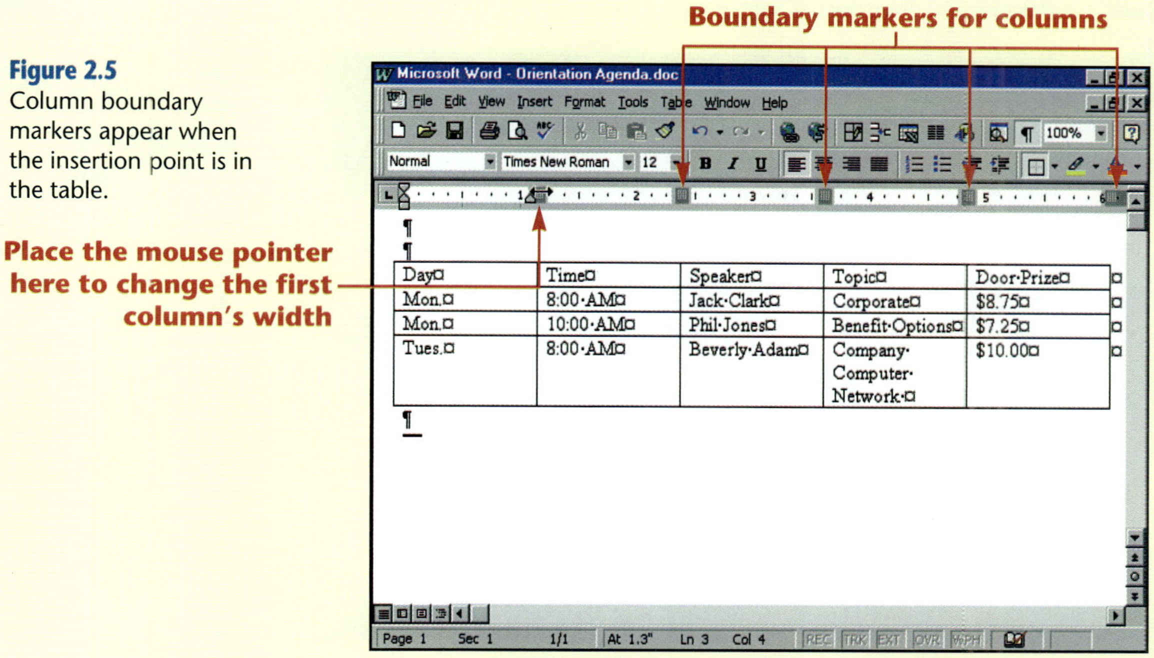

Figure 2.5
Column boundary markers appear when the insertion point is in the table.

Place the mouse pointer here to change the first column's width

The table shown in the figure:

Day	Time	Speaker	Topic	Door·Prize	
Mon.	8:00·AM	Jack·Clark	Corporate	$8.75	
Mon.	10:00·AM	Phil·Jones	Benefit·Options	$7.25	
Tues.	8:00·AM	Beverly·Adam	Company·Computer·Network·	$10.00	

2 **Place the mouse pointer on the boundary marker representing the right edge of the Day column.**

Figure 2.5 shows you where to place the mouse.

3 **Drag the marker to the left so that the column is about 1/2-inch wide.**

Figure 2.6 shows you where the first boundary marker should end. The ruler starts at zero. If you drag the marker halfway between 0 and 1 on the ruler, you make the column 1/2-inch wide. (Notice that the other boundary markers also move when you move this marker. Ignore that for now; you adjust each marker in turn.)

4 **Move the mouse pointer to the right boundary marker of the Time column. Drag the marker to the left so that the Time column is about an inch wide.**

The Time column is now approximately one inch wide. The Speaker column looks about right, so don't move it.

5 **Drag the Topic column's right boundary marker to the right so that the column is about two-inches wide.**

The Topic column is now about two-inches wide. The Door Prize column's boundary marker should be at 6 on the ruler, so you shouldn't have to move it. The column boundary markers and the table onscreen should now look like Figure 2.6. You might want to drag the column markers again to make minor adjustments, but don't fret if your boundaries don't align exactly as shown in Figure 2.6; just make sure that the table remains within the six-inch margin space.

continues

To Change a Column's Width   (continued)

Figure 2.6
The table with its new column widths.

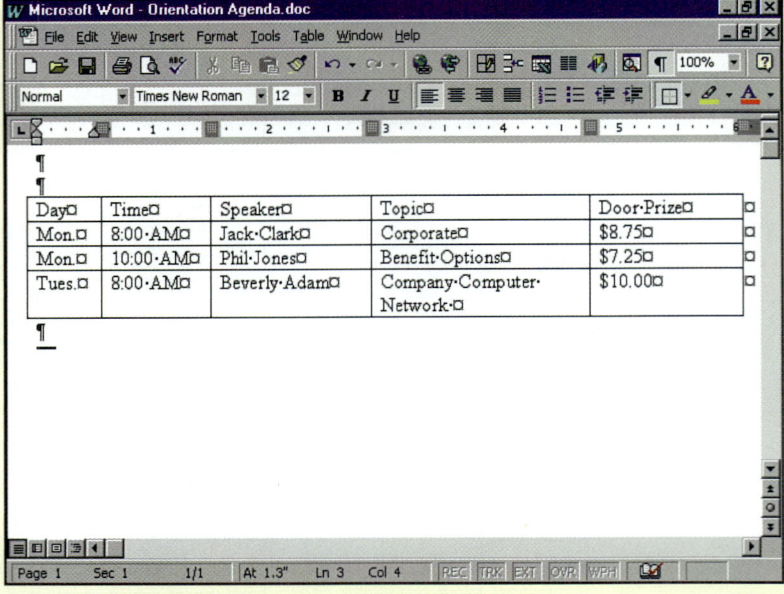

6 Save the file and leave it open for the next lesson.

When adjusting the column widths, do not select any cells or columns in the table. The column widths do not change properly if you have selected cells in a table.

Here's a trick that can save you a lot of time in the future. Instead of manually sizing columns—which you did in this lesson for the sake of learning—let Word do it for you with its AutoFit feature. Select the columns that you want to resize, then choose Table, Cell Height and Width. Click the Column tab, then choose AutoFit. Word resizes your columns based on the amount of text in each column. The trick is so easy, you'll think you did something illegal.

If you prefer to use the mouse, another method for resizing columns to best fit on the page is to place your cursor on the line between columns. When your cursor changes to a double-headed arrow, double-click your mouse.

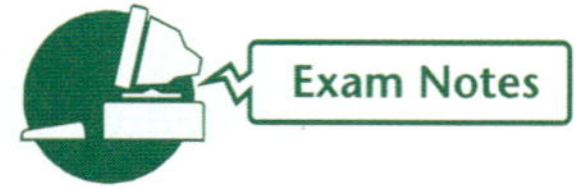

Just as you can change column width, you can change row height. By default, Word bases row height on the font size or the greatest number of lines in any cell in that row. You cannot individually set cell height, but should you decide you want the row height changed, you can do so by using the mouse or through the Cell Height and Width dialog box.

To change row height using the mouse, make certain that you are in Page Layout view, or Online Layout view, then:

- Point at the bottom border of the row whose height you want to change, or select several or all rows in the table. The mouse pointer changes to a pair of thin horizontal lines with arrowheads pointing up and down (see Figure 2.7). Drag the row border(s) to the desired height.

■ If you are in Page Layout view (see Figure 2.7), the vertical rulers show the row separators. You can change row height by pointing to the row separator, then when the mouse point becomes a two-headed arrow, drag the separator until the row is the desired height.

Figure 2.7
Drag the border of the row or the row separator on the ruler to adjust row height.

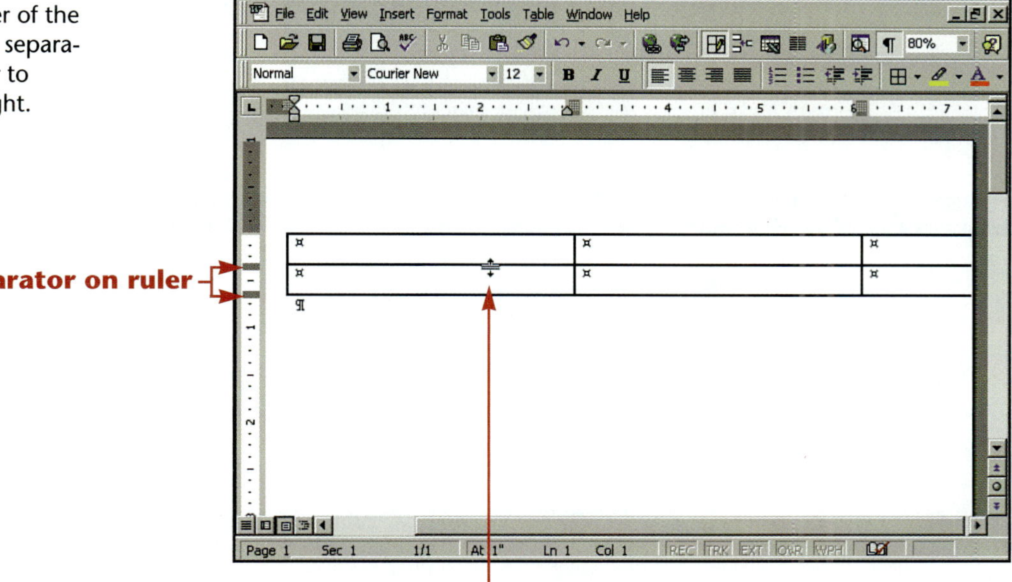

Mouse pointer for dragging the row height

To change the row height using the Cell Height and Width dialog box, select the row(s) you want to change and choose Table, Cell Height and Width from the menu. Select the Row tab (see Figure 2.8), choose from the Height of rows drop-down list and click OK. Table 2.1 describes the Height of rows choices found in the drop-down menu.

Figure 2.8
In addition to row height, you can set the alignment of the table on the page, indent the table from the left margin, or allow a row to break across pages.

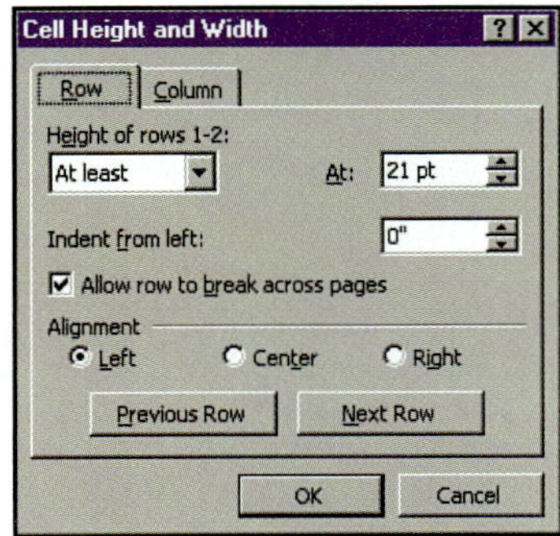

Table 2.1 Row Height Drop-down List Selections	
Select	To
Auto	Automatically adjust to the height of the tallest cell in the row
At least	Specify a minimum row height (entered in the At box, in points) that automatically adjusts to a large size to fit the row contents
Exactly	Specify a fixed row height (entered in the At box, in points). When making this selection, Word prints only the contents that fit in the specified height.

Lesson 4: Formatting Text in a Table

To emphasize text in a table, you can bold, underline, realign, and add other formatting to the text. You can format individual words, entire cells, entire rows, or entire columns. You can format the text in tables in many of the same ways that you format ordinary text in paragraphs.

In this lesson, you learn how to format the text in a row, a column, and a cell. You begin by making the row of column headers stand out by making the first row bold and changing the font size to 14 points.

To Format Text in a Table

1 **Select the table's first row.**

This time, instead of using the Table, Select Row command, use the mouse to highlight the row. Figure 2.9 shows you where to place the mouse; when the I-beam cursor changes to an arrow, click once to select the entire row.

Figure 2.9
Selecting the first row of the table for formatting.

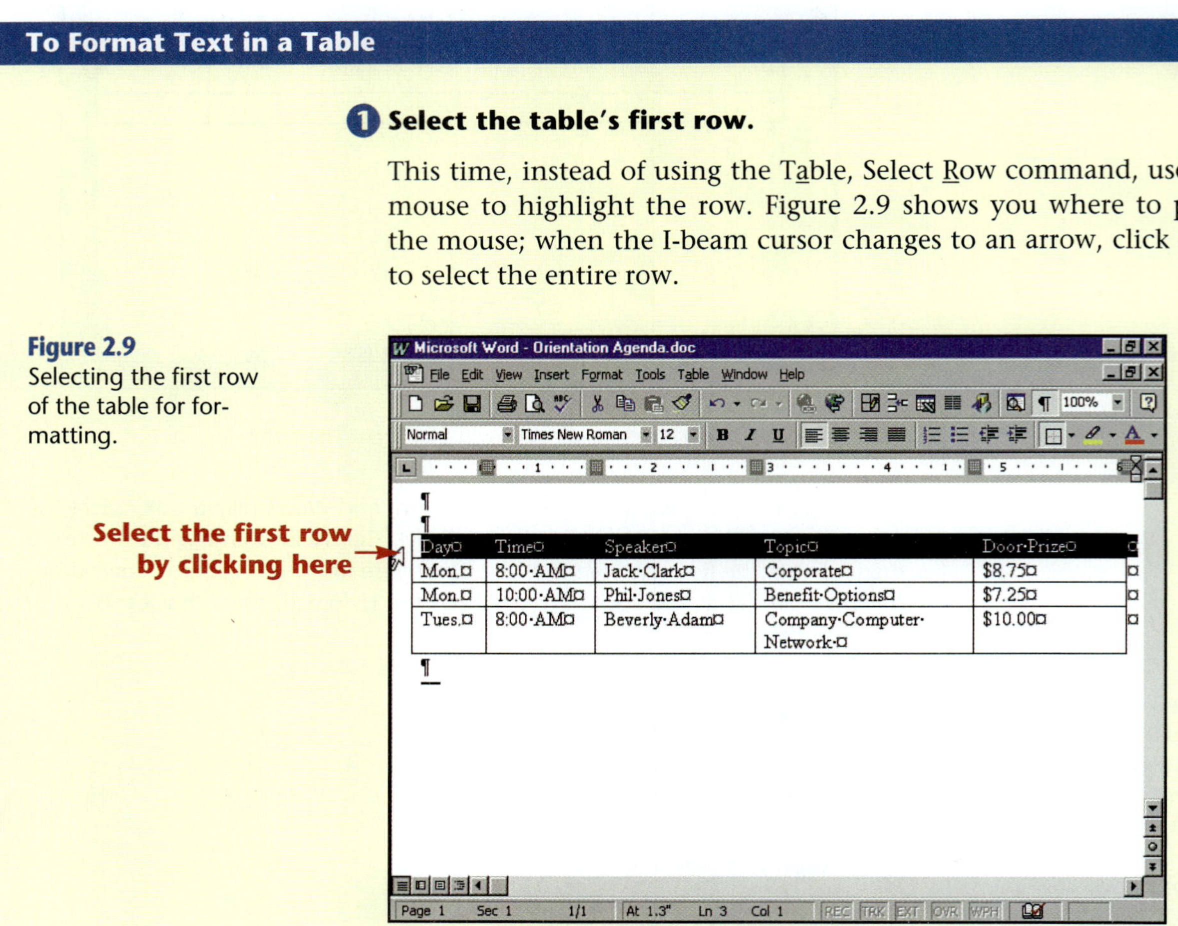

As with any kind of text in Word, you must first select the text before you format it. Because you want to format the entire first row, you must select all the text in the row before you can apply any formatting. Now you can make the text bold and change the font size.

2 **Click the Formatting toolbar's Bold button.**

All text in the first row is now bold.

3 **With the first row still selected, click the arrow next to the Formatting toolbar's Font Size button and select 14 as the new font size.**

The first row in the table should now be bold and sized to 14 points, as shown in Figure 2.10. Now change the Time column's alignment so that the AMs and PMs are right-aligned in the cells.

Figure 2.10
New formatting applied to the table's first row.

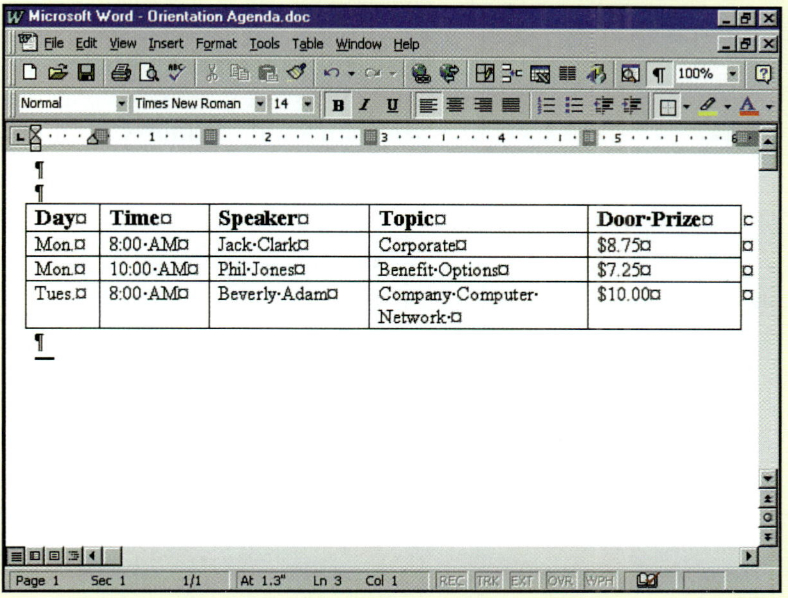

4 **Select the Time column.**

Figure 2.11 shows you where to place the mouse pointer to select the column by just clicking. Now you can right-align the text in this column.

Figure 2.11
Selecting the Time column for formatting.

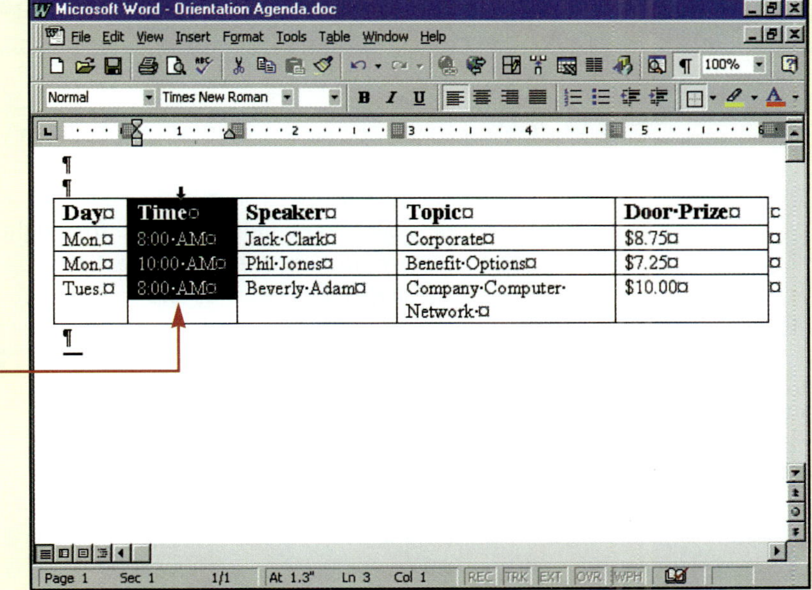

Word

To Format Text in a Table   (continued)

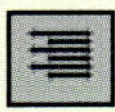

5 **Click the Formatting toolbar's Align Right button.**

The column's text is right-aligned, and the table should look like the one in Figure 2.12.

Even though you can align the text in a table's columns in different ways, a table usually looks more attractive if you format all its headings the same way. When you align some of the text differently within a table, you usually should center all the headings in their cells. Do that next.

Figure 2.12
The Time column right-aligned.

Day□	Time□	Speaker□	Topic□	Door·Prize□
Mon.□	8:00·AM□	Jack·Clark□	Corporate□	$8.75□
Mon.□	10:00·AM□	Phil·Jones□	Benefit·Options□	$7.25□
Tues.□	8:00·AM□	Beverly·Adam□	Company·Computer· Network·□	$10.00□

6 **Select the entire first row of the table.**

7 **Click the Formatting toolbar's Center button.**

The table's headings are centered inside their cells, and the table should now look like Figure 2.13.

Figure 2.13
The table with all headings centered.

Day□	Time□	Speaker□	Topic□	Door·Prize□
Mon.□	8:00·AM□	Jack·Clark□	Corporate□	$8.75□
Mon.□	10:00·AM□	Phil·Jones□	Benefit·Options□	$7.25□
Tues.□	8:00·AM□	Beverly·Adam□	Company·Computer· Network·□	$10.00□

8 **Save the file and leave it open for the next lesson.**

Table text can appear in a vertical orientation in your table. You may want to do this if horizontal space is at a premium. You can also merge cells and rotate text, creating a "header" effect in a row (see Project 6, Exam Note at the end of the project for more information). To rotate text, right-click in the cell whose text you want to rotate and choose Te**x**t Direction from the pop-up menu. The Text Direction dialog box appears as shown in Figure 2.14. Click the orientation you want. The Preview window shows you how the text looks. Click OK.

Figure 2.14
Select the vertical orientation for your text in the Text direction dialog box.

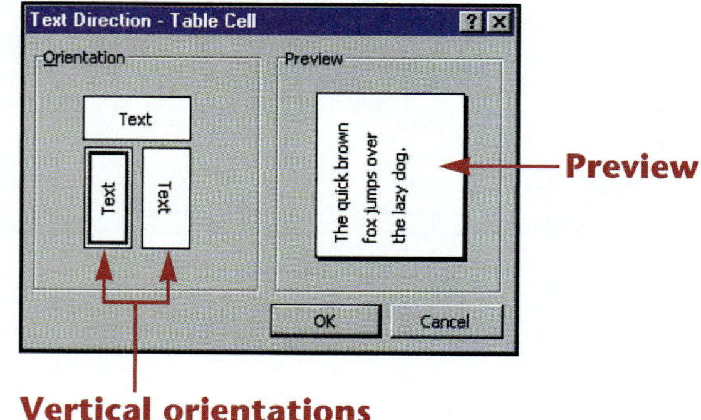

Lesson 5: Aligning a Column of Numbers on Decimal Points

Notice in the Door Prize column that the decimal points do not align. By default, the text in any column is left-aligned inside the cell. Numbers, however, often need a different alignment, especially if they contain decimal values. You should align those numbers on their decimal points to make columns neater and easier to read.

Decimal tab

A special tab that forces numbers beneath it to align along their decimal points.

You can align decimal points by placing a decimal tab on the ruler for the column that contains the numbers. This lesson shows you how to add a decimal tab to the Door Prize column.

To Align a Column of Numbers on Decimal Points

1 **Drag across the three cells below Door Prize to select them.**

2 **Click the tab button on the left side of the ruler until the decimal tab appears.**

Figure 2.15 shows you where to click and what the decimal tab looks like.

Click here to display the decimal tab...

Figure 2.15
Choosing a decimal tab on the ruler.

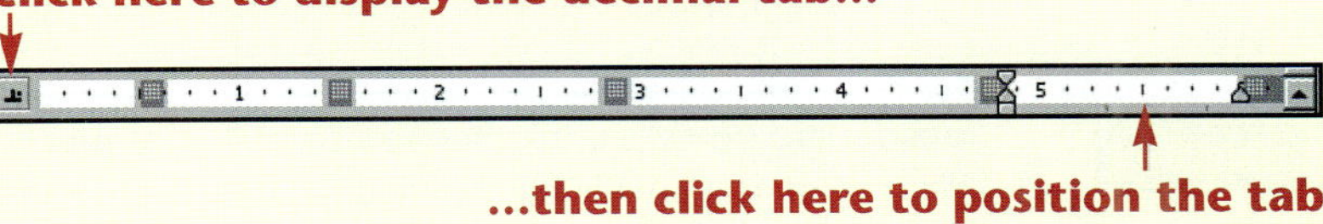

...then click here to position the tab

3 **Now click the 5.5-inch mark on the ruler.**

The ruler and Door Prize column should now look like those in Figure 2.16. As soon as you place the decimal tab on the ruler, all decimal points in the column align.

Figure 2.16
A decimal tab placed for Door Prize column.

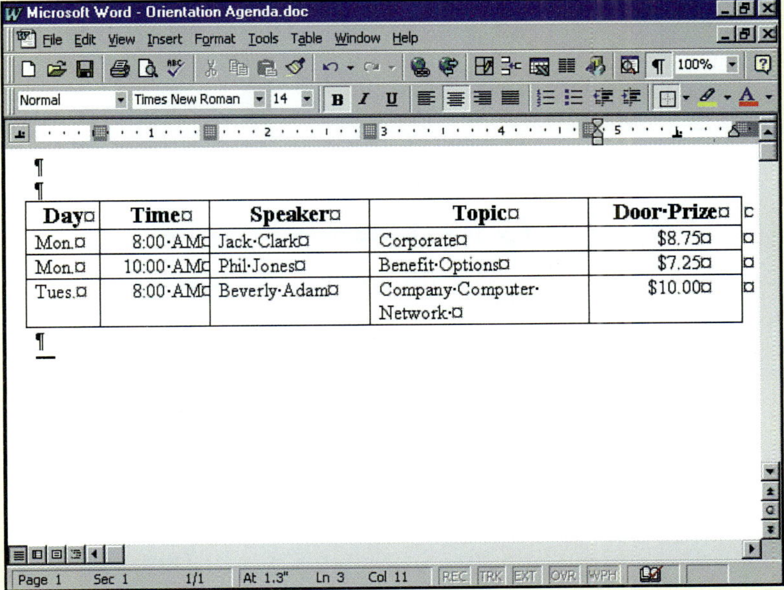

Day□	Time□	Speaker□	Topic□	Door·Prize□	□
Mon.□	8:00·AM□	Jack·Clark□	Corporate□	$8.75□	□
Mon.□	10:00·AM□	Phil·Jones□	Benefit·Options□	$7.25□	□
Tues.□	8:00·AM□	Beverly·Adam□	Company·Computer·Network·□	$10.00□	□

continues

To Align a Column of Numbers on Decimal Points   (continued)

4 **Save the file and leave it open for the next exercise.**

Setting the decimal tab on the ruler for a column of numbers aligns all types of numbers on their decimal points, regardless of how many numerals follow the decimal point.

After you place the decimal tab, you can drag it left and right on the ruler to change where the decimal points align in the column. Remember, however, to select the cells before you place the decimal tab on the ruler or before you drag it to change its position.

Lesson 6: Merging Cells in a Table

Merge

To combine multiple cells into a single cell.

Effective headings can really make a difference in tables. You can create a better-looking headline for the agenda by adding a major heading to the top of the table. To do so, add a new row at the top of the table and then merge the cells in that row into one giant cell. Then, when you type and center text in that row, the text flows across the entire top of the table.

Avoid merging cells until after you complete as much of the table as possible. After merging cells, you will have difficulty changing column widths in cells.

To Merge Cells in a Table

1 **Place the insertion point in the table's first cell.**

Add a new top row to the table.

2 **Choose Table, Insert Rows.**

Word inserts a new row above the row of headings. The inserted row picks up formatting from the row below it, so any text that you type in this row is bold, 14-point. The text is also centered because you centered all the headings in a previous lesson.

3 **Select the new first row.**

Now merge all the cells, so that the new row contains only one large cell.

4 **Choose Table, Merge Cells.**

All five cells merge into one cell. The row remains highlighted.

5 **Click the new merged cell.**

The row is no longer highlighted, but now contains the insertion point so that you can type the title. If the row remains selected, click the right side of the cell to unselect it.

6 **Type** `New Employee Orientation Agenda`.

Now change the height of the row to set it off from the rest of the table.

7 **Select the top row, then choose T<u>a</u>ble, Cell Height and <u>W</u>idth.**

The Cell Height and Width dialog box appears, as shown in Figure 2.17.

Figure 2.17
Use the Cell Height and Width dialog box to change the row height.

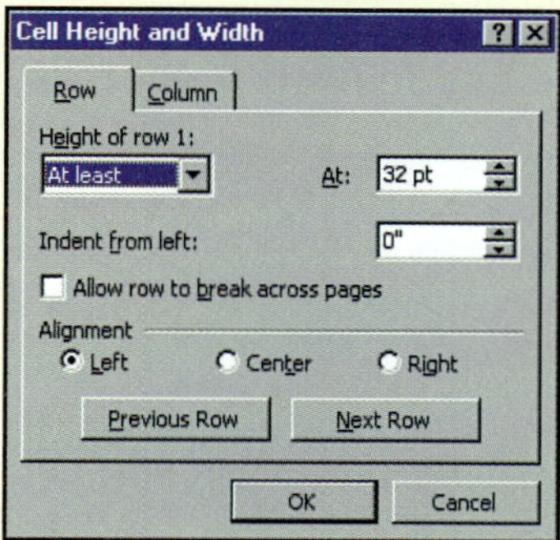

8 **With the <u>R</u>ow tab selected, click the down arrow below the H<u>e</u>ight of Row 1 option, and then select At Least.**

Selecting the At Least option specifies a minimum height for the row. If the text in the cell exceeds the height of the size that you specify, Word adjusts the row to fit the contents.

9 **Type** `32 pt` **in the <u>A</u>t text box and choose OK.**

The cell is now taller than the rest of the rows. When you deselect the row, your table should look like the one shown in Figure 2.18.

Figure 2.18
The completed table.

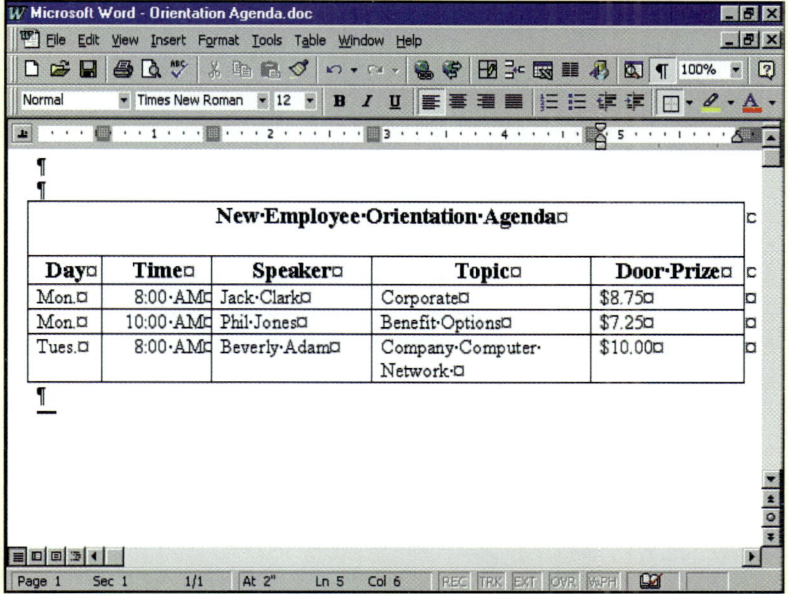

continues

To Merge Cells in a Table (continued)

Finally, designate the top two rows as table headings. Then, if the table spans more than one page, the top of each subsequent page repeats the headings.

10 Select the top two rows of the table and choose Table, Headings.

That's all there is to it. Now if your table spans across the next page, the top of the next page repeats the heading rows.

11 Save the file and leave it open for the next lesson.

Exam Notes

In this lesson, you learned to merge cells. You can also split cells by selecting the cell or cells that you want to split and choosing Table, Split Cells.

You can also merge cells to create a "header" type column on the left of a table, in which you can rotate text as shown in Figure 2.19. In this example, cells were selected and merged text was entered, rotated, and center aligned. The cell height was also adjusted.

Figure 2.19
Merging cells and rotating text can be valuable tools in creating tables such as this.

Day	Room	Time
Mon	Conf C	9–12
	Conf D	1–4
Tue	Conf C	9–12
	Conf D	1–4

Lesson 7: Adding Borders and Shading to a Table

By default, tables that you create have a 1/2-point, black, single-line border. In this lesson, you change some of these borders using the Tables and Borders toolbar.

Inside Stuff

The Tables and Borders toolbar gives you control of all borders that you add to tables. You might prefer, however, to let Word format tables automatically with AutoFormat.

Even after you use AutoFormat to dress up a table, you can make changes to it manually. The skills that you learn in this lesson can help you add borders to a table, whether unformatted or already AutoFormatted.

To Add Borders and Shading to a Table

1 Click the toolbar's Tables and Borders button.

The toolbar appears, as shown in Figure 2.20. If the Borders and Tables toolbar appears as a floating toolbar, drag its title bar near the top of the screen to place it below the Formatting toolbar.

Figure 2.20
The Tables and Borders toolbar.

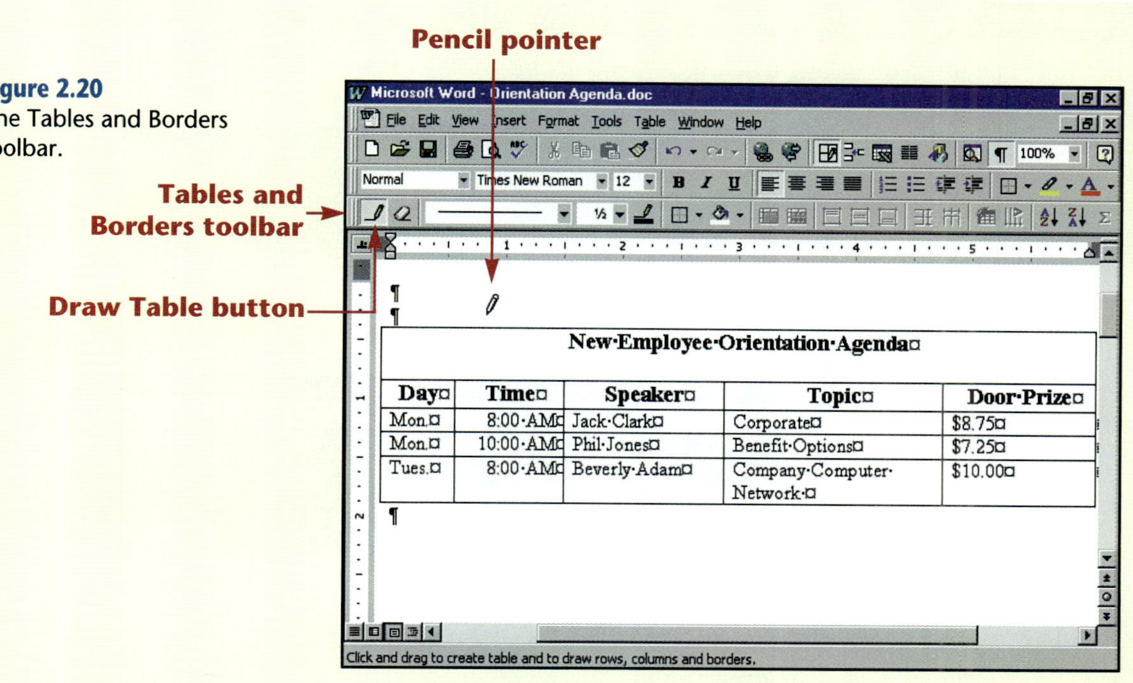

Notice that the mouse pointer turns into a pencil icon. Because you opened the Tables and Borders toolbar, Word thinks that you want to draw a table.

2 **Click the toolbar's Draw Table button to deactivate the Draw Table tool.**

Clicking the Draw Table tool (or pressing Esc) returns the mouse pointer to its normal I-beam shape.

3 **Click the anywhere inside the table and choose Table, Select Table.**

You have now selected the entire table so that you can change borders around its outside edges. Add a thick line around the table. First, you must select the type of line that you want to add and then select where you want to add the border.

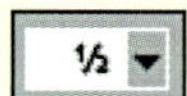

4 **Click the down arrow next to the Line Weight box on the Tables and Borders toolbar, and select the 1 1/2-point line.**

Next, select the outside border.

5 **With the table selected, click the down arrow next to the Border button and select the first item, as shown in Figure 2.21.**

continues

Figure 2.21
Add a thick line around
a table.

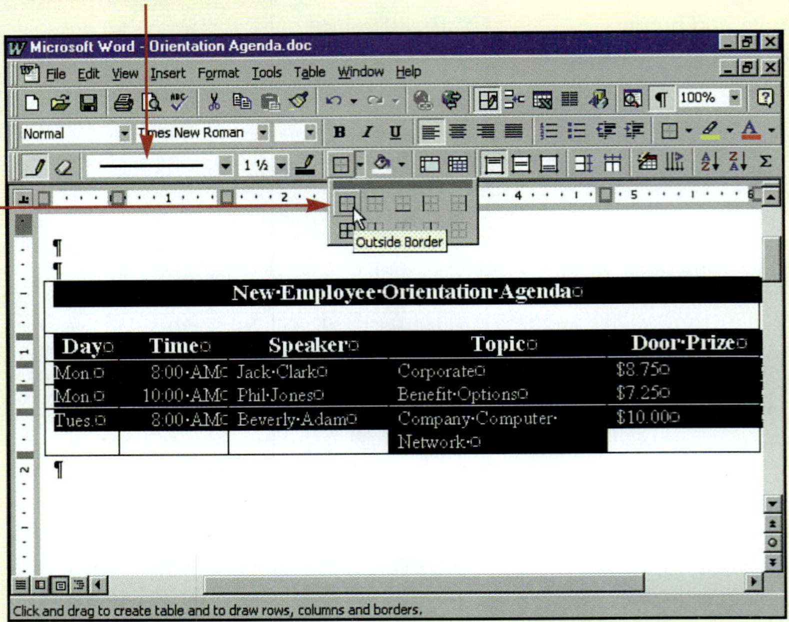

This option places a border all around the table, but doesn't change
the lines between cells. You can use this same tool to change outside borders or inside lines, or to remove all the lines in your table.
With the entire table selected, you cannot see the effect of the borders, so deselect the table.

6 Click the table's first cell.

The entire table is no longer selected. You can see that the thick
border surrounds only the outside of the table, while the default
single lines still remain inside the table. Now have some fun and
change some lines inside the table.

**7 With the thick line still selected, click the Tables and Borders
toolbar's Draw Table button.**

The pencil pointer appears. You can use this tool to draw lines in
your table. Remember that whatever line style and weight you
selected in the Tables and Borders dialog box is in effect when you
draw in your table.

**8 Use the drawing pointer to drag a thick line between the first
and second cells, as shown in Figure 2.22.**

Now that you've learned how to add borders, you next need to
learn how to remove them. When you experiment with tables, you
might often find that you want to remove borders so that you can
create a different look. Remove the horizontal lines in the table.

Figure 2.22
You can use the Draw Table button to draw lines in your table.

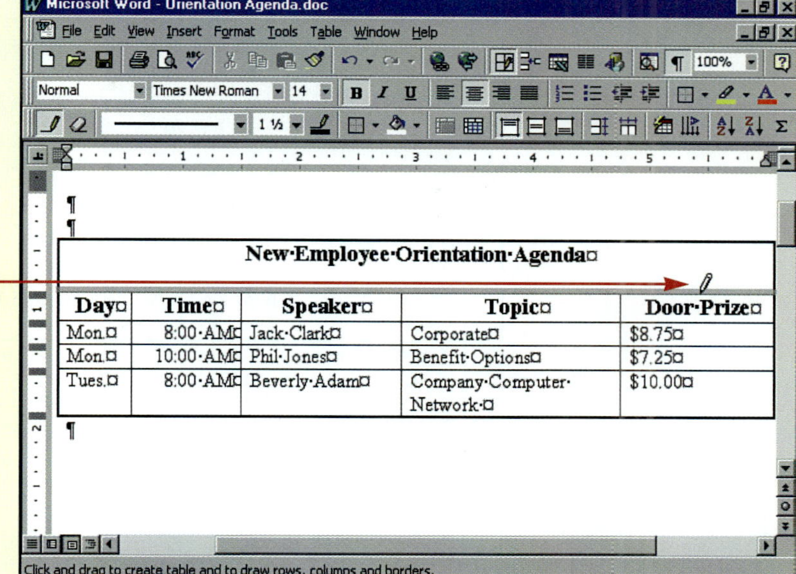

Pencil pointer

9 **Select No Border from the Line Style drop-down list in the Tables and Borders toolbar, then drag down the vertical lines one by one in the table below the first row.**

If you have problems...

If you drag the pointer down the middle of a column with the Draw Table feature selected, you split the cells in the column. Choose Edit, Undo, then drag down between columns to remove the lines.

When No Border is selected, dragging across the lines removes the border, leaving only the nonprinting gridline. (If you cannot see gridlines, choose Table, Show Gridlines.) Now replace the vertical lines with dotted lines.

10 **Select the dotted line from the Line Style drop-down list, and then drag down the vertical lines between columns one by one.**

Your table should look like Figure 2.23. To summarize, select the type of line and weight for your borders, then draw the lines in your table. Now add shading to the first row to make the major heading stand out even more.

11 **Click the Draw Table button to deactivate the pencil pointer, then select the table's first row.**

12 **Click the down arrow next to the Shading Color box, then choose the Gray-20% item from the drop-down palette.**

Hold the pointer over a color on the palette to view a tool tip that tells you the percentage of gray.

continues

To Add Borders and Shading to a Table   (continued)

Figure 2.23
Borders and lines added
to the table.

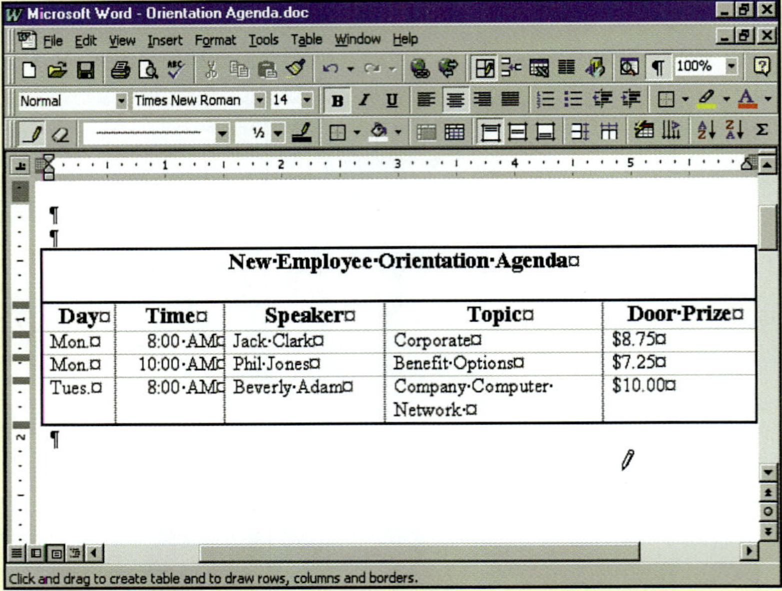

⓭ **Click the first cell to deselect the row.**

Now Word is applying shading. Make one more adjustment. The first row of the table looks better if vertically centered.

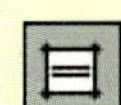

⓮ **With the insertion point in the first row, click the Tables and Borders toolbar's Center Vertically button.**

The table should now look like the one in Figure 2.24.

Figure 2.24
Shading applied to the
table's first row.

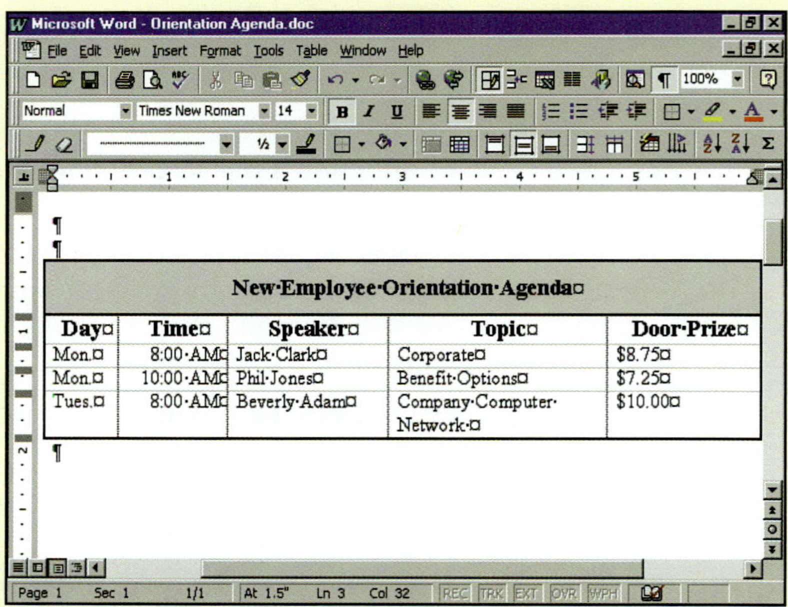

Now learn how to remove shading.

⓯ **Select the first row again, then open the Shading Color drop-down list and choose None.**

16 Click the first cell.

Word removes the shading. Now bring the shading back.

17 Click the Standard toolbar's Undo button to bring the shading back.

The row is highlighted again, so you cannot see the shading. Click the row again to deselect it.

18 Save and close the document.

If you can't select text because the mouse pointer has turned into a little pencil icon, click the Tables and Borders toolbar's Draw Table button (or press Esc) to deactivate it.

As mentioned earlier, the Draw Table feature enables you to create tables from scratch. If you have time at the end of class, click the Tables and Borders toolbar's Draw Table button, then drag across a blank area of a document. A table appears where you drag. Now drag the pointer inside the table to add rows and columns. When you're done drawing, click the Draw Table button again.

When you use this method to create a table, you might want to clean it up by making the rows the same height. To do so, select the rows, and choose the Tables and Borders toolbar's Distribute Rows Evenly button. A Distribute Columns Evenly button is also available for making columns the same width.

Lesson 8: Adding Figures and Sorting Rows in a Table

You often need to add figures to tables. Instead of tapping the figures into your calculator, you can let Word add your figures for you. In fact, Word lets you perform all sorts of complex formulas. However, for now, this lesson sticks to simple addition.

In this lesson, you add the figures in three columns of a sales results table. Then you change the order of the rows so that they are in alphabetical order.

To Add Figures and Sort Rows

1 Open the folder Project-02 and the file called Proj0202.doc from this book's companion CD, and save it as Sales Results.

This document contains a table reporting on the sales results for the first three months of the year. Now see how much money the sales representatives earned in January.

continues

To Add Figures and Sort Rows   (continued)

❷ Place the insertion point at the bottom of the January column in the TOTAL row.

❸ If the Tables and Borders toolbar is not displayed, click the Standard toolbar's Tables and Borders button.

When you click the Tables and Borders button, the Draw Table feature is active. Press Esc or click the Draw Table tool to turn off this option.

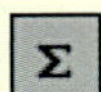

❹ Click the Tables and Borders toolbar's AutoSum button.

Word adds the figures in the column, as shown in Figure 2.25. You can use the AutoSum feature to add figures in rows as well as columns.

Figure 2.25
Let Word add figures for you.

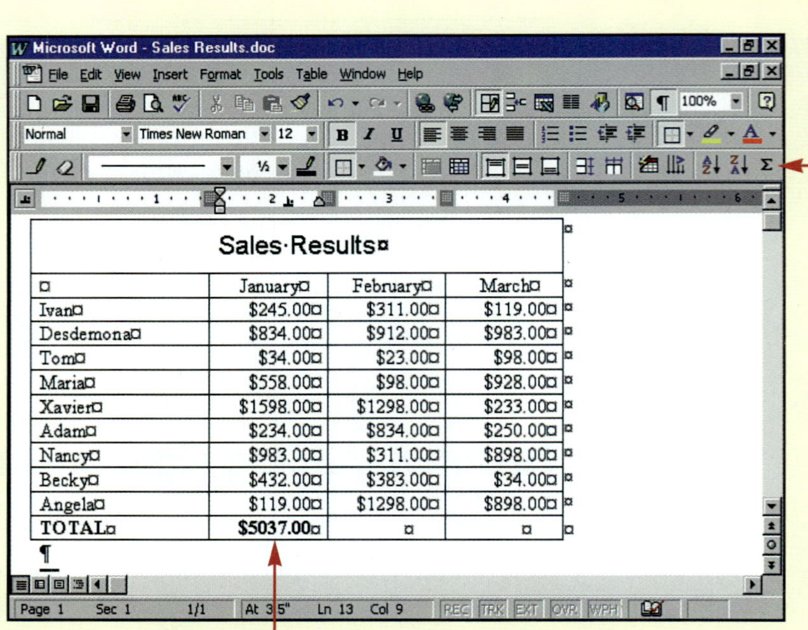

	January¤	February¤	March¤	
¤				
Ivan¤	$245.00¤	$311.00¤	$119.00¤	¤
Desdemona¤	$834.00¤	$912.00¤	$983.00¤	¤
Tom¤	$34.00¤	$23.00¤	$98.00¤	¤
Maria¤	$558.00¤	$98.00¤	$928.00¤	¤
Xavier¤	$1598.00¤	$1298.00¤	$233.00¤	¤
Adam¤	$234.00¤	$834.00¤	$250.00¤	¤
Nancy¤	$983.00¤	$311.00¤	$898.00¤	¤
Becky¤	$432.00¤	$383.00¤	$34.00¤	¤
Angela¤	$119.00¤	$1298.00¤	$898.00¤	¤
TOTAL¤	$5037.00¤	¤	¤	¤

Page 1   Sec 1   1/1   At 3.5"   Ln 13   Col 9   REC TRK EXT OVR WPH

❺ Use the AutoSum button to add the figures in the February and March columns.

The figures generated in the TOTAL row are called fields. They are similar to the special date fields that you insert and that Word updates automatically when you open the file later. Now change the figures in the column so that you can update the added total. You just discovered that, in January, Adam earned $1,234.00 rather than $234.00.

6 Change Adam's January sales to `$1234.00`.

Notice that the total remains the same, $5,037.00, even though a figure has changed in the column. If you were to close the file and reopen it, the field would be updated. However, a quicker way to update a field while you work is to press `F9`.

7 Click the field in the January TOTAL column and press `F9`.

You can instruct Word to update fields each time that you open or print the document. Choose Tools, Options and then click the Print tab in the Options dialog box. In the Printing section, select the Update Fields option, then choose OK.

Another way to update a field besides pressing `F9` is to right-click the field and choose Update Field from the shortcut menu.

The figure is now updated to $6,037.00. Now sort the names in the first column so that they are in alphabetical order.

8 Select only the names in the first column.

If you were to select the TOTAL cell in the column, Word would alphabetize the TOTAL row, which is something that you want to avoid.

9 Choose Table, Sort.

The Sort dialog box appears, as shown in Figure 2.26. Because you're sorting the names in the first column, you're ready to sort.

Figure 2.26
You can sort a table in alphabetical order.

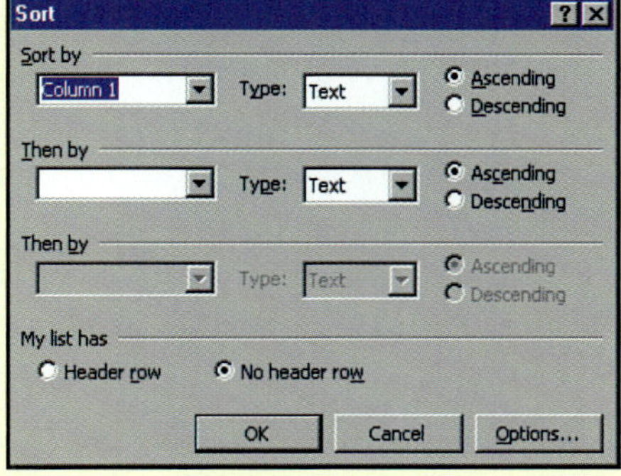

10 Choose OK to sort the selected cells in the first column.

The rows are now alphabetized in ascending order, starting with Adam and ending with Xavier, as shown in Figure 2.27.

continues

To Add Figures and Sort Rows   (continued)

Figure 2.27
Sorted rows.

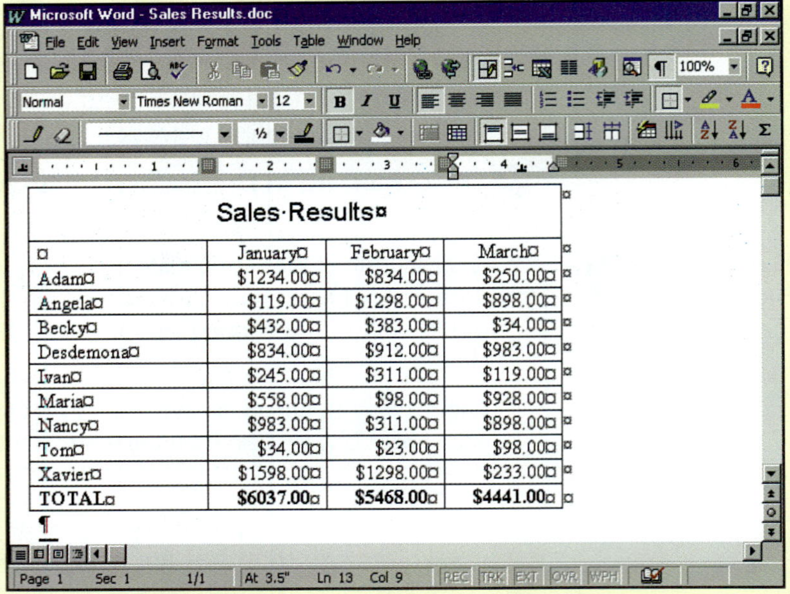

You might wonder why you aren't using the Tables and Borders toolbar's Sort Ascending button. Clicking this button sorts the entire first column, including the TOTAL column.

Next, sort the information in the March column in descending order, from highest to lowest.

11 Select the non-total figures in the March column, then choose Table, Sort.

First, notice that you're sorting by column 4 instead of column 1, and that the type is numbers rather than text (you can also sort by date). Notice the Ascending and Descending buttons on the right side of the Sort dialog box. Using these options, you can sort from higher numbers to lower numbers, or from lower numbers to higher numbers. Or, if you're sorting text, you can sort from A to Z or Z to A.

12 Choose Descending and then OK to sort the figures.

The figures in the March column are now sorted in descending order (from highest to lowest).

13 Click the Standard toolbar's Tables and Borders button to remove the Tables and Borders toolbar.

14 Save and close the document.

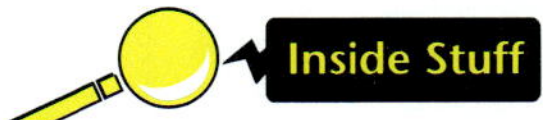

The table that you've been working on in this lesson is well suited for the AutoFormat feature. If you have time after class, place the insertion point anywhere in the table, then choose Table, AutoFormat. Select a format that you like, then choose OK.

In addition to creating tables and calculating table cell information, you can create a blank Excel worksheet in a Word table by embedding the worksheet. The advantage of embedding an Excel worksheet into a Word table is that you have the functionality of Excel, thus giving you more powerful formula and calculation capabilities. You learn more about embedding files and creating an Excel worksheet in a Word table in Project 14, "Using Word with Other Applications."

Project Summary

To	Do This
Select a row in a table	Click the row and choose Table, Select Row. You can also drag across the row or click just left of it (the pointer turns into a small arrow) to select the row.
Select a column in a table	Click the column and choose Table, Select Column. You can also drag down the column or click just above it (the pointer turns into a small down arrow) to select the column.
Insert a row in a table	Click anywhere in the row to insert a new row above it. Choose Table, Insert Rows.
Append a row	Click in the last cell of the table. Press the tab key. Word adds a new row to the end of the table.
Insert a column in a table	Select the column to insert a new column to the left of it. Choose Table, Insert Columns.
Append a column	Select the end of column markers located to the right of the last column of the table. After selecting, right-click the mouse and choose Insert column.
Delete a row in a table	Select the row to delete. Choose Table, Delete Rows.
Delete a column in a table	Select the column to delete. Choose Table, Delete Columns.
Change a column's width	Click the table. Go to the ruler and move the column boundary markers to the desired locations.

continues

To	Do This
Change a row's height	Click in the row. Go to the vertical ruler and move the row boundary marks to the desired height.
Apply formatting to text in a table	Select the text, cell, row, or column for formatting. Apply the formatting that you want.
Rotate text in a table	Right click the text. Choose Text Direction from the pop-up menu. Select the orientation and click OK.
Add a decimal tab to a column	Select the column in a table that contains the numbers. Select the decimal tab at the left edge of the ruler. Place the tab on the ruler by clicking once the desired point on the ruler.
Merge cells in a table	Select the cells. Choose Table, Merge Cells.
Split a merged cell	Select the cell or cells. Choose Table, Split Cells.
Display the Tables and Borders toolbar	Click the Formatting toolbar's Borders button.
Hide the Tables and Borders toolbar	Click the Formatting toolbar's Borders button.
Select a table	Click anywhere in the table. Choose Table, Select Table.
Add borders to a table	Use the Tables and Borders toolbar to add lines and borders.
Add shading to a row	Select the row. Choose the shading that you want from the Shading Color palette in the Tables and Borders toolbar.
Add predefined formatting to a table	Click the table. Choose Table, Table AutoFormat. Select the formatting that you want from the dialog box, then click OK.
Add figures in a column or row	Place the insertion point at the bottom of a column or the end of a row, then click the Tables and Borders toolbar's AutoSum button.
Sort rows in a table	Select the cells in the column that you want to sort, then choose Table, Sort.

Checking Your Skills

True/False

For each of the following statements, check *T* or *F* to indicate whether the statement is true or false.

__T __F   **1.** You must select a column before you insert a new column.

__T __F   **2.** You can create an entire table by using the Draw Table button.

__T __F   **3.** You can merge cells together, but you cannot split a cell into multiple cells.

__T __F   **4.** You can center text in a table using the toolbar's Center button.

__T __F   **5.** Calculations are automatically updated when you edit numbers in a table.

__T __F   **6.** You can only insert one row or column at a time.

__T __F   **7.** To delete a row, select it and press Del.

__T __F   **8.** Use the Cut and Paste commands to move a column or row.

__T __F   **9.** You can format text in a table using most of the same commands you use to format text not in a table.

__T __F **10.** Once you format a table with AutoFormat, you cannot change the formatting.

Multiple Choice

Circle the letter of the correct answer for each of the following:

1. How can you select an entire row?

   a. By dragging across the row with the mouse

   b. By choosing Table, Select Row

   c. By clicking just to the left of the row

   d. All the above

2. When you insert a row, where does the row appear?

   a. Below the current row

   b. Above the current row

   c. At the bottom of the table

   d. At the top of the table

3. When you insert a column, where does the column appear?

   a. To the left of the selected column

   b. To the right of the selected column

   c. On the left side of the table

   d. On the right side of the table

4. To remove all borders from the table, what do you do after selecting the table?

   a. Choose Table, Hide Gridlines

Word

b. Select No Border from a pop-up palette on the Tables and Borders toolbar

c. Set the border color to the same color as the page

d. Use the Hide Borders Wizard

5. How can you ensure that table headings are repeated at the top of the next pages in a long table?

   a. Select the entire table, then choose Format, Paragraph, Keep Lines Together

   b. Select the heading rows, then choose Table, Headings

   c. Use the Table Heading Wizard

   d. Copy and paste the heading to the top of the next pages as needed

6. What tool can you use to quickly total numbers in a row or column?

   a. AutoAdd

   b. AutoTotal

   c. AutoSum

   d. AutoCalculate

7. How many rows should you select when you want to insert three new rows?

   a. None

   b. One

   c. Two

   d. Three

8. What is the term for adding a column to the right side of a table?

   a. Insert

   b. Append

   c. Add-on

   d. Paste

9. In what view can you see the row separators on the vertical ruler?

   a. Normal

   b. Print Preview

   c. Page Layout

   d. Outline

10. What key or key combination do you use to align text in a table with a tab stop?

    a. Tab

    b. Shift+Tab

    c. Alt+Tab

    d. Ctrl+Tab

Completion

In the blank provided, write the correct answer for each of the following statements.

1. The toolbar that helps you draw lines in a table is called the _______________ toolbar.

2. Click the _______________ button to total numbers quickly.

3. Turning multiple cells into a single cell is known as _______________.

4. Placing table cells in alphabetical order is called _______________.

5. To make a cell taller, choose the menu item Table, _______________.

6. When you use the Draw Table tool, the mouse pointer looks like a ______________.

7. To insert a row or column using the mouse, you must first ______________ the row or column.

8. To append a row to the bottom of a table, position the insertion point in the last cell in the table and press ______________.

9. Column ___________ markers appear on the ruler when the insertion point is in a table.

10. Drag the border of the row to adjust row ________.

Matching

In the blank next to each of the following terms or phrases, write the letter of the corresponding term or phrase. (Note that some letters may be used more than once.)

a. AutoSum

b. Append

c. Merge

d. Header

e. Ascending

f. Descending

g. At Least

h. Split

i. Gridlines

j. Vertical Orientation

______ 1. Combining multiple cells into one cell

______ 2. Dividing one cell into multiple cells

______ 3. Term for adding a column to the right side of a table

______ 4. Feature that determines direction of text in a cell

______ 5. Nonprinting lines that show columns and rows onscreen

______ 6. Setting used to specify a minimum row height in the Cell Height and Width dialog box

______ 7. Button for totaling a row or column of numbers in a table

______ 8. Setting for arranging rows in alphabetical order A to Z

______ 9. Setting for arranging rows in alphabetical order Z to A

______ 10. The row(s) that will print at the top of any page on which the table is displayed

Applying Your Skills

Practice

The following exercises enable you to practice the skills you have learned in this project. Take a few minutes to work through these exercises now.

Setting Up and Sorting a Flight Timetable

In this practice lesson, you use Word's table formatting features to create and format a flight timetable.

To set up a flight timetable, follow these steps:

1. Open the file Proj0202 from the Project-02 folder on the CD, and save it in your `Practices` folder as `Timetable`.

2. Add a new column, between the Flt. Time and Cost columns; title the new column Notes.

3. Select the rows that contain flight information and sort them by cost in ascending order, so the least expensive flight is at the top and the most expensive is at the bottom.

4. With the rows still selected, sort them alphabetically by destination in descending order.

5. Format the first row text in bold, 11-point Arial, and center the headings in their cells.

6. Add a new row across the top of the table, then Merge the new row's cells to make one long cell, and type Charter Flights from Pittsburgh as the table's main title.

7. Designate the top two rows as header rows.

8. Highlight the four rows listing flight information (all the cells beneath the two rows of headings) and format the text in 10-point Times New Roman.

9. In the cells that contain flight numbers or flight times, center the text. In the cells that contain departure and arrival times, right-align the text.

10. In the cells that contain flight costs, set a decimal tab at approximately 5 3/4" on the ruler, then align the dollar amounts on the tab stop.

11. Increase the width of the Destination column so the text fits on one line.

12. Add internal and external border lines to the entire table, and 30% shading to the two header rows.

13. Insert a blank line in the document above the table and type the document title Outbound Flight Timetable in 24-point. Arial, centered. (Hint: Position the insertion point in the first row of the table and choose Table, Split Table.) Leave 24 points of blank space between the document title and the table.

14. Check the spelling and grammar in the document, preview it, then save it. If requested by your instructor, print it. Close it when you have finished.

Calculating Totals in a Sales Report

In this exercise, use Word's table formatting features to calculate totals in a sales report. You also modify and format the report.

To calculate totals in a sales report, follow these steps:

1. Open the file Proj0203 from the Project-02 folder on the CD, and save the file in your Practices folder as Sales.

2. Format the text in the first row in bold, 12-point Arial, and center the headings in their cells.

3. Resize the first column to make it about an inch wide.

4. Append a new column to the right side of the table by copying the January column. Change the title of the new column to `April`.

5. Rotate the text in the first row so it is displayed vertically, bottom to top. Adjust the height to exactly 65 points.

6. Enter formulas for totaling each month's sales.

7. Align all the dollar values in the table on decimal tabs.

8. Add a new row across the top of the table and set text direction to horizontal. Merge the new row's cells to make one long cell, and type `Monthly Sales by Salesperson` in 14-point bold Arial, centered as the table's main title. Set the row height to 18 points.

9. Designate the top two rows as header rows.

10. Select the rows with salesperson data, then sort them alphabetically in ascending order.

11. Apply internal and external borders to the entire table, and 20% shading to the TOTAL row.

12. Check the spelling and grammar in the document, preview it, and save it. If requested by your instructor, print it. When you have finished, close the file.

Formatting an Invoice Table

In this exercise, format the table in the invoice document you created in Project 1.

To format the invoice table, follow these steps:

1. Open the file Proj0204 from the Project-02 folder on the CD and save it in your `Practices` folders as `Invoice2`.

2. Insert a 1-point single line border around the first row, and apply a 5% gray shade to it. Change the font of the text in the first row to 18-point bold Arial.

3. Insert a 3/4-point double-line border across the top of the Total row, then apply a 5% gray shade to all cells in the last three rows, and make the data in the calculating cells bold.

4. Increase the paragraph spacing before the Total row in the table to 12 points so the text is not too close to the border above it. Do the same for the first and second rows in the table.

5. Insert a new row above the 5/29 row and enter data for a 5/22 1/2 hr. Piano lesson. Update the calculating fields. (You have to modify the formula for total piano lesson charges.)

6. Delete the 5/1 row, and update the calculating field cells again.

7. Right-align the dollar values in the third column.

8. Preview the invoice, check the spelling and grammar in the document, then save the document. If requested by your instructor, print it. Then close the document.

Modifying the Symposium Schedule

You can use the skills you learned in this project to modify and improve the symposium schedule you created in Project 1.

To modify the symposium schedule, follow these steps:

1. Open the file Proj0205 from the Project-02 folder on the CD and save it in your `Practices` folder as `Schedule2`.

2. Insert a column between Time and Monday and label it `Location`.

3. Center the column labels.

4. Move the last row up to the top of the schedule (before the 7:30-8:00 row). Change the Friday cell data for this row to `Free`.

5. Append a row to the bottom of the table for the 7:00 to 8:30 time frame. Copy the Monday through Friday data from the 5:30 to 7:30 row into the new row.

6. Increase the width of the Time column so the times can fit on one line. Do this without effecting the widths of the other columns in the table.

7. Apply a 10% shading to all cells containing the data Free and make the text bold.

8. Check the spelling and grammar in the document, preview it and save it. If requested by your instructor, print it. Close the document when you are finished.

Modifying Tables in the Loan Proposal

You have found some errors in the tables in the Loan Proposal document. Use the skills you have learned in this Project to correct the tables, then reformat them.

To modify tables in a loan proposal, follow these steps:

1. Open the file Proj0206 from the Project-02 folder on the CD and save it in your `Practices` folder as `Loan2`.

2. In the `Anticipated Expenses` table, insert a row between Demolition and Construction. Label it `Consulting` and enter a cost of $5,000.

3. Update the calculating fields, then align the third column on a decimal tab.

4. Sort the four rows of expense items alphabetically in ascending order.

5. Set the height of the first row to exactly 24 points.

6. Center the entire table on the page. (Hint: Select the table and click the Center button.)

7. Add a new first row to the second table in the document. Merge it into one cell and enter `Quarterly Net Profits`, centered.

8. Change the shading in the first two rows to 10% gray, and adjust the row height to 18 points.

9. Center the Quarterly Net Profits table on the page.

10. Check the spelling and grammar, preview the document and save it. If requested by your instructor, print it. Close it when you are finished.

Challenge

The following challenges enable you to use your problem-solving skills. Take time to work through these exercises now.

Modifying the Table in the Computer Training Concepts Letter

Modify the table in the letter sent to those who request information from Computer Training Concepts. Open the file Proj0207 from the Project-02 folder on the CD and save it in your Challenges folder as Cover Letter2.

Use manual formatting to improve the appearance of the table. For example, increase the paragraph spacing before the text in the first row. Increase the size of the font for the course names in the first column, and apply an underline to each name. Increase the width of the first column so the course names fit on one line each. Insert a row at the top of the table and enter the title Course Descriptions in the first cell. Format it in 18-point bold Arial, no underline. Merge the two columns in the new first row. Center the heading across the width of the table. Designate the first row as a header. Add a double-line border between the first and second rows.

Preview the document and adjust spacing as necessary. Check the spelling and grammar and save it. If requested by your instructor, print the letter. Close the file when you have finished.

Expanding the Table in the Business Proposal Document

In this exercise, you add more rows of budget items to the table in the Business Proposal document. Open the file Proj0208 from the Project-02 folder on the CD and save it in your Challenges folder as Proposal2.

Insert two new rows above the Travel row in the Proposed Budget table and type in the following two rows of data:

| Lodging | $15,000.00 |
| Miscellaneous | $5,000.00 |

Align the dollar values in the second column at a decimal tab. Update the total. Increase the size of the font in the first row to 14 points. Merge the two cells in the first row and center the text. Decrease the width of the first column so it is just wide enough to accommodate the text. Sort rows 2 through 6 numerically by the dollar value cost. Insert a border line between the first and second columns in rows 2 through 6, and across the bottom of row 6. Center the table on the page.

Check the spelling and grammar in the document, preview it, and save it. If requested by your instructor, print it. Close the document when you have finished.

Modifying the Computer Training Concepts Price List

Open the file Proj0209 from the Project-02 folder on the CD and save it in your `Challenges` folder as `Prices2`. Add a column titled `Length` between the Course column and Members column. Fill in the new column with the following data:

Excel I	5 days
Excel II	5 days
Excel III	7 days
Word I	5 days
Word II	5 days
Word III	7 days
Web Publishing I	2 days
Internet Explorer I	2 days
Microsoft Office	7 days

Move the Length column to the right side of the table. Move the Microsoft Office row so it is the first course listed. Move all of the Word rows above the Excel rows. Delete the Web Publishing course. Change the font of the text in the first row to 16-point bold Arial, no italics. Adjust the column widths so the text fits on one line. Center the text in the first row both horizontally and vertically. Right-align all pricing information. Remove the shading from all but the first column. Remove the shading from the cell at the top of the first column. Make sure there are internal and external borders for the entire table. Update all fields in the table.

Check the spelling and grammar in the document, preview it, and save it. If requested by your instructor, print it. Close the document when you have finished.

Modifying the Table in the Membership Renewal Document

You need to modify the table in the Membership Renewal. Open the Proj0210 from the Project-02 folder on the CD and save it in your `Challenges` folder with the name `Renewal5`.

Replace the date with the current date, and the text (Student's Name) with your own name. Add three rows and fill in the following data:

Type of Membership	Annual Dues	Annual Dues Less 10% Discount
Pool only	$300	$270
Summer only	$250	N/A
2-month trial	$100	N/A

Append a column to the table and title it `Family`. Leave it blank. Format the table using fonts, borders, and shading. Adjust column widths and row heights so the table is easy to read. Make row one a heading row so if the table splits across pages, the information on the second page is labeled, too. Align prices in each column on a decimal tab. Sort the membership types by full cost in ascending order.

Check the spelling and grammar and preview the document. Save it. If requested by your instructor, print it. Close the document when you are finished.

Modifying a Comparative Sales Report

You have a document with sales information by year listed in a table. You need to format and improve the table. Open the Proj0211 from the Project-02 folder on the CD and save it in your `Challenges` folder with the name `Comparison`.

Change the font and font size of the data in the first row so it is easier to read. Increase the font size of the rest of the data in the table. Make the state names bold.

Center the headings in each cell in the first row. Rotate the text in the first row so it is displayed vertically, bottom to top. Center it vertically. Make all columns 1.5" wide.

Append a row to the table and label it `Totals`. Enter formulas to total the yearly sales in each column of the new row. Append a column to the right of the table. Title it `Totals`. Make sure the formatting matches the other column titles. Enter formulas in each row of the new column for totaling the sales for each state. (Hint: You can enter the formula in the top row, copy it to all of the other rows using the Copy and Paste command, then, update the fields to adjust the totals correctly.) Adjust the column widths so all columns fit in the width of the page. Align all dollar values in the table on decimal tabs.

Add a title row to the table, merge the cells, set Text direction to horizontal and type `Three Year Sales Comparison` in 16-point bold Arial. Set the row height to 48 points and center the title horizontally and vertically. Make the top two rows heading rows. Sort the rows alphabetically by state in ascending order. Apply internal and external borders to the entire table, and 20% shading to the heading rows. Use the Split Table command to insert a line above the table. Type the document title `Sales Report for Computer Training Concepts` in 20 point Arial, centered. Leave 48 points of blank space between the title and the table.

Check the spelling and grammar in the document, preview it and save it. If requested by your instructor, print it. When you have finished, close the file.

You have completed the project and the associated lessons, as well as the "Checking Your Skills" and "Applying Your Skills" sections. Now use the PinPoint software evaluation mode to assess your comprehension of the specific exam tasks you have just learned. You can also use the PinPoint Trainer Mode and the Show Me tutorials to practice these specific exam tasks.

Project 3

Three

Working with Pictures

Sizing and Cropping a Picture

In this Project, you learn how to:

Objectives   **Required Activities**

➤ Size and Crop a Picture

➤ Position a Picture on the Page

➤ Change the Way Text Wraps Around a Picture

➤ Add a Border and Fill to a Picture

➤ Work with Text Boxes

➤ Create a Watermark   … … … … … … … … … … …   Create a Watermark

Why Would I Do This?

Pictures, such as clip art, scanned images, objects you draw your-self, or imported graphics, can add style to your documents. Graphics can support and clarify your text, make bold state-ments, and create a mood. You have already learned a great deal about using pictures and other graphics objects in a document if you worked with the MOUS Essentials: Word 97 Proficient book.

In this project, you learn how to use some of Word's more advanced capa-bilities to customize pictures in your documents. Specifically, you learn how to integrate pictures with document text and how to modify pictures to suit your documents. You also learn how to create a watermark.

Throughout most of this project, you use a document designed as a cover page for a product and price list for Oak Grove Garden Center. The docu-ment includes two clip art pictures that you modify in order to illustrate the text. Before you start the lessons, please be sure you are in Page Layout view, with both horizontal and vertical rulers displayed and the Zoom Control set to 100%. At times, you may be asked to change the Zoom set-tings; however, you should always use the setting with which you are most comfortable. You may notice that the figures use different Zoom settings to provide you with the best illustrations possible.

Size
To adjust the size and shape of an object.

Crop
To adjust the amount of an object you can view in a document.

Lesson 1: Sizing and Cropping a Picture

After you place a picture in your document, you can perform a variety of operations on it, including *sizing* and *cropping*. You first learned how to drag one of an object's sizing handles to change its size in Project 1. In this les-son, you learn how to set a precise size for a clip art image and how to crop an image so that only the part you want to use is visible.

To Size and Crop a Picture

❶ Open the folder Proj-03 and the file Proj0301 from this book's CD and save it as Catalogue Cover.

This document includes two pictures—a tree on page one and a bunch of tulips on page two. Each picture was inserted with its default image settings, but the results are vastly different, as Figure 3.1 shows. The tree seems about right in terms of size and shape, but the tulips are so large that Word forced them onto a second page.

Figure 3.1
The default settings for clip art may vary from picture to picture.

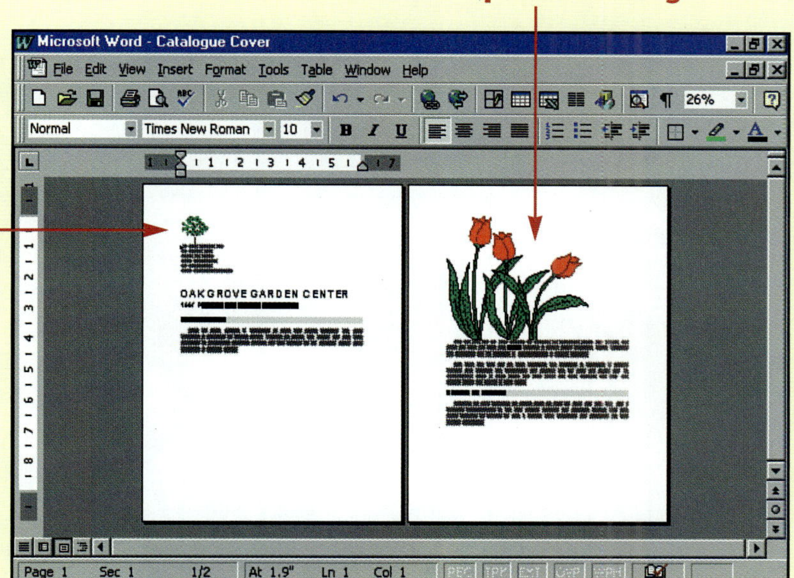

If you have problems...

If you can't see the graphics in the file, first make sure you have the document displayed in Page Layout view. If you are using Page Layout view, choose Tools, Options, click the View tab, and clear the Picture Placeholders check box.

In addition to the tulip picture being too large, you really don't need all three tulips to make the point in the document. Before you make the picture smaller, try cropping the right side to hide one of the tulips.

Bounding box
The rectangular area around an object. When the object is selected, the bounding box is sometimes referred to as the selection rectangle.

❷ Scroll down in the document and click the picture of the tulips.

This step selects the picture. You must select a picture before you can work with it. Eight sizing handles appear around the *bounding box*. In addition, when the picture is selected, Word displays the Picture toolbar, as shown in Figure 3.2.

If you have problems...

If the Picture toolbar doesn't appear automatically, choose View, Toolbars, Picture to display it.

Word

To Size and Crop a Picture   (continued)

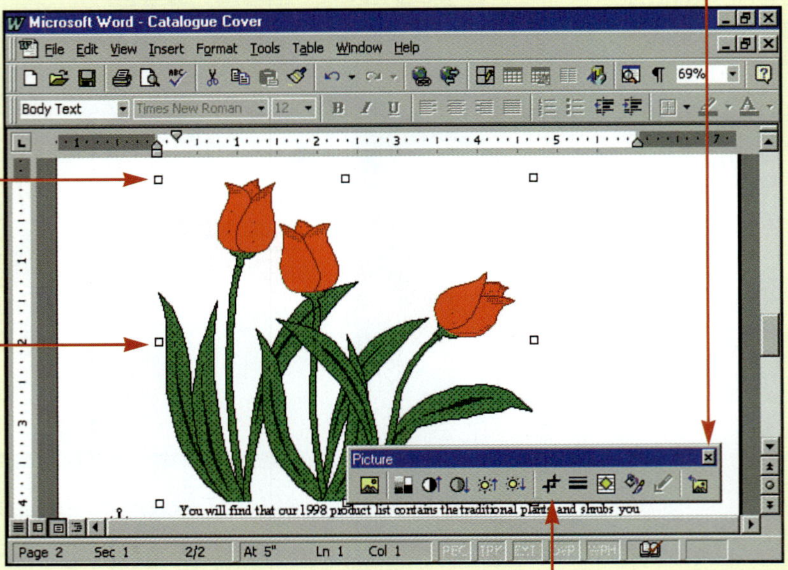

Figure 3.2
The Picture toolbar gives you easy access to the tools you need to format and modify graphics in a document.

Picture toolbar

Sizing handles

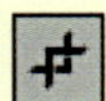

Crop button

If you have problems...

If the Picture toolbar blocks your view of the document, drag it out of the way. In the rest of the figures used to illustrate this project, the Picture toolbar has been docked at the right side of the document window.

3 **Click the Crop button on the Picture toolbar.**

Word changes the mouse pointer to the cropping tool, which looks like two Xs. As long as the mouse pointer is positioned outside the bounding box around the picture, it appears as the cropping tool. If you move the mouse pointer over the box, the mouse pointer changes to the four-headed arrow you use to move a picture.

4 **Position the cropping tool over the sizing handle in the middle of the right side of the picture; click and drag to the left about two inches.**

As you drag, the pointer changes to look like a vertical line with a handle pushing against the bounding box; the bounding box moves with the pointer. The bounding box appears as a dashed line, showing you how far you have cropped (see Figure 3.3).

5 **Release the mouse button when the bounding box shows that you have cropped off the tulip on the right.**

Word crops the picture, leaving just two tulips visible. (If Word moves the picture, you may have to scroll up in the document to find the picture again.) The area that is no longer visible hasn't been deleted—it's just hidden. Only the area within the bounding box is displayed.

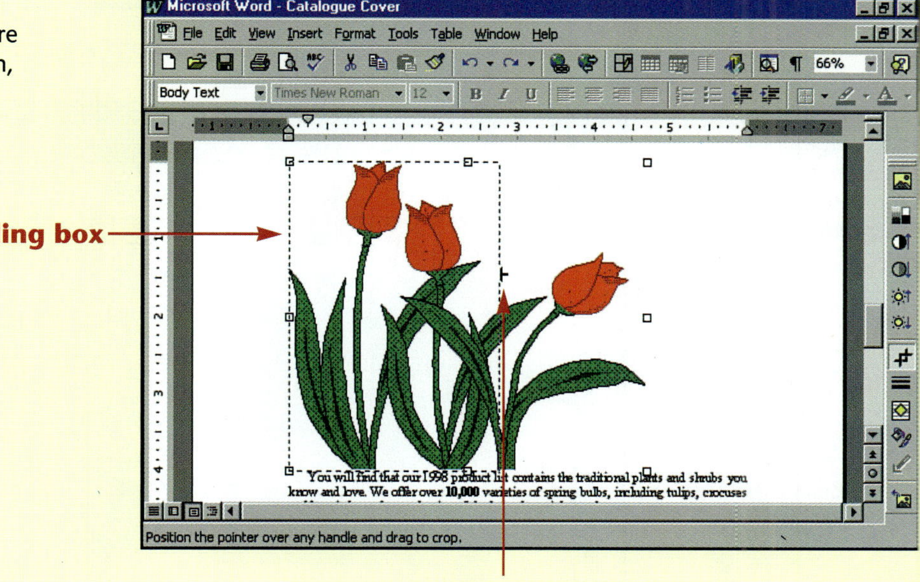

If you have problems...

If you crop too far, simply use the cropping tool to drag the bouncing box back out. Alternatively, choose Edit, Undo and try again.

When you crop or resize the tulip picture, Word may reposition the picture in the document. If Word moves the tulip picture, scroll up in the document until you see the picture again. For now, don't worry about the placement of the pictures. You learn more about fixing them in a particular location in Lesson 2.

Now use the Format Picture dialog box to set a precise size for the tulip picture so it fits nicely in the document.

6 Click the Crop button.

This action turns off the cropping tool.

7 Click the Format Picture button on the Picture toolbar.

The Format Picture dialog box appears, as shown in Figure 3.4. (You can also choose Format, Picture to open the dialog box.) In this dialog box, you can choose options and settings to format pictures in a document—including size, cropping, and position settings, as well as line and color enhancements.

8 Click the Size tab. In the Size and Rotate area, type 1.5 in the Height text box; then press Tab.

This step sets the height of the picture to 1 1/2 inches and automatically adjusts the width so the picture stays in proportion. Notice that the original size measurements are displayed at the bottom of the page; you can use the Reset button to revert to the default settings.

continues

To Size and Crop a Picture (continued)

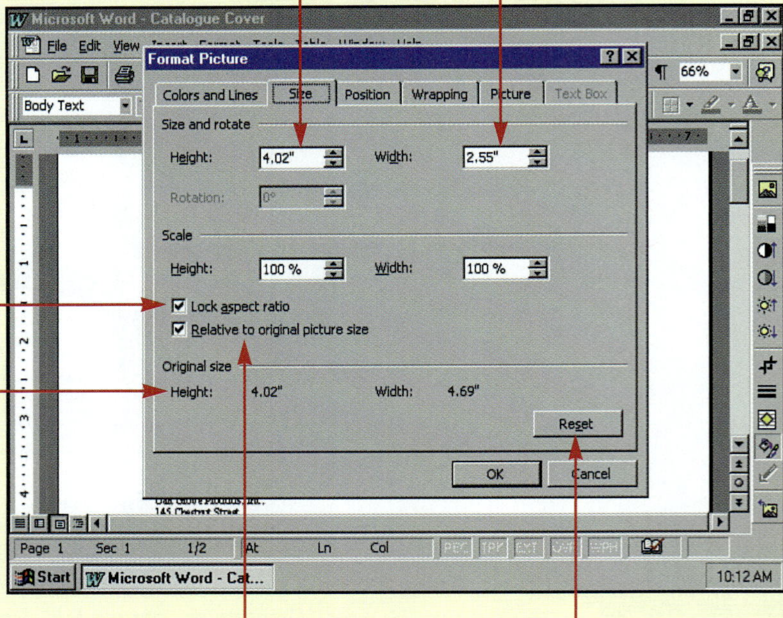

Figure 3.4
On the Size page of the Format Picture dialog box, you can set precise height and width measurements.

9 **Click OK.**

Word resizes the picture in the document so it's just about the same size as the tree picture. Again, don't worry about the placement of the pictures right now; you learn more about positioning pictures in Lesson 2.

10 **Save the document and keep it open.**

In the next lesson, you learn how to position a picture within a document.

To return a picture to its default size and crop settings, click the Reset Picture button on the Picture toolbar.

To resize a picture quickly, you can drag a sizing handle. Position the insertion point over a handle until it changes to a double-headed arrow, sometimes called a sizing tool. Drag the sizing handle in—toward the picture—to make the picture smaller; drag out—away from the picture—to make it larger. To change the width, drag one of the side handles. To change the height, drag one of the top or bottom handles. To change height and width proportionally at the same time, drag a corner handle.

Graphics such as pictures and drawing objects can slow down the response time of your computer considerably. If you are editing a document that contains a lot of graphics, you might want to hide the graphics to speed up scrolling. Simply choose Tools, Options, click the View tab, select the Picture Placeholders check box, and click OK.

Likewise, including graphics greatly increases the size of a document. You can save disk space by creating a link to a picture file instead of inserting the picture into your document. Position the insertion point in the document; then choose Insert, Picture, From File. In the Insert Picture dialog box, select the picture you want to insert and then select the Link to File check box and deselect the Save with Document check box. Click Insert. Word inserts the picture into the document. You learn more about linking objects into Word documents in Project 14.

Lesson 2: Positioning a Picture on the Page

Floating object

An object that can be positioned anywhere in a document, including header area, footer area, margins, or layered over text and other graphics.

Inline object

An object that is part of the document text.

Anchor

To keep an object on the same page as a particular paragraph.

By default, pictures are inserted into a document as *floating objects*. This means that the picture can be placed anywhere on the page—including the margins or header and footer area, or layered with text or other objects. You can adjust the position of a picture in a document in a few different ways:

- Simply drag it to the location where you want it to appear.

- Set a precise position for the picture by entering measurements on the Position page of the Format Picture dialog box.

- Set the picture to appear *inline* with the document text.

- Use the drawing tools to align the picture relative to the current page.

A picture is always *anchored* to a paragraph of text in the document and is always displayed on the same page as the anchor. By default, the picture is anchored to the nearest paragraph. However, you can move the anchor to any paragraph of text, even if it isn't the closest paragraph. This is useful if you want the picture displayed on the same page as a different paragraph. Finally, you can lock the anchor if you want to be sure it won't change even if you move the picture or edit the document.

In this lesson, you position and anchor the tulip picture in the document and then set the tree picture inline.

To Position a Picture on the Page

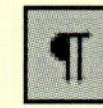

① **In the** Catalogue Cover **document, click the Show/Hide ¶ (Paragraph Marks) button on the Standard toolbar.**

This step displays hidden marks in the document, including anchor icons for selected objects, which appear in the left margin. By default, even though all pictures are anchored to the closest paragraph, the anchors aren't locked—when you move the picture, the anchor moves as well. Now drag the tulip picture where you want it placed in the document.

continues

To Position a Picture on the Page   (continued)

❷ Click the tulip picture to select it; then position the insertion point anywhere within the bounding box.

The mouse pointer changes to a four-headed arrow, as shown in Figure 3.5. You move pictures the same way you moved drawing objects in Project 1.

Figure 3.5
You can easily drag a floating picture any-where in a document.

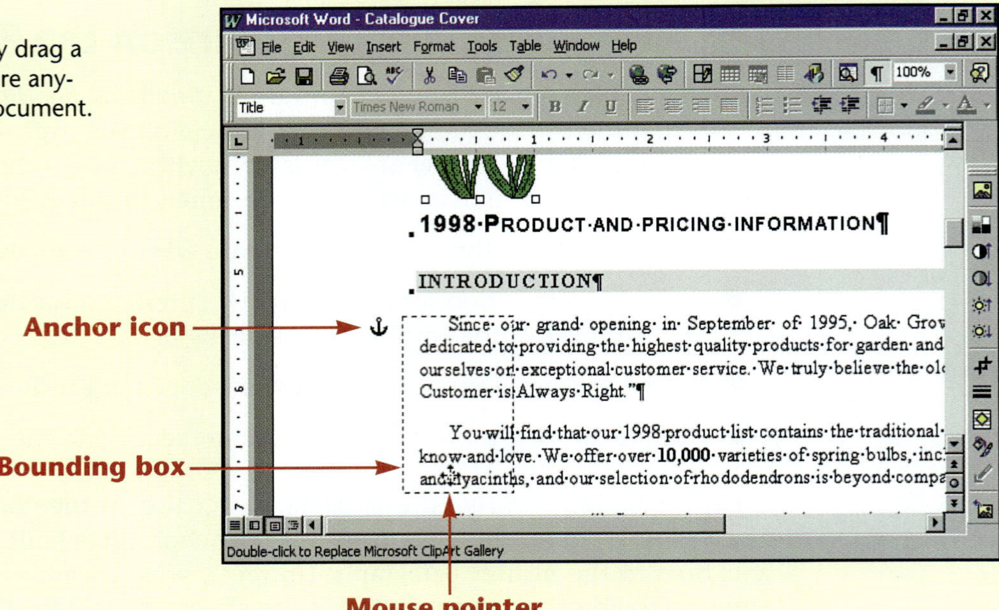

❸ Click and drag the bounding box down in the document.

As you drag, notice that the anchor icon in the left margin moves with the mouse pointer and bounding box.

If you have problems...

If the anchor icon doesn't appear on your screen, be sure that you have a picture selected in Page Layout view and that the Show/Hide ¶ button on the Standard toolbar is selected. If you still don't see the anchors, choose Tools, Options and select the View tab. In the Show group, select Object Anchors.

❹ When the anchor appears beside the first paragraph under the heading INTRODUCTION, release the mouse button.

Word moves the picture. The picture is now anchored to the first paragraph of the introduction; however, the anchor is free to move if you move the picture or add or delete text in the document. You have to lock the anchor to keep it from moving.

Now try positioning the picture precisely on the page and locking the anchor so the picture stays in position.

5 **Click the Format Picture button on the Picture toolbar and then click the Position tab.**

On the Position page of the Format Picture dialog box, you can set a precise position for the picture and choose anchoring options (see Figure 3.6). By default, the anchor is set to move with the text if you add or delete text in the document. You can deselect the <u>M</u>ove Object with Text option so that the picture stays anchored to the nearest paragraph, even if the text changes. Select the <u>L</u>ock Anchor check box if you want to keep the anchor with its current paragraph, even if the text in the document changes or the picture moves.

Figure 3.6
Use the Format Picture dialog box to position a picture and to adjust anchor settings.

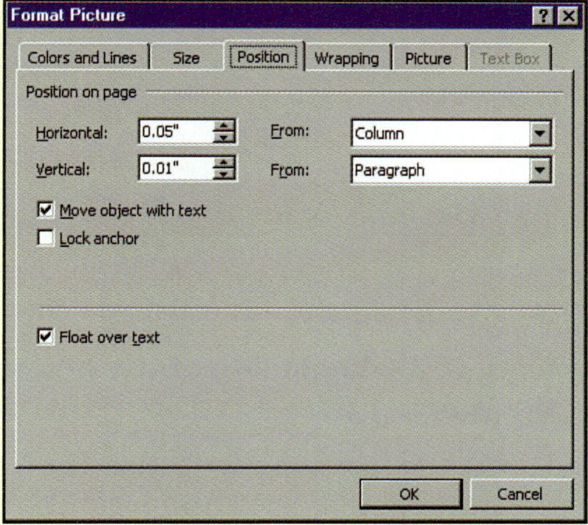

Now set a precise location for the picture, and lock the anchor so it remains with the current paragraph no matter how the document changes.

6 **Deselect the <u>M</u>ove Object with Text check box and select the <u>L</u>ock Anchor check box so the anchor will no longer move automatically. Type 3.5 in the <u>H</u>orizontal text box and select Page in the <u>F</u>rom drop-down list next to the Horizontal setting. Type 5.5 in the <u>V</u>ertical text box and select Page in the <u>F</u>rom drop-down list next to the <u>V</u>ertical setting. Then click OK.**

Word positions the picture 3 1/2 inches from the left edge of the page and 5 1/2 inches from the top of the page, as shown in Figure 3.7. The picture is still anchored to the same text; however, unless you move it again, it always appears at this precise location on the page where the text is located. Notice that a small lock icon appears beside the anchor icon in the document.

continues

Word

To Position a Picture on the Page   (continued)

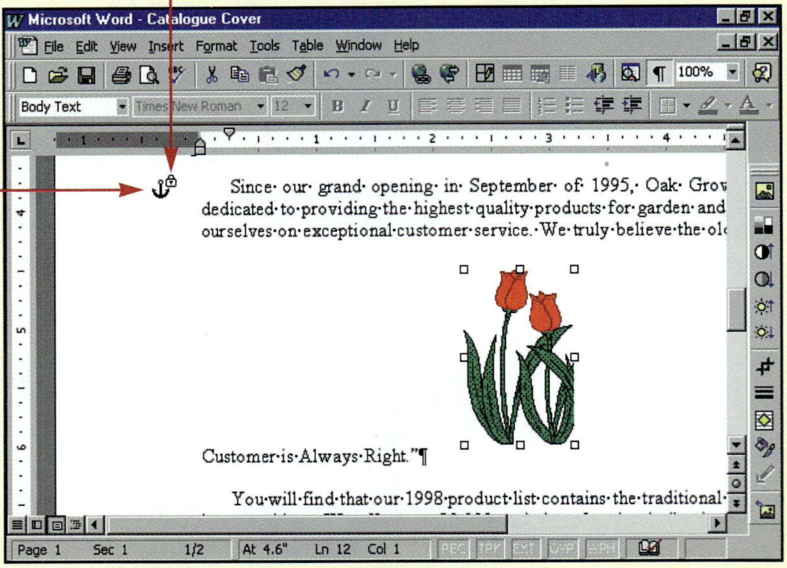

Figure 3.7
The picture appears precisely 3 1/2 inches from the left edge of the page and 5 1/2 inches from the top of the page.

Now see what happens when you change the document text.

7 **Click at the beginning of the first paragraph of text under the heading INTRODUCTION and then press Ctrl+⏎Enter.**

This action inserts a page break. The paragraph of text is forced onto the next page, as shown in Figure 3.8. The picture moves with the paragraph to which it's anchored, but it appears positioned on the new page in the same location it had been on the first page—3 1/2 inches from the left and 5 1/2 inches from the top.

Figure 3.8
A picture always appears on the same page as its anchor.

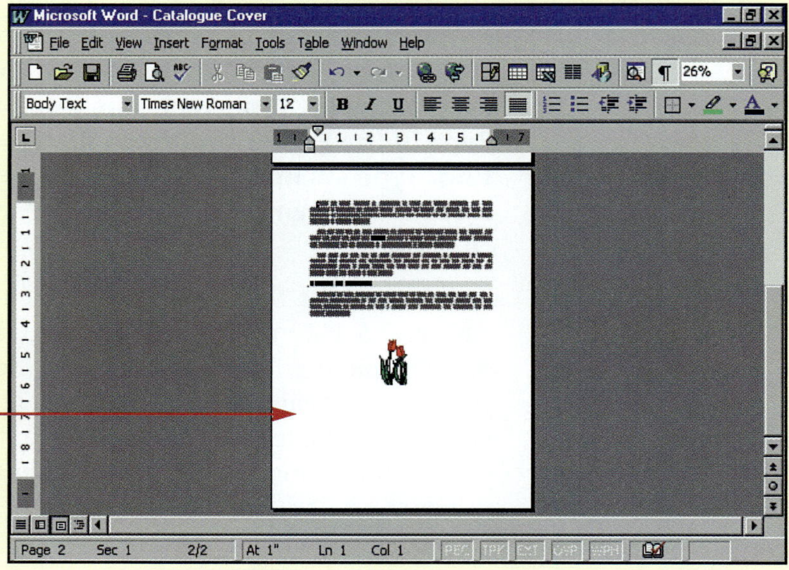

The picture is still 3 1/2 inches from the left edge of the page and 5 1/2 inches from the top

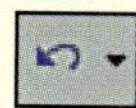

8 Click the Undo button on the Standard toolbar.

This step removes the page break. Now change the tree picture from floating to inline, so it's displayed as part of the document text.

9 Click the tree picture to select it and then the Format Picture button on the Picture toolbar.

The Format Picture dialog box opens.

10 Click the Position tab and then deselect the Float Over _T_ext check box.

This option determines whether the picture will be floating or inline. Notice that when this option is deselected the other options on the Position page become unavailable. That is because you position inline pictures just as you do regular text in a document.

11 Click OK.

Word changes the tree picture so it's inline with the document text, as shown in Figure 3.9. Notice that the picture appears at the beginning of the first line of text. The picture still has a bounding box and sizing handles that you can use to make it larger or smaller, but you can't drag it to move it.

Figure 3.9
The tree picture is now inline with the document text.

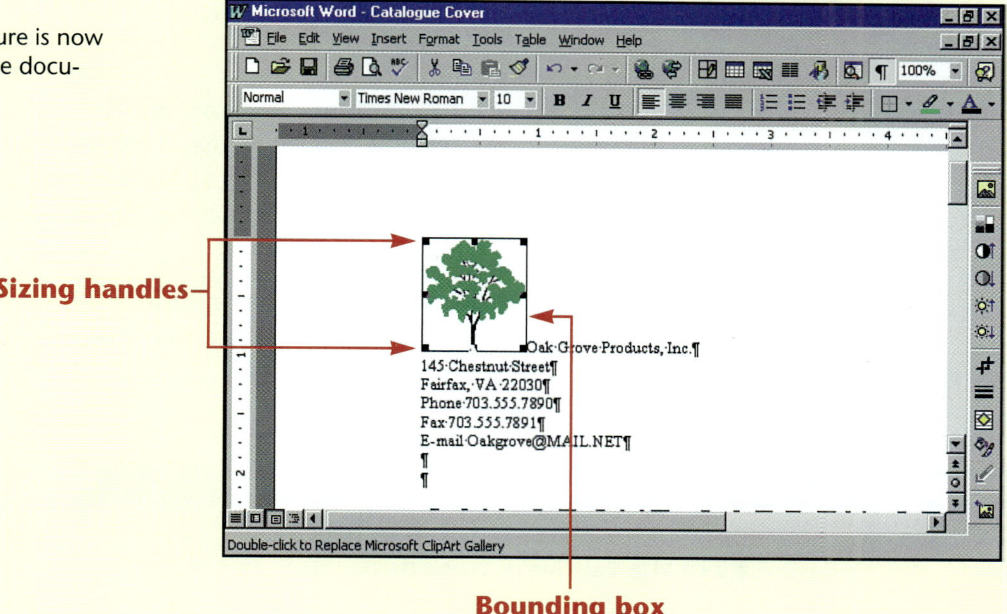

Sizing handles

Bounding box

Now see what happens if you insert characters in the document.

12 Press Ctrl + Home to move the insertion point to the beginning of the document; then press ↵Enter.

Word inserts a new line of text. Notice that the tree picture moved down with its line of text.

continues

Word

To Position a Picture on the Page   (continued)

⓭ **Press** `←Backspace` **to delete the blank line; save the Catalogue Cover document and keep it open.**

In the next lesson, you learn how to control the way text wraps around a picture.

You can also align a picture relative to the page by using options on the Drawing toolbar. First, select the picture you want to align. Click the Drawing button on the Standard toolbar to display the Drawing toolbar; then click the Draw button, point at Align or Distribute, and select Relative to Page. This action makes the alignment options available on the Align or Distribute submenu. Click Draw, point at Align or Distribute again, and select the alignment option you want to use.

You can move an anchor that isn't locked without moving the picture. Point at the anchor until the mouse pointer changes to a four-headed arrow and then drag the anchor to its new location. The picture stays put, but it's anchored to the new paragraph. If the paragraph moves to another page, so does the picture.

Lesson 3: Changing the Way Text Wraps Around a Picture

Text wrapping

The way text flows around a picture in a document.

When you insert a picture into a document, text moves out of the way to make room. By default, the text moves above and below the picture, but doesn't appear on the sides. The way that text appears around a picture is called *text wrapping*, and the default wrapping style is Top & Bottom. You can easily change the way that text wraps around a picture, and control the distance between the picture and the text.

In this lesson, you change the text wrapping around the tulip picture. (You can't change the text wrapping around the *tree* picture because it's now inline.)

To Change the Way Text Wraps Around a Picture

❶ **In the** `Catalogue Cover` **document, select the tulip picture.**

As you can see, the text wraps above and below the picture, but not along the sides. The quickest way to change the text wrapping is to use the Text Wrapping button on the Picture toolbar.

❷ **Click the Text Wrapping button on the Picture toolbar.**

A palette of wrapping styles pops up, as shown in Figure 3.10.

Figure 3.10
You can quickly select a text wrapping style from the pop-up list.

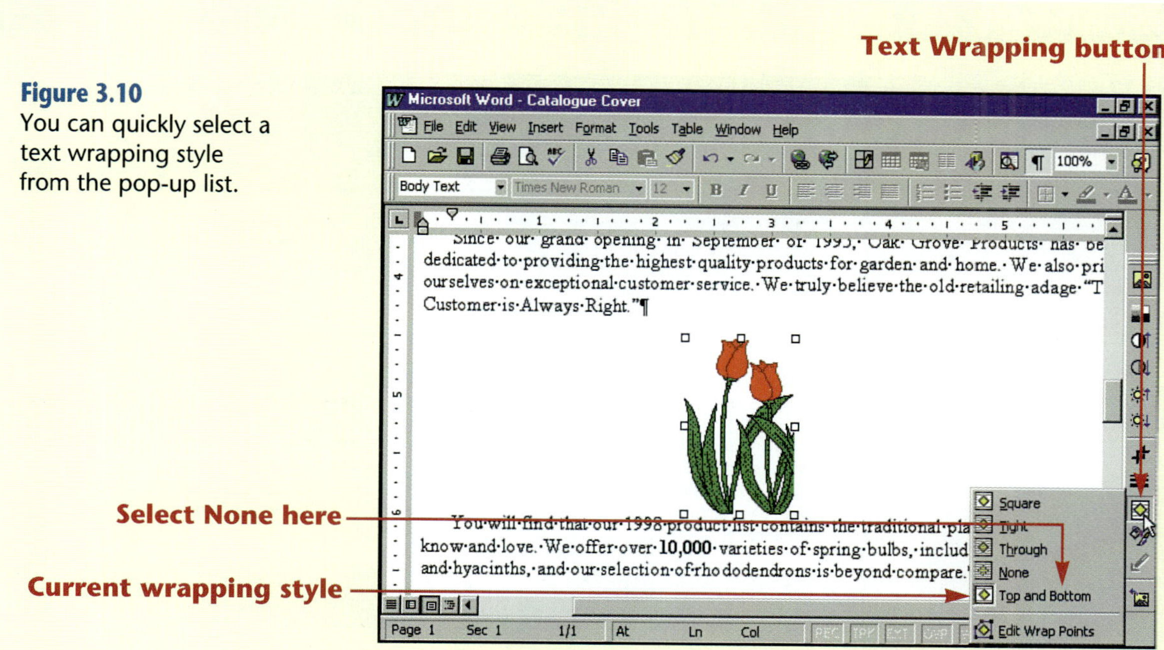

Select None here —

Current wrapping style —

First, see what happens when there is no text wrapping.

❸ Click the <u>N</u>one style.

Word removes all text wrapping, so the text simply continues as if there was no picture in the document at all (see Figure 3.11).

Figure 3.11
With no text wrapping, text flows right through the picture.

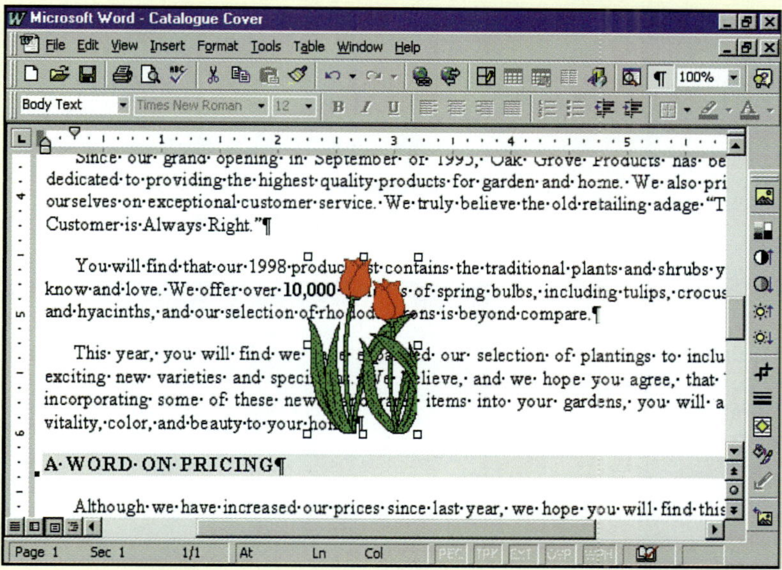

Try setting the text to wrap on all sides of the picture.

❹ Click the Text Wrapping button on the Picture toolbar. Then click the <u>S</u>quare style.

Word wraps the text around the picture so that it appears around all sides, as shown in Figure 3.12.

continues

To Change the Way Text Wraps Around a Picture   (continued)

Figure 3.12
Now the text wraps on
all sides of the picture.

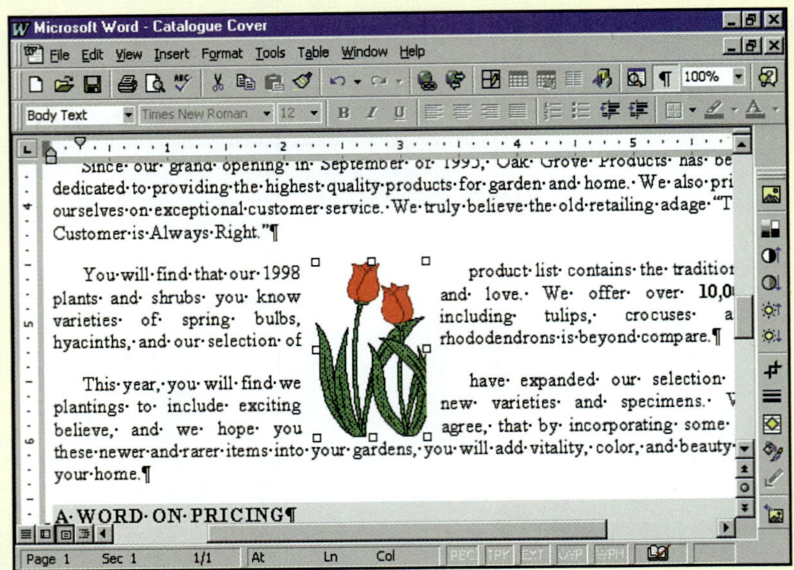

This time, use the Format Picture dialog box to change the text wrap.

5 **Click the Format Picture button on the Picture toolbar; then click the Wrapping tab in the Format Picture dialog box.**

On the Wrapping page of the Format Picture dialog box, you can select any of the text wrapping styles, and you can also customize some of the settings (see Figure 3.13). For example, notice that when the Square style is selected, you can specify whether you want to wrap text on the left, right, or both sides. You can also specify how far away from the picture you want the text to stop and start. These options are available when you select the Square, Tight, or Through wrapping style.

Figure 3.13
Use the Wrapping page
of the Format Picture
dialog box to fine-tune
the position of wrapped
text.

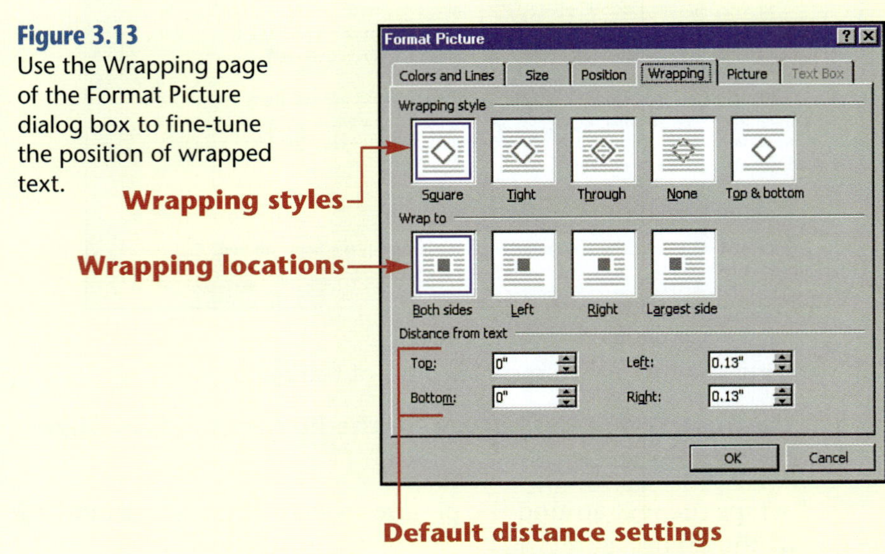

6 **Leave the Square Wrapping style selected for this example. Click Left in the Wrap To area and then click OK.**

Word changes the text wrapping so that text is wrapped on the left of the picture, but the right side of the picture is open. Now try adjusting the distance between the picture and the text.

7 **Click the Format Picture button on the Picture toolbar. Click the Wrapping tab; in the Distance From Text area, increase the value in the Left text box to .3.**

Because the text is wrapped only on the left side of the picture, this is the only value you have to change. Increasing the value increases the distance between the picture and the text.

8 **Click OK.**

Word adjusts the distance between the picture and the text. The text on the left side of the picture looks good now, but you really don't want to leave the right side open. Try using the Tight wrapping style to set the text to wrap around the contours of the picture, not just around the corners of the bounding box.

9 **Click the Format Picture button on the Picture toolbar and then click the Wrapping tab.**

The Wrapping options are now visible.

10 **Select the Tight wrapping style. Then select Both Sides in the Wrap To area, and increase the distance from the text to the picture on the right side to match the left side by entering .3 in the Right text box.**

These text wrapping settings help integrate the picture into the document, improving the overall page appearance.

11 **Click OK.**

Word changes the text wrapping again, as shown in Figure 3.14. This is the way you want the document to remain. To get a good look at the page, deselect the picture, or change to Print Preview.

12 **Save the changes you have made and keep the Catalogue Cover document open.**

In the next lesson, you learn how to add borders and fills to a picture.

continues

To Change the Way Text Wraps Around a Picture   (continued)

Figure 3.14
Now the text wraps tightly .3 inches from the picture.

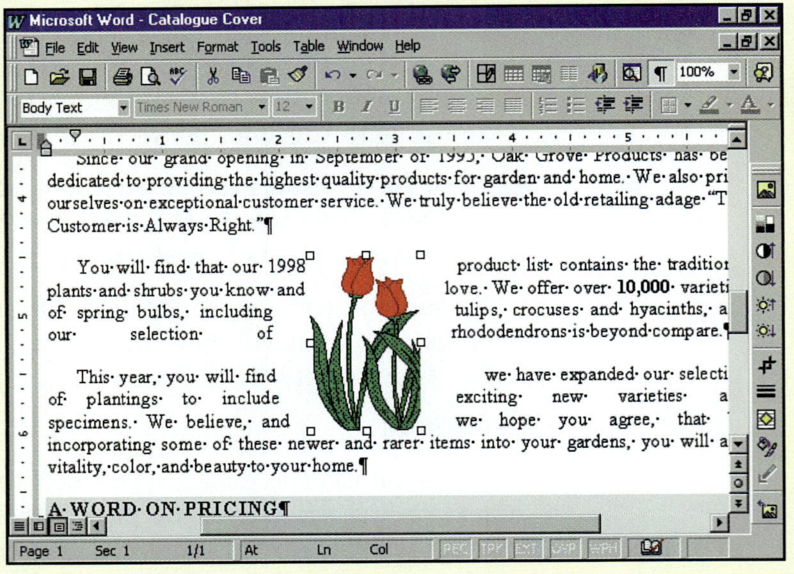

 **Inside Stuff**

If you have a picture with a lot of open areas in it, you may like the effect of the Through wrapping style. When you wrap text through a picture, the text contours are like those of the Tight style, but the Through setting also fills in any open areas within the picture.

Lesson 4: Adding a Border and Fill to a Picture

One of the easiest ways to modify the appearance of a picture is to add a border or a fill, or both. You can format the border with different line styles and colors. You can also fill the background area within the bounding box with a color or pattern.

In this lesson, you apply a border to the tulip picture and then fill the background of the picture with a pattern.

To Add a Border and Fill to a Picture

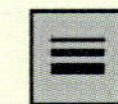

1 **In the `Catalogue Cover` document, select the tulip picture, if it isn't already selected, and then click the Line Style button on the Picture toolbar.**

A menu of line styles pops up.

2 **Click the 3 point double-line style on the pop-up menu.**

Word applies the border to the picture, as shown in Figure 3.15.

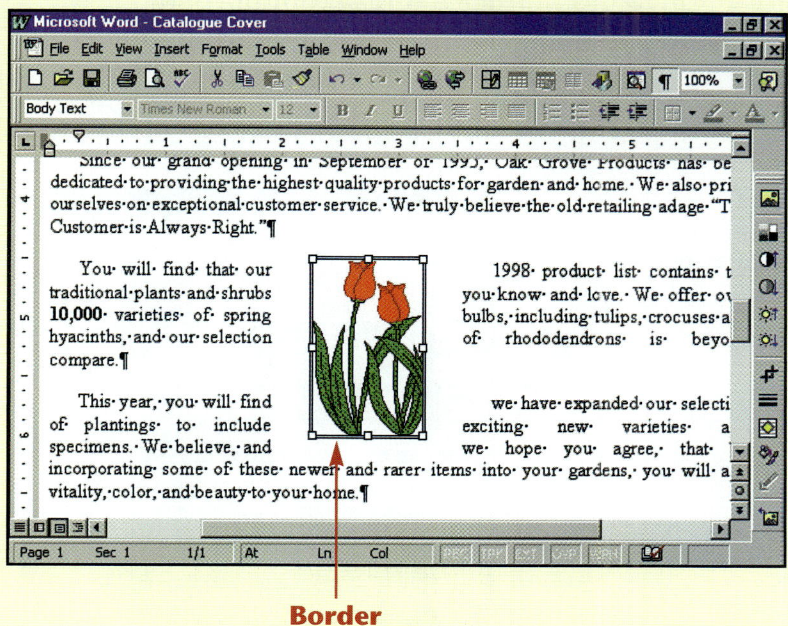

Now add a fill to the background.

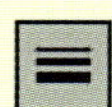

3 **Click the Line Style button on the Picture toolbar again. Then click More Lines.**

Word opens the Format Picture dialog box with the Colors and Lines page displayed, as shown in Figure 3.16. You can see the border color and line style you selected in the Line area of the dialog box.

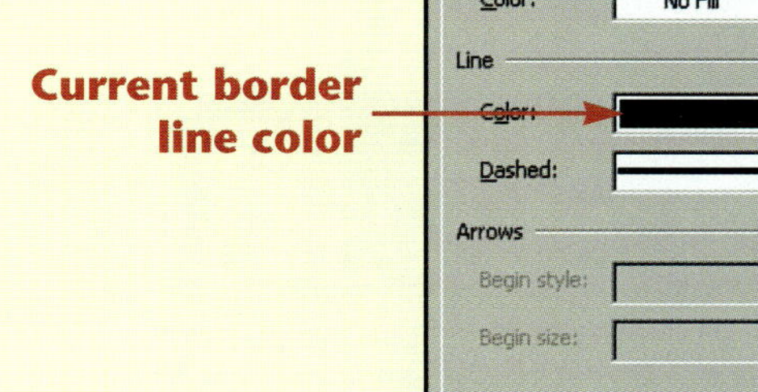

Now add a pattern fill to the picture.

4 **Click the arrow button for the Color option in the Fill area.**

This step opens the Fill Color palette.

continues

To Add a Border and Fill to a Picture   (continued)

5 **Select Fill Effects on the Fill Color palette.**

The Fill Effects dialog box opens (see Figure 3.17).

Figure 3.17
You can use colors, patterns, textures, or pictures as a fill.

Selected pattern →

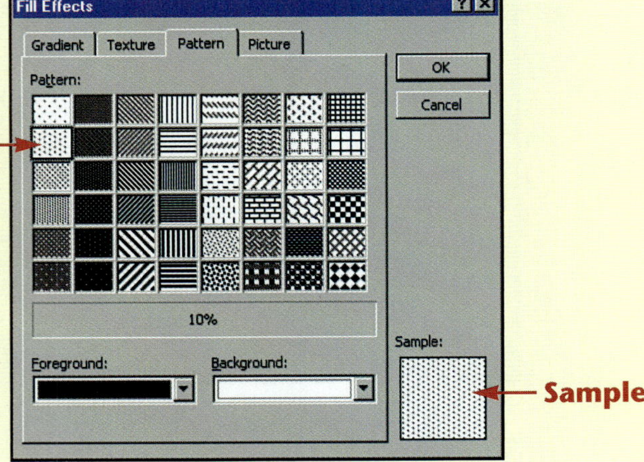

← **Sample**

6 **Click the Pattern tab; then select the first pattern in the second row—the 10% fill pattern.**

Word displays a sample of the selected pattern in the dialog box, as shown in Figure 3.17.

7 **Click OK.**

Word closes the Fill Effects dialog box and redisplays the Colors and Lines page of the Format Picture dialog box.

8 **Click OK.**

Word closes the Format Picture dialog box and applies the fill to the picture, as shown in Figure 3.18.

Figure 3.18
You can enhance a picture with a fill pattern.

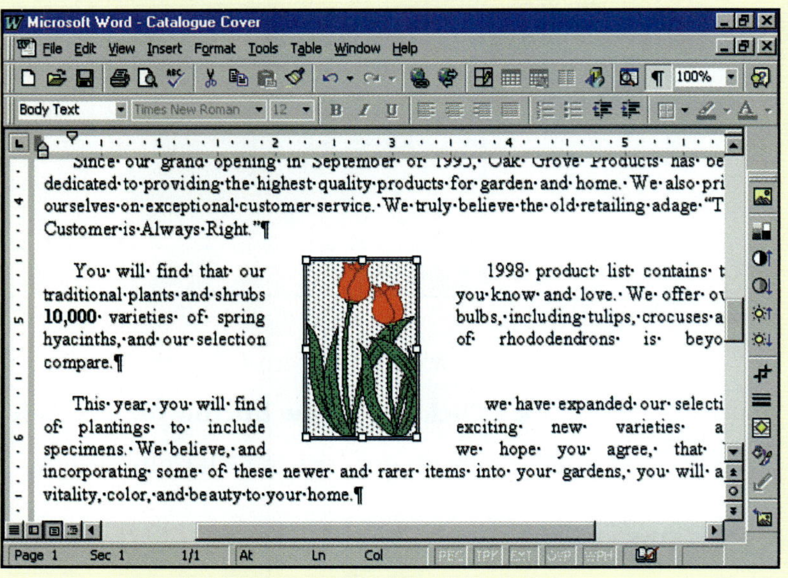

9 **Save the changes you have made to the `Catalogue Cover` document and keep it open.**

In the next lesson, you learn how to work with text boxes.

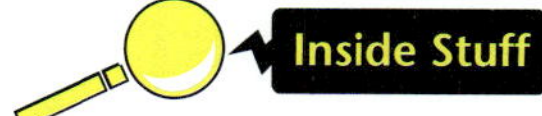

You can also format a picture in a document by using some of the drawing tools. For example, you can apply borders and fills using the Drawing toolbar, and you can apply shadow effects. If the picture is in metafile format (most clip art images are), you can even ungroup the objects in the picture and edit them individually.

With the tools on the Picture toolbar, you can adjust default picture settings that control the color of the picture. If you know you'll be printing the document on a black-and-white printer, for example, you may want to use the Image Control button to change the color style setting to Grayscale or Black and White, and then adjust the brightness or contrast settings to achieve the look you want. Feel free to experiment with these settings. You can always use the Undo button or the Reset button on the Picture toolbar to revert to the original picture settings.

Lesson 5: Working with Text Boxes

You can insert text box objects to help you format and position text or graphics in a document. Text boxes are useful for integrating text with graphics to create effects, such as a letterhead or logo, and for applying special formatting to text, such as rotating or flipping the text box and changing the orientation of the text from horizontal to vertical.

In this lesson, you insert the tree picture and the return address information into a text box and format it as a letterhead.

To Work with a Text Box

1 **Select the first six lines in the `Catalogue Cover` document.**

These lines include the tree picture and the return address information. You can place a text box around selected text automatically, or you can draw the text box first and then enter new text in it. Because the text already exists in the sample document, you'll simply place a text box around it.

2 **Choose Insert, Text Box.**

Word places a text box around the selected text and picture, as shown in Figure 3.19. The selected text box has a gray shaded border around it. Notice that the text box object is anchored to the first paragraph mark in the document (it only looks like the anchor is within the text box—it's actually to the left of the first paragraph mark).

continues

Word

To Work with a Text Box   (continued)

Figure 3.19
Use a text box to help you position text and graphics on a page.

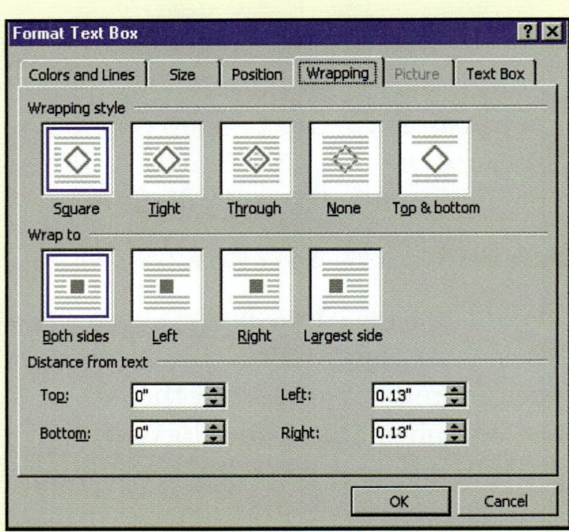

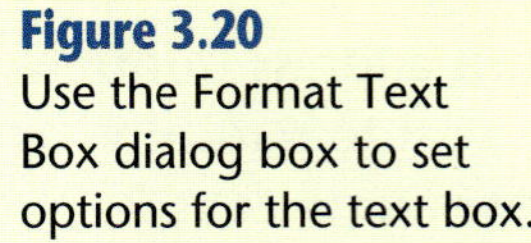

The text box is automatically sized at two inches square, which isn't quite large enough to contain all six lines of the text; some of the text seems to disappear below the bottom edge of the box! Don't worry—the text is still there, it's just hidden, as if it had been cropped. When you resize the box or the font size, you'll be able to see all of the text.

By default, the document text wraps square on all sides. Because you want the contents of the text box to appear as a letterhead on the page, first change the text wrapping.

❸ Choose Format, Text Box.

The Format Text Box dialog box appears, as shown in Figure 3.20. This dialog box is similar to the Format Picture dialog box except that the Text Box page is available instead of the Picture page.

Figure 3.20
Use the Format Text Box dialog box to set options for the text box.

4 **Click the Wrapping tab, select the T<u>o</u>p & Bottom Wrapping style, and click OK.**

Word changes the way the document text wraps around the text box, as shown in Figure 3.21. Because the object is at the top of the page, text appears only along the bottom in this example.

Figure 3.21
Now document text wraps on only the top and bottom of the text box.

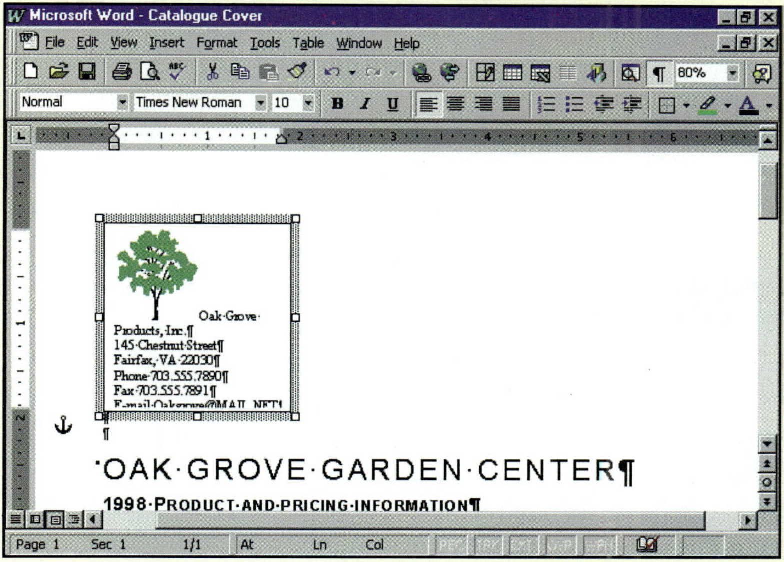

Now resize the text box.

5 **Drag the sizing handle in the middle of the right side of the text box to increase the width of the box from 2 inches to about 6 1/2 inches.**

When you release the mouse button, the text box is sized to fit from margin to margin across the page, as shown in Figure 3.22. Notice that all the text is now visible in the box.

Figure 3.22
You can resize and crop the text box just as you do pictures and other objects.

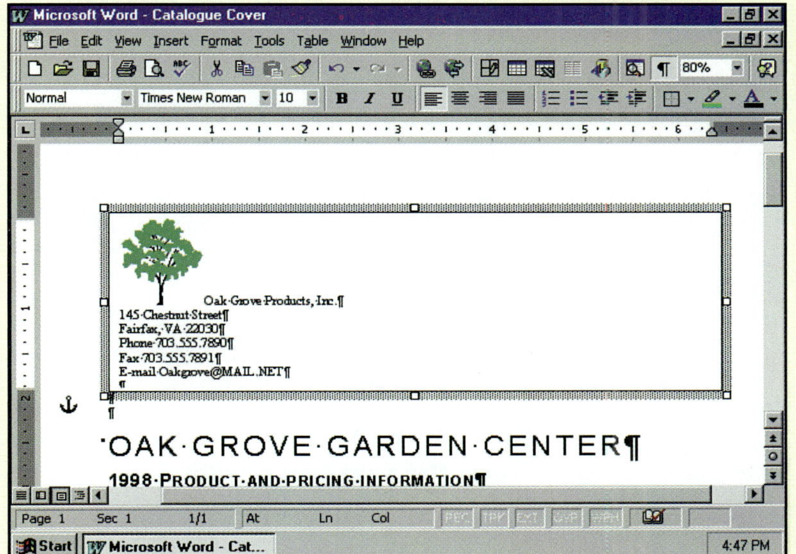

ccntinues

Try formatting the contents of the text box.

6 Click the Align Right button on the Formatting toolbar.

Word right-aligns everything in the text box. When the text box is selected, all formatting you select is applied to the entire contents of the text box. To format only some of the text, select it first.

Try changing the font and increasing the size of the company name.

7 In the text box, select the company name Oak Grove Products, Inc. **Then use the Formatting toolbar to change the font to Arial and increase the font size to 30 points.**

If you have problems...

If 30 isn't available in the Font Size drop-down list, simply type 30 in the Font Size box and press ↵Enter.

Word formats the text, as shown in Figure 3.23. As soon as you click inside the text box, Word changes to text-editing mode. Although the text box remains selected, notice that the bounding box changes to look like short black slashes. You can enter, edit, and format text in the text box by using the typical Word commands.

Figure 3.23
You can enter, edit, and format text in a text box.

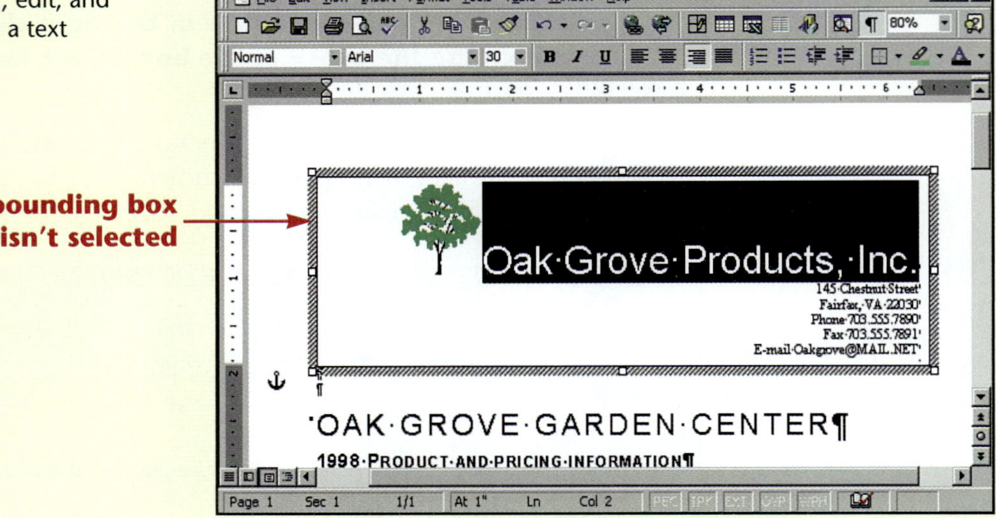

The bounding box isn't selected

The letterhead is looking good now. However, you would prefer to have no border around the text box. To make this change, begin by turning off the text-editing mode and selecting the text box.

8 With the four-headed arrow mouse pointer, click anywhere on the text box border.

Word turns off the text-editing mode. The insertion point is removed from the text box, and the slashes around the box change back to the gray border.

9 **Choose F̲ormat, Text B̲ox.**

The Format Text Box dialog box opens.

10 **Click the Colors and Lines tab; then open the C̲olor drop-down list in the Line area.**

A palette of colors drops down.

11 **Choose No Line at the top of the palette; then click OK.**

Word removes the border from the text box, as shown in Figure 3.24. To get a good look at it, click anywhere outside the text box.

Figure 3.24
The letterhead appears across the top of the document.

You have now finished creating the letterhead within the text box. In Whole Page view, it should look similar to the one in Figure 3.25.

Figure 3.25
In Whole Page view, you can get a good look at the way the pictures are integrated into the catalogue cover.

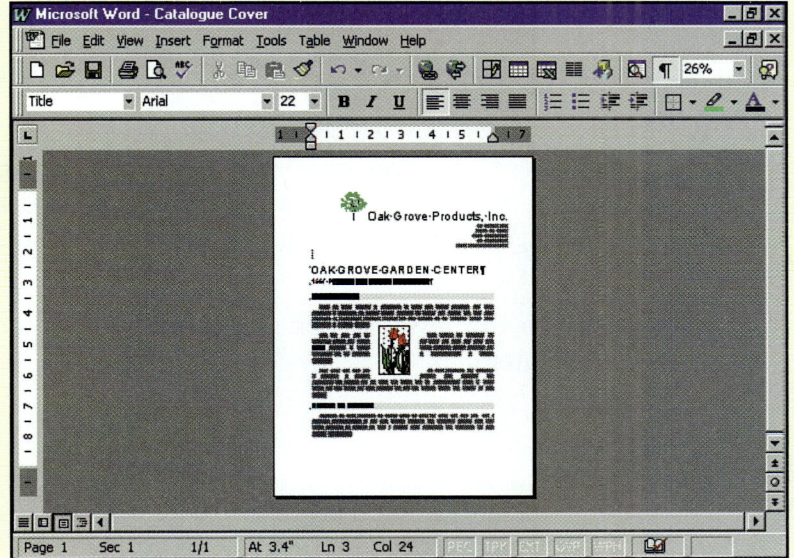

continues

To Work with a Text Box   (continued)

⑫ **Save the** `Catalogue Cover` **document and close it.**

You can format and position text boxes by using the drawing tools, as well as by using the Format Text Box dialog box. With the drawing tools, you can manipulate the text box object using such features as shadows and 3-D effects, as well as the Flip and Rotate commands. You can also use the alignment grid to position the text box, and you can group the text box with other objects.

You can change the orientation of text in a text box from horizontal to vertical up or vertical down. Vertical up text is aligned sideways on the left side of the text box, with the text reading from bottom to top. Vertical down text is aligned sideways on the right side of the text box, with the text reading from top to bottom. Choose Format, Text Direction to open the Text Direction - Text Box dialog box; then select the orientation you want and click OK.

In previous versions of Word, frames were used to position and format pictures, as well as text. If you are working with a document that contains frames, you can use the options in the Format Frame dialog box in place of the Format Text Box dialog box. Alternatively, you can remove the frame and replace it with a text box. To remove a frame, select it, choose Format, Frame, click the Frame tab, click the Remove Frame button, and then click OK.

You can insert a frame with Word 97 if you want, but you have to add the Insert Frame button to a toolbar; no menu command or key combination is available to insert a frame. Really, the only reason to use a frame instead of a text box is if the frame already exists in the document or if you want the frame to contain certain fields, such as those used to create numbered lists, tables of authorities, tables of contents, or indexes.

When you delete a text box, you delete the contents of the text box as well. To remove a text box without deleting its contents, use the Clipboard to cut and paste the contents outside of the text box; then delete the text box object.

Lesson 6: Creating a Watermark

A watermark is text or graphics that appears on the top of or behind document text. Watermarks are often found on pre-printed letters. You can create your own watermarks, such as a logo that appears centered on your page, or the word "confidential," which can appear behind the text of each page.

For this lesson, begin with a new, blank document and create a letterhead watermark.

To Create a Watermark

1 **With a new, blank document open, type a company name, address, and phone number at the top of the document. Choose font formatting and a font size to your liking. Center the text. Your letterhead might resemble that shown in Figure 3.26.**

Figure 3.26
Create a letterhead by starting with company information.

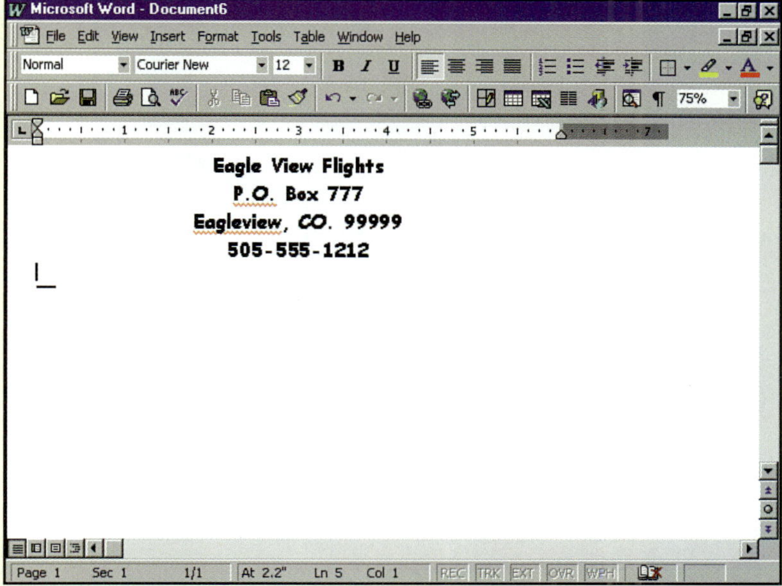

2 **Choose View, Header and Footer from the menu (watermarks begin in the header or footer of a document, even though the watermark displays centered on your page).**

3 **Click the Show/Hide Document Text button on the Header and Footer toolbar to hide the document text and to work with the graphic you are about to insert. If you don't click this button, you won't be able to select your graphic once you insert it into the document.**

4 **Choose Insert, Picture, Clip Art. Select a clip art item and click OK.**

5 **Clip art first appears in your document in the left side of your header (see Figure 3.27). You need to do some formatting to this clip art in order to turn the picture into a watermark. Right-click the clip art and choose Format Picture from the pop-up menu.**

6 **The Format Picture dialog box appears. Click the Picture tab. In the Image Control section, use the drop-down Color list to select Watermark. (See Figure 3.28.)**

continues

Word

To Create a Watermark   (continued)

Header area expands when you insert clip art

Figure 3.27
Start a watermark by inserting a picture into the header area.

Show/Hide document text button hides the company information you previously typed in the document

Figure 3.28
Select Watermark as the color, so your watermark appears faded on your document.

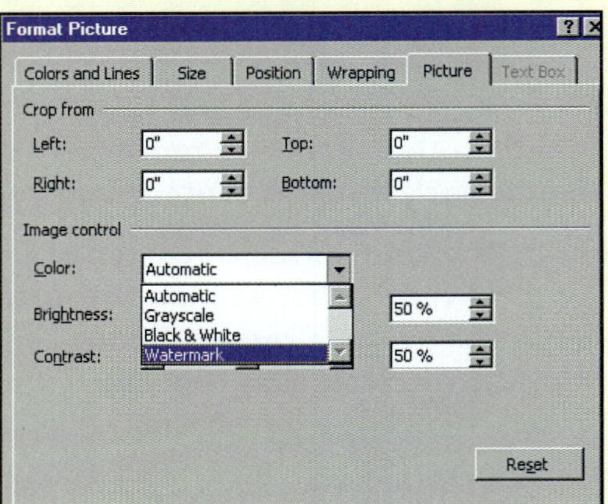

7 To be certain that the text you type on your new letterhead appears on top of the watermark, click the Wrapping tab of the Format Picture dialog box. Choose None as your wrapping option (see Figure 3.29). Click OK.

8 Your watermark graphic now appears on your document, outside of the header border as shown in Figure 3.30.

Figure 3.29
Disable wrapping so that text you type on your document appears on top of the watermark.

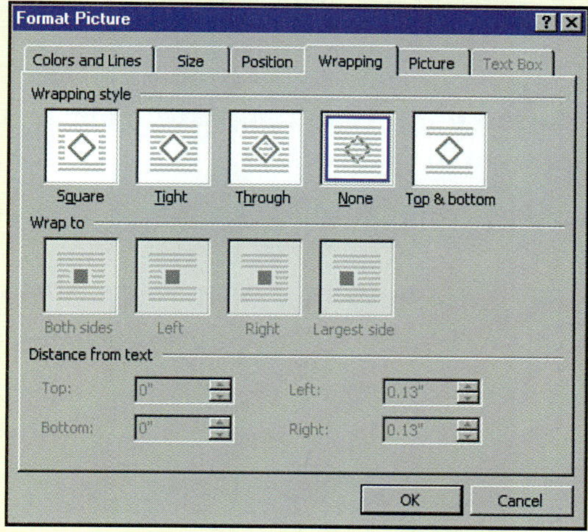

Figure 3.30
Once you have selected None as the wrapping option, the picture appears outside of the header.

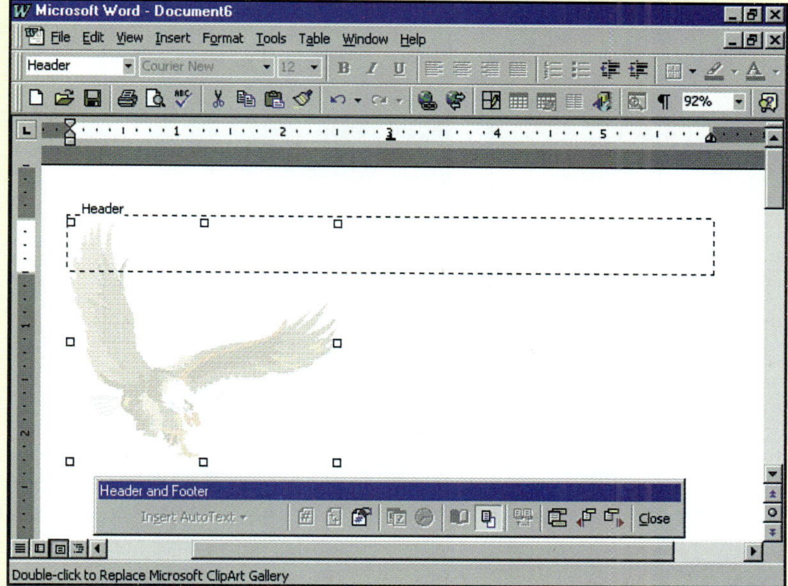

9 **Move and size the graphic until it is positioned where you want it on your document. To size the graphic, right-click the graphic and choose Format Picture. On the Size tab, increase the number in the Scale fields to increase the size of the object.**

10 **Click OK to close the Format Picture dialog box.**

11 **Click Close to close the Header and Footer toolbar.**

You must be in Page Layout view to see the watermark on your document. If you need to reposition or reformat the picture, choose View, Header and Footer.

continues

To Create a Watermark   **(continued)**

⑫ **Save your new letterhead as a template and create a letter based upon that template. Your letter might look like that shown in Figure 3.31.**

You learn more about templates in Project 6.

Figure 3.31
Company logos can make good-looking watermarks on letterheads. Here, an example is shown using clip art.

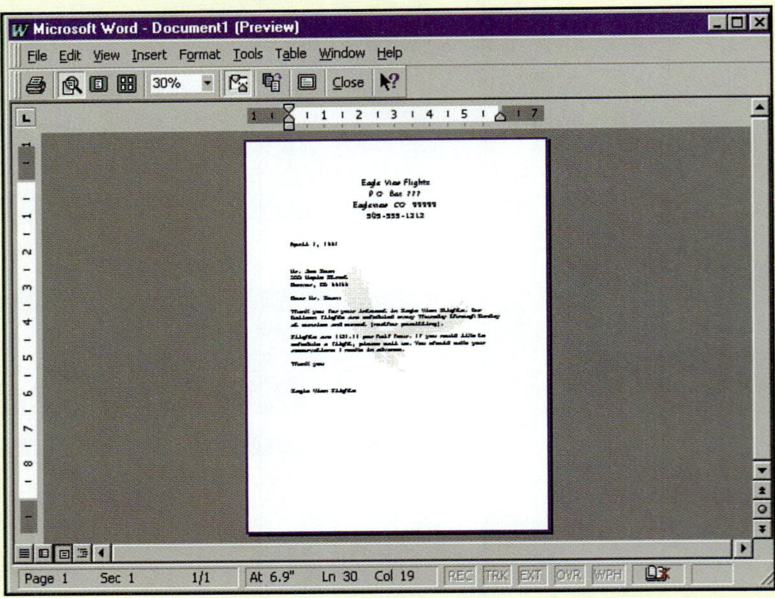

Exam Notes

To insert background text (such as the word "Draft") as your watermark, follow the preceding steps 1–3 and choose Insert, Text Box from the menu. Drag the rectangle shape in the approximate position where you want the text to appear on your letterhead. Type the watermark text in the box. To format the text, select it and choose Format, Font from the menu. Choose all of your formatting options. If you want to rotate the text within the box, choose Format, Text Direction from the menu and select the rotation option you want. Use the options on the Drawing toolbar (View, Toolbars, Drawing) to format the borders and background color of the text box.

You can also insert a WordArt object as a watermark. Choose Insert, Picture, WordArt from the menu.

Inside Stuff

If you find the watermark makes it difficult to read document text, try one of these steps to correct this situation:

- Lighten text in a text box by choosing a text color such as a light gray. (Click the Font Color button on the Formatting toolbar to select a color.)

- Lighten a WordArt object by right-clicking the object and choosing Format WordArt from the pop-up menu. Then select a lighter fill color on the Colors and Lines tab.

- Lighten drawing objects by right-clicking the object and choosing Format AutoShape from the pop-up menu. Then choose a lighter fill color from the Colors and Lines tab.

You have completed all of the lessons in this project. If you have completed your session on the computer, exit Word and Windows 95 before turning off your computer. Otherwise, continue with the "Checking Your Skills" and "Applying Your Skills" sections.

Project Summary

To	Do This
Resize a picture	Drag a sizing handle.
Resize a picture precisely	Click the Format Picture button on the Picture toolbar and then click the Size page tab. Enter the dimensions of the picture; then click OK.
Crop a picture	Click the Crop button on the Picture toolbar; then drag a sizing handle.
Change a picture from floating to inline	Click the Format Picture button on the Picture toolbar and then click the Position tab. Deselect the Float Over Text check box; then click OK.
Lock a picture's anchor	Click the Format Picture button on the Picture toolbar and then click the Position tab. Select the Lock Anchor check box; then click OK.
Add a border to a picture	Click the Line Style button on the Picture toolbar and select the line style.
Add a fill to a picture	Click the Line Style button on the Picture toolbar; then click More Lines. On the Colors and Lines page of the Format Picture dialog box, open the Color drop-down list in the Fill area. Select a color and then click OK, or click Fill Effects to select a pattern, gradient, or texture, and then click OK twice.
Set text wrapping	Click the Text Wrapping button on the Picture toolbar and select the text wrapping style you want to use.
Position a picture	Drag the picture to the new location.
Position a picture precisely	Click the Format Picture button on the Picture toolbar, click the Position tab, and enter the desired position relative to the page edges, a column, or the margins. Click OK.
Add a text box	Select the text; then choose Insert, Text Box.

continues

To	Do This
Format the contents of a text box	Select the text box contents and then specify the desired formatting.
Format the entire text box	Select the text box and specify the desired formatting.
Create a Watermark:	Choose View, Header and Footer to insert a graphic or text box, then apply formatting. For a picture, choose Watermark as the color in the Format Picture Dialog box. Position the text box or graphic and close the header and footer view.

Checking Your Skills

True/False

For each of the following statements, check *T* or *F* to indicate whether the statement is true or false.

__T __F   1. A picture always appears on the same page as its anchor.

__T __F   2. You must be in Normal view to change the placement of a picture.

__T __F   3. You can use a clip art image to create a watermark.

__T __F   4. You can't display text on all sides of a picture.

__T __F   5. You must use the tools on the Picture toolbar to add a border to a picture.

__T __F   6. Use the four-headed arrow pointer to resize a picture.

__T __F   7. A text box automatically expands to show all the text inside it.

__T __F   8. You must be in Page Layout view to see a watermark in a document.

__T __F   9. You cannot use text to create a watermark.

__T __F 10. You can use a WordArt object as a watermark.

Multiple Choice

Circle the letter of the correct answer for each of the following questions.

1. What element do you drag to increase or decrease the size of a picture?

   a. Sizing handle

   b. Bounding box

   c. Crop mark

   d. Line border

2. What must you do to keep an anchor from moving when the picture moves?

   a. Delete it

   b. Crop it

   c. Lock it

   d. Float it

3. What can you do to change the visible area of a picture?

   a. Delete it

   b. Crop it

   c. Lock it

   d. Float it

4. What type of pictures can you insert in a document?

   a. Clip art

   b. Scanned images

   c. Imported images

   d. All of the above

5. What text-wrapping style follows the contours of a picture?

   a. Top & Bottom

   b. Tight

   c. None

   d. Square

6. What type of objects can be positioned in the margin of a document?

   a. Inline objects

   b. Anchored objects

   c. Floating objects

   d. Cropped objects

7. What icon indicates that an anchor is locked in place?

   a. Anchor

   b. Safe

   c. Key

   d. Lock

8. Which text wrapping setting fills in open areas within a picture?

   a. Through

   b. Tight

   c. Square

   d. None

9. Where does a watermark appear in a document?

   a. In the letterhead

   b. On top of or behind the text

   c. In the footer

   d. Outside a text box

10. How do you change to editing mode when working with a text box?

    a. Click in the text box

    b. Click the text box border

    c. Click the Edit Mode button on the Standard toolbar

    d. Click the Edit Mode button on the Picture toolbar

Completion

In the blank provided, write the correct answer for each of the following statements.

1. You must use _______________ view if you want to see pictures in a document.

2. _______________ objects can be positioned anywhere in a document, including on top of text.

3. _______________ objects are part of the document text and move with the insertion point.

4. When you _______________ a picture, part of the picture is hidden outside the bounding box.

5. You can use the _______________ text-wrapping style to cause text to follow the contours of a picture.

6. A _______________ is text or graphics that appears on top of or behind the text in a document.

7. Lock the _______________ to keep a picture on the same page as a paragraph of text.

8. Use a _____ to apply color to the background of a picture.

9. Apply a _________ to outline a picture with a line.

10. Objects in a document are surrounded by a __________ box.

Matching

In the blank next to each of the following terms or phrases, write the letter of the corresponding term or phrase. (Note that some letters may be used more than once.)

a. Line style

b. Watermark

c. Bounding box

d. Cropping

e. Floating object

f. Page Layout

g. Text wrapping

h. Sizing

i. Inline object

j. Text box

1. Action that changes the height or width of an object

2. Action that changes the visible portion of a picture

3. Another term for selection rectangle

4. An object that is part of the document text

5. An object that can be positioned anywhere in a document

6. Text or graphics that appear behind or on top of text in a document

7. The way text flows around a picture in a document

8. The setting used to control the appearance of a border line

9. An object used to control the way text is positioned or formatted in a document

10. The view used when working with pictures

Applying Your Skills

Practice

The following exercises enable you to practice the skills you have learned in this project. Take a few minutes to work through these exercises now.

Illustrating an Invitation

In this practice lesson, you use the skills you learned in this project to enhance an invitation to a company picnic with a picture.

To illustrate the invitation, follow these steps:

1. Open the file Proj0302 from the Project-03 folder on the CD and save it in your `Practices` folder with the name `Picnic`.

2. Select the picture, choose F_ormat, _Picture, click the Size page tab, and set the picture width to 4" and the picture height to 2".

3. Open the Format Picture dialog box again, click the Position page tab, and set the Vertical alignment to 3" from the margins.

4. On the Wrapping page of the Format Picture dialog box, set the text wrapping to _Square.

5. On the Colors and Lines page of the Format Picture dialog box, select a black, solid, 1 point line border to go around the picture.

6. Preview the document and save it. If requested by your instructor, print it. Close the document when you have finished.

Formatting the picture in the Invoice document

In this exercise, you use the skills you learned in this project to size and position a picture in the invoice document you used in earlier projects.

To Format the Picture in the Invoice document, follow these steps:

1. Open the file Proj0303 from the Project-03 folder on the CD and save it in your `Practices` folder with the name `Invoice3`.

2. Select the picture, then drag the lower-right corner handle to resize the picture so it is approximately two inches square. (Hint: Use the rulers.)

3. If the Picture toolbar is not displayed, choose _View, _Toolbars, Picture to display it.

4. Crop the Treble Clef out of the picture by clicking the Crop button on the Picture toolbar, then dragging the sizing handle in the middle of the left side to the right until the Treble Clef is hidden. Alternatively, set the Crop from _Left setting on the Picture page of the Format Picture dialog box to .41".

5. On the Position page of the Format Picture dialog box, enter .1" in the _Horizontal text box, and change the _From setting to Margin. The _Vertical setting should be fine (.1" from the Paragraph).

6. Click the Text Wrapping button on the Picture toolbar and select Tight.

7. Increase the space between the picture and the text to .5" on the Wrapping page of the Format Picture dialog box.

8. Preview the document and save the changes you have made. If requested by your instructor, save the changes. Close the document when you have finished.

Formatting a Picture in the Flight Timetable

In this exercise, you use the skills you learned in this project to format a picture in the timetable document you used in an earlier project.

To format a picture in the Flight Timetable document, follow these steps:

1. Open the file Proj0304 from the Project-03 folder on the CD and save it in your Practices folder with the name Timetable2.

2. Drag the lower-left sizing handle up and to the right to resize the picture so it is approximately two inches square.

3. Drag the picture to position it centered horizontally on the page (approximately between two and four inches on the horizontal ruler).

4. Click the Text Wrapping button on the Picture toolbar and choose None.

5. Preview the document.

6. Drag the picture down below the table.

7. Apply a fill by selecting the 25% gray color from the Fill Color drop down palette on the Colors and Lines page of the Format Picture dialog box.

8. Preview the document again and save your changes. If requested by your instructor, print it. Close the document when you are finished.

Using a Text Box to Emphasize Information

In this exercise, you use the skills you learned in this project to add a text box to a report to call attention to an important fact.

To use a text box to emphasize information, follow these steps:

1. Open the file Proj0305 from the Project-03 folder on the CD and save it in your Practices folder with the name Interviews.

2. Select the second sentence of the third paragraph, then choose Insert, Text Box.

3. Drag the sizing handle in the middle of the right side of the text box to the right to increase the width of the text box to three inches. Alternatively, choose Format, Text Box to open the Format Text Box dialog box, click the Size page tab and set the Width to 3".

4. Drag the boundary box of the text box down and to the right to move the text box to the lower-right corner of the page so its right side is at the right margin, and its bottom is even with the last line of text. Alternatively, open the Format Text Box as in the previous step, click the Position page tab, and set the Horizontal position to 3.4" From the Column and the Vertical to 1.25" From the Paragraph.

5. On the Wrapping page of the Format Text Box dialog box, select the Square setting, and enter .3 inches in all the Distance from text boxes.

6. Increase the size of the text in the text box to 20 points and center it in the box.

7. Preview the document and save it. If requested by your instructor, print it. Close the document when you have finished.

Adding a Watermark to the Loan Proposal Document

In this exercise, you use the skills you learned in this project to create a watermark on the loan proposal document you worked with in earlier projects.

To add a watermark to the loan proposal document, follow these steps:

1. Open the file Proj0306 from the Project-03 folder on the CD and save it in your Practices folder with the name Loan3.

2. Choose View, Header and Footer, then click the Show/Hide Document Text button on the Header/Footer toolbar. If necessary, drag the toolbar to the top of the window so it isn't covering the document.

3. Choose Insert, Picture, Clip Art, and select a clip art image that relates to the theme of a restaurant, such as a cup of coffee or something. Try looking in the Food & Dining category, if available.

4. Open the Format Picture dialog box and make the following changes without closing the dialog box:

   On the Picture page, select Watermark from the Image Control Color drop down list.

   On the Wrapping page, select None.

   On the Position page, enter 1" in the Vertical text box.

   On the Size page, enter 6" in the Height text box.

5. Click OK.

6. Preview the document. Notice that the watermark appears on both pages of the document. That's because you inserted it in the header, so it appears on every page that the header is on.

7. Save the document. If requested by your instructor, print it. Close the document when you have finished.

Challenge

The following challenges enable you to use your problem-solving skills. Take time to work through these exercises now.

Formatting Pictures in a Presentation for Computer Training Concepts

Use the skills you have learned in this project to format the pictures in a company presentation. Open the file Proj0307 from the Project-03 folder on the CD and save it in your `Challenges` folder with the name `Presentation`. Change the picture of trees to inline format, and position it at the end of the line `As We Grew, So We Will Grow`. Crop Alaska and Hawaii off the map picture. Move the map into the middle of the last paragraph and anchor it. Set the text to wrap on both sides of the map picture. Preview the document and save it. If requested by your instructor, print it. Close the document when you have finished.

Creating a Personal Letterhead

Use the skills you have learned in this project to create your own personalized letterhead. Open a new blank document and save it in your `Challenges` folder with the name `Letterhead`. Insert a blank text box and type in your own name and address. Size and position the text box appropriately. Format the text. Add a logo to the Letterhead by inserting a picture on its own, or into the text box along with the text. If you insert a picture, choose one that is either descriptive of your name, address, or something that you like to do. Make sure you format the picture as part of the letterhead. Preview the document and make any necessary changes to the size, position, or formatting. Save the document. If requested by your instructor, print it. Close the document when you have finished. If you want to be able to use the letterhead to create new documents, save it as a template file. Alternatively, save it as AutoText so you can insert it into any document.

Formatting the Picture on the Deli Menu

In this exercise, format the picture you inserted on the sign for the Main Street Deli in an earlier project. Open the file Proj0308 from the Project-03 folder on the CD and save it in your `Challenges` folder with the name `Deli2`. Increase the width of the picture and position at the bottom of the document. Make sure text wrapping is set to Top and Bottom. Try out different borders or fills, such as a double line border, and a polka dot fill, and decide if you want to use them. Preview the document. Save it. If requested by your instructor, print it. Close the document when you have finished.

Formatting the Picture on the Health Club Letter

In this exercise, format the picture you inserted on the letter for the Health Club in an earlier project. Open the file Proj0309 from the Project-03 folder on the CD and save it in your `Challenges` folder with the name `Renewal3`.

Resize and position the picture so it appears on the left side of the document, starting at the top margin and extending down about 5 1/2". Remember to change the text wrapping option so it doesn't appear in the middle of the text. Preview the document. Save it. If requested by your instructor, print it. Close the document when you have finished.

Creating a Text Watermark for Computer Training Concepts Documents

In this exercise, you use the text DRAFT to create a watermark you can use on documents created for Computer Training Concepts, Inc. Open the file Proj0310 from the Project-03 folder on the CD and save it in your Challenges folder with the name Cover Letter3. View the Header area and hide the document text. Insert a text box into the header. Type the text DRAFT in the text box. Format and position the text box as a watermark that appears across the middle of the page. Make the font as large as possible and use a light color, such as 25% gray. You can apply a fill to the text box, also in a light color, and increase the size of the text to fill the whole page. That way, the fill fills the whole page. Preview the document. Save it. If requested by your instructor, print it. Close the document when you have finished.

You have completed the project and the associated lessons, as well as the "Checking Your Skills" and "Applying Your Skills" sections. Now use the PinPoint software evaluation mode to assess your comprehension of the specific exam tasks you have just learned. You can also use the PinPoint Trainer Mode and the Show Me tutorials to practice these specific exam tasks.

Project 4

Four

Working with Long Documents

Enhancing a Training Report

In this Project, you learn how to:

Objectives	Required Activities
➤ Move Through Long Documents	Use Bookmarks
➤ Add Footnotes and Endnotes	Create Footnotes and Endnotes Revise Footnotes and Endnotes
➤ Create Cross-References	Create a Cross-Reference
➤ Create a Table of Contents	Create and Modify a Table of Contents
➤ Add Headers and Footers to a Long Document	
➤ Create an Index	Create and Modify an Index

Why Would I Do This?

Well-prepared, long documents include special features to help readers locate information easily. Cross-references, for example, guide readers to other points in the document where they can find more information. A table of contents provides an idea of topics covered in the document. Headers and footers help readers keep track of the current location in the document, while an index helps readers find information on a specific word or topic.

You might not need Word's long document features very often, but when you do have to write a lengthy report, these special tools provide an easy way to enhance a document. In this project, you use these tools to improve the usability of a long report used to train managers in the science of interviewing prospective employees.

First, however, you need to understand how to move through a long document quickly.

Lesson 1: Moving Through Long Documents

Moving through a document can be a time-consuming chore. Fortunately, Word includes several features that help you navigate your documents more successfully. The Find feature provides an excellent way to find text, but you can also tell the Go To feature where you want to go in the document, and go there quickly. If you're working in one or two areas of your document most of the time, you might want to set bookmarks so that you can return to those places quickly. Best of all, you have the Select Browse Object, a versatile tool that helps you browse through different items in your document.

In this lesson, you experiment with different ways of browsing through your document. Familiarizing yourself with these tools helps you develop time-saving habits.

To Move Through Your Document

❶ Open the folder Project-04 and the file Proj0401 from the CD; save it as Interview Paper.

First, get a feel for the document's organization by turning on the Document Map feature.

Remember that you can change the document's magnification by selecting an option from the Zoom drop-down list on the Standard toolbar. You can select different zoom percentages depending on how much of the document you want to view. You can also type a different number (such as 90) in the Zoom box.

 As you go through the lessons in this project, you should display nonprinting characters so that you can see where spaces, tabs, and paragraph marks appear. Click the Standard toolbar's Show/Hide ¶ button to display nonprinting characters.

2 Choose View, Document Map.

A pane appears to the left of the document window, as shown in Figure 4.1. This pane includes the document's headings. You can click any of the headings in the left panel to jump quickly to that section.

Figure 4.1
Use the Document Map pane to move quickly through the document.

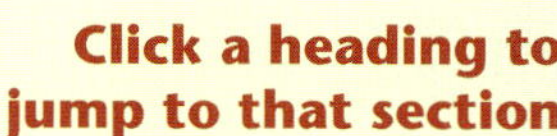

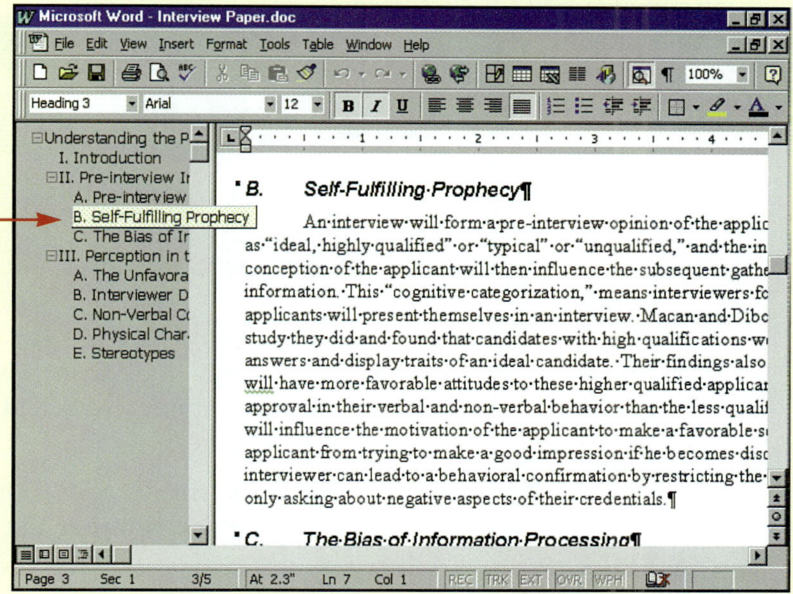

3 Click a heading in the Document Map pane to jump to that area.

When you click a heading in the Document Map pane, the insertion point jumps to that heading in the document.

4 Choose View, Document Map again to turn off the Document Map pane.

Now review some techniques for moving to the top or bottom of your document.

5 Press Ctrl+End to move to the end of your document. Press Ctrl+Home to move to the beginning of your document.

See Table 4.1 to review keystrokes for moving through the document. Now use the Go To feature to jump quickly to page 3.

6 Choose Edit, Go To.

The Find and Replace dialog box appears with the Go To tab selected, as shown in Figure 4.2. After you select how you want to browse

continues

Word

To Move Through Your Document   (continued)

in the G<u>o</u> to What list, the box to the right of the list instructs you to type a number for the category that you select.

You can also open the Find and Replace dialog box's G<u>o</u> To page by pressing [Ctrl]+[G] or by double-clicking the leftmost box on the status bar. You can also use the Select Browse Object tool at the bottom of the vertical scroll bar. This tool is discussed later in this lesson.

Figure 4.2
Use the Find and Replace dialog box's G<u>o</u> To page to move to a specific place in your document.

Where do you want to go today?

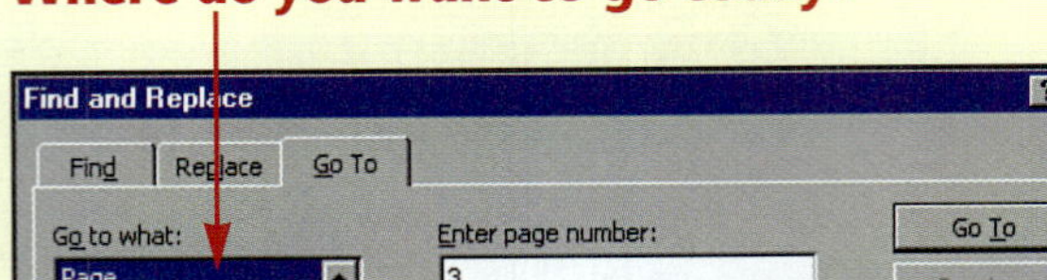

You can use the options in the Go to What list box to move through your document in different ways. For example, you can go to a specific footnote number, to a field that you've inserted, or to a heading. Now go to page 3.

❼ Make sure that Page is selected in the G<u>o</u> to What list, then type 3 in the <u>E</u>nter Page Number text box.

❽ Choose the Go <u>T</u>o button.

The insertion point jumps to the top of page 3.

❾ Choose Close to close the Find and Replace dialog box.

While on page 3, insert a bookmark at the beginning of the **Self-Fulfilling Prophecy** heading. If you plan to return to a section of your document frequently, setting a bookmark makes the section easy to revisit.

❿ Place the insertion point at the beginning of the Self-Fulfilling Prophecy heading, then choose <u>I</u>nsert, Boo<u>k</u>mark.

The Bookmark dialog box appears, as shown in Figure 4.3.

⓫ Type Prophecy, then choose <u>A</u>dd.

You now have a bookmark in your document. Now move to the top of the document, then return to the bookmark.

Figure 4.3
Adding bookmarks helps you return to frequently used sections.

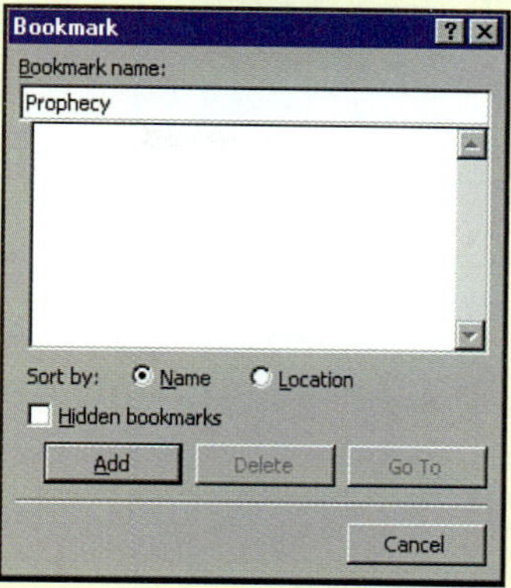

12 Press Ctrl+Home to move to the beginning of the document and then choose Edit, Go To.

The Find and Replace dialog box appears again with the Go To tab selected.

13 Select Bookmark in the Go to What list, make sure that Prophecy is selected, and choose Go To.

The insertion point jumps to the place where you set your bookmark.

14 Choose Close to close the Find and Replace dialog box's Go To page.

At this point, you might think it's a good idea to set bookmarks at all your main headings. However, the Select Browse Object feature provides a much easier way to move through headings.

When naming bookmarks, don't begin names with numbers and don't use symbols or spaces. These characters are unacceptable for bookmark names, and you won't be notified by Word that there is a naming problem. When you try to add a bookmark that contains an illegal name, the Add button becomes grayed out—but you receive no explanation that the problem lies within your bookmark name.

15 Click the Select Browse Object palette at the bottom of the vertical scroll bar.

A palette presenting several browse tools pops up, as shown in Figure 4.4. You can use this palette to browse through objects such as headings, footnotes, tables, and graphics.

continues

To Move Through Your Document (continued)

Figure 4.4
The Select Browse Object feature enables you to move through items in your document.

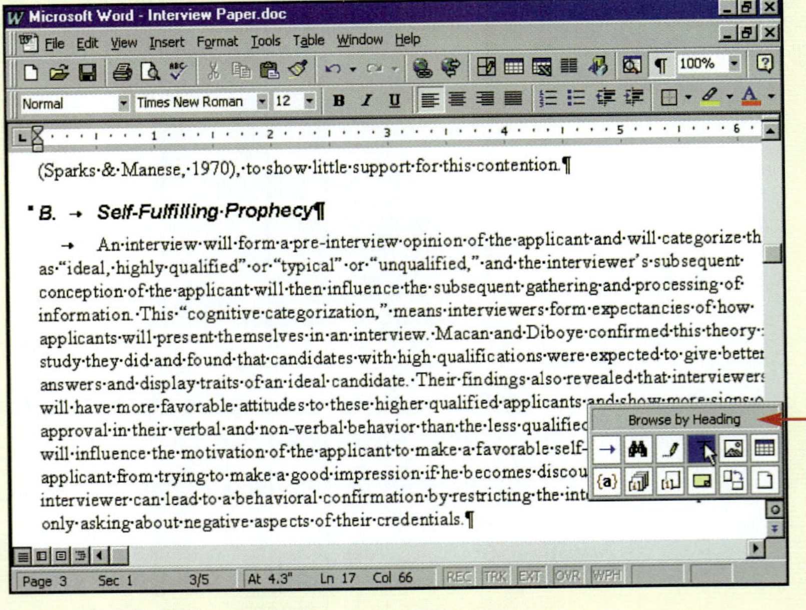

Select Browse Object —

16 **Click the Browse by Heading button.**

The insertion point jumps to the next heading in your document. At this point, notice that buttons with blue double arrows appear above and below the Select Browse Object feature. These buttons change roles, depending on the last browsing feature that you used in your document. If you don't select an item by which to move, clicking these buttons takes you to the next or previous page. After you search for text, these buttons let you jump to the next or previous occurrence of the search text.

Because you recently browsed to the next heading, clicking either the Next or Previous button takes you to the next or previous heading in your document.

17 **Click the Next button to move to the next heading. Continue to browse through the headings in your document.**

The Next and Previous buttons work not only for headings, but also for any type of browse action, such as searching for text or going to a bookmark. These buttons provide a good way to continue searching for text after you've closed the Find and Replace dialog box.

18 **Save the document and keep it open for the next lesson.**

Table 4.1 Keystrokes for Moving Through Documents	
Key(s)	Function
Home and End	Moves to the beginning or end of the line, respectively
Ctrl+Home and Ctrl+End	Moves to the beginning or end of the document, respectively
PgUp and PgDn	Moves one screen up or down, respectively
Ctrl+→ and Ctrl+←	Moves one word right or left, respectively
Ctrl+↑ and Ctrl+↓	Moves one paragraph up or down, respectively
Ctrl+PgUp and Ctrl+PgDn	Moves one page up or down, respectively

Lesson 2: Adding Footnotes and Endnotes

Footnotes explain or provide references for text in a document. When you add **footnotes** to your document, the footnote numbers are automatically numbered in sequence, so the order in which you insert your footnotes doesn't matter. You can also insert **endnotes** in your document. Footnote text appears at the bottom of the page, whereas endnote text appears at the end of a section or the end of the document.

Writers use footnotes and endnotes to provide references to source documents, to provide more detailed explanations or definitions of text without including them in the body of the document, and to make comments on the text. In this lesson, you create and edit a footnote.

There are two parts to each footnote or endnote: the reference mark and the note text. The note reference mark is a number, character, or combination of characters noting that additional information is contained in a footnote or endnote.

You can automatically number the reference marks or create your own custom marks. If you use automatic numbering, Word renumbers the note reference marks if you add, delete, or move notes.

The note text can be any length and format, and you can format the line that separates the notes from the body text of the document.

Figure 4.5 shows an example of both a footnote and an endnote. To view note text, rest the mouse pointer on the note reference mark. The note text appears in a pop-up above the mark, as shown in Figure 4.5. This works for both footnotes and endnotes. Double-click the note reference mark to display the note text in a note pane at the bottom of the screen. If you are in Page layout view, footnotes display at the bottom of the page and endnotes appear at the end of a section or at the end of the document, depending upon which option you selected.

Figure 4.5
Point to the reference
mark to see the endnote
text appear in a pop-up
above the number.

Endnote pop-up text

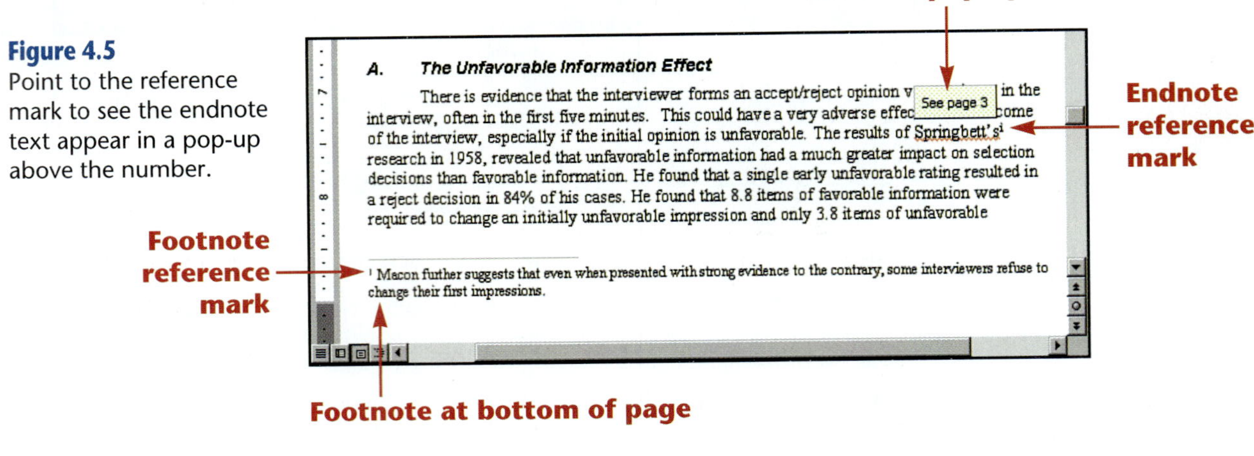

Endnote reference mark

Footnote reference mark

Footnote at bottom of page

Footnotes appear at the bottom of the printed page. If you want your notes to
appear at the end of the document or a section, you should insert **endnotes**
rather than footnotes. You can include both footnotes and endnotes in your document.

To Add a Footnote

❶ Choose View, Page Layout.

In Page Layout view, you can see footnotes at the bottom of the
page.

**❷ Place the insertion point at the end of the paragraph above
the heading III. Perception of the Interview (ending with and
disprove it).**

After working through Lesson 1, you should know how to move
through your document and locate headings.

❸ Choose Insert, Footnote.

The Footnote and Endnote dialog box appears, as shown in Figure
4.6. At this point, you can select to insert either a footnote or an endnote. You can also have Word number the footnotes automatically,
or you can add a custom number. In this lesson, you use automatic
numbering.

Figure 4.6
The Footnote and
Endnote dialog box.

**This option numbers your
footnotes automatically**

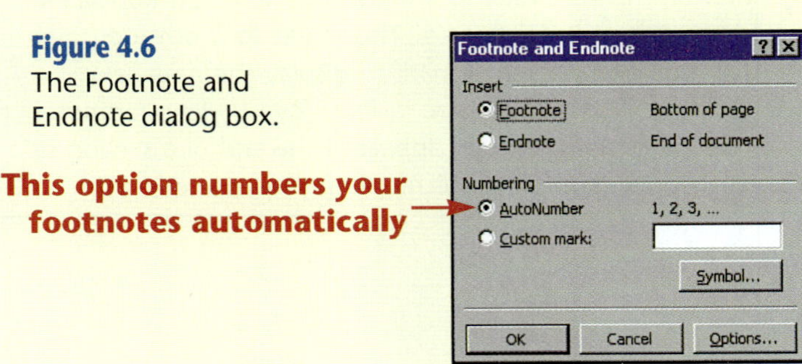

Word

4 Choose OK to insert a footnote.

A footnote number appears at the bottom of the page following a divider line. The insertion point appears next to the footnote number.

5 Type the following paragraph:

Macon further suggests that even when presented with strong evidence to the contrary, some interviewers refuse to change their first impressions.

The footnote appears at the bottom of the screen, as shown in Figure 4.7.

Figure 4.7
A footnote inserted in a document.

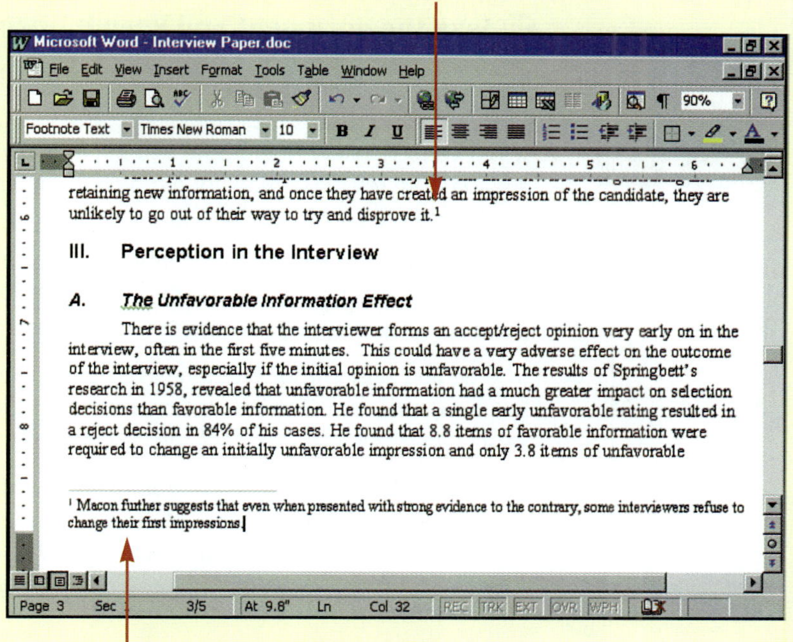

6 When you finish typing the footnote, click anywhere in the document window.

A footnote consists of two linked parts: the footnote reference mark and the corresponding footnote text. The reference mark appears in the body text where you placed the insertion point, and the footnote text appears at the bottom of the page.

Because you're in Page Layout view, you can still see the footnote at the bottom of the page. Switch to Normal view so that you can see how to work with footnotes even when you cannot see the note at the bottom of the screen.

continues

Word

To Add a Footnote   (continued)

7 **Choose View, Normal.**

Notice that you can no longer see the footnote text at the bottom of the page in Normal view. However, you can still see the footnote reference mark at the end of the paragraph in which you inserted it.

8 **Double-click the footnote reference mark.**

The footnote appears in a footnote pane at the bottom of the screen.

9 **Change** `some interviewers` **to** `many interviewers`**, then choose Close.**

You have now created and edited your footnote.

10 **Save the document and keep it open for the next lesson.**

If you want to read the footnote text in Normal view, hold the mouse pointer over the footnote reference mark for a moment. You can then read the note text above the footnote.

To move, copy, or delete a footnote or endnote, work with the note reference mark in the document, not the footnote text. If you have time after class, cut the footnote reference that you inserted, and paste it in a different location.

The default position for endnotes is at the end of the document. To change the position, click the Options button of the Footnote or Endnote dialog box and select where you want to place the note (end of page or end of section).

To change the appearance of footnotes or endnotes text or references, choose Format, Style, and then select All Styles from the List drop-down list. Select the Footnote or Endnote Text or Reference style from the Styles list, and choose Modify.

Lesson 3: Creating Cross-References

Cross-reference

A note, embedded in a document, that points readers to another section of the document where more related information is available.

Large documents often contain *cross-references* to other locations in the document. On one page, for example, you might find a reference such as "see page 15." The problem with cross-references is that after you type a reference on page 10, you might add or delete material, moving what was originally cross-referenced on page 15 to page 14 or 16.

If you try to update a document with many cross-references manually, you might not catch every reference, and you'll waste time. Fortunately, Word can handle cross-referencing for you. By using the Cross-Reference feature, you can create a reference to any item in a document and then let Word track its location as you edit the document; this way, the cross-reference remains accurate.

To Create Cross-References

1 In the sample document, go to the section titled `C. Non-Verbal Communications` **(on page 4). Place the insertion point just before the period at the end of the first sentence below the heading (ending with** `the first five minutes`**).**

This sentence refers to a point made earlier in the document in the section titled "The Unfavorable Information Effect."

2 Insert a space, then type `(page .`

Be sure to insert a space after the word *page*, as shown in Figure 4.8. After this space, Word automatically inserts the correct page number for the cross-reference. Do not put a close parenthesis at the end of the sentence yet. You do that after you finish setting up the cross-reference.

Figure 4.8
Setting up the cross-reference.

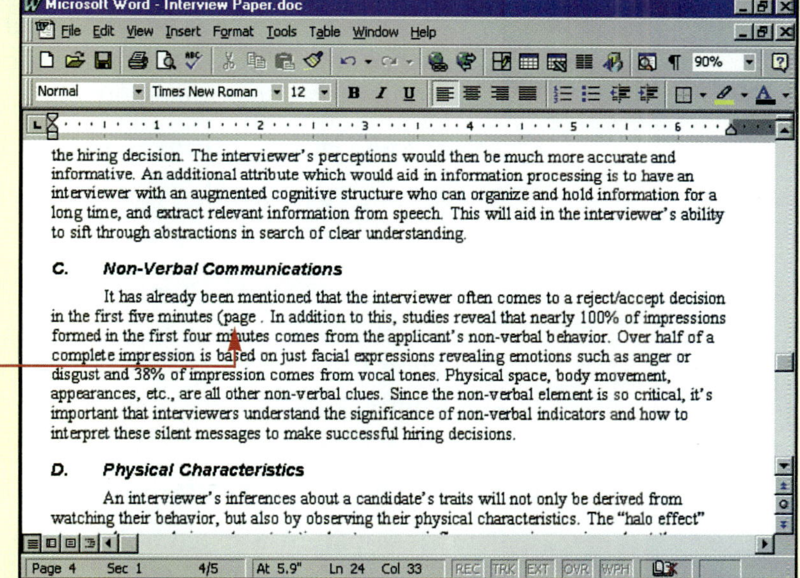

Prepare the text for the cross-reference

3 Choose Insert, Cross-reference.

The Cross-reference dialog box appears.

4 Select Heading in the Reference Type drop-down list.

When Heading is selected, the For Which Heading list box lists all headings in the report that are formatted with Heading styles (yet another good reason to use styles!). This list of headings makes it easy to select the heading to which to tie the reference (see Figure 4.9).

continues

To Create Cross-References (continued)

Figure 4.9
Use the Cross-reference dialog box to create cross-references.

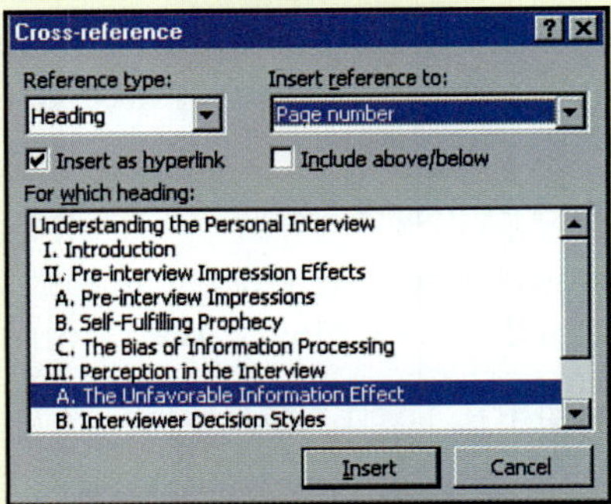

5 **Scroll down through the For <u>W</u>hich Heading list box and select A. The Unfavorable Information Effect.**

When the reader is in the section in which you placed the insertion point, you refer the reader to the section that you select in this list box. A cross-reference is most helpful when you provide a page number, so that readers can quickly turn back, review material, and then continue reading the report.

6 **Select Page Number from the Insert <u>R</u>eference To list box.**

By selecting Page Number, you tell Word to include the correct page number in the reference text.

7 **Choose the <u>I</u>nsert button, then choose Close.**

The Insert button inserts the page number for the cross-reference. Choosing Close clears the Cross-reference dialog box. Notice that the insertion point appears in a gray shade. This shade indicates that the insertion point is a field.

8 **Type a close parenthesis—)—at the end of the page reference.**

The close parenthesis completes the reference phrase that you added to this paragraph. Your cross-reference should look like Figure 4.10.

9 **Save the document and keep it open for the next lesson.**

Figure 4.10
A cross-reference in a document.

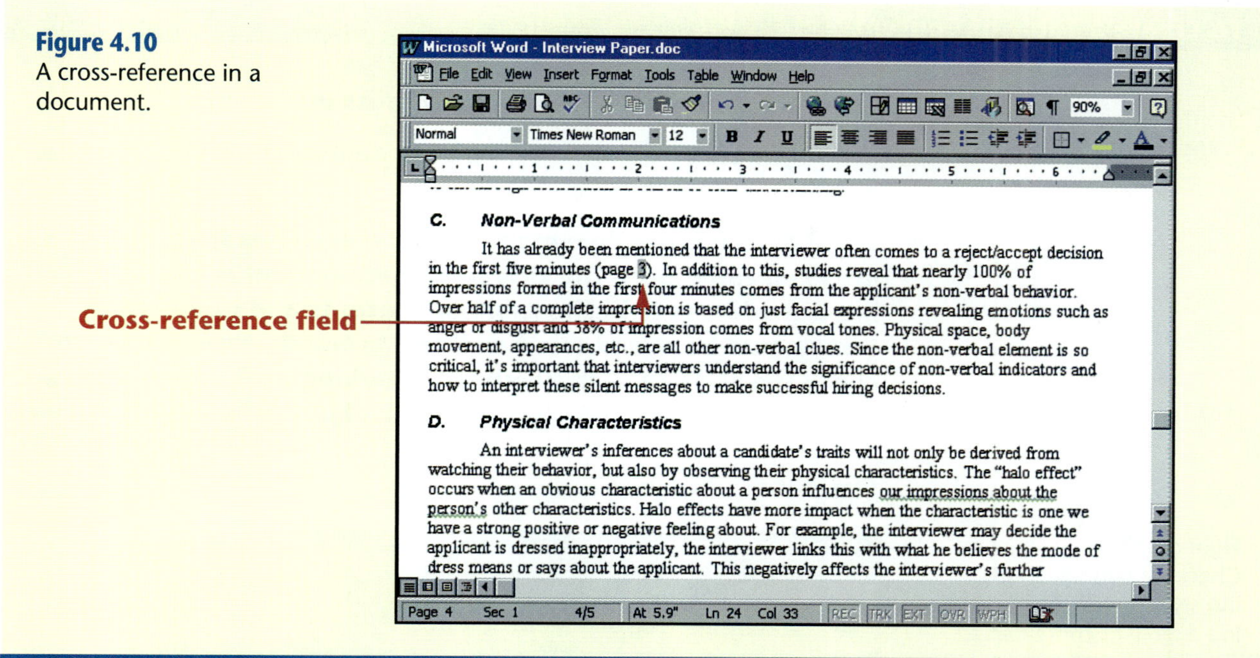

Cross-reference field

To create a reference to headings in a document, you must have assigned Word heading styles to the headings.

To update a cross-reference after you edit a document, select the reference field that you inserted and press F9. Word automatically updates all cross-references when you print or open the document.

Cross-references are active in the document. Therefore, you can click a cross-reference item to jump to the section that it references. Try this action by clicking the cross-reference number that you just inserted.

Lesson 4: Creating a Table of Contents

A table of contents provides readers with a guide to topics covered in a long document. Word makes creating a table of contents easy. All you have to do is select the headings to appear in the table of contents, make sure that you have assigned heading styles to the headings, and tell Word to create the table of contents for you.

You tell Word where to create the table and which format to use. Typically, a table of contents appears by itself on a page preceding a document's body. After you choose the format, Word compiles the table of contents using the headings that you styled.

To Create a Table of Contents

① **Go to the top of the document by pressing** Ctrl+Home.

Before you create the table of contents, double-check all headings to make sure that they are styled properly.

② **Scroll through the document, clicking each heading as you go. (You can ignore the title page because you aren't including any of its text in the table of contents and none of its text should be styled as a heading.) In the document's body, check the style of each heading by looking at the Style box on the Formatting toolbar (see Figure 4.11).**

Check the style here

Figure 4.11
Check for correct heading styles before building a table of contents.

Place the insertion point on each heading

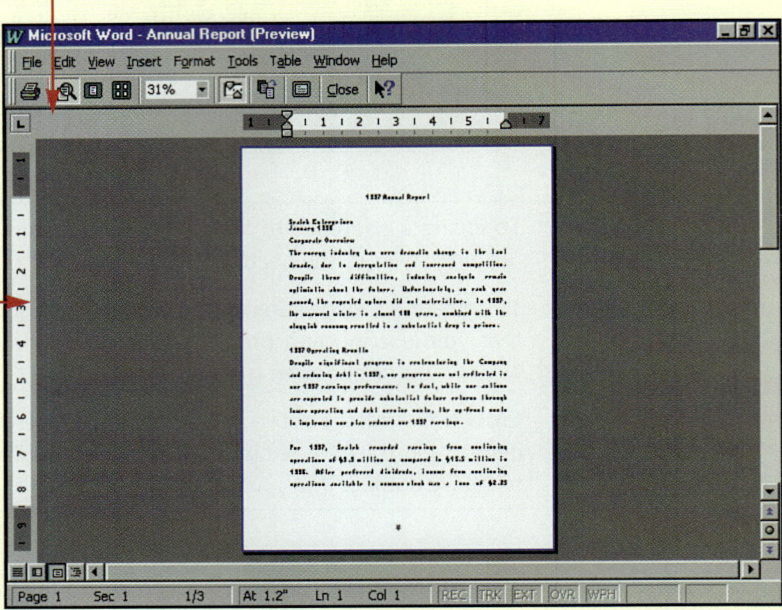

The document contains three types of headings: title, major headings, and subheadings. You should style the document's title with the Heading 1 style, major headings with the Heading 2 style, and subheadings with the Heading 3 style. If you improperly style any headings, apply the correct style before you continue.

When you finish checking the headings for proper styling, start setting up a new page for the table of contents.

③ **Place the insertion point at the top of page 2, on the blank line above** `Understanding the Personal Interview`**.**

Place the table of contents on a new page, between the title page and the first page of body text. To do so, create a new page between the title page and the body of the document.

④ **Press** Ctrl+⏎Enter**, then press** ↑**.**

Pressing Ctrl+⏎Enter inserts a page break, and pressing ↑ moves you to the new page that you just created.

5 **Press** ⏎Enter **once; then press** ⬆.

Pressing ⏎Enter creates a blank line for the title, and pressing ⬆ moves you to that line. Now create the title for the table of contents.

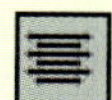

6 **Click the Center button on the Formatting toolbar.**

7 **Type** `Table of Contents`, **then press** ⏎Enter.

8 **Click the Align Left button on the Formatting toolbar, then press** ⏎Enter **again.**

Now you create the table of contents. The table of contents page should now look like Figure 4.12. Tell Word to build the table of contents.

Figure 4.12

Setting up the table of contents page.

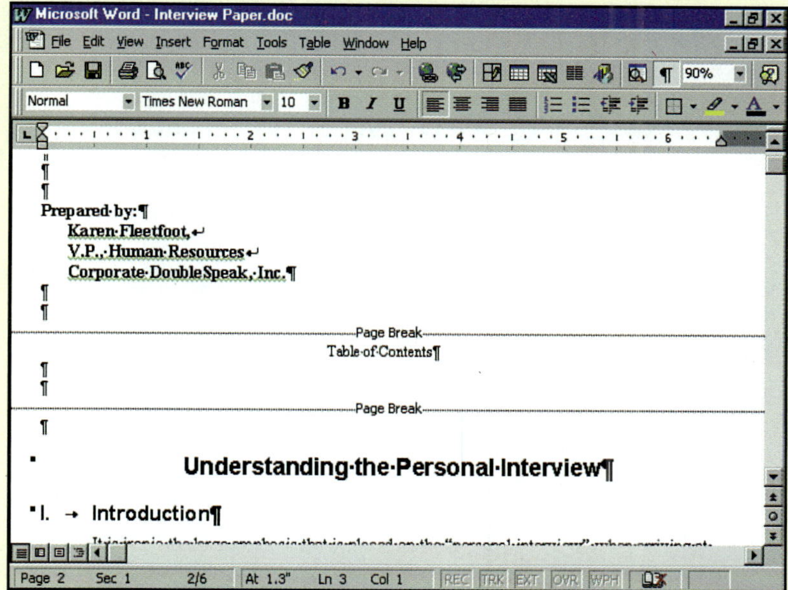

9 **Choose** **I**nsert, In**d**ex and Tables.

The Index and Tables dialog box appears.

10 **Click the Table of** **C**ontents tab.

Clicking the Table of **C**ontents tab switches to the dialog box's Table of Contents page (see Figure 4.13).

11 **Select Formal from the Forma**t**s list box.**

The Formal style aligns the page numbers flush right, as shown in the dialog box's Preview window.

12 **Make sure that the number 3 appears in the Show** **L**evels box.

The table of contents for this paper contains the title, major headings, and subheadings, so you need three levels for the table of contents.

continues

To Create a Table of Contents   (continued)

Figure 4.13
Use the Index and Tables dialog box to define a table of contents.

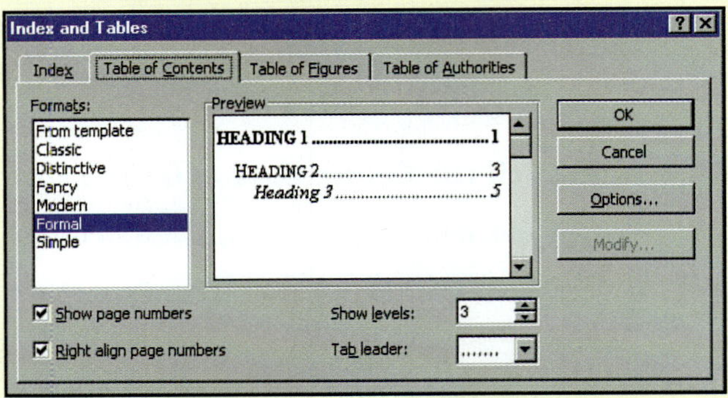

13 Choose OK.

Word now builds the table of contents. You should emphasize the Table of Contents heading at the top of the page to make it stand out better.

14 Select `Table of Contents` **at the top of the page and choose 14 from the Formatting toolbar's Font Size drop-down list.**

Your table of contents should look similar to the one in Figure 4.14.

Figure 4.14
The completed table of contents.

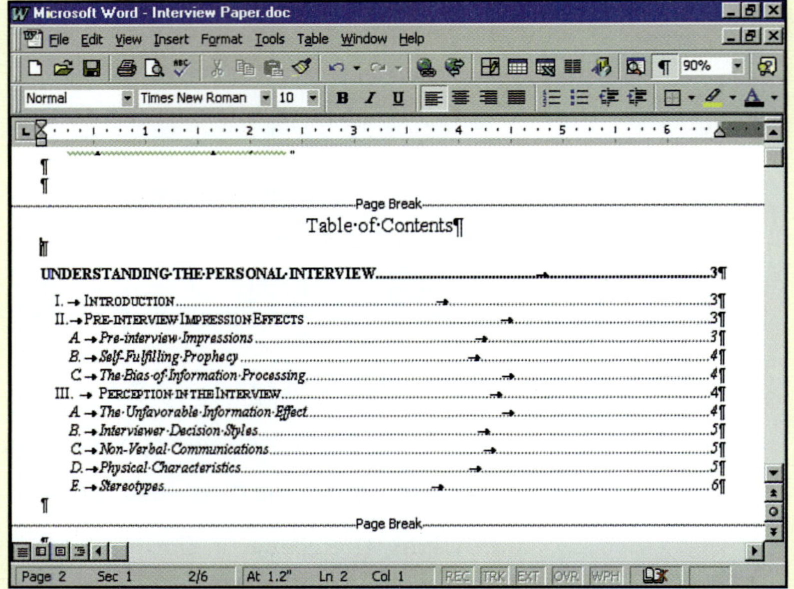

15 Save your work and keep the file open for the next lesson.

You can update a table of contents at any time by clicking the table of contents to select it and then pressing F9. The Update Table of Contents dialog box appears; you can then update just the page numbers or the entire table. If you add text to the document, you can simply update page numbers. If you add or delete headings that should appear in the table, however, you should update the entire table.

If you add new headings to a document and want them to appear in the table of contents, remember to apply a heading style to them.

If you format the title as Heading 1 in your document, the table of contents lists the title. Some people don't like to see this title in the table of contents. One way to avoid this is to use the heading styles to format only your main headings and subheadings, but not your title. If you've already formatted the title with a heading style, you can tell Word not to use the first heading level. To do so, select the table of contents, then choose Insert, Index and Tables and select the Table of Contents tab. Choose Options, then delete the 1 next to the Heading 1 style. Choose OK three times to return to your document and replace the table of contents.

You can use the table of contents as a way to move through your document. Just click a page number in the table of contents to jump to the section that it references.

Lesson 5: Adding Headers and Footers to a Long Document

In multiple-page documents, readers often appreciate landmarks that tell them the current page, the date the document was created, or other facts about the document. In extremely long documents, sometimes a reminder of the document's name or the section's title can be helpful. **Headers** and **footers** give you the opportunity to provide this kind of information to readers.

Headers or footers also can give a document a more professional and thoughtful appearance. They are especially useful in reports such as the one on which you are working. This lesson shows you how to add both a header and a footer to the sample document.

Headers and **footers** are simply formatting elements that repeat on each page of a document. Headers appear across the top of pages, and footers appear across the bottom. You can format headers and footers in many ways, using formatting for regular text.

If you talk to some long-time users of word processing programs, you might hear them use the terms running head or running foot rather than header or footer. These alternative terms are used because headers and footers "run" across the width of the page and throughout a document.

To Add Headers and Footers to a Long Document

1 Move to the top of the page that follows the table of contents page.

This is the page where you want headers and footers to start. (Word adds them to the title page as well, but you remove them later.) Actually, the insertion point can be anywhere in the document when you add headers or footers.

continues

2 Choose View, Header and Footer.

The Header and Footer command isn't under the Insert menu, as you might logically assume that it would be. Think of headers and footers as part of the document's view or appearance.

The Header and Footer toolbar appears, and other changes take place onscreen, as shown in Figure 4.15. The document's text turns gray, and an empty Header box with dashed lines appears at the top of the document. In this box, you create, edit, and format the header. Word also switches to Page Layout view if it isn't already in that view. You can use the tool tips to see each toolbar button's description.

Figure 4.15
The Header and Footer toolbar.

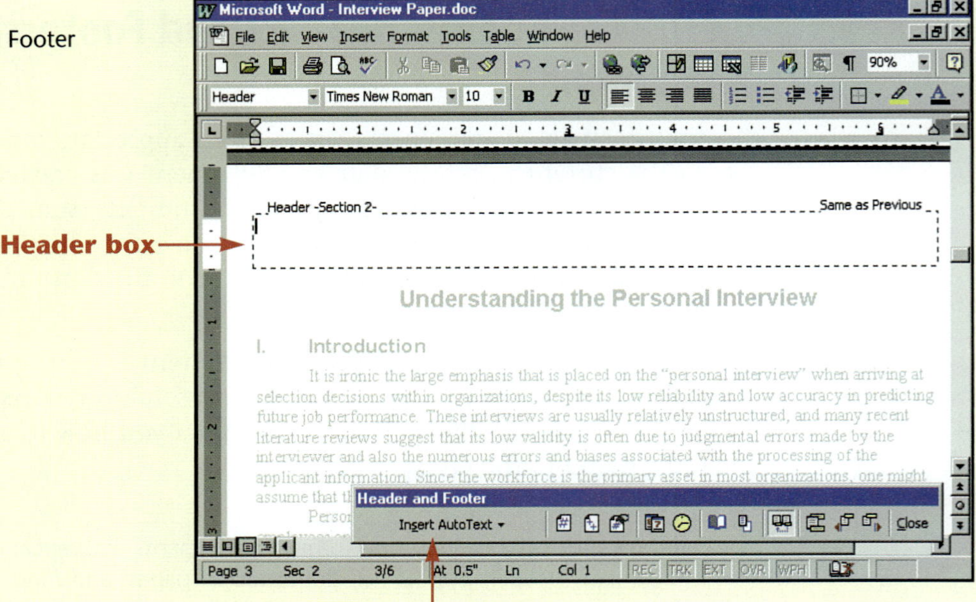

Header box

Header and Footer toolbar

Because the page is now set up for a header, create that first. This header is be simple, with the name of the document on the left and the page number on the right.

3 Type Understanding the Personal Interview **in the header box.**

4 Press Tab **twice.**

Pressing Tab twice moves the insertion point to the right end of the box. Note that the first tab stop places the insertion point at the center of the page. The header and footer boxes are set up so that you can quickly position information at the far left, center, and far right of the page.

5 Click the Header and Footer toolbar's Insert Page Number button.

Word inserts the page number. When you scroll through the document, you see that each page has its proper number assigned. If you edit the document to add or remove pages, Word automatically renumbers all pages correctly.

You're done with the header; now set up the footer. Again, the footer is simple, with the name of the company on the left and the current date on the right.

6 Click the Header and Footer toolbar's Switch Between Header and Footer button.

This action switches you from Header mode to Footer mode. Now the view changes as Word shifts to the bottom of the page and opens an empty footer box. If the Header and Footer toolbar covers the footer box, you can drag the toolbar's title bar to move the toolbar.

7 Type `Corporate DoubleSpeak, Inc.` in the footer box and press `Tab` twice.

The insertion point moves to the right side of the footer box. Next, add the date.

8 Click the Header and Footer toolbar's Insert Date button.

The date appears at the right end of the footer. Now check the headers and footers.

9 Click the Close button.

The Header and Footer toolbar disappears, and you return to Normal view. The easiest way to check headers and footers is to use Print Preview.

10 Click the Standard toolbar's Print Preview button.

In Print Preview mode, you can see not only the document text, but also headers and footers, as shown in Figure 4.16.

Scroll through the document to check every page. Notice that headers and footers are all in place. There is a problem, however—the title page has a header and footer, too. Usually, headers or footers don't appear on a title page, so remove them.

11 Click the Close button to exit Print Preview mode.

Return to Normal view so that you can resume working on the document. There's a very easy way to turn off headers and footers on the first page of a document.

continues

To Add Headers and Footers to a Long Document   (continued)

Figure 4.16
Check headers and footers in Print Preview mode.

Header ⟶

Footer ⟶

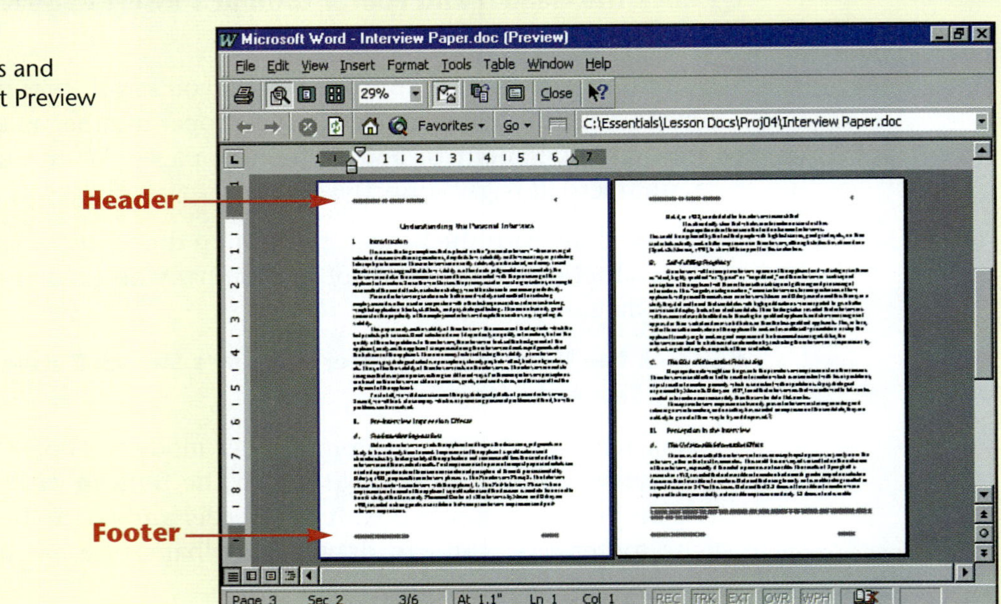

⑫ **Choose File, Page Setup, then choose the Layout tab.**

The dialog box should look like the one in Figure 4.17.

Figure 4.17
Using the Page Setup dialog box to turn off headers and footers on the first page.

Click here to remove headers and footers from the first page

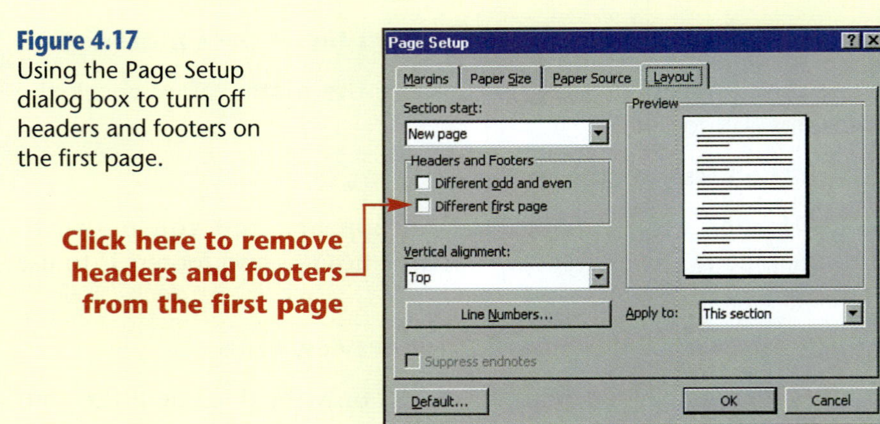

⑬ **In the Headers and Footers panel of the Layout page, select the Different First Page check box, then choose OK.**

This option ensures that the first page uses a different header and footer than other pages in the document. You aren't going to specify any text for this special header or footer, so none appears on the page.

⑭ **Go back to Print Preview mode and look at the pages again. Click Close when you're done.**

⑮ **Save the document and leave it open for the next lesson.**

Remember that, like many formatting elements in a document, headers and footers are largely matters of taste. Some people prefer only headers in their documents; others like footers. Many people think that using both in the same document is overkill, but others appreciate the additional information provided by both headers and footers.

When you add these elements to a document, consider readers. Do they need all the information that you are supplying, or would page numbers alone be enough? Do headers detract from the document's design, or are subtle footers the right touch?

Lesson 6: Creating an Index

An index is a listing of topics covered in a book or long document, along with page number references, that usually appears at the end of the book or document.

To create an index, start by marking words, phrases, or symbols you want to include in the index. Then choose an index design and generate a finished index, much like you generated a table of contents in Lesson 4. When the index is generated, Word collects the marked entries, sorts them alphabetically, references their page numbers, finds and removes duplicate entries from the same page, and displays the index.

In this lesson, you continue to work with your opened document from Lesson 5 and generate a small, representative sample index for this document.

To Create an Index

① **On page 3 of your document, locate the name Diboye. Select the word (double-click inside of the word) and choose Insert, Index and Tables from the menu. Click the Index tab (see Figure 4.18).**

Figure 4.18
The Index and Tables dialog box is the starting point for creating an Index or a Table of Contents.

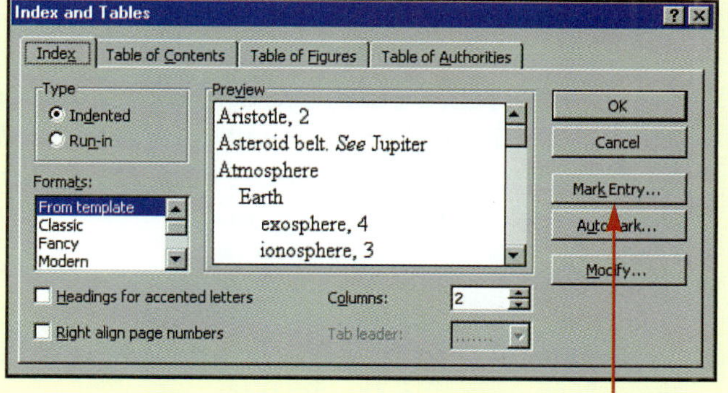

Click here to open the Mark Entry dialog box

continues

To Create an Index (continued)

2 **Click the Mark Entry button. The Mark Entry dialog box appears (see Figure 4.19). The text that you selected (Diboye) appears in the Main Entry box. You can edit the text, or enter new text if the selected text was not exactly what you wanted to appear in the text. Accept Diboye as the entry and click the Mark button.**

Figure 4.19
The Mark Entry dialog box remains open so you can mark additional entries in your document.

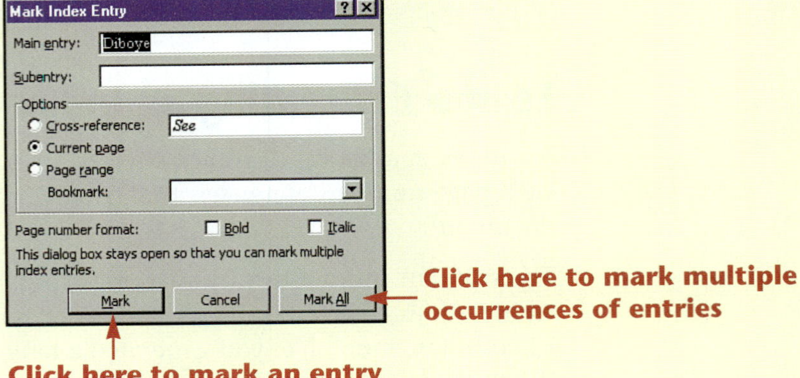

Click here to mark multiple occurrences of entries

Click here to mark an entry

Word marks each index entry by inserting a field immediately after the entry text in your document. If the field isn't visible (see Figure 4.20) click the Show/Hide button on the Standard toolbar.

Figure 4.20
Each marked index entry is followed by a field.

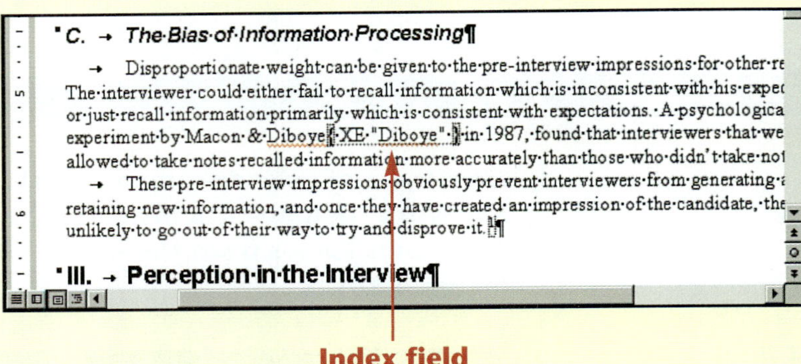

Index field

3 **The Mark Entry dialog box remains open so you can mark additional text in your document. Mark the following index entries and this time, click the Mark All button in the Mark Index Entry dialog box.**

Macan

Hakel

cognitive categorization

halo effect

4 **When you have completed marking the entries, close the Mark Index Entry dialog box. You're now ready to generate the index. Start a new page at the end of the document by inserting a hard page break at the end of page 5 (press Ctrl+↵Enter).**

5 **Place your cursor at the top of the new, blank page and choose Insert, Index and Tables from the menu. When the Index and Tables dialog box appears, select the Index tab (see Figure 4.21).**

Figure 4.21
Select from many pre-defined styles for your new index.

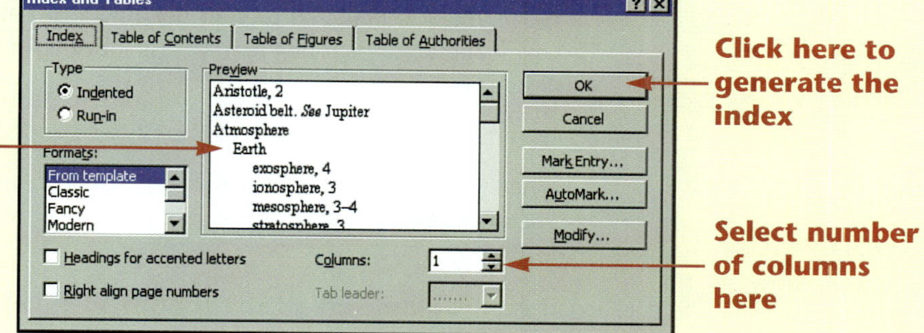

6 **Under Type, choose Indented or Run-in. When you choose a type, a sample appears in the Preview window.**

7 **Select from the predefined index formats in the Formats section. Formats also preview in the Preview window. Set the Columns option to 1.**

8 **Click OK to generate the index.**

Your index might look like the one shown in Figure 4.22, depending upon the formatting options you selected.

9 **Save your work and close the document.**

Figure 4.22
An example of a simple index whose formatting options were taken from the template.

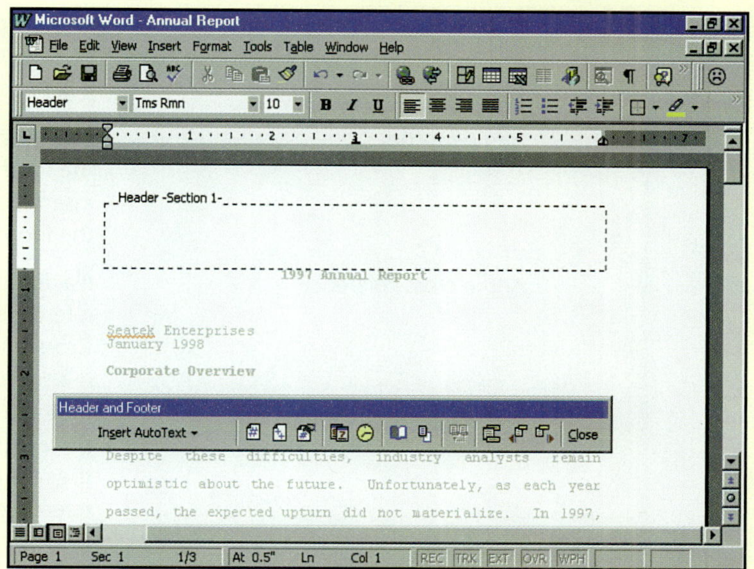

In this exercise, you added only a few items to the index. A "real" index would, of course, contain many entries.

You can create subordinate topics to a main index topic by typing the main topic in the Main entry box of the Mark Index Entry dialog box, and a subordinate topic in the Subentry box. For example, in a cookbook, the main entry might be "Pies" and the subentry might be "Apple."

If you need to create a third-level entry, add a colon at the end of the subentry text, followed by the text for the third-level entry. For example, a main entry might be "Desserts," a subentry "Pies," followed by "Apple."

To add formatting to page numbers in the index, select the Bold or Italic Page number format: options in the Mark Index Entry dialog box.

When you add new text to your document or new entries to your index once you have generated the index, update the index by placing your cursor anywhere in it. Press F9.

To remove an index entry, highlight its field code and press Del.

When you choose Mark All, only the first occurrence in each paragraph of your document exactly matches the text and case of the index entry will be marked.

You have completed all the lessons in this project. If you have completed your session on the computer, exit Word and Windows 95 before turning off your computer. Otherwise, continue with the "Checking Your Skills" and "Applying Your Skills" sections.

Project Summary

To	Do This
Move to a specific page	Choose Edit, Go To. Select Page in the Go to What list, type the page number, and choose Go To.
Browse the headings	Click the Select Browse Object palette at the bottom of the vertical scroll bar, then select Browse by Heading. Click the Next or Previous buttons to browse through headings.
Add a footnote	Place the insertion point where you want the footnote to appear, then choose Insert, Footnote. Choose OK, then type the footnote.
Add a cross-reference	Place the insertion point where cross-references will appear, then choose Insert, Cross-reference. In the Cross-reference dialog box, choose the type of reference that you want to make and then choose the exact text to which you want to tie the reference. Choose Insert to create the reference and close the dialog box.

To	Do This
Create a table of contents	Make sure that the document contains headings and that they have heading styles applied. Create a new page for the table of contents, then move the insertion point to the location at which you want to place the table of contents. Choose Insert, Index and Tables. Select a format for the table of contents and the number of heading levels that it should include. Choose OK to close the dialog box and create the table of contents.
Add a header or a footer to a document	Choose View, Header and Footer. In the Header and Footer toolbar, click the Switch Between Header and Footer tool to open a header or footer editing box. Type the text or use the tools to add a page number, date, or time. Choose Close to close the toolbar and return to Normal view of the document.
Remove a header or footer from the first page of a document	Choose File, Page Setup. In the Page Setup dialog box, choose the Layout tab and select the Different First Page check box. Choose OK to close the dialog box and remove the header and footer.
Create an Index	Mark index entries, place your cursor where you want the index to appear and choose Insert, Index and Tables. Select a format, type and number of columns for the index, and choose OK.
Update an Index or a Table of Contents	Place your cursor in the index or table of contents and press F9.

Checking Your Skills

True/False

For each of the following statements, check *T* or *F* to indicate whether the statement is true or false.

__T __F   **1.** You must type and format each footnote number when you create a footnote.

__T __F   **2.** Word updates cross-references and tables of contents automatically when you print or open the document.

__T __F   **3.** Headers apply to all pages in the section of a document, even if you begin typing on page 4.

__T __F   **4.** Applying styles to headings makes it easy to generate a table of contents.

__T __F   **5.** Footers and footnotes are synonyms referring to the same feature.

__T __F   **6.** When you click a cross-reference number, the insertion point jumps to the cross-reference destination.

__T __F   **7.** You can only see headers and footers onscreen in Print Preview.

__T __F   **8.** By default, endnotes are printed at the bottom of every page.

__T __F   **9.** You can include subordinate topics in an index.

__T __F **10.** When you edit a document, Word automatically updates the page numbers of entries in an index.

Multiple Choice

Circle the letter of the correct answer for each of the following:

1. On which menu can you find the Footnote command?

  a. View

  b. Insert

  c. Format

  d. Tools

2. Which feature helps you move through a long document?

  a. Go To

  b. Select Browse Object

  c. Document Map

  d. All the above

3. Which menu includes the Header and Footer command?

  a. View

  b. Insert

  c. Format

  d. Tools

4. When you create a cross-reference to a heading, you can insert the reference to what?

  a. The page number where the heading is located

  b. The heading text itself

  c. Both of the above

  d. None of the above

5. How can you open the Go To dialog box?

  a. By pressing Ctrl+G

  b. By selecting Go To from the Select Browse Object palette

  c. By double-clicking the leftmost box on the status bar

  d. All the above

6. Where does a footer appear in a document?

  a. At the bottom of every page

  b. At the top of every page

  c. Only on the first page

  d. Only on the last page

7. In Normal view, where do you type footnote text?

  a. At the bottom of the document

  b. Where you want the footnote number to be inserted

  c. In the Footnote pane

  d. In the Footnote text box

8. Where does Word create a table of contents?

    a. At the beginning of the document

    b. At the end of the document

    c. In the header

    d. At the insertion point location

9. What shortcut key updates an index?

    a. [F3]

    b. [F9]

    c. [F6]

    d. [F1]

10. What key combination moves the insertion point to the beginning of a document?

    a. [Ctrl]+[Home]

    b. [Ctrl]+[↑]

    c. [Ctrl]+[←]

    d. [Ctrl]+[PgUp]

Completion

In the blank provided, write the correct answer for each of the following statements.

1. If you want your notes to appear at the end of the document or a section, you should insert ___________ rather than footnotes.

2. To update a cross-reference field manually, select the field and press _______________.

3. The vertical pane along the left edge of the document window that outlines the document's structure is known as the _______________.

4. The option to place different headers and footers on the first page of your document is found on the _______________ page in the Page Setup dialog box.

5. Cross-reference notes are ___________ in a document.

6. Word creates a table of contents based on the _______ used to format the headings.

7. When you select the command to create a header or footer, Word changes to _____________ view.

8. To create a(n), _________ you must first mark the items you want to include.

9. To open the Footnote pane in Normal view, __________ the footnote reference mark.

10. If you plan to return to a section of your document frequently, setting a(n) _________ makes it easy to get back there quickly.

Matching

In the blank next to each of the following terms or phrases, write the letter of the corresponding term or phrase. (Note that some letters may be used more than once.)

a. Browse object

b. Table of contents

c. Header

d. Footer

e. Ctrl+End

f. Document map

g. Reference mark

h. Footnote pane

i. Cross-reference

j. Index

_______ 1. A number, character, or combination of characters noting that additional information is contained in a footnote or endnote

_______ 2. A listing of topics covered in a book or long document, along with page number references

_______ 3. Key combination to move to the end of a document

_______ 4. A note, embedded in a document, that points readers to another section of the document where more related information is available

_______ 5. Element that appears across the top of pages in a document

_______ 6. Element that appears across the bottom of pages in a document

_______ 7. Tool below the vertical scroll bar that helps you locate different items in your document

_______ 8. Pane along the left side of the document window in which headings are displayed

_______ 9. Where you type footnote or endnote text in Normal view

_______ 10. List of headings included in a document

Applying Your Skills

Practice

The following exercises enable you to practice the skills you have learned in this project. Take a few minutes to work through these exercises now.

Using Bookmarks and Navigating in a Document

In this practice lesson, you use the skills you learned in this project to insert bookmarks into a document and practice browsing through the document. You continue to use the same document throughout all of the Practice exercises.

To use bookmarks and navigate in a document, follow these steps:

1. Open the file Proj0402 from the Project-04 folder on the CD and save it in your `Practices` folder with the name `Report`.

2. Choose View, Document Map.

3. In the Document Map pane, click the heading `The New Deal`.

4. Choose Insert, Bookmark and then type the bookmark name `New_Deal` and click Add.

5. In the Document Map pane, click the heading `Effects on Prices`.

6. Choose <u>I</u>nsert, Boo<u>k</u>mark, then type the bookmark name `Prices` and click <u>A</u>dd.

7. Choose <u>V</u>iew, <u>D</u>ocument Map, then press Ctrl+Home.

8. Press Ctrl+G to open the <u>G</u>o To dialog box.

9. Select Bookmark in the G<u>o</u> to What list, then select Prices from the <u>E</u>nter bookmark name drop-down list.

10. Close the <u>G</u>o To dialog box, then click the Next Find/Go To button to go to the next bookmark -- New_Deal. (The blue down arrows below the Select Browse Object button.)

11. Click the Previous Find/Go <u>T</u>o button to go to the previous bookmark -- Prices.

12. Press Ctrl+Home, then save the document. If requested by your instructor, print it. Leave the document open to use in the next exercise.

Adding a Footer to a Document

In this exercise, you add a footer to the Great Depression report document.

To add a footer to a document, follow these steps:

1. In the `Report` document, choose <u>V</u>iew, <u>H</u>eader and Footer.

2. Click the Switch Between Header and Footer button on the Header and Footer toolbar.

3. Type your name flush left in the footer, then press Tab.

4. Type `Page`, press the Spacebar once, then click the Insert Page Number button on the Header and Footer toolbar.

5. Press Tab and click the Insert Date button on the Header and Footer toolbar.

6. Click the <u>C</u>lose button on the Header and Footer toolbar.

7. Save the document and preview it. Make sure the footer appears on every page.

8. If requested by your instructor, print the document. Leave it open to use in the next exercise.

Inserting Footnotes and Endnote

In this exercise, you insert footnotes and endnotes into the Report document.

To insert footnotes and endnotes in the document, follow these steps:

1. In the `Report` document, position the insertion point after the exclamation point at the end of the second sentence under the heading Chapter 1. Black Thursday (the sentence ends with $525!).

Word

2. Choose <u>I</u>nsert, Foot<u>n</u>ote. Select the <u>F</u>ootnote and <u>A</u>utoNumber options, then click OK.

3. Type the following footnote text—Meltzer, Milton, *Brother Can You Spare a Dime?*, Facts on File, 1991.

4. Position the insertion point after the period at the end of the second to last sentence in that paragraph (it ends with the word worthless), and choose <u>I</u>nsert, Foot<u>n</u>ote again. Select the <u>F</u>ootnote and <u>A</u>utoNumber options, then click OK.

5. Type the following footnote text—*World Book Multimedia Encyclopedia*, World Book, Inc., 1996.

6. Use Go To to go to the bookmark New_Deal, then position the insertion point after the first sentence in the paragraph under the heading The New Deal and choose <u>I</u>nsert, Foot<u>n</u>ote again. This time, select the <u>E</u>ndnote and <u>A</u>utoNumber options, then click OK.

7. Type the following endnote text—Meltzer, Milton, *Brother Can You Spare a Dime?*, Facts on File, 1991.

8. Double-click the endnote reference number, then move the insertion point to the end of that paragraph.

9. Choose <u>I</u>nsert, Foot<u>n</u>ote, select the <u>E</u>ndnote and <u>A</u>utoNumber options, then click OK.

10. Type Ibid.

11. Preview the document and save your changes. If requested by your instructor, print the document. Keep it open to use in the next exercise.

Creating a Cross-Reference in the Report Document

In this exercise, you add a cross-reference to the Report document.

To create a cross-reference in the report document, follow these steps:

1. In the Report document, click the Select Browse Object button and choose Footnote, then click the Previous Footnote button until the first footnote is displayed.

2. Double-click the footnote mark number to move the insertion point to the footnote reference mark in the document.

3. Position the insertion point after the fourth sentence in that paragraph, before the period, and type (for more information about how people reacted, see the section, . Don't forget to leave a space after the comma.

4. Choose <u>I</u>nsert, Cross-<u>r</u>eference. Select Heading from the Reference <u>t</u>ype list, select the heading Effects on People in the For <u>w</u>hich heading list, and select Heading text from the Insert <u>r</u>eference to: list.

5. Click <u>I</u>nsert, then click <u>C</u>lose. Type a close parenthesis to complete the cross-reference.

6. Click the cross-reference text.

7. Save the document. If requested by your instructor, print it. Keep the document open to use in the next lesson.

Creating a Table of Contents

In this exercise, you create a table of contents for the Report document.

To create a table of contents, follow these steps:

1. In the `Report` document, position the insertion point at the top of page 2 and press `Ctrl`+`Enter` to insert a page break. Press `↑` to move the insertion point on to the new page.

2. In 26-point Arial, type `Table of Contents`, then press `Enter` twice.

3. Choose Insert, Index and Tables, then click the Table of Contents page tab.

4. Select the Formal format and make sure the Show levels setting is 3.

5. Click OK.

6. Preview the document and save it. If requested by your instructor, print it. Leave the document open to use in the next exercise.

Creating an Index for the Report Document

In this exercise you create an index for the Report document.

To create an index for the report document, follow these steps:

1. In the `Report` document, select the word `stock` in the third sentence of the paragraph under the heading `Introduction`.

2. Choose Insert, Index and Tables and click the Index page tab.

3. Click the Mark Entry button. Make sure the entry text is correct, and that the Current page option button is selected.

4. Click the Mark All button.

5. Mark the following words in the document as index entries, too:

   `stock market`

   `Great Depression`

   `Black Thursday`

   `Dupont`

   `Prices`

   `Franklin D. Roosevelt`

   `Herbert Hoover`

   `depression`

   `New Deal`

   `congress`

   `Civilian Conservation Corp.`

6. Feel free to include other entries that you think are appropriate for an index for this document.

7. Press Ctrl+End to move the insertion point to the end of the document and press Ctrl+↵Enter to start a new page. In 26-point Arial, centered, type `Index` as a heading for the page.

8. Choose Insert, Index and Table and click the Index page tab.

9. Select Indented, and select the Formal Format, then click OK.

10. Save the document.

11. Go back and add the word `profits` to the index. To do this, locate and select the word, then choose Insert, Index and Tables, and click the Mark Entry button. Make sure the settings are correct, then click Mark All.

12. Select the index and press F9.

13. Try removing Congress from the index. Locate the word in the document and select the field code following it. Be sure to select the brackets and everything within them. Press Del.

14. Select the index and press F9.

15. Insert a page break before the heading `Recovery`, then update the index again.

16. Save the document. If requested by your instructor, print it. Close the document when you have finished.

Challenge

The following challenges enable you to use your problem-solving skills. Take time to work through these exercises now.

Inserting Bookmarks and Cross-references in an Annual Report

You have the annual report for Computer Training Concepts, Inc. In this exercise, use the skills you have learned in this project to insert bookmarks and cross references that you can use to locate information quickly. Open the file Proj0403 from the Project-04 folder on the CD and save it in your `Challenges` folder with the name `Annual`.

Start by browsing through the document using keyboard shortcuts. Move the end of the document and back to the beginning. Move to the first line of the third page, then to the first line of the second page. Display the document and use it to move quickly to different headings within the document. Insert a bookmark called `Expend` at the `Capital Expenditures` heading. Insert one called `Goals` at the `Goals for 2000` heading. Use Go To and the Object Browser buttons to move to each bookmark.

Insert a cross-reference to the heading Personnel Information after the phrase `hiring new management personnel` in the first sentence under the heading `1999 Operating Results`. See if you can reformat the cross-reference text to match the surrounding text. Use the cross-reference.

Save the document. If requested by your instructor, print it. Keep the document open to use in the next exercise.

Adding Footnotes and Endnotes to the Annual Report

In this exercise, add three footnotes and two endnotes to the Annual document. In the Annual document, insert a footnote after the first sentence in the second paragraph under the heading 1999 Operating Results. The footnote text should explain the decrease was an anticipated result of expansion efforts. Insert another footnote after the Capital Expenditures paragraph stating that these expenditures should lead to long-term growth. Insert a third footnote after the paragraph under the Corporate Overview paragraph, indicating that although growth was realized by the industry overall, it did not materialize at CTC.

Now, insert two endnotes. Put one after the first paragraph under Operating Results, and use it to reference last year's annual report. Put another endnote after the New CEO paragraph to explain that Ms. Stewart was on leave for ten months in 1992. Use the Browse Object button to browse through the footnotes and endnotes.

Preview the document. Adjust spacing and page breaks if necessary. Save the document. If requested by your instructor, print it. Keep it open to use in the next exercise.

Adding a Header and a Footer to the Annual Report

In this exercise, use the skills you learned in this project to add a header and a footer to the Annual document. Start by inserting a header on every page but the first. Include the page number. Insert a footer on every page but the first, also, and include your name and the date.

Preview the document. Save it. If requested by your instructor, print it. Keep the document open for the next exercise.

Adding a Table of Contents

In this exercise, use the skills you learned in this project to add a table of contents to the Annual document. Create a new blank page between the title page and the main document where you can insert the table of contents. Enter a heading on the page. Create the table of contents using three levels and a format that includes dot leaders before the page numbers. Try out a few different formats before picking one. Once you insert the table of contents, edit the Strategic Planning Information heading to Long Range Planning. Update the table of contents (select it and press F9).

When you are finished, preview the document. Save it. If requested by your instructor, print it. Keep the document open for the next exercise.

Adding an Index

In this exercise, use the skills you learned in this project to add an index to the Annual document. Mark the entries in the text, using your judgment as to which items are important enough to include. Try adding some subordinate entries such as `Chief Executive Officer` and `Chief Financial Officer` under `Personnel`. Try adding some cross-references such as `CFO, see Chief Financial Officer`.

When you have finished marking all entries, insert the index on the last page of the document (under create a new page with the heading INDEX) and insert the index. Try different styles and formats. You can always use <u>E</u>dit, <u>U</u>ndo to remove an index and try a different one. The marks remain in place.

Once you settle on an index, make some changes. Add an entry, delete an entry, and insert a page break in the document to change the page numbering. Update the index after the changes.

Save the document. Preview it. If requested by your instructor, print it. Close the document when you have finished.

You have completed the project and the associated lessons, as well as the "Checking Your Skills" and "Applying Your Skills" sections. Now use the PinPoint software evaluation mode to assess your comprehension of the specific exam tasks you have just learned. You can also use the PinPoint Trainer Mode and the Show Me tutorials to practice these specific exam tasks.

Project 5

Five

Advanced Formatting Techniques

Creating a Neighborhood Newsletter

In this Project, you learn how to:

Objectives	Required Activities
➤ Create Sections	
➤ Set Page Orientation	Change page orientation
➤ Add Borders Shading to a Paragraph	Create and modify page borders
➤ Create and Modify Page Borders	Apply paragraph and section shading
➤ Control Text Flow Options	Use text flow options (Widows/Orphans options and keeping lines together) Use non-breaking spaces
➤ Sort Paragraphs	Sort lists, paragraphs, and tables
➤ Create Alternating Headers and Footers	Format first page differently from subsequent pages
➤ Insert Special Characters	Insert special characters

Why Would I Do This?

ewsletters and similar documents, such as brochures and catalogs, require creative formatting to make them interesting and
easy to read. For a professional appearance, you want to take
advantage of many of the formatting features Word has available.

You'll be working on a newsletter in this project and this particular newsletter does not make use of columns, although columns are a very popular
way to present newsletters. You learn about columns in Project 10. Here,
you concentrate on some of the formatting tasks that help improve the
appearance of your document: creating sections to change page formatting,
changing the page orientation; applying borders to pages and paragraphs;
adding shading to paragraphs; controlling text flow; sorting paragraphs;
adding different headers and footers on the first page and alternating pages;
and inserting special characters

Lesson 1: Creating Sections

When you apply page numbering, headers and footers, page margins, page
orientation, and columns to a document, these features are referred to as
page formatting options and they affect the entire document. In order to
change to a different type of *page formatting* in the same document, you
have to create *sections*. The formatting is then assigned to a section, and the
next section can have entirely different formatting.

A document is divided into sections by section breaks, just as page breaks
divide a document into pages. There are four types of section breaks, as
shown in Table 5.1. Which type you use depends on where you want to
place the text that comes after the break.

Page Formatting

Formatting that applies to an entire page or document, as opposed to formatting that changes the appearance of only selected paragraphs or characters.

Section

A division of a document that allows different page formatting to appear in the same document.

Table 5.1 Section Breaks	
Type	Description
Next Page	The new section begins at the top of the next page. When you insert this type of section break, it adds a page break at the insertion point as well as the section break. This is useful for section beaks that coincide with major breaks in a document, such as a new chapter starting. It is necessary when you want to start a different page numbering style or start the page numbers with a different number.
Continuous	The new section continues on the same page as the preceding section. This is useful for using columns. A section that has a different number of columns can be separated from the preceding one but still be part of the same page.

Type	Description
<u>O</u>dd Page or <u>E</u>ven Page	The new section begins on the next even- or odd-numbered page. If an odd page section break falls on an odd page, a blank page is inserted to force the next available page to become an odd page (the same applies to an even page break on an even page). This is useful when a section break coincides with a major break, like a chapter in a document where each chapter must start on an odd page (or even page).

In Normal and Page Layout view, the location of section breaks is marked by a double-horizontal line with the label Section Break followed by the type of break. These markers don't appear in printouts and they don't show in Page Layout view if you aren't displaying nonprinting characters.

In the newsletter project, you add a section so you can change the page orientation at the end of the document in Lesson 2.

To Create Sections

❶ From the Project-05 folder on the CD, open the Proj0501 file and save it as Carpenter Cove.

The Carpenter Cove newsletter is a new publication developed for local bird and animal lovers interested in sightings and activities surrounding a local state park. The newsletter is a work in progress. Some of the articles have not been completed. Your job, however, is to work on the layout and formatting of the newsletter.

The first page of the newsletter has the title and a text box that contains the contents in a table (see Figure 5.1). The plan for subsequent pages is to have a graphic artist insert pictures. The final page of the newsletter will have a calendar.

You want different margins on the first page than you will use on the subsequent pages because you will be printing the first page on stationery that has a preprinted border on it. Therefore, the first page needs to be in a separate section to accommodate the different formatting. Because the final page of the newsletter will also have different formatting, you need to add a section break at the start of that page.

If you have problems...

If you can't see the title and the text box on the first page, you may be in Normal view. Choose <u>V</u>iew, <u>P</u>age Layout from the menu. When working with visual elements, such as page formatting and graphics, you should be working in the Page Layout view.

continues

To Create Sections   (continued)

Figure 5.1
This newsletter has a text box on the first page, a title, and articles.

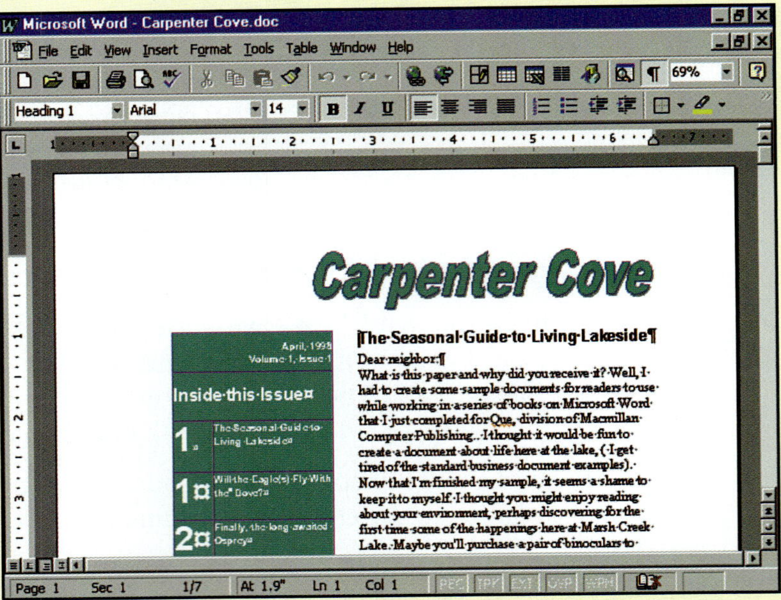

2 **Place your insertion point at the beginning of the line of the article title Will the Eagle(s) Fly with the Dove? and choose Insert, Break from the menu.**

The Break dialog box opens (see Figure 5.2).

Figure 5.2
By choosing a Next Page section break, you create the section and start a new page.

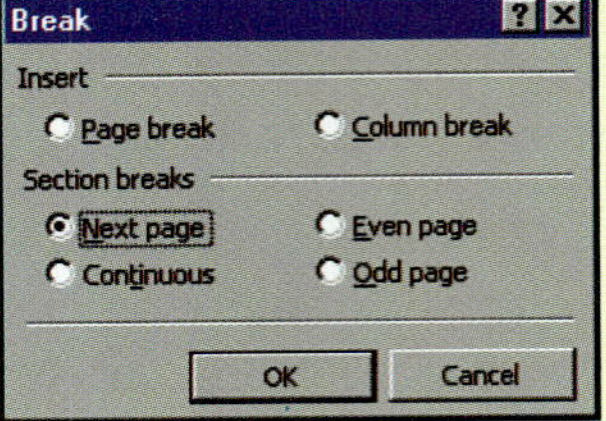

3 **Under Section breaks, click Next page and then choose OK.**

As shown in Figure 5.3, you see a double dotted line with the words `Section Break(Next Page)` at the end of the first article (if you can't see the section break, click the Show/Hide ¶ button on the Standard toolbar).

4 **Make sure your insertion point is in section 2 (the Status bar shows `Sec 2` after the page number). Then choose File, Page Setup.**

5 **Change the Top and Bottom margins to 0.75 inch and the Left and Right margins to 0.5 inch.**

Show/Hide ¶ button

Figure 5.3
The section break separates the first page from the second, so you can apply different formatting to each.

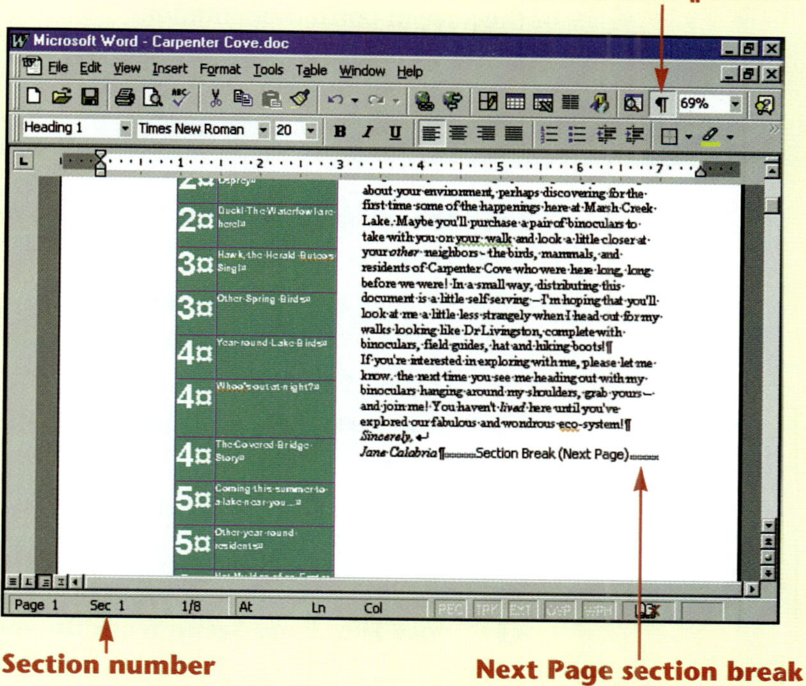

Section number

Next Page section break

6 From the **Apply to** drop-down list, select `This section` (if it's not already selected). Choose **OK**.

The second page is now formatted with smaller margins, but the first page still is set up with one-inch margins.

7 Save the document and leave it open for the next lesson.

Inside Stuff

You can add the section break and change the margins in one step. Place your insertion point where you want the new formatting to begin, and choose File, Page Setup. Specify your new margins. Then from the Apply to drop-down list, select `This point forward` and click OK. Word automatically adds the section break and changes the margins for the text following your insertion point.

Lesson 2: Setting Page Orientation

Portrait

The orientation in which the text runs parallel to the short edge of the paper.

Page orientation refers to the direction of the printing on the paper. In *portrait* orientation, Word prints the text with the narrow end of the paper at the top. In *landscape* orientation, the wide edges of the paper are the top and bottom. Most documents are printed in portrait, but you may want to use landscape orientation if you have a wide table or a considerable amount of text that runs across the page.

Landscape
Page orientation in which text runs parallel to the long edge of the paper.

In the newsletter, the editors plan to include a calendar of events on the last page. The calendar is a wide table, and it won't fit within the margins of the page in portrait orientation.

To Set Page Orientation

1 In the newsletter, press Ctrl+End **to move to the end of the document.**

To change the page orientation, you need to add a section break first. The section needs to start with the next page, so you specify a Next Page section break.

2 Choose Insert, Break from the menu. Select Next page and click OK.

By looking at the Status bar, you see that your insertion point is now in Sec 3 on Page 6. However, this page is still in portrait orientation.

3 Choose File, Page Setup from the menu. Click the Paper Size tab.

The Page Setup dialog box appears (see Figure 5.4).

Figure 5.4
The example in the Preview box shows how the orientation affects your document.

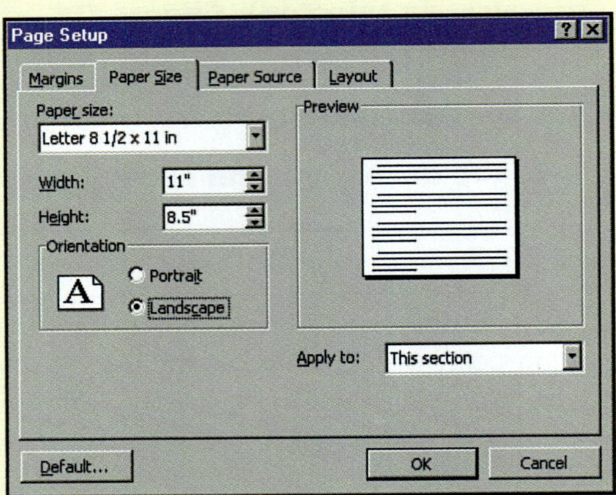

4 Under Orientation, click Landscape.

5 Make sure the selection in the Apply to box is This section.

6 Choose OK.

The last page is now in landscape orientation (you may have to change your Zoom percentage to verify that).

The page is now ready for the newsletter editors to add the calendar table.

7 Save the document but leave it open for the next lesson.

Lesson 3: Adding Borders and Shading to a Paragraph

To make your article headlines distinctive, it may help to add shading to the paragraphs. This is especially effective if your newsletter is being printed in color or read online. Where color is not available, or where you want less visibility, you may want to add a border to a paragraph to set it off from the other text around it.

In your newsletter, you're going to add shading to the article titles. The first article is a letter from the editor, so you want it to look different. You use borders to create a different look for that heading.

To Add Shading and Borders to Paragraphs

❶ In the newsletter, place your insertion point in the title of the second article (on page 2), titled `Will the Eagle(s) Fly with the Dove?`

Use the title of this article to specify the headline formatting you want to use for all the articles. This title is assigned the Heading 1 style, as are the other article titles in the newsletter.

❷ Choose F̲ormat, B̲orders and Shading from the menu.

The Borders and Shading dialog box appears (see Figure 5.5).

Figure 5.5
Use this dialog box to add borders and shading to a selected paragraph.

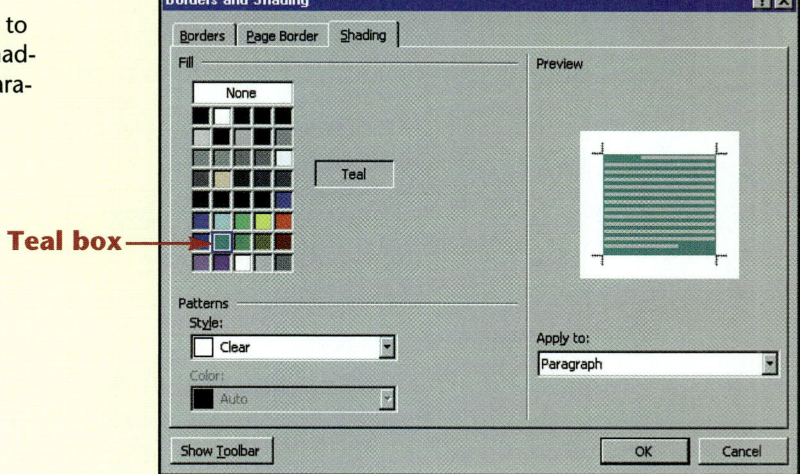

❸ Click the S̲hading tab.

❹ Under Fill, click the Teal color box (next to last row, second box from left). Then choose OK.

The entire paragraph has teal shading behind it.

❺ Select the entire title paragraph and choose F̲ormat, F̲ont from the menu.

continues

To Add Shading and Borders to Paragraphs   (continued)

6 **Change the <u>F</u>ont to Times New Roman, the Font style to Regular, the <u>S</u>ize to 20, and the <u>C</u>olor to White. Choose OK.**

You have now established the formatting that you want to use for all the article titles. The style applied to all the titles is Heading 1. In the next steps, you change the attributes of the Heading 1 style to match the paragraph you just formatted. In doing so, you automatically change all the article titles.

7 **Choose Heading 1 from the Style drop-down list on the Formatting toolbar.**

The Modify Style dialog box appears (see Figure 5.6). The dialog box lets you choose to update the style with your new changes or reapply the old style formatting.

Figure 5.6
The Modify Style dialog box appears when you change paragraph formatting and then select the same style already assigned that paragraph.

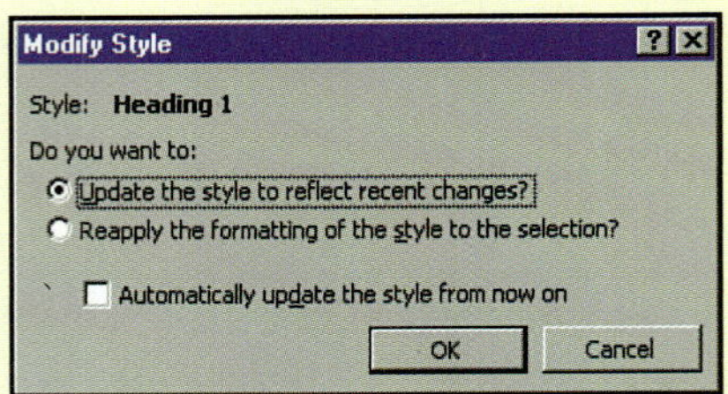

8 **Select <u>U</u>pdate the style to reflect recent changes and then choose OK.**

Check some of the other article titles in the newsletter. You see that the same formatting has been applied to those titles.

9 **Select the title The Seasonal Guide to Living Lakeside, which is the title for the first article.**

Because this article is really a letter to the readers, you want to set a different type of formatting for its title.

10 **Choose Heading 3 from the Style drop-down list on the Formatting toolbar.**

This gives the paragraph a different style from the other titles in the newsletter. Any changes to the formatting therefore do not affect the other titles.

11 **With the title still selected, choose Format, <u>F</u>ont from the menu. Select Arial as the <u>F</u>ont, bold Italic as the Font style, 18 points as the <u>S</u>ize, and Teal as the <u>C</u>olor. Choose OK.**

You have established the font characteristics of the title. Next, you add a border to the paragraph.

12 **With the paragraph still selected, choose Format, <u>B</u>orders and Shading from the menu. Select the <u>B</u>orders tab.**

The Borders and Shading dialog box appears (see Figure 5.7).

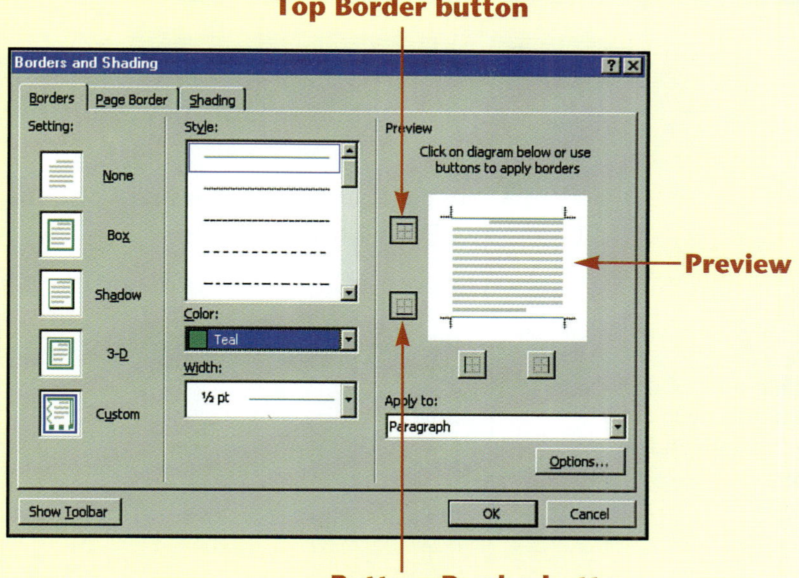

Figure 5.7
Select the line style, color, and width of the border for the selected paragraph.

13 **From the Style box, choose the first straight line. Select Teal from the Color drop-down list. Set the Width to $^1/_2$ point.**

14 **In the Preview box, click the Top Border button and then click the Bottom Border button.**

Instead of choosing one of the predefined settings, you customized your border by selecting only a top and bottom border.

15 **Choose OK.**

The article title for the letter has a unique format. To be able to use this format again, you need to incorporate it into the style assigned to the title paragraph, Heading 3.

16 **Choose Heading 3 from the Style drop-down list on the Formatting toolbar. Then click Update the style to reflect recent changes in the Modify Style dialog box and choose OK.**

17 **Save the newsletter file but leave it open for the next lesson.**

Lesson 4: Creating and Modifying Page Borders

Adding borders to paragraphs helps make the paragraphs stand out. By the same token, adding a border to a page would enhance the appearance of the page. Page borders are often used on report or proposal title pages or on awards or certificates.

In this lesson, you are going to add a border to the last page of the newsletter, where the calendar table eventually appears.

To Add a Page Border

1 **In the newsletter, press Ctrl+End.**

Your insertion point is now on page 6, the last page of the newsletter.

2 **Choose Format, Borders and Shading from the menu. Click the Page Border tab.**

The Borders and Shading dialog box appears (see Figure 5.8).

Figure 5.8
Word has a set of decorative borders you can apply to pages and paragraphs.

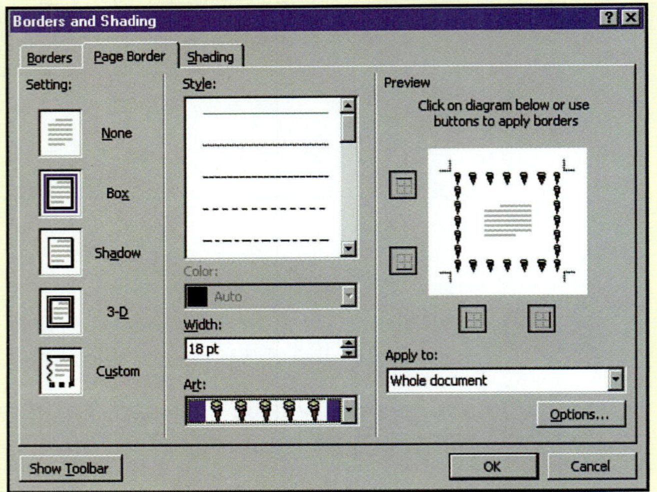

3 **Under Setting, select Box.**

This setting draws a border box around the entire page at the margins.

4 **From the Art drop-down list, select a decorative border.**

Word has a variety of decorative borders that you can apply. Check the Preview box after you make a selection, as some borders look different when you see them in a box.

5 **From the Apply to drop-down list, select This section.**

The last page is in a section of its own. By applying the border to only this section, you make sure the border appears only on the last page and not the rest of the pages.

6 **Choose OK.**

Preview the page to see the entire border. If it's not satisfactory, return to the Borders and Shading dialog box and choose a different decorative border or specify the line style, width, and color of a standard border.

7 **Save the file and leave it open for the next lesson.**

Lesson 5: Controlling Text Flow Options

Microsoft Word makes your text flow on the page, breaking lines automatically at the right margin and pages at the bottom margin. However, you may not always agree with how Word breaks lines, columns, or pages. You can control breaks manually or change option settings to make Word flow the text the way you want it. Table 5.2 describes some of the text flow options available to you in Word.

Table 5.2	Text Flow Options	
Option	Description	Do This
Automatic Hyphenation	Sets parameters to automatically hyphenate words that fall at the end of lines	Choose Tools, Language, Hyphenation. Click Automatically hyphenate document. In the Hyphenation zone box, specify the distance to leave between the end of a complete word and the right margin before hyphenating the word. Enter the number of consecutive lines you want to end with hyphens in the Limit consecutive hyphens to box. Click OK.
Hard Page Break	Starts a new page	Press Ctrl+Enter at the point where you want to start the new page.
Hard Return	Forces text to appear on the next line and starts a new paragraph	Press Enter where you want to start the new paragraph.
Keep Lines Together	Prevents a paragraph from being split by a line break	Select the paragraph. Format, Paragraph. Click the Line and Page Breaks tab. Select Keep lines together and then click OK.
Keep with Next	Prevents a page or column break from splitting two separate paragraphs	Click in the first paragraph. Format, Paragraph. Click the Line and Page Breaks tab. Select Keep with next and then click OK.
Line Break	Forces text to appear on the next line without starting a new paragraph	Press Shift+Enter at the point where you want the line to break.
Nonbreaking Hyphen	Prevents hyphenated words from being separated by automatic line breaks	Press Ctrl+Shift+- where you would normally type the hyphen.
Nonbreaking Space	Prevents two words from being separated onto different lines	Press Ctrl+Shift+Spacebar where you would normally type a space between the words.

continues

Table 5.2 (continued)		
Option	Description	Do This
Optional Hyphen	Defines where a long word should break when it falls at the end of a line; prevents a gap at the end of a line when the entire word moves down to the next line	Press Ctrl+- where you want to put the hyphen.
Widow/Orphan Control	Prevents the first or last line of a paragraph from being at the end or beginning of a page or column by itself	Choose Format, Paragraph. Click the Line and Page Breaks tab. Select Widow/Orphan control and then click OK.

In your newsletter, apply some of the text control options to make your text flow better.

To Apply Control Text Options

① Move to the beginning of the newsletter by pressing Ctrl+Home. Then click in the Dear Neighbor paragraph at the beginning of the first article.

First, you are going to set some specifications for the normal text in your newsletter.

② Choose Format, Style.

The Style dialog box appears (see Figure 5.9).

Figure 5.9
In the Style dialog box, you specify the font, paragraph, and other formatting that you want assigned to a style.

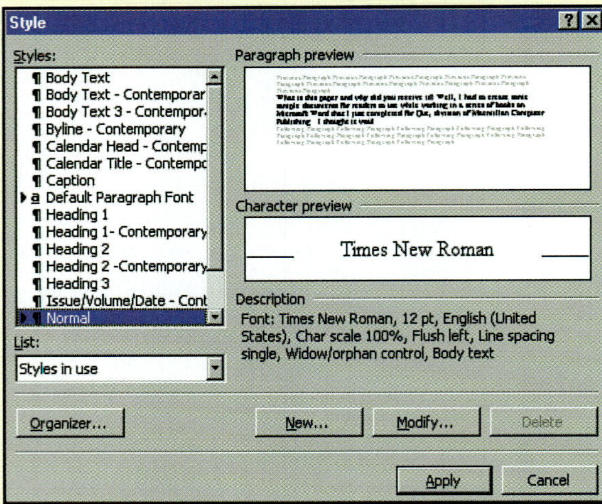

③ Select Normal from the Styles list. Click Modify.

④ Click Format and select Font. Change Size to 10 and click OK.

The Font dialog box is the same as the one you see when you choose Format, Font from the menu.

Orphan
The first line of the paragraph that appears by itself at the bottom of a page or column.

Widow
The last line of the paragraph that appears by itself at the top of a page or column.

Figure 5.10
Set line and page break options in the Paragraph dialog box.

5 **Click Format and select Paragraph. Click the Line and Page Breaks tab. Make sure Widow/Orphan control is selected.**

The Paragraph dialog box (see Figure 5.10) is the same box you see when you choose Format, Paragraph from the menu. Widow/Orphan control prevents the occurrence of *orphans* and *widows*, where a single line of a paragraph is separated from the remainder of the paragraph.

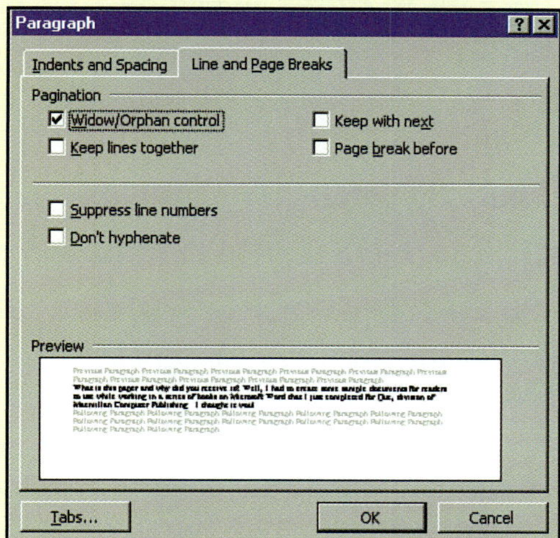

6 **Click the Indents and Spacing tab. Under Spacing, change After to 6 pt. Click OK.**

Adding space after the paragraph adds to the readability by giving some white space between the paragraphs.

7 **Click OK to close the Modify Style dialog box and then Apply.**

The newsletter looks a little cleaner with the extra white space between the paragraphs. Now you need to make an adjustment to the Heading 1 style.

8 **Go to the top of page 2. Select the paragraph** `Will the Eagle(s) Fly with the Dove?`

When using article titles, occasionally one of the titles is separated from its article by a page break. This may not appear to be a problem yet in your newsletter but you don't know what will happen when the graphics artist adds pictures and the authors of the articles complete their stories. To avoid having your article title on one page and the article on the next, change the paragraph formatting to keep the paragraphs together.

9 **Choose Format, Style. Make sure Heading 1 is the selected style. Then click Modify and choose Format.**

continues

Word

To Apply Control Text Options   (continued)

⑩ Choose Paragraph and select the Line and Page Breaks tab. Make sure Keep with next and Keep lines together are both selected. Click OK.

By selecting Keep with next, you ensure that an article title and its first paragraph won't be separated by page breaks. The Keep lines together option ensures that the title itself won't be split by a page break.

⑪ Click OK to close the Modify Style dialog box and then click Apply.

One of your tasks is to make the letter to the neighbors more distinctive.

⑫ Select the letter, from `Dear neighbor` through `eco-system`.

⑬ Change the font style to Italic and change the font size to `12`.

⑭ Choose Format, Paragraph. Click the Indents and Spacing tab. Under Indentation, change Left to `0.3` and Right to `0.3`. Click OK.

The words `Marsh Creek Lake` appear halfway down the letter. Your editors have made the policy that the name of this park should not be split onto separate lines. To keep the name on one line, you change the spaces between the words to nonbreaking spaces.

⑮ Delete the space between the words in `Marsh` and `Creek`. With your insertion point between the two words, press `Ctrl`+`⬆Shift`+`Spacebar`. Do the same thing to the space between `Creek` and `Lake`.

Small symbols appear between the words (if you are displaying non-printing characters), representing the nonbreaking spaces. The three words move as one down to the next line.

⑯ Save the newsletter and leave it open for the next lesson.

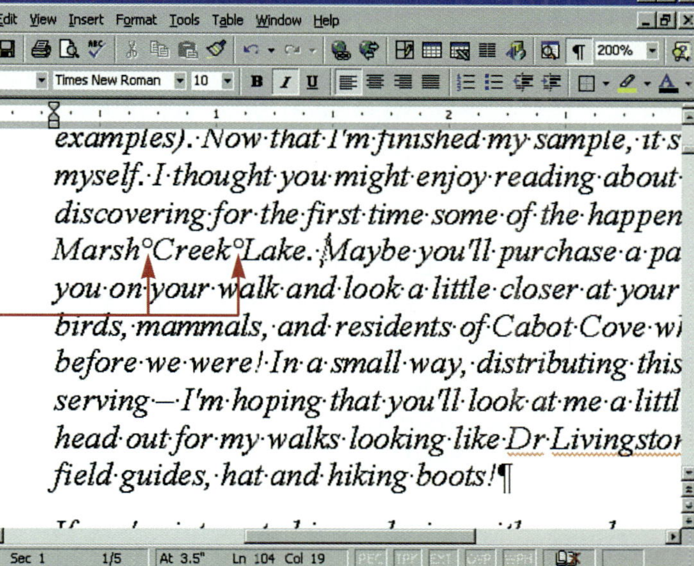

Figure 5.11
Small, nonprinting symbols replace the spaces to indicate where you inserted the nonbreaking spaces.

Exam Notes

You can also use the Insert menu to insert nonbreaking spaces, optional hyphens, or nonbreaking hyphens. To do so, choose Insert, Symbol. Click the Special Characters tab. Select the character you want from the list and then click Insert. Click Close to close the dialog box.

Lesson 6: Sorting Paragraphs

Putting paragraphs in alphabetical order can be a tedious task of cutting and pasting, if you try to do it manually. Word automates sorting for you.

There are some rules that govern sorting:

- You choose whether you want to sort alphabetically, numerically, or by date.

- You have a choice of sorting in ascending order (A to Z or 0 to 9) or in descending order (Z to A, 9 to 0).

- Paragraph marks (¶) separate items to be sorted (to see the paragraph marks, click the Show/Hide ¶ button on the Standard toolbar). Tabs separate *fields* within each item.

Field

A container or location that stores a particular type of data.

- Items beginning with punctuation marks or symbols (such as !, #, $, %, or &) are sorted first, followed by items beginning with numbers and then by items beginning with letters. Dates are treated as three-digit numbers.

■ If the sort is by numbers, all other characters are ignored. The numbers can be anywhere in a paragraph.

■ If the sort is by date, only the following are accepted as date separators: a hyphen (-), a forward slash (/), comma (,), and period (.). Only the colon (:) is recognized as a time separator. If the item isn't recognized as a date or time, Word puts the item at the beginning or end of the list (depending on whether the list is sorted in ascending or descending order).

■ When more than one item begins with the same character, Word looks to subsequent characters to determine the sort order.

Word sorts a list or a set of paragraphs by the first word in the paragraph, unless you have tabs separating columns of items. In that case, Word considers the tabs as field markers. The text in the first column is considered Field 1, the text in the second column is Field 2, and so on. That way it's possible to sort based on the second or subsequent column items instead of the first word of the line.

In one of the text boxes in your newsletter, you'll find a list of animals and birds seen around the lake. You are going to alphabetize that list in this lesson.

To Sort Paragraphs

❶ In the newsletter, go to page 5. Click inside the `Coming this Summer to a Lake Near You` **text box.**

This text box contains a series of paragraphs listing and describing some of the animals or birds an observer might soon see around the lake. You need to put this list in alphabetical order.

❷ Select the paragraphs from `Snapping Turtles` **through** `Goldfinches`.

These are the paragraphs you want to sort.

❸ Choose Table, Sort from the menu.

The Sort Text dialog box appears (see Figure 5.12).

Figure 5.12
In the Sort Text dialog box, specify the order you want to use in sorting the paragraphs.

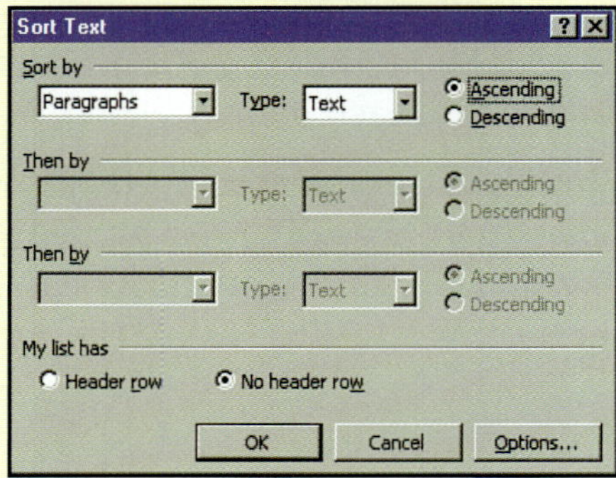

4 **From the <u>S</u>ort by drop-down list, select Paragraphs (if it's not already selected).**

Other choices from this drop-down list are a list of fields, the number of which corresponds to the number of tabbed columns in a paragraph. Since this list contains no tabbed columns, you are concerned only with sorting the paragraphs.

5 **Select Text as the <u>T</u>ype of sort you want to perform and click <u>A</u>scending to sort the list alphabetically from A to Z.**

6 **Choose OK.**

The list of paragraphs is now sorted alphabetically.

7 **Save your file and leave it open for the next lesson.**

Lesson 7: Creating Alternating Headers and Footers

Header

Information printed at the top of the page, such as document titles, author names, page numbers, logos, or graphics.

Footer

Information printed at the bottom of a page, such as page numbers, document names, logos, or graphics.

The newsletter still needs page numbers, and you would also like to add a *header* on each page that includes the name of the newsletter and its publication date. However, you don't want the header to appear on the first page. Also, because you want the page numbers to appear on the outside margin of the newsletter, you need to create *footers* that are different for the odd and even pages of your newsletter. Alternating headers and footers are headers and footers that are different on the odd and even pages of a document.

To Create Alternating Headers and Footers

1 **Go to page 1 of the newsletter.**

You don't have to start headers and footers from the top of your document. However, for your newsletter, it's best to start at the top because your first page is a different section than the remainder of the document. One way to set different headers and footers for different portions of a document is by using sections.

2 **Choose <u>V</u>iew, <u>H</u>eader and Footer from the menu.**

A dotted line box appears at the top of the first page with the label `Header - Section 1`. The Header and Footer toolbar also appears (see Figure 5.13).

To Create Alternating Headers and Footers   (continued)

Figure 5.13
A box appears at the top of the page that contains the text and/or graphics you want to include in the header.

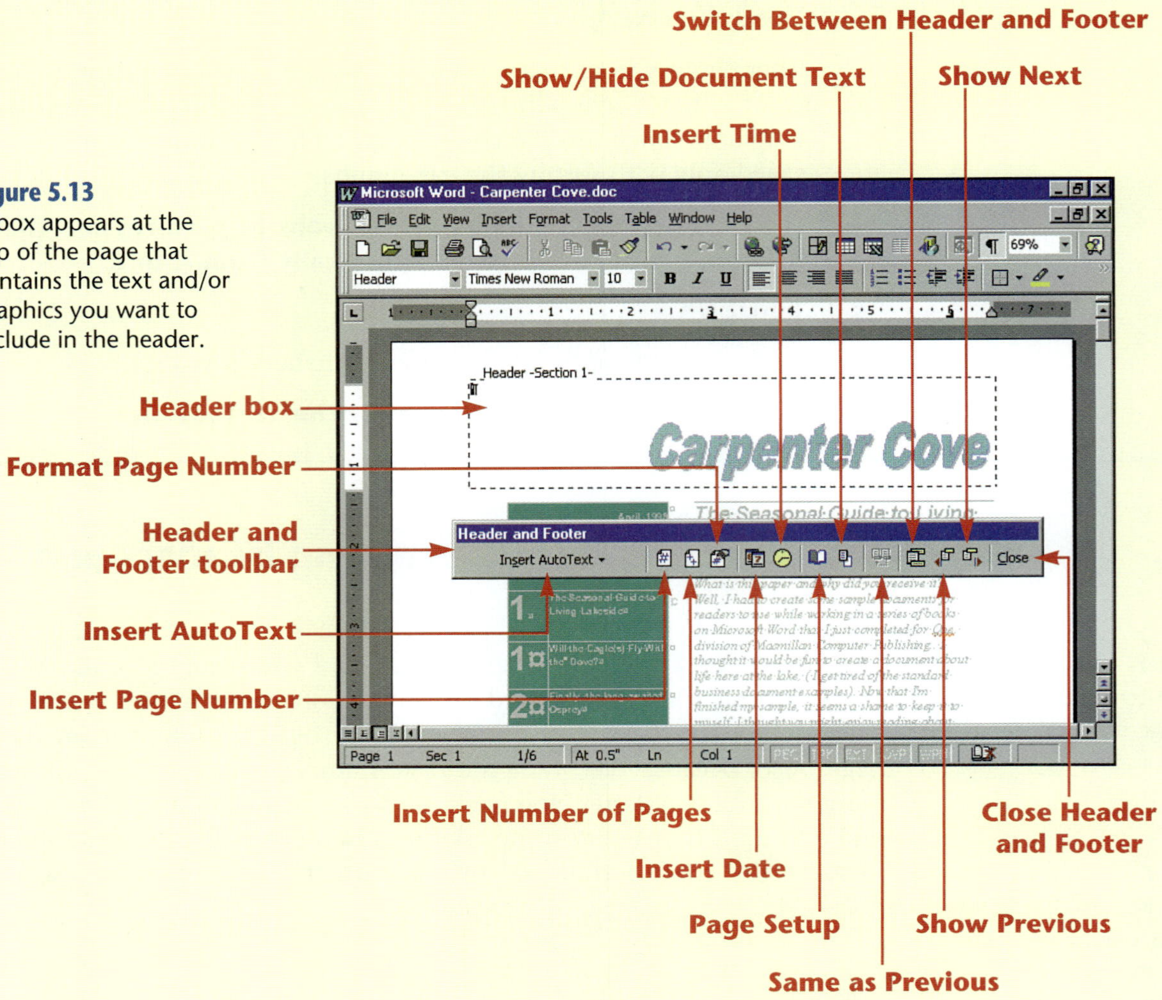

3 **You don't want to enter a header for the first page, so click the Switch Between Header and Footer button on the Header and Footer toolbar.**

Now you see the `Footer - Section 1` box at the bottom of the page.

4 **Type `Copyright Carpenter Cove Neighbors Association, April 1998`. Then press** `Tab` **and click the Insert Page Number button on the Header and Footer toolbar.**

A number 1 appears, but it has a gray background when you select it. This means that the page number changes, depending on which page you have open. You still need to format your footer, to keep your newsletter looking professional.

5 **Select the footer text (not including the page number) and change the font to 8-point Arial.**

6 **Select the page number and change its font to 18-point Times New Roman italic. Change the font color to Teal.**

The size and color of the page number text makes it stand out, while the copyright text remains small and unobtrusive. You may notice, however, that the page number isn't on the right margin. This means you have to adjust the tab setting.

7 **Click on the same line as the page number. On the ruler, drag the right-tab mark from 6 inches to 6.5 inches (or as near to it as possible).**

If your ruler is not visible, choose View, Ruler from the menu (see Figure 5.14).

Figure 5.14
Drag the right-tab mark on the ruler to adjust the tab setting.

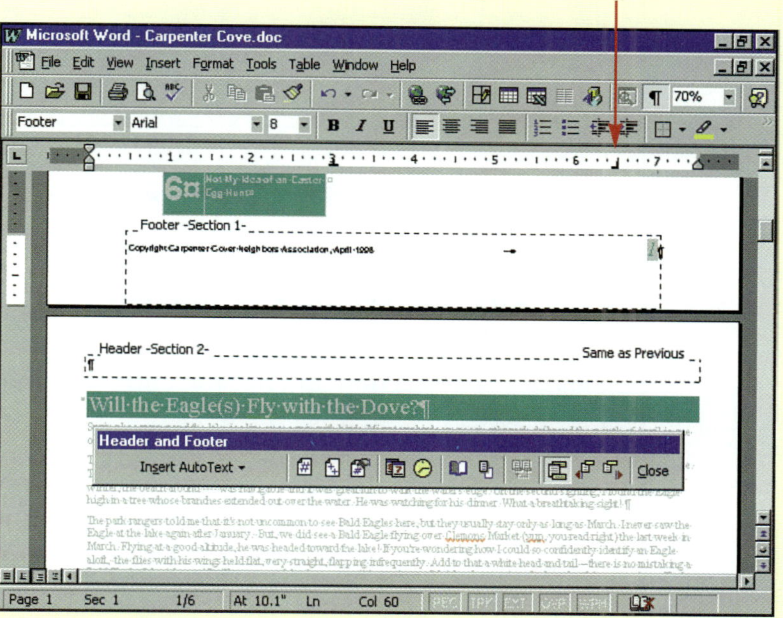

8 **Click Show Next on the Header and Footer toolbar.**

The Footer - Section 2 box appears. The label `Same as Previous` on the right side indicates that this footer is the same as the one you created for page 1. You don't want them to be the same.

9 **Click the Same as Previous button on the Header and Footer toolbar to turn it off.**

Now the Section 2 footer is independent of the Section 1 footer.

10 **Switch to the Section 2 header by clicking the Switch Between Header and Footer button on the Header and Footer toolbar. Then click the Same as Previous button to turn it off.**

The Section 2 header is now independent of the header on page 1.

continues

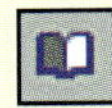

⑪ **Click the Page Setup button on the Header and Footer tool-bar.**

The Page Setup dialog box opens (see Figure 5.15), and the Layout tab should already be selected.

Figure 5.15
Use alternating headers and footers, by selecting Different odd and even Headers and Footers.

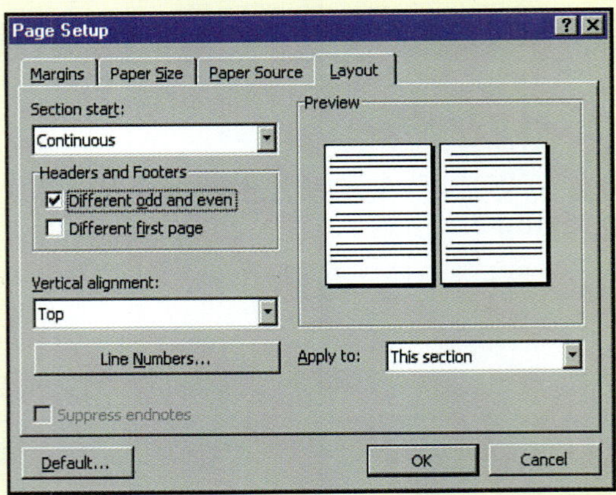

⑫ **Under Headers and Footers, select Different odd and even.**

This sets up the use of alternating headers and footers.

⑬ **From the Apply to drop-down list, select This section.**

You want the header and footer settings to apply only to the current section and not the entire document.

⑭ **Choose OK.**

The header box on page 2 is now labeled `Even Page Header - Section 2`. If `Same as Previous` appears, click the Same as Previous button on the Header and Footer toolbar to remove it.

⑮ **Type `Carpenter Cove` in the header box. Press ⬆Shift+⏎Enter and then type `April 1998`.**

⑯ **Select all the header text and set the font to 14-point Arial, bold, and italic. Then click the Align Left button on the Formatting toolbar.**

You have now set up your even page headers for the document. Your odd page headers are similar, so you need to copy the header text to the Clipboard.

⑰ **Select the header text and click the Copy button on the Standard toolbar.**

⑱ **Click Show Next on the Header and Footer toolbar.**

The Odd Page Header - Section 2 box appears.

19 **Click the Paste button on the Standard toolbar. Then click the Align Right button on the Formatting toolbar.**

The same text you had in the Even Page Header appears, but now you've aligned it with the right margin. Your headers are complete. Now you need to work on your footers.

20 **Click the Switch Between Header and Footer button on the Header and Footer toolbar.**

The text you used for the first page footer also appears in the Odd Page Footer - Section 2. You don't need the copyright text here.

21 **Delete** `Copyright Carpenter Cove Neighbors Association, April 1998` **and the tab from the footer. Then click the Align Right button on the Formatting toolbar.**

Only the page number remains, but it is flush right. You also need a page number for the even page footer but you need the formatting, too. So, copy the page number to the even page footer.

22 **Select the page number and click the Copy button on the Standard toolbar.**

23 **Click the Show Previous button on the Header and Footer toolbar.**

24 **Click the Paste button on the Standard toolbar and then the Align Left button on the Formatting toolbar.**

The page number appears with the same formatting as on the odd pages, but now it is aligned on the left. Your headers and footers are complete. All the even page headers and footers have their text left aligned; all the odd page headers and footers have their text right aligned.

25 **Click Close on the Header and Footer toolbar.**

Preview the newsletter and look through all the pages. Note that the page numbers appear at the outside margins of the newsletter (see Figure 5.16).

Figure 5.16
The header text and the page numbers appear on the outside margins.

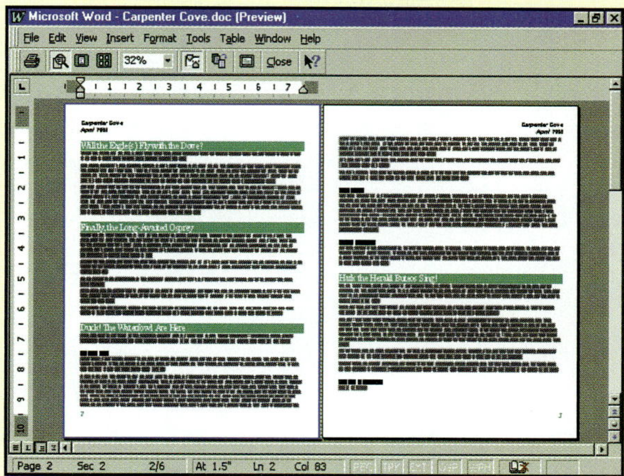

continues

<table>
<tr><td colspan="2">To Create Alternating Headers and Footers (continued)</td></tr>
<tr><td colspan="2">㉖ Save your newsletter and leave it open for the next lesson.</td></tr>
</table>

Exam Notes

You can set different headers and footers for your first page without including section breaks in a document. On the Layout tab of the Page Setup dialog box, select Different first page. The header and footer for the first page are then different from the headers and footers for the remainder of the document.

Lesson 8: Inserting Special Characters

Symbols such as letters with accents used in words from languages other than English, stars, bullets, happy faces, the copyright symbol, the registration mark, long (em) dashes, and Greek letters used in mathematical expressions don't appear on your computer keyboard. But you can still insert them into your documents. The variety of symbols you have to choose from in Word depends on the fonts you have installed on your computer, such as Wingdings.

What's the difference between symbols and special characters? Special characters also don't appear on your computer keyboard, and some items appear as both symbols and special characters. Special characters are more the type of characters needed by typesetters, such as the copyright symbol (©), ellipses (…), em spaces (wider than a normal space), and em dashes (—). Table 5.3 gives an example of or describes what the special characters are.

Table 5.3 Special Characters

Name	Description
Em dash	— a typographer's long dash (use instead of two hyphens)
En dash	– a typographer's dash (as opposed to a hyphen)
Nonbreaking hyphen	Keeps a hyphenated word from being split between two lines
Optional hyphen	Marks where a word should be hyphenated if it appears at the end of a line (it doesn't appear until the word needs to be broken at the end of a line)
Em space	A larger than normal space
En space	A larger than normal space, but not as large as an em space
Nonbreaking space	A space between words that prevents the words from being split between two lines
Copyright	©
Registered	®

Name	Description
Trademark	™
Section	§
Paragraph	¶
Ellipses	… (use instead of three periods)
Single opening quote	'
Single closing quote	'
Double opening quote	"
Double closing quote	"

In this lesson, you need to replace the word "copyright" in the footer on page 1 with the copyright symbol. You also want to insert a symbol at the end of each article to mark the close of the article.

To Insert Special Characters

❶ Go to page 1 of your newsletter and choose <u>V</u>iew, <u>H</u>eader and Footer from the menu.

You see the header box for Section 1, but you need to work with the footer.

❷ Click the Switch Between Header and Footer button on the Header and Footer toolbar.

The footer for Section 1 is now visible.

❸ Select the word `copyright` and press `Del`.

Instead of the word copyright, you are going to insert the copyright symbol.

❹ Choose <u>I</u>nsert, <u>S</u>ymbol from the menu. Click the S<u>p</u>ecial Characters tab.

The Symbol dialog box appears (see Figure 15.17).

Figure 5.17
Select the character you need from the <u>C</u>haracter list and click <u>I</u>nsert.

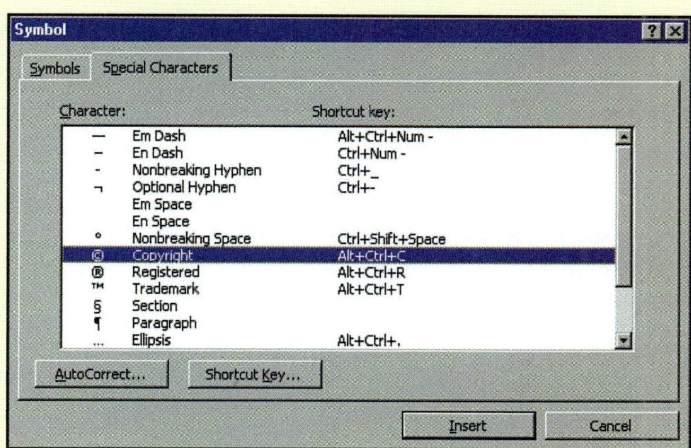

continues

Word

To Insert Special Characters   (continued)

5 **From the Character list, select Copyright. Then click Insert.**

Word inserts the copyright symbol at the insertion point. The Symbol dialog box stays open, so you may insert another symbol if needed.

6 **Click Close to close the dialog box.**

You may have to add a space after the symbol.

7 **Click Close on the Header and Footer toolbar**

You also want to add a symbol at the end of each article in the newsletter.

8 **Click after the last period in the** `Will the Eagle(s) Fly with the Dove?` **article.**

This is the location of the first article-ending symbol.

9 **Choose Insert, Symbol and click the Symbols tab.**

The Symbol dialog box opens (see Figure 15.18). A grid shows all the characters available in the font shown in the Font box.

Figure 5.18
Select a font and then click the symbol you want to insert.

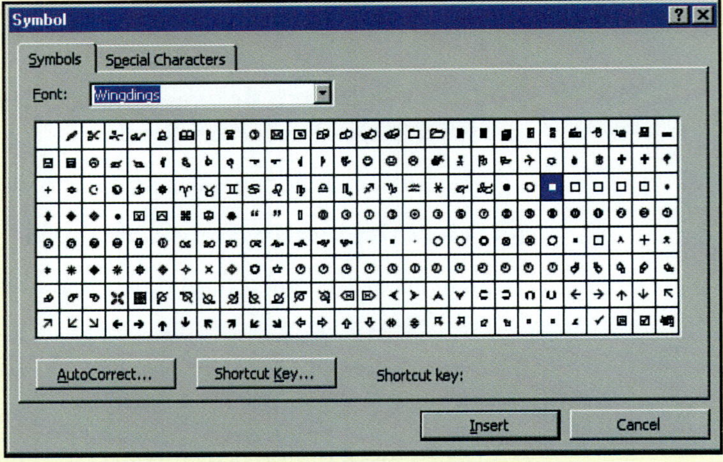

10 **From the Font list, select a font that contains symbols.**

Although most of your fonts have some symbols in their character set, there are special fonts that are made up only of symbols. Some of these fonts are Wingdings, Monotype Sorts, Zapf Dingbats, or Symbol. Your selection depends on the fonts you have installed on your computer.

⑪ Click the symbol you want to use.

When you click one of the symbols in the grid, you see a magnified version of the symbol. This helps you see clearly which symbol you want to select.

⑫ Click Insert.

The symbol you selected is inserted at the insertion point. Although you can leave the dialog box open and insert the symbol again and again, it's hard to work around the dialog box to place your insertion point where you need the symbol. It's much easier to copy and paste the symbol wherever you need it.

⑬ Click Close to close the dialog box.

 **⑭ Select the symbol and click the Copy button on the Standard toolbar.**

 **⑮ Go to the end of the next article and click the Paste button on the Standard toolbar.**

Continue to paste the symbol at the end of each article in the newsletter.

⑯ Save the document. Print two copies, if requested by your instructor. Close the document.

Some of the most commonly used symbols are available in AutoCorrect. They automatically appear in your text when you enter the text and press Spacebar. For example, typing (r) gives you the registered mark and :) gives you the happy face. To see what symbols are included in AutoCorrect, choose Tools, AutoCorrect from the menu. Check the listings under Replace text as you type.

You have completed all of the lessons in this project. If you have completed your session on the computer, exit Word and Windows 95 before turning off your computer. Otherwise, continue with the "Checking Your Skills" and "Applying Your Skills" sections.

Project Summary

To	Do This
Insert a section break	Position your cursor where you want the section to begin and choose Insert, Break, and choose the type of section break you want to insert (Next Page, Continuous, Even Page, Odd Page). Click OK.

continues

To	Do This
Change or set page orientation	Choose File, Page Setup from the menu. Click the paper Size tab. Select Landscape or Portrait in the Orientation section. If you want to change the orientation for a single page that is part of a multiple page document, set section breaks at the beginning and the end of the page, then set the page orientation for the single page.
Shade a paragraph	Select the paragraph and choose Format, Borders and Shading from the menu. Click the Shading tab. Select the Fill color you want and click OK.
Create a page border	Choose Format, Borders and Shading from the menu. Click the Page Border tab. Select the type of border you want and indicate whether you want the border to apply to sections or the whole document by choosing from the Apply to drop-down list.
Keep lines together (in a paragraph)	Select the paragraph. Choose Format, Paragraph from the menu. Click the Line and Page Breaks tab. Select Keep lines together and click OK.
Sort paragraphs	Select the paragraphs to be sorted. Choose Table, Sort from the menu. In the Sort by drop-down list, select Paragraphs. Choose Text as the Type of sort you want to perform and click Ascending or Descending. Click OK.
Insert a special character	Position your insertion point where you want to insert the special character. Choose Insert, Symbol from the menu. Select the character you want to insert from the Special Characters or Symbols tab. Click Insert, then click OK.

Checking Your Skills

True/False

For each of the following statements, check *T* or *F* to indicate whether the statement is true or false.

__T __F   **1.** You can apply different page formatting options to different sections in a document.

__T __F   **2.** The only way to get a different heading on the first page is to make the first page a separate section.

__T __F   **3.** Headers apply to all pages in the current section of a document, even if you begin typing on page 4.

__T __F   **4.** If a symbol does not appear on a key on your keyboard, you cannot insert it into a document.

__T __F   **5.** You can apply borders to pages as well as to paragraphs.

__T __F   **6.** The fastest way to put paragraphs in alphabetical order is to use the Cut and Paste commands.

__T __F   **7.** Section break markers show up onscreen in Page Layout view only if you have nonprinting characters displayed.

__T __F   **8.** Most standard letter documents are printed in landscape orientation.

__T __F   **9.** Word automatically breaks lines at the right margin.

__T __F **10.** There is no difference between special characters and symbols.

Multiple Choice

Circle the letter of the correct answer for each of the following:

1. A hard page break is used to do what?

   a. Create a new page at the insertion point.

   b. Create a new page at the bottom of the document.

   c. Create a new page that cannot be deleted.

   d. Create a blank page at the top of the document.

2. What type of break inserts both a page break and a section break at the same time?

   a. Column

   b. Continuous

   c. Next Page

   d. Chapter

3. On which menu do you find the Borders and Shading command?

   a. Format

   b. Tools

   c. Insert

   d. Edit

4. Which feature lets you apply gray behind an entire paragraph?

   a. Borders

   b. Shading

   c. Paragraph Spacing

   d. Change Case

5. Which of the following is not considered a special character?

   a. Paragraph mark

   b. Em dash

   c. Question mark

   d. Nonbreaking hyphen

6. What is the default symbol set displayed in the Symbol dialog box?

   a. Normal text

   b. Wingdings

   c. Symbol

   d. Marlett

7. What type of formatting do you apply to an entire page or document?

    a. Column formatting

    b. Font formatting

    c. Page formatting

    d. Paragraph formatting

8. What setting do you change if you want the text printed across the wide edge of the paper?

    a. Margins

    b. Paper size

    c. Vertical alignment

    d. Orientation

9. What text flow option prevents a paragraph from being split by a line break?

    a. Keep with Next

    b. Keep Lines Together

    c. Nonbreaking hyphen

    d. Nonbreaking space

10. What check box should you select to set up alternating headers and footers?

    a. Use <u>a</u>lternating

    b. Different <u>o</u>dd and even

    c. Different <u>s</u>ections

    d. Same as <u>P</u>revious

Completion

In the blank provided, write the correct answer for each of the following statements.

1. A line placed around a paragraph is called a ___________.

2. You can select a trademark symbol to insert in a document on the ________ Characters page of the Symbols dialog box.

3. You can divide a document into __________ so that you can have different page formatting in the same document.

4. In _________ orientation, Word prints the text with the narrow end of the paper at the top.

5. In _________ orientation, Word prints the text with the wide edge of the paper at the top.

6. Word has a variety of _________ borders that you may apply to pages.

7. ___________ headers and footers are headers and footers that are different on the odd and even pages of a document.

8. To sort paragraphs, you must _________ them first.

9. If you do not like where Word automatically breaks lines or paragraphs, you can change the ___ _____ options.

10. Press Ctrl+Shift+Spacebar to insert a ___________ space.

Matching

In the blank next to each of the following terms or phrases, write the letter of the corresponding term or phrase. (Note that some letters may be used more than once.)

a. Border

b. Ascending

c. Widow

d. Nonbreaking space

e. Orientation

f. Continuous

g. Ctrl+↵Enter

h. Orphan

i. Symbol

j. Shading

_______ 1. Shortcut key combination for inserting a hard page break

_______ 2. Effect that applies color or a gray screen behind a paragraph

_______ 3. Dialog box displaying list of special characters

_______ 4. Setting that affects which edge of the paper is the top

_______ 5. The first line of the paragraph that appears by itself at the bottom of a page or column

_______ 6. The last line of the paragraph that appears by itself at the top of a page or column

_______ 7. Command that prevents two words from being separated onto different lines

_______ 8. Line that runs around an entire page or paragraph

_______ 9. Section break that allows different formatting without starting a new page

_______ 10. Type of alphabetical sort that arranges paragraphs from A to Z

Applying Your Skills

Practice

The following exercises enable you to practice the skills you have learned in this project. Take a few minutes to work through these exercises now.

Formatting the Loan Proposal

Use formatting options to improve the appearance of the Loan Proposal document. You can set margins and line spacing, insert page and section breaks where necessary, control text flow, and add headers and footers.

To format a loan proposal, follow these steps:

1. Open the file Proj0502 from the Project-05 folder on the CD and save it in your Practices folder with the name Loan4.

2. Create a title page by inserting a Next Page section break after the line Indianapolis, Indiana.

3. Center the text on the title page vertically and horizontally, and change the font to 26-point Arial.

4. In the second section, starting at the top of page 2, change the top and bottom margins to 1.25 inches, double-space the lines, and justify the text.

5. Apply a 3-D 1/2-point border to every page in the document.

6. Create alternating headers starting on the second page of the document. On the odd pages, include the title Loan Proposal on the left. On the even pages, include your name on the right.

7. Insert a footer for every page but the first with the date on the left and the page number on the right.

8. Preview the document and insert page breaks, if necessary.

9. Check the grammar and spelling in the document, then save it. If requested by your instructor, print the proposal. Close the document when you are finished.

Formatting a Research Paper

Format a lengthy research paper for submission to a scholarly journal. Some of the techniques you can use to format the paper include justifying text, enhancing headings and subheadings, adjusting line spacing to improve readability, inserting page breaks and section breaks, and adding a header and a footer.

To format a research paper, follow these steps:

1. Open the file Proj0503 from the Project-05 folder on the CD and save it in your Practices folder with the name Interviews4.

2. Replace the text (Student's Name) on the fifth line of the document with your own name.

3. Insert a Next Page section break after the fifth line to create a title page that includes just the first five lines of the document. Center the title page vertically.

4. Set up the title page using the following formatting: Change the font of the first line to 16-point Arial. Change the second and third lines to 14-point Arial. Make all three lines bold and centered on the page. Change the font of the last two lines (Prepared by, and your name) to 12-point Arial. Make them bold and aligned on the right.

5. Change the margins starting with the second section of the document to 1.5" on all sides.

6. Change the font for the headings Introduction and I. Section 1 to 14-point Arial. Set the formatting so that there are always 18 points of white space after each heading.

7. Change the font size for the regular paragraph text in the rest of the document to 12-point. Justify the regular paragraph text and double-space it. Indent the first line of every paragraph .5 inch.

8. Insert a continuous section break between the Introduction and I. Section 1.

9. Change the orientation for the new section 3 to Landscape.

10. Apply a simple box border around the Introduction heading paragraph and the I. Section 1 heading paragraph.

11. Apply a double-line 1/2-point border to the top and bottom of the title page section.

12. Create a header that displays the date centered on every page of the document except the first page. Create a footer that displays on all pages. Include the report title (Personal Interviews), your name, and the page number.

13. Preview the document. Check the spelling and grammar in the document. Save the changes you have made, and, if requested by your instructor, print it. Close the document when you have finished.

Enhancing the Picnic Invitation

In this exercise, use borders and shading to enhance the appearance of the invitation to the company picnic.

To enhance the picnic invitation, follow these steps:

1. Open the file Proj0504 from the Project-05 folder on the CD and save it in your `Practices` folder with the name `Invitation`.

2. Apply a decorative border of flowers around the page.

3. Center the When? And Time? Lines on the page and apply a 3-point shadow border around them both, with a 15% gray shading.

4. Put a 15% gray shading behind the first paragraph — `It's Company Picnic Time`.

5. Insert a copyright symbol after the words `Grist Mill`.

6. Preview the document. Check the spelling and grammar in the document. Save the changes you have made, and, if requested by your instructor, print it. Close the document when you have finished.

Enhancing a Company Bulletin

In this exercise, you use the skills you learned in this projects to enhance the appearance of a document announcing new technology developments at Computer Training Association.

To enhance the company bulletin, follow these steps:

1. Open the file Proj0505 from the Project-05 folder on the CD and save it in your `Practices` folder with the name `Tech`.

2. Sort the three paragraphs in the section titled Implementation Strategy into alphabetical order by selecting all three, choosing Table, Sort, verifying that the options are set to sort paragraphs alphabetically in ascending order, and choosing OK.

3. Since this change causes a page break to fall in the middle of the three paragraphs (Installation), set text flows options to ensure the paragraph remains together. Select the Installation paragraph, choose Format, Paragraph, click the Line and Page Breaks tab, select the Keep lines together check box, and then choose OK.

4. Assume that more text is going to be added to the document. Set up a header for all odd pages that includes the page number on the right. Set up a header for all even pages that includes the date on the left. Set up a footer on all pages that includes your name on the left and the document title Technology Update on the right.

5. Preview the document. Check the spelling and grammar in the document. Save the changes you have made, and, if requested by your instructor, print it. Close the document when you have finished.

Improving a Thanks Letter

Even short documents can benefit from the formatting and editing techniques you have learned in this project. Use these skills to improve a thank you letter.

To improve a letter, follow these steps:

1. Open the file Proj0506 from the Project-05 folder on the CD and save it in the Practices folder with the name Thanks.

2. Change the date to the current date and replace the text (Student's Name) with your own name in both locations where it appears.

3. Apply a 3-point 3-D border with a 10% gray shading to the word MEMO.

4. Apply a 3-point shadow box border and a 5% gray shading to the indented quotation paragraph. Include the two lines attributing the quote to Jack Jackson.

5. Apply a 3-D, 1 1/2-point double-line border around the entire page.

6. Insert a trademark symbol after Word for Windows in the postscript.

7. Preview the document. Check the spelling and grammar and save it. If requested by your instructor, print it. Close it when you are finished.

Challenge

The following challenges enable you to use your problem-solving skills. Take time to work through these exercises now.

Improving the Appearance of the Computer Training Concepts Presentation

You want to use the formatting techniques you have learned to improve the appearance of the Computer Training Concepts presentation. Open the file Proj0507 from the Project-05 folder on the CD and save it in your Challenges folder as Presentation2.

Apply a 20% gray shade to the headings Sales History, Corporate History, Background Information, and Financial Statement. Sort the bulleted list of clients into alphabetical order. Set text flow so that the line introduction and the bulleted list remain on the same page as the first bulleted list item.

Set the Sales History section apart with section breaks so you can change the orientation so that the table will fit across the page.

Add alternating footers. Include your name and the page number on the even pages and the date and the page number on the odd pages.

Check the spelling and grammar and preview the document. Save it and if requested by your instructor, print the letter. Close the file when you have finished.

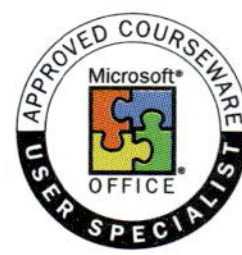

Formatting a Business Proposal for Computer Training Concepts

Use the skills you have learned to fine-tune to formatting of a corporate business proposal for Computer Training Concepts. Open the file Proj0508 from the Project-05 folder on the CD and save it in the Challenges folder with the name Proposal3.

Set up a title or cover page, including all the text up to the heading Overview. Adjust the spacing so that the three lines beginning with Proposal developed by are vertically centered on the page. Apply a page border to the cover page only.

Use another section break to set apart the portion of the document from the heading Proposal through the end of the text following the heading Conclusion. Increase the width of the margins in this new section to 1.5-inches and justify the text. Center all headings in this section and increase their font size. Sort the list in the Budget section alphabetically.

Preview the document and use page breaks and text flow controls to ensure that paragraphs, lines, and lists do not break at awkward spots.

Set up footers that print the company name and page number on all even pages, and the date and page number on all odd pages. Set up headers that print your name on every page. Preview the document again, check the spelling and grammar, and save your changes. If requested by your instructor, print the document and then close it.

Formatting a Course Descriptions Document

Use the formatting skills you have learned to improve the appearance of a course descriptions document for Computer Training Concepts. Open the file Proj0509 from the Project-05 folder on the CD and save it in your Challenges folder with the name Courses.

Center the headings Spreadsheet Courses, Word Processing Courses, Internet Courses, and Integration Courses, and apply a 10% gray shade to each. Apply a decorative page border to all pages in the document. Try out a few different geometric patterns and pick the one you think is most suitable.

Preview the document. Use text flow controls to ensure that none of the course descriptions is split between pages.

Add a header and footer to the second page only. Type Computer Training Concepts on the left side of the header, and Course Descriptions on the right side. Insert page numbers, centered, in the footer. Make sure you can see the header and footer within the page borders. Preview the document again. Check the grammar and spelling in the document and save it. If requested by your instructor, print it. Close the document when you are finished.

Formatting the Annual Report

Use the formatting skills you have learned to improve the appearance of a version of the annual report you worked with in the previous project. Open the file Proj0510 from the Project-05 folder on the CD and save it in your Challenges folder with the name Report2.

Set up a title page and apply a professional-looking border to it. Preview the document and identify where you need page breaks or text flow controls, and then apply them accordingly.

Apply a border and gray shade to the quotation paragraph. Sort the bulleted list in alphabetical order. Preview the document again, then check the spelling and grammar, and save your changes. If requested by your instructor, print the document, and then close it.

Formatting a Prospectus

You have been asked to format an overview of a prospectus for a money market fund. Use the skills you have learned to improve the appearance of the document and control the flow of text. Open the file Proj0511 from the Project-05 folder and save it in your Challenges folder as Prospectus.

Insert a plain box with a 10% gray shade around the company name at the top of the first page. Use a 3-point line and position it 12 points from the text. Use a break to force the section beginning with the heading Customer Profile to the next page.

Use text flow controls to be sure that none of the tables are split across pages. Put a plain box border with no shading around all pages.

Create an alternating footer that has your name and the page number on the odd pages, and the name of the fund and the page number on the even pages. Check the spelling and grammar in the document. Save it, preview it, and if requested by your instructor, print it. Close it when you have finished.

You have completed the project and the associated lessons, as well as the "Checking Your Skills" and "Applying Your Skills" sections. Now use the PinPoint software evaluation mode to assess your comprehension of the specific exam tasks you have just learned. You can also use the PinPoint Trainer Mode and the Show Me tutorials to practice these specific exam tasks.

Project 6

Six

Working with Templates

Using Predefined Documents

In this Project, you learn how to:

Objectives

Required Activities

- ➤ Use an Existing Template
- ➤ Use a Template Wizard
- ➤ Modify an Existing Template
- ➤ Create a New Template
- ➤ Change the Formatting in a Template

Why Would I Do This?

A template is a time-saving device. It is a document master that contains formatting information that you can use regularly to create documents of a similar kind. A template can contain titles, text, and graphics. When you open a new document in Word, you open it in the NORMAL.DOT template, which contains built-in specifications regarding fonts, margins, line spacing, justification, and paper size. The default NORMAL.DOT template comes with Word and is available when you install the program, but you can change the NORMAL.DOT template so that it conforms to your needs.

You can also use any of several other templates—ones that create different types of letters, faxes, reports, and memos—that accompany your Word software. In addition, you can create your own templates that meet the needs of your work or personal environment. In this project, you sample some of Word's built-in templates and create templates of your own.

Exam Notes

The Word Expert exam does not list specific requirements for using templates. However, Microsoft guidelines indicate that Expert users should master all skills required for the Proficient exam before taking the Expert exam. Although you do not need to take or pass the Proficient exam prior to taking the Expert exam, you do need to know about templates, which are a Proficient requirement. This lesson, therefore, is an important one in preparing to pass your Microsoft Expert User exam.

The Microsoft Expert exam does require that you know how to use a macro to create templates. This skill is covered in Project 9.

Lesson 1: Using an Existing Template

Begin by taking a look at some of Word's built-in templates. Some templates have wizards that accompany them. A wizard is a little program that prompts you for information that you need to fill in the template. Open and examine a template now.

To Open a Word Template

❶ Open a new, blank document by choosing File, New.

If you want to see Word's available templates (there are several), you need to choose File, New. The shortcuts for opening a new document—such as pressing Ctrl+N or clicking the Standard toolbar's New button—assume that you want to open the NORMAL.DOT template and don't give you the choice of opening other templates.

When you choose File, New, the New dialog box opens with a Blank Document icon displayed (see Figure 6.1). This icon represents the Normal.dot template. If you click the OK button, Word opens a new document in the Normal.dot template.

Figure 6.1
Choose File, New to
view Word's template
selection.

**If you click a template's
icon, you can see what
the template looks like
in the Preview window**

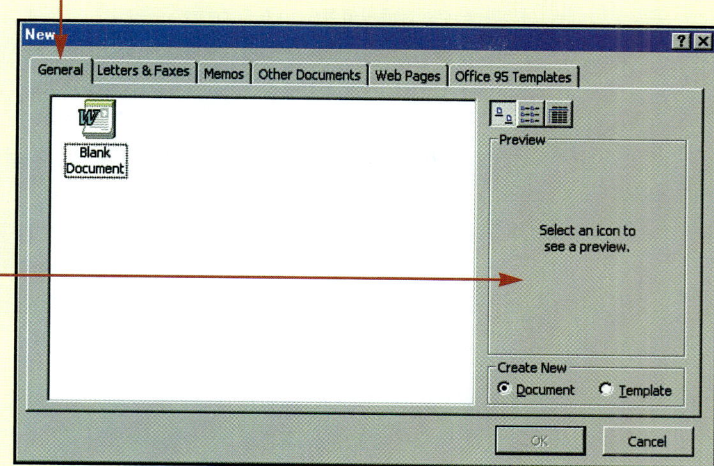

Note: The tabs for template selection might differ on your screen,
depending which templates you installed with Word.

**2 Click the Memos tab, and then click each of the icons once to
see a preview of the various memo options. Click the other
tabs and icons to see previews of all the templates available
to you.**

When you click one of the icons, Word displays a miniature preview of the template.

**3 In the Memos page, double-click the Contemporary Memo
icon to open a new document based on that template.**

The Contemporary Memo template opens as a new document.

4 Save this file as `Recycling Memo`.

To use the template, you can click the places labeled Click here and
type name. These items in brackets are called fields, which you
learned about in previous lessons.

**5 Click to the right of the To: heading, right on top of the text
Click here and type name. Then type your name.**

If you have problems...

When selecting a template field, such as the Click here and type name field
in the Contemporary Memo template, it is important that you click in the
correct place. If you click anywhere other than directly over the field, Word
places your insertion point incorrectly, or perhaps causes you to delete some
of the memo's text (as you do intentionally in step 6). Word highlights the
field in gray if you click and select it properly. Remember, if you delete something unexpectedly or type at an unintended location in the document, you
can always click the Undo button to cancel your actions.

Word replaces the entire field when you begin typing your name. If
you don't want to use a particular field in the template, you can

continues

simply select and delete it (see Figure 6.2). For example, if you don't want to send a copy of this memo to anyone, you can delete the CC: field, because you don't need it.

Figure 6.2
If the template includes any unneeded text, you can select and delete that text.

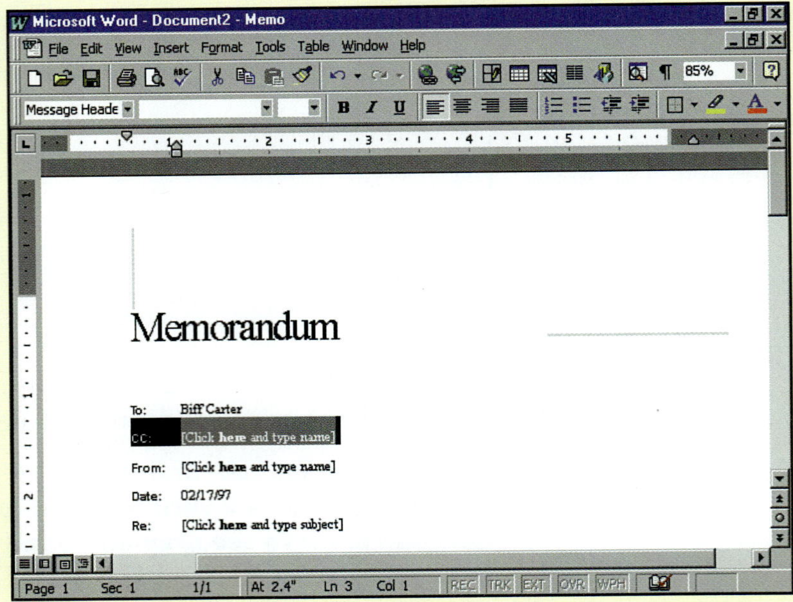

6 **Click in the margin to the left of the CC: heading to select the entire line; then press** Del.

Because you opened this template into a new document screen, deleting a line does not affect the original template. Now you can fill in the rest of the needed information at the top of the memo.

Some Word files end in .doc and others in .dot. The .doc files are document files and the .dot files are template files. When opening a template file, Word opens the file as a document file by default. Thus, any changes you make affect the document but not the original template.

7 **Click to the right of the other headings, on each field labeled Click Here, and enter the following information:**

From: Mr. Whitaker

Re: Company Recycling Program

Just as in any document, you can go back later and add or delete text. After you enter information in a Click Here field, the field designation disappears, and the text you type becomes regular text.

8 **To enter information in the body of the memo, simply select the text that appears onscreen (underneath the horizontal line) by dragging through it (see Figure 6.3). Replace the template text with the following sample text:**

```
It has come to the attention of management that you have been less
than enthusiastic in following the guidelines of the company's
recycling program. Please take the time to read the attached mate-
rial regarding the plan. It is assumed that you will make every
effort to participate fully in the plan from this point forward.
```

Figure 6.3
Drag through the template sample text to select it, then type your own text to replace the selection.

Replace selected text with your own memo

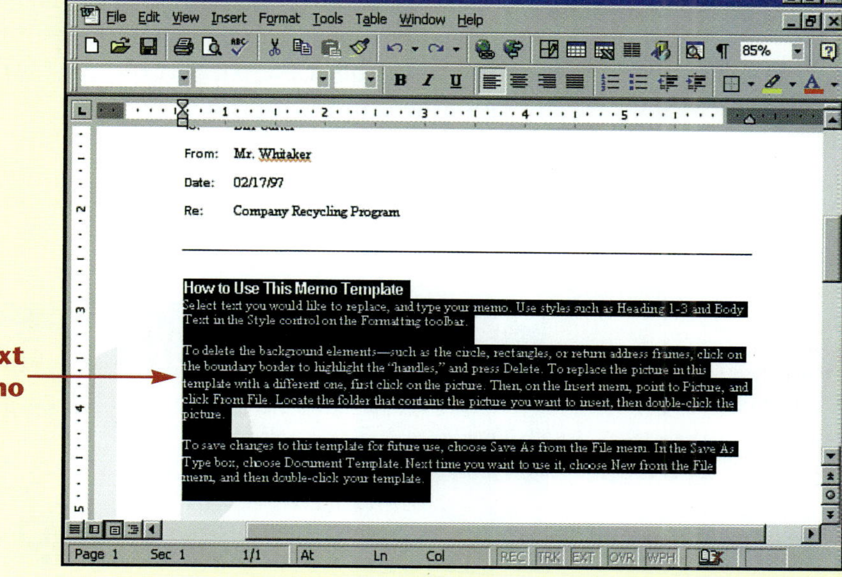

9 **Save the file and close it.**

Lesson 2: Using a Template Wizard

A wizard is a simple way to create a special type of document or to use a particular feature. Word provides wizards to help create templates. The wizard asks you questions and provides you with spaces in which you can fill in the answers. After you provide the information, the wizard uses it to create the document that you requested.

With some wizards, you can do more than just create a specific type of document. For example, although a fax template helps you create a fax cover sheet, a Fax Wizard actually helps you create a fax cover sheet, attach a document, and fax the whole thing from your computer. In this lesson, you learn more about the Fax Wizard.

Word

To Use a Template Wizard

Instead of making you select and replace information whenever you use a template, Word provides wizards to guide you through the completion of several of its templates. Fill in a template by using a wizard now.

1 Open the file named Proj0601 from the Project-06 folder of the CD and save it as `Pricing Breaks`.

This is the document that you will fax to an imaginary person.

2 Choose File, New. After the New dialog box appears, click the Letters & Faxes tab.

Several icons appear, representing different fax and letter templates. You can also find some wizards that can walk you through creating memos and letters.

3 Double-click Fax Wizard.wiz.

The Fax Wizard appears with a process overview of creating and sending a fax (see Figure 6.4).

Figure 6.4
The Fax Wizard overview lists the steps for sending a fax.

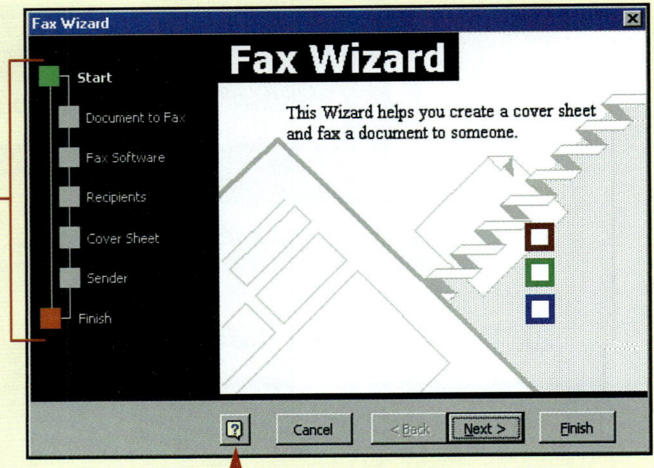

The wizard's steps are listed here

Click here when you need help

4 Choose the Next button.

This next panel asks which document you want to send (see Figure 6.5). If you have several documents open, you can click the down arrow to select the document.

5 If necessary, select the Pricing Breaks.doc file from the drop-down list.

6 Make sure that the With a Cover Sheet option is selected, then choose Next.

In the next wizard panel, you select how you want to send your fax. If your computer is set up with fax software, such as Microsoft Fax, you can fax the document straight from Word. However, if your system does not support faxing, you can print your cover sheet and document so that you'll be ready to fax it the old-fashioned way. Because you won't actually send the fax, just select the Microsoft Fax option.

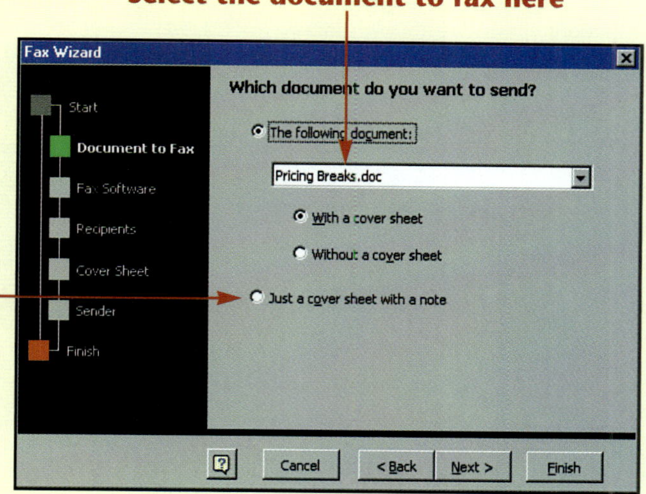

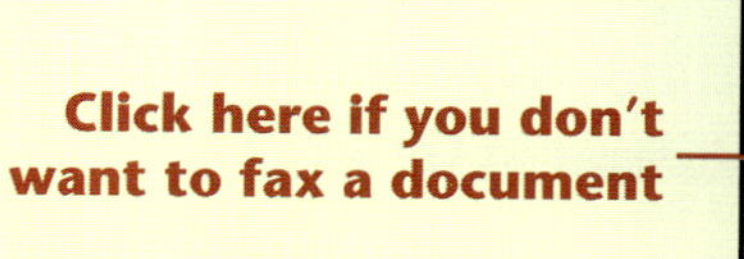
Figure 6.5
You can attach a document to fax.

7 **Select the Microsoft Fax option, then choose Next.**

Next, the wizard asks you who should receive the fax. If you've stored names and addresses in the Address Book, you can select the Address Book button, and select the person's name. Or, you can just type the name and fax number. You can fax the document to several people.

8 **Type Biff Loman in the text box below Name, and then 555-3984 in the text box below Fax Number. Choose Next.**

You won't actually send this fax, so the name and number that you enter aren't important. For future consideration, however, don't forget to use numbers that your business telephone system requires, such as a 1 for long-distance calls or a 9 to dial an outside line.

9 **When asked to pick a cover sheet, select Contemporary, then choose Next.**

The next panel asks for the sender's name and address. Depending on how Word is set up on your machine, the Fax template might already provide a name and address. You can accept these defaults or choose to overwrite them. To change these defaults, you can choose Tools, Options, User Information from the main menu.

10 **Make sure that your name and address are correct, then choose Next to proceed.**

You've answered all the questions to create a cover sheet and fax it along with a document that you opened. When working in a

continues

To Use a Template Wizard   (continued)

wizard, you can always choose the <u>B</u>ack button if you change your mind and want to return to the preceding dialog box.

In the final step of the Fax Wizard, you can choose <u>F</u>inish to print or send the fax, or you can cancel the process.

⑪ Choose <u>F</u>inish.

Word prepares your fax cover sheet and displays it onscreen. Figure 6.6 shows a completed fax cover sheet.

Figure 6.6
The finished fax form, based on the information that you entered in the Fax Wizard.

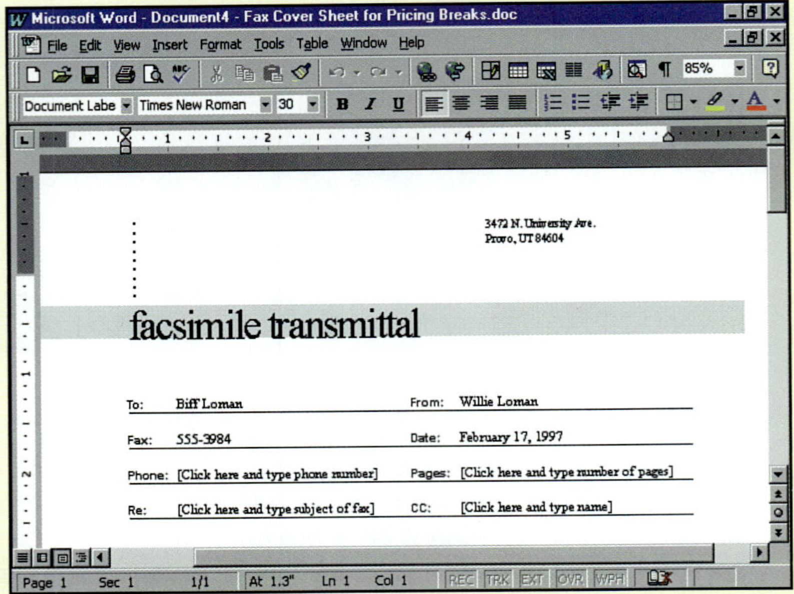

⑫ Close the file without saving it. Close the Pricing Breaks document as well.

After you have completed your fax form by using the Fax Wizard, you can change information simply by editing the text, as you would in any other document.

When you installed Word, you might not have installed all the templates and wizards available. You can rerun the setup program and click the <u>C</u>ustom button to install additional templates and wizards, many of which contain useful macros. If you have access to the Internet, you can also visit the Microsoft Office Web site and download free templates and wizards. For more information, choose <u>F</u>ile, <u>N</u>ew, click the Other Documents tab, and then double-click More Templates and Wizards.wiz.

Lesson 3: Modifying an Existing Template

Word might already contain templates that are similar to documents that you use regularly, but the templates might not be quite the same. Instead of creating an entirely new template, you can start with a Word template, use the pieces that you want, and then modify the rest to fit your needs. This lesson shows you how to change an existing template.

To Modify an Existing Template

1 Choose **File**, **New**. After the New dialog box opens, click once on the Contemporary Letter template in the Letters & Faxes page.

2 Select the **Template** option in the Create New panel of the New dialog box (see Figure 6.7).

A preview of the template you will open

Figure 6.7
Opening an existing template so that you can modify it.

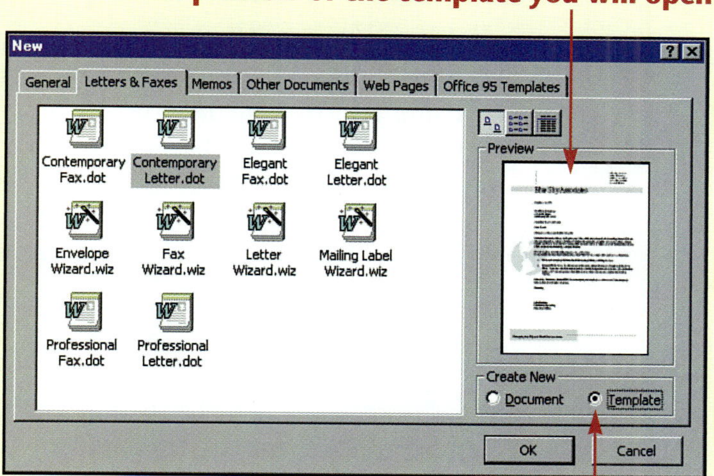

Click here to indicate that you want to open this template as a template rather than as a Word document (a .doc file)

The changes that you make to the template become part of the permanent master template.

3 Choose **OK** to open the memo as a template.

Notice that Word has named this Template1, similar to the way in which it names new documents (Document1, Document2, and so on).

4 Choose **File**, **Save As**, then type `Marketing Letter` in the File **Name** text box.

Always be sure to give your template a name that helps you recognize it in the future.

continues

Before saving the file, you must designate a folder. Save the file in the Letters & Faxes folder, which is located in the Templates folder.

5 Double-click the LETTERS & FAXES folder, then choose <u>S</u>ave.

Word saves the file as Marketing Letter.dot in the Letters & Faxes folder. Now edit the document so that a company is listed.

6 Select the text Company Name Here, then type Pranitis Athletic Equipment (or type your company's name).

7 Click the field in the upper-right box (Click here and type return address), then replace its contents with the following address (or your own):

Marketing Division

123 Westview Lane

Bean Blossom, Indiana   46260

Phone: (317) 555-2934

When you save this file, the new company name and address become part of your new template; thereafter, you won't have to type this information every time you create a letter. Figure 6.8 shows what your template should look like.

Figure 6.8
Change an existing template to conform to your needs.

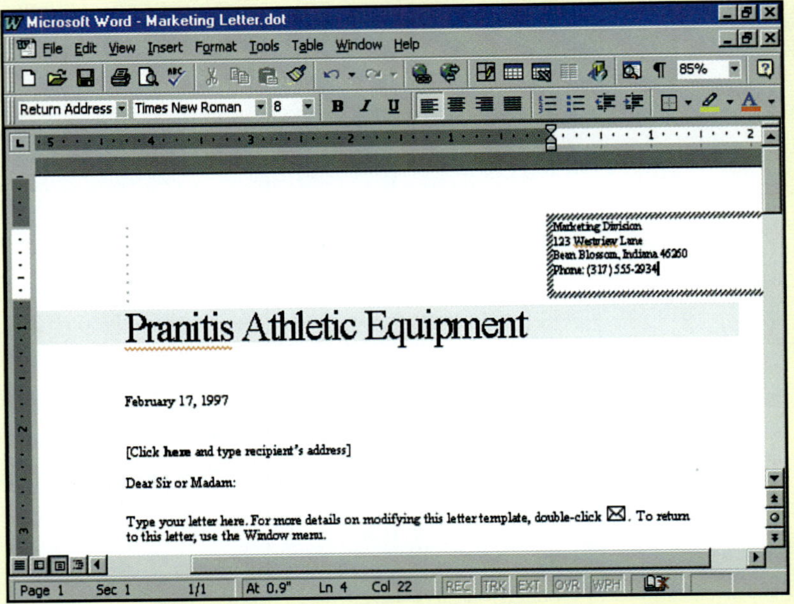

You can make editing changes in this document just as you would in any regular text document.

8 Replace the fields at the bottom of the letter (below Sincerely) with Harlan Pogue and Marketing Director.

9 **Save the template file, and close it.**

Now you can verify that your template is in place and that it is retrievable.

10 **Choose File, New. After the New dialog box appears, click the new Letters & Faxes tab.**

Your new template should be visible.

11 **Double-click the new template to open it as a new document (not as a template).**

Your new letter is formatted and nearly ready to be sent. Now all you have to do is replace the recipient's address field and type the letter.

12 **Close the document without saving it.**

You probably don't want the template that you just created to appear in your list of templates. To delete it, choose File, New, then select the Letters & Faxes tab. Right-click Marketing Letter.dot, then choose Delete. (When you finish this project, you might want to delete the templates that you are creating.)

Lesson 4: Creating a New Template

Instead of modifying an existing template, you might already have some documents of your own that you want to turn into new templates. Documents such as office reports, billing forms, and employment questionnaires lend themselves nicely to template design. In this lesson, you create a template based on a sample letter.

To Create a New Template

1 **Open the file Proj0602 from the Project-06 folder of the CD and save the file as Welcome Letter.**

A sample letter opens, as shown in Figure 6.9. To make this letter into a usable template, you simply select the items that change from one letter to the next (such as the name of the recipient and the date) and then set these items aside in such a way as to be readily recognizable when the template opens.

continues

Word

To Create a New Template (continued)

Figure 6.9
This sample letter is ready to be made into a template.

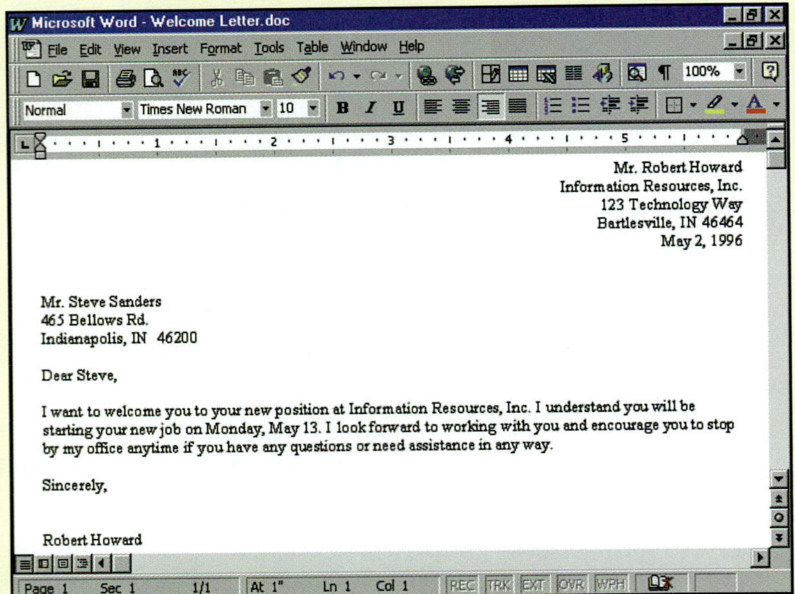

2 **Select the date near the top of the letter (below the return address) and replace this date with a date field code by choosing Insert, Date and Time. Select a format from the Available Formats list and choose OK.**

Make sure that the Date and Time dialog box's Update Automatically check box is selected (see Figure 6.10).

Figure 6.10
You can insert a date code in your template document so that it is updated when you create a document based on the template.

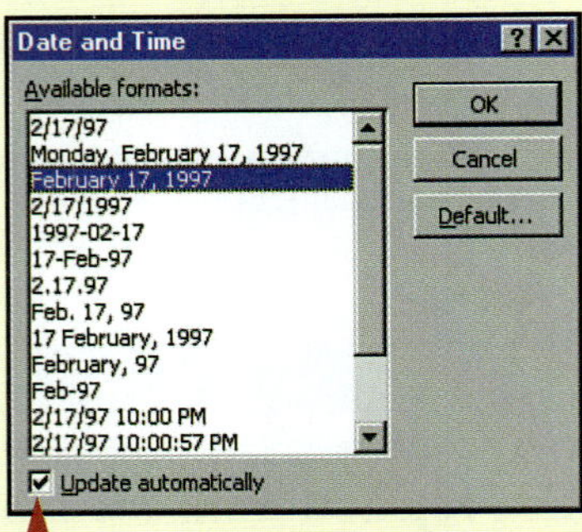

Select this check box to tell Word to update your date
each time you use your Welcome Letter template

When you create your own templates, you can borrow items from existing templates. Borrow an input field from the Contemporary Memo template that you looked at earlier.

3 **Choose File, New and click the Memos tab; then double-click the Contemporary Memo template.**

The Contemporary Memo template opens. Notice that the input fields ask you to click them and type a name.

4 Click once on a field that reads Click here and type name and then click the Standard toolbar's Copy button.

You have copied the field to the Clipboard.

5 Close the document created from the Contemporary Memo template without saving it.

You no longer need the memo template open because you've copied what you want from it.

6 In your Welcome Letter template, select the addressee's first line (`Mr. Steve Sanders`) and then click the Standard toolbar's Paste button to paste the Clipboard's contents in place of the line's current contents.

7 Continue by selecting each line of the address and then the recipient's first name in the salutation. After each selection, click the Paste button to replace the existing information with the input field that is in the Clipboard.

When you finish, your letter should look like the one in Figure 6.11. The Click here fields all refer to "name," but you can change that to read "address" or whatever description you prefer. You do so next.

Figure 6.11
Word has replaced the original text with Click here input fields.

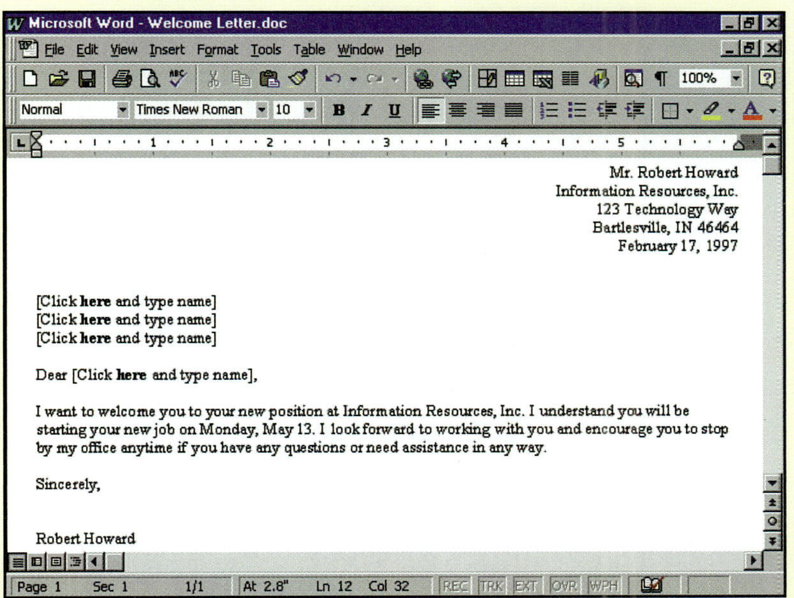

8 Right-click the second Click here and type name field code. When the shortcut menu appears, select Toggle Field Codes.

The field expands to display the entire field code (see Figure 6.12).

continues

Word

To Create a New Template (continued)

Figure 6.12
Word displays the entire field code. You can make changes to the code while it is in this form.

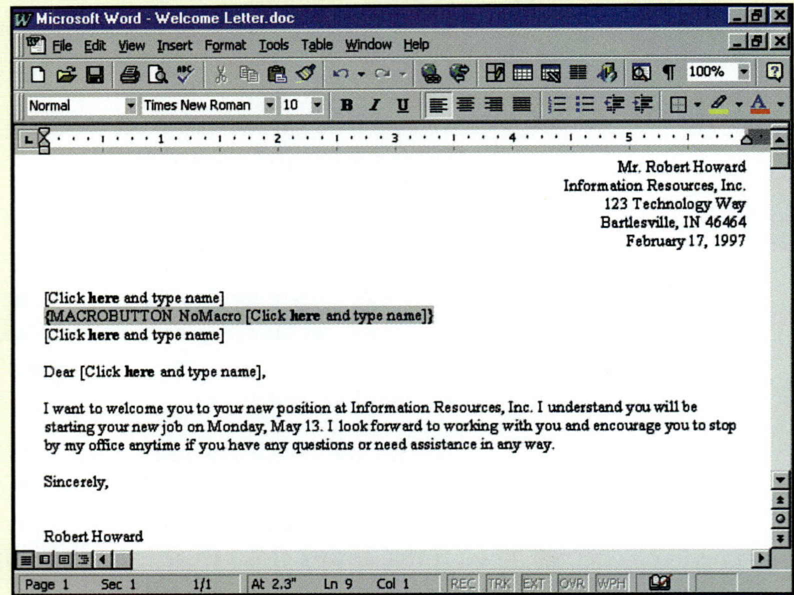

9 **Click once in the field code to place the insertion point next to the word** name **and change** name **to** address.

You can change the field code to include the information that is useful for your template.

10 **Right-click the field code again and select** **Toggle Field Codes.**

The field code returns to its original form, with address in the place of name.

11 **Repeat the preceding steps to change the third field code to read** Click here and type city, state, zip.

12 **Now change the fourth field code (the one in the salutation) to read** Click here and type first name.

Your completed template should look like Figure 6.13.

13 **To save your template, choose** **File, Save As,** **then select Document Template (*.dot) from the Save as** **Type drop-down list.**

The Templates folder is now open in the Save As dialog box, and the file name now has a .dot extension rather than a .doc extension.

14 **Double-click the Letters & Faxes folder so that you can save your template into the proper folder (see Figure 6.14). Then click the** **Save button to save your template.**

Figure 6.13
Your template is ready
to be saved.

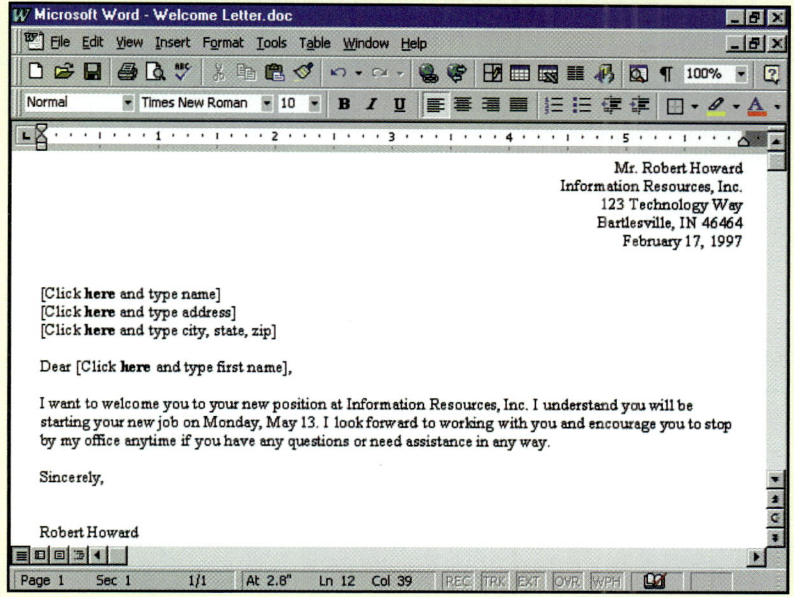

Save your template in this folder

Figure 6.14
Choose File, Save As to
save your template.

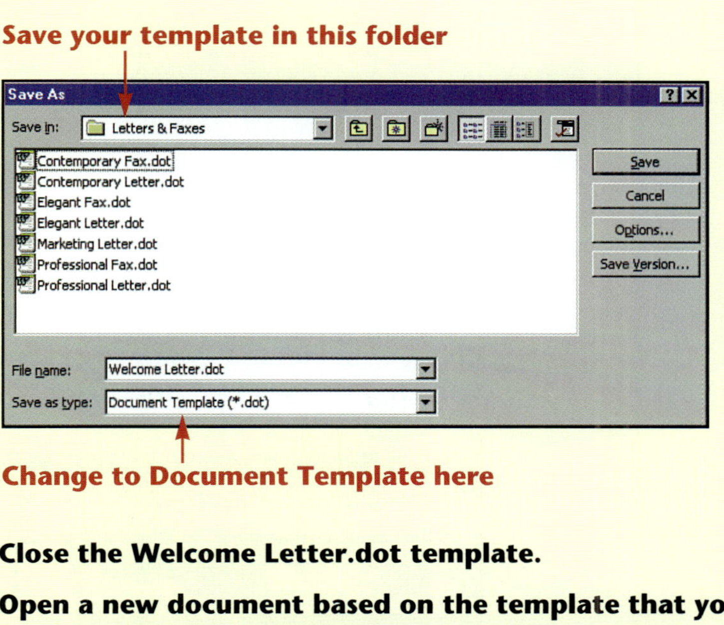

Change to Document Template here

15 **Close the Welcome Letter.dot template.**

16 **Open a new document based on the template that you just
created, then close the document without saving it.**

Lesson 5: Changing the Formatting in a Template

So far, you've changed only the text in the templates that you've edited
and created. However, you can also change a template's formatting so that
documents you create based on that template include that formatting.

The Normal.dot template contains all the default margin settings that are in place when a Word document opens. For example, the font is always 10-point Times New Roman, tabs are set every half inch, and text is left-aligned. You can edit the Normal.dot template to change these settings, as you learn in Project 14, "Customizing the Word Environment." Or you can create a new template that has different formatting settings.

In this lesson, you create a new template and then change its default font and margin settings.

To Change the Formatting in a Template

① **Choose File, New, then click the General tab.**

② **Choose the Template option in the Create New panel, then double-click Blank Document.**

The Blank Document icon is actually the same as the NORMAL.DOT template. Double-clicking this icon is the same as pressing Ctrl+N or clicking the Standard toolbar's New button. However, in this case, you're creating a new template based on the NORMAL.DOT template.

Next, give your template a name.

③ **Choose File, Save As, type Format Test, and choose Save.**

Word saves the Format Test.dot template in the Templates folder. Templates in the Templates folder appear in the General page when you choose File, New. Now change the default font.

④ **Change the default typeface by choosing Format, Font and selecting Univers font and size 11 (see Figure 6.15).**

Figure 6.15
Change the default font for the current template.

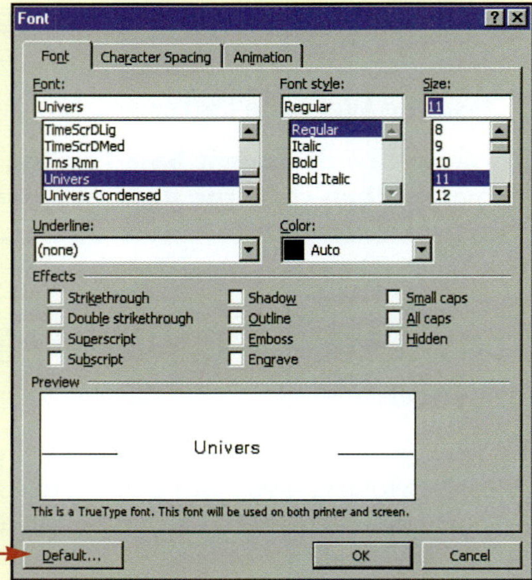

Choosing the Default button saves the changes to the current template

5 **Choose the <u>D</u>efault button.**

When you change the default typeface by clicking the <u>D</u>efault button in the Font dialog box, Word prompts you to accept this change to the Format Test template, as shown in Figure 6.16.

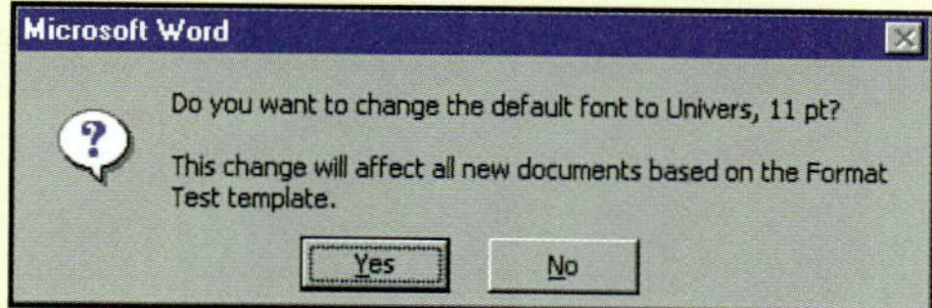

6 **Choose <u>Y</u>es to accept the changes.**

Next, change the default margin settings.

7 **Change the default margins to two inches on all four sides by choosing <u>F</u>ile, Page Set<u>u</u>p and making the changes.**

8 **Choose the <u>D</u>efault button and choose <u>Y</u>es to accept the change to the Format Test.dot template.**

That's enough formatting. Now test the new template.

9 **Close and save the template document.**

10 **Click <u>F</u>ile, <u>N</u>ew, click the General tab, then double-click Format Test.dot.**

A new document appears that is based on the Format Test.dot template. In the ruler, notice the changed margins.

11 **Type** `I like potted meat products`.

Notice that the font is 11-point Univers.

12 **Close the document without saving it.**

You have completed all of the lessons in this project. If you have completed your session on the computer, exit Word and Windows 95 before turning off your computer. Otherwise, continue with the "Checking Your Skills" and "Applying Your Skills" sections.

Project Summary

To	Do This
Open a Word template	Choose <u>F</u>ile, <u>N</u>ew and select the category of templates from which you want to choose. Then double-click the template that you want to open. You can see a preview of the template by clicking each template icon once.

continues

To	Do This
Use a template wizard	In the New dialog box, choose from several wizards that appear along with the various template icons. Double-click the wizard of your choice.
Modify an existing template	Choose File, New and choose the template that you want to modify. Select the Template option to open the template as a template rather than as a document and choose OK. Make the changes that you want to apply to this template and then save it, using the existing template name. Word saves the file as a new template, replacing the original template.
Create your own template	Create a document (or open an existing document) that contains the features that you want to save as a template. Save the document by choosing File, Save As. Type a name for the template. From the Files of Type drop-down list, select Document Template. Select the folder in which you want to save the template and choose OK.
Change a template's formatting	Create a new template or open an existing template as a template. Change any formatting options in the template document, then save the file as a template.

Checking Your Skills

True/False

For each of the following statements, check *T* or *F* to indicate whether the statement is true or false.

__T __F **1.** A template wizard is a little program that prompts you for information you need to complete the template.

__T __F **2.** Clicking the Standard toolbar's New button opens a document in the Normal.dot template.

__T __F **3.** When using a template wizard, you can't go back and make changes in your selections.

__T __F **4.** You can borrow items from existing templates when you create your own template.

__T __F **5.** Create a new template by choosing File, New, and then dragging the template name into the document.

__T __F **6.** Templates are listed in the Save dialog box.

__T __F **7.** Once you save a document as a template, you can't make changes to it.

__T __F **8.** Word comes with built-in templates for creating common documents.

__T __F **9.** To quickly create a document based on a letter template, press Ctrl+N.

__T __F **10.** Some templates include sample text that you can edit or delete.

Multiple Choice

Circle the letter of the correct answer for each of the following questions.

1. Which template contains formatting features that are default settings in Word?

   a. Default

   b. Normal

   c. New

   d. Wizard

2. What kind of documents can you create by using templates?

   a. Letters

   b. Faxes

   c. Memos

   d. All the above

3. To modify an existing template, you open the template as what?

   a. A document

   b. A new file

   c. A macro

   d. A template

4. What formatting settings does the Normal.dot template include?

   a. A typeface of 10-point Times New Roman

   b. Full justification

   c. Margins of 1" on all four sides

   d. Default tab settings at 1"

5. Which of the following can you include in a template that you create?

   a. A choice of font and font size

   b. Full justification

   c. Margin settings

   d. All the above

6. What button do you click in a template wizard when you are ready to have Word create the document?

   a. Next

   b. Back

   c. Finish

   d. Create

7. What file extension do Wizard templates have?

   a. .doc

   b. .wiz

   c. .dot

   d. .txt

8. How many steps does a template wizard have?

   a. 3

   b. 4

   c. 5

   d. As many as necessary

9. To save a new document as a template, what do you choose from the Save as <u>t</u>ype drop-down list?

    a. Document Template (*.dot)

    b. Word Document (*.doc)

    c. Template Wizard (*.wiz)

    d. Wizard Document (*.wzd)

10. In which folder should you save a template so it is available in the New dialog box?

    a. New

    b. Program Files

    c. Templates

    d. Office

Completion

In the blank provided, write the correct answer for each of the following statements.

1. Use a template ______________ to automate the process of inserting information in the template.

2. The Fax Wizard icon is on the ___________ & __________ page of the New dialog box.

3. To see a preview of a template, ______________ the template icon in the New dialog box.

4. The three-letter extension after files saved as template documents is

  .______________.

5. When selecting a template ________, such as Click here and type name, it is important that you click in the correct place.

6. Open a template as a new _________ if you do not want your changes to effect the original template.

7. Click the ________ button to move to the previous page in a wizard.

8. You can modify an ____________ template to create one customized for your own needs.

9. Use the Windows _________ to copy and paste items from an existing template into a new template.

10. You can ________ field codes on to display the entire field code in a template.

Matching

In the blank next to each of the following terms or phrases, write the letter of the corresponding term or phrase. (Note that some letters may be used more than once.)

a. Field

b. Template1

c. New

d. .dot

________ 1. Template that prompts you to answer questions

________ 2. The default template

________ 3. File extension for a template

________ 4. File extension for a wizard

Word

e. Wizard

f. Normal

g. Fax Wizard

h. <u>N</u>ext

i. .wiz

j. `Ctrl`+`N`

________   **5.** Dialog box where template icons are displayed

________   **6.** Button for moving forward through Wizard pages

________   **7.** Shortcut combination for creating a document based on the default template

________   **8.** Place holder for text that you can change or delete in a template

________   **9.** Template that helps you create a fax cover sheet, attach a document and fax the whole thing from your computer

________   **10.** Default name of the first template you create with Word

Applying Your Skills

Practice

The following exercises enable you to practice the skills you have learned in this project. Take a few minutes to work through these exercises now.

Creating and Formatting a Memo Using a Template

In this exercise, you create and format a memo document using a template.

To create and format a memo using a template, follow these steps:

1. In Word, choose <u>F</u>ile, <u>N</u>ew.

2. Click the Memos page tab.

3. Double-click the Professional Memo icon.

4. Save the document created by Word in your Practices folder with the name Tech Memo.

5. Replace the text Company Name Here with the text `Main Street Music.`

6. Click on the To: line where it says `Click here and type name`, and type `All Employees`

7. Click on the From: line where it says `Click here and type name` and type your own name.

8. Delete the CC: line.

9. Click on the Re: line where it says `Click here and type subject` and type `New Hours.`

10. Replace the text `How to Use This Memo Template` with the text `For Your Information.`

11. Read the paragraph about how to use the template, then replace it with the following sentence, followed by the bullet list: `Due to cus-tomer demand, we are expanding our store hours on Fridays, Saturdays, and Sundays. New hours are as follows:`

    - `Fridays:  10:00 a.m. - 10:00 p.m.`

    - `Saturdays:  10:00 a.m. - 10:00 p.m.`

   ■ Sundays   12:00 p.m. - 6:00 p.m.

12. Start a new, non-bulleted paragraph and type `Please let me know if you are interested in working this weekend.`

13. Press `↵Enter`, and type `Thanks for your cooperation and hard work,`

14. Press `↵Enter` four times and type your own name.

15. Check the spelling and the grammar and save the document. Preview it, print it if requested by your instructor, then close it.

Using a Template Wizard to Create a Memo

In this exercise, you use the skills you learned in this project to create a memo using a template wizard.

To use a template wizard to create a memo, follow these steps:

1. In Word, choose File, New.

2. Click the Memos page tab.

3. Double-click the Memo Wizard icon.

4. Click Next.

5. Select the Contemporary layout option button, then click Next.

6. Make sure the Yes options button is selected, then click Next.

7. Make sure the Name, Date, and Subject options are selected. Verify today's date in the Date text box, type your name in the Name text box, and type `Company Picnic` in the Subject text box, then click Next.

8. Enter `All Employees` in the To text box and deselect the Cc option button, then click Next.

9. Select the Attachments options button, then click Next.

10. Deselect the Confidential option, then click Next.

11. Click Finish. Word creates the memo according to your specifications and displays it onscreen. Click Cancel if the Office Assistant is displayed.

12. Click on the field `Click here and type`, and type the following text:

`Once again, it's time for our company picnic, and all of you old timers know there's no more fun than Main Street Music's company picnic!`

`This year we're planning volleyball, softball and some relay race events. As always, there'll be swimming in the pond and lots of great food.`

`So, pack up your kids, spouse, significant other, and the dog and head out to the old gristmill on Wayside Inn Road.`

`When?     June 6`

`Time?     2:30`

`If you need directions, ask Jill in personnel for a map.`

`See you there!`

13. Save the memo in your `Practices` folder with the name `Picnic2`.

14. Check the spelling and grammar in the memo and preview it. If requested by your instructor, print it. Close the document when you have finished.

Creating a New Template Based on an Existing Document

In this exercise, you use the skills you learned in this Project to create a new template based on the existing invoice document you worked with in earlier projects. You are able to use the template to create new invoice documents with common characteristics.

To create a new template based on an existing document, follow these steps:

1. Open the file Proj0603 from the Project-06 folder on the CD and save it in your `Practices` folder with the name `Invoice4`.

2. Choose File, Save As.

3. Change the File name to `Music Invoice`.

4. Select Document Template (*.dot) from the Save as type drop-down list.

5. Click Save. Word saves the new template in the Templates folder. It is displayed on the General page of the New dialog box.

6. If requested by your instructor, print the Music Invoice template document. Then close it.

Creating a New Document Based on the New Template

In this exercise, you use the skills you learned in this Project to create a document based on the new template you created in the previous exercise.

To create a new document based on the new template, follow these steps:

1. Choose File, New.

2. Click the General Page tab.

3. Double-click the Music Invoice template icon. Word creates a new invoice document.

4. Save the document in your practices folder with the name `Invcice5`.

5. In the invoice table, enter the following information:

Date	Description	Price
9/22/98	Studio Rental	$50.00
9/23/98	Studio Rental	$50.00

6. Delete the two blank rows from the table.

7. Update the calculating field in the last cell in the table.

8. Check the spelling and grammar in the document and save it. Preview it. If requested by your instructor, print it.

Creating a New Template Based on an Existing Template

In this exercise, you use the skills you learned in this project to create a new template based on the Music Invoice template.

To create a new template based on an existing template, follow these steps:

1. Choose File, New and click the General page tab, if necessary.

2. Select the Music Invoice template icon.

3. Click the Template option button in the Create New area, then click OK. Word creates a new template document based on the Music Invoice template.

4. Replace the text Invoice with the text Memorandum.

5. Delete the entire table.

6. Save the template with the name Music Memo in the Templates folder. Keep it open.

7. Choose File, New, click the Memos page tab, select the Professional Memo template icon, click the Template option button in the Create New area, and then click OK.

8. Select all lines beginning with the To: line to the end of the document, and click the Copy button on the Standard toolbar.

9. Close the Professional Memo template document.

10. Make sure the insertion point is on the last line of the Music Memo document, and click the Paste button on the Standard toolbar.

11. Word copies the information from the Professional Memo template into the Music Memo template.

12. Check the spelling and grammar in the Music Memo, then save it. Preview it. If requested by your instructor, print it. Close the document when you have finished.

13. Use Windows Explorer to move the Music Invoice.dot and Music Memo.dot files from the Templates folder into your Practices folder. For more information, ask your instructor.

Challenge

The following challenges enable you to use your problem-solving skills. Take time to work through these exercises now.

Using a Template to Create a Letter

In this exercise, you use one of Word's built-in letter templates to create a new document. Use the File, New command to open the New dialog box, then click the Letters & Faxes page tab. Select one of the Letter templates (not a wizard) and choose OK. To preview a template before opening it, click it. It is displayed in the preview area of the New dialog box. Save the letter document in your Challenges folder as Club.

Follow the instructions onscreen to create a letter from yourself as the Aquatics Director of the HealthFirst Health Club. This letter is to ask the manager of the Taste of China restaurant (located at 652 Chestnut Street, Marlborough, MA 01752) if you can reserve a function room for the swim team banquet on March 25 from 4:00 p.m. until 7:00 p.m. Propose an alternate date of April 8 and provide information on how and when to reach you to discuss the matter. Include information about the number of people and the type of menu you would like. Include at least two paragraphs in the letter. Don't forget to fill in the return address information at the bottom of the letter. (HealthFirst Health Club is located at 2950 Workout Lane, also in Marlborough, MA 01752. The phone number is 508-555-2516; the fax number is 508-555-2517.)

When you have finished, preview the letter, make any necessary adjustments to formatting, page setup, and spacing, then check the spelling and grammar in the document and save it. If requested by your instructor, print the letter. Close it when you have finished.

Using a Wizard to Create an Envelope

In this exercise, you use one of Word's built-in wizard templates to create an envelope document to use to mail the letter you created in the previous exercise. Use the File, New command to open the New dialog box, then click the Letters & Faxes page tab. Select the Envelope Wizard template icon and choose OK.

Select the option for creating a single envelope in the Office Assistant, then you can close the Office Assistant. Type the address for the Taste of China restaurant into the Delivery address text box. It is located at 652 Chestnut Street in Marlborough, MA 01752. Deselect the Omit check box above the Return address text box, and type in the address for the HealthFirst Health Club. It is located at 2950 Workout Lane, also in Marlborough. Click the Add to Document button, then save the document in your Challenges folder with the name Envelope. Check the spelling and grammar. If requested by your instructor, print the envelope. Close the document when you have finished.

Saving an Existing Document to Create a Template

In this exercise, you save the Computer Concepts proposal document that you worked with in earlier projects as a template. You then use the new template to create a new document.

Open the file Proj0604 from the Project-06 folder on the CD. Save it in the Templates folder as a document template with the file name Proposal Template. Replace the word "your" in the first sentence in the paragraph under the heading Proposal with Type Client Name Here. Delete the dollar values from the second column in the table, then save and close the document template.

Use the new template to create a new document. Save the new document in your Challenges folder with the name Proposal. Replace the text [Type Client Name Here] with the company name FairView Accounting. Enter the following dollar values in the second column of the table:

$7,500.00

$18,000.00

$75,000.00

$75,000.00

$100,000.00

Total the dollar values. Check the spelling and grammar in the document and save it. Preview it. If requested by your instructor, print it. Close the document when you have finished.

Modifying an Existing Template to Create a New Template

In this exercise, you modify the Proposal template to create a template you can use as general stationery for creating any type of draft documents for Computer Concepts, Inc. Use the New dialog box to locate and select the Proposal Template icon, but use it to create a new template file, not a new document file. Delete all information below the letterhead. All that remains is the letterhead and the watermark. Create a header that has the words `Draft Document` flush left, and the date flush right. Create a footer that has the page number centered. Save the template with the name `Draft Template`. Preview it. If requested by your instructor print it. Close it. If requested by your instructor, use it to create a new document.

When you have finished using the Proposal Template and the Draft Template, use Windows Explorer to move both files into your `Challenges` folder.

Creating Your Own Template

In this exercise, you create a new blank document template. Start by creating a new template based on the Normal.dot Blank Document template. Set the margins to two inches on all four sides. Set the vertical alignment to center. Set the default typeface to 36-point Arial. Set paragraph spacing to 18 points after. Set alignment to center. Save the template with the name `Announcements`. Check the spelling and grammar and save it. Preview it. If requested by your instructor, print it. Close it.

Use the Announcements template to create a new document. Type the following in the new document:

`Computer Concepts, Inc. Is Proud to Announce the Hiring of Janet McCall, PhD.`

Save the document in your `Challenges` folder with the name `McCall`. Check the spelling and grammar and save it. Preview it. If requested by your instructor, print it. Close it.

When you are finished using your Announcement template, use Windows Explorer to move it into your `Challenges` folder.

You have completed the project and the associated lessons, as well as the "Checking Your Skills" and "Applying Your Skills" sections. Now use the PinPoint software evaluation mode to assess your comprehension of the specific exam tasks you have just learned. You can also use the PinPoint Trainer Mode and the Show Me tutorials to practice these specific exam tasks.

Project 7

Seven

Using Merge

Setting Up a Mail Merge

In this Project, you learn how to:

Objectives

Required Activities

- ➤ Identify the Main Document
- ➤ Create the Data Source
- ➤ Enter Information Into the Data Source
- ➤ Create the Main Document
- ➤ Create an Envelope Main Document
- ➤ Merge the Files

Why Would I Do This?

When you want to send a personalized letter to a number of people, you can use Word's Merge feature. You can save time by setting up the letter as a form file and then merging the names and addresses of the recipients. The resulting personalized letter gives the impression that you typed each letter individually. In reality, you only typed the letter once.

For this Project, you send a letter to everyone who has registered for a Technology Training Conference. Using the letter as your sample document and the instructions provided in this Project, you learn how to use the Merge feature to create a letter and an envelope for each individual.

Merge

A feature that enables you to combine information, such as names and addresses, with a form document, such as a letter. The results of a typical merge are personalized letters and envelopes.

Lesson 1: Identifying the Main Document

A *merge* has two types of files: a **main document** and a **data source**. The main document contains the information that stays the same for all the recipients. The data source contains all the information for a person or an item (for example, address list and inventory list).

In this case, the main document is a letter. In the areas where you need to insert information from the data source, you insert merge **fields** into the main document that match the merge fields used in the data source. When you merge the two documents, Word matches the merge fields and inserts the information at the appropriate places in the main document.

You can create a main document from an existing document or you can start from scratch. In this case, the letter you need to send has already been created, so you need to identify the letter as the main document.

To Identify the Main Document

1 Open the Proj0701 file from the Project-07 folder on the CD. Save it as Registration Letter**.**

Registration Letter is the letter you want to send to all the conference participants.

2 Choose Tools, Mail Merge.

The Mail Merge Helper dialog box is displayed (see Figure 7.1). The Mail Merge Helper provides the steps for creating both the main document and the data source, and then merging these files.

3 Choose Create.

A drop-down list is displayed, showing the main documents you can create with the Mail Merge Helper. The Form Letters option is used to create a main document to be used in a merge where a new page is created for every record in the data source. The Labels option helps you set up a label form. The Envelopes option helps you set up an envelope form. Finally, the Catalog option is used in a merge where you want a list produced. Each record is placed on the current page, rather than on a new page.

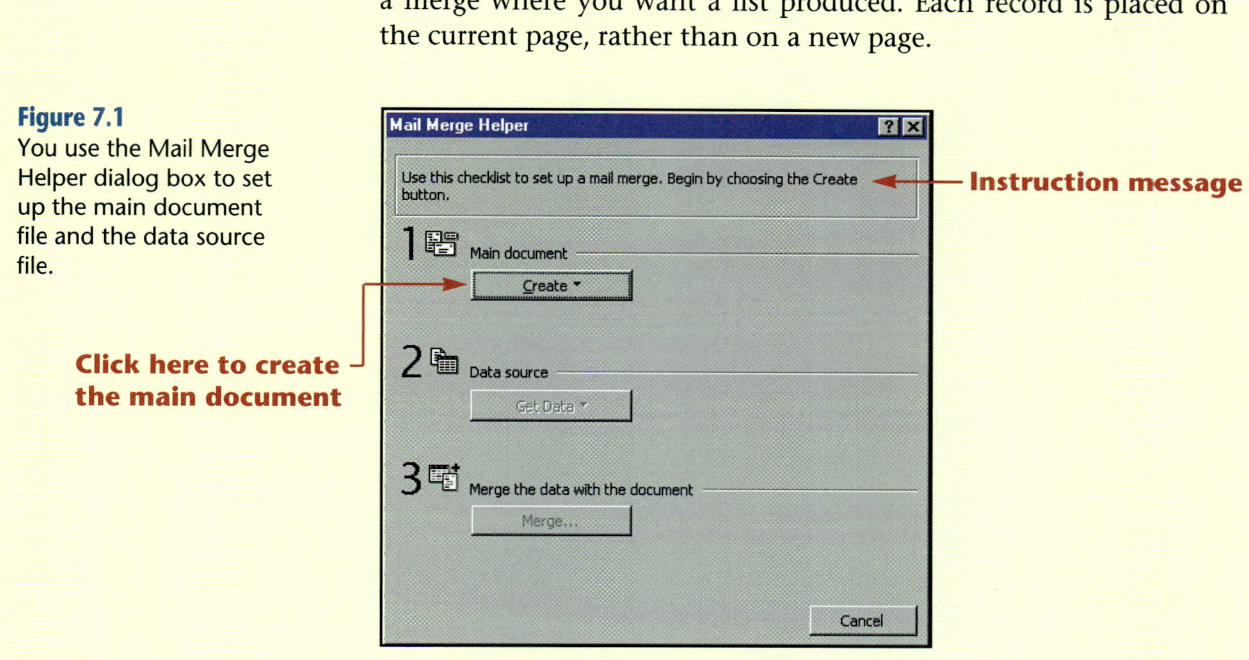

Figure 7.1
You use the Mail Merge Helper dialog box to set up the main document file and the data source file.

4 **Choose Form Letters.**

Word displays a message box asking whether you want to use the Registration Letter document in the active window or whether you want to start from scratch in a new main document.

5 **Choose Active Window.**

The Mail Merge Helper dialog box is now displayed with a message below the Main Document section, indicating a merge type of Form Letters. The name and location of the main document appear in the dialog box (see Figure 7.2).

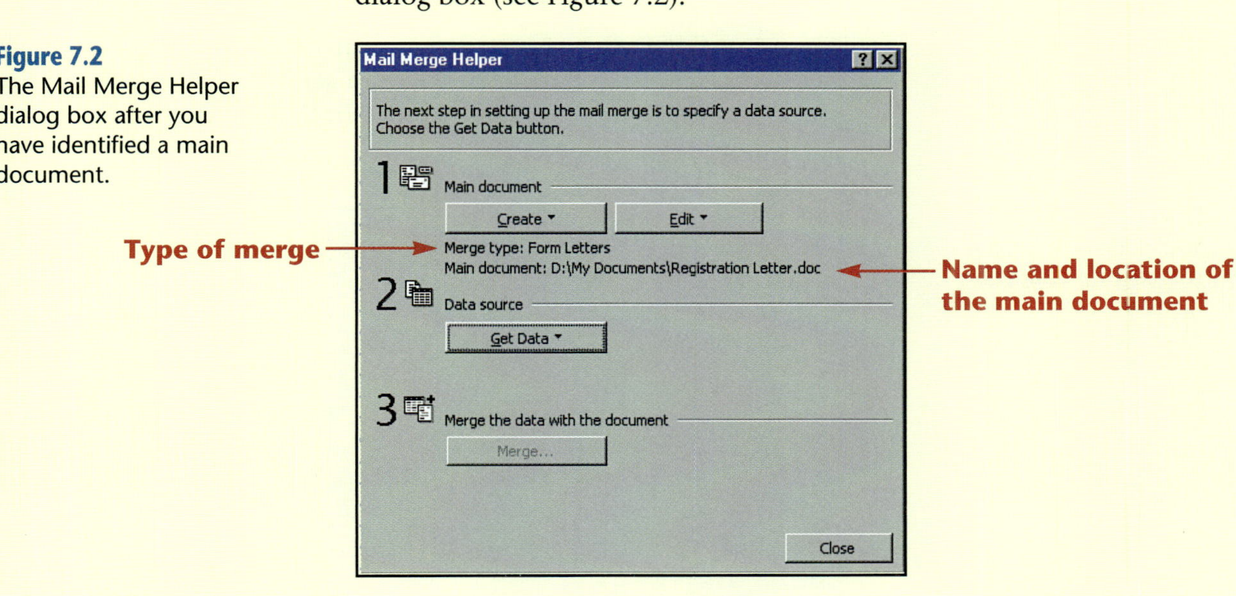

Figure 7.2
The Mail Merge Helper dialog box after you have identified a main document.

6 **Leave the Mail Merge Helper dialog box open so that you can use it in the next lesson where you create the data source for the form letter.**

Word

Word uses two files in a merge: the **data source** and the **main document**. The data source contains the information (such as names and addresses) that is inserted into the main document. The main document, sometimes called a form file, contains the information (such as a letter, a notice, or an invitation) that doesn't change from one person to the next. When you create the main document, you place merge fields—markers that indicate where you want to insert information from the data source—inside the document. These merge fields must match the merge fields used in the data source.

In the data source, each piece of information is called a **field**. A data source might have fields such as Name, Company, Address, City, State, and Zip code. You can have an unlimited number of fields in a record. A record is a collection of all the fields for an individual or item (for example, all the name and address information for one person). You can have as many records in the data source as you need. In the data source, a header row contains a list of all the merge fields.

Lesson 2: Creating the Data Source

The data source contains the information—in this case, the names and addresses—that you need to insert into the main document. The first step in creating the data source is to define how you want to organize the information. For this lesson, you separate the information into first name and last name fields to give you more flexibility when using the data.

Complete the following steps to define a data source for the conference participants.

To Create the Data Source

1 In the Mail Merge Helper dialog box, choose Get Data.

Choosing Get Data opens a drop-down list of options (see Figure 7.3). You can create a data source from scratch or you can identify an existing document as a data source. In this lesson, you create the data source from scratch.

Figure 7.3
You can create a data source from scratch or identify an existing file as the data source.

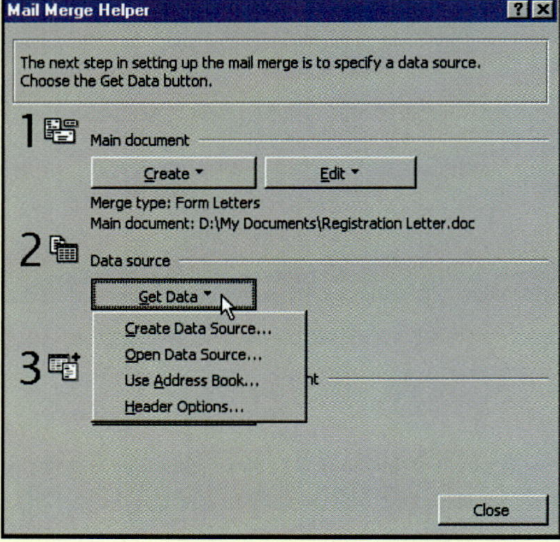

2 Choose Create Data Source.

The Create Data Source dialog box is displayed, as shown in Figure 7.4. Every data source has a header row that lists the merge fields used in the file. The first step in creating a data source is to identify the merge fields for the header row. The Create Data Source dialog box has a predefined list of merge fields you can use.

For this example, you remove the merge fields you won't use: Title, Company, Country, HomePhone, and WorkPhone. Because Title is the first field in the list, it is already selected. Remove this field name now.

Figure 7.4
You use the Create Data Source dialog box to specify the merge fields to be used in the data source file.

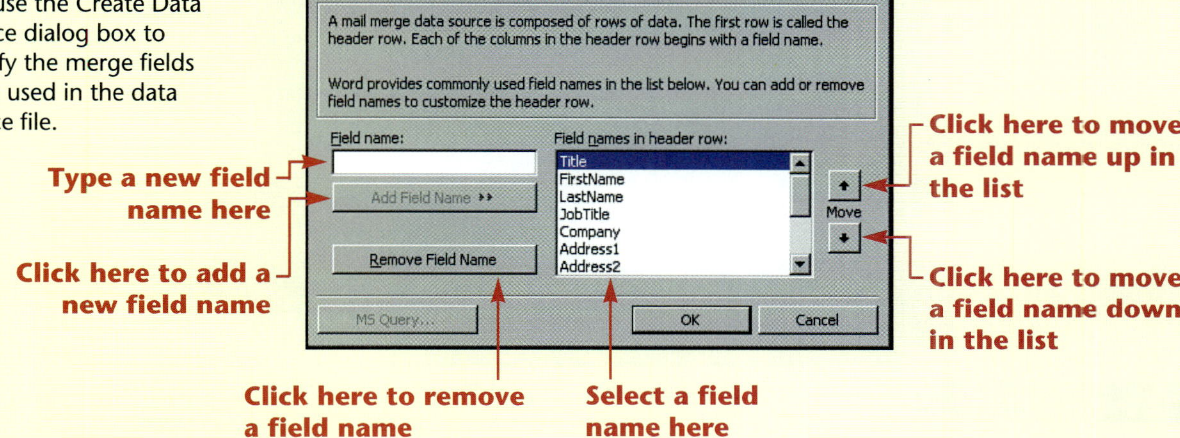

3 Choose Remove Field Name.

The Remove Field Name option takes the selected field name out of the Field names in header row list. The FirstName field becomes the first field name in the list. You can now remove the Company field name (merge field) as well.

4 Click Company and choose Remove Field Name.

Clicking a field name (merge field) selects that field name so that you can remove it or move it around in the list. Because the conference participants are all employees of EcoClean, you don't really need the Company field name.

Word 97 offers two address fields that you can use for multiline addresses—Address1 and Address2. Each address field holds only one line of information. You need to use both of these fields as well as the City, State, and PostalCode fields; however, you can remove the rest of the fields. Scroll down through the list of merge fields until you can see the Country and phone number (HomePhone and WorkPhone) fields.

5 Click Country and choose Remove Field Name.

You delete the Country field because everyone lives in the United States. The HomePhone field is now selected. You won't need to enter the participant's phone numbers for this mail merge, so go ahead and remove both phone number fields.

6 Choose Remove Field Name.

The HomePhone field was selected, so choosing Remove Field Name takes it out of the list. The WorkPhone field is now selected.

7 Choose Remove Field Name.

Both phone number fields are removed. The field names (merge fields) in the list box should now match the ones shown in Figure 7.5.

Figure 7.5
The Create Data Source dialog box with all the field names defined.

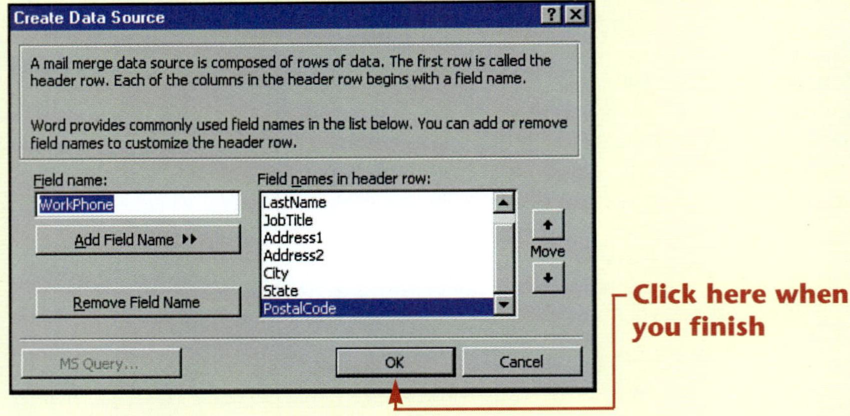

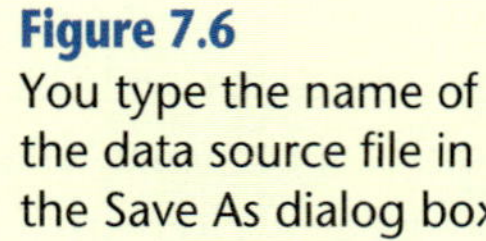

If your fields don't appear in the right order or if you accidentally remove a field, you should take care of this now. Although the fields don't have to be in any particular order for the merge, entering data in the data source is much easier if the field names are in the same order as the information you type.

If you need to reinsert a field name, type the name of the field in the Field name text box and choose Add Field Name. To move a field name, select it and use the Move arrows to insert it into the correct place in the list. Continue selecting field names (merge fields) and moving them around until they appear in the correct order.

8 Choose OK.

When you choose OK, the Save As dialog box opens (see Figure 7.6). You need to type a filename for the data source here.

Figure 7.6
You type the name of the data source file in the Save As dialog box.

Type the name of the data source file here

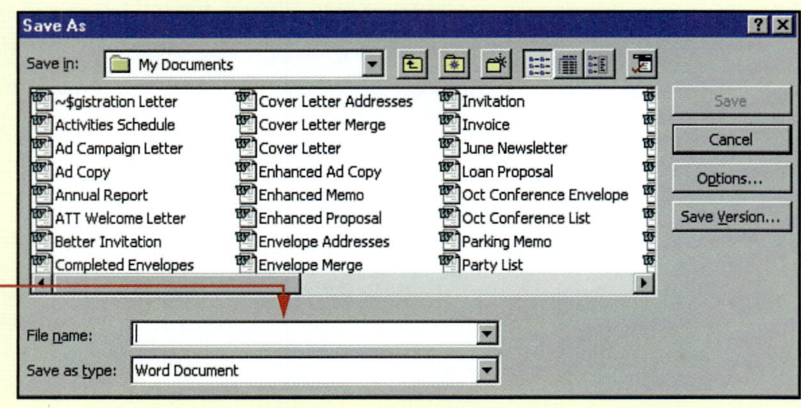

Word

9 **Type** `Oct Conference List` **in the file name text box and choose Save.**

Word saves the data source file and displays a message box indicating that you can add records to the data source or insert merge fields into the main document. Keep this message box open to use in Lesson 3, where you enter the name and address information for the conference participants.

Part of the preceding lesson involved removing the extra merge fields that you wouldn't use for the employees. That step is optional because you don't have to type any information in those fields. Entering the name and address information is easier, though, if you have to work with only the fields you will be using.

If you decide to include fields in a data source that won't be full for every record, you have the option to print (or not print) blank lines when fields are empty. In the Merge dialog box, choose Merge, and then place a check mark in one of the check boxes in the When Merging Records section.

Lesson 3: Entering Information into the Data Source

One benefit of creating the data source file is that you can use the file the next time you need to send something to these individuals. The effort you make now saves you time later.

In this lesson, you type the name and address information into the fields you defined. You should still have the message box displayed on your screen. Try entering the name and address information now.

To Enter Information into the Data Source

1 **Choose Edit Data Source in the message box.**

The Data Form dialog box is displayed, so that you can enter the name and address information for the employees (see Figure 7.7).

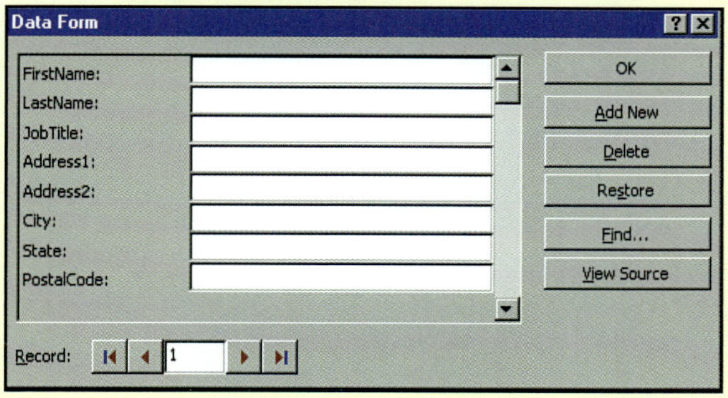

Figure 7.7
The Data Form dialog box with all the merge fields.

2 Type Jenna **in the FirstName text box and press** Tab.

The Data Form dialog box lets you quickly enter the name and address information in your data source. Pressing Tab after typing information in a field moves you to the next text box.

3 Type MacLaren **in the LastName text box and press** Tab.

Because you have broken the name into FirstName and LastName fields, you need only the last name here.

4 Type Benefits Coordinator **in the JobTitle text box and press** Tab.

5 Type 1603 Laurel **in the Address1 text box and press** Tab **twice.**

Because the address fills only one line, you need to press Tab one extra time to move past the Address2 text box. This field is used later when you have two-line addresses to enter, such as addresses that use a suite or apartment number.

6 Type Carmel **in the City text box and press** Tab.

Type only the name of the city here. Word has separate fields for the city, state, and zip code information.

7 Type Indiana **in the State text box and press** Tab.

In the next text box, Word uses the PostalCode field name for the zip code because other countries call this information a postal code, not a zip code.

8 Type 46033 **in the PostalCode text box.**

Before you move to the next record, check the information you have typed to make sure that its correct. Your information in the Data Form dialog box should match Figure 7.8.

Figure 7.8
The Data Form dialog box with the first record entered.

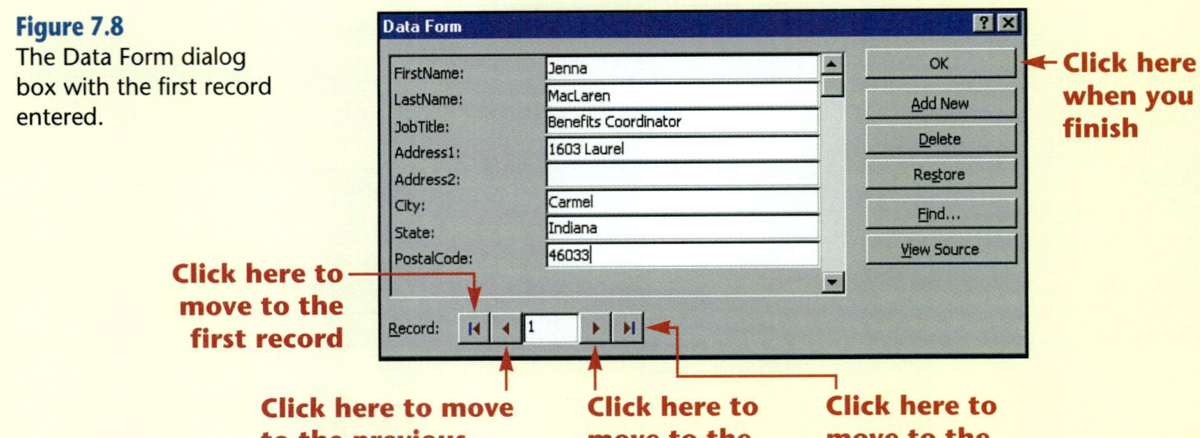

Click here when you finish

Click here to move to the first record

Click here to move to the previous record

Click here to move to the next record

Click here to move to the last record

If you need to fix mistakes in any of the fields, press ⏎Enter or Tab⇥ to move down a field name; press ⬆Shift+Tab⇥ to move up a field name. You can also click inside the text box in which you need to make the correction.

9 **Press** ⏎Enter.

Pressing ⏎Enter in the last field takes you to a new blank record.

10 **Using the preceding steps, enter the following names in the Data Form dialog box:**

```
MaryAlice Carr
Trainer
1105 Jimmy Drive
Apt. 304
Carmel, Indiana  46032

Christopher Woodmansee
Computer Technician
708 West Gibson
Indianapolis, Indiana 46230

Noah Sudanli
Researcher
8405 Jelson Blvd.
Apt. B
Beech Grove, Indiana  46055
```

11 **Choose** **V̲iew Source.**

Choosing V̲iew Source closes the Data Form dialog box and displays the data source information in the document window, along with a new toolbar—the Database toolbar. This toolbar has icons for common tasks you perform when working with merge files.

If you accidentally choose OK (rather than View Source), Word takes you back to the Registration Letter main document. To get to the data source file, click the Edit Data Source button (the last button on the right). In the Data Form dialog box, which is displayed, choose View Source.

Notice that Word places the data source information in a table (see Figure 7.9). Don't worry about the way the text wraps inside the table cells; it won't affect the way the text appears when you merge. You won't print this table, so you only need to adjust the table if the way it's displayed makes it difficult to read.

If the Database toolbar isn't displayed at the top of your document, right-click the Standard or Formatting toolbar and then choose the Database toolbar off the pop-up list.

To Enter Information into the Data Source   (continued)

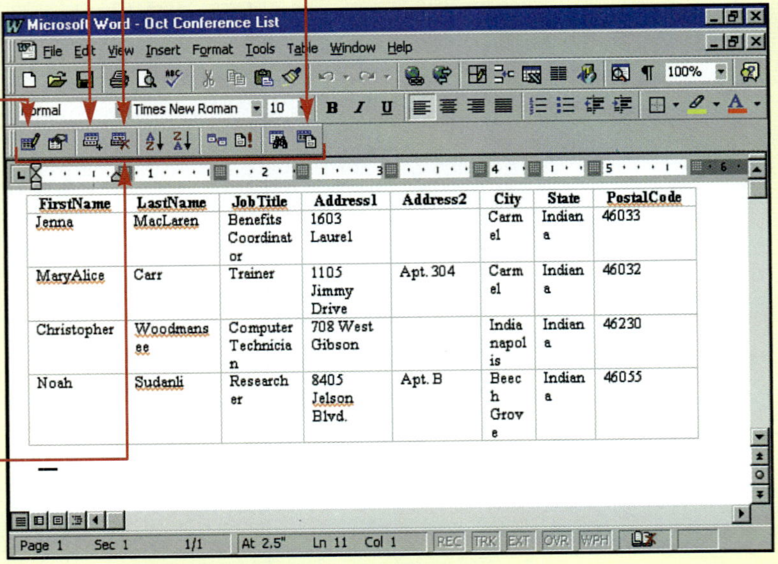

Click here to return to the Data Form dialog box

Click here to add a new record

Click here to delete a record

Click here to switch to the main document

Figure 7.9
The data source table filled in with the name and address information.

Database toolbar

FirstName	LastName	JobTitle	Address1	Address2	City	State	PostalCode
Jenna	MacLaren	Benefits Coordinator	1603 Laurel		Carmel	Indiana	46033
MaryAlice	Carr	Trainer	1105 Jimmy Drive	Apt. 304	Carmel	Indiana	46032
Christopher	Woodmansee	Computer Technician	708 West Gibson		Indianapolis	Indiana	46230
Noah	Sudanli	Researcher	8405 Jelson Blvd.	Apt. B	Beech Grove	Indiana	46055

12 Save your work and keep the Oct Conference List file open to use in the next lesson, where you learn to create the main document.

Lesson 4: Creating the Main Document

In Lesson 1, you identified the Registration Letter file as the file you use to create the main document file. You have taken only the first step in creating the main document, however. The second step is to insert the merge fields where you want the information from the data source to appear in the main document. Try inserting merge fields into the main document file now.

To Create the Main Document

1 In the Oct Conference List file, click the Mail Merge Main Document button on the Mail Merge toolbar.

Clicking the Mail Merge Main Document button switches to the main document file, the Registration Letter file (see Figure 7.10). Notice that the Mail Merge toolbar is displayed.

Figure 7.10
The main document with the Mail Merge toolbar displayed.

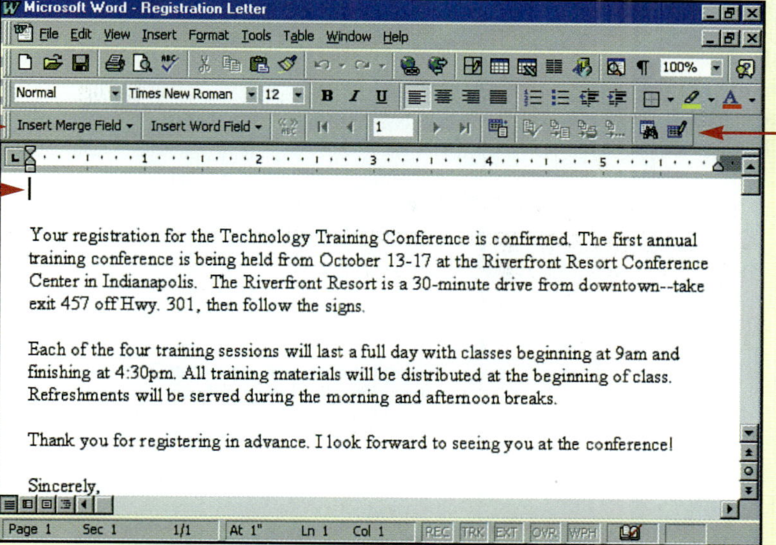

2 **Press** Ctrl+Home**; choose Insert, Date and Time.**

This opens the Date and Time dialog box, where you can choose from a wide variety of date and time formats.

3 **Click the third date format, then, if necessary, place a check mark in the Update automatically check box.**

The Update automatically option inserts the date as a code, so each time you perform a merge with this main document, the current date is inserted.

4 **Press** ↵Enter **four times.**

Pressing Ctrl+Home moves the insertion point to the top of the document where you want the date to appear. The letter should have the current date at the top, followed by the inside address and salutation. Pressing ↵Enter four times inserts blank lines between the date and the inside address.

5 **Click the Insert Merge Field button on the Mail Merge toolbar.**

The Insert Merge Field drop-down list is displayed below the button.

6 **Choose** FirstName**.**

Choosing FirstName inserts the field name with << >> on each side in the main document (see Figure 7.11).

If you have problems...

If you have the Field Codes option selected in the View page of the Options dialog box, your field is displayed like this:
{MERGEFIELD FirstName}.

To Create the Main Document (continued)

Figure 7.11
The main document with the FirstName merge field.

FirstName merge field ——→

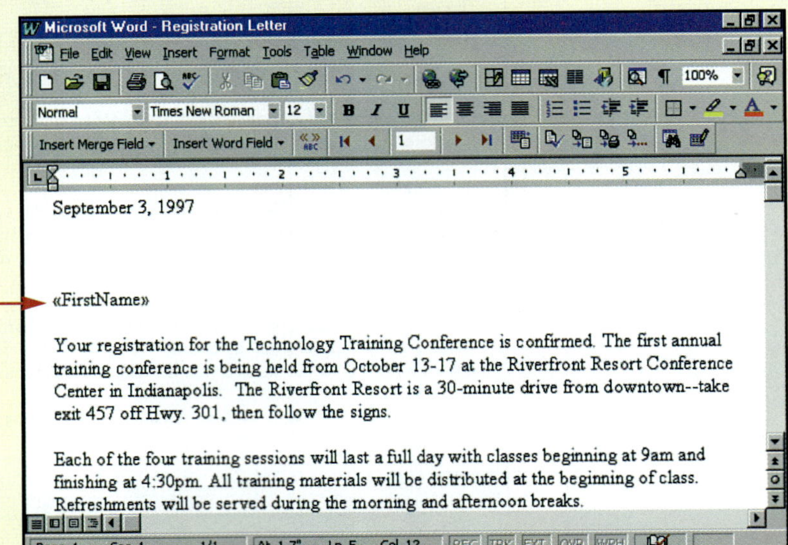

7 Press Spacebar **once.**

This inserts a space between the fields, so when you perform the merge, the first and last names will be separated by a space. All the formatting should be inserted in the main document, not in the data source.

8 Click the Insert Merge Field button on the Mail Merge toolbar, then choose LastName.

The last name field is inserted here.

9 Press ↵Enter.

The first and last names should be on a line by themselves, so you need to press ↵Enter to move down to a new line.

10 Use the Insert Merge Field drop-down list to insert the merge fields in the following format:

<<JobTitle>>
<<Address1>>
<<Address2>>
<<City>>, <<State>> <<PostalCode>>

Be sure to include the comma and blank space between the City and State fields and a space between the State and PostalCode fields.

11 Press ↵Enter **twice, type** Dear, **and press** Spacebar **once.**

This completes the inside address and begins the salutation line.

12 Click the Insert Merge Field button on the Mail Merge toolbar and choose FirstName.

This inserts the first name in the salutation line so that the recipient is addressed by his or her first name.

13 Type a colon (:).

The colon completes the salutation line. The Registration Letter should now look like the one in Figure 7.12.

Figure 7.12
The main document with the merge fields for the inside address and salutation.

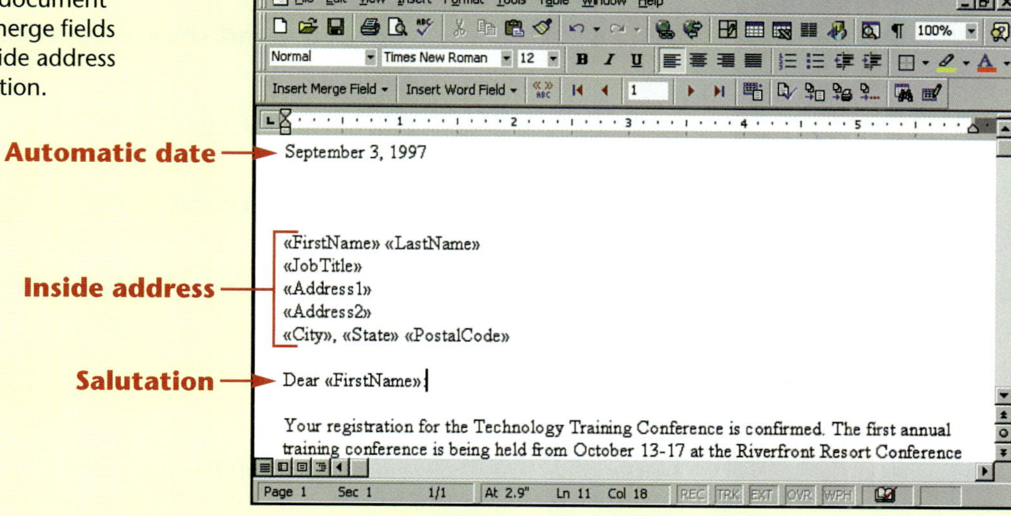

Automatic date
Inside address
Salutation

14 Save your changes in the Registration Letter file.

Switch to the Oct Conference List file (use the <u>W</u>indow menu) and save your changes. Switch back to the Registration Letter document. Leave Word in this state for the next lesson, where you learn to create envelope mailing addresses.

Lesson 5: Creating an Envelope Main Document

Because you need to mail these letters to the employees, you need to create an envelope main document that you can merge with the data source. The envelope main document contains merge fields for the members' names and addresses.

To Create an Envelope Main Document

1 In the Registration Letter, click the Mail Merge Helper button.

This opens the Mail Merge Helper dialog box, where you can create a new main document.

2 Choose Envelopes from the Create drop-down list.

Word displays a message box stating that you can create the envelope main document in the active window or in a new main document.

Word

To Create an Envelope Main Document   (continued)

❸ Choose New Main Document.

The Mail Merge Helper dialog box is displayed in a new document window. You now define the data source that you want to associate with this main document.

❹ Open the Get Data drop-down list and choose Open Data Source.

The Open Data Source dialog box is displayed. You need to specify the name of the data source file here.

❺ Type Oct Conference List **in the filename text box and choose Open.**

You can also double-click the Oct Conference List file in the file list, if you prefer that method. A message box is displayed, stating that Word needs to set up your main document.

❻ Choose Set Up Main Document.

The Envelope Options dialog box is displayed (see Figure 7.13). The settings in this dialog box represent the settings for a business size 10 envelope. You can choose another size from the Envelope Size list and Word shows you where the addresses appear on the preview envelope. If necessary, you can create a custom envelope size by choosing Custom Size and then entering the dimensions. Here again, Word shows you where the addresses appear.

Figure 7.13
You use the Envelope Options dialog box to set the options for the envelopes.

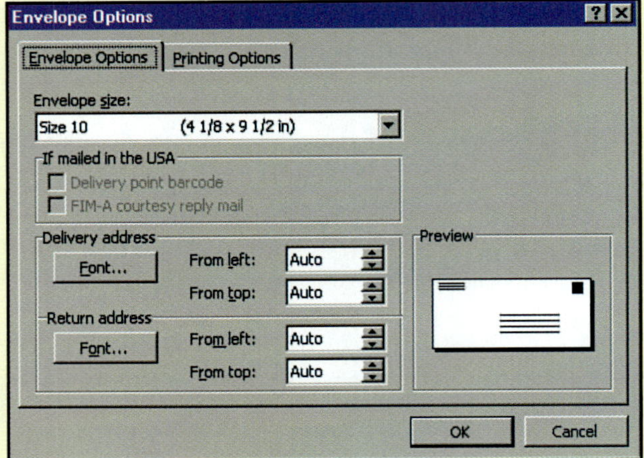

❼ Choose OK.

Choosing OK accepts the standard settings for the envelope. The Envelope address dialog box is displayed. You insert the merge fields for the envelope main document at this point.

8 **Use the Insert Merge Field drop-down list to insert the merge fields in the following format:**

```
<<FirstName>> <<LastName>>
<<JobTitle>>
<<Address1>>
<<Address2>>
<<City>>, <<State>> <<PostalCode>>
```

Make sure that you include the space between the FirstName and LastName, the comma and space between the City and State, and the space between the State and PostalCode. The Envelope address dialog box should now look like Figure 7.14.

Figure 7.14
The Envelope address dialog box with the merge fields in place.

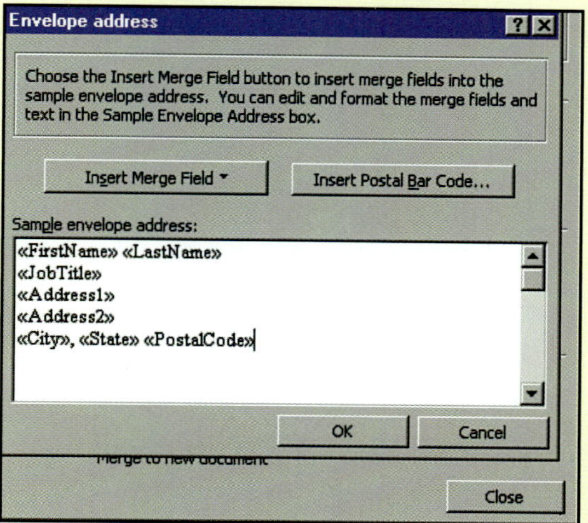

If you have problems...

If you forgot to insert spaces or commas (or you inserted too many), you can edit the sample address now. Simply click the Sample envelope address window and make your changes.

9 **Choose OK.**

Choosing OK closes the Envelope Address dialog box and returns you to the Mail Merge Helper dialog box. Leave this dialog box open so that you can merge the envelope main document and the data source in the next lesson. You also merge the form letter main document with the data source in the next lesson.

Lesson 6: Merging the Files

Merging the data source and main documents is by far the easiest part of the entire merge process. When you merge the data source and main documents, Word looks through each main document for any merge fields and then matches these merge fields with the merge fields in the data source.

When a match is found, Word pulls the information from the data source and inserts that information into the main document, replacing the merge

Word

fields. A new copy of the main document is created for each record in the data source. Because the envelope main document is currently the active document, merge it with the data source now. Then, switch to the October Registration Letter and merge it with the data source.

To Merge the Files

1 **In the Mail Merge Helper dialog box, choose Merge.**

The Merge dialog box is displayed (see Figure 7.15). The current settings merge all the records in the data source with the envelope main document to create a new document.

Figure 7.15
The Merge dialog box for the envelope main document.

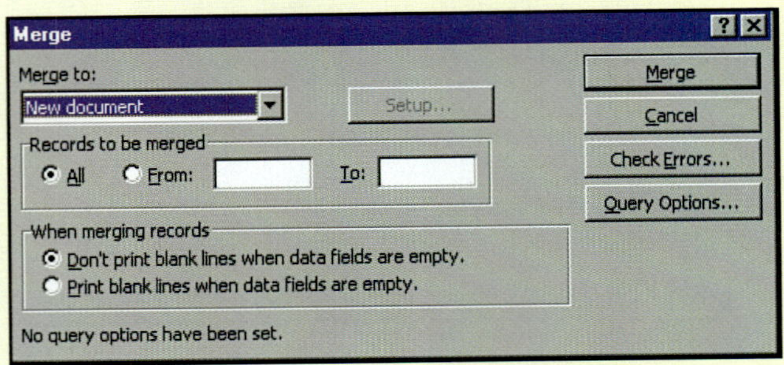

2 **Choose Merge from the Merge dialog box.**

When the merge finishes, the first envelope is displayed (see Figure 7.16). The return address on your envelopes may be different from the one shown in the figure. This information is pulled from the User Info page of the Options dialog box (accessed through Tools, Options). The user information, which is entered when the program is installed, can be edited in the User Information page of the Options dialog box.

Figure 7.16
The merged envelopes have the name and address information inserted.

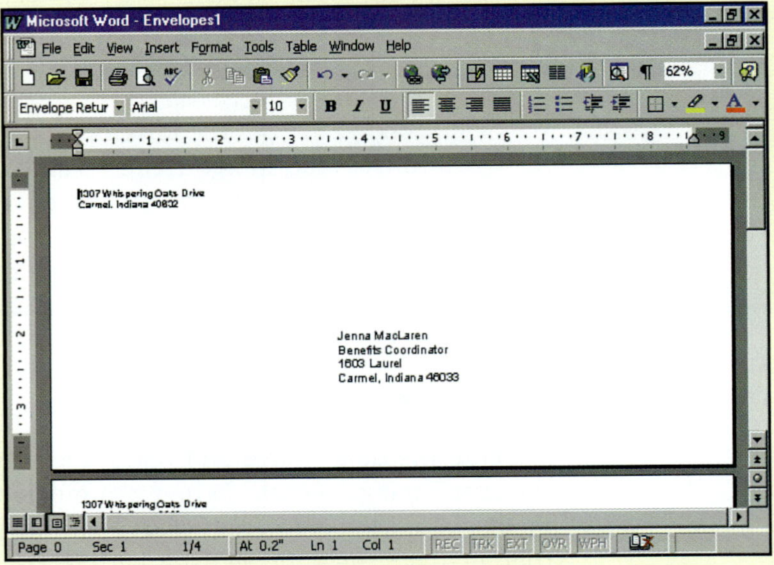

If a merge doesn't produce the results you want, just close the document that contains the results of the merge. (Don't save the document.) Make the necessary corrections in the data source and main documents; then perform the merge again.

First, make sure that you didn't accidentally delete part of the merge field in the main document—the << >> and the field names are very important. If you have deleted any part of the merge field, delete the rest of it; then reinsert the merge field. You can't type these codes from the keyboard.

Second, check that you have included the correct spacing and punctuation in the main document. All spacing and punctuation should be included in the main document, not in the data source.

Third, make sure that the merge fields in both files match exactly. If they don't, Word can't match the merge fields and insert the information.

❸ Click the Print button.

Clicking the Print button sends the envelopes to the printer. Most printers accept envelopes through a manual feed tray, so you have to insert the envelopes into the printer. If you don't have envelopes handy, use regular paper or print preview.

❹ Click the document Close button.

Clicking the document Close button closes the document window. Word prompts you to save your changes.

❺ Choose No.

In most cases, you don't need to save the results of a merge because you can always merge the two files again. Close and save the envelope main document now.

❻ If necessary, switch to the envelope main document.

Use the Window menu to switch to the envelope main document, which hasn't been saved and named yet.

❼ Click the Close button.

Clicking the Close button closes the document. Word prompts you to save your changes.

❽ Choose Yes.

Choosing Yes opens the Save As dialog box (because the document hasn't been named yet).

❾ Type Oct Conference Envelope in the filename text box and choose Save.

Now switch to the letter main document (Registration Letter) and merge it with the Oct Conference List data source file.

❿ Switch to the Registration Letter file.

To Merge the Files   (continued)

⓫ Click the Merge to New document button on the Mail Merge toolbar.

When the merge finishes, the member's first name has been inserted at the top of the letter, replacing the merge field (see Figure 7.17). Scroll through the letters; you should have a total of four individually addressed letters. Word automatically inserts a section break at the bottom of each merged letter to ensure that the letter prints on a separate page.

Figure 7.17
The completed letters are individually addressed.

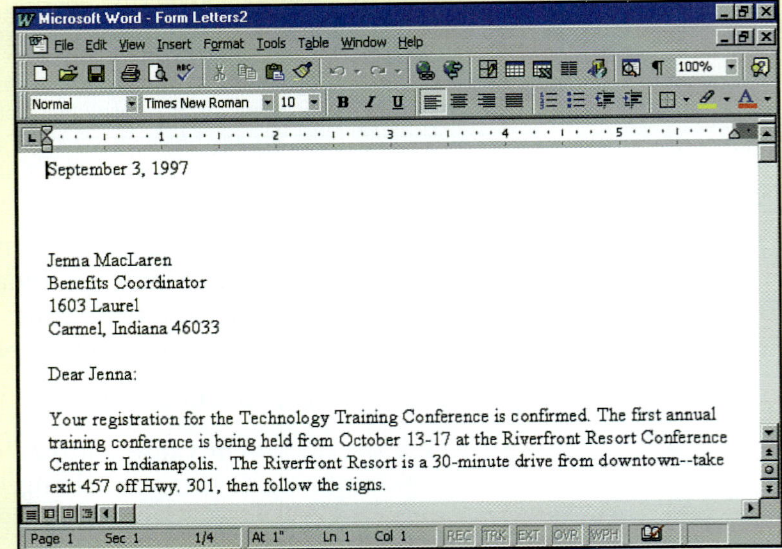

⓬ Click the Print button.

Clicking the Print button sends the letters to the printer. You may choose to Print Preview the documents.

⓭ Click the document Close button and choose No.

Now close and, if necessary, save the changes to Registration Letter.

If you have completed your session on the computer, exit Word for Windows and shut down Windows before turning off the computer. Otherwise, continue with the sections "Checking Your Skills" and "Applying Your Skills."

Project Summary

To	Do This
Identify a form letter as the main document	If necessary, open the main document file first. Otherwise, start from a new document window. Choose Tools, Mail Merge, Create, Form Letters, Active Window.
Create a data source	From the main document window, choose Tools, Mail Merge, Get Data, Create Data Source. If necessary, remove field names that you won't use. Choose OK. In the File Name text box, type a name for the data source file; then choose OK. Choose Edit Data Source. Type the names and addresses. Choose OK. Save your changes when you close the document.
Create the main document	In the main document window, click the Insert Merge Field button to insert the field names in their places in the main document. Include all formatting and punctuation in the main document. Save the changes to the document.
Create an envelope main window	In a new document window, choose Tools, Mail Merge, Create, Envelopes, Active Window. From another main document, choose Tools, Mail Merge, Create, Envelopes, New Main Document. Open the Get Data drop-down list and choose Open Data Source. Type the name of the data source file in the File name text box. Choose Set Up Main Document and choose OK. Click the Insert Merge Field button to insert the name and address field names. Choose OK.
Merge the main document and data source file	From either the main document or the data source file, choose Tools, Mail Merge to open the Mail Merge Helper dialog box. Choose Merge. If necessary, change the destination of the merge. Choose Merge.
Switch to another document	Choose Window; then choose the document name or number.

Checking Your Skills

True/False

For each of the following, check *T* or *F* to indicate whether the statement is true or false.

__T __F   1. Merge fields in the main document(s) and the data source must match exactly.

__T __F   2. The main document contains the information you insert into the data source.

__T __F   3. The Data Form dialog box lets you enter the merge fields you want to use in the data source.

__T __F   4. Each piece of information in the data source is called a record.

__T __F   5. You can create a main document from scratch or from an existing document.

__T __F   6. The fields in the data source must be in the same order as the fields in the main document.

__T __F   7. The main document is sometimes called a form file.

__T __F   8. You can have as many records in the data source as you need.

__T __F   9. Word offers three address fields that you can use for multiline addresses.

__T __F 10. You can leave some fields blank in a data source document.

Multiple Choice

Circle the letter of the correct answer for each of the following questions.

1. Which of the following contains the information you want to insert when you merge the files?

   a. Main document

   b. Data source

   c. File manager

   d. Data file

2. What is the name of the combination of a data source and a main document?

   a. Association

   b. File connection

   c. Merge

   d. File relationship

3. When you insert a field code into a form file, it looks like which of the following?

   a. F {FirstName}

   b. MergeField {FirstName}

   c. FIELD (FirstName)

   d. <<FirstName>>

4. You can create an envelope main document from which dialog box?

   a. Data Form

   b. Merge

   c. Mail Merge Helper

   d. Create Data Source

5. You must define which of the following before you can enter information in the data source?

    a. Field codes

    b. Merge fields

    c. Data fields

    d. Merge codes

6. The Mail Merge command is located on which menu?

    a. Format

    b. View

    c. Tools

    d. Insert

7. If you want a new page to be created for every record in the data source, use which option?

    a. Form Letters

    b. Labels

    c. Envelopes

    d. Catalog

8. What do you press to move up a field name in the Data Form dialog box?

    a. ⏎Enter

    b. Tab

    c. ⇧Shift + Tab

    d. a or b

9. What does pressing ⏎Enter in the last field in the Data Form dialog box do?

    a. Closes the dialog box, saving the information

    b. Takes you to a new blank record

    c. Closes the dialog box without saving the information

    d. Causes an error message to display

10. If you accidentally delete part of a merge field in the main document, what must you do to restore the field?

    a. Re-create the entire main document

    b. Delete the field, then reinsert it

    c. Type the codes and field name from the keyboard

    d. Start the entire merge process again

Completion

In the blanks provided, write the correct answer for each of the following statements.

1. When you merge a data source with a main document, a new document is created for every _______________ in the data source.

2. The _______________ file contains the variable information used in a merge.

3. You can create both data source and main documents from the _______________________________ dialog box.

4. In the data source, each piece of information is called a _________.

5. Every data source has a _____________ that lists the merge fields used in the file.

6. All spacing and punctuation must be entered in the _______________ _______________.

7. If you want a list of data records, use the _____________ option when creating the main document.

8. To edit information used for the return address of an envelope, choose the _____________ command from the Tools menu.

9. One person's name and address in a data source is an example of a(n) _______________.

10. When you choose View Source to display the data source file, the _____________ toolbar also displays.

Matching

In the blank next to each of the following terms or phrases, write the letter of the corresponding term or phrase. (Note that some letters may be used more than once.)

a. Mail merge main document

b. Merge

c. ⬆Shift+Tab⬍

d. Main document

e. Field

f. Data source

g. Record

h. Header row

i. Tab⬍

j. Merge fields

_______ 1. The merge file that contains the information inserted into the document

_______ 2. The merge document that contains the information that doesn't change

_______ 3. Markers that indicate where you want to insert information from a data source

_______ 4. A collection of all the fields for an individual item

_______ 5. Contains a list of all the merge fields

_______ 6. Clicking this button switches to the main document file

_______ 7. Enables you to combine information with a form document

_______ 8. Each piece of information, such as a name, in the data source

_______ 9. Press this to move down a field name in the Data Form dialog box

_______ 10. Press this to move up a field name in the Data Form dialog box

Applying Your Skills

Practice

The following exercises enable you to practice the skills you have learned in this project. Take a few minutes to work through these exercises now.

Merging a Cover Letter for Your Résumé

In this exercise you merge a cover letter for your résumé with a list of addresses.

To merge the cover letter, follow these steps:

1. In Word, open the file Proj0702 from the Project-07 folder on the CD and save it in your `Practices` folder as `Resume Letter`. Change the text Student's Name to your name. Keep the document open.

2. Open the file Proj0703 from the Project-07 folder on the CD and save it in your `Practices` folder as `Resume Addresses`; then close the document.

3. Identify the document Resume Letter as the main document for a Form Letter merge. Use the document Resume Addresses as the source document.

4. In the main document, insert merge fields to set up the recipient's address and greeting. Use these fields: Greeting, FirstName, LastName, JobTitle, Company, Address1, Address2, City, State, and PostalCode. Don't forget to leave spaces and add punctuation where necessary.

5. Merge the documents to a file so that you can preview the results.

6. If necessary, edit the data source and the main document, and then try the merge again.

7. Save the merge file in your `Practices` folder as `Resume Merged`. If requested by your instructor, print it.

8. Save the Resume Letter and Resume Addresses documents. Close all documents.

Creating Envelopes for Your Résumé

Now that you have created the form letters to be sent with your résumé, you need to print envelopes for these letters.

To create envelopes for your résumé, follow these steps:

1. Open a new document and identify it as the main document for an envelope merge.

2. Identify the Resume Addresses document as the data source.

3. Set up the main document, using the appropriate fields for an envelope.

4. Merge the envelopes to a document file so that you can preview them.

5. If necessary, edit the source document and the main document set up.

6. Save the envelope merge file in your `Practices` folder as `Resume Mail`. If requested by your instructor, print it.

7. Save the envelope main document in your Practices folder as Resume Envelopes. Close all the documents.

Creating Envelopes for an Invitation

In this exercise you use an address list to print envelopes for your party invitation.

To create the envelopes for an invitation, follow these steps:

1. Open the file Proj0704 from the Project-07 folder on the CD and save it in your `Practices` folder as `Invitation Addresses`.

2. Open a new document and identify it as the main document for an envelope merge.

3. Identify the Invitation Addresses document as the data source.

4. Set up the main document, using the appropriate fields for an envelope.

5. Merge the envelopes to a document file so that you can preview them.

6. If necessary, edit the source document and the main document set up. You can add your return address to the main document if you want. Try the merge again.

7. Save the merge document in your `Practices` folder as `Invitation` Mail. If requested by your instructor, print it.

8. Save the main document as Invitation Envelopes in your Practices folder. Save and close all documents.

Setting Up the CTA Letter for Use in a Merge

In this exercise you edit the CTA Letter so that it can be sent to all new members. Use mail merge to make it easy to customize these letters.

To set up the CTA letter for a merge, follow these steps:

1. Open the file Proj0705 from the Project-07 folder on the CD and save it in your `Practices` folder as `CTA Letter2`.

2. Open the Mail Merge Helper dialog box and identify this document as the main document for a Form Letter merge.

3. Create a new data source that contains the following fields:

   `Title`

   `FirstName`

   `LastName`

```
Address1

City

State

PostalCode
```

4. Save the data source in your `Practices` folder as `CTA List`.

5. Add the following records to the data source:

```
Mr. John Newsome
1305 S. Quincy Ave.
Westmont, IL   60559

Ms. Alicia Jackson
6075 Adams St.
Hinsdale, IL   60551

Ms. Karen Wilson
890 Elkhart Drive
Lombard, IL   60517
```

6. Insert the merge fields into the main document, CTA Letter2. Insert the `Title` and `LastName` fields into this salutation (following Dear).

9. Save CTA Letter2 again.

10. Merge the documents, and save the merge file in your `Practices` folder with the name `CTA Merge`. If requested by your instructor, print a copy of the file.

11. Save and close all the open documents.

Creating Envelopes for the CTA Letter

Now that you have created the form letters to be sent to CTA's new members, you need to print envelopes for these letters.

To create envelopes for the CTA letter, follow these steps:

1. Open a new document and identify it as the main document for an envelope merge.

2. Identify the CTA List document as the data source.

3. Set up the main document, using the appropriate fields for an envelope.

4. Merge the envelopes to a document file so that you can preview them.

5. If necessary, edit the source document and the main document set up.

6. Save the merge file in the `Practices` folder with the name `CTA Mail`. If requested by your instructor, print it.

7. Save the envelope main document as CTA Envelopes. Close all the documents.

Challenge

The following challenges enable you to use your problem-solving skills. Take time to work through these exercises now.

Customizing the Computer Training Concepts Letter

You want to use the Mail Merge feature to change the CTC Cover Letter so that more personal letters can be sent to people who request information from Computer Training Concepts. Open the file Proj0706 from the Project-07 folder on the CD and save it in your Challenges folder as Cover Letter4.

Set up this letter so that it merges with a data source you name CTC Names. Create five records for this data source that contain the following fields:

        Title

        FirstName

        LastName

        Company

        Address1

        Address2

        City

        State

        PostalCode

Select the option so that blank fields do not print when the files are merged. The salutation in the main document should contain Dear, then the person's title and last name.

Merge the letters, and save the merge file in your Challenges folder with the name CTC Merge. If requested by your instructor, print the file.

Save the main file and data source in your Challenges folder before closing them.

Creating Envelopes for the Customized Computer Training Concepts Letters

You need envelopes for the letters that you printed in the previous exercise. Merge an envelope main document with the CTC Names data source. Save the envelope merge file in your Challenges folder with the name CTC Mail. If requested by your instructor, print a copy of the CTC Mail file. Save the envelope main document in your Challenges folder as CTC Envelopes.

Customizing the Health Club Membership Renewal Letter

Now that you have learned to use the Mail Merge feature, you decide to take advantage of it to send customized letters to members regarding renewal of their health club memberships. Open the Proj0707 from the

Project-07 folder on the CD and save it in your `Challenges` folder as `Renewal45`.

Identify this document as the main document for a form letter merge. Create a data source for this document named Club List. Add four records to this document, using the following fields:

`Title`

`FirstName`

`LastName`

`Address1`

`City`

`State`

`PostalCode`

`Expiration`

Insert the `Expiration` field into the first paragraph, after If you renew your membership before it expires on. Also, insert the `FirstName` field somewhere within the body of the letter to make it seem more personal.

Merge the letters, and save the merge file in your Challenges folder with the name `Club Mail`. If requested by your instructor, print it. Save the data source and main document files in your Challenges file before closing them.

Customizing a Reunion Planning Letter

You decide to use Mail Merge to send customized letters to all your relatives regarding the planning of a family reunion. Open the Proj0708 from the Project-07 folder on the CD and save it in your `Challenges` folder as `Reunion`.

Print letters for five of your relatives, creating a data source named `Reunion Addresses`. You decide which fields to include.

Save the merged letters in your `Challenges` folder in a file called `Reunion Letters`. If requested by your instructor, print it. Also save the main document and data source files in your `Challenges` folder, then close these documents.

Creating Envelopes for the Customized Reunion Planning Letters

Print envelopes for the reunion letters you printed in the previous exercise. Create a new envelope main document, and merge it with the Reunion Addresses file. Save the merge file in your `Challenges` folder with the name `Reunion Mail`. If requested by your instructor, print it. Save the main document file as `Reunion Envelopes` in your `Challenges` folder. Close all open files.

Word

You have completed the project and the associated lessons, as well as the "Checking Your Skills" and "Applying Your Skills" sections. Now use the PinPoint software evaluation mode to assess your comprehension of the specific exam tasks you have just learned. You can also use the PinPoint Trainer Mode and the Show Me tutorials to practice these specific exam tasks.

Project 8

Eight

Advanced Merge Techniques

Working with Advanced Merges

In this Project, you learn how to:

Objectives   **Required Activities**

- ➤ Edit Records in a Data Source
- ➤ Edit Fields in a Data Source
- ➤ Sort a Data Source … … … … … … … … … … … … Sort records to be merged
- ➤ Filter Records for a Merge … … … … … … … … Merge a document using variable data
- ➤ Change the Filter Rules
- ➤ Customize a Main Document with Word Fields
- ➤ Use an Outlook Address Book as a Data Source

Why Would I Do This?

Sending out a mass mailing can be a tedious undertaking. First, you have to create a form letter, and then you have to generate one for each individual on your mailing list. Word simplifies the process by providing *merge* capabilities that let you create one form letter *main document* that can be customized automatically for everyone in the *data source* list. Using Word's merge capabilities, you can quickly notify everyone on your mailing list of important news.

You learned how to create a basic mass mailing by using the Merge feature in Project 7. In this project, you use a main document and a data source that have already been created to learn how to use some of Word's advanced merge capabilities to customize your mass mailings. You also learn how to use an address book you create in *Microsoft Outlook* as a data source. These skills help you use one data source for many types of mailings.

Lesson 1: Editing Records in a Data Source

When you create a merge data source in Word, you first specify the **fields** you want in the data source, and then enter information into the fields by using a *data form*. When you save the data source, Word creates a document with the information entered in a **table**. You can edit the information in the data source simply by editing the data in the table, or you can edit it using the data form. You usually use the table when you want to work with many records onscreen at once; you use the data form when you want to work with one record at a time.

In this lesson, you open a data source document in Word and learn how to edit records in the table and in the data form.

Merge
A Word feature that lets you insert information from a data source into a main document to create new, customized documents.

Main document
The Word document used in a merge that contains the information that doesn't change, such as the body of a letter.

Data Source
The Word document used in a merge that contains the variable information that is inserted into a main document, such as names and addresses of recipients.

Microsoft Outlook
An information management application that comes with Office 97.

Data form
A dialog box used to enter or edit one record of a data source document at a time.

To Edit Records in a Data Source

1 **Open the folder Project-08 and the file Proj0801 from this book's CD. Save it as** Employee Data**.**

This is a data source document containing information about employees at Oak Grove Products. When you display a data source document in Word, it's formatted as a table, as shown in Figure 8.1. If you're familiar with a database application such as Access, or even a spreadsheet application such as Excel, you recognize the table as a **database** or list. The first row, called the **header row**, contains the field names. Each subsequent row contains one **record** of data—in this case, the name, hire date, job title, address, and emergency contact information for one employee (see the Jargon Watch at the end of this lesson for more information).

Figure 8.1

A data source document in Word is formatted as a table.

Field names in the header row

One record per row

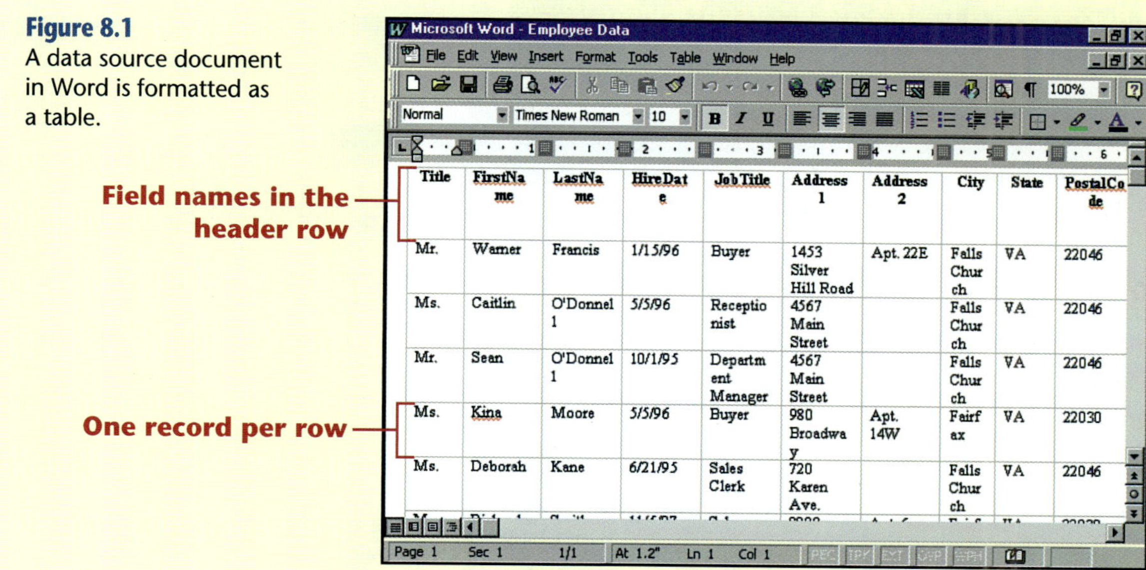

Title	FirstName	LastName	HireDate	JobTitle	Address 1	Address 2	City	State	PostalCode
Mr.	Warner	Francis	1/15/96	Buyer	1453 Silver Hill Road	Apt. 22E	Falls Church	VA	22046
Ms.	Caitlin	O'Donnel l	5/5/96	Receptio nist	4567 Main Street		Falls Church	VA	22046
Mr.	Sean	O'Donnel l	10/1/95	Departm ent Manager	4567 Main Street		Falls Church	VA	22046
Ms.	Kina	Moore	5/5/96	Buyer	980 Broadwa y	Apt. 14W	Fairf ax	VA	22030
Ms.	Deborah	Kane	6/21/95	Sales Clerk	720 Karen Ave.		Falls Church	VA	22046

Page 1   Sec 1   1/1   At 1.2"   Ln 1   Col 1

2 **Choose** **V**iew, **T**oolbars, Database.

This action displays the Database toolbar onscreen. The tools on the Database toolbar make it easy to edit and manage the information in the data source document.

If you have problems...

If the Database toolbar was displayed when you first opened the document in step 1, choosing View, Toolbars, Database in step 2 hides the toolbar. Simply repeat step 2 to display the toolbar again.

If table gridlines are not displayed onscreen, choose Table, Show Gridlines. It's easier to work in the table if you can see the boundaries between cells.

Now try editing records in the table. (To locate the cells referenced in the following steps, consider the header row to be row 1.)

3 **Click in the cell at the intersection of the third row and the fifth column and replace the text** Receptionist **with the text** Administrative Assistant.

This step changes Caitlin O'Donnell's job title, as shown in Figure 8.2. To edit data in a record in the table, you can use Word's table commands or the tools on the Database toolbar. For example, to delete a record, you could use the Table menu commands to select and delete a row from the table, or you could use the Delete Record button on the Database toolbar.

4 **With the insertion point still in the job title cell for Caitlin O'Donnell, click the Delete Record button on the Database toolbar.**

Word deletes the record in which the insertion point is currently located, without prompting you to confirm the deletion. (The insertion point can be in any cell in the record.)

continues

Word

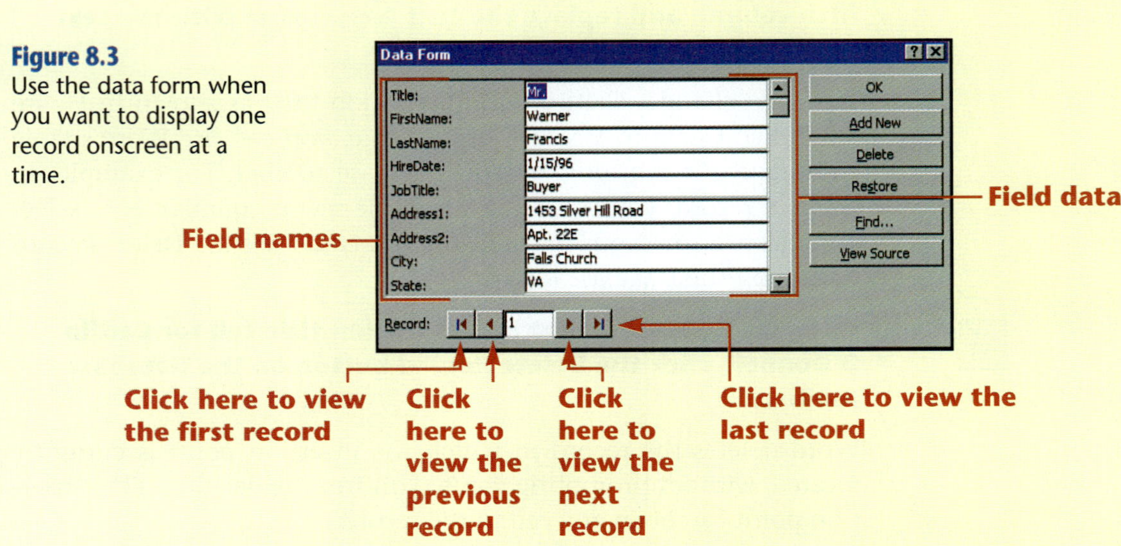

To Edit Records in a Data Source (continued)

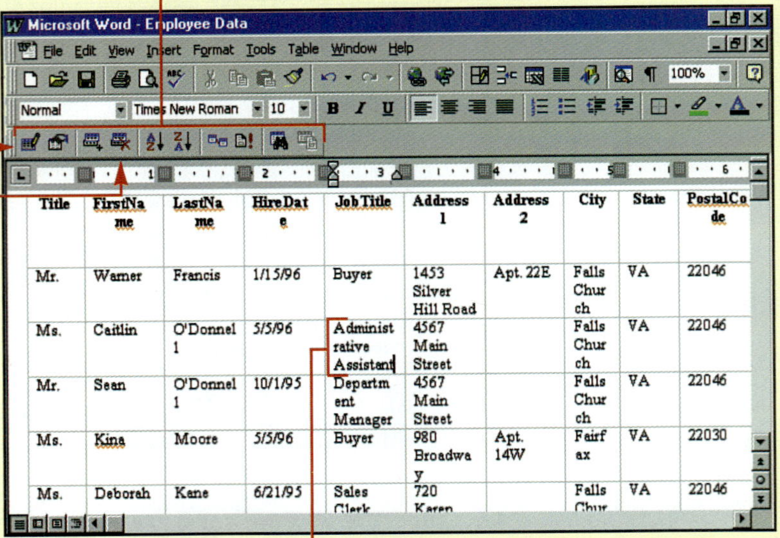

Figure 8.2
You can easily edit data directly in the data source document table.

Database toolbar

Data Form button

Delete Record button

Edited job title

5 **Click the Undo button on the Standard toolbar.**

Word replaces Caitlin O'Donnell's record.

Editing in the data source document table is easy, but if you have a lot of records in your data source, you may waste time trying to locate the record you want to edit. With the data form, you can quickly scroll through the records and find the record you need. Try using the data form to edit records in the data source.

6 **Click the Data Form button on the Database toolbar.**

Word opens the data form for this data source document with the first record displayed, as shown in Figure 8.3. The data form displays one record of information at a time, organized by field.

Figure 8.3
Use the data form when you want to display one record onscreen at a time.

Field names

Field data

Click here to view the first record

Click here to view the previous record

Click here to view the next record

Click here to view the last record

Lesson 2: Editing Fields in a Data Source

You can edit the fields in a data source to change a field name, add a new field, or remove a field you no longer need. As with records, you can edit fields in the data source document table, or you can use the Manage Fields dialog box, which you access by using the Database toolbar.

In this lesson, you learn how to edit fields in the data source using the data source document table and the Manage Fields dialog box.

To Edit Fields in a Data Source

1 In the Employee Data document, replace the text `PostalCode` **in the tenth cell in the header row with the text** `Zip`.

This step changes the field name, as shown in Figure 8.5.

Figure 8.5
The first row of the table contains the field names for the data source document.

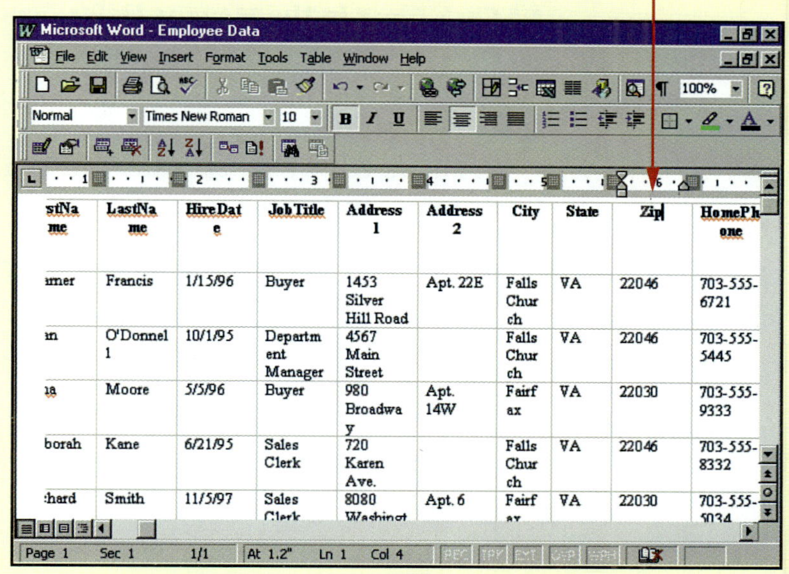

To add a field, simply insert a new column into the table and type the field name in the first row; to delete a field, delete the column. Keep in mind, however, that when you delete a field, you delete all the information entered in that field in each record of the database.

Now try editing fields by using the Manage Fields dialog box.

2 Click the Manage Fields button on the Database toolbar.

Word displays the Manage Fields dialog box, as shown in Figure 8.6.

continues

Word

To Edit Fields in a Data Source (continued)

Figure 8.6
You may find it easier to manage fields by using the Manage Fields dialog box.

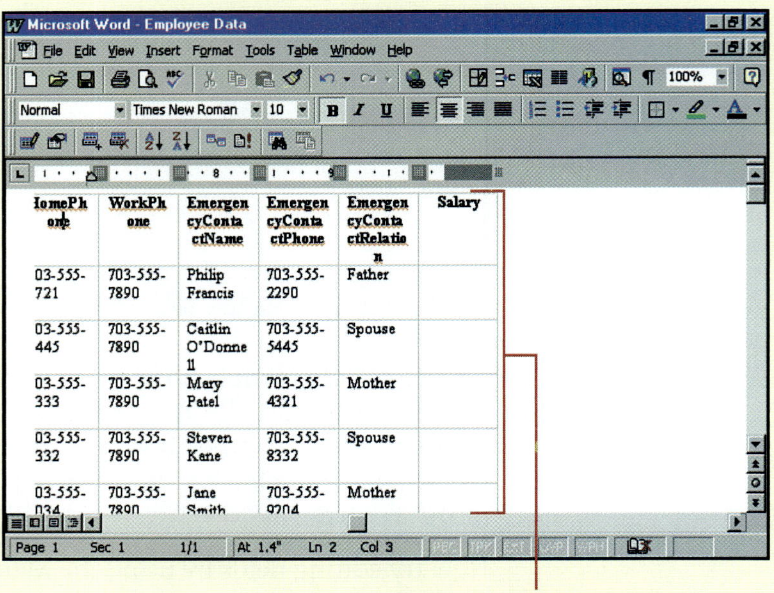

First, add a field.

3 **In the Field Name text box, type** `Salary`**; then click the Add button.**

Word adds the new field to the Field Names in Header Row list. Field names can be up to 40 characters long, must start with a letter, and cannot include spaces.

4 **Click Close in the Manage Fields dialog box. Then scroll over to the right side of the document.**

Word has added the Salary field to the table in the data source document (see Figure 8.7). Of course, there is no data for the new field in any record; you must enter the data by typing it in the table or by using the data form.

Figure 8.7
New fields are blank until you enter data for each record.

IomePhone	WorkPhone	EmergencyContactName	EmergencyContactPhone	EmergencyContactRelation	Salary
03-555-721	703-555-7890	Philip Francis	703-555-2290	Father	
03-555-445	703-555-7890	Caitlin O'Donnell	703-555-5445	Spouse	
03-555-333	703-555-7890	Mary Patel	703-555-4321	Mother	
03-555-332	703-555-7890	Steven Kane	703-555-8332	Spouse	
03-555-034	703-555-7890	Jane Smith	703-555-9704	Mother	

The new Salary field

Now try changing a field name and deleting a field with the Manage Fields dialog box.

5 **Click the Manage Fields button on the Database toolbar.**

Word opens the Manage Fields dialog box again. You change the name of the `Salary` field to `PayLevel`.

6 **Scroll down in the Field Names in Header Row list, select**
`Salary`**, and click the Rename button.**

Word opens the Rename Field dialog box, as shown in Figure 8.8.

Figure 8.8
You can easily rename
existing fields without
affecting field data.

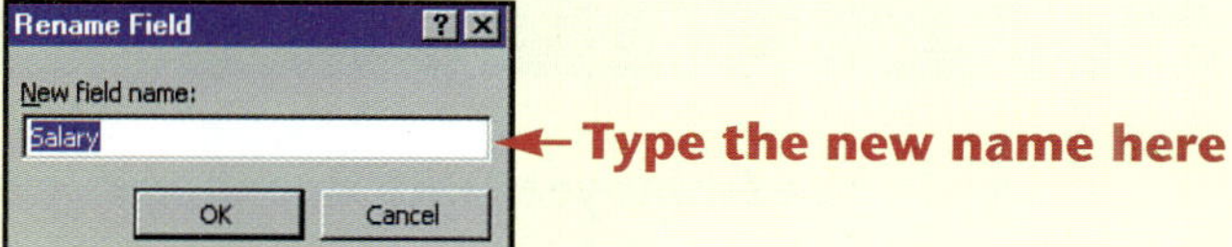

7 **In the New Field Name text box, type** `PayLevel`**; then click OK.**

Word changes the field name from `Salary` to `PayLevel`, as shown in
Figure 8.9.

Figure 8.9
You can see the new
field name in the
Manage Field dialog
box.

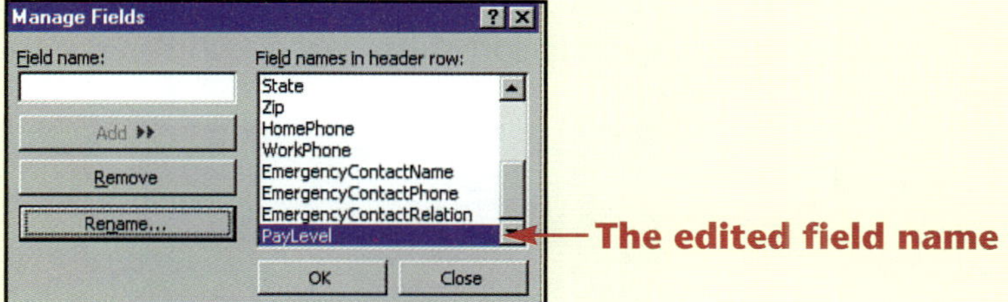

Now you decide not to include the PayLevel field in the data source
after all.

8 **In the Field Names in Header Row list, select** `PayLevel`**, if it's
not already selected; then click the Remove button.**

Word displays a confirmation box asking whether you're sure you
want to delete this field because all information in the field will be
deleted as well.

9 **Choose Yes.**

Word deletes the field from the list and from the data source. These
are all of the changes you make to the Employee Data data source
document for this lesson.

10 **Click Close in the Manage Fields dialog box.**

Word closes the dialog box.

11 **Save the Employee Data document and keep it open.**

In the next lesson, you learn how to sort the data source.

Lesson 3: Sorting a Data Source

The records in a data source appear in the order in which you enter them.
Likewise, that's the order in which they appear in the merge documents
when you conduct a merge. In other words, when you merge a data source
and a form letter, the first letter has the name and address from the first
record, the second letter has the name and address from the second record,

and so on. If you want the letters to appear in a different order, you can sort the data source before merging. Sorting is useful if you want the merge documents generated in alphabetical order, or according to ZIP code.

In this lesson, you learn how to sort the data source.

To Sort a Data Source

1 In the Employee Data document, click in any record in the LastName field (the third column).

First, try quickly sorting the data source alphabetically by last name.

2 Click the Sort Ascending button on the Database toolbar.

Word sorts the records alphabetically from A to Z, as shown in Figure 8.10. Using the Sort buttons on the Database toolbar, you can quickly sort the records according to the data in the current field.

Figure 8.10
The records are sorted alphabetically by employee last name.

Sort Ascending button

Sort Descending button

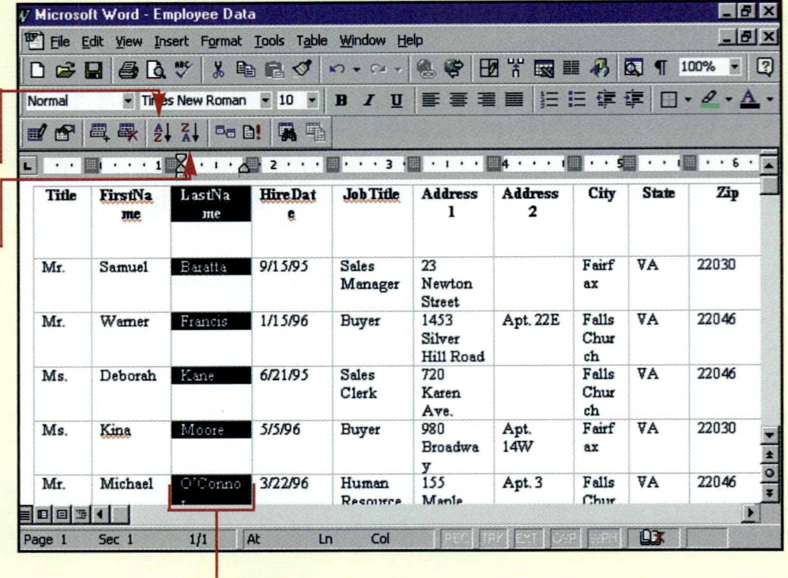

Sorted field

Now sort the data source according to hire date.

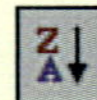

3 Click anywhere within the HireDate field; then click the Sort Descending button.

Word sorts the list again, this time in descending order by the data in the HireDate field (most recent date at the top). You can also use the Table, Sort command to sort the records according to the data in up to three fields. In other words, you can sort by ZIP code and then by last name; then, in case more than one person has the same last name, you can also sort by first name. Try it.

4 Click in any cell in the table to deselect the HireDate field. Then choose Table, Sort.

Word displays the Sort dialog box.

5 **In the Sort by drop-down list, select Zip.**

This step specifies that the first field you want to sort by is the ZIP field. By default, the type of sort setting is Number, and the sort order is Ascending. These settings are correct. Now select the second field you want to sort by.

6 **In the Then by drop-down list, select LastName.**

The default settings—text type in ascending order—are correct for this field.

7 **In the Then by drop-down list, select FirstName.**

You have now set up the specifications for the sort. The dialog box should look similar to the one in Figure 8.11.

Figure 8.11
Use the sort dialog box to sort by up to three fields.

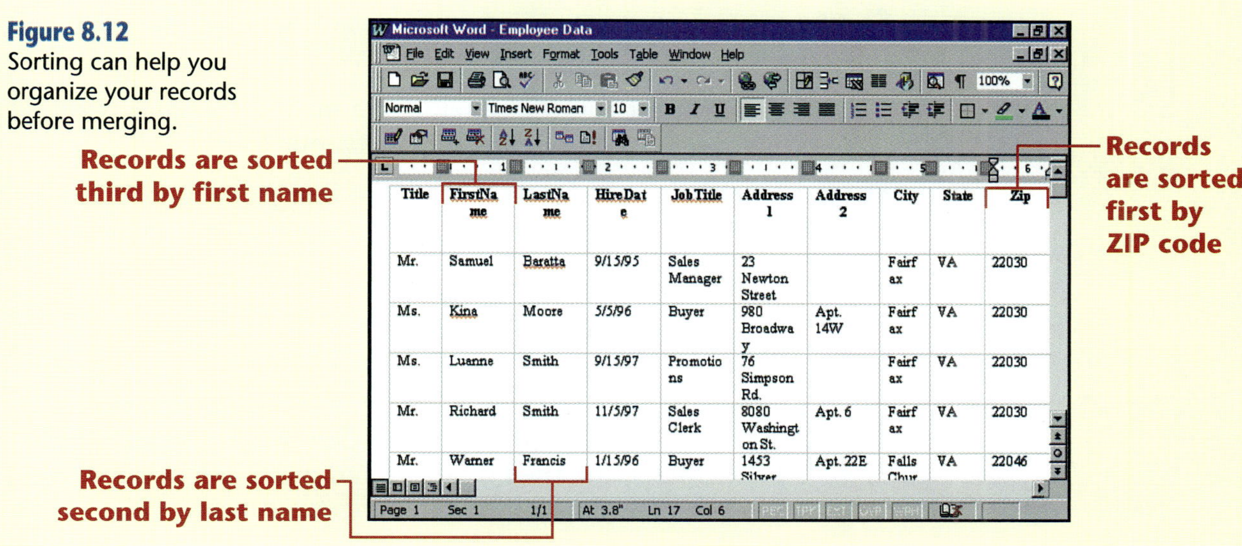

8 **Click OK.**

Word sorts the records in the data source, as shown in Figure 8.12. You also can view the records in the new sorted order in the data form. If you conduct a merge now, the merge documents appear with the records in the current order—sorted by ZIP code, then by last name, and then by first name.

Figure 8.12
Sorting can help you organize your records before merging.

To Sort a Data Source   (continued)

9 **Save the Employee Data document and close it. You can close the Database toolbar, too, if you want.**

In the next lesson, you learn how to filter records.

Lesson 4: Filtering Records for a Merge

Changing the sort order of the data source document is one way to control the way that merge documents are generated. You can also set conditions that *filter* records to determine which ones are actually used in a merge. For example, you might decide you want to send a form letter only to people living in a certain zip code or to people with a last name starting with the letter S. To specify which records are used in a merge, you set filter rules by which Word can filter the records. Word compares each record to the filter rules and then filters out the ones that don't match.

Filter

To set rules or conditions that Word uses to determine which records to include in a merge and which to leave out.

In this lesson, you set rules to filter records so that a form letter is sent only to employees who were hired in 1995. The steps in this lesson assume that you have already learned the basics of conducting a merge. If you haven't, ask your instructor for assistance.

To Filter Records for a Merge

1 **Open the file Proj0802 from the Project-08 folder in this book's CD and save it as** Lunch Letter**.**

This letter has already been set up with merge fields. However, you must identify the letter as a main document for a merge and the Employee Data document as the data source.

2 **Choose Tools, Mail Merge.**

Word opens the Mail Merge Helper.

3 **Click the Create button, select Form Letters and then choose Active Window.**

This step identifies Lunch Letter as the main document. Now, set the Employee Data document as the data source.

4 **Click the Get Data button in the Mail Merge Helper dialog box, select Open Data Source, select the Employee Data file, and then choose Open.**

The Mail Merge Helper should look similar to the one shown in Figure 8.13.

The documents are now ready to merge. If you wanted to generate a form letter for every employee in the data source document, you would click Merge and then go ahead and merge the documents. In this case, however, you want to filter the records first.

Figure 8.13
Use the Mail Merge
Helper to prepare a
main document and
data source for a
merge.

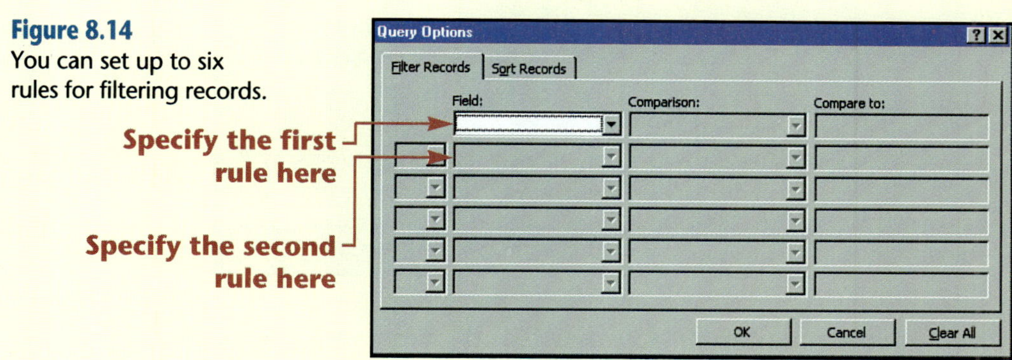

5 **In the Mail Merge Helper dialog box, click the <u>M</u>erge button.**

The Merge dialog box appears.

6 **Click the Query Options button.**

The Query Options dialog box opens, as shown in Figure 8.14. You
can set up to six selection rules that Word uses to filter the records.
Each rule includes the name of a field, a type of comparison, and a
value to which the data in the field will be compared.

Figure 8.14
You can set up to six
rules for filtering records.

7 **On the first line, select HireDate from the Field drop-down
list.**

This action tells Word that you want to filter the records based on the
data in the HireDate field. Notice that as soon as you select a field,
Word enters a default comparison—Equal to—in the Comparison text
box, and a default operator—And—in the operator box between the
first rule and the second rule.

8 **From the Comparison drop-down list, select Less than.**

This step tells Word that you want to include the records that are
less than the value you specify, and filter out all other records.

continues

9 In the Compare To text box, type 1/1/96.

This is the value Word uses for the comparison. If the date in the HireDate field is less than (earlier than) 1/1/96, Word includes the record in the merge. If the data doesn't match, Word filters out the record. To make sure that you get only records from 1995, you can specify another rule for records greater than or equal to 1/1/95.

10 Leave the operator set to And. In the second row, select HireDate from the Field drop-down list, select Greater than or equal from the Comparison drop-down list, and type 1/1/95 **in the Compare To text box.**

This step sets the second rule for the filter. Now the filter is set to include records dated on or after January 1, 1995 but before January 1, 1996—in other words, all records for 1995. The Query Options dialog box should look similar to the one shown in Figure 8.15.

Because you're using the And operator between the first and second rules, the conditions of both rules must be met. You change the And to Or if you want to set a filter for either one rule or another (you use the Or operator in Lesson 5).

Figure 8.15
These rules filter out all records that don't have a hiring date in 1995.

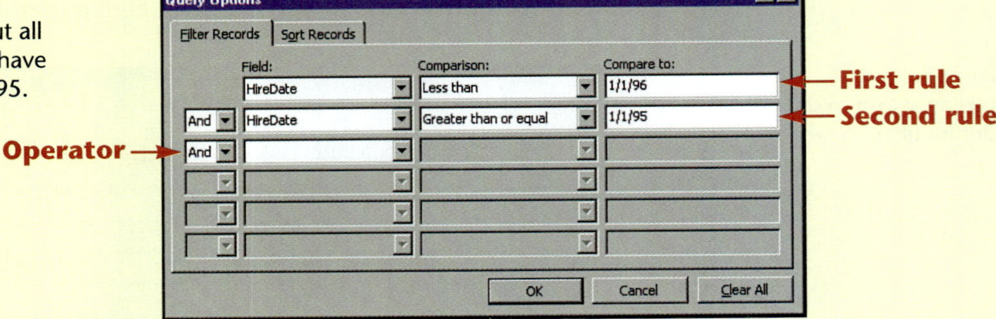

Now see what happens when you merge the documents to a new file.

11 In the Filter Records dialog box, click OK.

Word closes the dialog box and redisplays the Merge dialog box. Notice that a message line tells you that query options have been set for the merge process.

12 Choose Merge.

Word merges the documents and displays them in a new file called Form Letters1. If you scroll through the document, you see that only three records met the rules; all others were filtered out.

13 Save the Form Letters1 document as Merge1 **and then close it.**

14 Save the Lunch Letter document and keep it open.

You have completed the lesson on setting filters. In the next lesson, you learn how to clear the current filter rules and set new rules.

You can sort a data source at the same time that you set filter rules. If you click the Sort Records tab in the Query Options dialog box, you see sort options similar to those in the Sort dialog box (displayed by choosing the Table, Sort command). You can sort by up to three fields, in either ascending or descending order. For more information, refer to Lesson 3.

Lesson 5: Changing the Filter Rules

Word remembers the filter rules from one merge to the next; the next time you merge the Lunch Letter document with the Employee Data data source, the same filters are in effect. You can change the filter to use different records in the merge, or, if you want all records, you can clear the filter completely.

In this lesson, you clear the filter and then enter new filter rules.

To Change the Filter Rules

① In the Lunch Letter document, click the Mail Merge button on the Merge toolbar.

Word displays the Merge dialog box. Notice that the message line near the bottom of the dialog box indicates that query options have been set. It's a good idea to check for query options before you generate a merge, so that you don't filter out records you want to include.

② Click the Query Options button.

Word opens the Query Options dialog box. The rules from the previous merge are still in place.

③ Click the Clear All button.

Word clears all the filter conditions from the dialog box. If you generate the merge now, all records are included. This time, however, you include records for all employees who live in Falls Church or Alexandria.

④ From the Field drop-down list in the first row, select City.

This is the field you compare. Word has automatically entered Equal to in the Comparison list box, which is the correct comparison for this rule.

⑤ In the Compare To text box, type Falls Church.

This action sets the first rule. Now add the rule to include employees living in Alexandria.

⑥ Click the operator arrow button between the first and second rules and choose Or.

For this filter, you need to include records for employees who live in Falls Church *or* Alexandria. If you use the And operator, the City

continues

Word

To Change the Filter Rules   (continued)

field will have to contain *both* Falls Church *and* Alexandria for the record to be included in the merge.

7 **From the second Field drop-down list, select City. Leave Equal to in the Comparison list box, and type** Alexandria **in the Compare to text box.**

This step sets both rules for the filter you want to use, as shown in Figure 8.16.

Figure 8.16
These rules filter out all employees who don't live in either Alexandria or Falls Church.

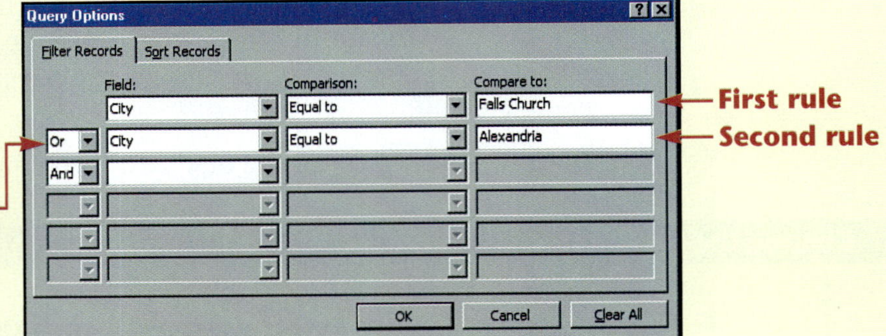

First rule

Second rule

Make sure the operator is Or

8 **Click OK.**

Word closes the Query Options dialog box and redisplays the Merge dialog box.

9 **Choose Merge.**

Word creates a new document called Form Letters2 and displays it onscreen. This time, six records meet the filter rules.

10 **Save the Form Letters2 document as** Merge2 **and then close it.**

You have now completed the lesson on changing filter rules. Before continuing, clear the rules.

11 **Click the Mail Merge Helper button on the Merge toolbar. Then click Query Options.**

This step opens the Mail Merge Helper and then the Query Options dialog box. You can open the Query Options dialog box from either the Merge dialog box or the Mail Merge Helper dialog box.

12 **Click the Clear All button and then click OK.**

This step clears the rules for filtering the records, and then closes the Query Options dialog box.

13 **Close the Mail Merge Helper; then save the Lunch Letter document and keep it open.**

In the next lesson, you learn how to use Word fields to customize a main document.

Lesson 6: Customizing a Main Document with Word Fields

For many form letters, simply customizing the name and address information is enough. However, sometimes you may want the recipient to receive specialized information, even though you're using a form letter. For example, you may want to include a note to the recipients living in a certain zip code if you're planning a trip to visit them soon.

To customize form letters, you can use Word fields to specify when to include additional information. For example, the ASK and FILLIN fields prompt you for information during the merge, and the IF...THEN...ELSE fields let you specify a condition that must be met for the information to be included in the merge document. You insert the field in the main document, and then Word customizes the merge document during the merge.

In this lesson, you use Word fields to customize the Lunch Letter document.

To Customize a Main Document with Word Fields

1 **In the Lunch Letter document, delete the word** Tuesday **from the first sentence in the second paragraph of text.**

There is one luncheon on Tuesday for employees who have been with Oak Grove since 1995, and another on Wednesday for all other employees. You can use an IF field to specify that employees who have been at Oak Grove since before 1/1/96 should receive a letter saying the luncheon is on Tuesday, but that all other employees should receive a letter saying that the luncheon is on Wednesday.

2 **Position the insertion point where the word Tuesday originally was (be sure to leave a space between the word on and the period at the end of the sentence), and click the Insert Word Field button on the Merge toolbar.**

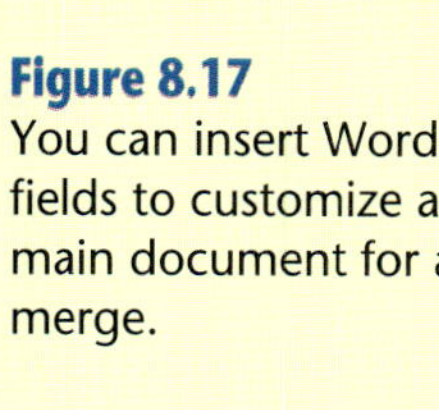

A list of available Word fields drops down, as shown in Figure 8.17.

Figure 8.17
You can insert Word fields to customize a main document for a merge.

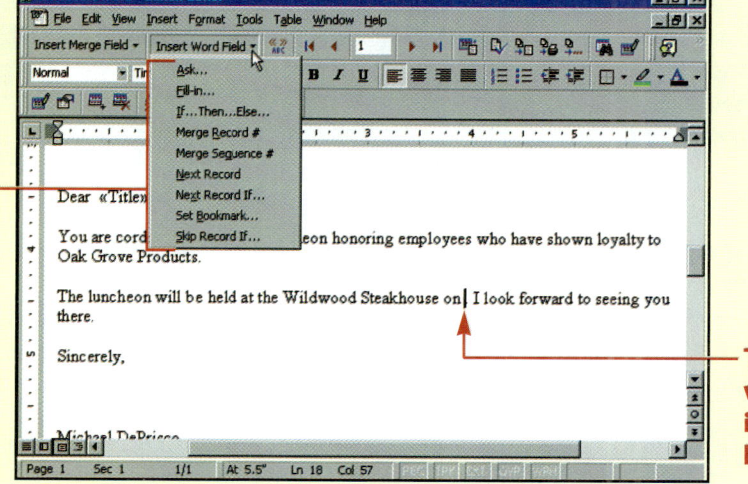

Select a field here

The field will be inserted here

continues

To Customize a Main Document with Word Fields   (continued)

Table 8.1 describes the Word fields that you can use to customize a form letter mail merge main document.

Table 8.1 Word Fields for Customizing Main Documents

Field	Description
ASK	Displays a prompt as each record is merged, asking for information; then assigns your response as the value for a bookmark. The response is in the main document at the location where you inserted the bookmark. You can insert the bookmark in more than one place in the main document.
FILL-IN	Displays a prompt as each record is merged, asking for information; then enters your response at the FILL-IN field location in the main document.
IF...THEN...ELSE	Displays information in the main document based on whether a record meets specified criteria.
MERGE RECORD #	Displays the data source number of the record (the order in which the records are stored in the data source).
MERGE SEQUENCE #	Displays the print order number of the record (the order in which the records are printed).
SET BOOKMARK	Assigns a value to a bookmark and then displays the value at each location of the bookmark field in the main document.
SKIP RECORD IF	Causes the current record not to merge if specified criteria are met.

3 Click If...Then...Else.

Word displays the Insert Word Field: IF dialog box (see Figure 8.18). First you set a rule that specifies a condition that must be met.

Figure 8.18
Setting an IF condition is similar to setting a rule for filtering records.

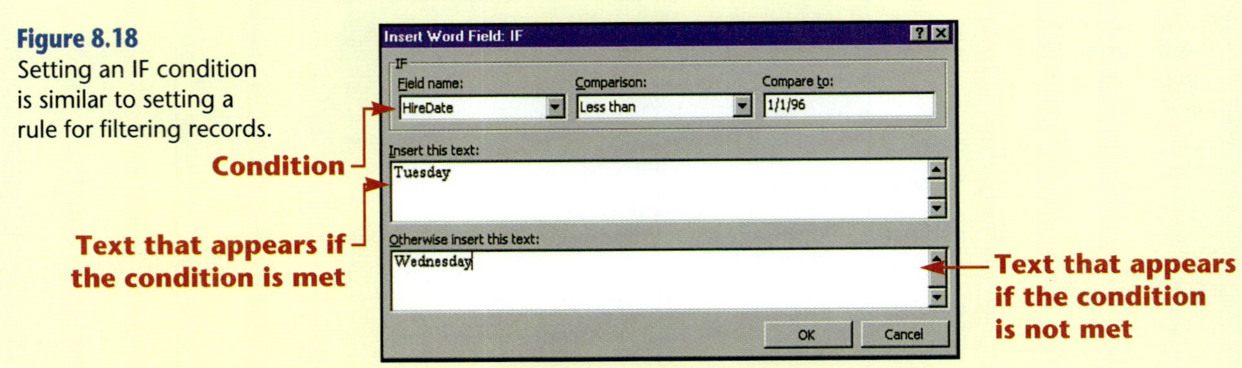

Condition

Text that appears if the condition is met

Text that appears if the condition is not met

4 Select HireDate from the Field Name drop-down list.

This is the field that Word compares.

5 Select Less than from the Comparison drop-down list and type 1/1/96 in the Compare To text box.

This step sets the condition for the IF field. Now you specify the text that should be entered in the document if the condition is met.

6 In the Insert This Text text box, type Tuesday.

This is the text to be displayed if the date in the HireDate field is less than (earlier than) 1/1/96.

7 In the Otherwise Insert This Text text box, type Wednesday.

This is the text to be displayed if the date in the HireDate field is 1/1/96 or later. The dialog box should look similar to the one in Figure 8.18.

8 Click OK.

Word inserts the field at the insertion point location. When you merge the documents, it displays text according to whether the condition you specified is met in each record. By default, the field displays the text that appears in the first record. Try merging the documents now.

9 Click the Merge to New Document button on the Merge toolbar.

Word displays the merge documents in a new document named Form Letters3. Notice that some of the letters say the luncheon is Wednesday and some say the luncheon is Tuesday, depending on the hire date information in the employee record.

10 Save the Form Letters3 document as Merge3 and close it.

11 Save the Lunch Letter document and close it.

In the next lesson, you use a different main document to learn how to use an Outlook Address Book as a data source.

Lesson 7: Using an Outlook Address Book as a Data Source

Word 97 comes with an information manager application called Outlook. One of the features of Outlook is an address book (or contact list) that you can maintain to keep track of information about people you contact during your workday. You can use the Outlook Address Book as a data source for a Word mail merge.

In this lesson, you learn how to use your Outlook Address Book as a data source. The steps in this lesson assume that you already have entered data in Outlook in either the Address Book or the Contact List. If you have an address book in a different application, these steps should work as well.

Word

To Use an Outlook Address Book as a Data Source

1 Open the file Proj0803 from the Project-08 folder on the CD and save it as Address Book Letter**.**

This document has already been set up with mail merge fields (see Figure 8.19). However, you must identify the document as a merge main document and select the data source for the merge. Notice that the field names are different from the field names in a typical Word data source. These field names correspond to the field names used in the Outlook Address Book.

Figure 8.19
The field names in the main document correspond to the Outlook Address Book field names.

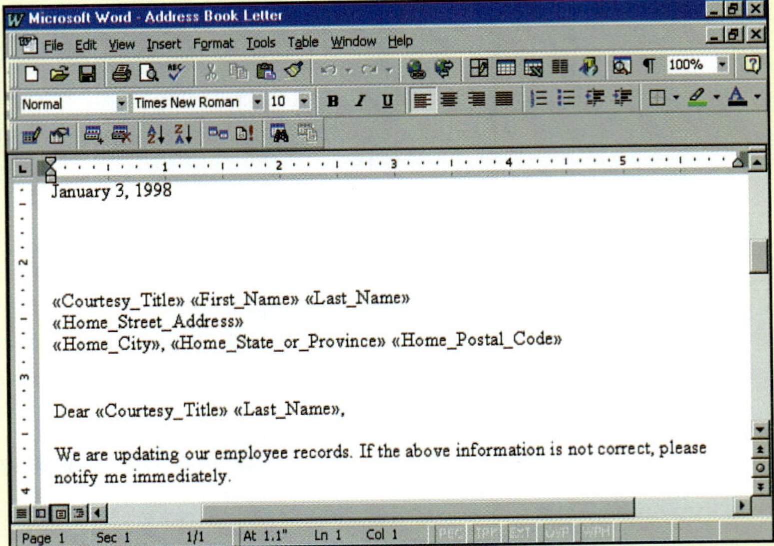

If you have problems...

If you're using a different Address Book, the merge field names in your data source may not be the same as those in the Address Book Letter document. Once you get the data source for the merge, you can edit the main document to replace the merge fields in the Address Book Letter document with the merge fields in your data source. If you need assistance, ask your instructor.

2 Choose Tools, Mail Merge.

Word displays the Mail Merge Helper.

3 Click Create, select Form Letters, and click the Active Window button.

This step identifies Address Book Letter as the main document.

4 Click the Get Data button; then select Use Address Book.

Word displays a list of available address book files, as shown in Figure 8.20. This list varies, depending on the applications and files you have installed on your computer.

Figure 8.20
You can select any one of the address book files you have set up on your computer as a data source for a mail merge.

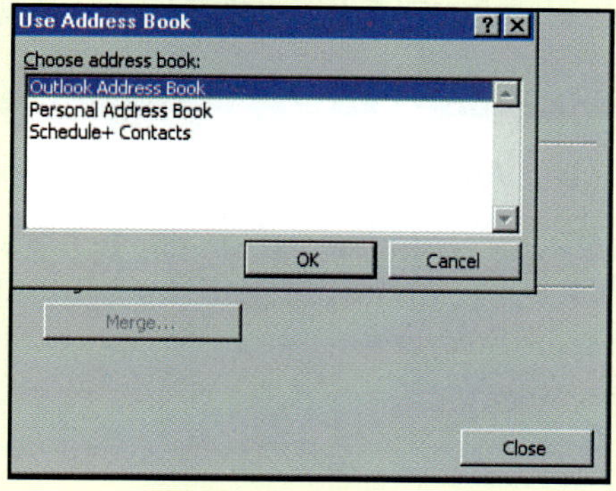

5 **Select the address book you want to use—in this case, Outlook Address Book—and then click OK.**

Word starts converting the data in the address book file. If you selected an Outlook Address Book, it displays the Choose Profile dialog box, as shown in Figure 8.21.

Figure 8.21
When you use Outlook, you can select the profile that contains the file you want to use.

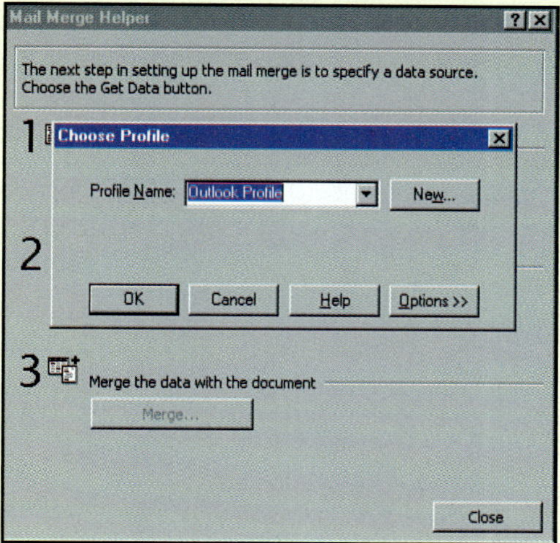

6 **Select the Profile file you want to use and then click OK.**

Word finishes converting the address book file so you can use it in Word as a data source, and then displays the Mail Merge Helper dialog box. The address book is temporarily saved as a virtual file, not an actual Word file. You can view the data source by using the data form, just as if it were a Word document, but you can't edit the file or save it.

7 **Click the Merge button in the Mail Merge Helper dialog box.**

The Merge dialog box opens.

8 **Click Merge.**

Word merges the Address Book Letter document with the Outlook Address Book data, and displays it in a new document called Form Letters4.

continues

Word

To Use an Outlook Address Book as a Data Source   (continued)

⑨ Save the Form Letters4 document as `Merge4` and then close it.

⑩ Save the Address Book Letter document and close it.

You have completed all of the lessons in this project. If you have completed your session on the computer, exit Word and Windows 95 before turning off your computer. Otherwise, continue with the "Checking Your Skills" and "Applying Your Skills" sections.

Exam Notes

You can perform a merge with other data files, including Microsoft Access. In the Mail Merge dialog box, click the Get data button. Change to the drive and folder where the Access file is stored, and choose All Files from the Files of Type drop-down list. Select your database file and click Open. You can now merge with the Access database.

Project Summary

To	Do This
Edit a data source record	Open the data source document and use the table or the data form to make the necessary changes.
Delete a data source record	Open the data form and find the record you want to delete. Then choose <u>D</u>elete. Alternatively, position the insertion point in the record row in the table and click the Delete Record button on the Database toolbar.
Rename a field	Type the change in the data source table; or click the Manage Fields button on the Database toolbar, select the field name, click Re<u>n</u>ame, type the new name, and click OK.
Add a field	Insert a column in the data source table and type the field name in the header row; or click the Manage Fields button on the Database toolbar, type the new field name, and click <u>A</u>dd.
Remove a field	Delete the column from the data source document's table; or click the Manage Fields button on the Database toolbar, select the field name and click <u>R</u>emove.
Sort records	Position the insertion point in the field to sort by and click the Sort Ascending or Sort Descending button on the Database toolbar.

To	Do This
Sort records by more than one field	Choose Table, Sort, select the first field to sort by, the second field to sort by, and the third field to sort by, and then click OK.
Set filter rules	Click Query Options in the Mail Merge Helper or Merge dialog box. Select the field and the comparison type for the first rule; then type the data to compare in the Compare To text box. If necessary, set additional rules on each subsequent line. Click OK.
Clear filter rules	Click Query Options in the Mail Merge Helper or Merge dialog box. Click Clear All. Set new rules or click Close.
Add Word fields to a main document	Position the insertion point in the main document; then click the Insert Word Field button on the Merge toolbar and select the field to insert. If necessary, type prompt or text information; then click OK.
Use an Address Book as a data source	Use the Mail Merge Helper to create a main document; then choose Get Data. Select Use Address Book. Select the Address Book file and profile you want to use. If necessary, edit the main document to insert the merge fields.

Checking Your Skills

True/False

For each of the following statements, check *T* or *F* to indicate whether the statement is true or false.

__T __F **1.** In a Word document, data source information is formatted as a table.

__T __F **2.** You can't change the name of a field in a data source.

__T __F **3.** You can sort data source records by up to three fields.

__T __F **4.** You can filter data source records by up to six rules.

__T __F **5.** Filtering rules are cleared automatically once the merge is complete.

__T __F **6.** When you rename a field, all data currently entered in the field is deleted.

__T __F **7.** By default, records appear in a merge document in alphabetical order.

__T __F **8.** When you use the And operator between two filter rules, the conditions of both rules must be met.

__T __F **9.** You can sort a data source at the same time that you set filter rules.

__T __F **10.** Word fields are exactly the same as merge fields.

Multiple Choice

Circle the letter of the correct answer for each of the following questions.

1. Which toolbar lets you edit a data source or data source fields?

    a. Merge

    b. Sort

    c. Database

    d. Datasource

2. In a data source table, what is the first row called?

    a. Field row

    b. Header row

    c. Record row

    d. Data row

3. What Word 97 application comes with an address book feature that you can use as a merge data source?

    a. Access

    b. Excel

    c. PowerPoint

    d. Outlook

4. What should you use to display the data source when you want to see only one record at a time?

    a. A data form

    b. A table

    c. A Word field

    d. An address book

5. What type of sort should you use to list records by date?

    a. Numerical

    b. Alphabetical

    c. Ascending

    d. Descending

6. Which toolbar button automatically sorts records alphabetically from A to Z?

    a. Sort Descending

    b. Sort Alphabetically

    c. Sort A-Z

    d. Sort Ascending

7. What do you do to the data source to specify which records are used in a merge?

    a. Edit it

    b. Filter it

    c. Sort it

    d. Open it

8. What is the default comparison in a filter rule?

    a. Greater than

    b. Less than

    c. Equal to

    d. Not equal to

9. Which operator should you use between filter use if you want to set a filter for either one rule or the other?

    a. And

    b. Or

    c. Else

    d. Other

10. To include all records in a merge, what do you have to do to the filter?

    a. Clear it

    b. Delete it

    c. Copy it

    d. Query it

Completion

In the blank provided, write the correct answer for each of the following statements.

1. Use the _______________ Word field to print specified text only on the records that meet certain criteria.

2. Set rules to _______________ out the records you don't want to include in a merge.

3. To change a record, edit the merge _______________ _______________.

4. In the data source, field names appear in the _______________ _______________ of a table.

5. When you want to filter records that match either of two rules, you must use the _______________ operator.

6. When you want to filter records that match two rules, you must use the _______________ operator.

7. You can _______ through the data source to find and display the record you want to edit

8. The _______ _______ displays one record of information at a time.

9. If you want to change the order of letters in a merge, you can _______ the data source before merging.

10. Set filter selection rules in the _______ Options dialog box.

Matching

In the blank next to each of the following terms or phrases, write the letter of the corresponding term or phrase. (Note that some letters may be used more than once.)

a. Table

b. Header row

c. And

d. Rule

e. Sort Descending

f. Outlook

g. Or

h. Restore

i. Data Form

j. Skip Record If

_______ **1.** Specification for filtering records

_______ **2.** Operator for filtering according to more than one rule

_______ **3.** Operator for filtering according to either of two rules

_______ **4.** Location of field names in data source

_______ **5.** Method of showing one record of a data source at a time

_______ **6.** Method of showing all records of a data source at a time

_______ **7.** Word field that causes the current record not to merge if specified criteria are met

_______ **8.** Information manager application that comes with Word 97

_______ **9.** Button that reverses changes made to a record in a data source

_______ **10.** Button that sorts numerical fields from 9 to 0

Applying Your Skills

Practice

The following exercises enable you to practice the skills you have learned in this project. Take a few minutes to work through these exercises now.

Modifying a Data Source for a Customer Mailing List

In this exercise, use the skills you have learned to customize the data source for a customer mailing list.

To modify the data source, follow these steps:

1. Open the file Proj0804 from the Project-08 folder on the CD and save it in your Practices folder as CTA List2.

2. Change the Title field name to Salutation.

3. Delete the record for Deborah Kane.

4. Sort the records alphabetically by company name.

5. Save the file and, if requested by your instructor, print it. Close the document.

Filtering Records for a Merge

In this exercise, use the skills you have learned in this project to filter records for a merge.

To filter records, follow these steps:

1. Open the file Proj0805 from the Project-08 folder on the CD and save it in your Practices folder as CTA Letter3.

2. Use the Mail Merge Helper to make CTA Letter3 a main document.

3. Use the Mail Merge Helper to open the CTA List2 from the previous skill as the data source.

4. Set query option rules so that only customers who work at Smithson Co. or Angier Lane, Inc. receive the mailing.

5. Merge the records to a new document and save it as CTA Merge2 in your Practices folder.

6. If requested by your instructor, merge the records to the printer.

7. Save and close all open files.

Customizing the CTA Mailing

In this exercise, use the skills you have learned in this project to customize the form letters to your customers.

To customize the CTA mailing, follow these steps:

1. Open the file Proj0806 from the Project-08 folder on the CD and save it in your Practices folder with the name CTA Letter4.

2. Set up the CTA Letter4 document for a form letter merge, using the CTA List2 document as a data source.

3. Edit the CTA Letter4 document to insert an If...Then...Else field on a blank line below the closing.

4. Specify that if the records are from Fairfax, Word should print the following line:

   ```
   P.S. I'm planning to be in town next month and will give you a
   call.
   ```

5. Clear all query options, merge the records to a new document, and save the merge document in your Practices folder as CTA Merge3.

6. If requested by your instructor, merge the records to the printer.

7. Save and close all open files.

Sorting and Filtering Your Résumé Mailing

In this exercise, use the skills you have learned in this project to sort and filter the data source for your cover letter mailing.

To sort and filter your résumé mailing, follow these steps:

1. Open the file Proj0807 from the Project-08 folder on the CD and save it in your Practices folder with the name Resume Letter2.

2. Open the file Proj0808 from the Project-08 folder on the CD and save it in your Practices folder with the name Resume Addresses2.

3. Sort the Resume Addresses2 document numerically by zip code, then alphabetically by last name, then alphabetically by first name.

4. Set up the Resume Letter2 document for a form letter mail merge, using the Resume Addresses2 document as the data source.

5. Set query options to print letters only for companies in Indiana or Massachusetts.

6. Merge the records to a new document, and save it in your Practices folder as Resume Merge2.

7. If requested by your instructor, print the merge file.

8. Save and close all open documents.

Using an Address Book as a Data Source

If you have an Address Book in another application, try using it as a data source for a mail merge.

To use an address book as a data source, follow these steps:

1. Open the file Proj0809 from the Project-08 folder on the CD and save it in your Practices folder with the name New Letter.

2. Use the Mail Merge Helper to make the New Letter document a main document.

3. Use the Mail Merge Helper to set your address book as the data source.

4. Edit the main document to insert the merge fields for the customer's name and address where necessary.

5. Merge to a new document; then save the document in your `Practices` folder as `Letter Merge`.

6. If requested by your instructor, print the merge documents. Then save all open files and close them.

Challenge

The following challenges enable you to use your problem-solving skills. Take time to work through these exercises now.

Sorting and Filtering the CTC Mailing

In this exercise, you use the skills you have just learned to sort and filter the Computer Training Concepts mailing. Open the file Proj0810 from the Project-08 folder on the CD and save it in your `Challenges` folder as `Cover Letter5`. Then open the file Proj0811 from the Project-08 folder on the CD and save it in your `Challenges` folder as `CTC Names2`. Use these two documents to create a mass mailing in alphabetical order by last name, going only to customers in Chicago. Save the resulting merge file in your `Challenges` folder as `CTC Merge2`. If requested by your instructor, print the merge file, then save and close all open documents.

Changing the Filter for the CTC Letter

In this exercise, use the same main document and data source files you used in the previous lesson. Open the Cover Letter5 document, then change the filter so that you print letters for companies in Indiana and Illinois, sorted alphabetically by company name, then by last name, then by first name. Save the resulting merge file in your `Challenges` folder as `CTC Merge3`. If requested by your instructor, print the merge file, then save and close all open documents.

Sorting and Filtering the Health Club Renewal Mailing

In this exercise, you use the skills you have just learned to sort and filter the health club renewal mailing. Open the file Proj0812 From the Project-08 folder on the CD and save it in your `Challenges` folder as `Renewal5`. Open the file Proj0813 From the Project-08 folder on the CD and save it in your `Challenges` folder as `Club List2`. Set up the two files for a merge. Sort the data source alphabetically by city, then by last name, then by first name. Filter the data source so letters print only for members with last names beginning with letters falling between G and R in the alphabet. Save the resulting merge file in your `Challenges` folder as `Club Merge2`. If requested by your instructor, print the merge file, then save and close all open documents.

Changing the Sort and Filters for the Health Club Renewal Mailing

In this exercise, you use the same files you used in the previous exercise to create a different mailing for the health club. Open the Renewal5 document. Change the Query Options so that you can print letters for people whose memberships expire in June or July. Sort the letters by ZIP code, then by last name, then by first name. Save the resulting merge file in your `Challenges` folder as `Club Merge3`. If requested by your instructor, print the merge file, then save and close all open documents.

Sorting and Filtering the Family Reunion Mailing

In this exercise, you use the skills you have just learned to sort and filter the family reunion mailing. Open the file Proj0814 From the Project-08 folder on the CD and save it in your `Challenges` folder as `Reunion2`. Open the file Proj0815 From the Project-08 folder on the CD and save it in your `Challenges` folder as `Reunion Addresses2`. Set up the two files for a merge. Sort the data source alphabetically by first name, then by last name. Filter the data source so letters print only for relatives who do not live in Indiana. Save the resulting merge file in your `Challenges` folder as `Reunion Merge2`. If requested by your instructor, print the merge file, then save and close all open documents.

You have completed the project and the associated lessons, as well as the "Checking Your Skills" and "Applying Your Skills" sections. Now use the PinPoint software evaluation mode to assess your comprehension of the specific exam tasks you have just learned. You can also use the PinPoint Trainer Mode and the Show Me tutorials to practice these specific exam tasks.

Project 9

Nine

Automating Your Work

Using AutoText, AutoFormat, and Macros

In this Project, you learn how to:

Objectives   ## Required Activities

➤ Create AutoText Entries

➤ Insert and Modify an AutoText Entry

➤ Delete an AutoText Entry

➤ Use AutoFormat to Clean Up a Document

➤ Record and Run a Macro … … … … … … … … … …Record and run macros

➤ Edit Macros … … … … … … … … … … … … … … … …Edit Macros
Copy, rename, and delete macros

Why Would I Do This?

t's frustrating when you have to type the same passage of text over and over. You can probably think of several examples from your work: your company's name and address, the standard closing of a form letter, or even an entire paragraph in a contract. These commonly used pieces of text can require lots of time to type, format, and check the spelling. It would be helpful if you could create them once, make sure that they were perfect, and then reuse them when you need them, in any document that you create.

Word includes several features that can help you automate tasks such as reusing text and formatting text while you type. For example, with AutoText, you can create a special entry that permanently stores the text. You can then recall the text at any time and insert it into any document—spell-checked, formatted, and ready to go.

This project shows you how to use AutoText, AutoCorrect, and AutoFormat. You also learn to automate and simplify common word processing tasks by creating macros. Taking the time now to learn these automation techniques saves you lots of time in the future.

Lesson 1: Creating AutoText Entries

Imagine that you must write many business letters. Each time that you create a particular letter, you type some of the same text, such as your company's name and a standard signature block. It would be handy if you could save these frequently used bits of text in a special location so that you could use them when you wanted, without actually typing them. Word's **AutoText** feature enables you to do just that. AutoText is a stored piece of text, or a graphic image of any size, that you can instantly insert into any document.

You can create separate AutoText entries for your company's name, standard signature block, or any other passage that you type frequently. Word can store AutoText so that it always retains its original formatting, or you can save an entry as "plain text" to be formatted when inserted into a document. You can even store some kinds of graphic images and formatted tables as AutoText entries, and then quickly add them to a document without cutting and pasting them from another program.

This lesson shows you how to create AutoText entries. You open an existing, finished letter, and borrow text from it to create AutoText entries for your company's name and for the signature block. Later in this project, you learn how to insert those AutoText entries into other letters.

AutoText is a very powerful (and underused) feature of Word. It enables you to store many different pieces of text and retrieve them instantly, whenever you want. Experienced Word users take full advantage of AutoText. If you talk to "old-time" Word users, you might hear them mention using "glossaries" in Word. In older versions of Word, AutoText entries were called glossaries.

To Create an AutoText Entry

❶ In a blank document, start typing the salutation, `To Whom It May Concern:`.

By the time that you finish typing **To Whom**, a ScreenTip appears that says To Whom It May Concern:, as shown in Figure 9.1. You can press either ⏎Enter or F3 to complete the phrase. Or you can just keep typing and the ScreenTip goes away.

Figure 9.1
A ScreenTip enables you to insert a phrase quickly.

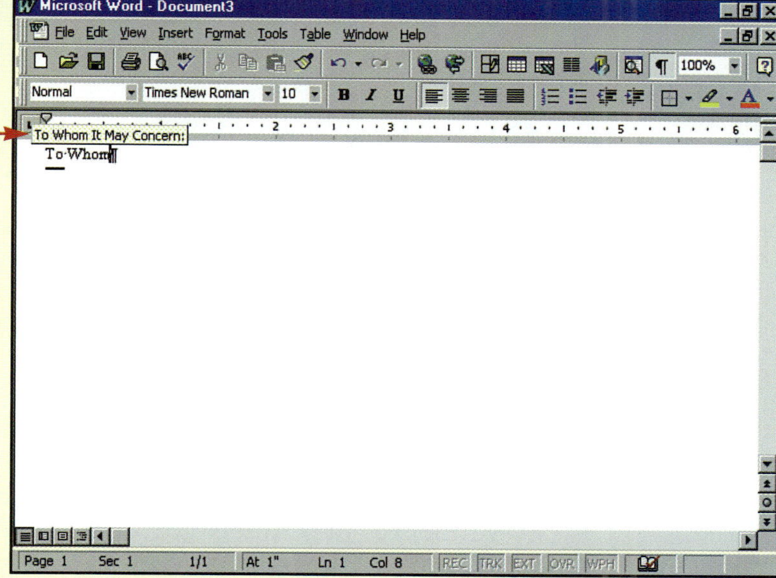

❷ Press ⏎Enter **to insert the rest of the phrase To Whom It May Concern:.**

"To Whom It May Concern:" is one of about 40 AutoText entries that come with Word 97. To view a list of AutoText entries, you can choose Insert, AutoText, then browse through the categories.

If you have problems...

If a ScreenTip does not appear when you begin typing To Whom It May Concern:, the feature is turned off. Choose Insert, AutoText, AutoText, then select the Show AutoComplete Tip for AutoText and Dates check box.

Inside Stuff

AutoText is just one aspect of a new feature called AutoComplete. AutoComplete helps you insert several other items, such as the current date, your name, or a day of the week. For example, if you begin typing the current date (on October 15, 1998), typing `Octo` displays the ScreenTip "October." Pressing ⏎Enter or F3 inserts the rest of October. Pressing the Spacebar brings up another tip, October 15, 1998. Press ⏎Enter or F3 to insert the whole date, or just keep typing.

Create an AutoText entry in a real situation.

continues

To Create an AutoText Entry **(continued)**

3 **Close the document without saving it, then open the file Proj0901 in folder Project-09 from this book's CD. Save it as** `Marshall Letter`.

First, make sure that you display any nonprinting characters (such as spaces and paragraph returns).

4 **If nonprinting characters do not appear, turn them on by clicking the Standard toolbar's Show/Hide button.**

Use the company name in this letter to create the first AutoText entry.

5 **In the body of the letter, select Reising Star Production Company by dragging across it with the mouse.**

Don't select the space after the word Company. When creating AutoText entries, pay attention to such details as spaces and punctuation, or you might insert characters that you want—or don't want. This text becomes your first AutoText entry.

6 **Choose Insert, AutoText, New.**

The Create AutoText dialog box appears, as shown in Figure 9.2. The first part of the selected text appears in the Please name your AutoText entry text box. Word uses this text as the name for the AutoText entry unless you change it. Names of AutoText entries should be short and easy to remember so that you can use them quickly. The name can be as short as one character or as long as 32 characters, including spaces and special characters.

You give this AutoText entry a shorter name.

Figure 9.2
The Create AutoText dialog box.

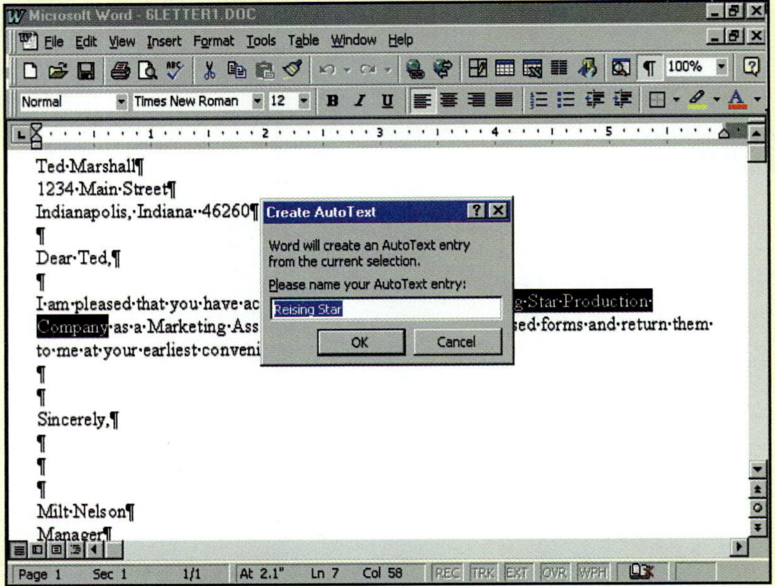

7 **Type** r **to replace** Reising Star **in the box, then choose OK.**

You just renamed the AutoText entry with a very short name. Its new name is r. Word adds this new entry to its list of AutoText entries.

You have created your first AutoText entry. You can now add your company's name to any document just by typing one letter and pressing F3. Now create an AutoText entry from the letter's signature block.

8 **Select the entire closing of the letter, beginning with the word** Sincerely, **and down through the blank paragraph mark at the end of the document, as shown in Figure 9.3.**

You use all this text for the next AutoText entry.

Figure 9.3
Selecting the letter's signature block.

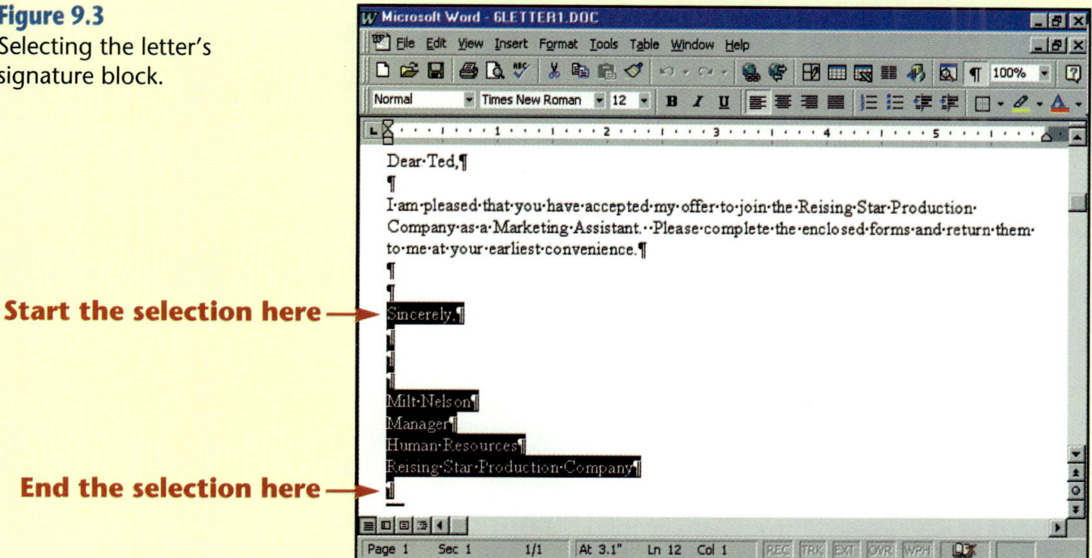

Start the selection here →

End the selection here →

9 **Choose** Insert, AutoText, New.

To create a new AutoText entry for selected text quickly, press Alt+F3.

The Create AutoText dialog box opens again. Sincerely, appears in the box. Now give the signature block a shorter name.

10 **Type** sig **in the box, then choose OK.**

The signature block entry's new name is sig. You just created a second AutoText entry.

11 **Close the document without saving.**

You do not have to save the document to save the AutoText entries. They are automatically saved and ready for use in any document.

If you plan to create or insert many AutoText entries, you might want to use the AutoText toolbar. To display this toolbar, choose View, Toolbars, AutoText. When you're finished using the AutoText toolbar, choose View, Toolbars, AutoText again to turn it off.

AutoCorrect looks for common typing and spelling mistakes in your document and automatically corrects them as you type (once you press Spacebar). For example, AutoCorrect replaces teh with the. It also fixes common capitalization mistakes.

AutoText enables you to define and store frequently used sections of text or graphics, then insert them into a document as needed. For example, you could define an AutoText entry containing your complete name and address, and then insert it into a document with a few keystrokes.

When you do create text automation entries, be certain that your AutoText shortcut is not an abbreviation with multiple uses. For example, using MS as a shortcut for Microsoft may cause problems when you have to send letters to Ms. Brown.

Lesson 2: Inserting and Modifying an AutoText Entry

Two new AutoText entries are now available to insert into any document that you open or create from scratch. In this lesson, you open an unfinished letter and put the finishing touches on it by inserting the two new AutoText entries. Then you learn to modify an AutoText entry.

To Insert and Modify an AutoText Entry

1 **Open the folder Project-09 and the file Proj0902 from this book's CD. Save it as** Fisher Letter.

The first paragraph is not complete. Insert the company's name at the end of the line and complete the paragraph.

2 **Place the insertion point after the last space at the end of the incomplete paragraph.**

By placing the insertion point after the space, you ensure that the spacing is correct when you insert the AutoText entry.

3 **Type the letter r, then press F3.**

Word inserts the first AutoText entry, replacing the r that you just typed. (Remember: r is the name of the AutoText entry for the company's name.) Because the AutoText entry is only one letter and no ScreenTip appears, you needed to press F3 rather than ↵Enter to insert the AutoText entry.

If you have problems...

If Word didn't insert the company name, you might have pressed Spacebar after typing r and before pressing F3. Delete the r, type it again, and then press F3 immediately after you type r. If Word still doesn't insert the company name, you might have given the AutoText entry a different name—or you might not have actually created it. To check, choose Insert, AutoText. Scroll through the list of names until you find the one for the company name. If you do not have an entry for the company name, go back to Lesson 1 and create one.

4 **Finish the sentence by adding a space and typing** `as Assistant Controller.` **(Make sure you add the period at the end of the sentence.) Then type** `Please complete the enclosed forms and return them to me at your earliest convenience.`

This sentence finishes the paragraph.

5 **Press** `↵Enter` **three times.**

Now insert the signature block AutoText entry at the end of the letter.

6 **Type** `sig` **and press** `F3`.

Word inserts the signature block at the end of the letter. Your document should now look like the one in Figure 9.4.

Figure 9.4
The completed Fisher letter.

Signature block inserted with AutoText

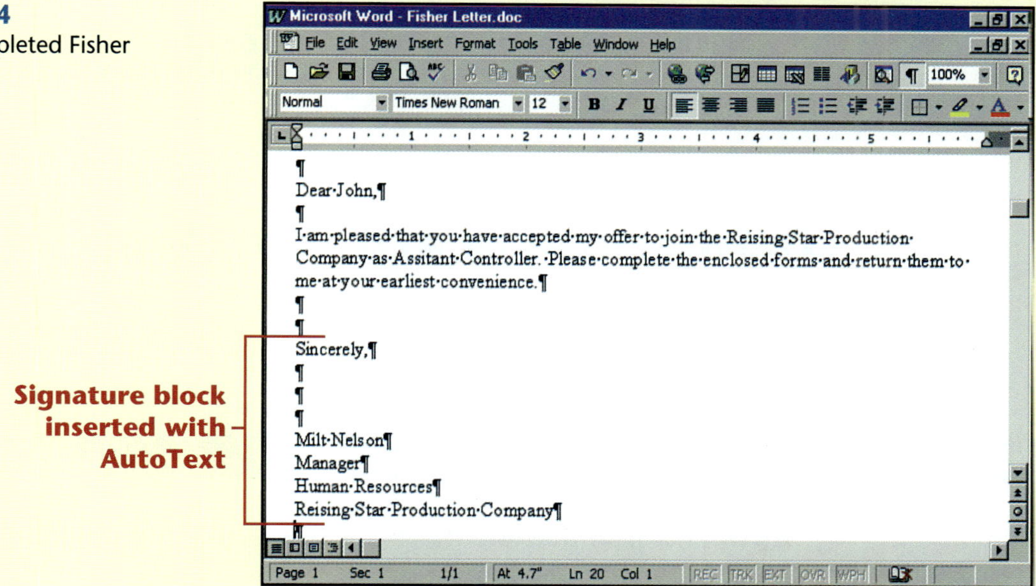

Milt Nelson has earned a promotion. He is now a director rather than a manager, so the AutoText entry for his signature block needs to be modified. Next, you learn to modify an AutoText entry.

7 **In the closing, change the word Manager to** `Director`.

8 **Select the entire signature block, starting with the word** `Sincerely` **and including the last blank paragraph mark.**

This is the original signature block, but with the modification.

9 **Choose Insert, AutoText, New.**

The Create AutoText dialog box appears.

10 **Type** `sig` **and choose OK.**

11 **When asked to redefine the AutoText entry, choose Yes.**

The warning box disappears, and Word redefines the old AutoText entry by overwriting it with the new text that you selected. The

Word

To Insert and Modify an AutoText Entry (continued)

AutoText entry keeps its old name, but now contains the modified information.

Now make sure that the modified AutoText entry works.

12 Move the insertion point to the bottom of the document, then type sig and press F3.

Word inserts the modified AutoText entry.

13 Click the Standard toolbar's Undo button twice.

Clicking the Undo button the first time deletes the AutoText entry. Clicking Undo the second time deletes sig. Now you have only one letter closing.

14 Save and close the document.

You are saving the document because you changed it, not because you need to save the AutoText entry. Remember that Word automatically saves AutoText entries.

Lesson 3: Deleting an AutoText Entry

You just learned that Milt Nelson has been fired. That's the last letter that you ever have to type for him! Therefore, you can delete the AutoText signature block that bears his name.

To Delete an AutoText Entry

1 Open a new document.

2 Choose Insert, AutoText, AutoText.

The AutoCorrect dialog box opens with the AutoText tab selected as shown in Figure 9.5. You can use this dialog box to add, delete, and insert AutoText entries.

Figure 9.5
The AutoCorrect dialog box displays all AutoText entries.

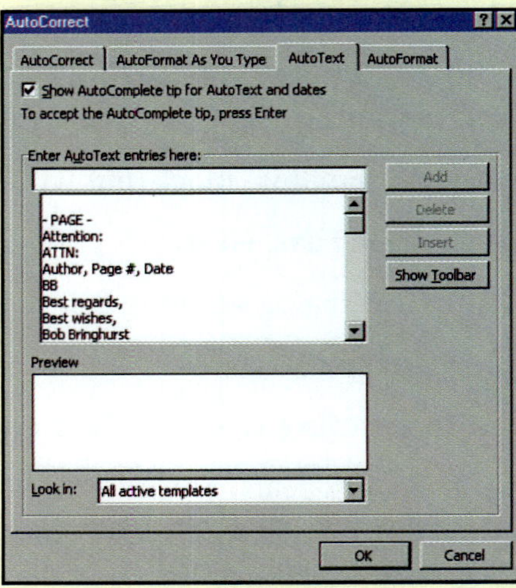

3 **Type** sig **in the Enter AutoText entries here text box.**

This action selects the signature block AutoText entry.

4 **Click the Delete button.**

You have deleted the entry. Go ahead and delete the company name entry, too.

5 **Type** r **in the Enter AutoText entries here text box, then click Delete.**

You have deleted the r entry. While you're in the AutoCorrect dialog box, take a look at the AutoCorrect feature to see what happens while you type.

6 **Click the AutoCorrect tab in the AutoCorrect dialog box.**

AutoCorrect options appear, as shown in Figure 9.6. Like the AutoText feature, the AutoCorrect feature helps you type what you intend to type, fixing many misspellings and typos. For example, if you type teh rather than the, Word changes the misspelling to the— while you type. Or, if you type (c), Word changes it to © after you add a space (if you really want (c) rather than ©, press ⬅Backspace) or click Undo).

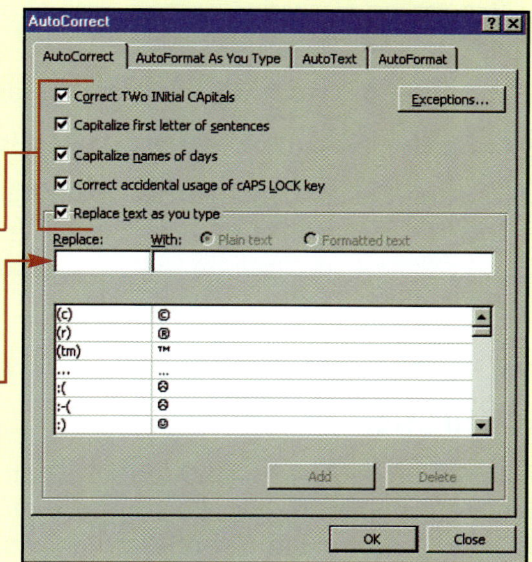

Figure 9.6
AutoCorrect automatically fixes certain misspellings and typos on the spot.

When selected, these options are applied as you type

You can insert new AutoCorrect entries here

7 **Click the AutoFormat As You Type tab.**

The AutoFormat As You Type page appears, as shown in Figure 9.7. Like the AutoCorrect feature, the AutoFormat As You Type feature works behind the scenes, fixing your text while you type. When you type 1/2, for example, Word converts it to the ½ symbol after you add the next space.

8 **Click the Close button to close the AutoCorrect dialog box.**

Now explore how these various AutoCorrect features work.

To Delete an AutoText Entry   (continued)

Figure 9.7
The options of the
AutoFormat As You
Type page.

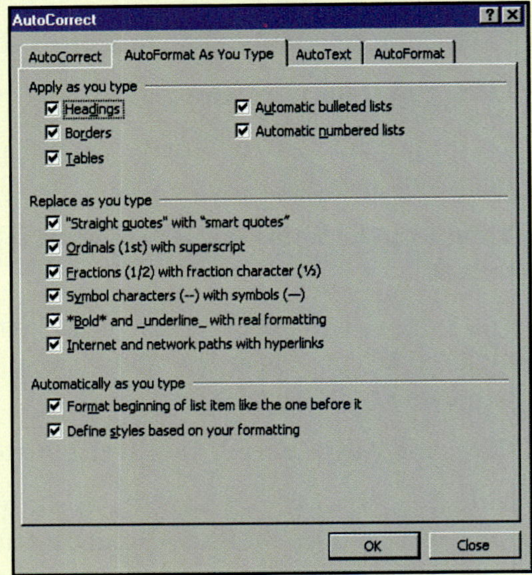

9 **In the blank document, type the following sentence, including the typing mistakes. Notice the changes that occur while you type.**

STar Gazer(tm) executives made none of teh "important" changes we discussed—I don't know why.

The AutoCorrect feature fixes your typing while you type.

10 **Close the document without saving it.**

Deleting the AutoText entries doesn't affect the document, so you don't need to save it.

Lesson 4: Using AutoFormat to Clean Up a Document

Face it: You probably write and receive 10 times as many email messages as letters. You frequently have to copy text from these email messages and other word processors into your Word documents. When you do, your document might be missing such formatting as copyright symbols, curly quotation marks, and long dashes, or even simple formatting such as bold and italics. You can use the AutoFormat feature to clean up documents that haven't benefitted from the AutoFormat and AutoCorrect features.

In this lesson, you open a document copied from an email message and use AutoFormat to reformat it automatically.

❶ Open the folder Project-09 and the file Proj0903 from the book's CD. Save it as `Mime Backlash`**.**

This file was copied from an email message into Word (see Figure 9.8).

Figure 9.8
Unformatted text from an email message.

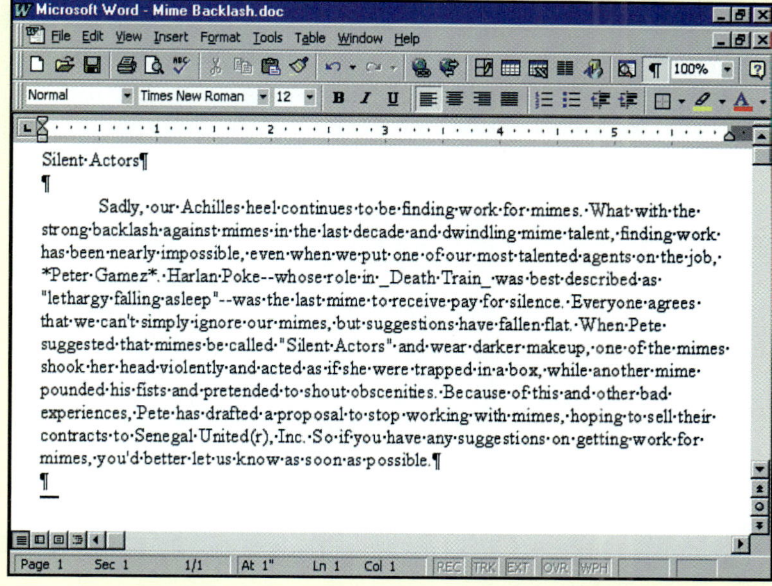

Notice that this document contains formatting that you need to clean up. When writing email messages, people use underscoring and asterisks before and after phrases for emphasis. Dashes are made with double hyphens (--) rather than long dashes (—). Notice also the straight quotation marks (""). If you had typed this text into Word, the AutoFormat As You Type feature discussed in the previous lesson would have formatted this text for you. But it's not too late to fix.

❷ Choose F̲ormat, A̲utoFormat.

The AutoFormat dialog box appears, as shown in Figure 9.9. Now explore what occurs during the AutoFormat.

Figure 9.9
Using AutoFormat to clean up text from an email message.

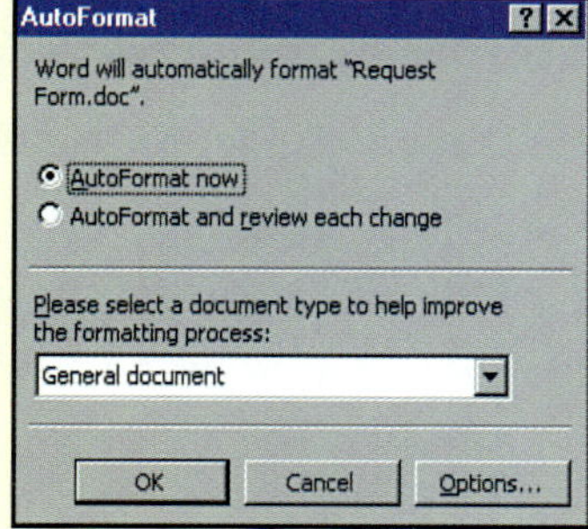

❸ Choose O̲ptions.

The AutoCorrect dialog box appears with the AutoFormat tab selected (see Figure 9.10). Many of these options also appear in this dialog

ccntinues

To Use AutoFormat   (continued)

box's Format As You Type page. Selecting options in the AutoFormat page doesn't affect the text that you type; instead, they affect existing text in an unformatted document, such as the one that you have open.

Figure 9.10
The AutoFormat page lists several options that you can reformat.

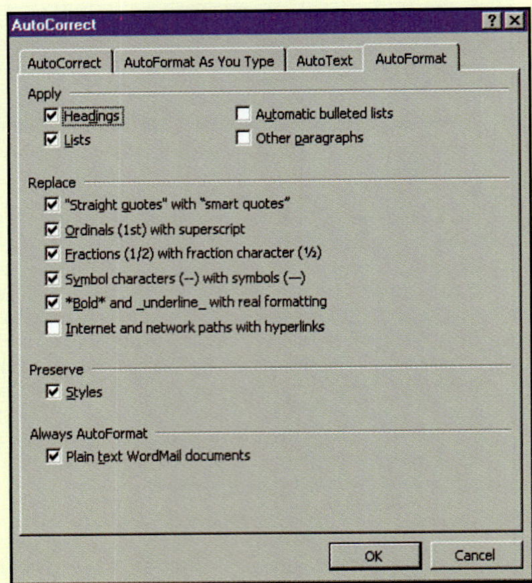

4 **In addition to any other options selected, make sure that you select the following check boxes:**

```
Headings
"Straight Quotes" with "Smart Quotes"
Symbol Characters (--) with Symbols (—)
*Bold* and _Underline_ with Real Formatting
```

These options clean up the document that you have open.

5 **Choose OK.**

The AutoFormat dialog box appears again. Review the changes made to the document.

6 **Select the AutoFormat and Review Each Change option.**

7 **Select General Document from the drop-down list, then choose OK.**

Word makes all the formatting changes in the document. The AutoFormat dialog box provides a list of options. Now review the changes.

8 **Choose Review Changes.**

Word highlights the changes and displays the Review AutoFormat Changes dialog box, as shown in Figure 9.11. By clicking the Find buttons, you can review the changes one by one and accept or reject them. However, by examining the marked revisions, you can see that all these changes are desirable.

Figure 9.11
Reviewing the displayed
AutoFormat changes.

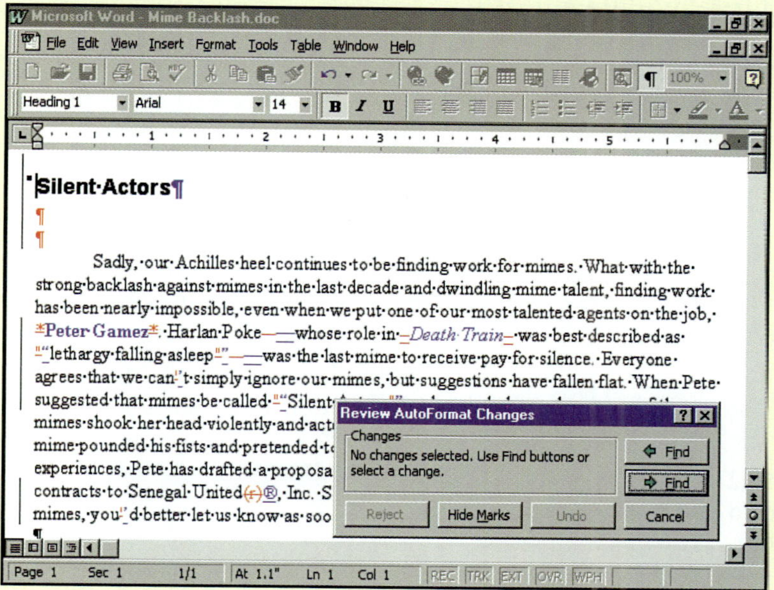

> **9** **Choose Cancel to close the Review AutoFormat dialog box, then choose Accept All.**
>
> Word changes the formatting in your document. Silent Actors is now a heading, and straight quotation marks are now curly quotation marks. AutoFormat has also made other formatting improvements.
>
> **10** **Close and save the document.**

Lesson 5: Recording and Running a Macro

A *macro* is a small computer program that you can write in Word to speed up repetitive tasks. Macros are typically created by recording a series of keystrokes and mouse actions. In this lesson, you create a simple macro that generates a standard return address.

Creating a macro in Word is like making a tape recording. When you record a song with a tape recorder, you insert a tape, press the Record button, and record the song as it plays on the radio. To listen to the song again, you insert the tape, press Play, and listen as the song plays from the tape.

When you create a macro in Word, you simply tell Word to record your actions (keystrokes and command selections). For example, you can tell Word to record your keystrokes and commands as you type your company name, insert page numbers, or set up the format for a formal report. When you finish, you can tell Word to "play back" those recorded keystrokes and commands to repeat the task. Try recording a simple macro now.

Macro

A small program that enables you to group together multiple Word commands to simplify everyday tasks. You can put macros on a drop-down menu or a toolbar, or you can assign them to shortcut keys. This way, they are as easy to use as any of the built-in Word commands.

To Record and Run a Macro

❶ In a new document window, choose Tools, Macro, Record New Macro.

The Record Macro dialog box appears (see Figure 9.12). Give your new macro a name. A macro name can consist of up to 80 characters, including upper- and lowercase letters, but no spaces. For example, if you were to create a macro that formats the margins on your page to one inch on each side and changes your entire document to the Arial font, you might name that macro Margin1Arial. At this point, you could assign a macro to a toolbar or a keystroke, although you don't do so in this lesson.

Figure 9.12
The Record Macro
dialog box.

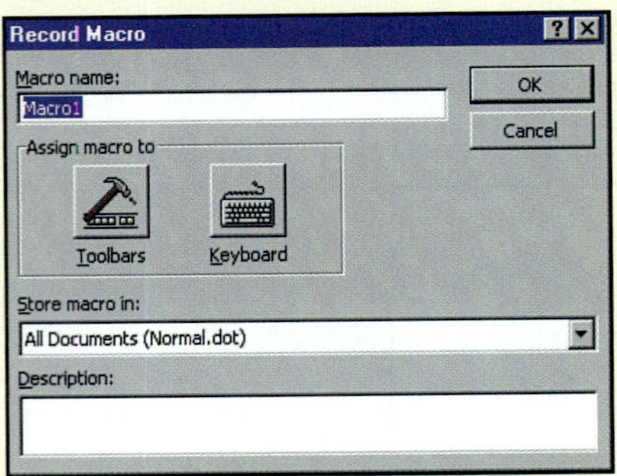

❷ Type `ReturnAddress` **in the Record Macro Name box, then choose OK.**

Word assigns the macro the name ReturnAddress. The Record Macro dialog box closes, and you return to the document window. A small Macro Record toolbar with two buttons appears onscreen, and the REC (RECord) indicator on the status bar becomes bold. The mouse pointer has a tiny cassette tape icon attached to it.

❸ Type your name and address.

Type your name and address as you want them to appear when you play the macro in a letter or envelope document. Traditionally, your name and street address appear on separate lines; city, state, and zip code information appear on the same line. Figure 9.13 shows a sample return address. Notice the Record Macro mouse pointer below the address.

After you finish recording your macro, turn off the macro recorder. If you forget to turn off the recorder, Word continues to record keystrokes until you exit Word or turn the recorder off. The next step shows you how to stop the recorder.

If you have problems...

If you make a mistake, don't worry about it; just backspace over the mistake and then type the correct information.

When you record a macro, don't include unnecessary cursor movements. For example, if you press Ctrl+Home before typing your return address while you record the macro, the macro performs that keystroke when it runs. Therefore, the macro automatically moves the insertion point to the top of the document and inserts the return address. If you include unnecessary cursor-movement actions in the macro, stop recording the macro (see the following steps) and start over.

Figure 9.13
Recording a return address macro. Note the tools that appear onscreen as you record keystrokes.

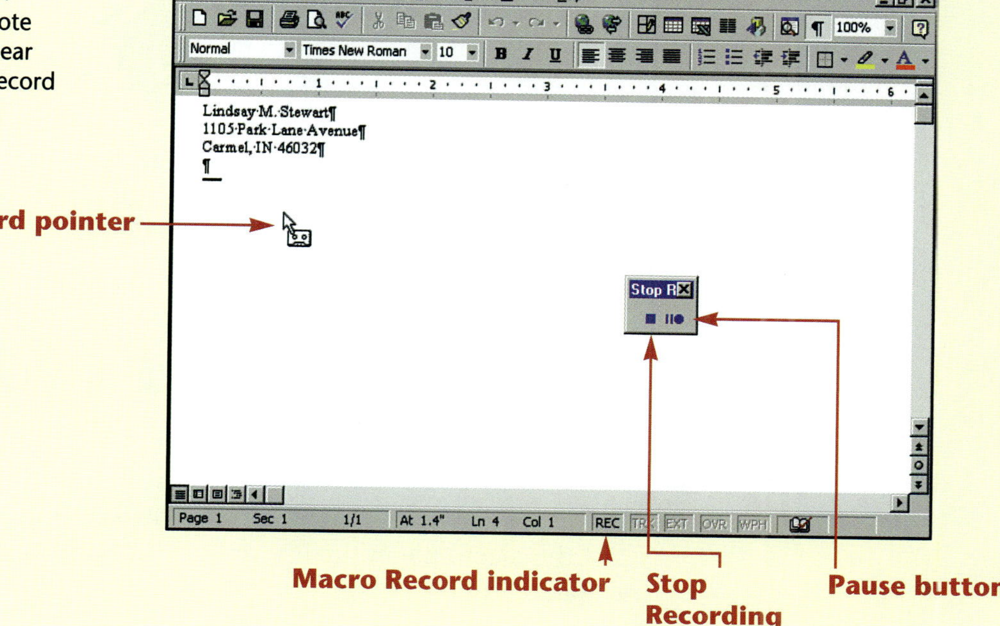

Macro Record pointer

Macro Record indicator   **Stop Recording button**   **Pause button**

4 **After you type your name and address, click the Macro Record toolbar's Stop Recording button.**

Clicking the Stop Recording button, shown in Figure 9.13, immediately stops the recording of your macro and stores it for future use in whichever templates were indicated when you started recording the macro. Word stores the macro with the name that you assigned to it earlier. The mouse pointer returns to its normal state.

5 **Close the current document without saving it.**

You don't need to save the document; the macro is already recorded in the Normal.dot template. Now open a new document to see how the macro that you created is available in any new documents.

6 **Open the folder Project-09 and the practice document Proj0904 and rename it** `Macro Practice`**.**

In this document, you see a typical letter advising friends that you have moved to a new address. Now run the macro that you created to insert your new return address into the document.

7 **Click the second line after the paragraph that begins with** `I've moved to a new address` **(see Figure 9.14).**

You must move the insertion point at which you want the macro to put the return address.

To Record and Run a Macro   (continued)

Figure 9.14
Click where you want the return address to appear in the document.

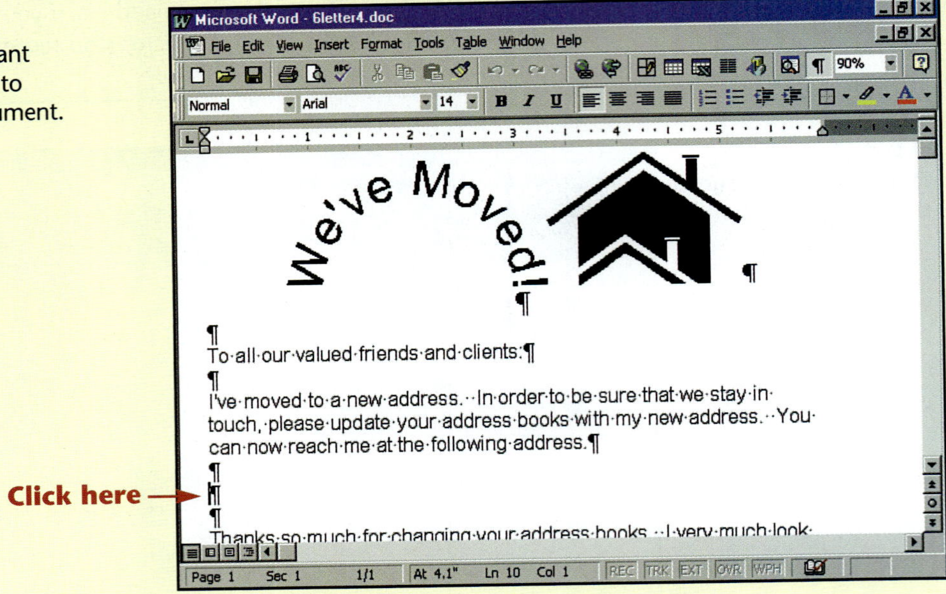

8 **Choose Tools, Macro, Macros.**

The Macros dialog box appears, as shown in Figure 9.15. You can select the macro file in the list, or you can type the macro's name in the Macro Name text box.

Figure 9.15
Select ReturnAddress and choose Run.

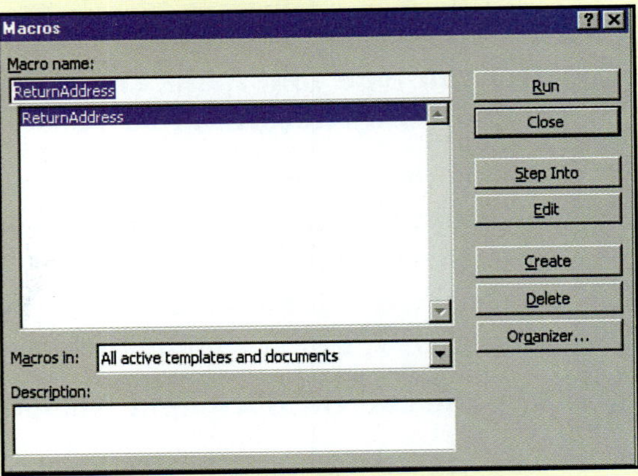

9 **Select the ReturnAddress macro in the Macro Name list box, then choose Run.**

Your address is inserted into the document. Your screen should now look like Figure 9.16.

10 **Save the document and keep it open for the next lesson.**

Word

Figure 9.16
Your document with the return address automatically inserted.

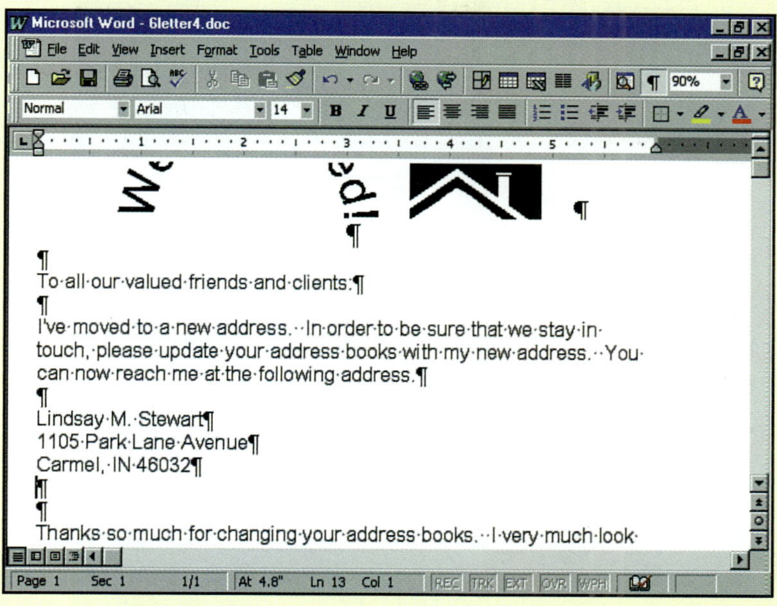

Notice that when you inserted the text, it automatically adopted the font information from the current document. This happened because when recording the macro, you didn't supply any specific font information. If, while recording the macro, you selected the text and applied font information to it, Word would use that font information whenever you inserted the text. Most of the time, however, you want the text to take on the current document's font and formatting information.

Lesson 6: Edit, Copy, Rename, and Delete Macros

There are times when you need to edit a macro. For example, if you relocate, you need to change the address macro you created in Lesson 5. If it's a simple macro, such as the address macro, you can either re-record it, or edit it in a program called Visual Basic, which contains a powerful programming language that enables you to create your own mini-applications within Word—if you know how to program.

In this lesson, you learn how to edit the address macro while working in Visual Basic. At the end of the lesson is an Exam Note which describes the method for copying, renaming, and deleting a macro. You learn about using Macros to create templates in Project 12.

Editing a Macro

With your document open from Lesson 5, edit the ReturnAddress macro.

❶ Choose Tools, Macro, Macros from the menu.

The Macros dialog box appears. Select the macro you want to edit and click the Edit button. The Visual Basic code window appears as shown in Figure 9.17.

Word

Editing a Macro (continued)

Figure 9.17
Edit the macro by changing your street address.

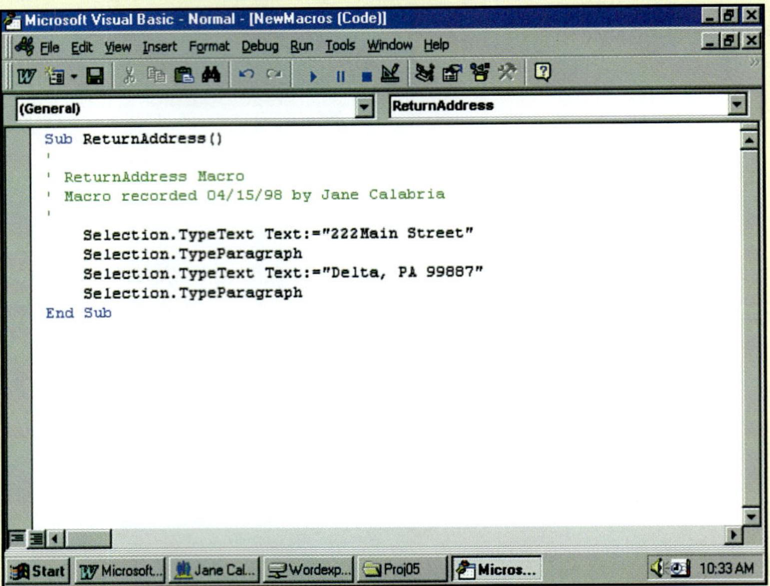

② **Highlight the street address text and change the street address to some other address (see Figure 9.18).**

Figure 9.18
Edit the street address as you would edit any text in Word; highlight the text and type the new address.

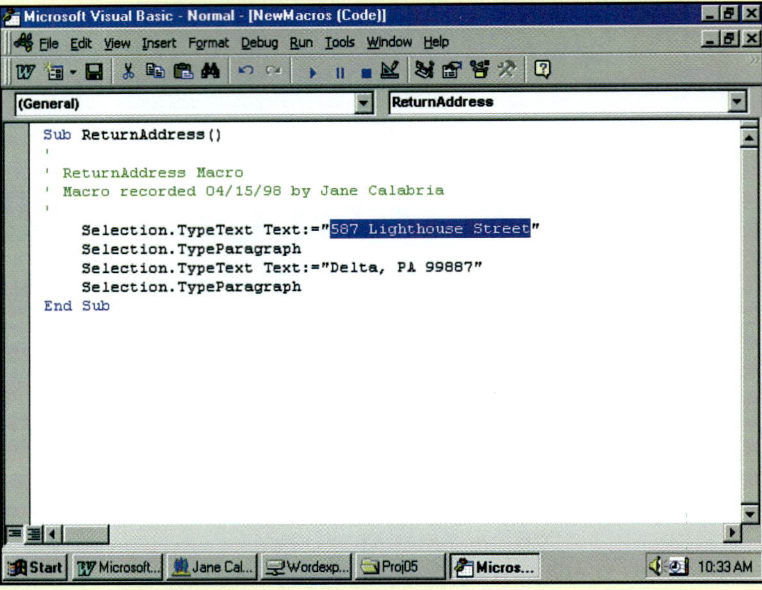

③ **Choose File, Close and Return to Microsoft Word.**

④ **Delete the address from your document and test the macro by running it again. You see your changes.**

Once the Microsoft Visual Basic window is open, the individual lines of code involved in the macro appear in the Code window on the right of the screen. Although it's helpful to have a knowledge of the Visual Basic programming language and how it works (especially if you want to add steps and conditional statements), there are some simple things you can do to the macro code to correct or adjust the steps you recorded.

One adjustment you can make to increase the speed and efficiency of your macro is to remove unnecessary properties. For example, when you record a macro that selects an option from a dialog box, the macro recorder records all the settings in the dialog box. You can remove the unnecessary properties from the recorded macro by deleting those lines of code. When editing your macro, be sure to test it along the way as you make changes.

The following lines of code are for a recorded macro that changes the selected text to the color blue: (lines that begin with a ' are comment lines, not commands—they help you to understand what the macro is doing).

```
Sub BlueText()

'

' BlueText Macro
' Macro recorded July 30, 1997 by Dorothy Burke

'

    With Selection.Font
                .Name = "Courier"
                .Size = 12
                .Bold = False
                .Italic = False
                .Underline = wdUnderlineNone
                .StrikeThrough = False
                .DoubleStrikeThrough = False
                .Outline = False
                .Emboss = False
                .Shadow = False
                .Hidden = False
                .SmallCaps = False
                .AllCaps = False
                .ColorIndex = wdBlue
                .Engrave = False
                .Superscript = False
                .Subscript = False
                .Spacing = 0
                .Scaling = 100
                .Position = 0
                .Kerning = 0
                .Animation = wdAnimationNone
        End With
    End Sub
```

There are several lines of code that are unnecessary to the macro and can be deleted. The macro could be as simple as:

```
Sub BlueText()

'

' BlueText Macro

' Macro recorded July 30, 1997 by Dorothy Burke

'

    With Selection.Font

        .ColorIndex = wdBlue

End With

End Sub
```

You could even change wdBlue to wdGreen to get green text.

When the macro recorder records a method, it also includes the values of all the arguments. The following recorded macro opens a file called WordTOC.doc. The resulting macro includes all the arguments for the Open method:

```
Sub OpenTOC()

'

' OpenTOC Macro

' Macro recorded July 30, 1997 by Dorothy Burke

'

        ChangeFileOpenDirectory "C:\QUE\CSWord\"

        Documents.Open FileName:="Wordtoc.doc",

                            ConfirmConversions:=False,

                            ReadOnly:=False,

                            AddToRecentFiles:=False,

                            PasswordDocument:="",

                            PasswordTemplate:="",

                            Revert:=False,

                            WritePasswordDocument:="",

                            WritePasswordTemplate:="",

                            Format:=wdOpenFormatAuto

End Sub
```

The arguments that are not needed can be removed, such as the arguments set to an empty string (marked by the double quotes, ""). The resulting macro would look like this:

```
Sub OpenTOC()

'

' OpenTOC Macro

' Macro recorded July 30, 1997 by Dorothy Burke

'

        ChangeFileOpenDirectory "C:\QUE\CSWord\"

        Documents.Open FileName:="Wordtoc.doc",

                            ConfirmConversions:=False,

                            ReadOnly:=False,

                            AddToRecentFiles:=False,

                            Revert:=False,

                            Format:=wdOpenFormatAuto

End Sub
```

For more information on using Visual Basic with Word macros, choose <u>H</u>elp, <u>C</u>ontents and Index. Select the Contents tab and then refer to the Microsoft Word Visual Basic Reference topic.

Copying a macro to another document or template, renaming a macro, or deleting a macro can all be done from the Organizer. You reach the Organizer through the Macros dialog box:

1. Choose <u>T</u>ools, <u>M</u>acro, <u>M</u>acros from the menu to open the Macros dialog box.

2. Click the Organizer button.

3. The Organizer dialog box appears with the Macro Project Items tab selected (see Figure 9.19).

Figure 9.19
Use the Organizer to copy, delete, or rename macros.

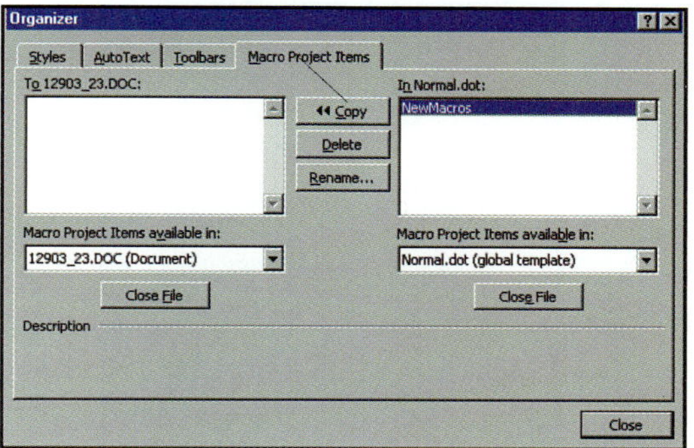

4. There are two boxes in the dialog box: The box on the right displays the macros in the Normal document template and the box on the left displays the macros used in the document you have open. From either list, select the macro you want to copy, rename, or delete.

   If the macro is in another template that's attached to the current document, select that template from the Macro Project Items available in drop-down list.

   If the document you want isn't listed, click the Close File button and then click the Open File button. Select the file you want to use and then click Open. Its macros appear in that box.

5. Click the appropriate button for the action you want to perform:

   Copy. Copies the macro from one box to the other, thus copying it from the Normal template to the current document or vice versa, depending on where the macro was stored.

   Delete. Deletes the selected macro (to delete more than one macro, hold down Ctrl and click each one you want to delete before clicking Delete).

   Rename. Enter the new name for the macro and click OK.

6. Click Close.

Supplied Macros. The Macros8.dot template contains macros that you may find useful in your daily work or as samples to review and modify. To use the macros,

Word

choose File, Open from the menu and then change to the Microsoft Office\ Office\Macros folder. From the Files of Type drop-down list, select All Files. Then double-click the Macros8.dot. Run the macros you want and then copy any you need to other documents using the Organizer.

You have completed all of the lessons in this project. If you have completed your session on the computer, exit Word and Windows 95 before turning off your computer. Otherwise, continue with the "Checking Your Skills" and "Applying Your Skills" sections.

Project Summary

To	Do This
Create an AutoText entry	Select the text, graphic, or symbol for the entry. Choose Insert, AutoText, New. Type a name for the entry, then choose OK.
Insert an AutoText entry	Position the insertion point where you want to insert the entry. Type the name of the AutoText entry, then press F3.
Modify an AutoText entry	Insert the original AutoText entry into a document. Make the desired modifications to the text, then select the text that you just modified. Choose Insert, AutoText, New. Type the name of the entry, then choose OK. Choose Yes to replace the old entry.
Delete an AutoText entry	Choose Insert, AutoText, AutoText. Select the entry's name, choose Delete, then choose Close.
Record a macro	Choose Tools, Macro, Record New Macro. Type the macro's name, then choose OK. Execute the series of keystrokes and menu commands that you want to record in the macro. When finished, click the Macro toolbar's Stop Recording button.
Run a macro	Place the mouse at the point in your document where you want to launch the macro. Choose Tools, Macro, Macros. Select the macro that you want to run, then choose Run.
Edit a macro	Choose Tools, Macro, Macros and select the macro you want to edit. Make your changes to the macro and choose File, Close and Return to Microsoft Word.
Rename a macro	Choose Tools, Macro, Macros from the menu to open the Macros dialog box. Click the Organizer button and select the Macro Project Items tab from the Organizer dialog box. Select the macro and click the Rename button to perform the action, then click the Close button.
Delete a macro	Choose Tools, Macro, Macros from the menu to open the Macros dialog box. Click the Organizer button and select the Macro Project Items tab from the Organizer dialog box. Select the macro and click the Delete button to perform the action, then click the Close button.

Copy a macro	Choose Tools, Macro, Macros from the menu to open the Macros dialog box. Click the Organizer button and select the Macro Project Items tab from the Organizer dialog box. Select the macro and click the Copy button to perform the action, then click the Close button.

Checking Your Skills

True/False

For each of the following statements, check *T* or *F* to indicate whether the statement is true or false.

__T __F **1.** You can use AutoText to automatically format text in a document.

__T __F **2.** You can use AutoFormat to automatically format text in a document.

__T __F **3.** Word comes with some built-in common AutoText entries.

__T __F **4.** AutoText entries can be up to 100 characters long.

__T __F **5.** Once you create an AutoText entry, you cannot change it.

__T __F **6.** You can review formatting changes made by AutoFormat to accept or reject them.

__T __F **7.** Macros are useful for automating common word processing tasks.

__T __F **8.** You cannot rename a macro.

__T __F **9.** All macros must be stored in the Normal.dot template.

__T __F **10.** You can copy macros from one document to another.

Multiple Choice

Circle the letter of the correct answer for each of the following questions.

1. What feature is useful for automatically substituting regular keystrokes with symbols?

   a. AutoText

   b. AutoCorrect

   c. AutoFormat

   d. AutoSymbol

2. What feature is useful for saving a series of keystrokes and commands for future repetition?

   a. AutoText

   b. Macros

   c. Styles

   d. Fields

3. What feature is useful for automatically inserting a selection of text or a graphics image into a document?

   a. AutoText

   b. AutoFormat

   c. AutoInsert

   d. AutoSymbol

4. What shortcut key can you use to insert an AutoText entry?

   a. F1

   b. F2

   c. F3

   d. F4

5. What element is usually displayed when you type an AutoText name in a document?

   a. Office Assistant

   b. What's This? pointer

   c. AutoText dialog box

   d. ScreenTip

6. What icon appears with the mouse pointer while you record a macro ?

   a. The letter M

   b. A cassette tape

   c. A microphone

   d. Earphones

7. In which dialog box do you copy a macro?

   a. Macros

   b. Organizer

   c. Record

   d. Copy Macros

8. What program comes with Word for use in editing macros?

   a. Visual Basic

   b. Basic Macros

   c. Macro Codes

   d. Macro Outlook

9. In which template does Word store new macros by default?

   a. Invoice.dot

   b. Memo.dot

   c. Macro.dot

   d. Normal.dot

10. What dialog box is used to delete an AutoText entry?

   a. Create AutoText

   b. Delete AutoText

   c. AutoFormat

   d. AutoCorrect

Completion

In the blank provided, write the correct answer for each of the following statements.

1. _______________ is a stored piece of text or a graphics image of any size that you instantly insert into a document.

2. The __________ As You Type feature works behind the scenes, fixing your text while you type.

3. A _________ is a small computer program that you can write in Word to speed up repetitive tasks.

4. Click the _______________ button when you have finished entering macro keystrokes and commands.

5. When you type the _________ of an AutoText entry, a ScreenTip usually displays the complete entry.

6. You can store text and __________ in an AutoText entry.

7. In Visual Basic, you can see and edit the macro _______.

8. You can assign a ___________ key combination for quickly playing a macro.

9. Use the _____________ dialog box to copy and rename macros.

10. Use AutoFormat to automatically apply ___________ formatting to ordinals throughout a document.

Matching

In the blank next to each of the following terms or phrases, write the letter of the corresponding term or phrase. (Note that some letters may be used more than once.)

a. Macro toolbar

b. Code window

c. AutoFormat

d. Organizer

e. AutoText

f. F3

g. AutoCorrect

h. Insertion point

i. Alt+F3

j. Macro

_______ **1.** The part of the Visual Basic screen where the macro code is displayed.

_______ **2.** Keystroke for inserting an AutoText entry.

_______ **3.** Feature used for copying and renaming macros.

_______ **4.** Feature used for recording and playing back commands and actions.

_______ **5.** Element that displays the Stop Recording and Pause buttons.

_______ **6.** Feature that applies formatting to existing text.

_______ **7.** Feature that stores selected text or graphics for future insertion in a document.

_______ **8.** Feature that fixes common spelling errors.

_______ **9.** Key combination for quickly turning selected text into an AutoText entry.

_______ **10.** Where an AutoText entry is inserted.

Applying Your Skills

Practice

The following exercises enable you to practice the skills you have learned in this project. Take a few minutes to work through these exercises now.

Creating AutoText Entries to Automate a Cover Letter

In this practice lesson, you create AutoText entries that you can use to automate the process of creating cover letters for the Computer Training Association.

To create AutoText entries to automate a cover letter, follow these steps:

1. Open the file Proj0905 from the Project-09 folder on the CD and save it in your `Practices` folder with the name `CTA Letter5`.

2. Replace the Student's Name return address information with your own name and address information. Also replace the text Student's Name in the closing with your own name.

3. Create an AutoText entry for the picture, called Logo.

4. Create an AutoText entry for the CTA name and address information to the right of the picture, called `CTA`.

5. Create an AutoText entry for your name and return address, called `Return`.

6. Create an AutoText entry for the seven lines that comprise the body of the letter, called `Welcome`.

7. Create an AutoText entry for the Closing and the signature line, called `Close`.

8. Save the document. If requested by your instructor, print it. Close the document when you have finished.

Using AutoText Entries to Create a Cover Letter

In this practice lesson, you use the AutoText entries that you created in the previous exercise to create a cover letter for the Computer Training Association.

To use AutoText entries to create a cover letter, follow these steps:

1. Create a new document and save it in your Practices folder with the name `CTA Letter6`.

2. Insert the AutoText entry `logo`.

3. Insert the AutoText entry `CTA`.

4. Insert the current date as an updating field and format it in 12-point Times New Roman.

5. Leave four blank lines and insert the AutoText entry `return`.

6. Type the following name, address and salutation in 12-point Times New Roman:

```
Mr. James LeRoc
45 S. 102nd St.
Indianapolis, IN 46290

Dear Mr.LeRoc,
```

7. Leave one blank line, then insert the AutoText entry `Welcome`.

8. Insert the AutoText entry `Close`.

9. Check the spelling and grammar in the document and preview it. Save the document. If requested by your instructor, print it. Close it when you have finished.

Creating a Macro to Sort a List of Names

In this practice lesson, you record a macro that sorts a list of names alphabetically in ascending order, then use it to sort a list.

To create a macro to sort a list of names, follow these steps:

1. Open the file Proj0906 from the Project-09 folder on the CD and save it in your `Practices` folder with the name `Names`. This document includes two tables of names.

2. Choose Tools, Macro, Record New Macro.

3. Name the macro Sort and click OK.

4. Select the first table of names in the Names document.

5. Choose Table, Sort.

6. Click the Sort by drop-down arrow and select LastName.

7. Make sure that the sort is set for text ascending.

8. Choose OK.

9. Click the Stop button on the Macro toolbar. Now, use the macro to sort the second table of names.

10. Position the insertion point anywhere in the second table.

11. Choose Tools, Macro, Macros.

12. Select Sort in the list of Macros, then click Run.

13. Save the Names document. If requested by your instructor, print it. When you are finished, close it.

Editing the Sort Macro

In this practice lesson, you use Visual Basic to edit the Sort macro so it sorts alphabetically by Company name. Then you use it to sort a list.

To edit a macro to sort a list of names, follow these steps:

1. Open the file Proj0907 from the Project-09 folder on the CD and save it in your `Practices` folder with the name `Names2`. This document is a version of the document you used in the previous exercise.

2. Choose Tools, Macro, Macros.

3. Select Sort in the list of macros, then click Edit. The Visual Basic Editor opens, with the macro code displayed. To change the macro so it sorts by Company Name instead of by Last Name, you have to designate column 3 as the sort field instead of column 2.

4. Locate the text FieldNumber="Column 2" on the first line of the macro code.

5. Change the 2 in "Columm 2" to a 3.

6. Choose File, Close and Return to Microsoft Word. Now, try out the new macro.

7. Position the insertion point anywhere in the first table.

8. Choose <u>T</u>ools, <u>M</u>acro, <u>M</u>acros.

9. Select Sort in the list of Macros, then click <u>R</u>un. The list is now sorted alphabetically by Company Name. The second list is still sorted by Last Name.

10. Save the Names2 document. If requested by your instructor, print it. When you are finished, close it.

Copying and Renaming a Macro

In this practice lesson, you copy the sort macro to a document created with a different template, then rename it.

To copy and rename a macro, follow these steps:

1. Open the file Proj0908 from the Project-09 folder on the CD and save it in your `Practices` folder with the name `Tech Memo2`.

2. Choose <u>T</u>ools, <u>M</u>acro, <u>M</u>acros.

3. Click the <u>O</u>rganizer button.

4. Make sure the Macro Item page tab is selected, then select the macro name NewMacros in the list on the right side of the Organizer dialog box. This macro contains any new macros stored in the Normal.dot template, including the Sort macro you just created.

5. Click the <u>C</u>opy button. This copies the macro to the current document.

6. Select the NewMacros macro in the list on the left side of the Organizer dialog box.

7. Click the <u>R</u>ename button.

8. Type `NewMacros2` in the Rename dialog box, then click OK.

9. Click Close to close the Organizer dialog box.

10. Any new macros including the Sort macro are now available in the Tech Memo document.

11. Save the Tech Memo document. If requested by your instructor, print it. When you are finished, close it.

Challenge

The following challenges enable you to use your problem-solving skills. Take time to work through these exercises now.

Creating AutoText Entries for Computer Training Concepts Documents

Use the skills you have learned in this project to create AutoText entries from an existing document that you can use to quickly create new documents.

Open the file Proj0909 from the Project-09 folder on the CD and save it in your `Challenges` folder as `Cover Letter6`. Replace the text Student Name with your own name. Create AutoText entries for the letterhead, the body of the letter, and the closing. Save the document and, if requested by your instructor, print it. Close it when you have finished.

Using AutoText Entries to Create a Document for Computer Training Concepts

Use the AutoText entries to quickly create a new document. Create a new blank document and save it in your `Challenges` folder as `Cover Letter7`. Use the AutoText entries you created in the previous exercise to create a new letter. Insert the date as an updating field. On the last line of the document, insert the UserInitials field. Save the document and, if requested by your instructor, print it. Close it when you have finished.

Creating a Macro to Search for and Replace a Company Name

In this exercise, you create a macro that can be used to change the name of the company Computer Training Concepts, Inc. to Training Concepts Unlimited, Inc. wherever it appears in a document.

Open the file Proj0910 from the Project-09 folder on the CD, and save it in your `Challenges` folder with the name `Macro`. Create a new macro called `Replace`, and record the keystrokes and commands necessary to replace the text Computer Training Concepts, with the text `Training Concepts Unlimited`. Stop recording when the process is finshed.

Save the Macro document. If requested by your instructor, print it. Close it when you have finished.

Using a Macro to Search for and Replace a Company Name

In this exercise, you use the macro that you created in the previous exercise. Open the file Proj0911 from the Project-09 folder on the CD, and save it in your `Challenges` folder with the name `Macro2`. Play the macro. Save the document. If requested by your instructor, print it. Close it when you have finished.

Editing a Macro

In this exercise, you edit the macro that you created in exercise 3. Instead of changing the name to Training Concepts Unlimited, you want to change it to Conceptual Training Unlimited. Open the file Proj0912 from the Project-09 folder on the CD, and save it in your `Challenges` folder with the name `Macro3`. Open the Macros dialog box and select the Replace macro. Open the Visual Basic Editor, locate the replacement text `Training Concepts Unlimited` in the macro code, then change it to `Conceptual Training Unlimited`. Close the Visual Basic Editor. Run the macro in the Macro3 document. Save the document. If requested by your instructor, print it. Close it when you have finished.

You have completed the project and the associated lessons, as well as the "Checking Your Skills" and "Applying Your Skills" sections. Now use the PinPoint software evaluation mode to assess your comprehension of the specific exam tasks you have just learned. You can also use the PinPoint Trainer Mode and the Show Me tutorials to practice these specific exam tasks.

Project 10

Working with Columns

Creating and Using Columns

In this Project, you will learn how to:

Objectives

Required Activities

➤ Designate Columns Before Entering Text

➤ Type in Columns

➤ Assign Columns to Previously Typed Text

➤ Resize Columns

➤ Master Insertion Point Movement in Columns

➤ Insert Column Breaks and Section Breaks … … … … Balance Column Length
Keep Text in Columns Together

Why Would I Do This?

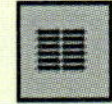

Word's Column feature enables you to create appealing, professional-looking documents that flow and read easily, and that keep the text from looking too wordy. Columns are an excellent tool to use when you design newsletters, brochures, advertising material, or any documents that lend themselves to an attractive presentation.

Use columns to make text stand out. You can separate the page into sections, enabling you to display text in multiple columns and full-page text all on the same page. Break columns part of the way down the page if you don't want them to continue all the way to the bottom of the page. Columns are easy to set up, either before you type text or after you have entered the text.

When you set up text in columns, the text begins in the left column and continues down that column to the end of the page (or partially down the page if you have selected a column length that is less than a full page). Then the text continues at the top of the next column on the same page, much like a newspaper article. In fact, this type of text flow in a column structure is referred to as newspaper-style columns.

When you need side-by-side columns, such as those in a phone list, invoice, or list of figures, use Word's table feature (see Project 7, "Using Merge").

Lesson 1: Designating Columns Before Entering Text

To enter text into columns, you must tell Word how many columns you want. By default, Word separates the columns so that each column is the same width and all columns have the same amount of space separating each other. When you enter text, the text fills the first column to the bottom of the page and then jumps to the top of the second column.

In this lesson, you practice designating columns before entering text.

To Designate Columns

❶ Open Word or, if Word is already open, open a new document. Save the blank document as Columns.

Use a blank document so that you can designate columns; then the columns are in place before you begin typing. (Later in this project, you learn how to divide existing text into columns.)

❷ Click the Standard toolbar's Columns button and hold down the mouse button.

When you click the Columns button, a grid divided into four columns appears.

3 **Drag the mouse pointer across the grid until you highlight three columns and see 3 Columns at the bottom of the box, then release the mouse button (as shown in Figure 10.1).**

Figure 10.1
Use the Columns grid to designate the number of columns you want.

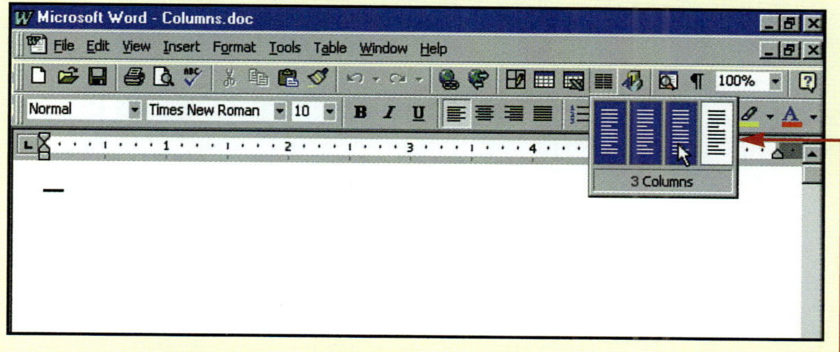

Drag the mouse arrow across the columns in the grid

Don't worry if you select the wrong number of columns; you can always bring the mouse back to the correct number of columns.

4 **If the ruler is not showing onscreen, choose View, Ruler to display the ruler.**

Notice that the ruler is now divided into sections; between each section is a column marker. The markers show the space between the columns. The ruler should now look like the one in Figure 10.2. Notice, too, that Word has switched to Page Layout view.

Figure 10.2
You can see the column widths on the ruler.

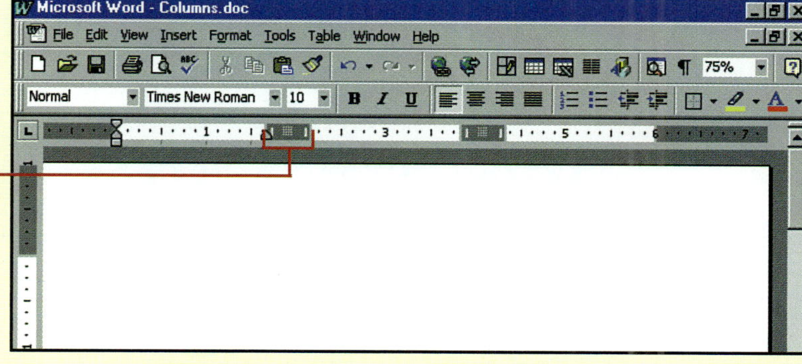

This space is left between the column

5 **Now change the number of columns from three to two by clicking the Columns button and dragging across two columns.**

You can easily change the number of columns later if you want. Notice the change on the ruler when you switch to two columns.

6 **Save this file and leave it open for the next lesson.**

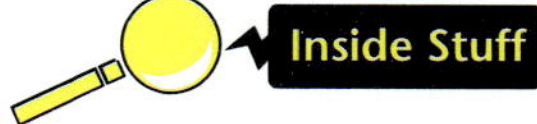

Clicking the Standard toolbar's Columns button is the quickest way to set up columns in the document. Sometimes, however, the quickest way isn't the best way. You can create columns by choosing Format, Columns. The Columns dialog box opens to give you more choices than just how many columns you want (see Figure 10.3).

Figure 10.3
Open the Columns dialog box by choosing Format, Columns.

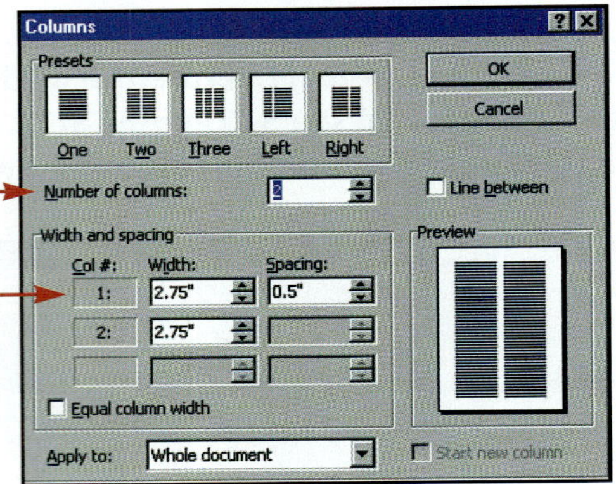

In the Columns dialog box, you can select the number of columns you want to use, and the specific widths of the columns and the spaces that separate them. You can also place a line between the columns.

Exam Notes

The columns dialog box provides five predefined column layouts. They are as follows:

- One column

- Two equal width columns

- Three equal width columns

- Two unequal width columns with the wider column on the left

- Two unequal width columns with the wider column on the right

Columns that you create using the Columns button on the toolbar are always columns of equal length.

Lesson 2: Typing in Columns

Having columns is nice, but what you really want to do is put something into the columns. In this lesson, you add text to the columns that you created in Lesson 1.

Word should be displaying the `Columns` file that you created in Lesson 1. Currently, you have two columns designated.

To Type in Columns

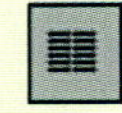

1 Click the Columns button and select three columns.

You've told Word that you want to type in three columns. On the ruler, you see the margins for the three columns. If the ruler were not displayed, you wouldn't see any difference onscreen when you change the number of columns.

2 Begin typing at the top of the page. Type the following sample text to see how the text wraps:

IntroVision United, Inc. is pleased to announce the Annual
Technology Training Conference on March 19-25. The conference will
be held at the Journey Inn Convention Center in Springfield,
Missouri.

Notice that the text that you type goes only about a third of the way across the screen before reaching the right margin of the column and then wrapping to the next line (see Figure 10.4).

Figure 10.4
Entering text in a column.

The right margin of the column

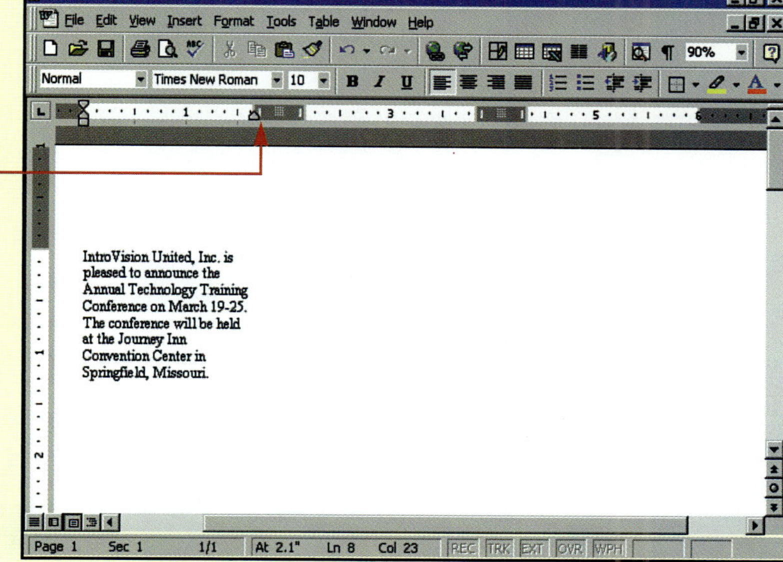

3 **Press ↵Enter twice to move to a new line, then choose Insert, File and insert the file Proj1001 found in folder Project-10 from the CD.**

Inserting this text fills in the rest of the first column and wraps to the next column. Now see what columns look like in Normal view.

4 **Choose View, Normal. Place the insertion point at the end of the text.**

Notice the vertical measurement on the status bar at the bottom of the screen. In Normal view, Word adjusts the text measurement on the status bar as if you were typing on one extremely long page (see Figure 10.5).

If you switch to Page Layout view, you can see how the columns really fall on the page.

5 **Choose View, Page Layout or click the Page Layout View button in the lower-left corner of the screen.**

That's more like it! Figure 10.6 shows the typed columns in Page Layout view.

continues

To Type in Columns   (continued)

Figure 10.5
You're still on page 1, but look how long the column is!

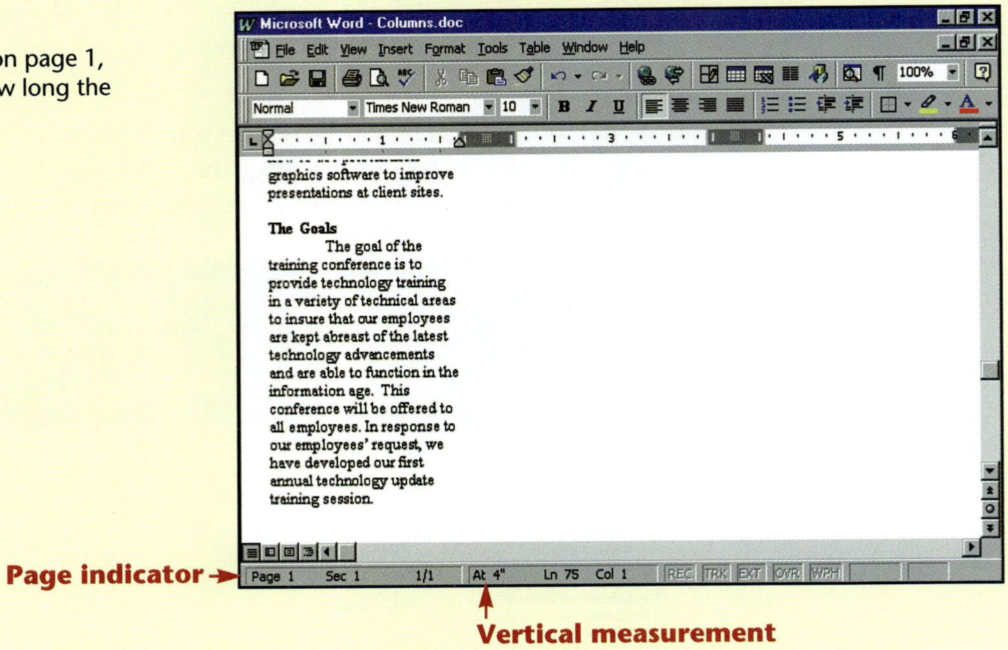

Page indicator →

Vertical measurement

Figure 10.6
Page Layout view shows columns the way they're supposed to look.

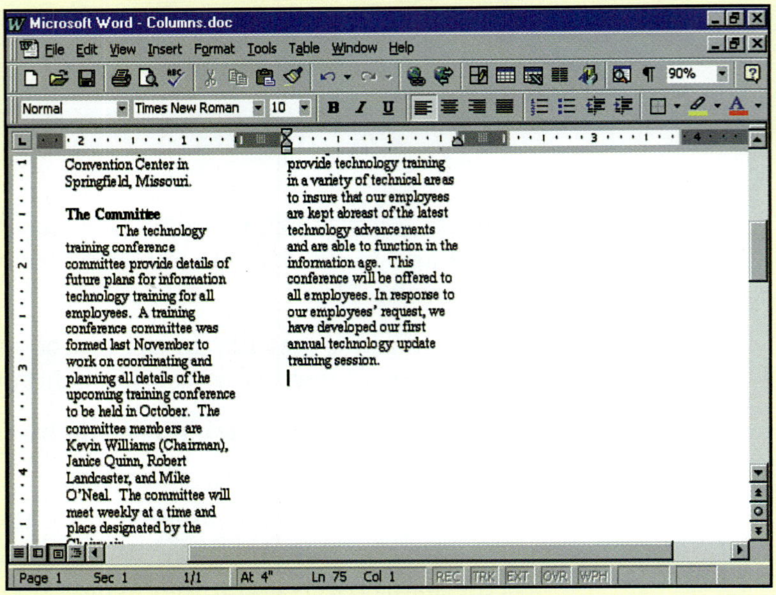

If you continue typing, the columns keep up with you. The text wraps around to the top of the next column until you reach the bottom of the third column. Then the text continues on the next page at the top of the leftmost column again.

6 Save this file and close it.

Lesson 3: Assigning Columns to Previously Typed Text

If you know how many columns you want to have before you start typing, you can designate columns first, as you did in Lesson 2, and then begin typing the columns. Sometimes, however, you can't be sure how many columns you need, or even if you need columns, until you get some text onscreen. Setting columns after you've typed text is as easy as it is before you begin typing.

To Assign Columns to Previously Typed Text

❶ Open the folder Project-10 and the file Proj1002 from the CD and save the file as Cost Containment.

A text file appears onscreen. This file has not been formatted for columns, so you can set up two columns for this document.

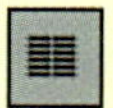

❷ Click the Columns button and select two columns from the grid.

Word switches to Page Layout view and splits the entire document into two columns. You can change your mind and choose a different number of columns.

❸ Place the insertion point anywhere in the document, then click the Columns button and select three Columns.

Word now displays the document in three columns (see Figure 10.7). Notice that changing the columns affects the entire document, regardless of where you place the insertion point. Next, remove the columns from the document.

Figure 10.7
Word places the entire document in columns.

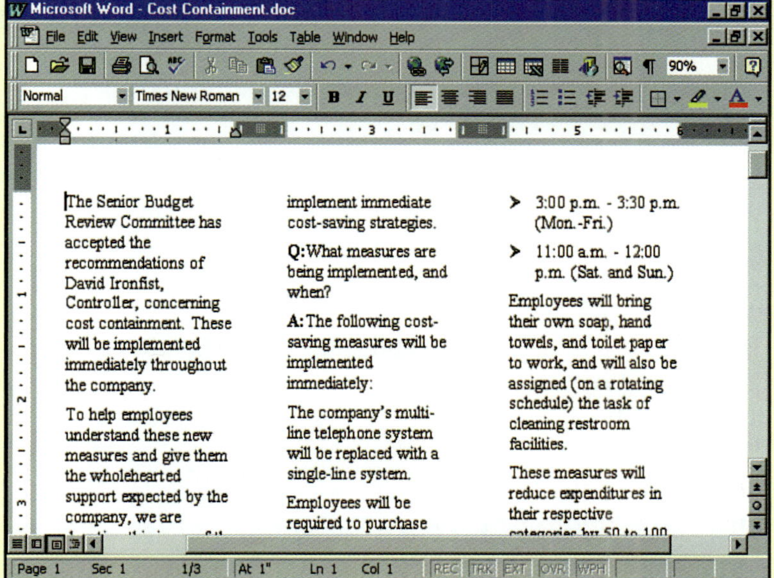

continues

Word

To Assign Columns to Previously Typed Text   (continued)

4 **Click the Standard toolbar's Columns button and select one column.**

In Word, selecting a one-column document is the same as not using any columns at all. The document returns to a full-page, margin-to-margin display.

5 **Save this file and leave it open for the next lesson.**

Lesson 4: Resizing Columns

When you set up columns, Word gives you columns that are all the same size, with one-half-inch **gutters** between the columns. Word also has a few standard uneven column settings from which you can choose, or you can set specific widths for each of the columns and the gutters.

I thought a gutter was that leaf-filled, metal thing on the edge of my roof! In the world of word processing, the term has a different meaning altogether. A gutter is the blank space that separates columns. You can control a gutter's width by dragging its edges on the ruler or by choosing Format, Columns and specifying a width. You can make the gutter very wide or extremely thin, and you never have to worry about cleaning out the leaves.

If you are working in two columns and you want them to be of unequal width, you can use Word's preset left and right column options. Choosing one of these options saves you a bit of time that you can otherwise spend measuring and estimating what the column widths should be.

To Resize Columns

1 **Choose Format, Columns.**

The Columns dialog box appears, as shown in Figure 10.8. Notice the Presets area at the top of the dialog box. The first three settings represent the one-, two-, and three-column settings that you used earlier in this project. The Left and Right presets, however, enable you to set up two columns of unequal widths.

Figure 10.8
You can control column widths in the Columns dialog box.

Standard one-, two-, and three-column widths

Uneven column widths

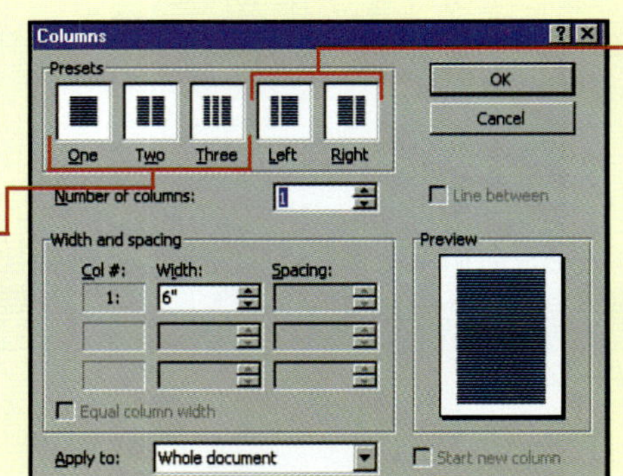

2 **Choose the <u>L</u>eft preset option and then click OK.**

This option formats the text in two columns, with the left column half as wide as the right column.

3 **Open the Columns dialog box again and then choose the <u>R</u>ight preset option. Click OK.**

Choosing this option formats the text with the right column half as wide as the left column.

When you use the <u>L</u>eft and <u>R</u>ight preset options, you can further adjust the column widths by moving column markers on the ruler. You can practice using the ruler to adjust column widths now.

4 **Display the ruler if it is not currently in view.**

If you look closely at the ruler's column marker (as shown in Figure 10.9), you can see that it contains three smaller, fainter markers within it. You can use these markers to adjust both the column and the gutter widths.

If you click the middle of the column marker (that is, the spot that looks like a faint grid), you can drag the entire marker left or right to change the width of the columns. If you click one of the faint lines near the left or right edge of the column marker, you can drag the line to make the gutter wider or narrower.

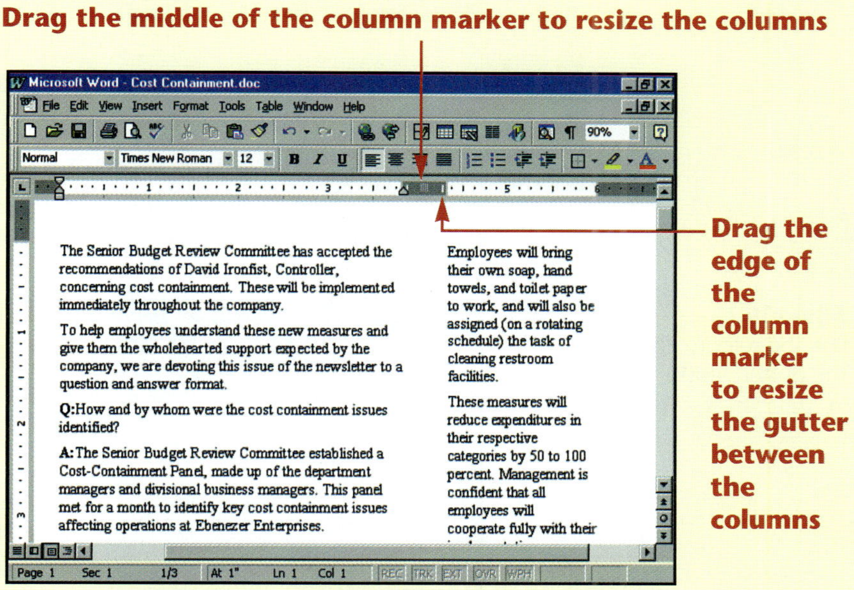

Figure 10.9
The ruler features tools that enable you to adjust columns and gutters on the fly.

Drag the middle of the column marker to resize the columns

Drag the edge of the column marker to resize the gutter between the columns

5 **Place the mouse pointer over the grid in the middle of the column marker.**

The mouse pointer turns into a double-headed horizontal arrow. When you see this arrow, you can drag the column marker to relocate the gutter and resize the columns.

continues

Word

To Resize Columns   (continued)

6 **Widen the right column by dragging the grid marker an inch or so to the left on the ruler. Release the mouse button.**

When you drag the marker, you see a vertical, dashed line in the text, which indicates where the middle of the gutter will fall after you release the mouse button (see Figure 10.10).

Figure 10.10
Change column widths by using the ruler.

The vertical line shows you where the gutter is after you release the mouse button. Drag here to change the column width

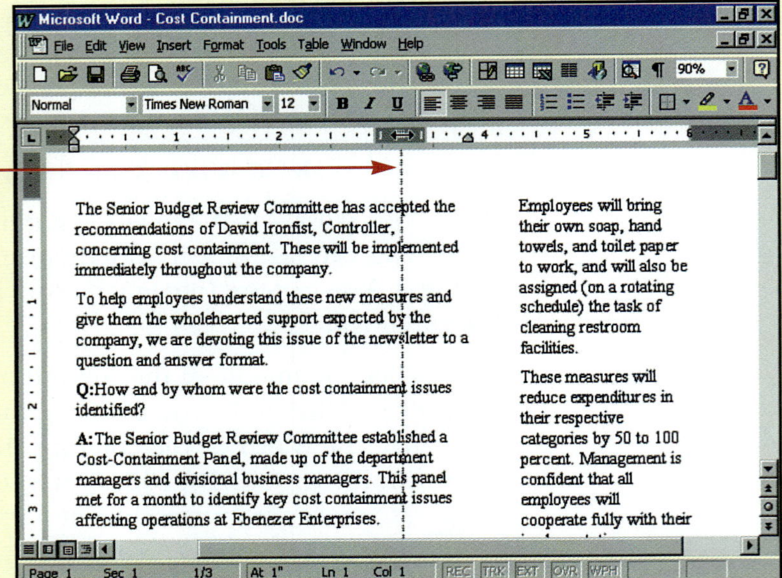

You also can use the column marker to adjust the width of the gutter between the columns. You make this adjustment next.

7 **Now change the gutter width by dragging the faint line near the right edge of the column marker a half inch or so to the right (as shown in Figure 10.11). Release the mouse button.**

Figure 10.11
Use the ruler to change the gutter width.

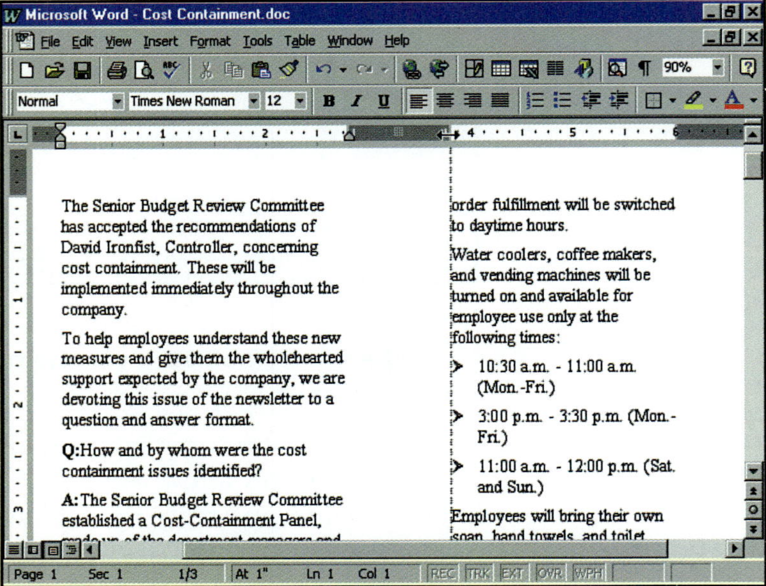

Word automatically adjusts the text to fit within the new measurements. You can make the gutter marker quite large (almost the width of the paper, if you have only two columns), or you can shrink the gutter to a width of zero.

Inside Stuff

Use the Columns dialog box if you want to reset column widths with precise measurements instead of dragging the column marker along the ruler. Make sure that the Equal Column Width check box is not selected, then type the measurements that you want for each column. You can activate the Columns dialog box by double-clicking the column marker on the ruler.

Although you're learning about Word's column features, you're not making the columns any more attractive. Use the Columns dialog box to clean up the mess.

8 **Choose F̲ormat, C̲olumns to open the Columns dialog box.**

9 **Type** 3 **in the N̲umber of Columns box.**

10 **Select the E̲qual Column Width check box.**

11 **Type** .25" **in the S̲pacing box.**

This setting narrows the gutter between the columns.

12 **Select the Line B̲etween check box.**

The dialog box's Preview window shows you how the page looks with the settings that you have chosen.

13 **Choose OK.**

The columns are now set at an equal width with quarter-inch gutters and a vertical line in between, as shown in Figure 10.12.

Figure 10.12
Equal-width columns with a line between them.

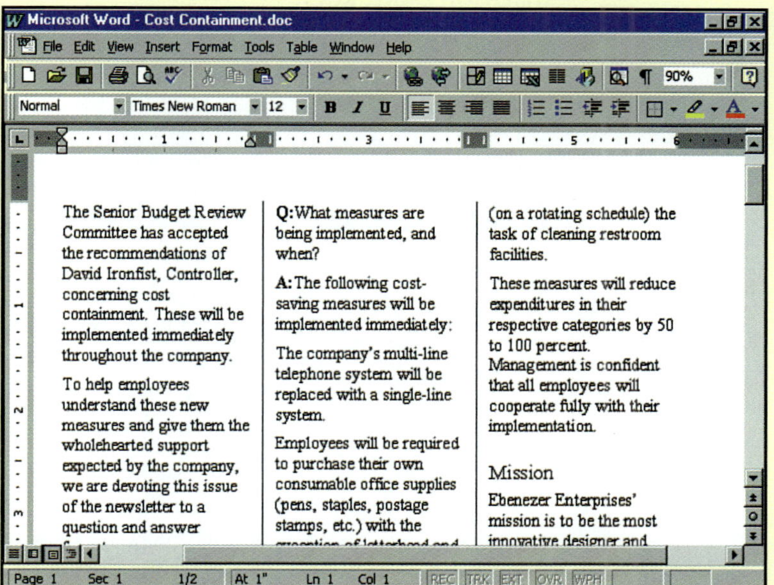

Word

To Resize Columns   (continued)

But what if you want a line between only one pair of columns and not anywhere else? You can use Word's Line Draw feature to place an individual line anywhere you want on the page, including between columns. To draw a line, right-click any toolbar and select Drawing. Click the Line button, then drag down the column gutter to where you want to insert the line. To remove the Drawing toolbar, right-click it and choose Drawing.

14 **Save this file and keep it onscreen for the next lesson.**

You can change the number and formatting of columns at any time. To change from three columns to four, for example, click anywhere inside any of the columns and use the Columns button on the toolbar to highlight four columns. You can also reduce the number of columns using this method.

To delete columns and return to a single column (there is always one column in a document, even a letter), place your cursor in your column structure and, using the Columns button on the toolbar, set the columns at 1.

Lesson 5: Mastering Insertion Point Movement in Columns

You can always use the mouse to relocate the insertion point when you're working in columns. But what about keyboard movement? When you work in Normal view, the insertion point moves normally when you use such navigation keystrokes as Ctrl+PgDn or ↓. But how does the insertion point move from one column to the next in Page Layout view when you use the insertion point keys?

Table 10.1 describes the ways in which the insertion point moves when you use columns in Page Layout view.

Table 10.1 Insertion Point Movement in Columns in Page Layout View	
Arrow	**Movement**
↓	The insertion point moves down through the current column to the bottom of the page and then continues down through the same column on the following page, and so on. On reaching the bottom of the column on the document's last page, the insertion point stops and does not proceed to the top of the next column.
↑	The insertion point moves up through the current column to the top of the page and then continues up through the same column on the preceding page, and so on. On reaching the top of the column on the document's first page, the insertion point stops and does not proceed to the top of the prior column.

Arrow	Movement
→	The insertion point moves through the text in one column, one line at a time, left to right. At the bottom of the page, the insertion point continues to the top of the next column on the same page. At the bottom of the last column on a page, the insertion point goes to the top of the first column on the next page.
←	The insertion point moves through the text in one column, one line at a time, right to left. At the top of the page, the insertion point continues to the bottom of the preceding column on the same page. At the top of the first column on the page, the insertion point goes to the bottom of the last column on the preceding page.
Alt+↑	The insertion point moves to the top of the previous column on the current page and continues to cycle through each column from right to left, never leaving the current page.
Alt+↓	The insertion point moves to the top of the next column on the current page and continues to cycle through each column from left to right, never leaving the current page.

Experiment now with the keyboard insertion point movements for columns.

To Master Insertion Point Movements in Columns

❶ Using the Columns button, select three equal columns for the column display and make sure that you are using Page Layout view.

The columns should appear side-by-side, three across the page.

❷ Referring to Table 10.1, practice moving the insertion point with the keyboard insertion point keys until you are comfortable with the movements.

❸ Experiment with other key combinations with which you are probably already familiar, such as Ctrl+↑ and Ctrl+↓ (up and down one paragraph at a time) and Ctrl+PgUp and Ctrl+PgDn (move the insertion point to the next or previous page).

❹ Save and close the file, but do not exit from Word.

Lesson 6: Inserting Column Breaks and Section Breaks

The real fun in working with columns comes when you want to have columns on only part of the page or when you want the text to break and head for the top of the next column before it gets to the bottom of the page. Figure 10.13 shows one way in which you can break columns to create interesting features.

Word

You might remember that when you designate two columns, three columns, or specific column measurements, these choices apply to the entire document. If you want to apply different column features to different parts of a document, you must designate sections in the document. When you start a new section, you can apply a column feature to one section without affecting any other section of the document.

Try working with sections and columns in a document now.

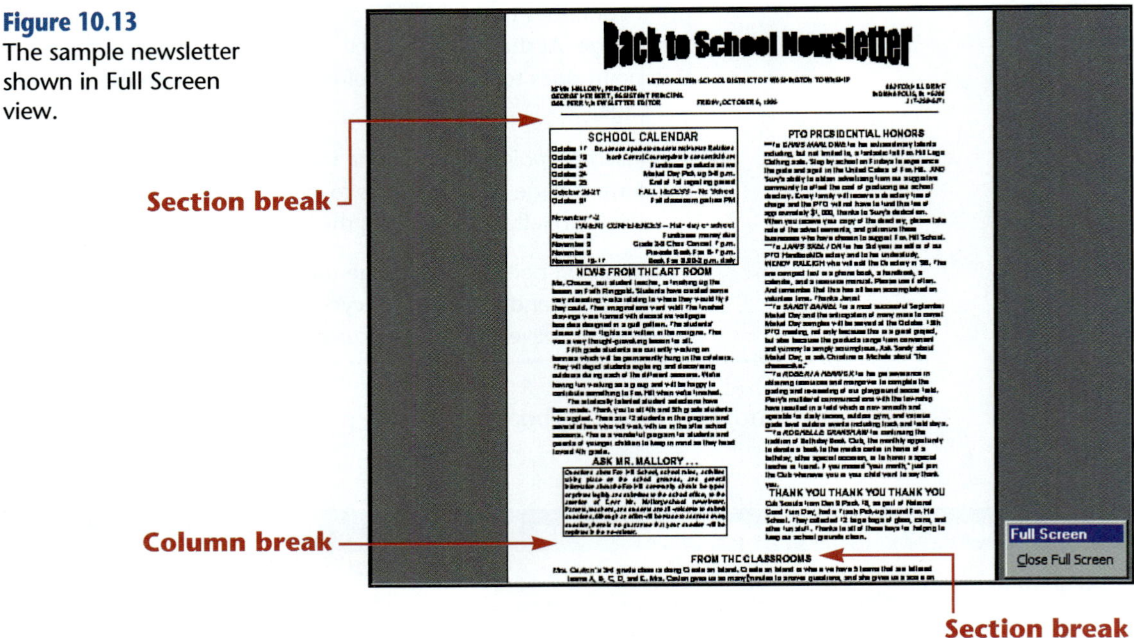

Figure 10.13
The sample newsletter shown in Full Screen view.

Section break

Column break

Section break

To Insert Column and Section Breaks

❶ **Open the folder Project-10 and the file Proj1003 from the CD and save the file as** Newsletter**.**

It is often easier to type an entire document before applying columns. This way, you can see how much material you have and then decide how best to present it. The newsletter with which you are working has been typed for you, but it needs columns to break up the material and make it easier to read. In this newsletter, you want to retain the masthead across the top of the page (one column), but then break the text beneath the masthead into two columns.

❷ **Place the insertion point on the blank line after the dashed line that separates the masthead from the body of the newsletter.**

When inserting breaks into a document, place the insertion point at the precise place where you want the break to occur.

❸ **Choose Insert, Break.**

The Break dialog box appears, as shown in Figure 10.14. In this dialog box, you can designate the type of break that you want to place in the document.

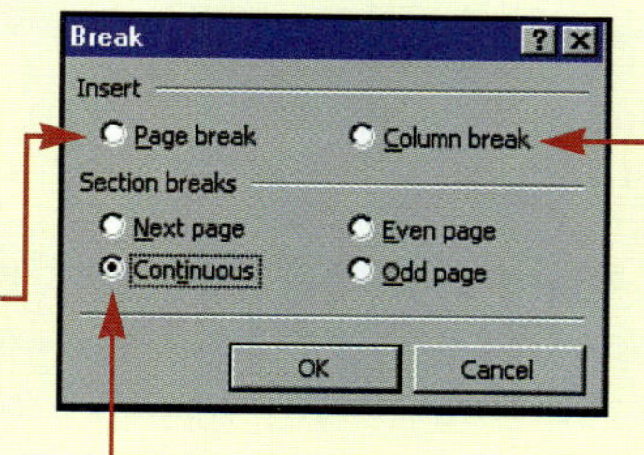

Figure 10.14
Tell Word to place a break in the document.

The Page Break option starts a new page

The Column Break option stops the text at the insertion point and resumes the text at the top of the next column

A section break places a nonprinting separator in the text so that each section can be addressed independently of the others

4 **In the Section Breaks panel, choose the Continuous option and then OK.**

A continuous section break places a nonprinting break in the text at the insertion point. In the status bar, you should now see that the insertion point is in section two.

5 **With the insertion point in section two, designate two columns for this section of the document.**

When you designate two columns for this section, the text in section two appears in columns, but the masthead (which is in section one) remains in one column, which spans the width of the page.

Currently, the text goes all the way to the bottom of the page in two columns. But you want to stop the columns part of the way down the page and then resume using one-column text. To make this change, you first must break the column part of the way down the page and have the text wrap to the second column at a specific point.

The story entitled PTO PRESIDENTIAL HONORS should start in this newsletter's second column, so you can put another break just before that story.

6 **Place the insertion point on the line above** PTO PRESIDENTIAL HONORS.

The insertion point is at the point where you want the text to break and continue in column two.

7 **Choose Insert, Break.**

This time, you don't want to end the section; you just want to stop the column. So don't choose a section break, but a column break.

8 **Choose the Column Break option and click OK.**

The text should now be split into two columns, with the story PTO PRESIDENTIAL HONORS heading up the second column.

9 **Click the Print Preview button to see how the whole page looks.**

The text breaks properly in column one and carries over to column two. Finally, you want to release the Column feature part of the

continues

To Insert Column and Section Breaks   (continued)

way down column two so that you can go back to full text across the bottom of the page.

10 **Choose <u>C</u>lose to exit Print Preview, then place the insertion point in the second column on the same line as the column break in column one, on the blank line at the end of the story titled** THANK YOU THANK YOU THANK YOU **(see Figure 10.15).**

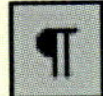

To help you see the actual column break, make sure that, if necessary, you display non-printing characters by clicking the Show/Hide button.

Figure 10.15

A column break moves the text below the insertion point to the next column.

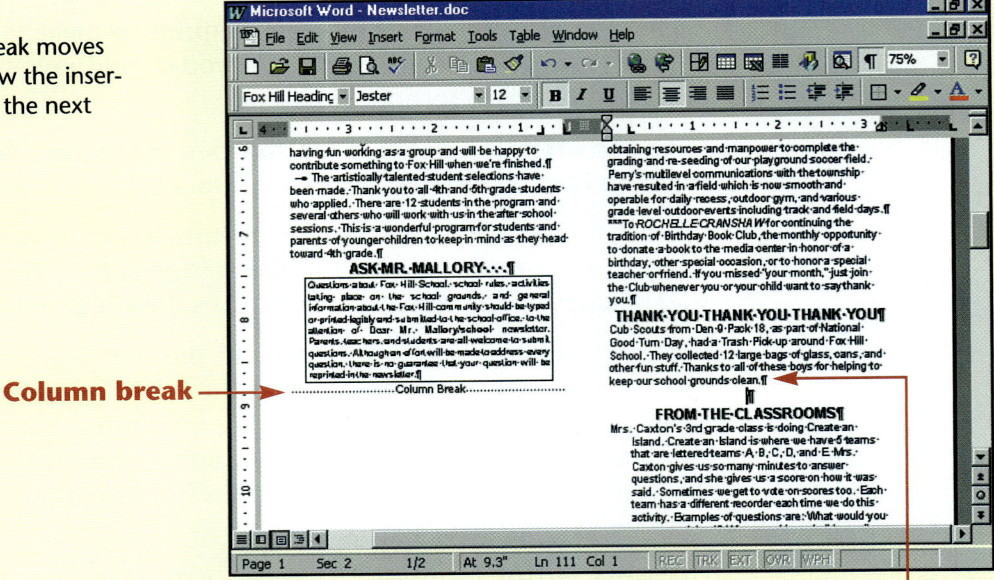

Before you can go back to full text rather than two columns, you must insert another section break.

11 **Choose <u>I</u>nsert, <u>B</u>reak. After the Break dialog box opens, click the Con<u>t</u>inuous option and click OK.**

12 **Make sure that the insertion point is in section three and then designate one column.**

The text at the bottom of the page spans the space between the page margins. Now finish the newsletter by breaking the final story into two columns.

13 **Place the insertion point at the beginning of the story titled MUSIC NOTES and insert a continuous section break.**

Exam Notes

Selecting a continuous section break results in balanced column lengths.

14 **Designate two columns for the** MUSIC NOTES **story in section four.**

Depending on exactly where the insertion point was when you placed breaks in the newsletter, you might have to adjust line spacing between some stories. The finished newsletter should look like the one in Figure 10.13.

You have completed all of the lessons in this project. If you have completed your session on the computer, exit Word and Windows 95 before turning off your computer. Otherwise, continue with the "Checking Your Skills" and "Applying Your Skills" sections.

Exam Notes

If you're not worried about balanced columns, but you would like to ensure that specific text does not get split from one column to the next, keep the text together by forcing the start of a new column with a column break. This technique is useful for placing headings and headlines at the top of a column. Insert a column break just before the heading or headline text.

Project Summary

To	Do This
Designate columns	With the insertion point anywhere in the section of the document in which you want to have columns, click the Standard toolbar's Columns button and drag across the grid until you reach the number of columns that you want.
Resize columns	Choose Format, Columns and enter the measurements for the columns. Choose OK when you're done.
Change the width gutter spaces	On the ruler, drag the edge on either side of a gutter marker to increase or decrease the size.
Move the insertion point in columns	In Page Layout view, press → to move the insertion point from the bottom of one column to the top of the next. Press ← to move the insertion point from the top of one column back to the bottom of the preceding column. Pressing ↑ and ↓ keeps the insertion point in the same column and moves you from page to page.
Insert a section break	Choose Insert, Break and then choose Continuous and click OK.
Insert a column break	Choose Insert, Break, choose Column Break, and click OK.

Checking Your Skills

True/False

For each of the following statements, check *T* or *F* to indicate whether the statement is true or false.

__T __F **1.** The space separating your columns must be the same for all the columns in your document.

__T __F **2.** If you designate more columns than you want, you can click the Columns button again to change the number of columns.

__T __F **3.** You can see the margins of your columns if you display the ruler.

__T __F **4.** You can force text to move to the top of the next column before it reaches the bottom of the page.

__T __F **5.** If you want your columns to start at the beginning of the document, your insertion point must be at the beginning of the document when you select the Columns feature.

__T __F **6.** You must divide a document into columns before you enter text.

__T __F **7.** You can drag a column marker on the ruler to change a column's width.

__T __F **8.** When the insertion point is in the top line of a right-hand column, press ⬆ to move to the last line of the column to the left.

__T __F **9.** You can use section breaks to format a document with different numbers of columns.

__T __F **10.** You can only see columns onscreen in Print Preview.

Multiple Choice

Circle the letter of the correct answer for each of the following questions.

1. What do you call the space between the columns?

    a. Alley

    b. Septic tank

    c. Gutter

    d. Sewer

2. The status bar tells you that you are typing in which of the following?

    a. Column

    b. Document

    c. Font

    d. Format

3. Which option do you select to place a line between your columns?

    a. Border between

    b. Line between

    c. Separate columns

    d. You can't place a line between columns

4. When columns are displayed in Page Layout view, where does the insertion point move when you press (Alt)+(↑)?

    a. To the top of the previous column on the same page

    b. To the bottom of the previous column on the same page

    c. To the top of the next paragraph on the next page

    d. To the top of the same paragraph on the next page

5. To display text in two columns in part of your document and three columns in another part of the same document, what kind of break can you use?

    a. Column

    b. Continuous section

    c. Page

    d. Any of the above

6. What type of break should you use to force text from the bottom of one column to the top of the next column?

    a. Column

    b. Next page section

    c. Page

    d. Any of the above

7. What view does Word use to display columns?

    a. Normal

    b. Outline

    c. Page Layout

    d. Print Preview

8. Which does Word display onscreen when you drag a column marker to resize columns?

    a. The gutter

    b. A four-headed arrow

    c. An I-beam

    d. A vertical, dashed line

9. By default, how many columns are created in a new, blank Word document?

    a. One

    b. Two

    c. Three

    d. None

10. What options should be on if you want to see column breaks onscreen?

    a. Show/Hide Columns

    b. Show/Hide Breaks

    c. Show/Hide Layout

    d. Show/Hide ¶

Completion

In the blank provided, write the correct answer for each of the following statements.

1. Set precise column widths in the _____________ dialog box.

2. In ___________-style columns, text flows from the bottom of one column to the top of the next column.

3. Use a(n) _____________ break to stop the text before it reaches the bottom of the page and start it at the top of the next column.

4. By default, Word creates columns so that each column is the same
   ________________.

5. When you type in ______________ view, all your columns appear as if
   they are one long column on the left side of the page.

6. Column ________ on the ruler show where each column boundary is
   placed.

7. Space between columns is called the __________.

8. Choose Word's preset _________ column option to create two columns
   with the left column half as wide as the right column.

9. Choose Word's preset _________ column option to create two columns
   with the right column half as wide as the left column.

10. Press (Alt)+_________ to cycle the insertion point to the top of the next
    column on the current page, left to right.

Matching

In the blank next to each of the following terms or phrases, write the letter
of the corresponding term or phrase. (Note that some letters may be used
more than once.)

a. (Alt)+(↓)

b. (Alt)+(↑)

c. Page Layout

d. Column markers

e. Gutter

f. Section break

g. Grid

h. Column break

i. Line between

j. Newspaper-style

________ 1. Element used to control the length of text in a column

________ 2. Element used to allow different numbers of columns in the
           same document

________ 3. Element that drops down from the Columns button so you
           can specify the number of columns to create

________ 4. Elements that display the borders between columns on the
           ruler

________ 5. Space between columns

________ 6. View Word uses to display columns onscreen

________ 7. Key combination used to cycle through each column from left
           to right, never leaving the current page

________ 8. Key combination used to cycle through each column from
           right to left, never leaving the current page

________ 9. Columns in which text flows from the bottom of one column
           to the top of the next column

________ 10. Option used to insert a visual border between columns

Applying Your Skills

Practice

The following exercises enable you to practice the skills you have learned in
this project. Take a few minutes to work through these exercises now.

Creating a Brochure Formatted in Columns

In this practice lesson, you create a brochure for the New Food Café. You create a new document, format it into multiple columns, and enter some text.

To create a brochure formatted in columns, follow these steps:

1. Create a new, blank document in Word and save it in your `Practices` folder with the name `Cafe Brochure`.

2. Use the Columns button on the Standard toolbar to format the document in two columns of equal width.

3. On the first line, in 16-point Arial, type `New Food Café`, then press `⏎Enter`.

4. On the next line, in 14-point Arial, type `Where those in the know come to dine!` (Notice how the text wraps within the first column.)

5. Type the following information in 14-point Arial. Leave a blank line between each paragraph.

New Food Café is an avant-garde restaurant that has recently opened on Main Street in Carmel. New Food offers a diverse and eclectic menu that appeals to a diverse and eclectic clientele.

The décor is homey and inviting, yet surprisingly sophisticated. Original artwork is displayed on every wall, adding a charming feeling to the already warm environment. A large fireplace takes up the back wall, while the front windows provide a frame for the activity on the street outside.

The owner, Janice Dumais, is a newcomer to the restaurant scene. Previously, she operated a folk-art gallery. Ms. Dumais has vowed to maintain the integrity of the New Food Café vision. She makes herself available to her customers and can usually be found table-hopping through the dining room.

The chef, Sam Dumais, is the owner's brother. His love of food and his willingness to experiment are evident in the interesting specials he prepares daily. Mr. Dumais' talents are numerous—in addition to the daily specials, he is responsible for the fresh baked breads and pastries that grace the tables.

The New Food Café is open from 11:30 a.m. to 10:00 p.m. Tuesday through Saturday. On Sundays, the hours are 9:30 a.m. to 10:00 p.m. The charming Sunday brunch should not be missed.

The New Food Café also has a private room that can be reserved for parties and functions.

Following is a list of lunch items available on a daily basis:

Turkey Club

Hamburger

Cheeseburger

Fish and Chips

Soup of the Day

Pasta of the Day

Stop by and find out why the New Food Café is where those in the know come to dine!

6. Check the spelling and grammar in the document and save it. Preview it. If requested by your instructor, print it. Close the document when you have finished.

Editing a Document Formatted in Columns

In this practice lesson, you format and edit text in a version of the brochure document you created in the previous exercise.

To edit a document formatted columns, follow these steps:

1. Open the file Proj1004 from the Project-10 folder on the CD and save it in your `Practices` folder with the name `Café Brochure2`.

2. Format the list of lunch items as a bullet list. Use a simple dot as the bullet marker.

3. Cut the list and the paragraph preceding it from its current location and paste it between the paragraph that introduces the food and the paragraph that introduces the décor.

4. Insert the following text at the end of the paragraph that mentions the private room: `The room has a fireplace, and accommodates up to 25 people.`

5. Apply bold to all occurrences of the restaurant name.

6. Insert a line between the two columns.

7. Check the spelling and grammar in the document and preview it. Save the document. If requested by your instructor, print it. Close the document when you have finished.

Applying Columns to an Existing Document

You believe that if you use columns, you can fit the Interview scholarly report on one page. In this practice lesson, you practice formatting the document into different numbers of columns, using different column and gutter widths.

To apply columns to an existing document, follow these steps:

1. Open the file Proj1005 from the Project-10 folder on the CD and save it in your `Practices` folder with the name `Interviews5`.

2. Replace the text Student's Name with your name, then use the Columns button to format the document into three columns of equal width.

3. Use the Columns button to change back to single-column formatting. (Hint: Select only one column in the drop-down grid.)

4. Use the Format, Columns command to format the document into two columns of unequal width. Set the width of the left column to 3".

5. Use the ↓ key to move the insertion point down to the end of the document. You can see that the document still does not fit on one page.

6. Change the margins to 1.25" on all sides. Now the document fits on one page.

7. Use the Columns button to change the layout to one column, then use it to change the layout to two columns of equal width.

8. Change the gutter width to .75".

9. Preview the document. If requested by your instructor, print it. Close the document when you have finished.

Changing Column Formatting

In this practice lesson, you modify column formatting and use column breaks to improve the appearance of the Interview report.

To change column formatting, follow these steps:

1. Open the file Proj1006 from the Project-10 folder on the CD and save it in your Practices folder with the name Interviews6.

2. Use the Format, Columns command and apply the Left preset layout to the document.

3. Drag the column marker on the ruler to move the right border of the left column just a bit to the right. This should increase the width of the column just enough so that no words in the title are split onto two lines.

4. Scroll down to the bottom of the page. You think the document might look better if the last paragraph in the left column moved to the top of the right column.

5. Insert a column break before the subheading Question of Validity.

6. Cut the last paragraph in the document, including its subheading, and move it before the column break. Notice that the column break moves to make room for the pasted text, so it now falls near the top of the right-hand column, forcing the text after it onto the next page.

7. Delete the column break. (Hint: Position the insertion point on the column break and press Del.)

8. Insert a column break before the subheading First Impressions Count.

9. Insert a line between the two columns.

10. Preview the document and save it. If requested by your instructor, print it. Close the document when you are finished.

Using Different Column Formatting in the Same Document

In this practice lesson, you insert section breaks so that you can use different column formatting in the same document.

To use different column formatting in the same document, follow these steps:

1. Open the file Proj1007 from the Project-10 folder on the CD and save it in your Practices folder with the name Technology2.

2. Format the document into two columns of equal width. The letterhead and logo do not look right in a narrow column format.

3. Change back to single-column formatting.

4. Position the insertion point at the beginning of the line with the `I. Implementing New Technology.`, and insert a continuous section break.

5. Now, leave the letterhead section in one column and format the second section into three columns of equal width.

6. Insert a column break before the sentence `Applications will be gradually introduced over a three-phase period` that falls at the bottom of the first column.

7. Insert a line between the columns.

8. Preview the document and save it. If requested by your instructor, print it. Close the document when you have finished.

Challenge

The following challenges enable you to use your problem-solving skills. Take time to work through these exercises now.

Creating a Newsletter

Use the skills you have learned in this project to format a document as a company newsletter.

Open the file Proj1008 from the Project-10 folder on the CD and save it in your `Challenges` folder as `Newsletter`. The document contains the material for a company newsletter, but it has all been entered in one column. Start by inserting a section break between the banner heading and the first headline, `Welcome`. Apply a two-column format to the second section.

Justify the text in the columns. Center the sales table in the right column. (Hint: Select the table and click the center button on the Formatting toolbar.) Notice that the heading `Sales Sources` falls at the bottom of a column. Insert a column break to move it to the top of the next column. Notice that this causes one sentence of text to move onto a third page. Decrease the width of the gutter between the columns to .3". This should provide enough space so that the document fits on two pages.

Preview the document and save it. If requested by your instructor, print it. Close the document when you have finished.

Creating a Flyer with Columns

Use the skills you have learned in this project to format a document with columns. Separate the document into different sections so you can change the number of columns in each section. Control the flow of text using column breaks.

Open the file Proj1009 from the Project-10 folder on the CD and save it in your `Challenges` folder as `Flyer`. Use section breaks to divide the document so that all text up to and including the heading `Q & A` is the first section, formatted in a single column. The Q & A section should end before the `Cost Saving Measures` heading. It should be formatted in two columns. Use a column break to align the text as evenly as possible. The third section should begin with the `Cost Saving Measures` heading and continue through the `Other News Around the Company` heading. It should be formatted in one column. The remaining section of the document should be formatted in two columns. Use a column break to position each article in a different column. Make the right column narrower than the left column so that the text appears to be approximately the same length in both columns.

Create a footer for the document that has the company name flush left, the page number in the middle, and the date in an updating field on the right.

Preview the document and save it. If requested by your instructor, print it. Close the document when you are finished.

Formatting the Proposal into Columns

Use the skills you have learned in this project to format the proposal document you have been working with into columns. Pay attention to the different elements such as the letterhead, bullet lists, and table that may require different column widths or spacing.

Open the file Proj1010 from the Project-10 folder on the CD and save it in your `Challenges` folder as `Proposal6`.

Format the document so that the letterhead remains in single-column format. You want the `Overview` heading centered over a section on the first page, and the `Proposal` heading centered over a section on the second page. Under each heading, format the document in two columns. Make sure the entire table fits within a column so you can read all of the data. Also, use column breaks as well as column and gutter width to ensure that no subheadings are too close to the bottom of a column, and so that no bullet list is split across columns or pages. If the `Financial Statement` ends, being the only text on the third page, format it in a single column.

Creating a Catalogue Page

Use the skills you have learned in this project to create a new document that you will use as a page in the course catalogue for `Training Concepts Unlimited`.

Create a new document and save it in your `Challenges` folder as `Catalogue`. Set it up in two columns, with the left column half as wide as the right column. Type `Course List`, then press ⏎Enter twice and type the following information. Put each course on a separate line, and leave a blank space between the categories of courses. For example, leave a space between the Excel courses and the Word courses.

`Type in Excel 1, Excel 2, Excel 3, Word 1, Word 2, Word 3, Access 1, Access 2, Access 3, PowerPoint, Internet Explorer 1, Internet Explorer 2, Internet Explorer 3, Outlook Express, Web Page Authoring.`

Type the heading `Introduction`, then press ⏎Enter twice and continue typing the following: `Welcome to the wonderful world of Training Concepts Unlimited! This catalogue is designed to provide you with all of the information you need to make a smart decision about corporate training. We include detailed descriptions of all the courses we offer, as well as pricing information and class locations.`

As you may know, Training Concepts Unlimited offers a membership plan designed to save you money. When you enroll as a member, you receive preferential treatment in all areas of training, including scheduling, locations, and, of course, costs. You also receive special notifications about new course offerings and other interesting activities.

Type the heading Support Materials Available, press ⏎Enter twice and continue typing Also included with this catalogue are pages and pages of items that we also offer for sale, including books and supplies. Although the name Training Concepts Unlimited is associated with corporate training, you may be pleased to know that we also sell support materials. We can even custom order many items, including pencils, T-shirts, and coffee mugs.

Check the spelling and grammar in the document and save it. Go back and format the headings in 16-point Arial. Format the regular text in 14-point Times New Roman. Apply bold face to every occurrence of the company name. Justify all text. At the beginning of the document set up a new section formatted in a single column and type the company name, centered in 24-point Times New Roman. Leave 18 points of space after the company name. Check the spelling and grammar again, then save the document. If requested by your instructor, print it. Close the document when you have finished.

Modifying the Catalogue

Use the skills you have learned in this project to improve the appearance of the catalogue page.

Open the file Proj1011 from the Project-10 folder on the CD and save it in your Challenges folder as Catalogue2. Insert a column break before the heading Introduction. Change the width of both columns, decreasing the width of the left column to 2" and increasing the width of the right column to 3.5". Insert a line between the columns. Preview the document. Save it, and if requested by your instructor, print it. Close the document when you have finished.

You have completed the project and the associated lessons, as well as the "Checking Your Skills" and "Applying Your Skills" sections. Now use the PinPoint software evaluation mode to assess your comprehension of the specific exam tasks you have just learned. You can also use the PinPoint Trainer Mode and the Show Me tutorials to practice these specific exam tasks.

Collaborating on Documents

Working with Workgroup Editing

In this Project, you learn how to:

Objectives	Required Activities
➤ Highlight Key Points in a Document	
➤ Insert Comments in a Document … … … … … … …	Insert Comments in a Document Add Comments to the File Properties
➤ Review and Edit Comments in a Document	
➤ Track and Review Changes to a Document … … …	Track Changes to a Document Route Documents
➤ Compare Documents	
➤ Protect Documents … … … … … … … … … … …	Protect Documents
➤ Save Different Versions of a Document … … … …	Create Multiple Versions of a Document
➤ Create a Master Document … … … … … … … …	Create Master Documents

Why Would I Do This?

t is a rare event today when a single individual is responsible for planning, developing, writing, and editing any serious document. Usually, many people are involved—submitting ideas, providing comments and feedback, reviewing, and rewriting. With hard copy printouts, this process can result in confusion, wasted paper, and a lot of time spent incorporating other people's changes into your version.

Word 97 includes many features designed to help people work together to create documents. Word takes charge of the organizational tasks involved in collaboration, such as tracking changes made by different people, dating different versions of the same document so you always know which is the most current, and identifying the source of comments inserted in the text. You and your coworkers are free to focus on the important things, such as actually writing and preparing the document.

In this project, you learn how to develop a report worked on by many people. You use the tools involved in collaborating to learn how to highlight key points in a document so that others can easily find important items. You insert and edit comments and track changes. You learn how to save different versions of a document, how to route a document, and how to compare versions of a document and mark the differences between them. You also protect a document to prevent unauthorized people from making changes. Lastly, you learn how to create a master document.

Lesson 1: Highlighting Key Points in a Document

You can easily highlight the key elements in a Word document that you want someone else to review. Highlighting is useful when you need someone to look at only a few parts of a document, or when you want the main topics to stand out.

Highlight
To surround data with a different color so that it stands out in the document.

When you *highlight* text or graphics in a document, Word applies a colored shading to the selection. By default the shading is yellow, but you can change the color whenever you want. You can even use different colors within the document. For example, you can highlight main topics that you want someone to review in yellow and highlight topics that you need to expand in pink. Or you can color code the highlighting according to the reviewer; one person can highlight in green, another in blue, and so on.

In this lesson, you learn how to highlight parts of a report document using the default highlight color. You then learn how to change the highlight color.

To Highlight Key Points in a Document

1 **Open the folder Project-11 and then the file Proj1101 from this book's CD and save it as** `Cost Containment Report.`

This document is a report that's being developed by the Cost Containment Panel for the company Oak Grove Products, Inc. You use it throughout this project. First, display the Reviewing toolbar, which provides buttons to quickly access most of the tools you use in this project.

2 **Choose View, Toolbars, Reviewing.**

Word displays the Reviewing toolbar (see Figure 11.1). Now, to draw immediate attention to the major sections of the document, try highlighting headings.

3 **Select the first heading in the document—**`Mission`**—and then click the Highlight button on the Reviewing toolbar.**

Word highlights the selected text, as shown in Figure 11.1.

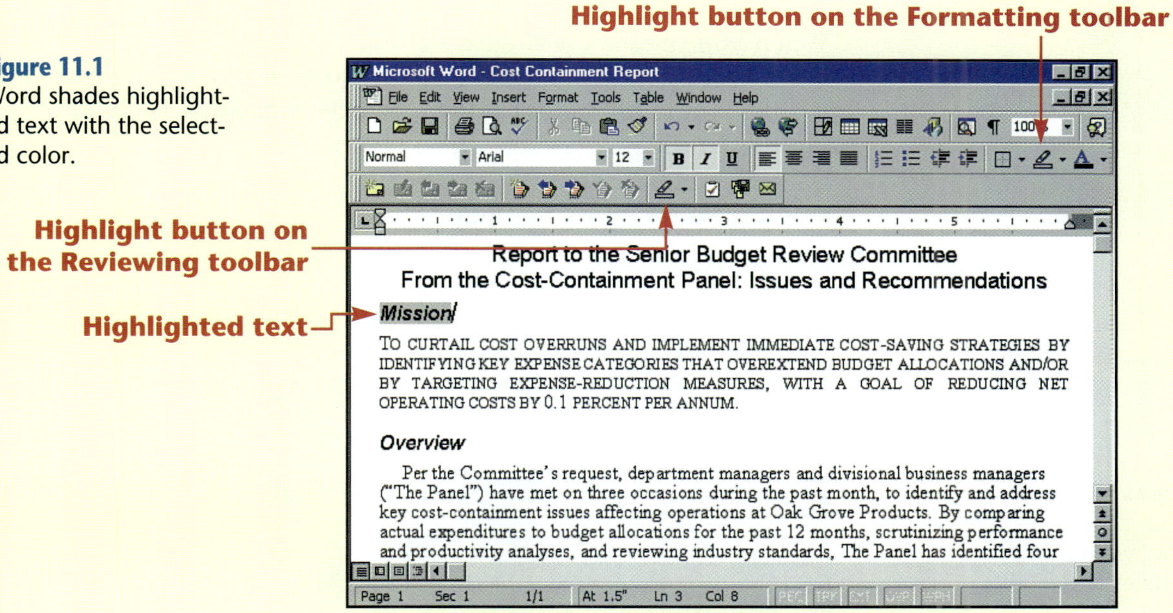

Figure 11.1
Word shades highlighted text with the selected color.

If you have problems...

If you don't have the Reviewing toolbar displayed, you can use the Highlight button on the Formatting toolbar. It performs exactly the same function.

If the highlight color does not appear in your document, you may have highlighting hidden. Choose Tools, Options, click the View tab, select the Highlight check box, and then click OK. If it still does not appear, someone may have set the highlight color to None. Also, the default highlighting shade is yellow, which may not show up very well on a monochrome monitor or when printed on a standard black-and-white printer. You learn how to change the highlight color later in this lesson.

continues

Word

To Highlight Key Points in a Document   (continued)

You can move the Reviewing toolbar to any location on the screen. In the figures used for this project, the Reviewing toolbar is displayed across the top of the document window, between the Ruler and the Formatting toolbar.

To remove the highlighting, you simply repeat the procedure.

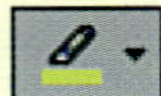

4 Select the `Mission` **heading again and click the Highlight button again.**

Word removes the highlighting from the text.

When you want to highlight multiple items in succession, you can toggle the highlighter so it remains on. When the highlighter is on, any text that you select with the mouse becomes highlighted.

5 Click the Highlight button.

The button appears pressed in. The highlighting feature will remain on until you click the button again.

6 Click and drag across the `Mission` **heading.**

When you release the mouse button, Word highlights the selected text. Highlighting stays on (active), so that you can continue to highlight text in the document. Notice that when highlighting is on, the mouse pointer becomes a pen marker attached to an I-beam (see Figure 11.2). With this highlighter tool, you select any text or graphics you want to highlight.

7 Double-click the `Overview` **heading.**

Word highlights the heading. Now both the Mission heading and the Overview heading are highlighted, as shown in Figure 11.2. The highlighter tool is still active, so you can highlight the last heading in the document.

Figure 11.2
With the highlighter tool, you can highlight a series of elements.

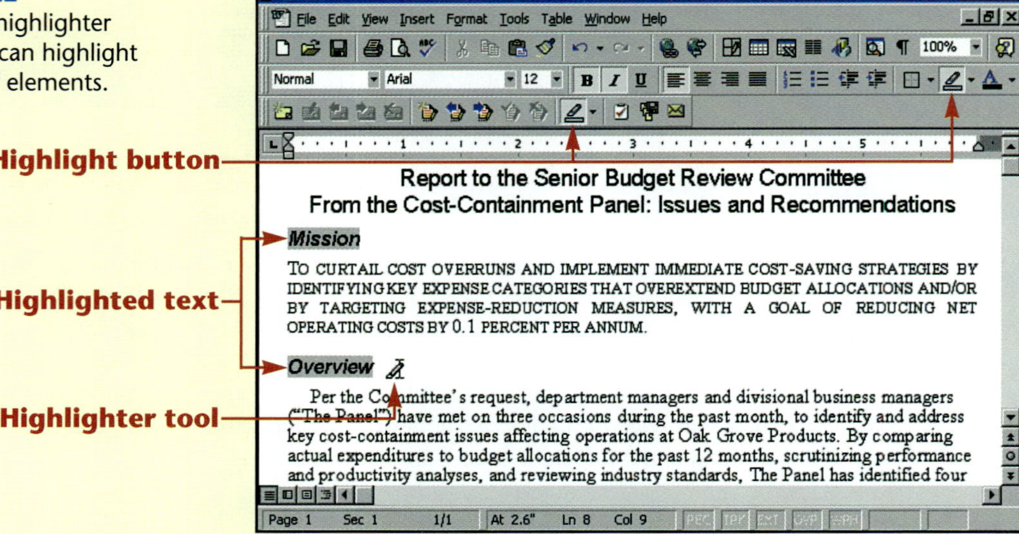

Highlight button
Highlighted text
Highlighter tool

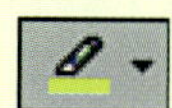

8 **Scroll down in the document, select the heading** `Targeted Expense Categories`**, and click the Highlight button.**

Word highlights the heading and turns off the highlighter. The button no longer appears pressed in. Now try changing the highlight color.

9 **Click the arrow button on the right side of the Highlight button.**

Word displays the highlight color palette, as shown in Figure 11.3. You can select any color from the palette.

Figure 11.3
Click a color on the palette to change the highlight shade.

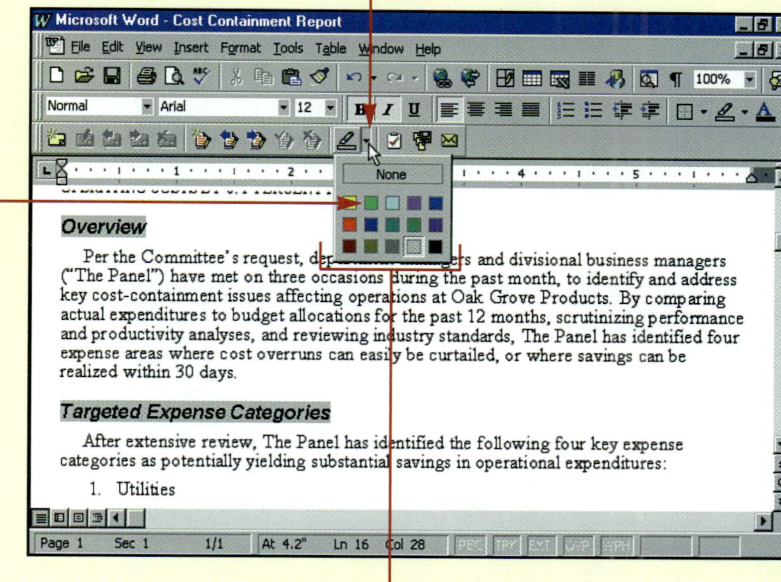

10 **Click Bright Green.**

This step changes the highlight color to bright green and turns on the highlighter tool. Any text you select now is highlighted in green.

To remind yourself to fill in the budgetary figures for this example, highlight the caption for Table 1.

11 **Select the** `Table 1` **caption.**

Word highlights the caption in green, as shown in Figure 11.4, and the highlighter remains active.

continues

Figure 11.4
You can use different highlight colors in one document.

The table caption is highlighted in green

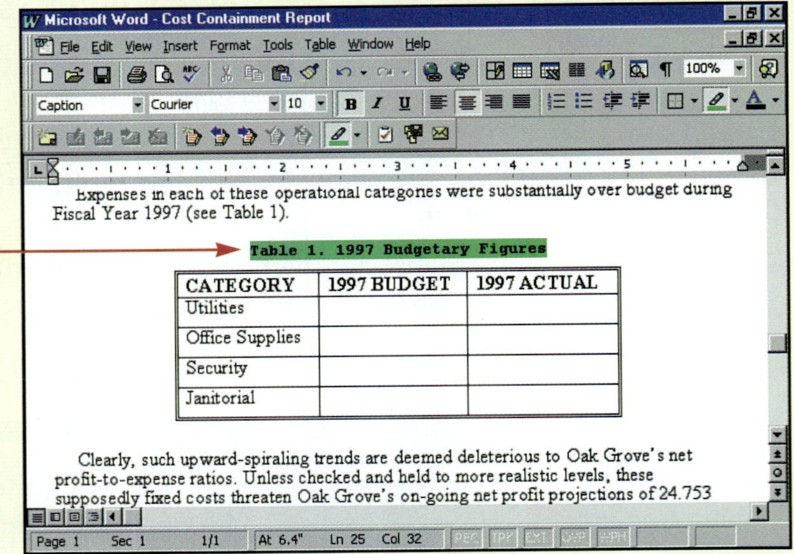

CATEGORY	1997 BUDGET	1997 ACTUAL
Utilities		
Office Supplies		
Security		
Janitorial		

You have now highlighted all the items you need to highlight in the document, so you can turn off the highlighter.

12 Click the Highlight button on the Formatting toolbar.

This step turns off the highlighter.

13 Save the Cost Containment Report document and leave it open.

In the next lesson, you learn how to insert comments into a document.

Inside Stuff

You can turn off the highlighter quickly by typing new text in the document. The highlighter tool changes back to a regular insertion point, and the new text appears without highlighting.

Highlighting works best when a document is going to be reviewed online. Unless you use a color printer, highlighted text prints as shaded text. If you plan to print a document with highlighting, you should use a very light color for shading.

To print highlights, set the options in the Highlight Changes dialog box by choosing Tools, Track Changes, Highlight Changes from the menu. In the Highlight Changes dialog box, select Highlight changes in printed document to print changes; deselect this option to turn off printing highlights.

To remove highlighting in a large portion of a document, select as much text as you want and choose None from the highlight palette. When you want to highlight again, simply select the highlight color you want to use from the highlight palette before you select the items to highlight.

Lesson 2: Inserting Comments in a Document

With Word, you can make suggestions to an author by inserting comments into a document. This is the equivalent of writing notes in the margins of a printed document. Word marks the location in the document where the comment is inserted and displays the comments in a separate window pane. Comments are numbered and identified by reviewer. If you are familiar with using Word's footnotes or endnotes feature, you will see that inserting comments is similar.

In this lesson, you learn how to insert *comments* into a document.

Comment

A note or other text inserted in a document, but displayed in a separate pane or ScreenTip.

To Insert Comments in a Document

1 **In the** Cost Containment Report **document, position the insertion point at the end of the sentence under the** Mission **heading.**

You will insert a comment suggesting changes to the mission statement.

2 **Click the Insert Comment button on the Reviewing toolbar.**

Word highlights the word preceding the insertion point in the document, inserts a comment mark, and opens the Comment pane, as shown in Figure 11.5. The insertion point is in the Comment pane, next to the corresponding comment mark. Each comment mark consists of the reviewer's initials and a number, enclosed in brackets.

Figure 11.5

Enter comment text in the Comment pane.

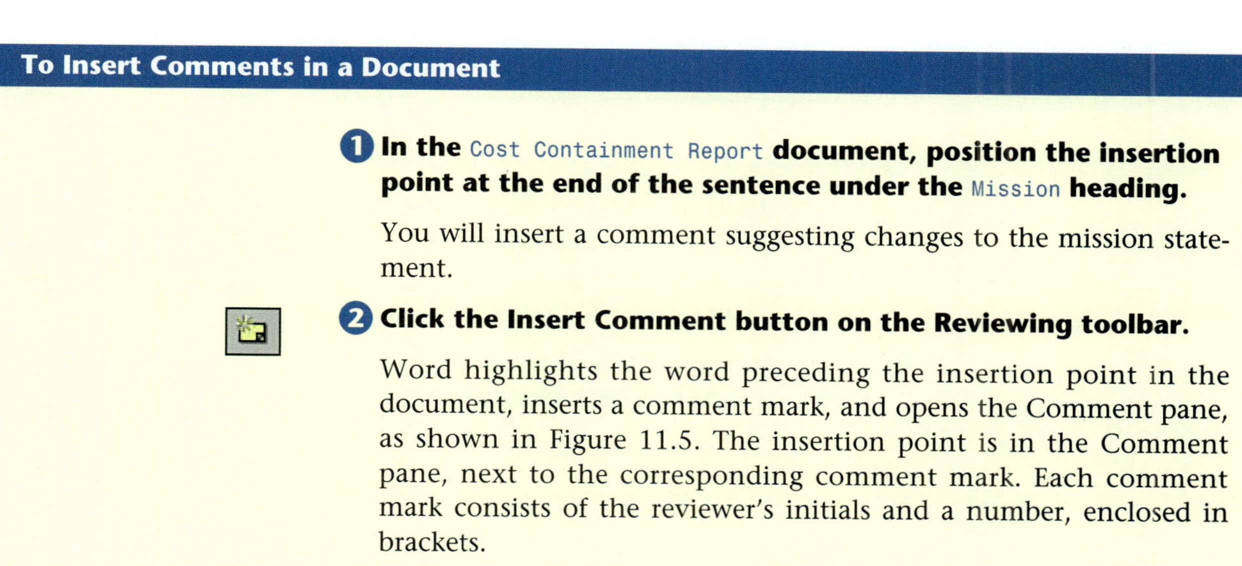

Comment mark in the document

Comment pane

Comment mark in the Comment pane

continues

Word

To Insert Comments in a Document (continued)

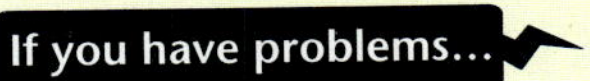

If Word does not highlight the text in yellow, you do not have it set to display ScreenTips. Choose Tools, Options, click the View tab, select the ScreenTips check box, and click OK.

On monochrome monitors, you may have trouble seeing the yellow highlight onscreen. To identify the location of comments when you can't see the highlighting, you can display the comment marks in the document by displaying hidden text. To display hidden text (including comment marks), choose Tools, Options, click the View tab, select the Hidden Text check box, and then click OK. If you display all hidden text, the comment marks are displayed as well. Simply click the Show/Hide ¶ button on the Standard toolbar to hide or show marks.

3 **Type** `Verify target goal with upper management..`

This is the comment text. You can continue working in the document with the Comment pane open, or you can close the pane until you are ready to insert, review, or edit comments. Before you close the pane, add one more comment.

4 **In the document window, position the insertion point in the word** `three` **in the first sentence under the** `Overview` **heading.**

You insert a comment here.

5 **Click the Insert Comment button on the Reviewing toolbar.**

Word inserts another comment mark and moves the insertion point into the Comment pane.

6 **Type** `I thought we met four times..`

You now have two comments entered in the document, as shown in Figure 11.6.

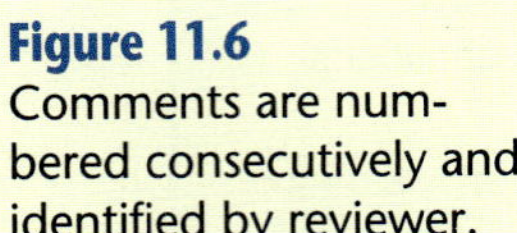
Figure 11.6
Comments are numbered consecutively and identified by reviewer.

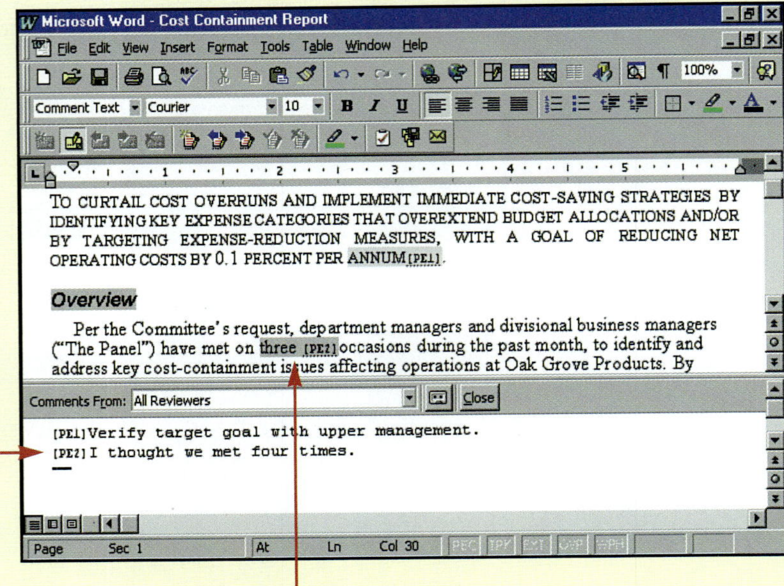

Corresponding mark in Comment pane

Comment mark in document

Now close the Comment pane.

7 Click the Close button in the Comment pane.

Word closes the Comment pane and hides the comment marks. The locations of the comments are highlighted in the document text in a pale yellow (see Figure 11.7).

Figure 11.7
Text that has comments attached appears highlighted in pale yellow.

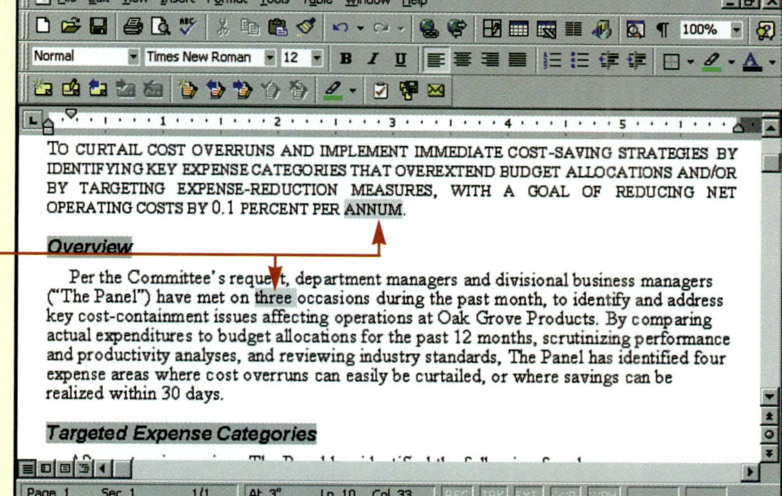

Comment mark highlighting

If you have problems...

If Word displays comment marks in the document even when the Comment pane is closed, it just means that you have hidden text displayed. You can keep it displayed or hide it. To hide hidden text (including comment marks) choose Tools, Options, click the View tab, deselect the Hidden Text check box, and then click OK. If you display all hidden text, the comment marks are displayed as well. Simply click the Show/Hide ¶ button on the Standard toolbar to hide or show marks.

8 Save the changes you have made to the Cost Containment Report and keep it open.

In the next lesson, you learn how to review and edit comments.

Inside Stuff

You can also insert comments using menu commands. Position the insertion point where you want to insert a comment and then choose Insert, Comment.

Exam Notes

You can also store comments about a document in the document Summary. Different than inserting comments into the document itself, the Document summary contains important information about each document. You can search for a document on the basis of this information, or incorporate some of this information into the document itself. If your document is used by others, including the document Summary information could be most useful.

continues

To insert comments into the Document Properties dialog box, open the document and choose File, Properties. Select the Summary tab and add your comments to the Comments field. An example of the kind of information you might include in the Comments field is `draft copy of the ABC proposal - for review`. Click OK to save the document properties.

To include Document Properties information in the document itself, place a field in the document. You learned how to place fields into Word documents; choose Insert, Field and in the Categories list box, select Document Information. A list of document information fields appears in the Filed Names dialog box; choose which of the document properties you want to include (such as the Comments field). Click OK.

Lesson 3: Reviewing and Editing Comments in a Document

After comments are entered into a document, you can review them and edit them at any time. The easiest way to review the comments is directly onscreen, while you are working with the document. You can also read them and edit them in the Comment pane.

In this lesson, you learn how to review comments onscreen and in the Comment pane. You also learn how to edit and delete comments.

To Review and Edit Comments in a Document

1 **In the Cost Containment Report document, click the word** ANNUM **at the end of the text under the** Mission **heading; leave the mouse pointer so it is touching the highlighted word.**

This text is associated with a comment. When you point at it with the mouse, a Comment icon flashes next to the mouse pointer and a ScreenTip appears, displaying the name of the reviewer and the comment text (see Figure 11.8).

If you have problems...

If a ScreenTip does not appear when you point at the comment highlight in the document, check two things. First, make sure that you are not moving the mouse pointer at all. Second, make sure that ScreenTips are turned on.

2 **Click the Next Comment button on the Reviewing toolbar and leave the mouse pointer touching the button.**

Word moves the insertion point to the next comment in the document and displays a ScreenTip with the comment and the reviewer's name. Try editing this comment.

Figure 11.8
Comment ScreenTips display the name of the person who created the comment, as well as the comment text.

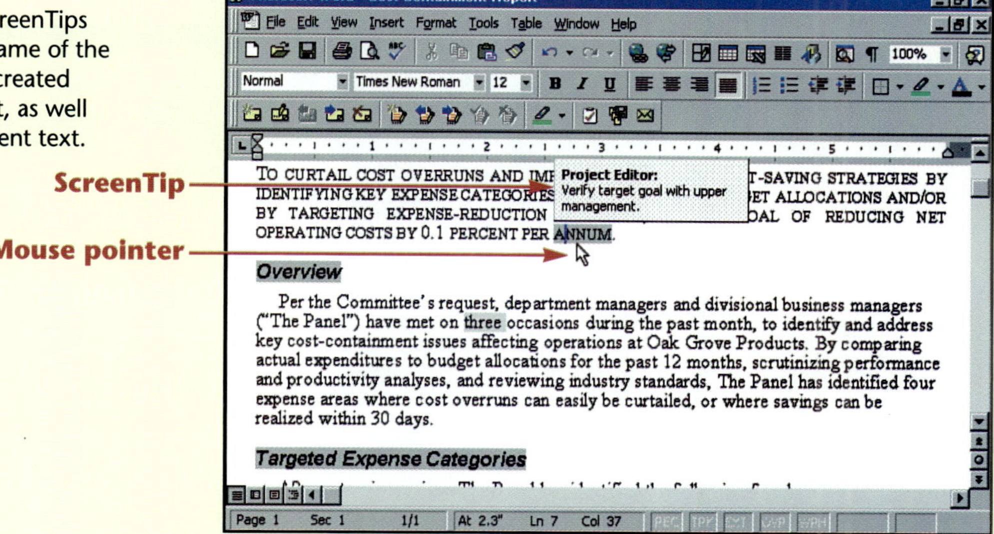

ScreenTip

Mouse pointer

③ Click the Edit Comment button on the Reviewing toolbar.

Word opens the Comment pane, displaying the list of comments in the document. You can edit the text of any comment in the Comment pane.

④ Change the text of comment 2 to `I thought we met five times.`

The text is changed. When you point at the comment with the mouse pointer, you can see the change in the ScreenTip. You can insert or delete comments with the Comment pane open or closed. Now, with the Comment pane still open, try deleting a comment.

⑤ Scroll up in the document window and click the word ANNUM.

You delete the comment associated with this text.

⑥ Click the Delete Comment button on the Reviewing toolbar.

Word deletes the comment and removes the highlight from the document text. Then Word automatically renumbers the remaining comments in the document, as shown in Figure 11.9.

⑦ Click the Close button in the Comment pane.

Word closes the pane, leaving only one comment in the document.

⑧ Save the Cost Containment Report document and keep it open on your screen.

In the next lesson, you learn how to track changes to a document by using revision marks.

continues

To Review and Edit Comments in a Document (continued)

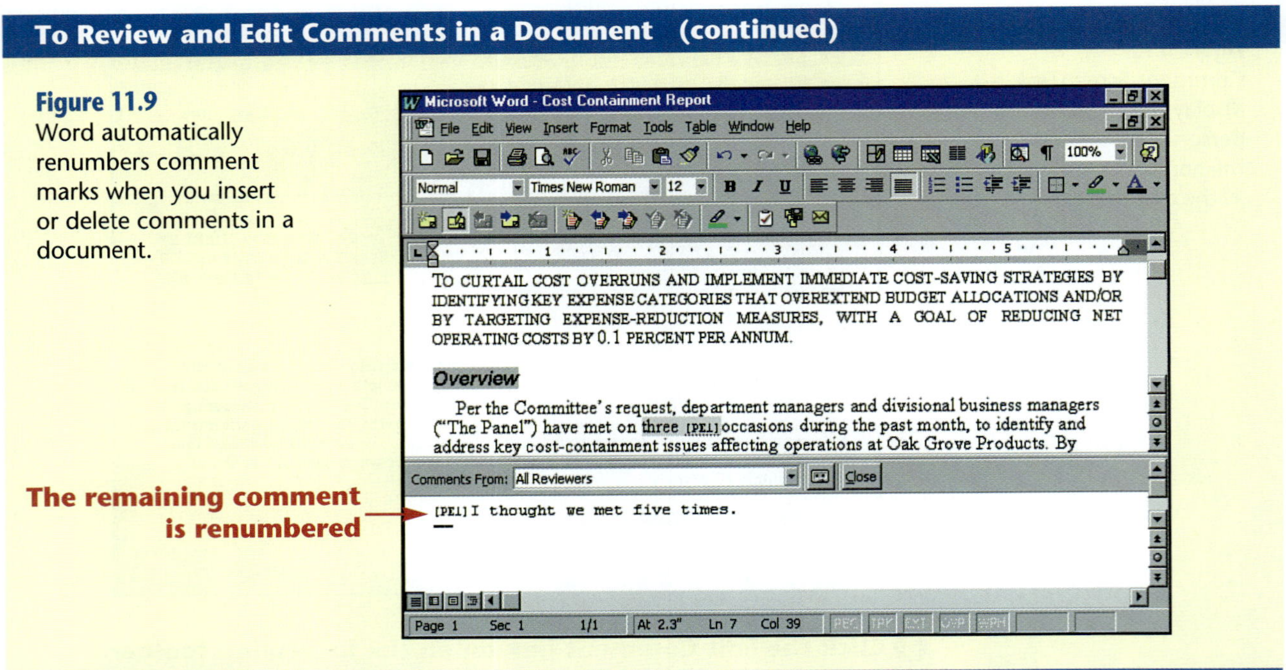

Figure 11.9
Word automatically renumbers comment marks when you insert or delete comments in a document.

The remaining comment is renumbered

The name and initials assigned to comments come from the user information you enter when you set up Microsoft Word or Microsoft Office. You can change the initials used to identify comments that you insert by changing your user information, which is useful if multiple reviewers use the same computer system. Choose Tools, Options, and click the User Information tab. On the User Information page, type the name you want to appear in comments in the Name text box, type the initials you want in the Initials text box, and click OK. New comments entered after this change will appear with the new name and initials; existing comments in the document are not changed. The user information is the same for all Office applications that you use.

You can select to display only certain reviewer's comments in the Comment pane. By default, All Reviewers is selected in the Comments From drop-down list. You can select the name of a single reviewer to display only those comments in the pane.

If you have a sound card and microphone connected to your computer, you can record voice comments. Click the Insert Comment button, click the Insert Sound Object button in the Comment pane, and record your voice comments using your sound recorder application. To play back the comment, double-click the sound button in the Comment pane.

You can print a document with or without comments. To print the comments with the file, choose File, Print and click the Options button. In the Print Options dialog box, select the Comments check box and click OK. To print only the comments, select Comments from the Print What drop-down list in the Print dialog box.

If comment marks are displayed, you can quickly open the Comment pane by double-clicking a comment mark.

To incorporate text from a comment into a document, copy the text in the Comment pane to the Clipboard; then paste it into the document.

Lesson 4: Tracking and Reviewing Changes to a Document

To help you monitor revisions to a document, you can track changes while you edit. When you track changes, Word indicates all changes made to a document by applying noticeable formatting called *revision marks*. By default, insertions are marked with underline, and deletions are marked with strikethrough.

Revision marks

Formatting applied to insertions and deletions in a document so that you can quickly see what changes have been made.

After changes are marked, you can scroll through them and decide whether you want to accept the change and incorporate it into the document, or reject the change and delete it from the document.

In this lesson, you learn how to turn on the tracking feature, track changes, and accept or delete changes.

To Track and Review Changes to a Document

❶ In the Cost Containment Report document, click the Track Changes button on the Reviewing toolbar.

This turns on the Track Changes feature. Notice that the TRK indicator on the status bar is displayed in bold (see Figure 11.10). By default, Word will highlight changes onscreen and in printed documents.

❷ Select the `Mission` **heading and replace it with the text** `Goal Statement`**.**

Word applies the default revision mark formatting, as shown in Figure 11.10. Instead of removing deleted text from the document, Word changes the font color and applies strikethrough formatting. Inserted text appears in a different color and underlined. Notice the black vertical line in the left margin, indicating the lines where changes have been made.

If you have problems...

The color and formatting of revision marks on your computer may differ from those on other computers. (Changing the revision mark color and formatting is covered in the next lesson.) Word may also assign a specific color to different reviewers who work on the same document.

Now make a few more edits.

❸ In the Overview paragraph, change the numeral `12` **to the written number** `twelve` **and the numeral** `30` **to the written number** `thirty`**.**

Word applies revision marks to the changes.

continues

To Track and Review Changes to a Document   (continued)

Figure 11.10
Revision marks indicate where changes have occurred in a document.

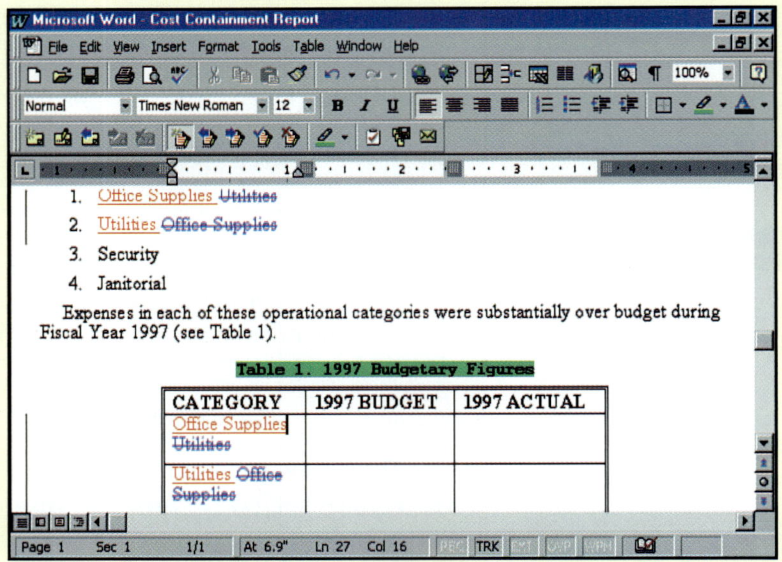

4 **Rearrange the first two categories in the numbered list and the table so that** `Office Supplies` **is listed before** `Utilities`.

Word applies revision marks to the changes. The document should look similar to the one in Figure 11.11.

Figure 11.11
Revision marks are applied to all changes in a document, including changes to tables, headers, footers, comments, and other elements.

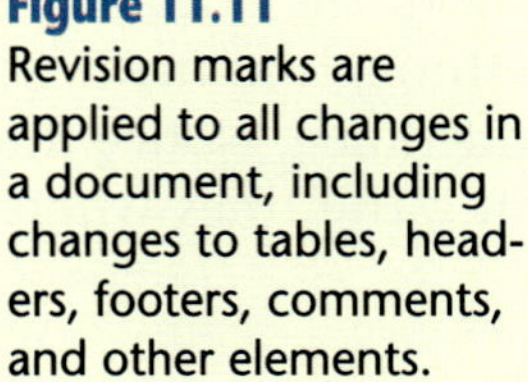

Now use the Reviewing toolbar to scroll one by one through the changes and decide whether you want to accept or reject them.

5 **Click the Next Change button on the Reviewing toolbar until the third row in the table—where the label** `Office Supplies` **has been replaced by the label** `Utilities`**—is selected.**

You can use any of Word's selection methods to select marked text, or you can use the Next Change and Previous Change buttons on the Reviewing toolbar.

6 **Click the Accept Change button on the Reviewing toolbar.**

Word incorporates the change into the document and removes the revision marks. The row remains selected. Once you select a change, you can choose whether you want to accept it or reject it, or leave it marked in the document. In this step, you have accepted the change.

7 **Click the Previous Change button on the Reviewing toolbar.**

Word selects the previous change—the second row in the table. (Click the Previous Change button to move from the insertion point up in the document; click the Next Change button to move from the insertion point down in the document.)

8 **Click the Accept Change button on the Reviewing toolbar.**

Word incorporates the change into the document text and removes the revision marks. In Figure 11.12, you can see how the table looks with all changes accepted.

Figure 11.12
When you accept a change, Word incorporates it into the document and removes the revision marks.

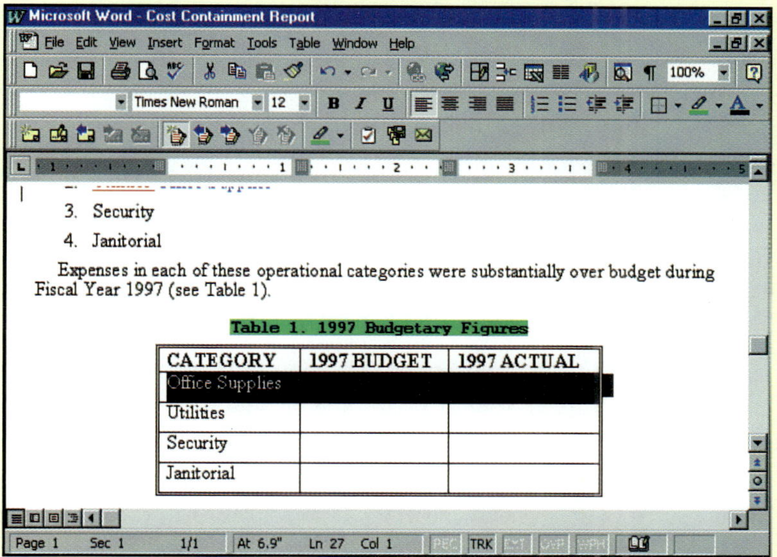

9 **Repeat steps 7 and 8 to accept the changes you made to the numbered list and to replace the numerals** `30` **and** `12` **with text. Stop when the inserted heading title** `Goal Statement` **is selected.**

For this example, do not replace the Goal Statement heading.

continues

To Track and Review Changes to a Document   (continued)

If you have problems...

If Word reaches the end or the beginning of the document while selecting changes, it displays a message box asking whether you want to continue. Choose OK to continue or Cancel to stop. If other elements in the document include changes, such as a Comment pane, an endnote or footnote pane, or headers and footers, Word asks whether you want to select changes in those areas.

To restore the original wording for the Goal Statement heading, you must reject the insertion and then reject the deletion.

⑩ Click the Reject Change button on the Reviewing toolbar and then click the Previous Change button.

Word removes the inserted text and selects the deleted text.

⑪ Click the Reject Change button.

Word reverts to the original heading title and removes the revision marks. You have reviewed and accepted or rejected all revisions in the document. There is no sign that changes had been made.

⑫ Click the Track Changes button on the Reviewing toolbar.

This turns off the Track Changes feature so you can edit the document without revision marks.

⑬ Save the document and close it.

In the next lesson, you learn how to compare documents to mark changes automatically.

You can also turn on the Track Changes feature by using menu commands. Choose Tools, Track Changes, Highlight Changes, select the Track Changes While Editing check box, and then click OK.

You can double-click the TRK tracking indicator button on the status bar to toggle the Track Changes feature off and on.

With ScreenTips, you can view information about each marked change, including who made the change and when, and what type of change it is. Simply move the mouse pointer to touch the revision marks; Word displays the ScreenTip.

To change the color or formatting of revision marks, choose Tools, Options and click the Track Changes tab. You can select a color and a formatting mark to use for inserted text, deleted text, changed formatting, and changed lines. To set Word to change the color for each reviewer automatically, set all the color options to By Author.

By default, Word displays revision marks onscreen. If you want to hide the marks, choose Tools, Track Changes, Highlight Changes, deselect the Highlight Changes on Screen check box, and then click OK. To hide changes in printed documents, deselect the Highlight Changes in Printed Document check box as well.

One method of having several people make revisions and comments to the same document is to route the document. In order to route a document, Word must be mail-enabled—that is, you must have an email system installed and Word must be configured to send information to your email program. In a classroom environment, it is possible that email is not configured, but routing documents is a requirement for the Word Expert exam. Therefore, we have included the routing documents instructions in this Exam Note so you can practice routing in the classroom or at home, depending upon your mail setup.

When a document is routed, it's sent as an attachment to an email message. As one person finishes his revisions to the document, he sends the document on to the next person, and so forth, until it returns to the originator.

To route a document, you must first prepare a routing slip by completing the following steps:

1. Open the document you plan to route.

2. Choose File, Send To, Routing Recipient from the menu to open the Routing Slip dialog box (see Figure 11.13).

   If you haven't set up Microsoft Exchange on your system, a wizard appears to help you specify your Exchange server, the mail software you'll be using, the name and location of your mailbox file, any passwords you need to open your mail software, and the location of your address book. Once you finish with the wizard, the Routing Slip dialog box appears.

Figure 11.13

Set up routing options from the Routing Slip dialog box.

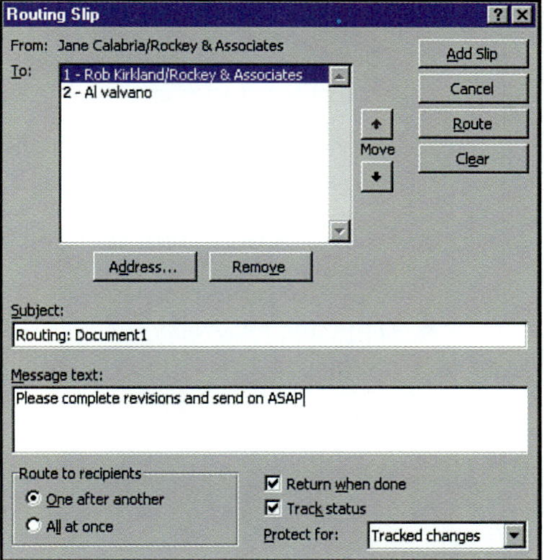

3. Click the Address button to select the recipients of the document (see Figure 11.14).

4. In the Type Name or Select from List box, enter the recipient's name or select the recipients from the list of people in your address book (hold down Ctrl while clicking names to select more than one name). Avoid selecting groups because Word treats the group as if it were one person and sends the document to all people in the group at once rather than routing it to each one in turn.

5. Click the To button and then OK.

continues

Word

Figure 11.14
Enter the names of the recipients or select them from the list of names in your address book.

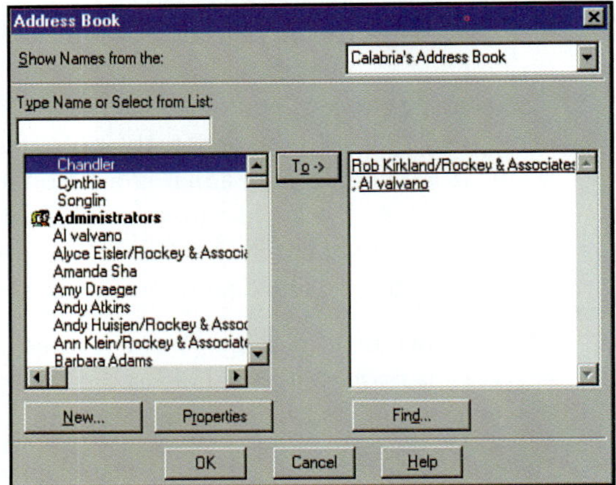

6. To set the order of names in the routing list, click a person's name and then click the up or down move arrows to move the name up or down the list.

7. Select the One After Another option to have the document routing to the first person on the list, and then to the second, then the third, and so on.

8. Select Return When Done to have the document routed back to you after everyone on the list is finished with it.

9. Select the Track Status option to receive a message whenever someone forwards the document on to the next person on the routing list.

10. From the Protect For drop-down list, select one of the following options:

   ■ Comments: lets reviewers insert comments but not change the contents of the document

   ■ Tracked Changes: turns on revision marking to track all changes the reviewer makes in the document

   ■ Forms: routes a form that you want recipients to complete without modifying the form itself

   ■ None: the reviewer's changes are not tracked, so you can't highlight or merge changes

11. Click Route to route the document.

Click Add Slip to close the dialog box without routing the document. When you're ready to route the document later, open the document, choose File, Send To, Next Routing Recipient.

When you receive an email message with a routed document attached, open the attachment as per the instructions in your email software (in most cases, you double-click the attachment icon). Make your changes, revisions, or comments and send the document to the next person by choosing File, Send to, Next Routing Recipient from the menu.

If you want to route the document to someone who isn't on the routing list, choose, File, Send To, Other Routing Recipient from the menu.

Lesson 5: Comparing Documents

One way to control the changes made to documents is to retain the original document and send a copy to reviewers. Reviewers can make changes to the copy and then send it back to you. To quickly discover what changes reviewers have made, you can compare the copy with the original. Word automatically highlights the changes with revision marks.

Comparing documents is also useful if you have been working with two copies of the same document and cannot remember how they differ.

In this lesson, you work with a document that is similar to the Cost Containment Report except that it has been reviewed and edited by someone in Oak Grove's controller's office. You compare the reviewed document to the Cost Containment Report document that you have been using to see the differences. You then learn how to review, accept, and reject many changes all at once.

To Compare Documents

① Open the folder Project-11 and the file Proj1102 from this book's CD and save it as `Reviewed Report`**.**

This file is based on the same document as the Cost Containment Report, but it has been reviewed and edited. In particular, you may notice that dollar amounts have been inserted in the table. Compare the two documents to see the differences.

② In the Reviewed Report document, choose Tools, Track Changes, Compare Documents.

The Select File to Compare With Current Document dialog box is displayed, as shown in Figure 11.15.

Figure 11.15
You can select any document to compare to the current document.

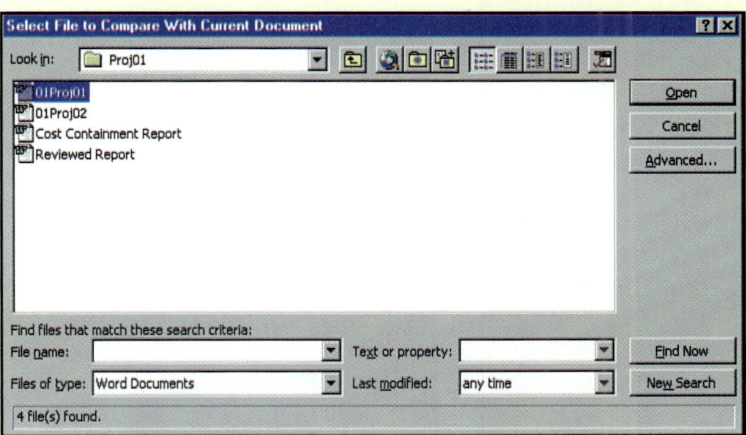

continues

To Compare Documents **(continued)**

❸ Select the Cost Containment Report in the list and click the <u>O</u>pen button.

Word compares the two documents and highlights the differences between the two by displaying revision marks in the Reviewed Report document (see Figure 11.16). The effect is as if you had tracked the changes while editing—text that appears in the Cost Containment Report document but not in the Reviewed Report document is marked as a deletion, while text that appears in the Reviewed Report document but not in the Cost Containment Report document is marked as an insertion.

Now use the Accept or Reject Changes dialog box to indicate which changes to accept and which to delete.

❹ Choose <u>T</u>ools, <u>T</u>rack Changes, <u>A</u>ccept or Reject Changes.

Word displays the Accept or Reject Changes dialog box. Using the Find (forward) and Find (back) buttons, you can scroll through the changes in the document one by one, just as you did with the toolbar buttons in the preceding lesson.

Figure 11.16
Word highlights the differences between the two documents with revision marks.

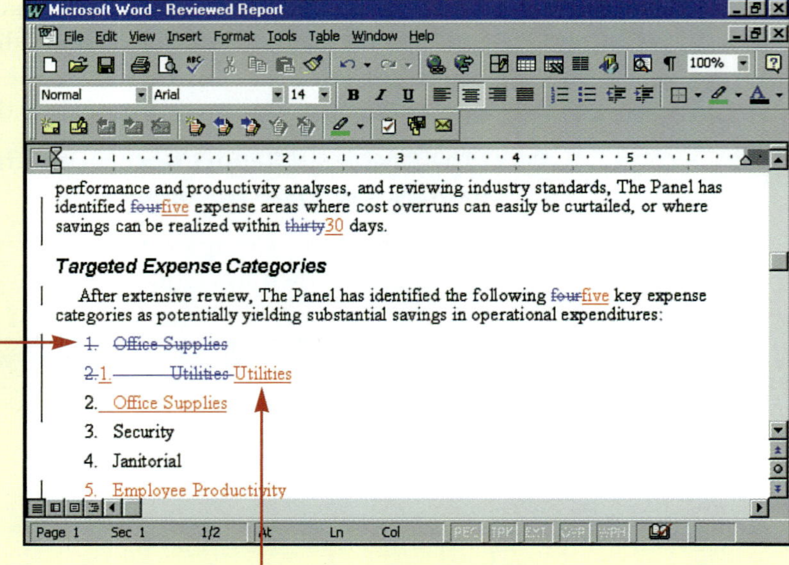

Deleted text appears in Cost Containment Report, but not in Reviewed Report

Inserted text appears in Reviewed Report, but not in Cost Containment Report

❺ Click the <u>F</u>ind button.

Word selects the next change in the document (in this case, the first change). The Accept or Reject Changes dialog box shows information about the selected change, including who made it, when it was made, and what type of change it is (see Figure 11.17).

Figure 11.17
You can accept or reject changes and preview the way the document will look by using the Accept or Reject Changes dialog box.

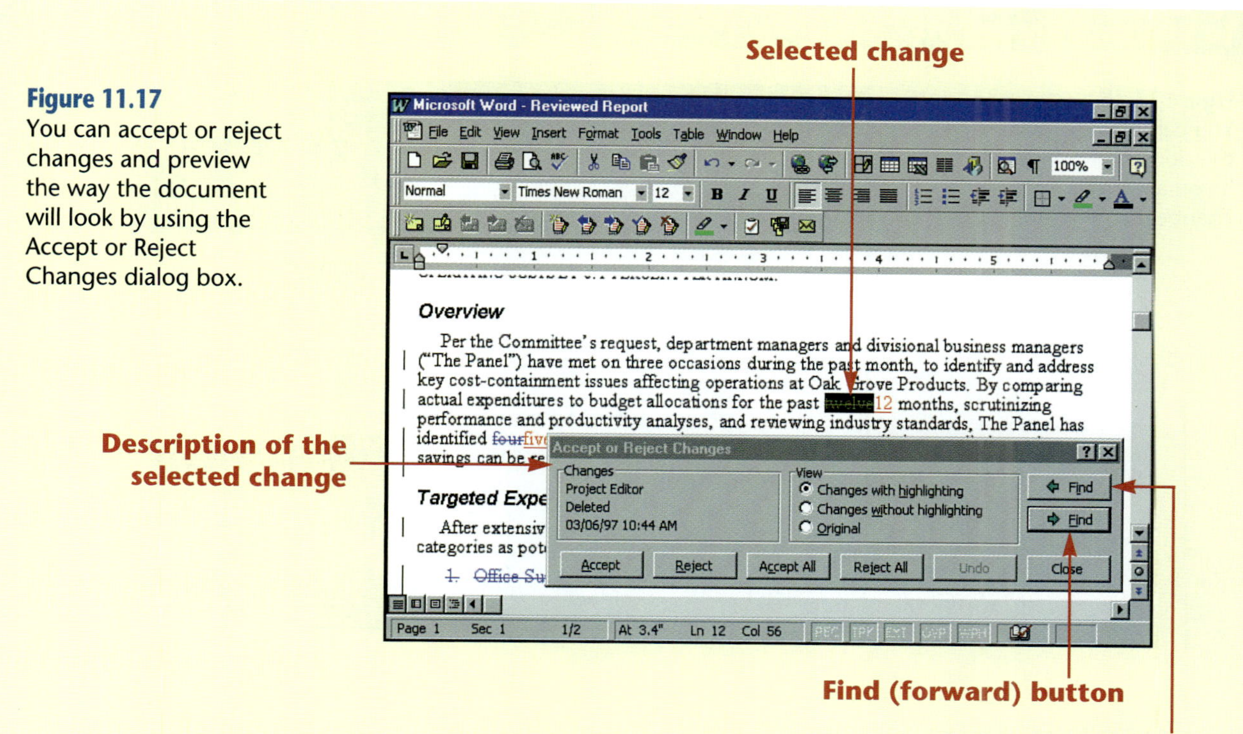

6 **Click the Accept button.**

Word accepts the change, removes the revision marks, and selects the next change in the document. To reject the change, you would click the Reject button. You can use these steps to move one by one through the differences in the document to see which ones you want to accept and which you want to reject.

However, if the reason you are comparing documents is not to see which individual changes you prefer, but rather which version of the document you want, you can quickly accept or reject all of the changes. Before you do this, you can preview the document to see which option is appropriate. First, preview the document as it will look if you accept all the changes.

7 **Click the Changes Without Highlighting option in the Accept or Reject Changes dialog box.**

Word displays the document as it would look if you accepted all the changes, and keeps the dialog box open. You can move the dialog box out of the way and scroll through the document to see what you think. Notice that, in this version, the document includes the table data (see Figure 11.18).

continues

Figure 11.18
You can preview how the document will look if you accept all changes.

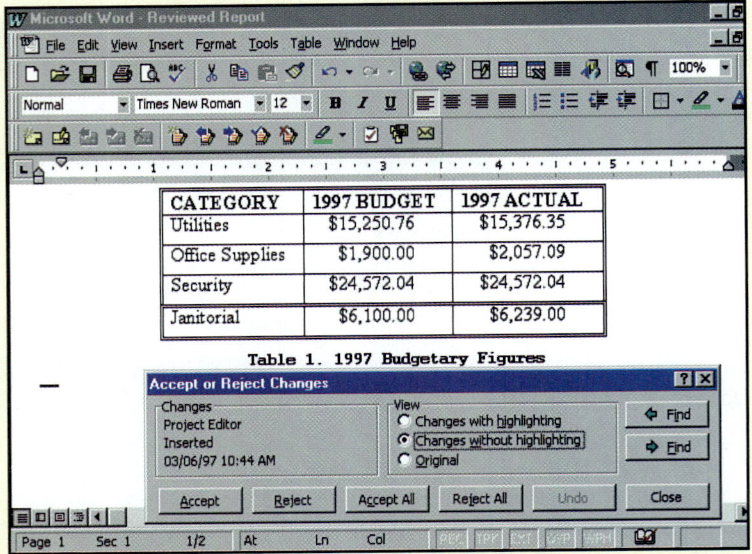

Now preview the document as it will look if you reject all the changes.

8 **Click the Original option in the Accept or Reject Changes dialog box.**

Word displays the document as it would look if you rejected all changes. For this example, you accept all changes.

9 **Choose Accept All.**

Word displays a message box asking whether you want to accept all the changes without reviewing them.

10 **Click Yes.**

Word accepts all changes in the document and removes all revision marks. The Accept or Reject Changes dialog box remains open. If you regret your decision, you can choose Undo.

11 **Click the Close button in the dialog box.**

Word closes the dialog box.

12 **Save the changes you have made to the Reviewed Report document and keep it open on your screen.**

In the next lesson, you learn how to protect your document from unauthorized editing.

Lesson 6: Protecting Documents

There are times when you need to be able to control when and how people make changes to a document. For example, if you are the primary author or the project manager responsible for keeping track of all the contributions, you need a way to be sure that no unauthorized changes are made. With

Word, you can protect a document so that unauthorized users cannot change the contents of a document.

You can control access to a document in three ways:

- You can set Word so that reviewers can enter comments in a document but cannot change the document text.

- You can set Word so that all changes made by reviewers are tracked using revision marks. That means that you see immediately if any text or graphics have been moved, deleted, or inserted.

- You can set Word to protect a document so changes can be made only in form fields.

In this lesson, you learn how to protect your document for comments or tracked changes. You learn how to work with forms in Project 12.

To Protect Documents

1 In the Reviewed Report document, choose Tools, Protect Document.

The Protect Document dialog box opens, as shown in Figure 11.19. You use this dialog box to select the type of protection you want for the document, and to set a password, if necessary.

Figure 11.19
Use the Protect
Document dialog box
to control unauthorized
changes to a document.

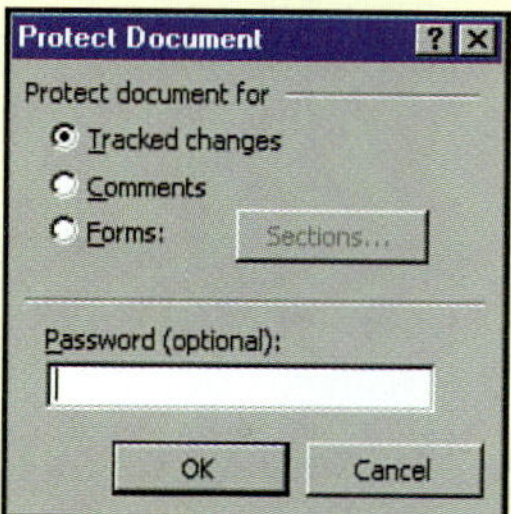

2 Select the Tracked Changes option and click OK.

Word protects the document by tracking changes. Notice that the TRK indicator on the status bar appears in bold, indicating that tracking is active. When a document is protected for tracked changes, you can insert and delete text, graphics, comments, and other elements, but all the changes will be indicated with revision marks.

Now see what happens when you delete some text.

3 Select the title of the document and press Del.

Instead of removing the title from the document, Word tracks the change using revision marks.

continues

To Protect Documents (continued)

4 Click the Undo button on the Standard toolbar.

Word undoes the deletion and removes the revision marks.

Now try protecting the document for comments.

5 Choose Tools, Unprotect Document.

Word removes the Track Changes protection.

6 Choose Tools, Protect Document, click the Comments option, and then click OK.

Word protects the document so that only comments can be inserted. Notice that many toolbar buttons and menu commands are no longer available and that the TRK button appears in bold. No one—including you!—can make editing changes.

Now see what happens when you try to delete text.

7 Select the report title and press Del.

Nothing happens. You cannot edit the document when it is protected for comments, except to insert comments.

8 Position the insertion point in the Mission **heading and click the Insert Comment button on the Reviewing toolbar.**

Word inserts a comment and opens the Comment pane, as shown in Figure 11.20. Notice that the comment is inserted with revision marks—the inserted text appears in color and underlined.

Figure 11.20
When a document is protected for comments, comments are inserted with revision marking turned on.

Comment mark appears in color and underlined

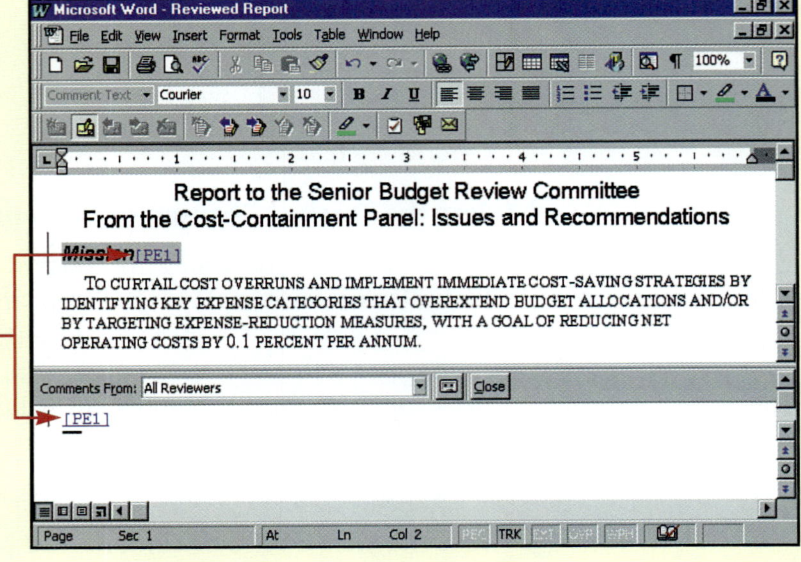

9 Type Verify goal with upper management **and then click the Close button in the Comment pane.**

Word closes the Comment pane. Now unprotect the document.

⑩ Choose Tools, Unprotect Document.

Word removes the document protection. Changes you made with protection turned on remain highlighted with revision marks.

⑪ Save the Reviewed Report document and keep it open.

In the next lesson, you learn how to save multiple versions of a document.

You can use the Highlight feature to highlight text and graphics in a protected document.

If you want to make sure that unauthorized users cannot remove document protection and change a document, you can add password protection. Choose Tools, Protect Document to open the Protect Document dialog box. Select the type of protection you want and then type a password in the Password (Optional) text box and click OK. Word displays the Confirm Password dialog box; retype the password—exactly the way you typed it the first time—and click OK. Word protects the document. When you next choose Tools, Unprotect Document, Word displays the Unprotect Document dialog box. You must enter the correct password to remove the protection.

Another way to protect a document is to assign a password. By password protecting a document, only those who know the password can open the file. To assign a password, open the document, choose File, Save As from the menu. In the Save As dialog box, click the Options button. Figure 11.21 shows the Save dialog box in which you can assign passwords. You can assign a password to open the file, which controls who may read the file. To restrict who may edit the document, enter a password in the Password to Modify box.

Passwords can be up to 15 characters long and can include letters, numbers, symbols, and spaces. As you enter a password, only asterisks appear in the box. This keeps anyone from reading the password over your shoulder.

Figure 11.21
Enter passwords in the File Sharing section of the Save As dialog box.

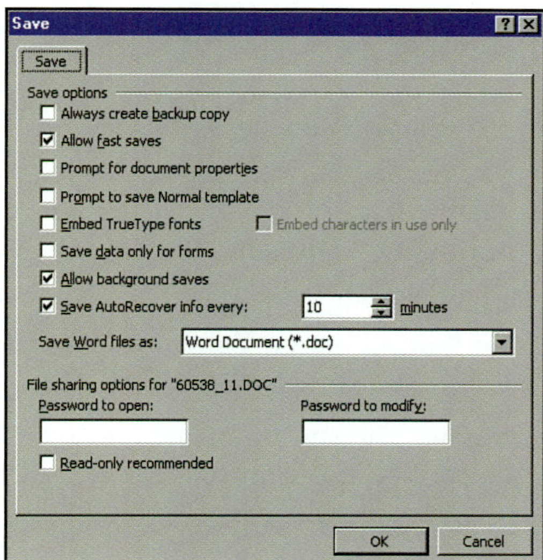

Lesson 7: Saving Different Versions of a Document

When you want to save a copy of a document in Word, you use the File, Save As command to save the file with a new name. You then have two unique files that may or may not be identical, depending on how much editing you do. In Word 97, you can save multiple versions of a document as part of the original file.

Saving versions of a file is useful for keeping track of documents that are passed around for reviewing. Each version is marked with the name of the person who saves it, as well as the date and time that the version was saved. Using versions, for example, you can keep copies of your original version, the version edited by reviewers, and the version that incorporates the reviewers' changes. You can also have Word automatically save versions of a document each time the document is closed. This can help you keep track of who is working with a file and when, as well as what types of changes are being made.

In this lesson, you learn how to save a version of a file and how to open and view a version of a file.

To Save Different Versions of a Document

1 In the Reviewed Report document, click the Save Version button on the Reviewing toolbar.

The Save Version dialog box appears, as shown in Figure 11.22. The dialog box displays the name of the person who saved the version, along with the date and time when the version was saved.

Figure 11.22
You can include comments to help you differentiate between versions of a document in the Save Version dialog box.

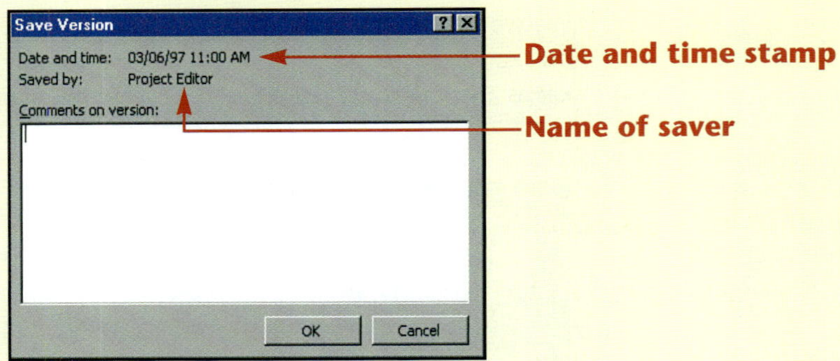

You can enter comments to help you keep track of which version this is.

2 In the Comments on Version text box, type Changes have been incorporated and click OK.

Word saves the version of the file, and keeps the original file open onscreen. You can continue editing or close the file. Changes that you make now will not be included in the version that you just saved.

❸ In the document title, replace `Issues and Recommendations` **with** `Targeted Expense Categories`**.**

This version of the document now has a different title from the version you just saved. Now make one more change.

❹ Delete the comment attached to the `Mission` **heading and save the document.**

Now open and view the version you saved in step 2.

❺ Choose <u>F</u>ile, Ve<u>r</u>sions.

The Versions in Reviewed Report dialog box is displayed, as shown in Figure 11.23. All versions of this document that have been saved are listed in the dialog box. You can open them, delete them, and display the full comment text.

Figure 11.23
Select the version you want to open or delete.

List of saved versions ➔

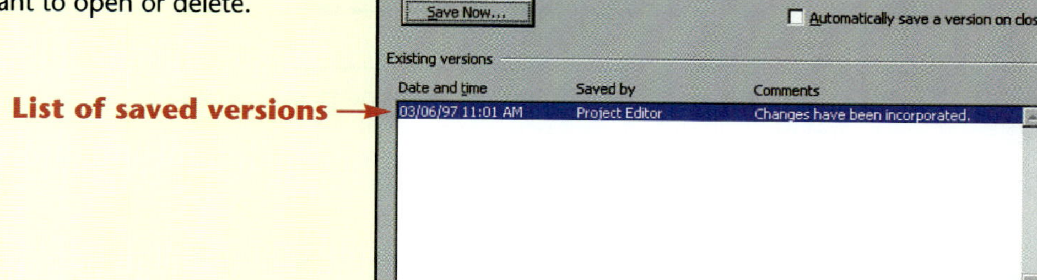

Because only one version has been saved in this example, it is already selected.

❻ Click the <u>O</u>pen button.

Word opens the version and displays it in split-screen view along with the regular document, as shown in Figure 11.24. The saved version is active. Notice the date stamp in the title bar, as well as the difference between the two versions—the original has the new report title that you typed in step 3, and the comment highlighting is gone.

❼ Choose <u>F</u>ile, <u>C</u>lose to close the saved version; then maximize the remaining document window.

Word closes the version and saves it along with the file.

❽ Save the Reviewed Report document and close it.

continues

To Save Different Versions of a Document   (continued)

Figure 11.24
You can compare the original document with the saved version.

Original document →

Saved version →

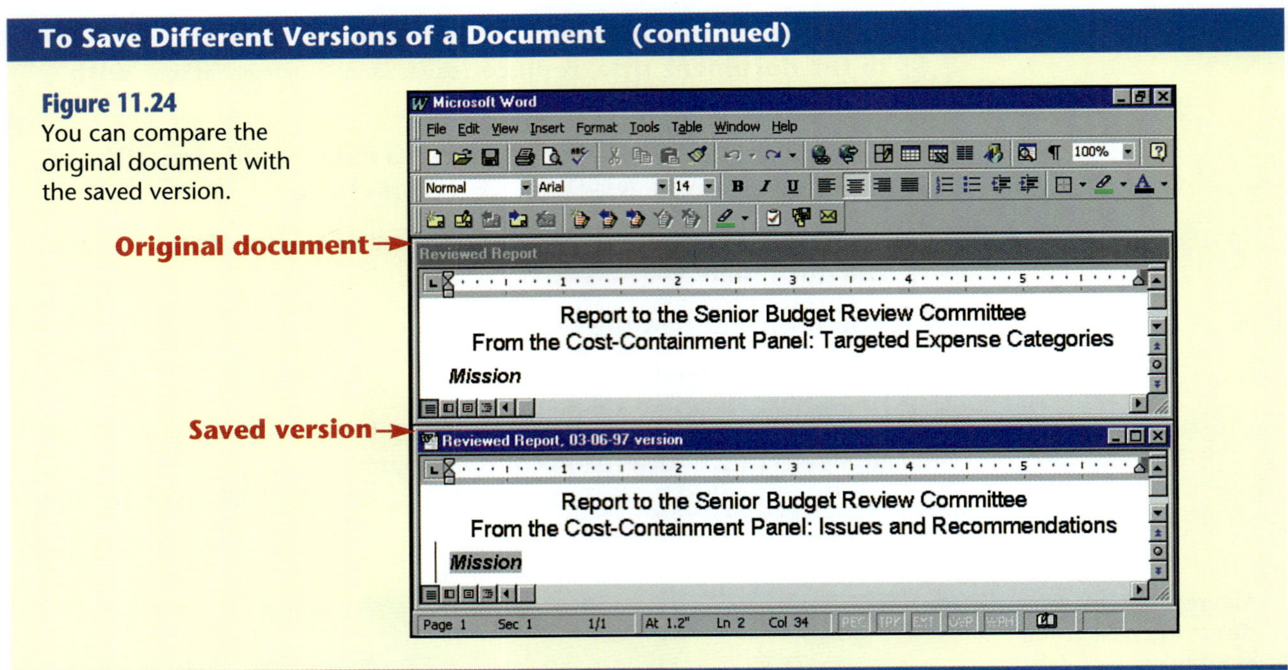

You can open the Save Version dialog box by using menu commands. Choose File, Save As and then click the Save Version button.

To delete a version of a file, choose File, Versions, select the version to delete, and then choose Delete. Word asks whether you are sure you want to delete the version because it cannot be recovered once it is gone. Choose Yes to delete the version. Choose No to leave it in place.

To set Word to save a version of a file automatically every time the file is closed, choose File, Versions, select the Automatically Save a Version on Close option, and then choose Close.

If you want to compare a version of a document with the original, you must save the version as a new document. Open it using the File, Versions command; then use the File, Save As command to save it with a new name.

If you have a document saved with multiple versions and you want to distribute only the most recent version, you can either delete all other versions or use the File, Save As command to save the most recent version with a new name. The versions will remain with the original file, and you can then distribute the new file.

Lesson 8: Creating Master Documents

Working with long documents can be cumbersome, particularly if more than one person is editing the document. Frequently, you end up working with a set of smaller documents to manage the work. But separating documents causes problems when you want to join them all together again— such as in an annual report where you want consecutive page numbers, headers and footers, a table of contents, maybe even an index.

Word's solution to the problem of longer documents is the master document, which acts as a binder for a set of separate files called subdocuments. The master document helps manage all the subdocuments that are its components. A master document can be created and worked on by one person, or it can be a part of a cooperative effort where several people work on their own subdocuments.

You can create a master document from scratch (including all of the subdocuments) in the Master Document view. You can also can create a master document by adding existing files as subdocuments (as explained in the Exam Note at the end of this lesson).

In this lesson, you learn how to create a master document.

To Create a Master Document

1 **Start a new document.**

2 **Choose View, Master Document from the menu to switch to the Master Document view.**

You create an outline for the master document to serve as its skeleton. Use Word's built-in heading styles or use the Promote and Demote buttons on the Outlining toolbar to set the outline levels (see Figure 11.25).

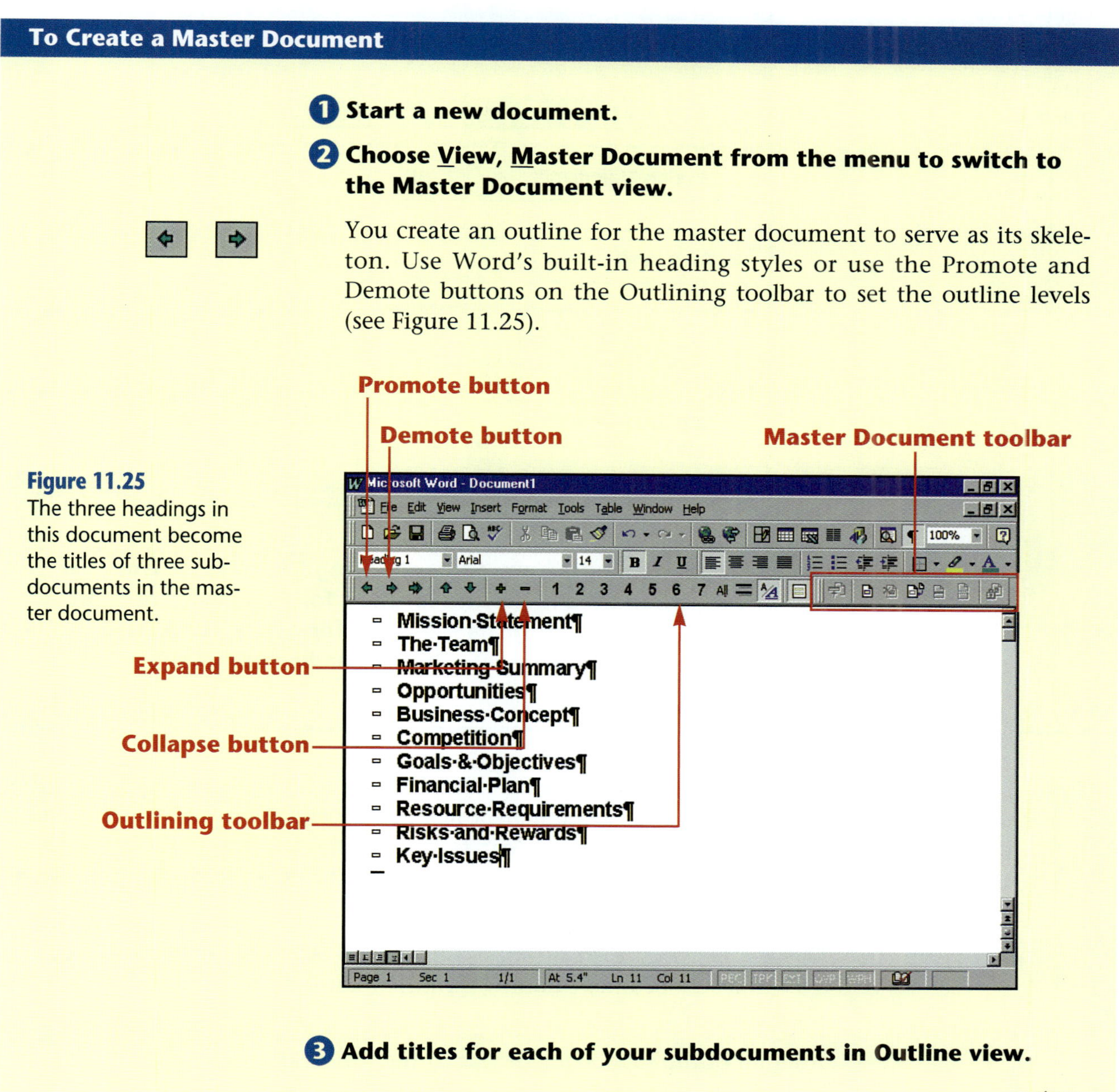

Figure 11.25
The three headings in this document become the titles of three subdocuments in the master document.

3 **Add titles for each of your subdocuments in Outline view.**

continues

Word

To Create a Master Document (continued)

④ **Select the headings and text you want to divide into subdocuments. The first heading in the selection must be formatted with the heading style or outline level that you want to use to create the beginning of each subdocument (for example, Heading 1).**

⑤ **Click the Create Subdocument button on the Master Document toolbar (see Figure 11.26).**

Figure 11.26
The Master Document inserts section breaks between the subdocuments.

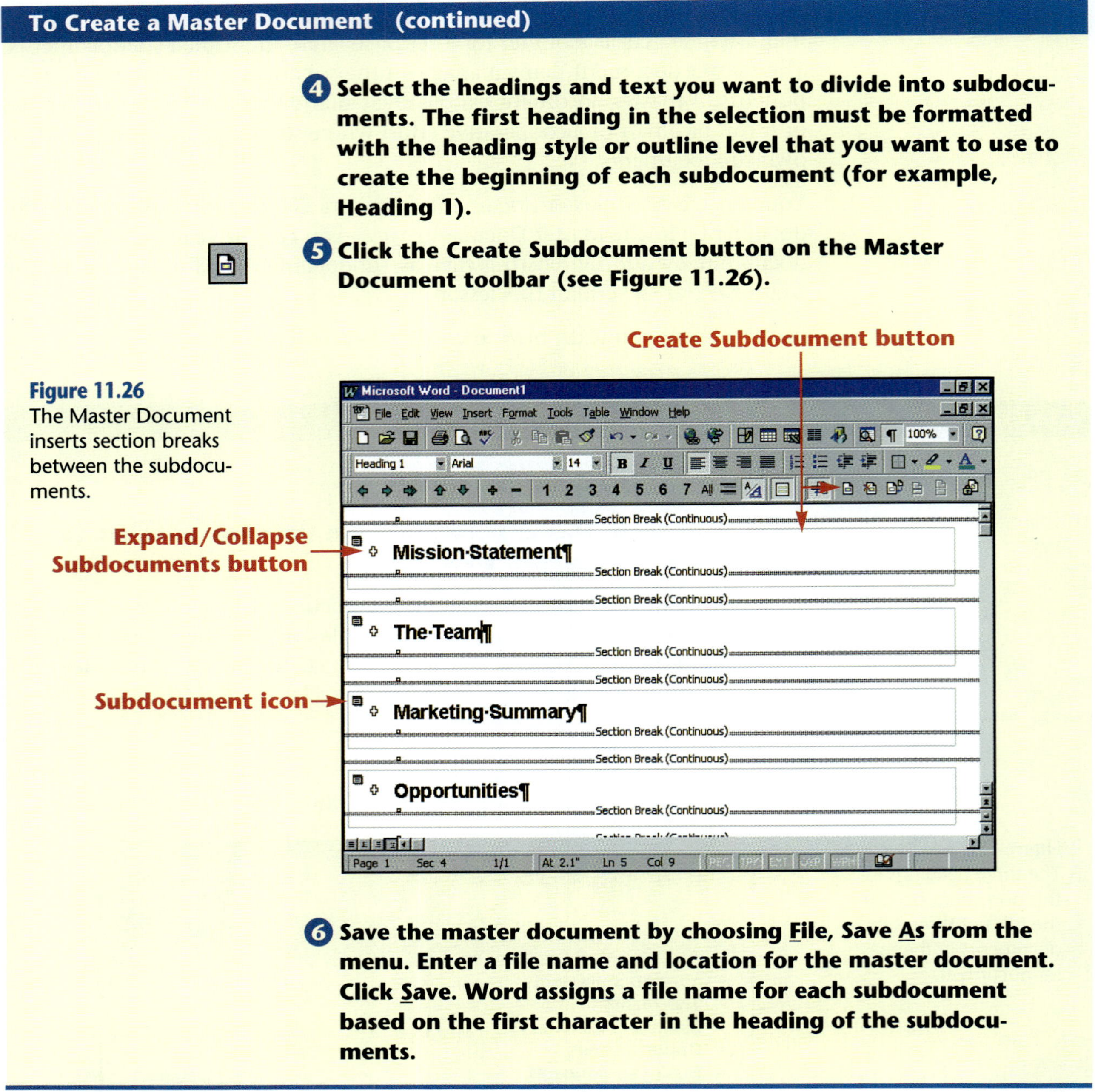

⑥ **Save the master document by choosing <u>F</u>ile, Save <u>A</u>s from the menu. Enter a file name and location for the master document. Click <u>S</u>ave. Word assigns a file name for each subdocument based on the first character in the heading of the subdocuments.**

Normally, all subdocuments are collapsed (you only see the titles) when you open a master document. Click the Expand Subdocuments button on the Master Document toolbar to see all the text in a subdocument. Of course, in this case, you only have title text so you won't see any expansion. The Expand Subdocuments button becomes the Collapse button when subdocuments are expanded.

To edit a subdocument from within the master document, expand the subdocument first.

After all of the subdocument text in the master document is complete, you can add headers and footers as well as a table of contents and an index to create a professional, complete set of documents ready for binding.

By the time you decide to create a master document, some of the documents you need for subdocuments may already be in progress, or you may have a set of existing documents that you want to add to the master document.

To insert an existing document into the master document, follow these steps:

1. Open the master document in the master document view.

2. Expand the subdocuments by clicking on the Expand Subdocuments button on the Master Document toolbar.

3. Place your insertion point where you want to insert the existing document. This should be in a blank line between existing subdocuments.

4. Click the Insert Subdocument button on the Master Document toolbar.

5. In the Insert Subdocument dialog box, enter the filename of the document you want to add. Click Open.

If you have created a document that you wish to convert to a master document:

1. Open the document you want to convert to a master document.

2. Choose View, Master Document to open the Master Document view.

3. Apply Word's built-in heading styles or specify outline levels to set up the outline of the master document.

4. Select the headings and text you want to divide into subdocuments. Remember to format the first heading you select with the heading style or outline level that you want to use to designate the beginning of each subdocument.

5. Click the Create Subdocument button on the Master Document toolbar.

6. Save the master document by choosing File, Save As from the menu. Enter a filename and location for the master document. Click Save. Word assigns a filename for each subdocument based on the first characters in the heading for the subdocument.

You have completed all the lessons in this project. If you have completed your session on the computer, exit Word and Windows 95 before turning off your computer. Otherwise, continue with the "Checking Your Skills" and "Applying Your Skills" sections.

Project Summary

To	Do This
Highlight key points	Select the key point; then click the Highlight button on the Reviewing toolbar.
Highlight a succession of key points	Click the Highlight button on the Reviewing toolbar; then select each key point.

continues

To	Do This
Change the highlight color	Click the Highlight drop-down arrow button and select a color from the palette.
Insert a comment into a document	Position the insertion point, click the Insert Comment button on the Reviewing toolbar, and then type the comment text.
Delete a comment	Position the insertion point within the highlighted text and click the Delete Comment button on the Reviewing toolbar.
Review comments	Point at the highlighted text onscreen to view the comment in a ScreenTip, or click the Edit Comment button on the Reviewing toolbar to view a list of comments in the Comment pane.
Track changes	Click the Track Changes button on the Reviewing toolbar.
Review changes	Click the Next Change or Previous Change button on the Reviewing toolbar to select a change. Click the Accept Change button to incorporate the change into the document, or click the Reject Change button to revert to the original document text.
Compare documents	Open the document in which you want changes displayed. Then choose Tools, Track Changes, Compare Document. Select the document you want to compare to the open document; then choose Open.
Accept all changes	Choose Tools, Track Changes, Accept or Reject Changes. Click the Accept All button.
Reject all changes	Choose Tools, Track Changes, Accept or Reject Changes. Click the Reject All button.
Protect a document from all changes except comments	Choose Tools, Protect Document, select the Comments option, and then click OK.
Protect a document to track changes	Choose Tools, Protect Document, select the Tracked Changes option, and then click OK.
Unprotect a document	Choose Tools, Unprotect Document.
Save a version of a document	Click the Save Version button on the Reviewing toolbar, type the comments, and then click OK.
Open a version of a document	Choose File, Versions, select the version, and choose Open.

Checking Your Skills

True/False

For each of the following statements, check *T* or *F* to indicate whether the statement is true or false.

__T __F   **1.** You can highlight text only in pink.

__T __F   **2.** You can color-code revision marks by author.

__T __F   **3.** Revision marks appear in the Revision Mark pane.

__T __F   **4.** You can protect a document so that all changes are tracked with revision marks.

__T __F   **5.** Saved versions of a file are stored with a different name in a different folder from the original file.

__T __F   **6.** You can only print highlights if you have a color printer.

__T __F   **7.** You can store comments in the document summary.

__T __F   **8.** You must have Word set up to use with an email system in order to route documents.

__T __F   **9.** You cannot assign passwords to control access to specific documents.

__T __F **10.** Only the person who creates a master document can edit the subdocuments.

Multiple Choice

Circle the letter of the correct answer for each of the following questions.

1. On which toolbar do you find most of the tools you use to collaborate on documents?

   a. Standard

   b. Formatting

   c. Reviewing

   d. Merge

2. What color is used to highlight text where comments are inserted?

   a. Gray

   b. Red

   c. Green

   d. Yellow

3. Where does Word display a list of all comments in a document?

   a. Document window

   b. Comment dialog box

   c. Comment pane

   d. Status bar

4. What command do you use to incorporate a single change into a document?

   a. Accept

   b. Reject

   c. Compare

   d. Merge

5. By default, what mark does Word place in the left margin to indicate where lines have been edited when tracking changes?

   a. A question mark

   b. A vertical black line

   c. An arrow

   d. An exclamation point

6. On which tab of the Document Properties dialog box can you add comments?

   a. General

   b. Summary

   c. Statistics

   d. Contents

7. Who specifies the recipients on a routing slip for documents?

   a. The network administrator

   b. The project manager

   c. The routing originator

   d. The last person to edit the document

8. What do you call a file in a master document?

   a. Master document file

   b. Outline document

   c. Separate document

   d. Subdocument

9. What view do you use to set up a master document?

   a. Outline view

   b. Page Layout view

   c. Master Document view

   d. Normal view

10. What type of break does Word use to separate subdocuments within a master document?

   a. Section break

   b. Page break

   c. Master document break

   d. Column break

Completion

In the blanks provided, write the correct answer for each of the following statements.

1. To keep an unauthorized user from changing a document, you must _______________ it.

2. By default, Word marks deletions with _______________ format when tracking changes.

3. When you open a version of a file, it appears with the original in _______________ _______________ view.

4. When you compare documents, Word shows the differences using _______________ _______________.

5. If you cannot see comments onscreen, you need to turn on _______________.

6. To include Document Properties information in a document, place a _______________ in the document.

7. To _________ a document, Word must be configured to send information to your email program.

8. A _________ ____________ acts as a binder for a set of separate files.

9. To edit a subdocument you must ___________ it first.

10. When a document is routed, it's sent as an __________ to an email message.

Matching

In the blank next to each of the following terms or phrases, write the letter of the corresponding term or phrase. (Note that some letters may be used more than once.)

a. Document Summary

b. Yellow

c. ScreenTip

d. Routing slip

e. Email

f. Subdocument

g. Master Document view

h. Expand Documents

i. Revision marks

j. Asterisk

________ 1. File within a master document

________ 2. Character that is displayed when you type a password

________ 3. Formatting applied to changes made to a document when changes are being tracked

________ 4. List of people to route a document to

________ 5. Software required to route a document

________ 6. View used to create a master document

________ 7. Default color for highlighting and comments

________ 8. Feature used to display comments in a document

________ 9. Feature that includes important information about a document

________ 10. Button used to display all the text in a subdocument

Applying Your Skills

Practice

The following exercises enable you to practice the skills you have learned in this project. Take a few minutes to work through these exercises now.

Adding Comments to a Document

In this exercise, practice the skills you have learned in this project by adding comments into a version of the Café Brochure document and adding comments to the document's file properties.

To add comments to a document, follow these steps:

1. Open the file Proj1103 from the Project-11 folder on the CD and save it in your Practices folder with the name Café Brochure3.

2. Insert a comment after the line `Following is a list of lunch items available on a daily basis`, questioning if all the items are available daily. Indicate in the comment that you think fish and chips are available only on Fridays.

3. Insert a comment after the first reference to the owner, indicating that you think the last name might be spelled incorrectly.

4. Insert a comment after the paragraph about the private function room, indicating that you think it can hold only 20 people.

5. Delete the second comment.

6. Add a comment to the document's file properties, indicating that you believe the spelling of the owner's last name should be verified.

7. Save the document. If requested by your instructor, print a copy, including the comments, and then close the document.

Tracking Changes to an Agenda

Use the skills you learned in this project to track changes to a training seminar document.

To track changes to an agenda, follow these steps:

1. Open the file Proj1104 from the Project-11 folder on the CD and save it in your `Practices` folder as `Agenda`.

2. Choose <u>T</u>ools, <u>T</u>rack Changes, <u>H</u>ighlight Changes.

3. Make sure that all check boxes in the Highlight Changes dialog box are selected, then choose OK.

4. Move the times of all three meetings back one hour.

5. Switch the speaker for the first meeting on Monday with the speaker for the meeting on Tuesday.

6. Add a row to the table for a tour of the facilities at 11:00 a.m. on Tuesday with Sue Ward.

7. Save the document. If requested by your instructor, print the document, including the revision marks. Then close the document.

Comparing Versions of a Report, Reviewing Changes, and Protecting the Report

Use Word to compare an original copy of a report with a copy that has been reviewed and edited. Review the differences to decide which ones to accept and which to reject. Finally, protect the report document so unauthorized changes cannot be made.

To compare versions of a report, review changes, and protect the report, follow these steps:

1. Open the file Proj1105 from the Project-11 folder on the CD, save it in your `Practices` folder as `Interviews7`, and close it.

2. Open the file Proj1106 from the Project-11 folder on the CD, save it in your `Practices` folder as `Edited Interviews`, and keep it open.

3. Choose Tools, Track Changes, Compare Documents, and select to compare the Interviews7 document to the Edited Interviews document.

4. Choose Tools, Track Changes, Accept or Reject Changes, review the changes in the document and accept or reject them as follows:

   - Accept the first change (deletion of `????????, Introduction`, and `I. Section 1`" heading)

   - Accept the second change (insertion of name and title of preparer, report subtitle, and heading title)

   - Reject the third change (insertion of the word "relatively")

   - Accept the fourth and fifth changes (insertion of `recent` and `numerous`")

   - Accept the sixth and seventh changes

   - Reject the eighth change

5. Choose Changes without highlighting in the Accept or Reject Changes dialog box to preview the document as it would look if you accept the remaining changes; then choose Original to preview it as it would look if you reject the remaining changes.

6. Accept All remaining changes.

7. Save the document, then choose Tools, Protect Document, OK to protect it so that any new changes are highlighted with revision marks.

8. Choose File, Save As and click the Options button to enter a password so that the document can only be opened or modified with the password `Interview` (it's permissible to use the same password for both features). Be careful to enter the correct password twice for each option.

9. Test the password protection by closing the document and reopening it, then try to edit it.

10. Save the document. If requested by your instructor, print the document and then close it.

Saving Different Versions of a Document

Use Word to save different versions of the same document. If you have an email system, try routing the document to other people for review.

To save different versions of a document, follow these steps:

1. Open the file Proj1107 from the Project-11 folder on the CD and save it in your `Practices` folder as `Technology3`.

2. Choose File, Versions, then click the Save Now button.

3. Type `Original, no changes`, then click OK.

4. Change the heading `Implementing New Technology` to `New Technology Arriving Soon`.

5. Change the heading `Implementation Strategy` to `Strategy for Implementing New Technology`.

6. Choose File, Versions, then click the Save Now button.

7. Type `Trying out new headings`, then click OK.

8. Choose File, Versions, select the first version and click Open so you can see both versions at the same time and compare them.

9. Close the original version.

10. If you have email, route the most recent version——the one with the new headings——to three people for reviewing.

11. Save the document. If requested by your instructor, print it. Close the document when you are finished.

Creating a Master Document

Use Word to create a Master Document from scratch, then add existing documents to a master document file.

To create a master document, follow these steps:

1. Open the file Proj1108 from the Project-11 folder on the CD, save it in your `Practices` folder as `Café Brochure4`, then close it.

2. Open the file Proj1109 from the Project-11 folder on the CD, save it in your `Practices` folder as `Loan5`, then close it.

3. Open the file Proj1110 from the Project-11 folder on the CD and save it in your `Practices` folder as `Master`. Keep it open.

4. Move the insertion point to the blank line at the end of the document and click the Promote button on the Outlining toolbar.

5. Type `Sample Menu`.

6. With the insertion point still on the line with the heading Sample Menu, click the Create Subdocument button on the Master Document toolbar. You now have one subdocument in the Master document. Try adding existing files as subdocuments.

7. Move the insertion point to the blank line at the end of the document, then click the Insert Subdocument button on the Master document toolbar.

8. Locate and open the document `Café Brochure4`. Word adds it to the Master document.

9. Move the insertion point to the blank line at the end of the document, click the Insert Subdocument button, then locate and open the `Loan5` document.

10. Save the Master document.

11. Collapse the subdocuments.

12. Expand the subdocuments.

13. Save the Master document again. If requested by your instructor, print it. Close the document when you have finished.

Challenge

The following challenges enable you to use your problem-solving skills. Take time to work through these exercises now.

Highlighting Text and Inserting Comments in a Prospectus

You are reviewing a prospectus for a coworker. Highlight the headings you think need expanding, and insert comments to question facts. Open the file Proj1111 from the Project-11 folder on the CD and save it in your Challenges folder as Prospectus2.

Highlight the headings Total Net Assets, Redemptions, and Minimum Purchase in pink. Highlight the Customer Profile heading in green. Insert a comment after August 1, 1983, questioning the date; indicate in the comment that you think it was July 1, 1984. Insert a comment after the minimum purchase price, indicating that you think it is $1,500. Insert a comment after the public offering price, indicating that you think it is $5.00 per share.

Delete the second comment. Add a comment to the file properties requesting an investigation into the minimum purchase price.

Save the Prospectus2 document. If requested by your instructor, print a copy, including the comments, and then close the document.

Tracking Revisions

Edit a version of the Computer Training Concepts course list so it is appropriate for the Spring semester, then review the changes and either accept them or reject them.

Open the file Proj1112 from the Project-11 folder on the CD and save it in your Challenges folder with the name Courses2. Turn on revision marks so you can track the changes you make.

Change the season at the top of the document to Spring 2000. Increase all non-member pricing by $5.00. Delete the Excel 3 course, which will not be offerered. Change the name of the Web Publishing 1 course to Web Publishing with Word 97.

Review the changes you have made. Reject all pricing changes, but accept all other changes. Save the document. If requested by your instructor, print it. Close it when you have finished.

Saving Versions of a Presentation

While you are working on the presentation for Computer Training Concepts, you save versions so that you can keep track of how it has changed. Open the file Proj1113 from the Project-11 folder on the CD and save it in your Challenges folder with the name Presentation3.

Save a version of the presentation with the comment Saved before edits. Change the subtitle from "As We Grew, So We Will Grow" to "History Points to Our Future." Save another version with the comment Trying out a new subtitle. Set Word to save a version automatically whenever the document is closed.

If requested by your instructor, print the most recent version of the document. Close it when you have finished.

Protecting an Annual Report Document

You want to be certain that no one makes unauthorized changes to an annual report document. Protect the document using passwords and other available tools.

Open the file Proj1114 from the Project-11 folder on the CD and save it in your `Challenges` folder with the name `Report3`. First, set it so that any changes are made with revision marks. Test the protection by changing the date to 2000.

Add password protection for both opening and modifying the document. Use the password Report3 for opening the document, and the password Training for modifying the document. Save and close the document.

Test the password protection by opening the document. Once it is open, change the date back to 1999. Save the document. If requested by your instructor, print it. Close it when you have finished.

Creating a Master Document

You want to add all your Computer Training Concepts documents to the presentation you have been creating. To do so, add them into a master file.

Open the file Proj1115 from the Project-11 folder on the CD and save it in your `Challenges` folder with the name `CTC Master`. Insert the following documents as subdocuments into the CTC Master file: `Presentation3`; `Courses2`; and `Report3` (you need to use the passwords to open it). Save the CTC Master document. If requested by your instructor, print it. Close it when you have finished.

You have completed the project and the associated lessons, as well as the "Checking Your Skills" and "Applying Your Skills" sections. Now use the PinPoint software evaluation mode to assess your comprehension of the specific exam tasks you have just learned. You can also use the PinPoint Trainer Mode and the Show Me tutorials to practice these specific exam tasks.

Project 12
Twelve

Creating Basic Forms

Creating a Form Template

In this Project, you learn how to:

Objectives

Required Activities

➤ Create a Form Template … … … … … … … … … … … …   **Create and Modify Forms**
Use Macros to Create Templates
Create Catalogs and Lists

➤ Create a Printed Form

➤ Insert Text Form Fields   … … … … … … … … … …   **Insert Fields**

➤ Insert Form Fields in a Table   … … … … … … … …   **Insert Fields**

➤ Set Text Form Field Options for Dates … … … … … …   **Insert Fields**

➤ Set Options for Other Form Fields   … … … … … …   **Insert fields**

➤ Perform Calculations in a Form

➤ Use an Online Form

Why Would I Do This?

Form
A document designed for use in collecting and tabulating information.

Forms are a simple method of collecting information. They are so common in everyday life that we hardly notice them. You use forms when you register a new software program, apply for a job, open a bank account, or fill out a purchase order or invoice. The types and variations of common forms are nearly endless.

On most forms, you can enter information in a variety of ways. For example, you can simply write or type information, such as your name and address, in blank spaces; you can select a check box to provide information, such as your marital status or gender; sometimes you can select from a list of choices. With Word, you can create forms that accept information entered in these three ways. The forms can be designed to be filled out online using Word, or to be printed and filled out the old-fashioned way—with pencil and paper.

Form field
An area in an onscreen form where users can enter information by typing, selecting from a drop-down list, or marking a check box.

In this project, you learn how to design, create, and use simple forms that can be printed or filled out online. You learn how to create and customize the three basic types of *form fields*: text, check box, and drop-down list. You also learn how to automate some online fields by using bookmarks and calculations.

Lesson 1: Creating a Form

In Word, forms are stored as templates. To use a form, you create a document based on the template, which you then can fill out online or print and fill out manually. There is one major difference between a form and a template, however. Templates are designed so that you can customize them to suit your needs, but forms are *protected* so that you can enter data only in form fields. Protecting a form template ensures that the form won't be changed accidentally by the person filling it out or printing it.

Form protected
Marked as read only so that users can enter and edit data only in form fields. Text and graphics not in form fields cannot be changed at all until the form is unprotected.

Word forms contain two types of information:

- Standard text and graphics appear on the form to provide information such as labels, or what the user should enter. This information does not change from form to form.

- Form fields appear where the user enters the information online. Although the form fields appear on each form, the information in the fields is variable and may change depending on who fills out the form.

When you create a form, it is a good idea to take some time to plan the form layout before you begin. It helps to have a paper form that you can use as a guide or an existing document that you can easily convert into a form. It is also a good idea to make use of tables and graphic elements in a form, both to improve the appearance of the form and to make it easier to organize the standard text and form fields on the page.

In this lesson, you open a document, edit it so that it can be used as a form, protect it, and save it as a form template.

1 Open the folder Project-12 and the file Proj1201 from this book's companion CD and save it as `Invoice`.

This document is a regular Word document, set up as an invoice (see Figure 12.1). As it stands, it can be used once or copied and edited with Word for use again and again. However, turning this invoice into a form saves a lot of time and effort.

This document is well-designed to be saved as a form template. If you scroll down in the document or display it in Whole Page view as shown in Figure 12.1, you can see that it includes standard elements such as the return address and logo, as well as text labels and graphic lines. It also has data organized in a table. Once the document is saved as a template, you can use it to quickly create forms that you can print and fill out manually. Alternatively, you can add form fields to the template so that users can fill it out online.

Figure 12.1
An invoice is a good example of a document that can easily be set up as a form.

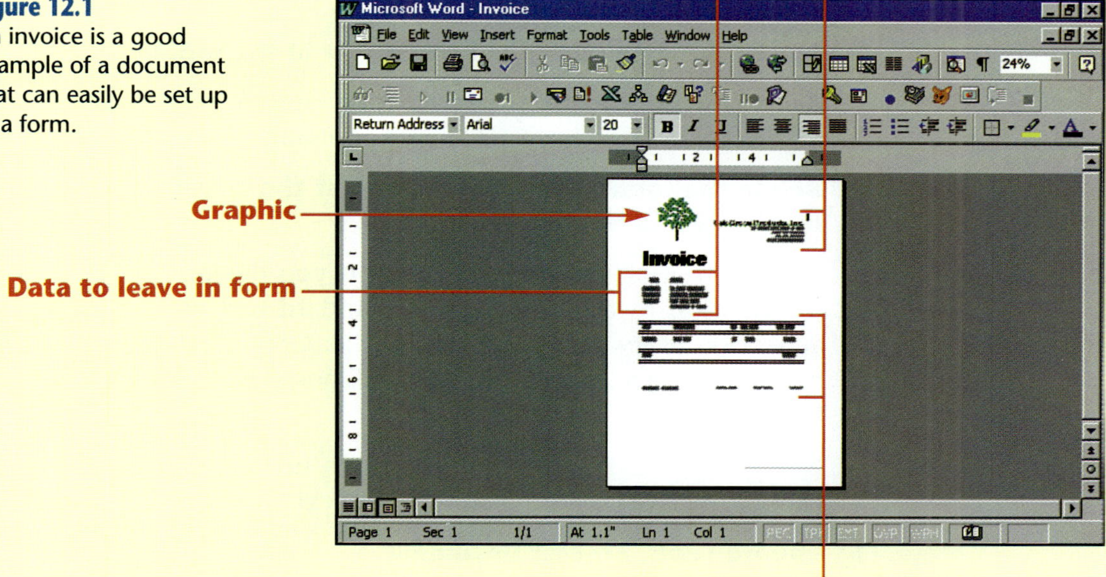

The first step in creating the form template is to delete the variable data that, in the finished form, is entered into form fields.

2 In the Invoice document, delete the date, the name of the addressee, and the text on the three address lines. In other words, delete the following information (shown on the next page):

continues

To Create a Form Template   (continued)

3/15/98
Mr. Jacob Wentworth
Wentworth Enterprises
6060 South Street
Indianapolis, IN 46290

This information changes on each invoice form that is filled out. You should not delete the label text, however, because that remains standard on the invoice form. Also, do not delete the paragraph marks on the address lines. You want to preserve the layout of the invoice as much as possible.

If you have problems...

If you have trouble identifying where to select data and where to leave data in place, try displaying paragraph marks and table gridlines. To display paragraph marks, click the Show/Hide ¶ button on the Standard toolbar. To display table gridlines, choose Table, Show Gridlines.

It may also help to display the document in a larger zoom setting. Try zooming to 100%.

3 Delete the data from the second row of the table.

Again, this information changes from invoice to invoice. Do not delete any rows from the table or the column labels in the first row.

4 Delete the total price from the cell at the intersection of the third row and the fifth column.

This is the last variable information you delete. The remaining information in the document is standard text and graphics that appear on every invoice issued by Oak Grove Products. The main body of the Invoice document should look similar to the one shown in Figure 12.2.

Now protect the document so that an unauthorized user cannot change the basic layout, graphics, and text.

5 Choose Tools, Protect Document.

The Protect Document dialog box is displayed, as shown in Figure 12.3. You can protect the document for three types of editing:

- Tracked changes—users can edit only with revision marks

- Comments—users can add comments but cannot edit the document

- Forms—users can enter and edit data only in form fields

Figure 12.2
Once the variable information has been deleted, the document can be protected and saved as a template.

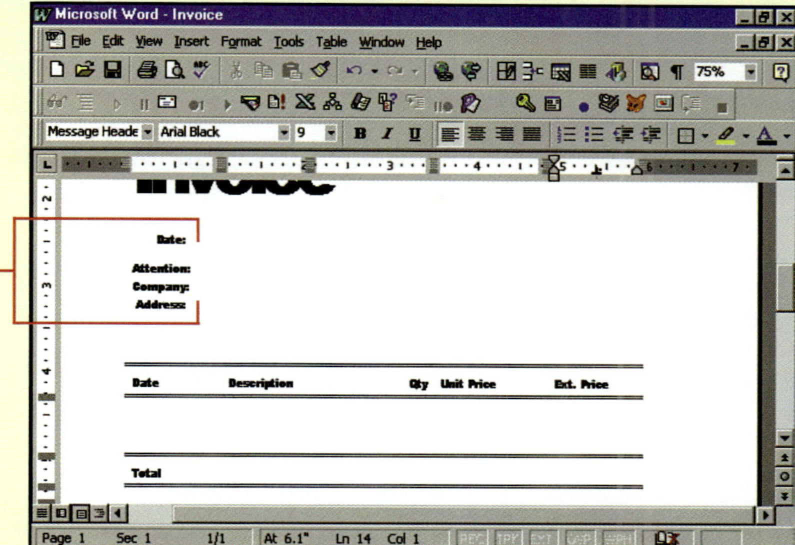

Data has been deleted

Figure 12.3
Use the Protect Document dialog box to protect the form from unauthorized editing.

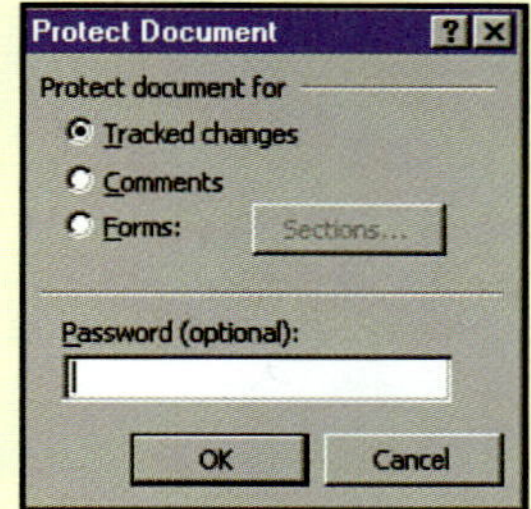

You can also set up password protection so that the document cannot be unprotected unless the user enters the correct password. You need to protect this document so that users can enter and edit data only in the form fields.

6 Click the Forms option button; then click OK.

Word protects the Invoice document so that the standard text, graphics, and layout cannot be edited. Because no form fields are entered in the document yet, you cannot edit the document at all.

7 Try moving the insertion point anywhere within the existing text.

No matter where you click the mouse or what keys you press, you cannot position the insertion point or edit the document. Now save the document as a template.

8 Choose File, Save As.

The Save As dialog box is displayed.

continues

Word

To Create a Form Template (continued)

9 **From the Save as _Type_ drop-down list, select Document Template.**

Word changes the Save _In_ folder to Templates and displays all the template subfolders, as shown in Figure 12.4.

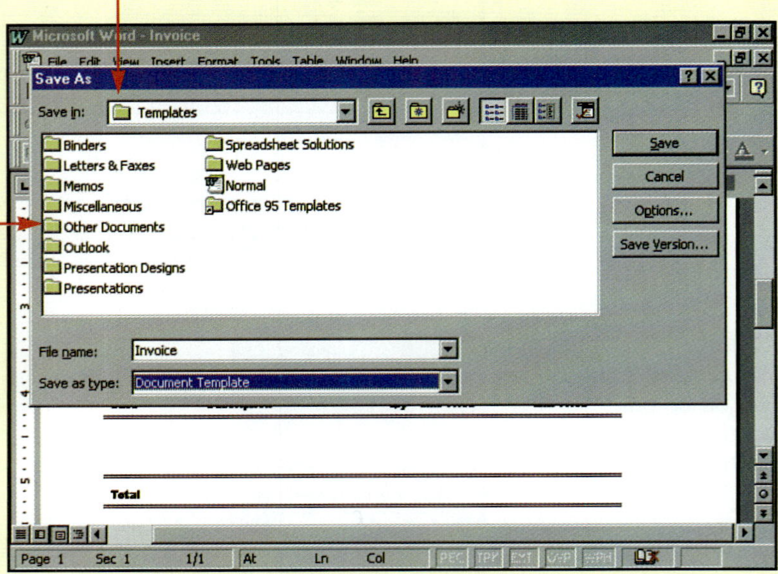

Figure 12.4
By default, Word saves templates in the Templates folder.

Other Documents subfolder

10 **Change the File _Name_ to `Invoice Form`, change the Save _In_ folder to the Other Documents subfolder, and then choose _Save_.**

Word saves the document as a template in the Other Documents subfolder.

11 **Save the Invoice Form template and close it.**

In the next lesson, you learn how to use it to create a printed form.

If you want to make sure that no one unprotects a form and edits it, you can add password protection at the same time that you protect the form. In the Protect Document dialog box, type a password in the _Password_ text box and click OK. Word displays the Confirm Password dialog box so you can reenter the password. When you click OK, the document becomes password-protected. When anyone (including you!) attempts to unprotect the document, Word displays the Unprotect Password dialog box. You must enter the password correctly to be able to edit the document.

Macros are a powerful tool when combined with templates. They can automate the task of completing document created with a template and are particularly useful when working with online forms.

When you create a template for an online form , you insert fields on that form. Any macro in the form template can run automatically when the insertion point enters or exits a form field.

To automate a template by adding macros, you must first create the macros you want to run in the template. Then do the following:

1. Create or open the form template that you want to automate.

2. If protection has been applied to the form, click the Protect Form button on the Forms toolbar or choose Tools, Unprotect Document from the menu.

3. Create the macros you want to use in the template and store them in the template.

4. Add the form fields you need in the template.

5. For each form field to which you want to attach a macro, double-click the form field to see the Field Options dialog box (this box differs slightly depending on the type of field you're working on).

6. Under Run Macro On (see Figure 12.5), select the macro you want to use with that field from the Entry drop-down list if you want the macro to run when the insertion point enters the field. If you want the macro to run when the insertion point exits the field, select the macro from the Exit drop-down list.

7. Click OK. Test the template to see that your macros work properly.

Figure 12.5
Select an existing macro from either the Entry or Exit drop-down lists.

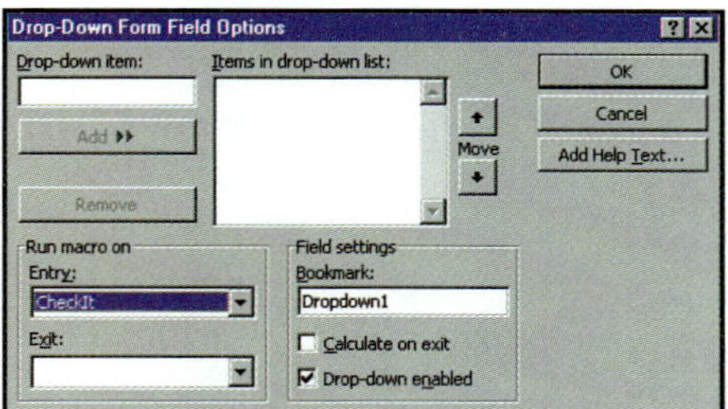

Word has a mail merge feature that also involves fields. These are "merge" fields designed to pull unique pieces of information from a data source (database) file. However, this same system allows you to create a catalog, membership directory, parts list, or similar document. For more information on using mail merge, refer to Project 8, "Advanced Merge Techniques." We have placed this Exam Note in your forms lesson because Microsoft lists the required activity, "Create catalogs and lists," under the skill set "Use Forms" on the Microsoft Word 97 Expert User Skills Roadmap.

There may not be sufficient time for your instructor to work with this skill, but you can practice it on your own. There is also a practice review at the end of this chapter for creating catalogs and lists.

To create a catalog or list, follow these instructions:

1. Choose Tools, Mail Merge from the menu to open the Mail Merge Helper dialog box.

2. Under step 1, Main Document, click the Create button.

3. From the menu that appears, select Catalog. With a catalog main document, all of the merged data is placed in one resulting merged document and the text you add to the main document is repeated for each set of data.

continues

4. Once you make the selection, a dialog box appears asking whether you want to use the active document window when you create the document or a new document window. Click Active Window to turn the document you currently have open into your main document for the mail merge.

5. Under step 2, Data Source, click the Get Data button.

6. From the menu that appears, select Create Data Source. Set up the fields you want to use. Click OK and then click Edit Data Source to enter the data to create the data source.

7. In the main document, insert the text and graphics you want repeated with each data record. Where you want to put data from the data source, click Insert Merge Field on the Mail Merge toolbar and choose the field name that you want to insert.

8. Return to the Mail Merge Helper by clicking on the Mail Merge Helper button on the Mail Merge toolbar. Under step 3, Merge the Data with the Document, click the Merge button. From the Merge To drop-down list, select New Document.

9. Under Records to Be Merged, select All or From. If you choose From, enter the record numbers in the From box and the To box that you want to merge. If you only want to merge specific records or records of a certain type, click Query Options and set conditions on the merge.

10. Under When Merging Records, select Don't Print Blank Lines When Data Fields Are Empty if you don't want any blank lines in your letters, labels, or envelopes because there was no entry in a particular field (such as the field Company where a person is self-employed and doesn't have a company name).

11. Click Merge.

12. When the catalog document appears, add headers, footers, or any additional text you need. Then print the document as you would any other Word document.

Lesson 2: Creating a Printed Form

If you plan to use a form in printed format instead of online, you do not need to add form fields. Once you set up the document, protect it, and save it as a template, you can use it to create and print form documents.

In this lesson, you use the Invoice Form template to create a printed form that you can fill out manually.

To Create a Printed Form

1 **In Word, choose File, New.**

The New dialog box is displayed.

2 **Click the Other Documents tab.**

The templates stored in the Other Documents folder are listed in the dialog box, as shown in Figure 12.6.

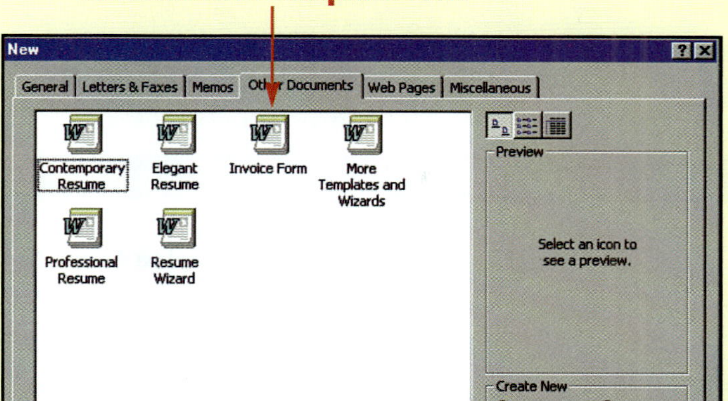

Figure 12.6
The Invoice Form template is stored with other templates in the Other Documents folder.

3 **Select the Invoice Form template; then click OK.**

Word creates a new document based on the Invoice Form template. Because the document is based on a protected template, the document is protected as well; you cannot edit the existing text. To create printed forms, all you have to do is print the document.

4 **Click the Print button on the Standard toolbar.**

Word prints the Invoice Form template. You can manually enter the variable data to complete the form.

5 **Close the open document.**

Word closes the document. You do not have to save the document; whenever you want to print more forms, you simply create a new document based on the form template.

Keep Word open for the next lesson, where you learn how to add text form fields to a form template.

In many cases, you will want to print multiple copies of the form so that you have a stack on hand when you need them. To print more than one copy of the form, you must use the File, Print command to open the Print dialog box. Enter the number of copies in the Number of Copies text box; then click OK.

Lesson 3: Inserting Text Form Fields

If you want users to be able to fill out a form online, you must add form fields to the form template. As mentioned earlier, there are three basic types of form fields:

■ Text form fields, in which users can enter text or numbers

■ Check box form fields, which users can select or deselect to mark an item

- Drop-down form fields, which display a list from which users can select an option

In this lesson, you add text form fields to the Invoice Form template so that users can type data into the form online.

To Insert Text Form Fields

❶ In Word, open the Invoice Form template document and choose Tools, Unprotect Document.

Word unprotects the document so that you can edit it.

If you have problems...

If you have trouble locating the Invoice Form template document, ask your instructor for assistance. You may find it in the list of files at the bottom of the File menu, or you may have to wade through a maze of folders and subfolders to find it. It should be stored in the Other Documents folder in the Templates folder, which is usually found in the Microsoft Office folder. The Microsoft Office folder should be in the Program Files folder on your hard disk.

❷ Choose View, Toolbars, Forms.

Word displays the Forms toolbar, as shown in Figure 12.7. Notice that the toolbar floats onscreen and is not anchored to the top, bottom, or either side. You can move it if you want.

Figure 12.7
You use the Forms toolbar to insert form fields into a document, to set form field options, and to modify the appearance of the form.

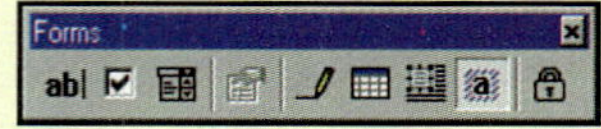

❸ Position the insertion point at the first left tab stop after the label Date on the line under the banner Invoice (see Figure 12.8). Then click the Text Form Field button on the Forms toolbar.

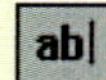

Word inserts a text field at the insertion point location, as shown in Figure 12.8. The field is created with default settings so that it will accept any number of characters of typed data. The field is lightly shaded in gray onscreen.

If you have problems...

If the form fields you insert into your document do not appear shaded, click the Form Field Shading button on the Forms toolbar.

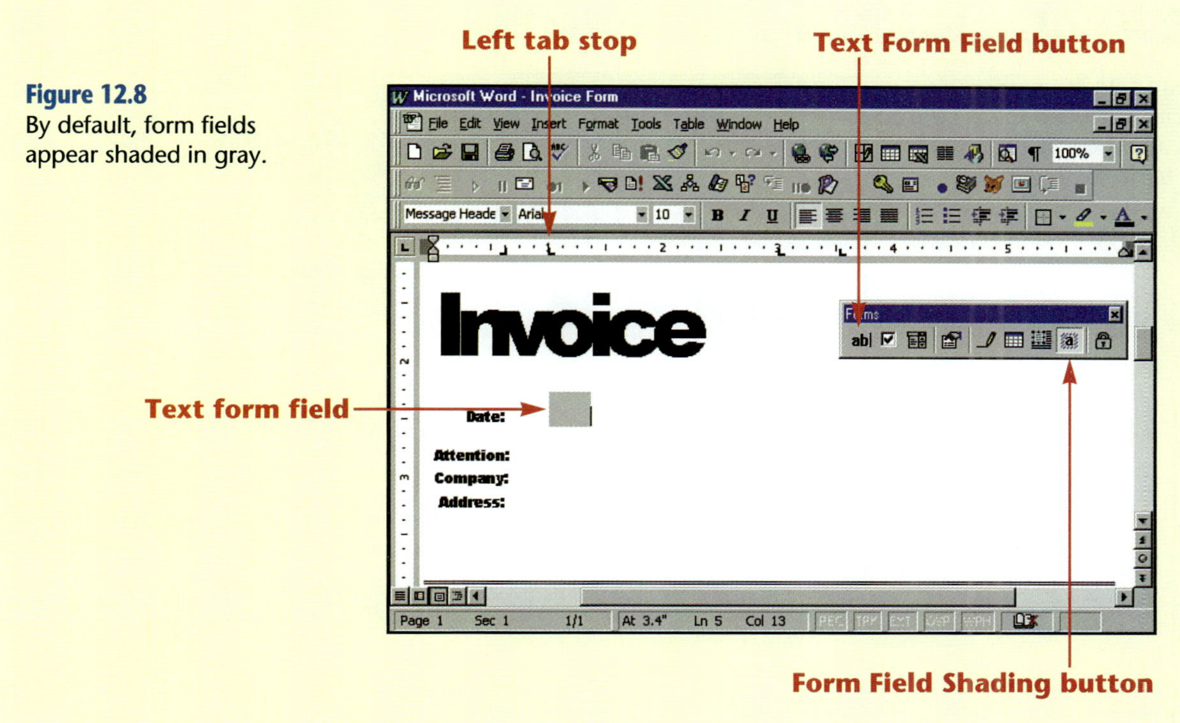

ab|

④ Press ⬇ to move to the left tab stop after the word Attention; then click the Text Form Field button on the Forms toolbar.

Word inserts a text form field at the location of the insertion point.

ab|

⑤ Press ⬇ to move to the left tab stop on the Company line; then click the Text Form Field button.

Word inserts a Text form field at the insertion point location.

⑥ Repeat step 5 three times to insert text form fields on the three address lines.

When you are finished, the top of the Invoice Form template document should look similar to the one in Figure 12.9.

⑦ Save the Invoice Form template and keep it open on your screen.

In the next lesson, you insert form fields into the table in the Invoice Form template.

continues

Word

To Insert Text Form Fields (continued)

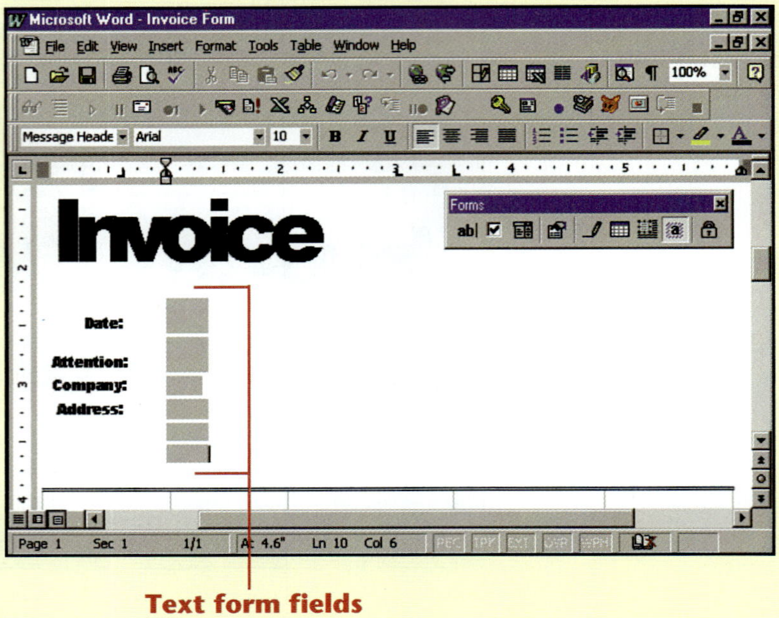

Figure 12.9
You can insert text form fields anywhere in a form template.

Text form fields

When you fill out an online form, Word moves through the fields in the order in which you insert them in the document. For this reason, you should give some thought to the way you want users to fill out the form fields before you actually insert them into the document. If you want the user to move from left to right across the page, you should insert the form fields from left to right across the page. If you want the user to move up and down the page, you should insert the form fields up and down the page. You learn more about filling out online forms in Lesson 8.

Lesson 4: Inserting Form Fields in a Table

Using a table in a form template helps you align fields so that they look good and makes the form easier for users to fill out. In addition, you can use Word's Table features to format and manipulate the fields and data in the table to improve the form. For example, in Lesson 7, you learn how to create calculating form fields in the table.

To insert form fields in a table, you use the same steps that you use to insert form fields in a regular text area. In this lesson, you insert text, drop-down, and check box form fields in the table in the Invoice Form template document.

This book assumes that you are familiar with Word's Table features. If you are not, ask your instructor for information. Using tables is covered in Project 1.

To Insert Form Fields in a Table

1 **If gridlines are not already displayed in the Invoice Form template document, choose Table, Show Gridlines. Then move the insertion point into the first cell of the second row in the table—the cell under the label Date.**

You need a text form field in this cell. Editing with gridlines displayed helps you to position the insertion point where you want to insert fields.

2 **Click the Text Form Field button on the Forms toolbar.**

Word inserts a text form field in the cell.

3 **Press** Tab.

The insertion point moves to the cell under the Description label. This is where you insert a drop-down form field so that users can select from a list of available products.

4 **Click the Drop-Down Form Field button on the Forms toolbar.**

Word inserts a drop-down form field in the cell; it looks just like a text form field. In Lesson 5, you learn how to set form field options to customize each type of field.

5 **Press** Tab **and insert a text form field in the cell under the** Qty **label.**

This is the field where users can enter the number of items purchased.

6 **Repeat step 5 twice to insert text form fields in the cells under the** Unit Price **and** Ext. Price **labels.**

These two form fields are used to display the cost information. Now add a text form field for the total invoice amount.

7 **Press** ↓ **to position the insertion point on the row labeled** Total, **in the cell under the** Ext. Price **label, and insert a text form field.**

Now you insert check box form fields next to the three payment method options.

8 **Click in the cell containing the text** Money Order, **in the last row of the table; then click the Check Box Form Field button on the Forms toolbar.**

Word inserts a check box form field in the cell, to the left of the text. Users can mark the check box form field next to the payment method they want to use for an invoice.

continues

To Insert Form Fields in a Table

⑨ Click in the cell containing the text `Bank Check`; then click the Check Box Form Field button on the Forms toolbar.

Word inserts a check box form field to the left of the text. Now insert the last form field into the template document.

⑩ Click in the cell containing the text `Visa/MC`; then click the Check Box Form Field button on the Forms toolbar.

These are all the form fields you need in the Invoice Form template. The bottom half of the document should look similar to the document shown in Figure 12.10.

⑪ Save the changes you have made to the Invoice Form template document and keep it open on your screen.

In the next lesson, you learn how to use form field options to control the information entered in form fields.

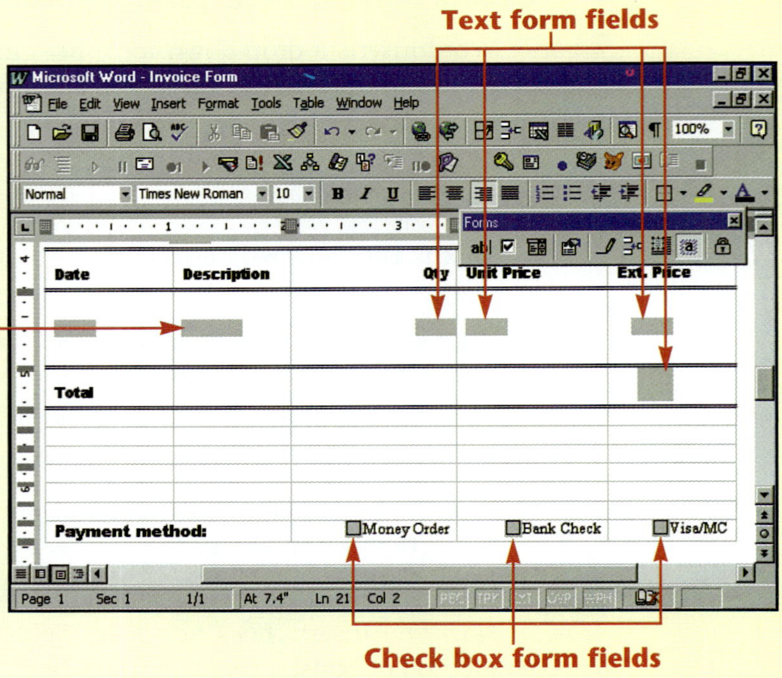

Figure 12.10
The bottom half of the Invoice Form template includes all three types of form fields.

Inside Stuff

Form fields are created with the basic default form field settings. In some cases, these default settings are all you need in your form template. Once you insert the form fields, you can protect the document template, close it, and use it online, as described in Lesson 8, or create printed, blank forms, as described in Lesson 2. However, in most cases, you want to set the form field options in order to customize the form. Lesson 5 covers setting form field options for all three types of form fields.

Lesson 5: Setting Text Form Field Options for Dates

Inserting form fields in a document is quite easy, as you learned in Lessons 3 and 4. However, by default, each type of form field is created with only basic, standard settings. For example, text form fields are created to accept any type of regular text and an unlimited number of characters. Although the default settings may be appropriate for some form fields, if you want to customize the form fields for your form, you must set the form field options.

In this lesson, you learn how to set form field options for date fields, so that two of the text form fields in the Invoice Form template accept only valid dates.

To Set Text Form Field Options for Dates

1 **In the Invoice Form template document, click in the first field in the document (the text form field on the Date line). Then click the Form Field Options button on the Forms toolbar.**

Bookmark

A descriptive name that you can assign to items in a Word document. You can use bookmarks to locate and reference the items in other operations.

The Text Form Field Options dialog box opens, as shown in Figure 12.11. In this dialog box, you can specify such settings as the type of text that the field accepts, how many characters the field accepts, and the format in which you want the text to appear. You can assign the field a descriptive *bookmark* name that you can use to reference the field in other operations. (In Lesson 7, you use bookmarks to set up calculating fields.) You can also enter default data that appears in the field for all new documents created with that form template; the user can leave the default data in place or replace it with new data.

This first text form field in the Invoice Form template is where the user will type the invoice date. You can set the field options to specify that the field should accept only date information, and you can specify how you want the date displayed.

Figure 12.11

Use the Text Form Field Options dialog box to customize text form fields.

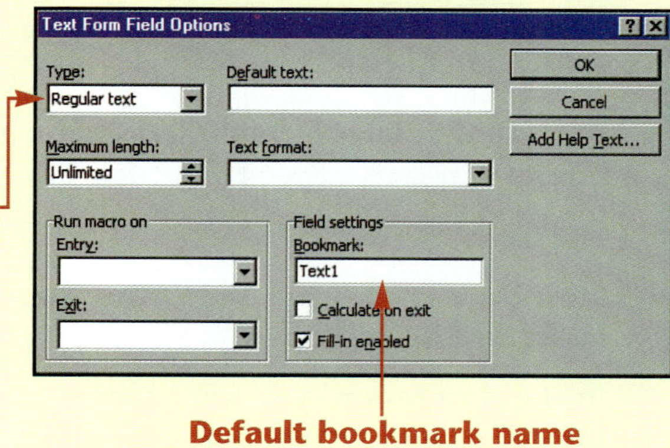

Default text type

Default bookmark name

continues

To Set Text Form Field Options for Dates   (continued)

2 Click the Type arrow button to open the drop-down list, and then select Date.

When you open the Type drop-down list, it displays the available settings for the type of text that can be entered in the selected form field. The list includes Regular Text (the default setting), Number, Date, Current Date, Current Time, and Calculation. Selecting Date in this step specifies that only valid dates can be entered in this field.

3 Open the Date Format drop-down list and select the MMMM,d,yyyy format.

This step specifies that you want the date to be displayed in the field in a month, date, year format, such as September 9, 1997.

4 Replace the default name in the Bookmark text box with the name InvoiceDate.

Bookmark names can be up to thirty characters long but cannot include spaces. These are all the options you need to set for the selected field.

5 Click OK.

Word closes the dialog box. The default settings are appropriate for the rest of the text form fields at the top of the document. Now try setting options for the product information form fields in the table.

6 Click in the text form field in the cell under the Date label; then click the Form Field Options button on the Forms toolbar.

The Text Form Field Options dialog box appears. You also set this field to accept only date entries, but you need to use a different format.

7 Select Date from the Type drop-down list; then select M/d/y from the Date Format drop-down list.

This step formats the field to display dates in numerical format; for example, 9/9/97.

8 Change the default bookmark name in the Bookmark text box to TransactionDate; then click OK.

The dialog box closes.

9 Save the changes you have made to the Invoice Form document and keep it open.

In the next lesson, you learn how to set options for other type of text form fields, as well as for drop-down form fields and check box form fields.

Lesson 6: Setting Options for Other Form Fields

The options in the Form Field Options dialog box change, depending on the current form field. There are more options available for text form fields than for the other two types of form fields. However, you can specify bookmark names for all types of fields. When you set form field options for drop-down fields, you enter the items you want displayed in the drop-down list. When you set form field options for check box fields, you specify how large you want the check box to appear and whether it should start out blank or marked with an X.

In this lesson, you continue setting options for the form fields in the Invoice Form template document.

To Set Options for Other Form Fields

1 **Click in the drop-down form field under the Description label on the product information line; then click the Form Field Options button on the Forms toolbar.**

The Drop-Down Form Field Options dialog box is displayed, as shown in Figure 12.12. You must enter the choices you want displayed in the drop-down form field.

Figure 12.12

Use the Drop-Down Form Field Options dialog box to specify the items you want displayed in the drop-down list.

Type the item name here

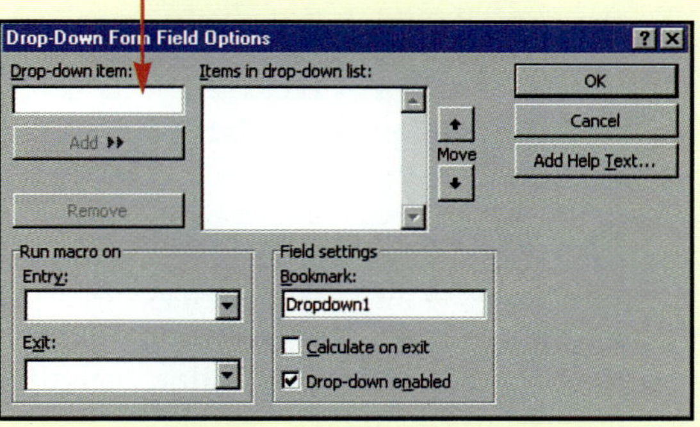

2 **In the Drop-Down Item text box, type `Tulip bulbs`; then click the Add button.**

Word adds the item `Tulip bulbs` to the Items in Drop-Down List box. It is displayed when a user selects the field. Now add three more items to the list.

3 **In the Drop-Down Item text box, type `Hyacinth bulbs`, click Add, type `Crocus bulbs`, click Add, type `Day Lily bulbs`, and click Add.**

There are now four items in the drop-down list, as shown in Figure 12.13.

continues

To Set Options for Other Form Fields (continued)

These are all of the items you need. There are no other options to set for the drop-down form field.

Figure 12.13
You can view the items you have added to the list in the Drop-Down Form Field Options dialog box.

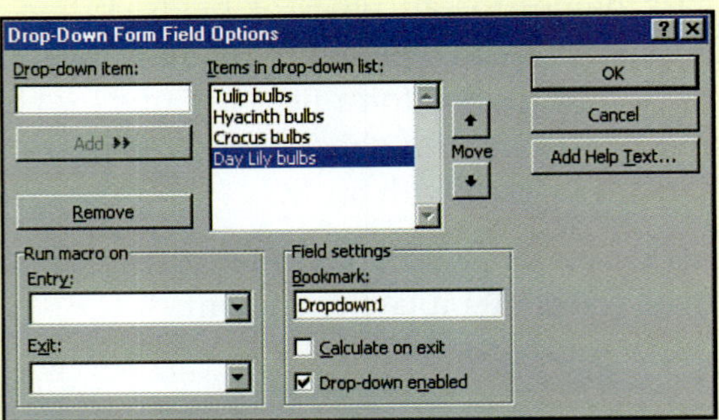

4 Click OK.

The dialog box closes. Notice that the first item in the list appears in the field in the table (the drop-down arrow appears only when the field is selected for data entry). Now set the options for the `Qty` and `Unit Price` text form fields.

5 Click the text form field in the cell under the `Qty` label; then click the Form Field Options button on the Forms toolbar.

This field needs to be set to accept only numbers, and to use 10 as the default, which is the minimum value for orders.

6 In the Text Form Field Options dialog box, select `Number` from the Type drop-down list; then enter `10` in the Default Number text box.

Now specify a number format and enter a descriptive bookmark name that you can use to set up a calculating field in Lesson 7. Because you reference the bookmark name in calculations, you also need to tell Word to update calculations whenever new data is entered in this field.

7 Select `#,##0` from the Number Format drop-down list, replace the default Bookmark name with `Quantity1`, select the Calculate on Exit check box, and then click OK.

This step specifies that you want the number displayed in a standard format with a comma between the thousands and hundreds columns, that you want the bookmark name to be Quantity1, and that you want Word to update the automatic calculations after data is entered. When the dialog box closes, notice that the default number appears in the field. It appears in all new documents until the user replaces it.

Enter the bookmark name as Quantity1, not just Quantity. If you then add rows to the invoice form for additional product items, you can set unique bookmark names for each field in the Qty column by increasing the number in the bookmark name. For example, in the second row, you could name the bookmark Quantity2, and so on.

Now set options for the Unit Price field.

8 **Click the text form field in the cell under the Unit Price label and then click the Form Field Options button on the Forms toolbar. Select Number from the Type drop-down list, enter the number 0 in the Default Number text box, and then select $#,##0.00($#,##0.00) from the Number Format drop-down list.**

This step sets the field to display data as dollar values. You also reference this field in a calculation in Lesson 7, so you need to enter a descriptive bookmark name and tell Word to update calculations when the data in this field changes.

9 **Change the default Bookmark name to UnitPrice1; then click the Calculate on Exit check box and click OK.**

Now set options for the Money Order check box field.

10 **Click the Money Order check box form field; then click the Form Field Options button on the Forms toolbar.**

The Check Box Form Field Options dialog box appears, as shown in Figure 12.14.

Figure 12.14
Use the Check Box Form Field Options dialog box to specify a check box size and to indicate whether to mark the check box field automatically.

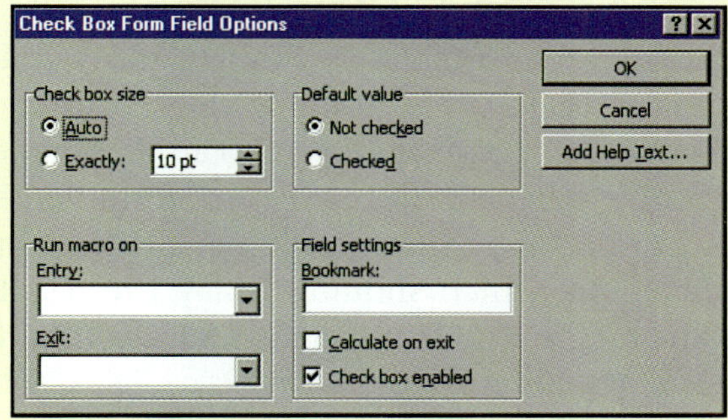

By default, check boxes are automatically sized according to the current font, and are not checked. You can set a precise size in the Exactly text box; select the Checked option if you want the box to appear selected (with an X in it). For this example, the Money Order check box should be selected because that is the preferred method of payment.

11 **Click the Checked check box; then click OK.**

The dialog box closes, and Word marks the Money Order check box form field in the Invoice Form template document.

continues

Word

12 Save the changes you have made to the Invoice Form template document and keep it open.

In Lesson 7, you learn how to set form fields in a table to perform automatic calculations.

Items in a drop-down form field appear in the order in which you enter them. If you want the items to appear in a different order, you can rearrange the list in the Drop-Down Form Field Options dialog box. Simply select the item you want to move in the Items in Drop-Down List box; then click the Move arrow button that points up to move the item up in the list, or the arrow button that points down to move the item down in the list. To delete an item from the list, select it and then click the Remove button.

You can add help text to any form field. Help can appear in the status bar when the field is selected, or can create a pop-up box that appears when a user presses F1 when the field is selected. To add help text to a form field, select the field; then open the Form Field Options dialog box and click the Add Help Text button.

To enter help on the status bar, make sure that the Appear on Status Bar page tab is selected. To enter pop-up help, select the Press Help Key (F1) page tab. Then type the help text in the space provided. If the text already exists as an AutoText entry, click the AutoText entry button and then select the entry in the list box.

Lesson 7: Performing Calculations in a Form

If a form uses a table, you can take advantage of Word's Table features to perform calculations automatically in form fields, using values entered in other fields. For example, you can automatically calculate sales tax or outstanding balances. In the invoice form you have been creating throughout this project, two fields could benefit from automatic calculations: the Ext. Price field, which should display the result of multiplying the Qty field value by the Unit Price value, and the Total field, which should display the result of adding all of the Ext. Price fields in the table together.

When calculating in a table or in a form field, you can use standard mathematical operators as well as some built-in functions. Table 12.1 describes the mathematical operators. For information on available functions, consult the Word Help program under the topic Formulas, Fields.

Table 12.1 Mathematical Operators

Operation	Operator
Add	+
Subtract	–
Multiply	*
Divide	/
Exponentiate (raise to a power)	^
Less than	<
Less than or equal to	<=
Greater than	>
Greater than or equal to	>=

In this lesson, you set options for calculating fields.

To Perform Calculations in a Form

1 In the Invoice Form template document, click the text form field in the cell under the Ext. Price label; then click the Form Field Options button on the Forms toolbar.

The Text Form Field Options dialog box is displayed.

Expression

A mathematical statement, consisting of formulas and operators.

2 Choose Calculation from the Type drop-down list.

Word displays an *Expression* text box in the dialog box and enters an equal sign (=) in it. The equal sign is the symbol used in Word and other Microsoft applications to specify that you are creating a mathematical *formula*.

Formula

A specific calculation such as adding or subtracting two numbers.

3 In the Expression text box, type Quantity1*UnitPrice1.

This formula indicates that to get the value you want to display in this field, Word will multiply the value in the Quantity form field by the value in the UnitPrice form field. (Although you can reference the table cells by using column letters and row numbers, using the form field bookmarks makes it easier to enter the correct expression.)

4 From the Number Format drop-down list, select the setting $#,##0.00($#,##0.00) and then click OK.

Notice that Word immediately displays $0.00 in the Ext. Price field (see Figure 12.15). It calculates this result by multiplying the default value of 1 in the Qty field by the default entry 10 in the Unit Price field. Now set up a formula for calculating the invoice total.

continues

Word

To Perform Calculations in a Form (continued)

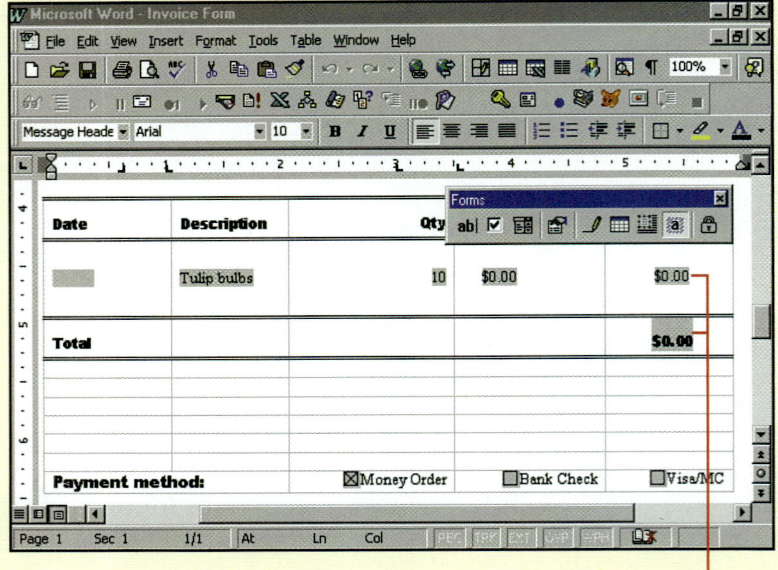

Figure 12.15
You can easily set up Word to perform automatic calculations in form fields in a table.

Calculating fields

⑤ Click the text form field in the Total row under the Ext. Price field label, and then click the Form Field Options button on the Forms toolbar.

Function

A predefined mathematical statement built into Word and other Microsoft applications.

For this calculation, you want Word to add all the values in as many fields as appear in the Ext. Price column of the table. However, you do not know in advance how many rows of items will be entered, so you cannot enter an expression referencing each field you want to add. Luckily, Word comes with some built-in *functions* (predefined formulas) that you can use. In this case, you simply tell Word to add together all the field values that appear in the column above the current field.

⑥ From the Type drop-down list, select Calculation; then click in the Expression text box and type SUM(ABOVE).

This expression indicates that, to get the result to display in the current field, Word will add together all the values that appear in the column above.

⑦ From the Number Format drop-down list, select the setting $#,##0.00($#,##0.00); then click OK.

This step formats the field to display the result as a dollar value, and then closes the dialog box. The form should look similar to the one shown in Figure 12.15.

You have now completed setting up the Invoice Form template document. Before you close it, you must save the changes and protect the document.

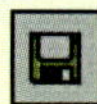

8 **Click the Save button on the Standard toolbar; then click the Protect Form button on the Forms toolbar.**

The form template is now saved and protected.

9 **Close the Forms toolbar and the Invoice Form document.**

When you close the document, save the changes if prompted. In the next lesson, you learn how to use the form template to create an online form.

Using the table format to perform calculations is a very basic way of automating a form. If you want to create more complex, interactive online forms that include more options for entering data, selecting choices, and recording feedback, you should use the ActiveX controls that come with Word. For more information, ask your instructor or consult the Word Help program.

You can edit a form template at any time. Simply open the template document, unprotect the document, make the changes, protect the document, and then save and close it. New documents based on the template reflect the changes.

Lesson 8: Using an Online Form

Once you have the form template saved and closed, you can use it to create forms that can be filled out and saved online with Word.

In this lesson, you use the Invoice Form template to create and fill out an invoice.

1 **In Word, choose File, New.**

The New dialog box appears.

2 **Click the Other Documents tab, select the Invoice Form template, and then click OK.**

Word creates a new document based on the Invoice Form template. By default, the first form field is selected.

3 **Save the new document with the name Garden Club Invoice.**

You do not always have to save online forms; sometimes you fill them out, print them, and then close the file without saving. However, in this case, save the file so that you have it for reference at the end of the lesson.

continues

To Use an Online Form   (continued)

❹ Scroll down so that you can see the first field. Then type 3/18/98 and press Tab.

Word enters the date in the field in the format you specified when setting form field options and moves to the next form field. Pressing Tab in a form always moves to the next field. Pressing ◆Shift+Tab moves to the previous field. You can also click a field to select it.

You can tell which form field is selected because it appears in a darker gray. Also, a selected text form field has a bold black underline, a selected drop-down form field displays the drop-down list arrow button, and a selected check box form field has a bold black border around it.

If you have problems...

Word moves through the fields in the order in which you inserted them in the document, which may not always be the order in which they appear in the document. If you press Tab in a form and Word moves to a field that you don't think is the next field in the form, chances are that you didn't insert the fields in a left-to-right, top-to-bottom progression.

❺ Type Ms. Samantha Jones and press Tab.

Word enters the name in the field and moves to the next form field. Notice that the field expands to let you enter as much text as you want. That's because you set the form field option to unlimited length. Now enter the company name and address.

❻ Type Garden Club Designs, press Tab, type 5050 Lantern Rd., press Tab, type Hanover, NH 03755, and press Tab.

Now all of the address information is filled in, and the last text field in the address area is selected. You do not have to fill in every form field. Simply leave the field blank and move to the next field.

❼ Press Tab, type 3/3/98, and press Tab again.

Word enters and formats the date and moves to the Description field. The drop-down arrow button appears to the right of the field (see Figure 12.16).

❽ Click the arrow button and select Day Lily bulbs from the drop-down list; then press Tab.

Word enters Day Lily bulbs in the Description field and then moves to the Qty field.

❾ Type 50, press Tab, type 1.50, and press Tab.

As soon as you press Tab to move out of the Unit Price field, Word automatically calculates the Ext. Price and the Total. It fills in the two calculating fields, and moves forward in the form to the Money Order check box field (see Figure 12.17).

Figure 12.16
Drop-down form field lists work just like drop-down lists in Windows applications.

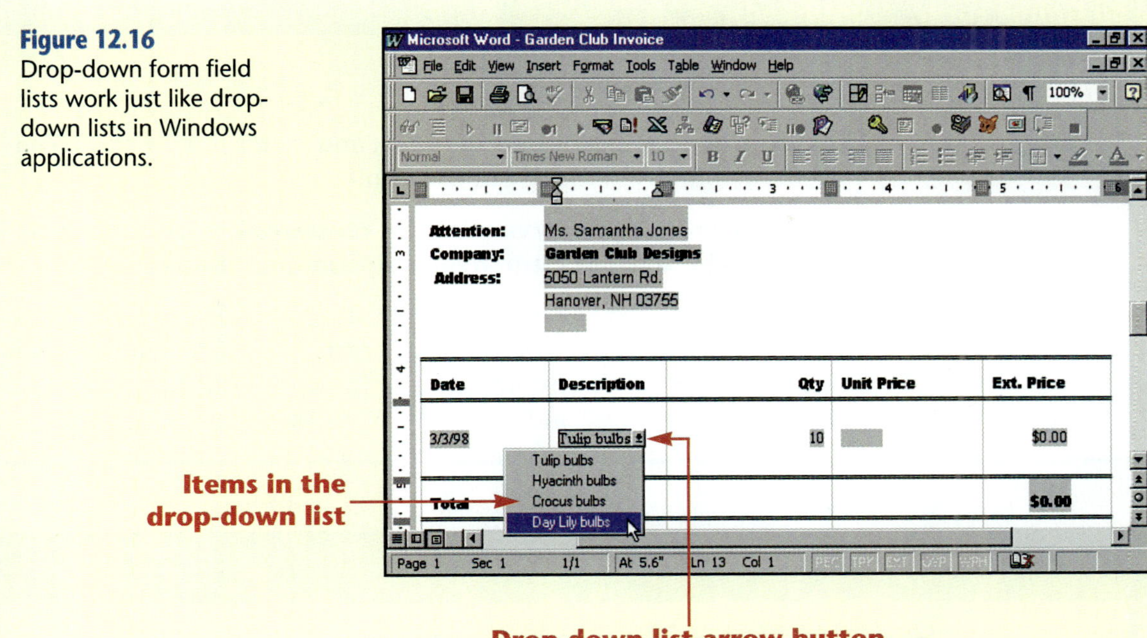

Figure 12.17
Word automatically updates the values in the calculating fields.

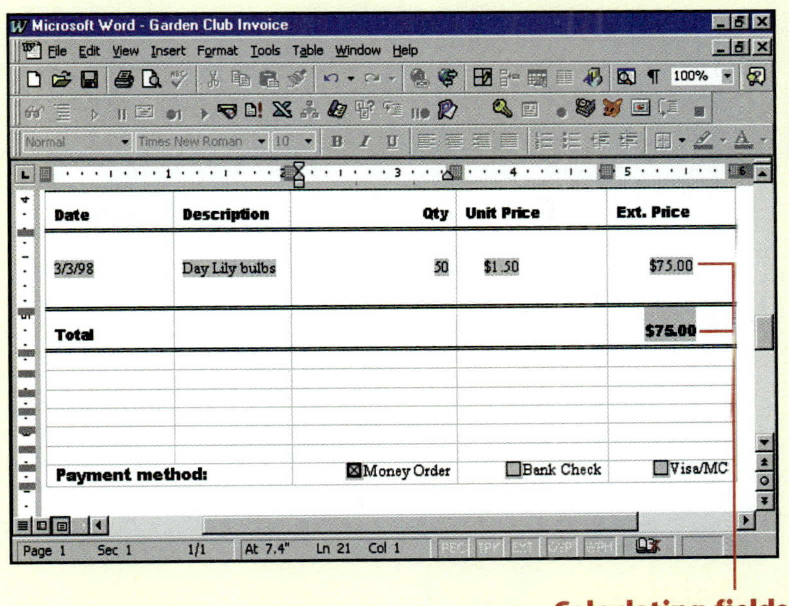

You set the Money Order check box to appear checked by default, but in this case you want the addressee to pay by bank check.

10 Press Spacebar.

Word unmarks the Money Order check box. You can mark or unmark check box fields by pressing Spacebar or by clicking the field with the mouse.

continues

Word

To Use an Online Form   (continued)

11 Press `Tab` **and then** `Spacebar`.

This moves to the `Bank Check` check box and marks it with an X. You have now completed filling out the form.

12 Save the changes you have made. If requested by your instructor, print the Garden Club Invoice document; then close it.

You have completed all the lessons in this project. If you have completed your session on the computer, exit Word and Windows 95 before turning off your computer. Otherwise, continue with the "Checking Your Skills" and "Applying Your Skills" sections.

Project Summary

To	Do This
Create a simple form	Open a new document and enter the fields, form fields, and unchanging text and graphics. Protect the document and save it as a template.
Insert a text form field	Unprotect the form template. Position the insertion point; then click the Text Form Field button on the Forms toolbar.
Insert a drop-down form field	Unprotect the form template. Position the insertion point; then click the Drop-Down Form Field button on the Forms toolbar.
Insert a check box form field	Unprotect the form template. Position the insertion point; then click the Check Box Form Field button on the Forms toolbar.
Set form field options	Click in the field. Click the Form Field Options button on the Forms toolbar. Set options in the dialog box; then click OK.
Print a blank form	Choose File, New and create a new document based on the form template. Print as many copies of the form as you need.
Fill out an online form	Choose File, New and create a new document based on the form template. Enter data in the fields, pressing `Tab` to move forward to the next form field. When complete, save the document and print it.
Toggle gray shading on or off form fields	Click the Form Field Shading button on the Forms toolbar.

To	Do This
Toggle field codes	Press ⬆Shift+F9.
Protect a form	Click the Protect Form button on the Forms toolbar or choose Tools, Protect Document, Forms, and then click OK.

Checking Your Skills

True/False

For each of the following statements, check *T* or *F* to indicate whether the statement is true or false.

__T __F   **1.** You can use a Word form only once.

__T __F   **2.** Text form fields can accept text, numbers, and other data you type using the keyboard.

__T __F   **3.** There are three types of form fields.

__T __F   **4.** You cannot include tables in form templates.

__T __F   **5.** When a form is protected, you must use a password to fill out the form fields.

__T __F   **6.** You can use macros to automate forms.

__T __F   **7.** By default, you cannot see blank form fields onscreen.

__T __F   **8.** Press Spacebar to select or deselect a check box form field.

__T __F   **9.** Bookmark names can be up to 30 characters long, including spaces.

__T __F   **10.** Dates entered in a form field are always displayed in the mm/dd/yy format.

Multiple Choice

Circle the letter of the correct answer for each of the following questions.

1. Which toolbar do you use to insert form fields?

   a. Standard

   b. Formatting

   c. Forms

   d. Merge

2. By default, how do form fields appear onscreen?

   a. Shaded gray

   b. Outlined in red

   c. Shaded blue

   d. Outlined in gray

3. To perform a calculation in a form, which type of field must you insert?

   a. Check box

   b. Date

   c. Drop-down

   d. Text

4. When filling out a form, which key do you press to move to the next field?

    a. Esc

    b. ↵Enter

    c. Tab

    d. Spacebar

5. Which type of form field should you use when you want to provide users with a list of choices?

    a. Drop-down

    b. Text

    c. Check box

    d. Date

6. Which type of field should you use when you want users to select an option?

    a. Text

    b. Check box

    c. Drop-down

    d. Merge

7. What feature do you use to create a Catalog?

a. Table

b. Mail Merge

c. Bookmark

d. Macros

8. What feature do you use to automate a template?

    a. Table

    b. Mail Merge

    c. Bookmark

    d. Macros

9. Where can you enter data in a protected form?

    a. The header

    b. The footer

    c. The form fields

    d. Nowhere

10. Where should you insert a form field you want to perform calculations?

    a. Anywhere

    b. In a table cell

    c. At the end of the document

    d. At the beginning of the document

Completion

In the blank provided, write the correct answer for each of the following statements.

1. To keep an unauthorized user from changing a form, you must ______________ it.

2. You can reference ___________ names to make it easier to set up calculating fields in forms.

3. Press ______________ to mark or unmark a check box field.

4. To use a form again and again, save it as a ______________.

5. Forms can be filled out ______________ or printed and filled out manually.

6. Use _________ to automate a template.

7. Use _________ fields to set up a catalog main document.

8. To run a macro when the insertion point first moves into a form field, select the macro from the ___________ drop-down list.

9. To run a macro when the insertion point moves out of a form field, select the macro from the ___________ drop-down list.

10. A selected _________ form field has a bold black border around it.

Matching

In the blank next to each of the following terms or phrases, write the letter of the corresponding term or phrase. (Note that some letters may be used more than once.)

a. ⬆Shift + Tab⇥

b. Macros

c. Merge field

d. Gray

e. Text field

f. Check Box field

g. Tab⇥

h. Bookmark

i. Drop-down List field

j. Functions

_______ 1. Form field where you can enter any keyboard character

_______ 2. Form field you mark by pressing the spacebar

_______ 3. Form field from which you select an option

_______ 4. Field used to create a catalog or list

_______ 5. Default color of a blank form field

_______ 6. Key used to move from one form field to another

_______ 7. Key combination used to move backwards from one form field to another

_______ 8. Feature used to automate templates

_______ 9. Feature used to reference form fields for calculations

_______ 10. Predefined formulas used for calculations

Applying Your Skills

Practice

The following exercises enable you to practice the skills you have learned in this project. Take a few minutes to work through these exercises now.

Creating a Visitor's Check-In Form

In this exercise, practice the skills you have learned in this project by creating a printed form that you can keep at a receptionist's desk to keep track of people visiting the company.

To create a visitor's check-in form, follow these steps:

1. Open the file Proj1202 from the Project-12 folder on the CD and save it as a template in your `Practices` folder with the name `Visitor Form`.

2. Delete all variable information in the form.

3. Save the form.

4. Choose <u>T</u>ools, <u>P</u>rotect Document, select the <u>F</u>orms option button, then choose OK.

5. If requested by your instructor, print the form.

6. Close the template document when you have finished.

Creating a Fax Cover Sheet Form

Create a simple form that people in your office can use as a fax cover sheet by filling it out online or by printing it and filling it out manually.

To create a fax cover sheet form, follow these steps:

1. In Word, open the file Proj1203 from the Project-12 folder on the CD and save it in the `Other Documents` folder as a template named `Fax Form`.

2. Choose <u>V</u>iew, <u>T</u>oolbars, Forms to open the Forms toolbar.

3. Delete all variable information in the document.

4. Insert form fields where the variable information should be entered, as described below.

   Insert text form fields for entering the information in all eight cells of the table.

   Insert five check box form fields for selecting the level of importance of the fax.

5. Set options for the form fields. For example, format text fields for numbers, dates, or regular text. If necessary, limit the number of characters that can be entered or enter default values.

6. Format the document, enhancing fonts and adding borders, shading, and graphic elements to improve its appearance.

7. Save, protect, and close the form.

8. Create a new document based on the Fax Form template.

9. Save the new document in your `Practices` folder with the name `Fax Sheet`.

10. If requested by your instructor, print a blank copy of the Fax Sheet document to fill out manually.

11. Fill out the Fax Sheet form online, and save it. If requested by your instructor, print the form and close it.

12. If requested by your instructor, use Windows Explorer to move the Fax Form template into your Practices folder.

Creating a Catalog of Client Names and Addresses

In this exercise, use Mail Merge and merge fields to create a catalog list of client names and addresses.

To create a catalog of client names and addresses, follow these steps:

1. Open the file Proj1204 from the Project-12 folder on the CD and save it in your `Practices` folder with the name `Catalog`. Keep it open.

2. Open the file Proj1205 from the Project-12 folder on the CD and save it in your `Practices` folder with the name `Client Data`. Close it.

3. With the Catalog document open, choose Tools, Mail Merge.

4. Click the Main Document Create button and choose Catalog.

5. Click the Active Window button.

6. Click the Get Data button and choose Open Data Source.

7. Select and open the file `Client List` in your `Practices` folder.

8. Save the Catalog document.

9. Click the Merge to New document button on the Mail Merge toolbar.

10. Save the resulting merge document in your `Practices` folder with the name `Client List`. If requested by your instructor, print both the Catalog document and the Client List document. Close all open documents when you have finished.

Automating a Template Using Macros

In this exercise, use macros to automate a request form template, so that users who ask for information can also fill out an order form.

To automate a template using macros, follow these steps:

1. Open the file Proj1206 from the Project-12 folder on the CD and save it in the `Other Documents` folder as a template with the name `Request Form.dot`. This document is already set up as a form, including form fields. You might want to take a minute to scroll through it. Keep it open.

2. Open the file Proj1207 from the Project-12 folder on the CD, choose Tools, Protect Document, select the Forms option button, and click OK. Save the document in the Other Documents folder as a template with the name `Order Form.dot`. This document is also set up as a form, including form fields. You can scroll through it if you want, then close it.

3. In the Request Form.dot template, record a macro named Ordering, saved in documents created with the Request Form.dot template only. Record the macro to create a new document based on the Order Form.dot template and to save the new document with the name `My Order` in your Practices folder. After you stop recording the macro, close the My Order document.

4. Back in the Request Form template, double-click the Check Box form field to the right of the text `I would like to order information`.

5. From the Exit drop down list, select Ordering, then click OK.

6. Choose Tools, Protect Document, select the Forms option button, and click OK.

7. Save the changes to the Request Form document. If requested by your instructor, print it. Close the document when you have finished.

Using the Automated Template to Create and Fill Out Forms

In this exercise, use the automated template you created in the previous exercise to create and fill out an information request form. If the macro was stored correctly with the template, you also create and fill out the My Order information order form.

To use the automated template to create and fill out forms, follow these steps:

1. Create a new document based on the Request Form template and save it in your Practices folder with the name Request1.

2. Fill in the form fields with the date, your name, and address.

3. Press Tab to move to the first check box, then press Spacebar to select it.

4. Press Tab to move to the next check box. If you automated the template correctly in the previous exercise, the My Order form should open.

5. Fill in the My Order form, then save it in your Practices folder with the name My Order2. If requested by your instructor, print it, then close it.

6. Save the Request1 document. If requested by your instructor, print it, then close it.

7. If requested by your instructor, move the Request Form and Order Form templates into your Practices folder.

Challenge

The following challenges enable you to use your problem-solving skills. Take time to work through these exercises now.

Creating and Using an Evaluation Form

Create an evaluation form that managers can use online or printed.

Open the file PROJ1208 from the Project-12 folder on the CD and save it as a template Form in the Other Documents folder named Evaluation.

Delete all variable data. Format the data in the document to improve its appearance. Enter form fields where variable data is entered. Set form field options. Save, protect, and close the template. Create a new document based on the Evaluation Form template and save it in your Challenges folder as First Evaluation. If requested by your instructor, print a blank copy of the First Evaluation document; then fill out the form online and if requested by your instructor, print a copy of the filled-out form and close it. If requested by your instructor, move the Evaluation Form template into your Challenges folder.

Creating a Receipt Form

Design and create a form that you can use as a receipt for payments received. Create a new, blank document based on the Normal template, and save it as a template in the Other Documents folder called Receipt Form. Design a simple form, either by looking at a paper receipt form or by using your imagination. Set up the form using a table. You should include standard elements such as a return address for yourself or your company; a logo or graphic image; and text labels for areas such as the date, the amount received, a description of what the payment was for, and the name and address of the person who made the payment. You can include other information as well.

Insert the appropriate form fields in the template document. Include a calculating field for totaling the amounts received. Set options for the form fields. Protect, save, and close the template document. Create a new document based on the Receipt Form template, save it in your Challenges folder as First Receipt. If requested by your instructor, print a blank copy of it. Fill it out; then, if requested by your instructor, print it again. Save it and close it. If requested by your instructor, move the Receipt Form document into your Challenges folder.

Creating a Health Club Membership List

Use Mail Merge and Merge fields to create a membership list for the health club. Open the file Proj1209 from the Project-12 folder on the CD and save it in your Challenges folder as Member List. Open the file Proj1210 from the Project-12 folder on the CD and save it in your Challenges folder as Member Data. Then close it.

Use Mail Merge to make the Member List document a Catalog main document for a merge. Use the Member Data document as the data source. Insert merge fields so that the member's name, address, phone numbers, and expiration date print in the merge document. Merge the documents. Save the merge document in your Challenges folder with the name Member Merge. If requested by your instructor, print the document. Close all open documents.

Creating an Invoice Form

Create an invoice form for Computer Training Concepts based on an existing invoice document. Open the file Proj1211 from the Project-12 folder on the CD and save it as a template in the Other Documents folder with the name CTC Invoice. Modify it as necessary to create a form. Replace variable information with form fields. Use all three types of form fields and use a calculating field. Set Form Field Options as necessary. Protect and save the template. Use it to create a new form document, save it in your Challenges folder with the name CTC Invoice1. Fill it out. If requested by your instructor, print it. Close it when you have finished. If requested by your instructor, move the CTC Invoice template into your Challenges folder.

Automating a Template

Create a template that adds a paragraph of text to a document if a certain check box is selected when a form created with the template is filled out.

Open the file Proj1212 from the Project-12 folder on the CD and save it as a template in the `Other Documents` folder with the name `Registration Form`. Create a macro named `Color` that is stored only with the Registration Form template. Record the macro to move the insertion point to the last line of the document, insert a blank line and type the following text in blue: `We can help you purchase an inkjet printer at a substantial discount! Please contact Liz Jefferson at extension 222 for more information!`

Delete the text from the template document when you have finished recording the macro.

In the Registration Form template, double-click the check box form field to the right of the text Color Printer. Choose Color from the E̲xit drop-down list, then click OK.

Protect the Registration Form template, then save it and close it. Use it to create a new document in your `Challenges` folder with the name `Registration1`. Fill out the form. Select the Color Printer check box, then press Tab⇥. The paragraph should be inserted at the end of the document, in blue. If requested by your instructor, print it. Close it when you have finished. If requested by your instructor, move the Registration Form template into your Challenges folder.

You have completed the project and the associated lessons, as well as the "Checking Your Skills" and "Applying Your Skills" sections. Now use the PinPoint software evaluation mode to assess your comprehension of the specific exam tasks you have just learned. You can also use the PinPoint Trainer Mode and the Show Me tutorials to practice these specific exam tasks.

Project 13

Thirteen

Creating Charts

Working with Charts

In this Project, you learn how to:

Objectives	Required Activities
➤ Create Charts … … … … … … … … … … … … …Create and Modify Charts
➤ Modify Charts   … … … … … … … … … … … …Create and Modify Charts
➤ Import Data into Charts … … … … … … … … …Import Data into Charts
➤ Copy Data from Other Applications … … … … … …Import Data into Charts

Why Would I Do This?

harts and graphs, such as pie charts or column graphs, are valuable tools in illustrating data. Often, reports such as a business annual report contain charts illustrating data such as sales and profits. Word doesn't create charts, but uses a program called Microsoft Graph 97, which is packaged with Word.

There are several ways to include charts in a Word document:

- Create a chart while working in Word, using Microsoft Graph 97.

- Paste a chart from another application into a Word document.

- Import data or a chart from other programs (such as Microsoft Excel or Lotus 1-2-3) into a Microsoft Graph 97 chart.

- Paste a chart or insert a chart file from another application into your Word document but link it back to the original file and application so that the chart in your document updates when changes are made to the original.

- Embed a chart object from another application (such as a Microsoft Excel chart) into your document.

In this project, you create a chart in Word to display data from a market study and use existing data to create another chart to show quarterly profits. You modify the charts to improve their appearance. Finally, you import data from another application to create a chart.

Lesson 1: Creating Charts

You have been asked to add a pie chart to a memorandum about the results of a marketing study. Create the chart from Word, using Microsoft Graph 97.

To Create a Chart

1 **From the Project-13 folder on the CD, open the Proj1301 file and save it as** `Pie Chart`**.**

You are going to add a pie chart to this memo.

2 **Place your insertion point in the memo in the paragraph immediately following** `Here is how we stack up.`

The chart appears at the insertion point.

3 **Choose Insert, Object from the menu. Click the Create New tab if it's not already selected.**

The Object dialog box opens (see Figure 13.1).

Figure 13.1
Select the type of object you want to insert in your document and click OK.

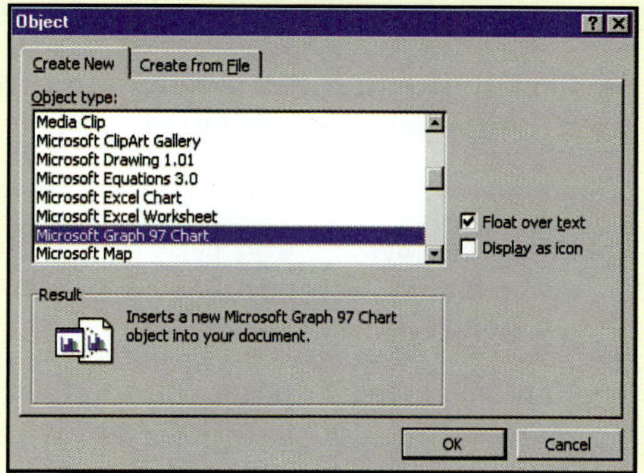

4 **From the <u>O</u>bject type list, select Microsoft Graph 97 Chart. Choose OK.**

A column chart and a datasheet window appear in your document (see Figure 13.2). The datasheet contains sample data that you replace to create your own graph. The chart is transformed automatically as you add your data and select formatting options, until it becomes the chart you want.

To replace the sample data, click in the cell in the datasheet where you want to put new data and then type your own data there. Press ↵Enter to accept the data and move down one row; press Tab to move one cell to the right and ◆Shift+Tab to move one cell to the left (the arrow keys also help you navigate in the datasheet).

Figure 13.2
The datasheet contains the data that generates the graph.

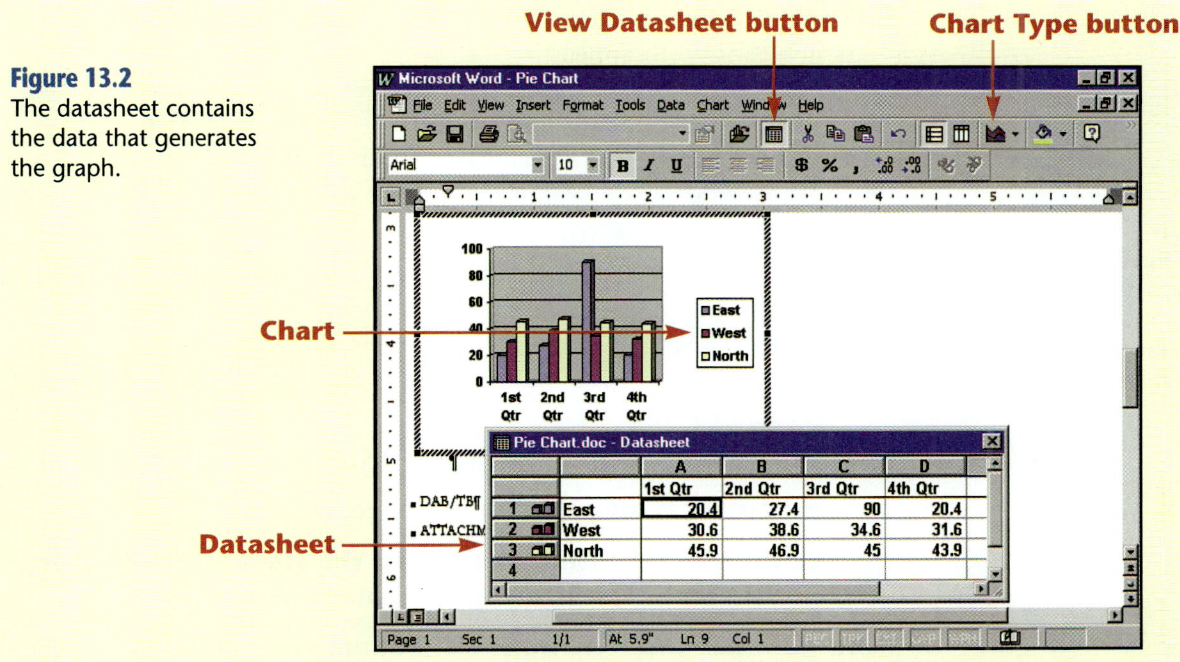

continues

Word

5 Click in the first cell in column A, where it currently says 1st
Qtr. **Type** Naturelle **and press** Tab.

You are entering the labels for the slices in the pie chart.

6 Where it says 2nd Qtr, **type** Fantasm **and press** Tab. **Type** Chiffon
and press Tab, **type** Tigre **and press** Tab, **and type** Forever **and**
press Enter.

Now you need to enter the number for each fragrance's market
share.

If you have problems...

Don't panic if you don't see Naturelle after you type Forever. That column
has simply scrolled off the datasheet window. Click the horizontal scroll bar
arrows to see missing columns.

7 Press ← **until the cell below Naturelle is highlighted. Type** 19
and press Tab. **Below Fantasm, type** 24 **and then press** Tab.
Type 13 **below Chiffon and press** Tab, **type** 30 **below Tigre and**
press Tab, **and type** 14 **below Forever and press** Enter.

You have entered all the values for the pie slices. You don't need the
next two rows of sample data.

8 Click on the cell where you see the word West, **hold down the**
left mouse button, and drag down to the cell that says North.
Release the mouse button.

The two cells are selected. You are going to delete the two rows in
which those cells appear.

9 Choose **E**dit, **D**elete **from the menu.**

The Delete dialog box appears (see Figure 13.3).

Figure 13.3
Use the Delete dialog
box to delete rows or
columns from the
datasheet.

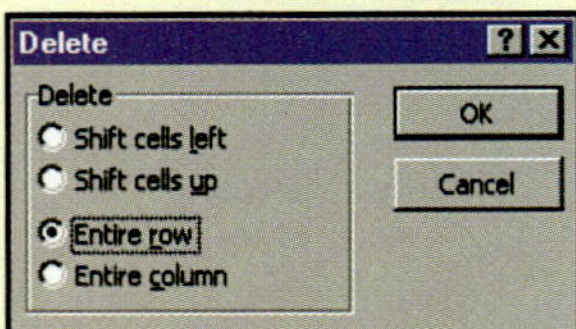

10 Click Entire **r**ow **and then choose OK.**

The datasheet is complete. You no longer need to see it.

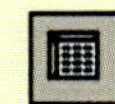

11 Click the View Datasheet button on the Standard toolbar or
click the Close (X) button on the Datasheet window.

As you click the View Datasheet button, notice that the toolbars
have changed. As long as the graph is active, these toolbars appear.

If you need to change or add data to the Datasheet, click the View Datasheet button again to make the datasheet reappear.

Did the graphing tools disappear? If you are seeing the regular Word toolbars, you may have clicked outside the chart window, defined by the chart border, in part of the document. To reactivate the chart, double-click in the middle of the graph.

12 Click outside the chart border in an open area of your document.

13 Save the file but leave it open for the next lesson.

Your Word menus and toolbars return. If you need to move or size the chart, click on it once to select it. Drag the chart to move it. Drag its handles (small, hollow boxes) to size it.

Lesson 2: Modifying Charts

After you create the chart, you realize that you need to enhance its appearance or change the data that you used to create the chart. All you have to do is double-click in the middle of the chart to reactivate the Microsoft Graph 97 program. All the graphing tools and menus become visible again. This happens because the chart is *embedded* in your document.

To Modify a Chart

1 In the Pie Chart document, double-click in the middle of the pie chart.

Now you can see the menus and toolbars you need for graphing.

2 Click the down arrow on the Chart Type button.

You see a palette of available chart types (see Figure 13.4).

Embedded object

Data (such as a chart) from one document that is placed into a second document. After the data is embedded, it becomes a part of the second document but still retains a separate identity for editing.

3 Click the 3-D Pie Chart (middle, next to last row).

The chart has been transformed from a column chart to a three-dimensional (3-D) pie chart. A pie chart is useful for showing the parts of a whole, or percentages.

4 Choose Chart, Chart Options from the menu.

The Chart Options dialog box appears (see Figure 13.5).

Note that the menu also changes when you are working with charts and graphs.

continues

To Modify a Chart (continued)

3-D Pie Chart

Figure 13.4
A palette of available chart types appears when you click the arrow next to the Chart Type button.

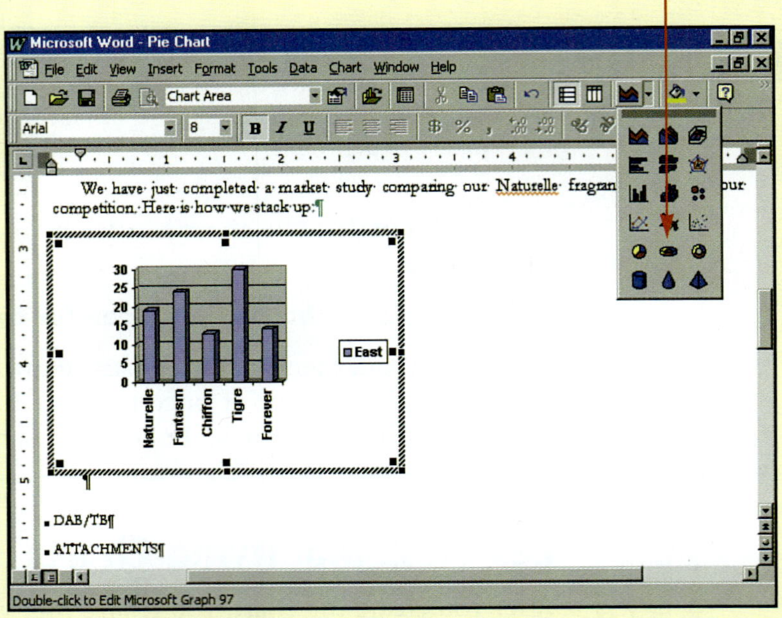

Figure 13.5
You can modify the chart in the Chart Options dialog box.

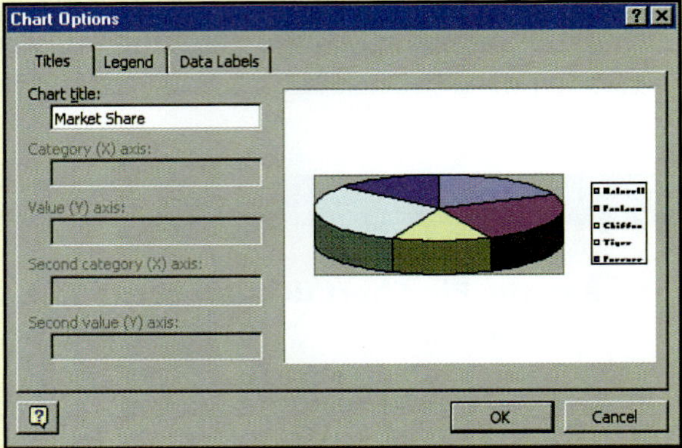

❺ Click the Titles tab and type `Market Share` **in the Chart title text box.**

As you can see from the sample in the dialog box, the chart title appears above the chart. It defines the chart.

Legend
List that has small symbols or color boxes to tell you what the lines or bars represent.

❻ Click the Legend tab. Deselect ṣShow legend.

Pie charts don't normally have *legends*. They usually use slice labels.

❼ Click the Data Labels tab. Click Show ḷabel.

Labels for the fragrances appear next to the slices representing their share of the market.

❽ Choose OK.

You need to emphasize the slice that represents Naturelle.

9 **Click once in the middle of the pie and then click once in the Naturelle slice.**

The first click selects all the pie slices. The second click selects only the Naturelle slice. Handles (small black boxes) appear around the slice to indicate that it's selected.

10 **Point in the middle of the selected slice and drag it away from the center of the pie for a short distance.**

This is called cutting, or exploding, the slice. It serves to emphasize that slice.

11 **Choose Chart, 3-D View from the menu.**

The 3-D View dialog box appears (see Figure 13.6).

Figure 13.6
The 3-D View controls the tilt of the chart and also allows you to rotate the slices for better position.

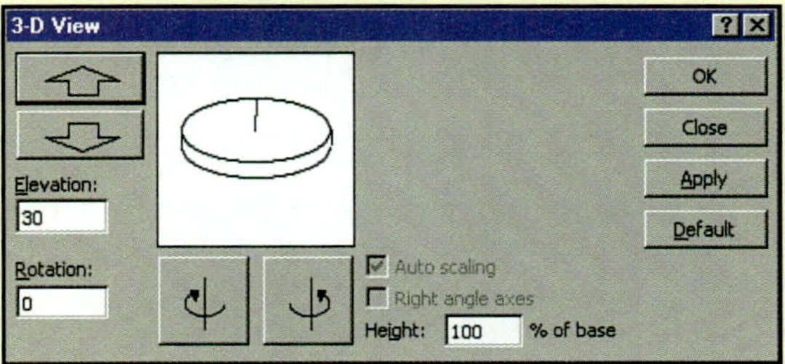

12 **Change the Elevation to 30 and click OK.**

This tilt shows more of the pie chart face toward you.

13 **Click outside the chart border in another area of your document.**

The graphing tools and menus are replaced by the Word tools and menus.

14 **Save the file. Print two copies if requested by your instructor. Close the file.**

As you selected the Naturelle slice, you can select other elements in the chart for modification. If you right-click a selected element, you see a shortcut menu of commands that helps you modify the element. If you double-click an element, a dialog box appears with formatting options for that element.

Lesson 3: Importing Data into Charts

You don't always have to type your data into the datasheet. One of the easiest ways to bring data into the chart is to use an existing table of data. If the table is set up similarly to the datasheet (labels in the top row and left column, numbers in all other cells), all you have to do is select the table before you insert the chart object.

Word

❶ From the Project-13 folder on the CD, open the Proj1302 file and save it as `Column Chart`.

In this memo, a table displays figures relating to quarterly sales. As useful as this table is, a column chart would more clearly illustrate how well the company is doing in the fourth quarter compared to the previous three quarters of the year. Rather than retype the information from the table into the chart datasheet, you are going to use the table as the basis for your chart.

❷ Click in one of the table cells and choose Ta**ble, Select T**a**ble from the menu.**

All the cells in the table are now selected. If you are working with a table that includes totals, you don't always want to select all the cells because you don't need to include the totals in the chart. However, you should make sure to include the labels in the top row and left column.

❸ Choose Insert**, O**bject **from the menu. Click the C**reate New **tab.**

The Object dialog box appears.

❹ From the Object **type list, select Microsoft Graph 97 Chart. Click OK.**

When the graph appears, the data from your table automatically appears in the Datasheet (see Figure 13.7).

Figure 13.7
The table data you selected appears in the chart's datasheet.

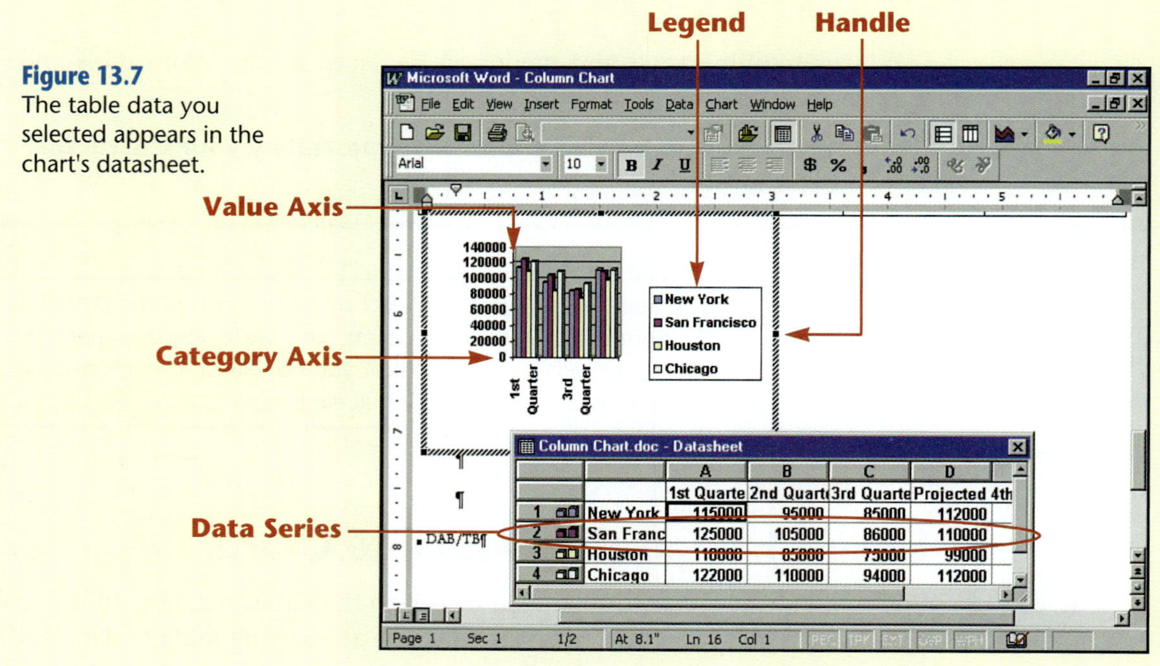

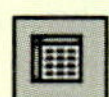

5 **Click the View Datasheet button on the Standard toolbar.**

You won't need to add data, so you can close the datasheet. Now you want to enlarge the chart area.

6 **Point to one of the sizing handles (little black boxes) on the right side of the graph border and drag to the right to make the chart wider.**

Making the chart wider makes it easier to work with and read. You can also drag one of the bottom handles to make the chart taller.

7 **Right-click in the legend and choose Format Legend from the shortcut menu.**

The Format Legend dialog box appears (see Figure 13.8). Using this dialog box, you change the position and orientation of the legend by placing it below the chart running horizontally instead of vertically.

Figure 13.8
The Format Legend dialog box has options to control the position, font, and box type of the legend.

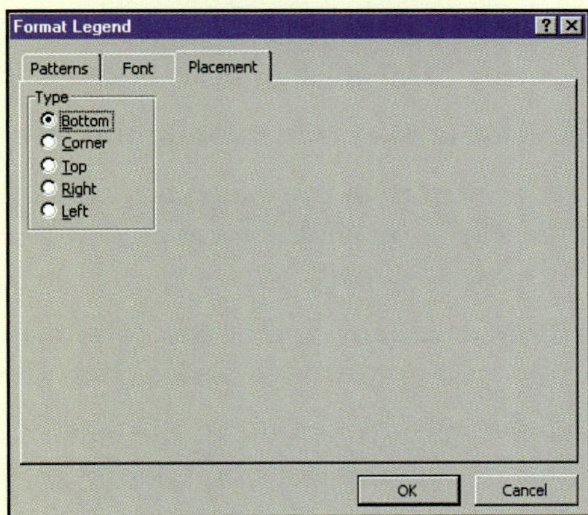

8 **Click the Placement tab and select Bottom. Choose OK.**

The legend moves underneath the graph. Your next step is to format the numbers on the Value Axis to appear as currency.

9 **Double-click any number on the Value Axis.**

The Format Axis dialog box appears (see Figure 13.9).

10 **Click the Number tab. Select Currency from the Category list. Change the number of Decimal places to 0.**

The numbers on the Value axis are too close to each other, so you need to space them farther apart.

11 **Click the Scale tab. Change the value in the Major unit box to 25000 and the Maximum value to 150000. Then choose OK.**

The font size of the labels along the Category axis is a little large, and the labels are almost running into each other.

continues

To Import Data into Charts   (continued)

Figure 13.9
Although the numbers in the table had no dollar signs, the Currency number format adds the dollar sign and commas to separate the thousands.

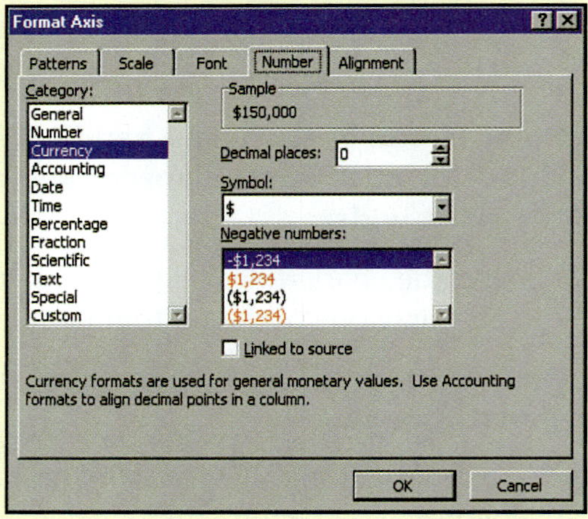

12 **Double-click one of the labels on the Category Axis.**

The Format Axis dialog box appears. It's a little different from the Format Axis dialog box for the Value axis because the Category axis usually has text labels instead of values to format.

13 **Click the Font tab. Change the Size to 6 and click OK.**

The Font tab of the dialog box closely resembles the dialog box you see when you choose F**o**rmat, **F**ont to change the appearance of text in your document.

Data Series
A row of data in a Datasheet that produces a line on a line chart, a set of columns or bars that share a color on column or bar charts, or an area on an area chart.

14 **Right-click any one of the columns representing Houston. Choose F**ormat Data Series **from the shortcut menu.**

A *data series* is usually all the data in one row of the Datasheet, in this case all the Houston sales for each quarter. In the Format Data Series dialog box (see Figure 13.10), you can change the color of all the Houston columns.

Figure 13.10
In the Format Data Series dialog box, you can set the color, pattern, and shape of the columns for one data series.

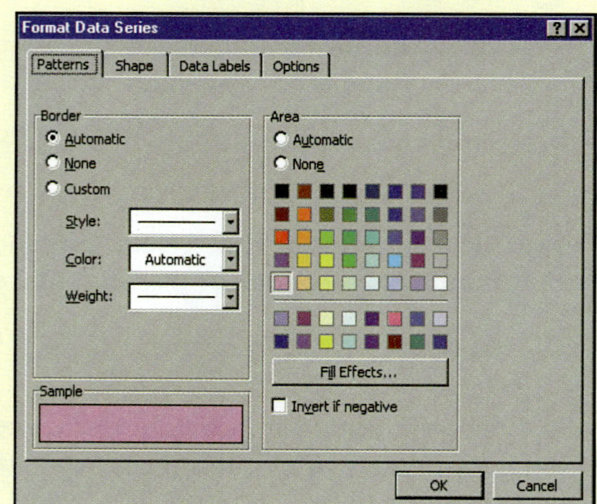

15 **Click the Patterns tab (if necessary). Under Area, click one of the color swatches. Choose OK.**

The new color you chose is applied to all the columns in the Houston data series. Note that the color in the legend has also changed.

16 **Choose Chart, Chart Options from the menu. Click the Titles tab if necessary.**

The Chart Options dialog box appears (see Figure 13.11).

Figure 13.11
Enter the titles for the chart and axes in the Chart Options dialog box.

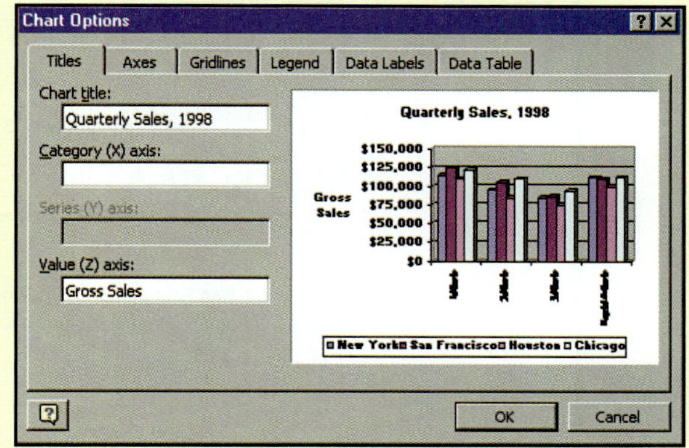

17 **In the Chart title box, type** Quarterly Sales, 1998. **Type** Gross Sales **in the Value (Z) axis box. Choose OK.**

Adding titles defines what the chart and its values represent.

18 **Right-click the** Gross Sales **title for the Value axis. Select Format Axis Title from the shortcut menu.**

The axis title would look much better if it were vertical, so change the text alignment of the title to 90 degrees. You do this in the Format Axis Title dialog box (see Figure 13.12).

Figure 13.12
You change the alignment of the axis by dragging the red orientation pointer or by entering the number of degrees.

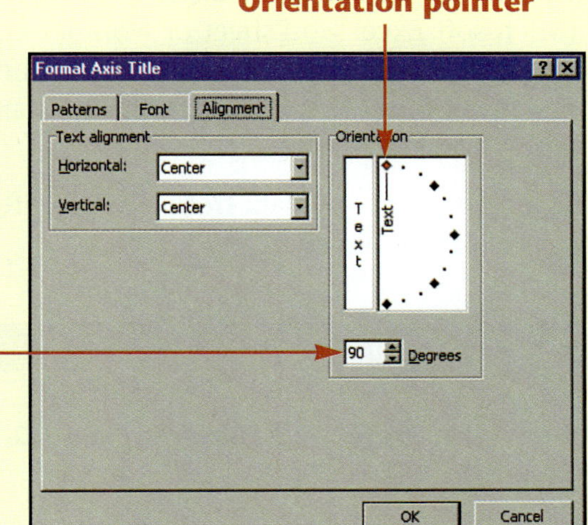

To Import Data into Charts (continued)

19 **Click the Alignment tab. Change the number in the Degrees text box to 90. Choose OK.**

The chart is now complete, as shown in Figure 13.13.

Figure 13.13
Your final chart is similar to this.

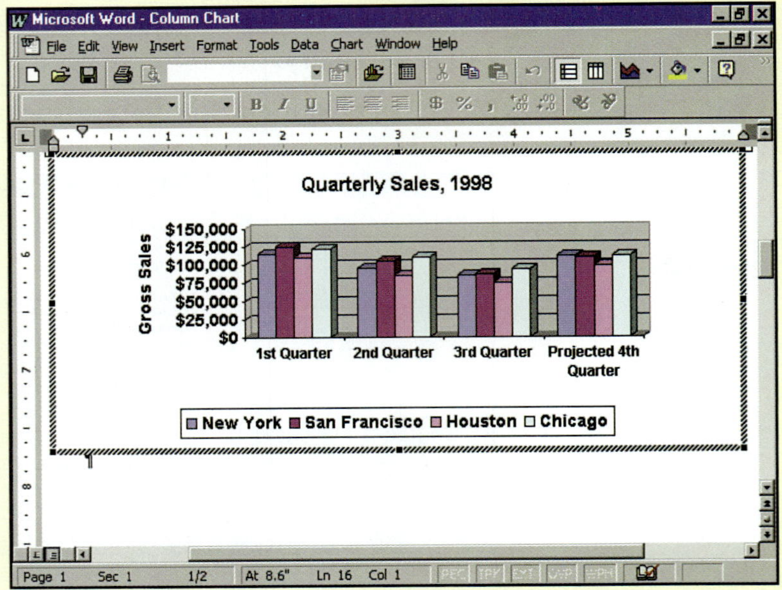

20 **Click outside the chart border. Save the document. Print two copies if requested by your instructor. Then close the file.**

Lesson 4: Copying Data from Other Applications

The data that you use to generate a chart may already exist in an application other than Word, such as in spreadsheet or from a *delimited text file*.

Delimited Text File

A file where the text is separate by tab characters, commas, or spaces to indicate

Microsoft Graph 97 can import data from files that have the following file extensions: TXT or CSV (delimited text files), WKS or WK1 (Lotus 1-2-3), XLS (Microsoft Excel worksheet or workbook), XLC (Microsoft Excel 4.0, or earlier, chart), or SLK (SYLK, or symbolic link files). If you have data in another type of file, check your application and see if it can save the file in one of the listed formats.

In this lesson, you copy data from a Microsoft Excel spreadsheet into a document to create a line chart.

To Copy Data from Another Application

1 **From the Project-13 folder on the CD, open Proj1303 and save it as Line Chart.**

This document is the beginning of a proposal to sell sales training to a corporation. Expertise, Inc., is making the proposal and has already done some work for a small division of the corporation.

Using that track record, Expertise wants to create a training program for the corporation's entire sales force. You are going to create a chart in the proposal showing how the training improved sales in the division Enterprise already trained.

2 Press Ctrl + End.

Your insertion point is now at the end of the document, where you place the chart.

3 Choose Insert, Object from the menu and click the Create New tab.

4 Select Microsoft Graph 97 Chart from the Object type list and click OK.

The datasheet and the sample column chart appear.

5 Click in the upper-left cell in the Datasheet, above East and to the left of 1st Qtr.

This sets the cell where you want the upper-left corner of the copied data to appear.

6 Click the Start button on the taskbar and choose Programs, Microsoft Excel (or follow your instructor's directions to find Excel).

The Microsoft Excel Program opens.

7 Choose File, Open from the menu. Select the Project-13 folder on CD drive from the Look in list.

8 Click the Proj1304 file and choose Open.

The worksheet that opens contains the quarterly sales figures for all the salespeople in the Reading Division (see Figure 13.14).

Figure 13.14
Select the labels and the data, but not the totals, as the range you want to graph.

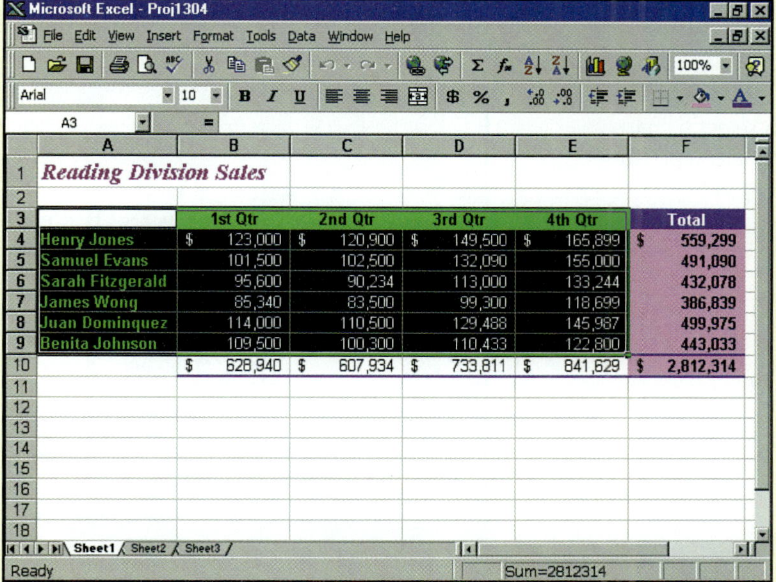

Microsoft Excel - Proj1304

	1st Qtr	2nd Qtr	3rd Qtr	4th Qtr	Total
Reading Division Sales					
Henry Jones	$ 123,000	$ 120,900	$ 149,500	$ 165,899	$ 559,299
Samuel Evans	101,500	102,500	132,090	155,000	491,090
Sarah Fitzgerald	95,600	90,234	113,000	133,244	432,078
James Wong	85,340	83,500	99,300	118,699	386,839
Juan Dominquez	114,000	110,500	129,488	145,987	499,975
Benita Johnson	109,500	100,300	110,433	122,800	443,033
	$ 628,940	$ 607,934	$ 733,811	$ 841,629	$ 2,812,314

Sum=2812314

continues

To Copy Data from Another Application   (continued)

9 Select the range A3:E9.

Click the cell above `Henry Jones` and drag down and across to the cell that has the figure `122,800` to select the range. When you're selecting the data to import, don't include blank rows, columns, or any columns or rows that have totals in them.

10 Choose Edit, Copy from the menu.

A copy of the data is placed in the Clipboard.

11 Click the Microsoft Word button on the Taskbar to switch to your document and the Datasheet.

You are now ready to place the data in your Datasheet.

12 Choose Edit, Paste.

To have the chart update automatically when the original data is modified, choose Edit, Paste Link when you paste the data into the datasheet.

The data you copied from the Excel worksheet overwrites the existing sample data in the datasheet.

13 Click the View Datasheet button on the Standard toolbar.

Now that the data has been pasted, you no longer need the datasheet to work on the chart. Note that the currency formatting from the worksheet carries over to the chart (there are dollar signs on the Value axis labels).

14 Choose Chart, Chart Type from the menu.

To get more options in choosing your chart types, use this menu command instead of the Chart Type button. In the dialog box (see Figure 13.15), you can choose not only a chart type but a sub-type, or variation, of that chart type.

Figure 13.15
You can select a chart type and sub-type from the dialog box.

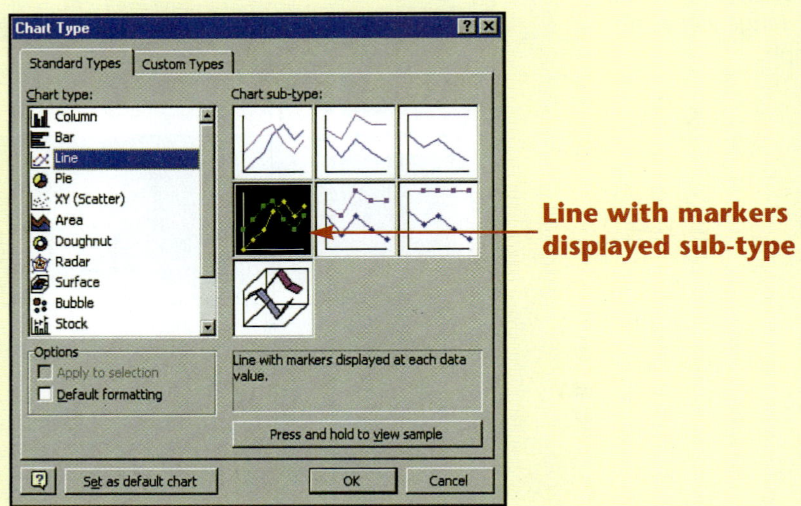

15 **From the Chart type list, select Line. Then select the Line with markers displayed Chart sub-type (the first sub-type in the second row). Choose OK.**

You may want to apply some of the chart modification skills to your chart to make it more professional looking.

16 **Drag one of the handles on the right side of the chart border to the right to increase the size of the chart.**

17 **Double-click the legend. Click the Placement tab and select Bottom. Choose OK.**

18 **Double-click one of the value labels on the Value axis. Click the Scale tab. Change Minimum to 75000 and Maximum to 175000. Choose OK.**

19 **Click outside the chart border.**

The chart is now complete (see Figure 13.16).

Figure 13.16
The completed chart as it appears in the document.

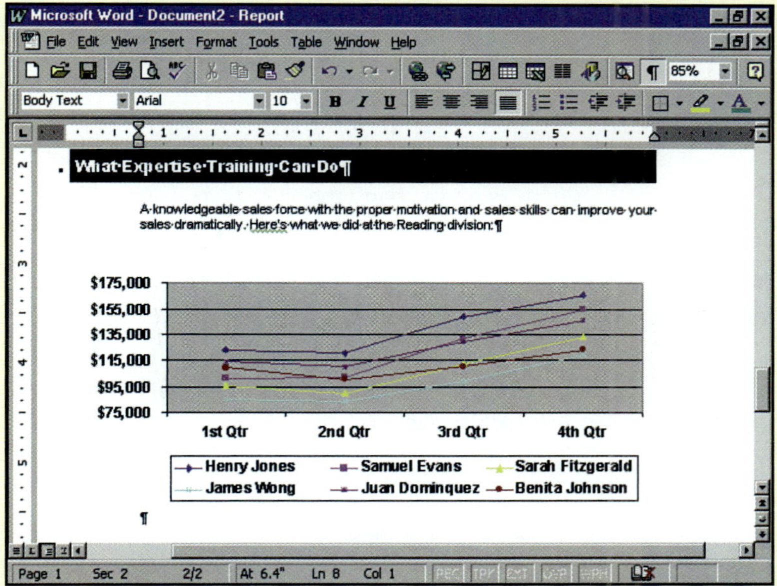

20 **Save the document. Print two copies if requested by your instructor. Close the document.**

21 **Click the Microsoft Excel button on the taskbar to switch back to Excel. Choose File, Exit and don't save the file.**

You can import data directly from a file into the datasheet when you create your chart. Click in the cell where you want the upper-left corner of cell of your imported data to appear. Choose Edit, Import File from the menu. In the Import File dialog box that appears, select the file you want to import (choose the location from the Look in drop-down list). From the Files of type drop-down list, select the file format of the file. Choose Open.

continues

If the file you import is a text file, the Text Import Wizard opens. Follow the steps in the wizard to specify how the imported data is organized and how you want it arranged in the datasheet.

If the file you are importing is a spreadsheet, the Import Data Options dialog box appears. Specify which sheet you want to use (for an Excel workbook). Choose to import the entire worksheet or a range (you enter the range reference or range name). Select <u>O</u>verwrite existing cells to replace all the current data in the datasheet. Choose OK.

You have completed all of the lessons in this project. If you have completed your session on the computer, exit Word and Windows 95 before turning off your computer. Otherwise, continue with the "Checking Your Skills" and "Applying Your Skills" sections.

Project Summary

To	Do This
Insert a chart	Place your insertion point where you want the chart to appear. Choose <u>I</u>nsert, <u>O</u>bject from the menu. Click the <u>C</u>reate New tab, and select Microsoft Graph 97 Chart from the Object type list. Click OK.
Change a chart type	Click inside the chart. Choose <u>C</u>hart, Chart <u>T</u>ype from the menu. Select the new chart type you want and click OK.
Replace sample data in a chart	Click in the cell in the datasheet and type your data. The sample data is replaced.
Delete a row or column from a datasheet	Select the cells to be deleted and choose <u>E</u>dit, <u>D</u>elete from the menu. Choose Entire <u>r</u>ow or Entire <u>c</u>olumn. Click OK.
Add Data Labels	Click inside of the chart. Choose <u>C</u>hart, Chart <u>O</u>ptions from the menu. Click the Data Labels tab. Click Show <u>l</u>abel. Choose OK.
Explode a pie chart slice	Select the slice you want to explode and drag it away from the center of the chart a short distance.
Copy data into a chart from a table or list in another application	Insert a chart into your Word document. Switch to the application from which you want to copy the data. Open the file whose data you want to copy in its native application. Highlight the data and copy it. Switch back to Word. Paste the data into the datasheet of the chart in your Word document.

Word

To	Do This
Import data into a chart	Create a chart in Word. Click in the first cell of the datasheet. Choose Edit, Import File from the menu. Select the file you want to import and select the file format of the file you are importing. Choose Open. If the file is a spreadsheet, specify which sheet or a range for the spreadsheet. Select Overwrite existing cells to replace all the sample data in the datasheet.

Checking Your Skills

True/False

For each of the following statements, check *T* or *F* to indicate whether the statement is true or false.

__T __F **1.** You can import data to create a chart from files that have a .txt extension.

__T __F **2.** Pie charts usually include a legend.

__T __F **3.** A datasheet is made up of columns and rows, similar to a table.

__T __F **4.** You create charts using the program Microsoft Chart 97.

__T __F **5.** Once a chart is created, you cannot change it in any way.

__T __F **6.** Graphing tools and menus are displayed when the chart is selected.

__T __F **7.** You can create a chart from data already stored in a Word table.

__T __F **8.** You can import data directly from a file stored in .xls format into a Datasheet.

__T __F **9.** You can only create pie charts or line charts.

__T __F **10.** A chart title is the name of the file in which the chart is stored.

Multiple Choice

Circle the letter of the correct answer for each of the following questions.

1. What is the name of the program you use to create charts for Word documents?

   a. Microsoft Chart 97

   b. Microsoft Graph 97

   c. Microsoft Datasheet 97

   d. Microsoft Table 97

2. Which file format can be imported for use as a chart?

   a. .slk

   b. .rtf

   c. .pcx

   d. .tif

3. In what window do you type new chart data?

   a. Table window

   b. Graph window

   c. Datasheet window

   d. Column window

4. What chart type is good for depicting trends over time?

   a. Pie chart

   b. Line chart

   c. Scatter chart

   d. Doughnut chart

5. Which element is never included as part of a chart?

   a. Legend

   b. Title

   c. Value axis

   d. Caption

6. How do you reactivate the chart window?

   a. Double-click the chart

   b. Drag a sizing handle

   c. Choose File, Reactivate

   d. Click the Reactivate Chart button

7. Which chart is useful for showing percentages of a whole?

   a. Pie chart

   b. Line chart

   c. Scatter chart

   d. Column chart

8. What chart element is used to label the entire chart?

   a. Legend

   b. Title

   c. Value axis

   d. Category axis

9. When you are done working with a chart, how do you display the Word tools and menus again?

   a. Click the Word Tools button

   b. Double-click the chart

   c. Click anywhere outside the chart border

   d. Close the Chart document and open a Word document

10. What dialog box do you use to change the axis title alignment?

    a. Alignment

    b. Format Chart

    c. Chart Options

    d. Format Axis Title

Completion

In the blank provided, write the correct answer for each of the following statements.

1. Charts are __________ objects in a Word document.

2. Type new data for a chart in the __________ window.

3. You can ______data from other programs such as Microsoft Excel to create a chart.

4. The chart __________ is a list that has small symbols or color boxes to tell you want the lines or bars represent.

5. To see more of the face of a pie chart you can change the ____________ setting.

6. To increase the size of a chart, drag one of the _______ handles.

7. Usually all of the data in one row of a datasheet is translated in a _____ _____ in a chart.

8. The default chart type is _________.

9. To emphasize a slice of a pie chart you can cut or _______ it.

10. The _______ axis shows the text labels used to identify information in a chart.

Matching

In the blank next to each of the following terms or phrases, write the letter of the corresponding term or phrase. (Note that some letters may be used more than once.)

a. Data series

b. Embedded object

c. Chart Type

d. Microsoft Graph 97

e. Chart border

f. Chart

g. Column

h. Axis

i. Title

j. Legend

_______ 1. The program used to create charts for Word documents

_______ 2. One row of a datasheet

_______ 3. An object used to illustrate data

_______ 4. Chart element that defines the entire chart

_______ 5. Default chart type

_______ 6. Data from one document that is placed into another document

_______ 7. Chart element that tells you what the chart date represents

_______ 8. Element that defines categories or values in a chart

_______ 9. Line that is displayed around the outside of a chart in a Word document

_______ 10. Button used to change from a column chart to a pie chart

Applying Your Skills

Practice

The following exercises enable you to practice the skills you have learned in this project. Take a few minutes to work through these exercises now.

Charting Business Expenses

In this exercise, practice the skills you have learned in this project by creating a pie chart to compare expenses for the New Food Café.

To chart business expenses, follow these steps:

1. Open the file Proj1304 from the Project-13 folder on the CD and save it in your `Practices` folder as a template with the name `Café Chart`.

2. Press `Ctrl`+`End` to move the insertion point to the last line in the document.

3. Open the Insert menu and choose Object.

4. Select Microsoft Graph 97 Chart, then click OK.

5. Replace the labels 1st Qtr, 2nd Qtr, 3rd Qtr, and 4th Qtr with the names of the following expense categories: `Food`, `Labor`, `Supplies`, and `Overhead`.

6. In the cells directly below each category label, type the following dollar values: `$1,500`, `$2,500`, `$3,000`, `$3,500`.

7. Select and delete the remaining two rows of sample data in the datasheet.

8. Click the Chart Type drop down arrow on the Charting toolbar and select the Pie Chart icon.

9. Click the View Datasheet on the Charting toolbar.

10. Click anywhere in the document outside the chart border.

11. Save the document. If requested by your instructor, print it. Close the document when you have finished.

Modifying a Chart

In this exercise, modify the chart you created in the previous exercise to make it easier to read.

To modify a chart, follow these steps:

1. In Word, open the file Proj1305 from the Project-13 folder on the CD and save it in your `Practices` folder with the name `Café Chart2`.

2. Single-click the chart, then drag the sizing handle in the lower-right corner down and to the right to increase the size of the chart to fill the width of the document page.

3. Double-click the chart.

4. Click the View Datasheet button on the Charting toolbar to close the datasheet window.

5. Choose <u>C</u>hart, Chart <u>O</u>ptions.

6. On the Titles page, type `Weekly Expenses` in the Chart <u>t</u>itle text box.

7. Click the Legend page tab and deselect the <u>S</u>how legend check box.

8. Click the Data Labels page tab and select the Show label <u>a</u>nd percent option button.

9. Click OK.

10. Choose <u>C</u>hart, Chart <u>T</u>ype, then select the Exploded Pie with 3-D visual effect chart type (it's in the middle of the second row).

11. Click OK.

12. Click anywhere outside the chart border.

13. Save the document. If requested by your instructor, print it. Close the document when you have finished.

Import Data to Create a Chart

In this exercise, use existing table data to create a chart comparing sales for Computer Training Association.

To import data to create a chart, follow these steps:

1. Open the file Proj1306 from the Project-13 folder on the CD and save it in your `Practices` folder with the name `CTA Chart`.

2. Select rows 2 through 6 in the chart. Do not select the first row or the last row.

3. Choose <u>I</u>nsert, <u>O</u>bject, select Microsoft Graph 97 Chart, then click OK.

4. Click the View Datasheet button to close the datasheet.

5. Drag the lower-right sizing handle down and to the right to increase the height and width of the chart.

6. Click anywhere outside the chart border.

7. Save the document. If requested by your instructor, print it. Close the document when you have finished.

Modifying the Chart

In this exercise, modify the chart you created in the previous exercise.

To modify the chart, follow these steps:

1. Open the file Proj1307 from the Project-13 folder on the CD and save it in your `Practices` folder with the name `CTA Chart2`.

2. Double-click the chart.

Word

3. Right-click any number on the Value Axis (the dollar values) and choose F̲ormat Axis.

4. Click the Number page tab and set the D̲ecimal places to 0, then click OK.

5. Right-click the Category Axis (the months) and select Format Axis.

6. On the Alignment page, rotate the text orientation to 30 D̲egrees, then click OK.

7. Choose C̲hart, Chart O̲ptions and type `Sales Comparison` in the Chart t̲itle text box, then click OK.

8. Click anywhere outside the chart border.

9. Single-click the chart, then drag it down so it appears in the document below the line of text `This chart might make the data more clear:`.

10. Save the document. If requested by your instructor, print it. Close the document when you have finished.

Copying Data from Another Application to Create a Chart

In this exercise, copy data from a Microsoft Excel spreadsheet into a Word document to create a chart.

To copy data from another application to create a chart, follow these steps:

1. Open the file Proj1308 from the Project-13 folder on the CD and save it in your `Practices` folder with the name `Technology4`.

2. Press Ctrl+End.

3. Choose I̲nsert, O̲bject, select Microsoft Graph 97 Chart, and click OK.

4. Click in the upper-left cell in the Datasheet, above the label East and to the left of the label 1st Qtr.

5. Click the Start button on the taskbar and choose Programs, Microsoft Excel (or follow your instructor's directions to open Excel).

6. Choose F̲ile, O̲pen, then locate and open the file Proj1309 from the Project-13 folder on the CD, just as you would using Word 97.

7. Select the range A2:E5 by clicking in the first cell in row 2 (to the left of the label Phase 1 and above the label Hardware) and dragging to the cell with .3 in it (the fifth cell in the Training row).

8. Click the Copy button on the Standard toolbar, then choose F̲ile, E̲xit to close Excel.

9. Back in the datasheet window, click the Paste button on the Standard toolbar.

10. Click the View Datasheet button on the Charting toolbar to close the datasheet.

11. Click the Chart Type button and select the Bar Chart type.

12. Drag the sizing handles to increase the size of the chart in the document.

13. Choose Chart, Chart Options and type Technology Implementation Costs in the Chart title text box, then type `Costs in millions` in the Value (Y) axis text box, then click OK.

14. Right-click any value on the Value axis and select Format Axis.

15. Click the Number page tab, select Currency, set the Decimal place to 1, then click OK.

16. Click anywhere outside the chart border.

17. Save the document. If requested by your instructor, print it. Close the document when you have finished.

Challenge

The following challenges enable you to use your problem-solving skills. Take time to work through these exercises now.

Creating and Formatting a Chart from Scratch

In a memo to company trainers, create a chart showing registration numbers for Computer Training Concepts courses.

Open the file Proj1310 from the Project-13 folder on the CD and save it in your `Challenges` folder with the name `CTC Chart`. Insert a chart object at the end of the document. Use the following data to fill in the datasheet:

Excel 1	Excel 2	Excel 3	Word 1	Word 2
45	35	25	58	60

Select the chart type that best represents the data. Add a chart title, and make sure the chart labels are informative and easy to read. Use any other formatting techniques you want to improve the appearance of the chart. Save the document. If requested by your instructor, print it. Close the document when you have finished.

Creating a Chart from Existing Data

Use the data in a table in a Word document to create a chart showing Sales trends. Open the file Proj1311 from the Project-13 folder on the CD and save it in your `Challenges` folder with the name `Sales Chart`. Use the data in the table to create a chart that shows the trends in sales over a four-month period. Format the chart to make it easy to read and interpret. Save the document. If requested by your instructor, print it. Close the document when you have finished.

Modifying an Existing Chart in a Word Document

Modify an existing chart to make it easier to read and interpret. Open the file Proj1312 from the Project-13 folder on the CD and save it in your Challenges folder with the name Member Chart. Change the chart type to one that best shows off the data. Modify the formatting to improve the appearance of the chart. Add titles and labels, and change colors where necessary. Use any other techniques you think will make the chart look better. Save the document. If requested by your instructor, print it. Close the document when you have finished.

Using Excel Data to Create a Chart in a Word Document

Use data that is saved in an Excel worksheet to create a chart in a Word document. Open the file Proj1313 from the Project-13 folder on the CD and save it in your Challenges folder with the name Reunion Chart. Your cousin has kept a log of how many reunion responses have been received. Use the data in the Excel file Proj1314 to create a chart in the Word document that tracks the number of responses received over the past four months. Format the chart to best depict the data. Be sure to include titles and labels, and a legend if necessary. Save the document. If requested by your instructor, print the document. Close the document when you have finished.

Importing a File Directly into a Datasheet

Try importing data from an Excel worksheet directly into a datasheet to create a chart. Your cousin tracked the states where reunion responses came from in addition to the number of responses. Import the worksheet into a Word chart so you can graph that information in the document, as well.

Open the Word file Proj1315 from the Project-13 folder on the CD and save it in your Challenges folder with the name Reunion Chart2. Start Microsoft Graph 97 and display the sample datasheet. Click in the top right hand cell in the datasheet. Choose Edit, Import File. In the Import File dialog box, locate and open the Excel worksheet file Proj1315.xls from the Project 13-folder on the CD. Import the entire sheet1 worksheet by overwriting the existing cells.

Format the chart to best depict the data represented. Save the document when you have finished. If requested by your instructor, print it. Close the document.

You have completed the project and the associated lessons, as well as the "Checking Your Skills" and "Applying Your Skills" sections. Now use the PinPoint software evaluation mode to assess your comprehension of the specific exam tasks you have just learned. You can also use the PinPoint Trainer Mode and the Show Me tutorials to practice these specific exam tasks.

Project

14 Fourteen

Using Word with Other Programs

Switching from One Application to Another

In this Project, you learn how to:

Objectives

Required Activities

➤ Switch from One Application to Another

➤ Copy Data Between Applications ... ... Create Worksheets in a Table

➤ Link Data Between Applications ... ... Import Worksheets in a Table

➤ Control Links ... ... Modify Worksheets in a Table

➤ Work with Embedded Data

➤ Share Data Across Different Applications

Why Would I Do This?

Y ou might frequently use data from one application in another. For example, you might use data from an Excel spreadsheet in a report you're writing in Word. Or you might write a letter in Word and need a phone number and address that are stored in a database program. Perhaps you have seen some great clip art in a drawing program that would help you make a point in a presentation. Fortunately, the barriers between spreadsheet programs, art programs, presentation programs, and word processors grow fainter with each new generation of software.

Multitasking

The execution of more than one program or task at a time on a computer system.

Integration

Using two or more software applications together to create a single document.

Windows programs share information and basic functionality with one another; they let you work electronically in much the same way that you work in real life. In real life, you typically do many things at once. The most current Windows software lets your computer do many things at once, too. For example, you can have a spreadsheet, a schedule program, and a word processor all running at the same time, and you can switch from one program to another whenever you want, without closing one application to start another. This process is called *multitasking*. In addition to this capability, Windows applications can easily share and exchange data. Using *integration*, you can copy pictures from an art program into a word processor or text from a word processor into a spreadsheet. In this project, you learn how to take advantage of these capabilities with Word and other programs.

In this project, you come across many terms that have to do with integrating data from one application into a file in a different application.

The common Windows platform allows many Windows applications to share data easily. This feature goes by the catchy names **OLE**, which stands for **object linking and embedding**, and **DDE**, which stands for **dynamic data exchange**.

DDE uses **linking** to set up a connection between two files. When you update the file where the data was created originally (called the **source** file), the **target** file (the file where the data has been pasted) is updated as well. The link can be from one document to another in the same application, or across applications. (You can also call the two files in a linked relationship the **client** and the **server**. The server is the source file, where the original data is located. The client is the target file, where the data has been pasted.)

OLE uses **embedding** to create an object in the target file by copying data from the source file. With embedding, the object is not linked to the source file in any way, but it is linked to the source application. You can edit the object in the target file by using the source application features, but the changes do not affect the original data.

Another applicable term to sharing information is **importing**. Import is a more generic term—a file inserted into a Word document using the menu bar (Insert, File) or data pasted into a Word document is considered to be imported.

Lesson 1: Switching from One Application to Another

Windows makes it very easy to switch among applications running on your computer. You can launch (start) applications in a variety of ways, but the most popular method is to use the Start button on the taskbar. The number of applications you can run simultaneously depends on the speed of your computer and the amount of memory it has.

In this lesson, you learn how to open several applications so they run simultaneously. Then practice three different methods for switching from one application to another. Before you start to work through the steps in this lesson, you should close all open applications.

To Switch from One Application to Another

① Start Word, open the folder Project-14 and the file Proj1401 from this book's CD and save it as UP Marketing Plan.

This document contains a marketing plan being developed for the UP company.

② Click the Start button on the taskbar and slide the mouse pointer up to the Programs folder.

The Start menu pops up from the Start button, and a list of programs installed on your computer appears as a submenu, as shown in Figure 14.1.

Figure 14.1
In Windows 95, you can start programs by using the Start button and the Programs submenu.

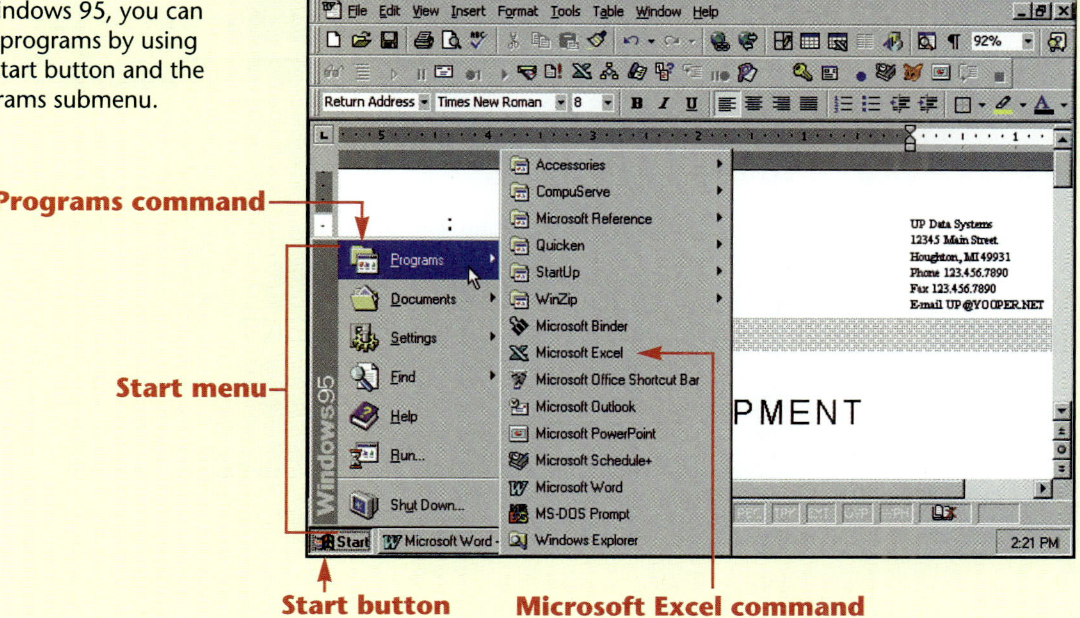

continues

To Switch from One Application to Another   (continued)

If you have problems...

If the taskbar does not appear at the bottom of your screen, it may have been moved to a different edge of your screen, or it may be hidden. If you see it along a different edge of the screen, you can leave it there or drag it back to the bottom. If it does not appear at all, simply move the mouse pointer down to the bottom of the screen to see whether the taskbar appears. If you want the taskbar to be visible all the time, you can change the taskbar properties. Ask your instructor for more information about using Windows properties.

3 **Click Microsoft Excel on the Programs submenu (refer to Figure 14.1).**

Excel launches, as shown in Figure 14.2. Notice that when Excel starts, it becomes the active window. Word is still running, but the Excel window overlaps the Word window. On the taskbar, you can see buttons for both Word and Excel. Because Excel is active, its button appears pressed in (selected). Also, notice the difference in the shades of the title bars in Figure 14.2. The title bar for Excel, which is the active window, is darker than the title bar for Word, which is not active.

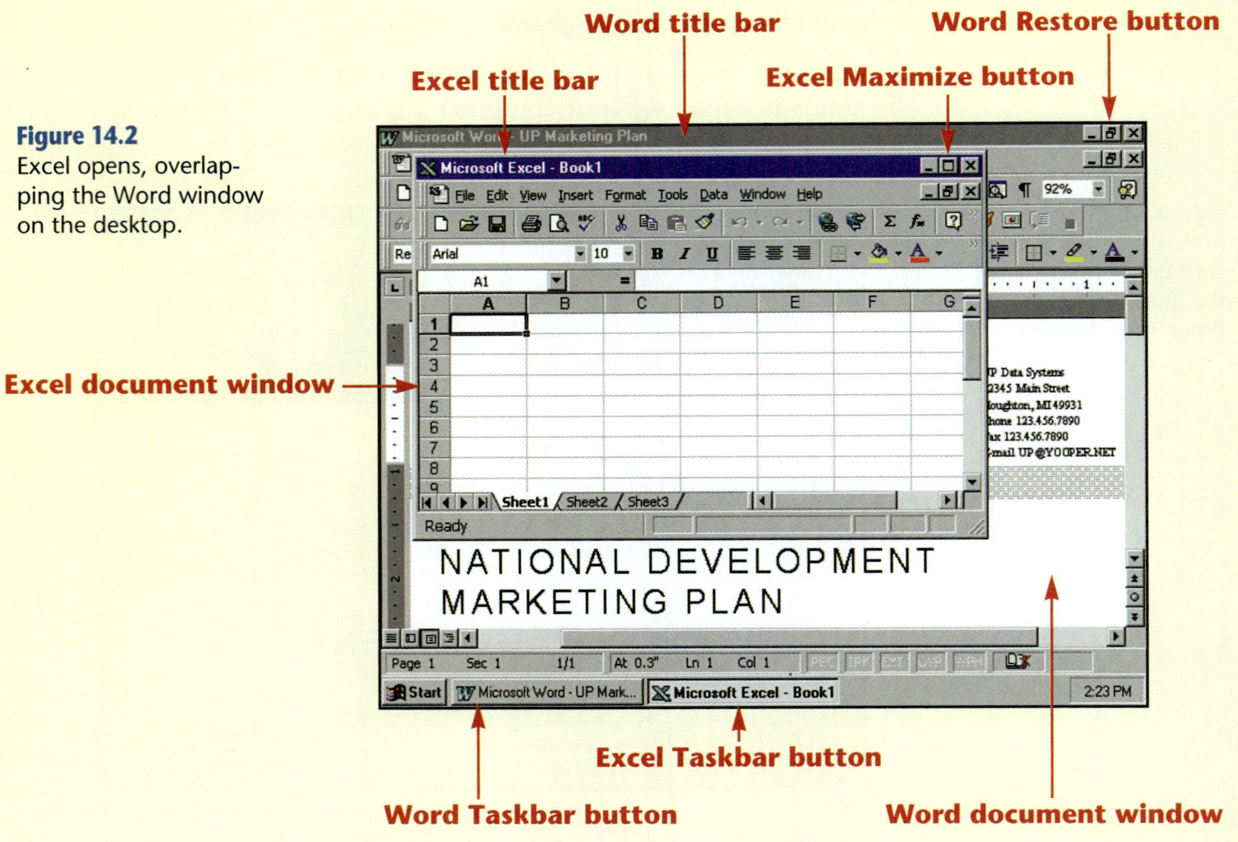

Figure 14.2
Excel opens, overlapping the Word window on the desktop.

If you have problems...

In the figures used to illustrate this lesson, the Excel window is not maximized. If your Excel window starts maximized, click its Restore button to make it smaller. Likewise, in the preceding figure, the Word window is maximized. If your Word window is not maximized, click its Maximize button. If you are not familiar with the Maximize and Restore buttons, refer to Figure 14.2, and ask your instructor for information about using Windows.

Excel is a popular spreadsheet program used frequently with Word. If you cannot find Excel in your system's Programs list, your classroom may not be set up for Excel, or Excel may be located in a different submenu. If you do not find it, check with your instructor. If your classroom is not equipped with Excel, this project works equally well with most Windows applications, such as the Paint program, which you can find listed under Accessories in the Programs list.

4 Click the Microsoft Word button on the taskbar.

Clicking the Word button makes Word active. The Word window moves in front of the Excel window on the desktop. Because the Word window is maximized, you no longer can see the Excel window, but it is still there. Now the Word title bar is dark, and the Word taskbar button appears to be pressed in.

5 Click the Microsoft Excel button on the taskbar.

Clicking the Excel button makes Excel active again.

You can also use the keyboard to switch from one program to another. Try using the keyboard shortcuts to switch programs now.

6 Press Alt+Esc.

Word becomes active. This keyboard shortcut cycles through open application windows, one by one. The active window moves to the front.

7 Press and hold down Alt and press Tab once; do not release Alt.

This shortcut opens a small window or dialog box in the middle of the screen that displays icons for the open applications (see Figure 14.3). If you release Alt, the icon with the blue box around it becomes active.

If you have problems...

You must continue to hold down Alt, or the window disappears. Press and hold Alt and tap Tab. Don't release Alt until you select the program you want to switch to (see the next step).

continues

Word

To Switch from One Application to Another   (continued)

Figure 14.3
Pressing (Alt)+(Tab)
opens a small window
in the middle of the
screen where you can
select the application
you want to make
active.

Word icon

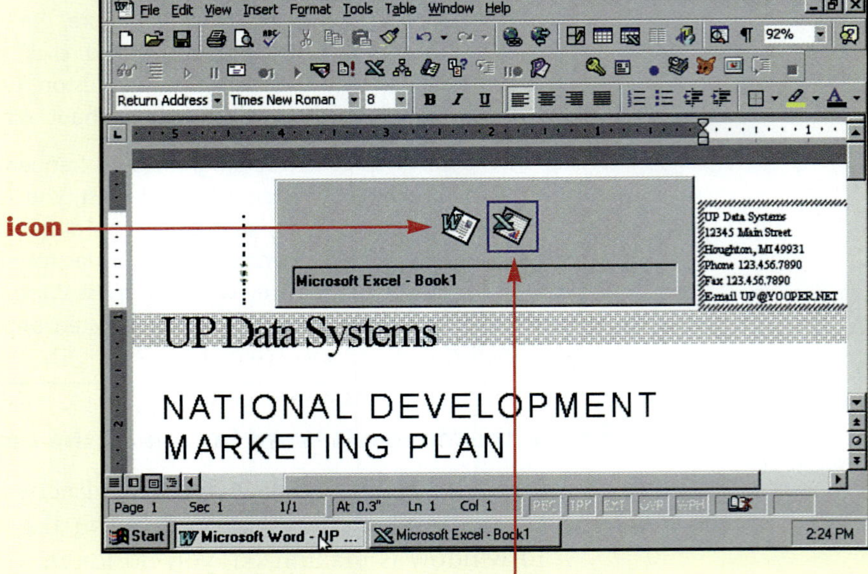

Excel icon

8 While you continue to hold down (Alt), press (Tab) twice.

Pressing (Tab) moves the blue box from icon to icon. When the box
encloses the icon for the program you want, release (Alt); that program becomes active. This method of changing applications is useful when you have several programs open at the same time. (Alt)+(Esc)
works well to toggle back and forth when you have two open programs.

9 When the Excel icon is selected, release (Alt).

The Excel window becomes active.

Now try one more method for switching to an application—clicking
in the window to activate it.

10 Click anywhere inside the Word window.

Clicking inside the Word window switches you to Word. As long as
part of the window you want to make active is visible on the screen,
you can click within the window to switch to that application.

11 Make Excel active; click its Maximize button.

You can switch to Excel using any of the techniques described in
this lesson. Leave the Excel window active and maximized to fill the
desktop. You use Excel and Word in the next lesson to learn how to
copy data from one application to another.

If the Microsoft Office 97 suite of applications is installed on your computer, you may have the Microsoft Office shortcut bar visible onscreen. You can use this toolbar to switch among Office 97 applications. Simply click the toolbar button corresponding to the application you want to make active.

If you have several applications open, the buttons on the taskbar may become too small to read. If this happens, you can increase the height of the taskbar. To do this, place the mouse pointer over the top border of the taskbar. The mouse pointer changes to a double-headed arrow. Click and drag up to increase the height of the taskbar. Release the mouse button when the taskbar is the size you want.

Lesson 2: Copying Data Between Applications

Anyone who has worked with computers has experienced the frustration of entering information in one program (such as a database of customer information), only to have to reenter the information—for example, in a letter. "If it's already in the computer somewhere," you might ask, "why should I have to reenter it?" This is a fair question, and one addressed in many ways by Windows. The rest of this project explores a few ways that programs share data in Windows.

In this lesson, you learn how to copy data from one program to another. You copy spreadsheet data from Excel into a marketing report created in Word. To copy information from one application to another, you use the Cut, Copy, and Paste commands found in most Windows applications. These commands (available from the Edit menu, shortcut menus, or toolbar buttons) enable you to cut or copy information you select from one place and then paste the information somewhere else.

Before you begin this lesson, Excel should be open, and it should be the active window, maximized on your screen. If it is not, open Excel and maximize it, or ask your instructor for assistance.

Although it is not the purpose of this book to teach you how to use a spreadsheet program, it will help you to complete the lessons in this project if you are familiar with some basic Excel terminology.

A **workbook** is an Excel document file. A **worksheet** is one page of an Excel workbook file. Worksheets are organized in a grid of **columns** and **rows**. The rectangular areas where columns and rows intersect are called **cells**. All data in a worksheet is entered in cells.

Columns are identified by letters from the left end of the worksheet to the right; and rows are identified by numbers from the top of the worksheet to the bottom. A cell is identified by the letter of the column containing the cell, followed by the number of the row containing the cell. So, the cell in the top left corner of the worksheet is called cell A1. In Figure 14.4 (shown on the following page), cells A1 through E6 are selected.

To Copy Data Between Applications

1 **In Excel, use the File, Open command to open the folder Project-14 and the file Proj1402 from this book's CD; use the File, Save As command to save the file as UP Data.**

This Excel worksheet contains data and charts for historic and pro-jected sales data. Don't worry if you have never used Excel before; you should be able to follow the steps easily to complete this lesson. First, you must select the data in Excel that you want to copy to Word.

2 **Click the cell in the upper-left corner of the worksheet where the text Historic Data appears (cell A1); then hold down the left mouse button, drag across to column E and down to row 6 (cell E6), and release the mouse button (see Figure 14.4).**

This selects cells A1 through E6, which contain the data you want to copy.

Figure 14.4
You must first select the Excel data so you can copy it to Word.

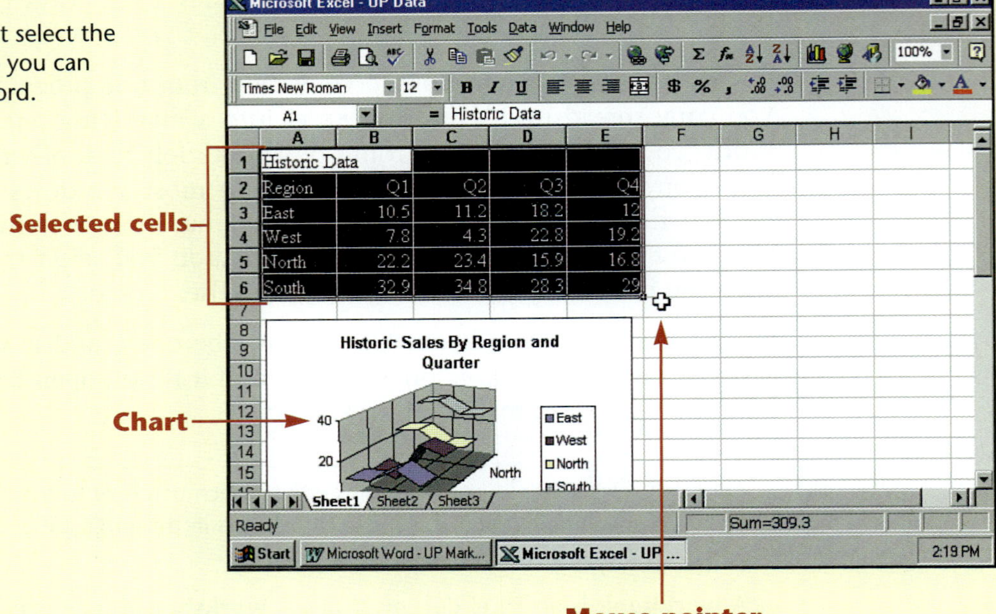

3 **In Excel, click the Copy button on the Standard toolbar.**

This step copies the data to the Windows **Clipboard**. You might notice a flashing dotted line around the data in Excel; it indicates that the selection is stored on the Clipboard. Windows applications use the same basic buttons in all applications; this feature makes learning new applications easier. Notice that Excel's **Copy** button looks exactly like Word's Copy button. (You can also choose Edit, Copy, if you prefer.)

4 **Click the Word button on the taskbar to switch to Word.**

The Word window becomes active, with the UP Marketing Plan document open.

5 **Press** Ctrl+End.

This action moves the insertion point to the bottom of the Word document. Notice that there is a blank line at the end of the document; this is where you **paste** the Excel data.

6 **In Word, click the Paste button on the Standard toolbar.**

Word makes a copy of the data that you copied earlier to the Clipboard and **pastes** it into the document at the location of the insertion point, as shown in Figure 14.5. (Be patient; it may take a few seconds.) Virtually any information can be pasted from one Windows application to another, or from one document to another by using the Clipboard, including art, data, and charts.

Notice that the worksheet data is formatted in Word as a table. You can use Word's T̲able menu to format and edit the data, just as you would format or edit a table that you create in Word.

Figure 14.5

Spreadsheet data can be pasted from Excel into Word to help illustrate historical trends.

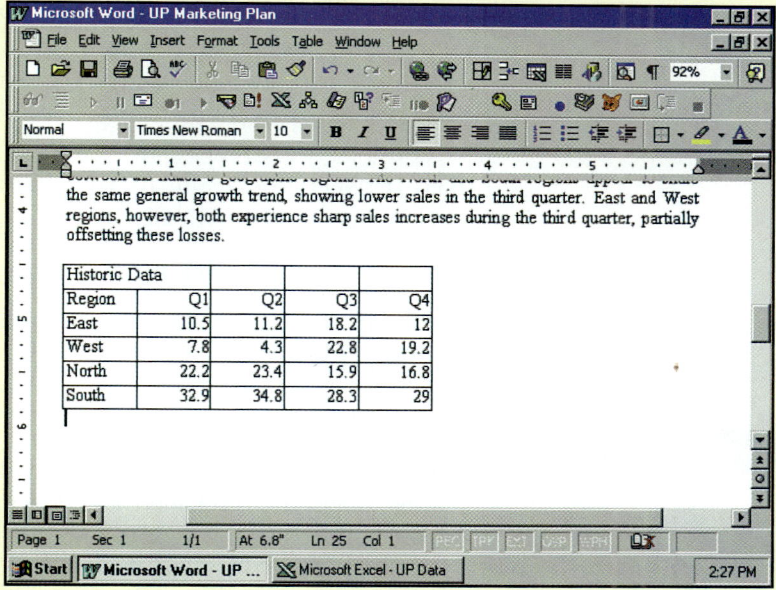

Historic Data				
Region	Q1	Q2	Q3	Q4
East	10.5	11.2	18.2	12
West	7.8	4.3	22.8	19.2
North	22.2	23.4	15.9	16.8
South	32.9	34.8	28.3	29

7 **Save both the Word document and the Excel worksheet.**

Leave the applications open to use in the next lesson, where you learn how to link data between applications.

Lesson 3: Linking Data Between Applications

Link

To paste data as an object in a document, so that it is dynamically connected to the file where it was originally created.

Object linking and embedding (OLE)

A feature of Windows applications that allows you to link and embed data between compatible applications.

How good is a report if it is based on outdated information? Have you ever tried to create a report based on partial information, only to have the missing data become available at the last minute? Wouldn't it be great if you could create a report in Word that used information from Excel, and if it could automatically update the report at the same time that the information in Excel is updated?

With Windows, you can *link* information across several programs dynamically, which means that the information is updated in every program where it appears, if it is changed at the source. This feature is part of *object linking and embedding* (OLE). Although OLE sounds complicated, it is actually very easy to use, and it can help you keep data updated continuously, across many different files. In this lesson, you learn how to use OLE to link data between the two documents you used in the preceding lesson.

To Link Data Between Applications

❶ In the Word document, click anywhere within the table. Choose Table**, Select T**able**; then choose T**able**, **Delete** Rows.**

This step deletes the worksheet data you copied into your report in the preceding lesson. That data was simply a "snapshot" of what the worksheet looked like at that moment. Because the data in the worksheet is likely to change, you need to link the Excel data to the Word document instead of simply pasting it. Once the data is linked between the applications, changes made in the Excel worksheet are made automatically in the Word document as well.

❷ Switch to Excel by clicking the Excel button on the taskbar.

The data in the UP Data worksheet should still be selected from the preceding lesson.

If you have problems...

> If the data in the worksheet is not selected, follow the instructions in step 2 of Lesson 2 to select it. Click the upper-left cell, hold down the mouse button, drag over to column E and down to row 6, and then release the mouse button.

❸ Click the Copy button on the Standard toolbar.

You just placed a copy of the data in the Clipboard.

❹ Switch back to Word and press Ctrl+End.

This step ensures that the insertion point is at the bottom of the UP Marketing Plan document.

❺ Choose **Edit, **Paste** Special.**

The Paste Special dialog box appears (see Figure 14.6). With this dialog box, you are going to paste a linked, dynamic copy of the data, instead of a static copy. That way, when data changes in Excel, the data automatically updates in the Word report.

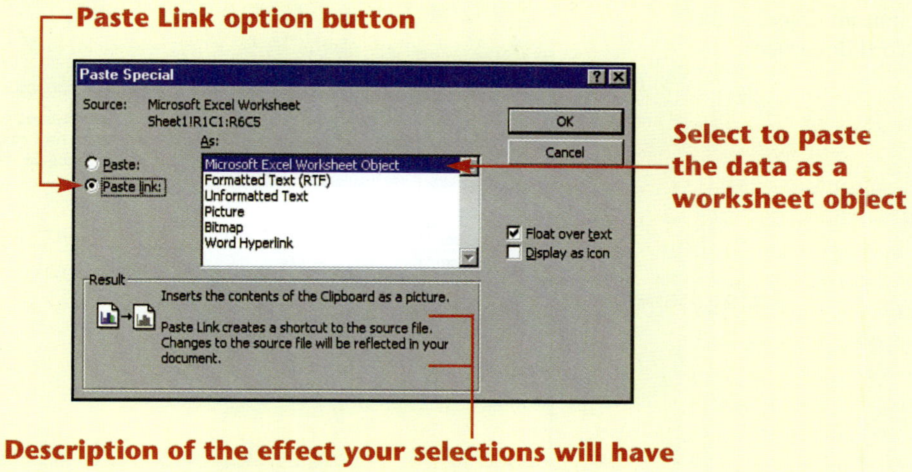

—Paste Link option button

Figure 14.6
Use Paste Link to link data between applications.

Select to paste the data as a worksheet object

Description of the effect your selections will have

6 **Select the Paste Link option button.**

This step specifies that you want to link the Excel data to the Word document, instead of simply pasting it.

7 **Select `Microsoft Excel Worksheet Object` from the As list of data types.**

This tells Word that you want to link the data as an actual Excel object. Notice that a description of the results of your selections appears in the Result area of the dialog box (refer to Figure 14.6).

8 **Click OK.**

The data is once again pasted into the document, as shown in Figure 14.7. This time, however, the data is linked as an *object*, which means that it is an independent item within the Word document. You cannot edit a linked object in Word by using Word features, as you could when the Excel data was pasted as a table. You must use the source application—in this case, Excel—to edit the data. However, you edit the worksheet object by using some of the features about editing graphic objects you already know. For example, you can resize the object, add borders, or drag the object to a new location in the document.

Notice the sizing handles that indicate that the object is selected in the Word document. To see how linking works, try making a change in the original Excel file now.

9 **Switch to Excel, click cell D3 in the Excel worksheet, type 30, and press ⏎Enter (see Figure 14.8).**

This increases the East region's third quarter sales. Notice that Excel automatically updates the corresponding chart when the worksheet data changes.

continues

To Link Data Between Applications   (continued)

Figure 14.7
The linked data is pasted as an object in the Word document.

Figure 14.8
When you edit the source file in Excel, the changes appear in the target file in Word.

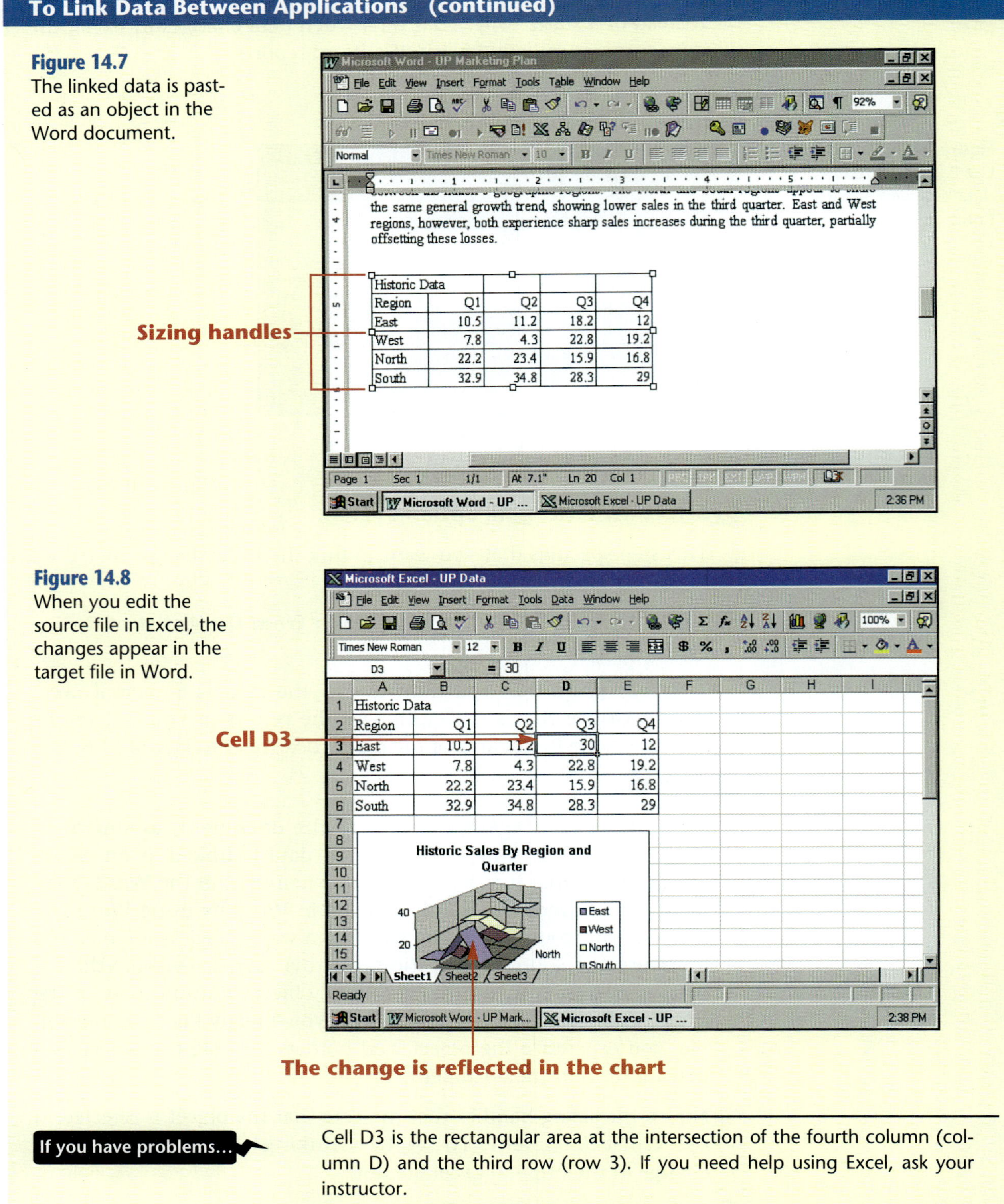

If you have problems... Cell D3 is the rectangular area at the intersection of the fourth column (column D) and the third row (row 3). If you need help using Excel, ask your instructor.

10 Switch to Word.

In your Word document, notice that the object has changed to reflect the new data in the Excel worksheet (see Figure 14.9). Every time you open or switch to the Word target document, the link to the source document is refreshed, and the chart in the document is updated.

If you have problems...

If the object in Word does not update automatically, you may not have it selected. When both the source and target applications are open, the object must be selected in the target file for the update to occur. To update the link manually, select the object in Word and press F9.

Figure 14.9
The object in Word reflects the changes made in Excel.

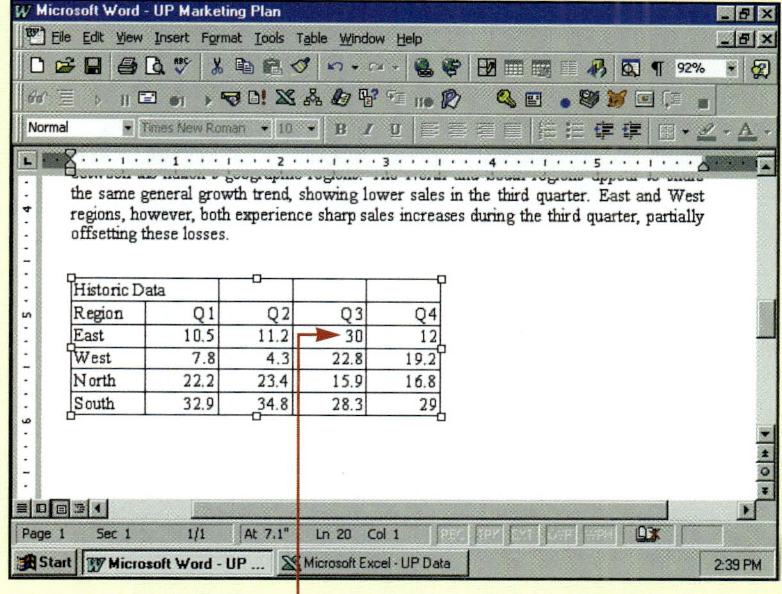

The East's third quarter sales have changed

11 Switch back to Excel and use the File, Exit command to close the application. When prompted, choose Yes to save the changes you have made to the UP Data worksheet.

When Excel closes, the Word document remains open on the desktop.

12 Save the changes you have made to the Word document and leave it open.

In the next lesson, you learn how to control links.

When you delete a file that is linked to another file, you permanently break the link, but you do not harm the data in the remaining document.

You can quickly launch the source application and open the source document from a linked object. Simply double-click the object; or select the object and choose Edit, Linked Worksheet Object, and then choose Open Link from the submenu.

If you do not need to display the linked data in the target document, you can save disk space by inserting it as an icon instead of as an actual object. For example, you may only need to provide access to the data instead of displaying it in full in a report. To insert the object as an icon, copy the data from the source file to the Clipboard; then switch to the target file and choose Edit, Paste Special. In the Paste Special dialog box, select Paste Link, select the object type, check the Display as Icon check box, and click OK. You can still access the source file directly from the target file by double-clicking the icon to launch the source application and open the source file.

Lesson 4: Controlling Links

As you have learned, links between documents are updated automatically whenever you open or switch to the target document. Sometimes, however, you might not want links to be updated right away. For example, if you use a lot of linked objects, updating significantly slows down the response time of an application. Likewise, if you are doing a lot of editing, you might want to wait until you have finished the editing and then update all the links in the target document at once.

You can also change the source of a link easily. Changing the source is useful if new data becomes available in a different file, or even in the same file; you can change the source without having to delete the linked object and link a new object.

In this lesson, you learn how to control the way in which a link is updated and how to change the source of a link. You also learn how to break a link permanently.

To Control Links

1 In the UP Marketing Plan document in Word, choose Edit, Links.

The Links dialog box opens, as shown in Figure 14.10. In this dialog box, all the links in the current document are displayed. In this case, there is only one link—to the UP Data worksheet. In the dialog box, you can see the exact reference to the cells that are the source of the link. Notice that the default Update option—Automatic—is selected.

Figure 14.10
You can change settings in the Links dialog box to control the way in which Word updates linked data.

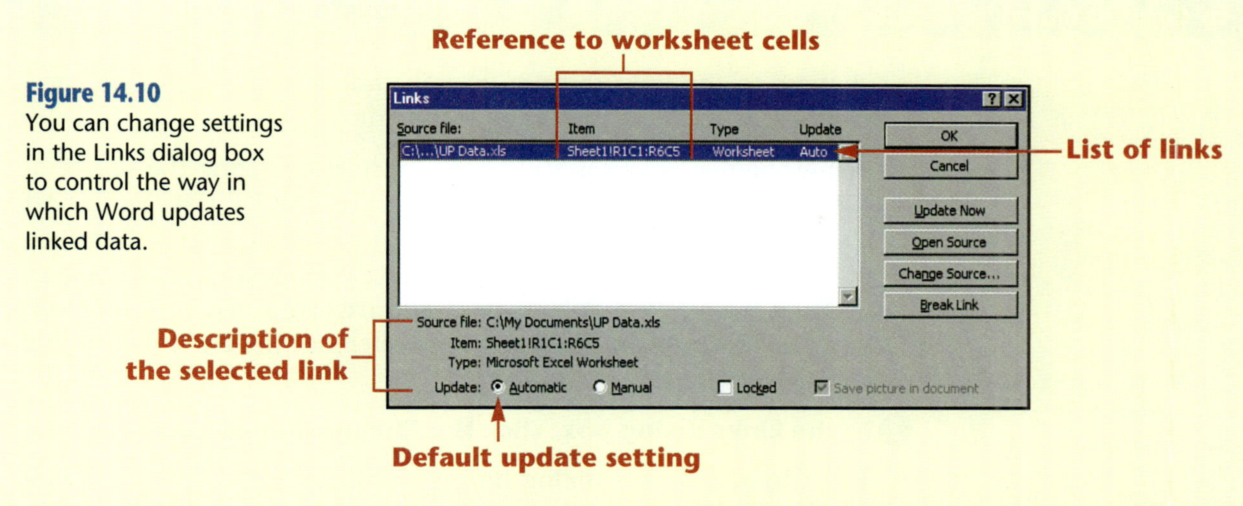

If you have problems...

If you are editing links in a document that contains more than one link, be sure to select the link you want to edit in the Links dialog box. You can edit more than one link at a time: Select the first link and then hold down Ctrl while you click additional links.

Now change the Update option to Manual so that the link is not automatically updated every time a change is made to the source document.

2 Click the Manual option button and then OK.

This step changes the link update setting, so that changes made to the source file do not immediately affect the target file. Now see what happens when you make a change to the source file.

3 Double-click the table in the Word document.

This starts or switches to Excel. You can quickly launch or switch to a source application by double-clicking the linked object. The source document, UP Data, is now open. Maximize it if necessary.

4 Click cell E6, type 15, and press Enter. (To find cell E6, locate the rectangular area at the intersection of the fifth column—column E—and the sixth row.)

This reflects a dramatic drop in the fourth quarter results for the South region. Notice the change in the chart.

5 Click the Word button on the Taskbar.

Because the link is set for manual updating, the table in the Word document has not changed. When you want to update the table, you must select the Update Now command.

6 Choose Edit, Links; then click the Update Now button.

Word closes the Links dialog box so that it can update the link. When it has finished, you see the change in the worksheet object; Word then displays the Links dialog box again. You can make other

continues

To Control Links   (continued)

changes to the links settings, or you can close the dialog box and continue working in the Word document.

While the dialog box is still open, consider changing the source of the data in the linked object. For example, the UP Data worksheet also includes projected sales data, which you could reference instead of the historic data in the UP Marketing Plan document. Instead of deleting the existing linked object and pasting a new linked object, you can simply change the source to reference the other data in the UP Data worksheet.

7 In the Links dialog box, click the Change Source button.

The Change Source dialog box is displayed, as shown in Figure 14.11. This dialog box is similar to the Open dialog box; however, in addition to being able to select the source file, you also specify the exact position within the source file where the data is located.

Select the source file here

Figure 14.11
Use the Change Source dialog box to link different data to an existing object.

Specify the location of the source data here

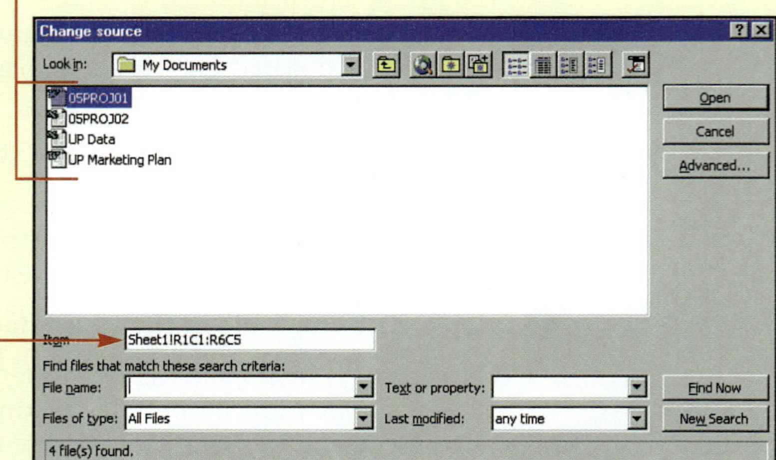

In this example, you will specify different cells in the same worksheet file.

8 In the Change Source dialog box, select the UP Data file.

This step identifies the source file for the link. Now you must identify the exact location of the data in the file. The projected sales data is located in cells A22 through E27 in the worksheet. However, you must use a specification that Word can understand.

9 Edit the text in the Item text box to say Sheet1!R22C1:R27C5.

This setting identifies the source of the data as being on sheet 1— the same worksheet as the historic data—starting in the 22nd row in the first column (R22C1) and ranging to the 27th row in the fifth column (R27C5). In other words, cells A22 through E27.

⑩ Choose Open.

Word closes the Change Source dialog box and displays the Links dialog box, as shown in Figure 14.12. The new link source is referenced in place of the original.

Figure 14.12
The new link source information appears in the Links dialog box.

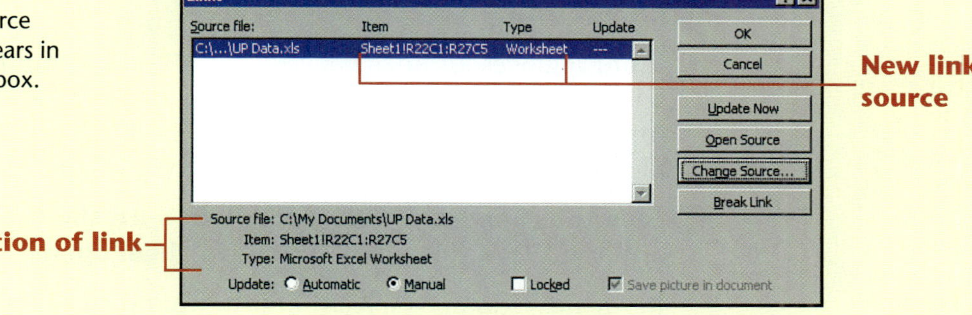

New link source

Description of link

⑪ Click OK.

Word changes the source of the object data and updates the link. Be patient; this may take a while. When the change is complete, the object in the Word document should look similar to the one in Figure 14.13.

Figure 14.13
The object changes to reflect the new data source.

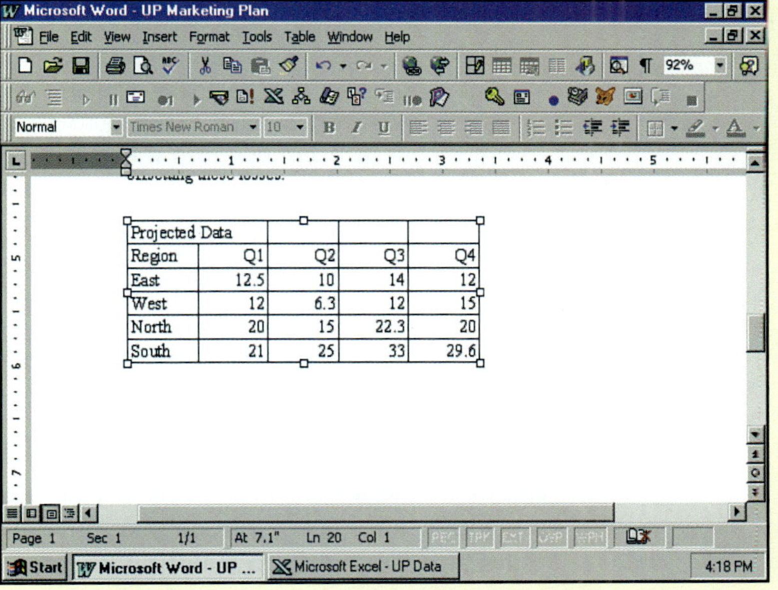

Now consider what would happen if you had to give an electronic copy of the marketing plan to someone to whom you did not want to provide access to the worksheet data. Luckily, you can easily break a link so that there is no connection between the source file and the target file. Try breaking the link between the UP Marketing Plan document and the UP Data worksheet now.

continues

To Control Links (continued)

⑫ **Choose Edit, Links and click the Break Link button in the Links dialog box.**

Word displays a message box asking whether you are sure you want to break the links.

⑬ **Choose Yes.**

Word removes all links between the UP Marketing Plan document and the worksheet. The object remains in the Word document—but instead of being a linked worksheet object, it is now an embedded picture object. You can edit it by using Word's drawing tools.

⑭ **Save the changes you have made to both the Excel document and the Word document and keep them open.**

In the next lesson, you learn how to work with embedded data.

When you open a file with links set to update manually, Word may display a prompt asking whether you want to update the links. Choose Yes to update the links or No to keep the target file unchanged, even if changes have been made to the source file. You can manually update the links whenever you want.

To manually update links without opening the Links dialog box, select the linked object and press F9.

When you want to temporarily keep a link from updating, you can lock it. Locking a link is useful if you are not sure who else has access to the source file or if you want to verify changes made to the source file before the link is updated. To lock a link, choose Edit, Links and then select the Locked check box. When you are ready to update the links, deselect the Locked check box and continue with either a manual or an automatic link update.

Lesson 5: Working with Embedded Data

There may be times when you don't want a link between files. For example, you may want to keep the source file and the target file separate so that you can experiment with the effects of possible changes in data, or so that you can format the object to look good in your Word document, without worrying about how the formatting changes affect the original data in the source file. In cases such as these, you should embed the data instead of linking it.

When you embed an object in a Word document, you can edit the object by starting the source application from within Word. The changes you make affect the object in the Word document, but not the original data in the source file. Likewise, changes you make to the source data do not affect the embedded object. In other words, when you embed an object, it is linked to the application you used to create it but not to the file it was originally saved in.

In this lesson, you delete the projected sales data from the Word document and then embed the historical sales chart. Next, you edit the chart in the Word document, using Excel features.

To Work with Embedded Data

1 Click the object in the Word document to select it and then press Del.

This deletes the object from the document. Now try embedding a chart.

2 Switch to Excel and scroll the worksheet until you see the chart titled Historic Sales by Region and Quarter.

This is the chart you will embed in the UP Marketing Plan document. As usual, you must first select it and copy it to the Clipboard.

3 Position the mouse pointer over the blank area in the upper-left corner of the chart until the ScreenTip says Chart Area; **then click (see Figure 14.14).**

This selects the entire chart. The chart is selected when sizing handles appear around the outside edge of the chart, and the words Chart Area appear in the name box, as shown in Figure 14.14.

Figure 14.14
You must select the chart in order to copy it to the Clipboard.

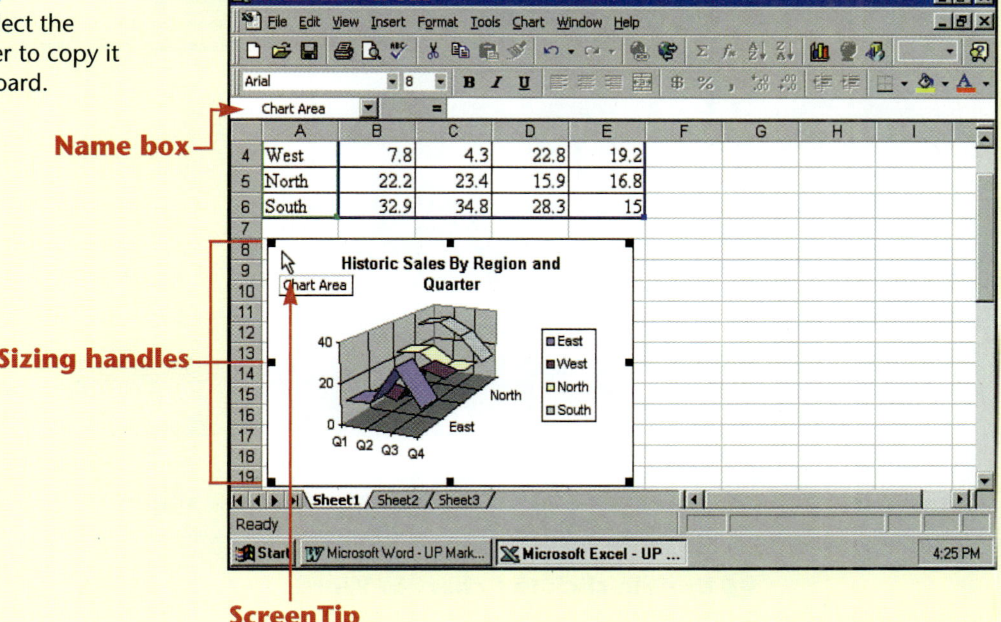

If you have problems... If you double-click the chart, Excel opens a formatting dialog box. Click Cancel and try selecting the chart again.

continues

To Work with Embedded Data (continued)

If you click one of the chart's many individual parts, you select just that part. For example, if you click the legend, handles appear around just the legend. To copy the chart, you must select the entire chart area. Before you click, make sure that you are pointing at the chart area.

4 **In Excel, click the Copy button on the Standard toolbar.**

This step copies the chart you want to embed to the Clipboard.

5 **Switch to Word and choose Edit, Paste Special.**

The Paste Special dialog box appears.

6 **Click the Paste option button—not the Paste Link option button—and make sure that `Microsoft Excel Chart Object` is selected in the As list; then click OK.**

Word embeds the chart in the document, as shown in Figure 14.15. The chart is not linked in any way to the source data in the UP Data worksheet. However, to edit it, you must use Excel.

Figure 14.15
The chart is embedded in the Word document.

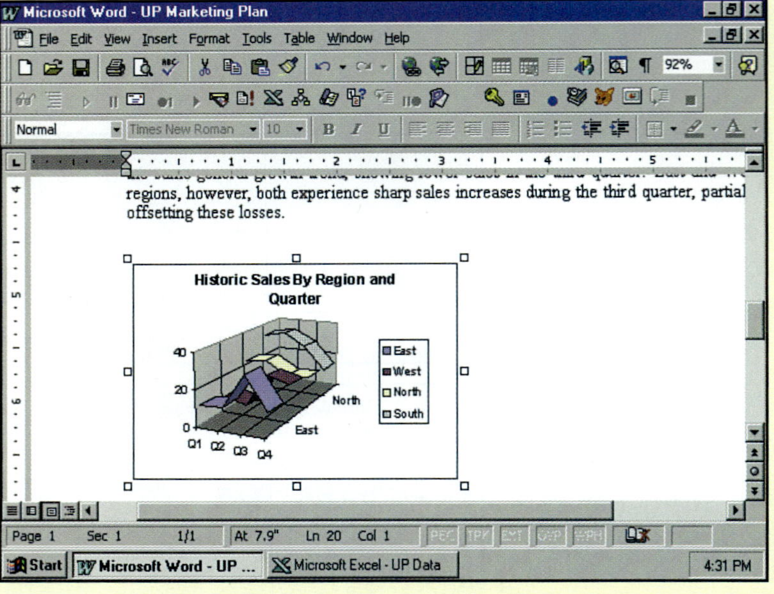

Now try editing the chart from Word to improve its appearance in the document.

7 **Double-click the chart in Word.**

This opens the object's source application within Word—in this case, an Excel window opens and displays the chart, as shown in Figure 14.16. (If you prefer to use menu commands, choose Edit, Linked Worksheet Object; then choose Edit from the submenu.) Although the application title bar tells you that you are still in Word, notice that the menu bar and toolbars have changed to display Excel commands and options.

Figure 14.16
You edit embedded objects from within the current application, using features of the source application.

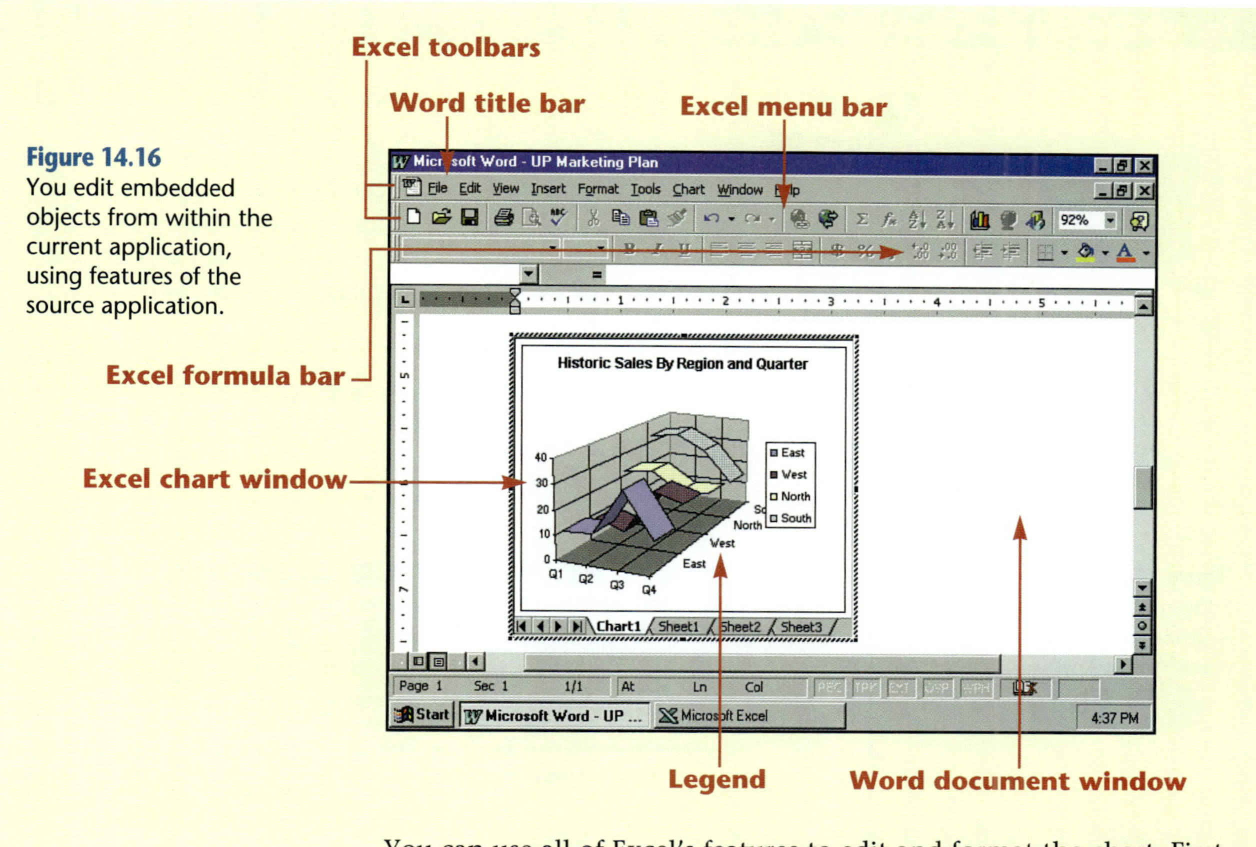

You can use all of Excel's features to edit and format the chart. First, try moving the legend so that it doesn't obscure the labels in the chart.

8 Choose <u>C</u>hart, Chart <u>O</u>ptions.

This step opens Excel's Chart Options dialog box (see Figure 14.17).

Figure 14.17
You use Excel's chart options features to move the legend in the chart object in the Word document.

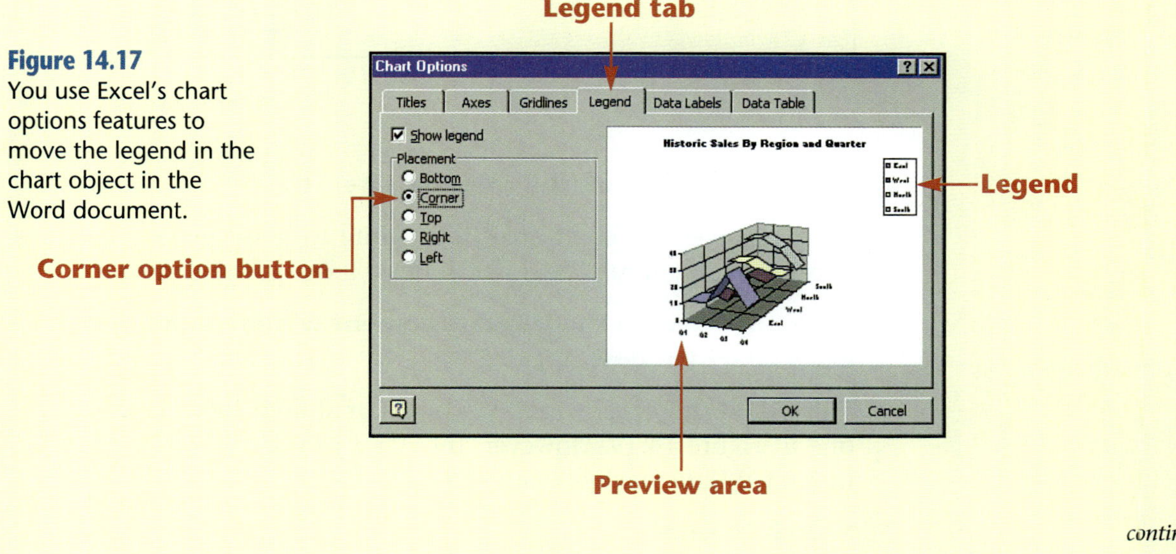

continues

Word

To Work with Embedded Data (continued)

9 Click the Legend tab; then click the C̲orner option button and then OK.

This step tells Excel to move the chart legend to the upper-right corner of the chart area, and closes the Chart Options dialog box. You can see a preview of the way the chart will look in the Chart Options dialog box before you click OK (refer to Figure 14.17).

Now try changing the background color of the chart.

10 Click the Fill Color arrow on the Formatting toolbar.

The Fill Color palette is displayed, as shown in Figure 14.18.

Figure 14.18
Editing fill color in Excel is similar to editing fill color in Word.

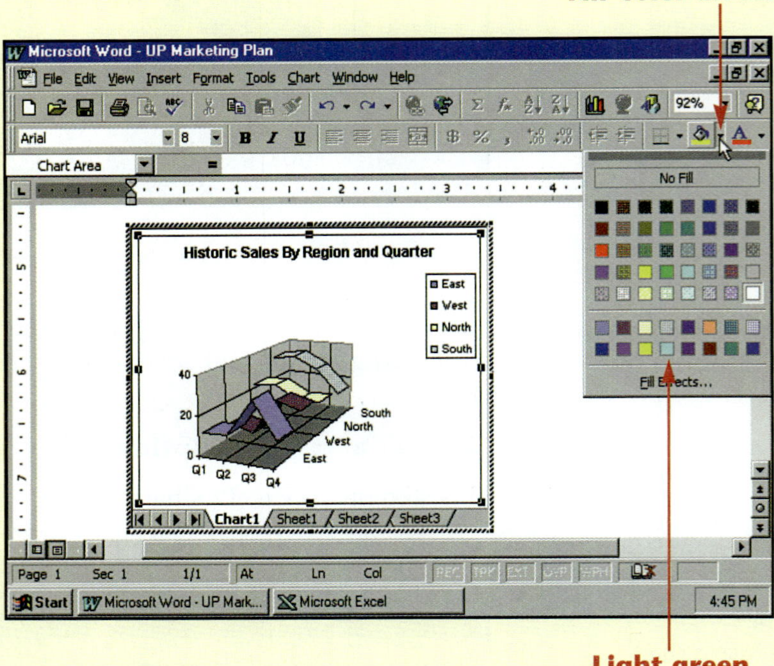

11 Click Light Green on the color palette.

Excel changes the chart area from white to light green. Now close Excel so that you can see how the chart looks in the document.

12 Click anywhere in the Word document window outside the Excel chart window.

This closes the Excel window. The chart should look similar to the one in Figure 14.19. However, the chart in the original Excel document, UP Data, has not been changed at all.

13 Switch to Excel.

You can see that the changes you have made in the Word document have not affected the original chart in the UP Data worksheet at all.

Figure 14.19
The changes you made enhance the appearance of the chart in the Word document.

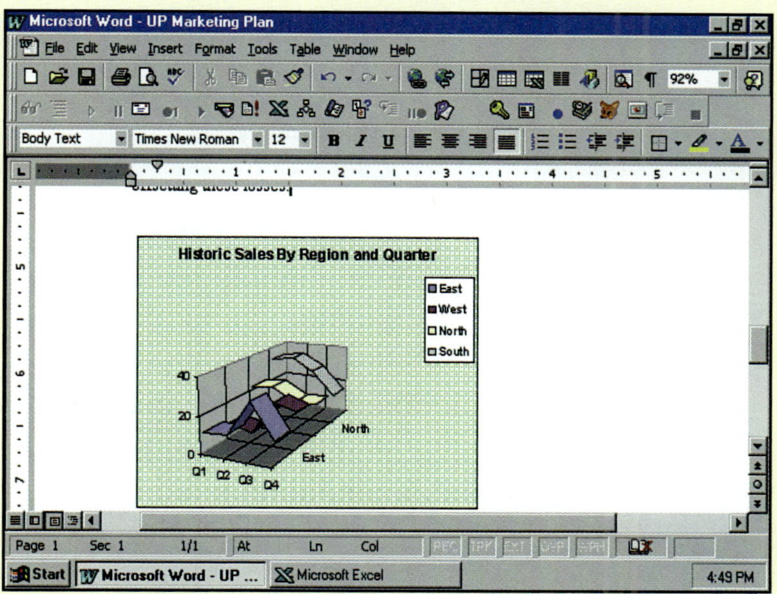

⑭ **Save the UP Data worksheet and close Excel; then save the UP Marketing Plan document in Word, and leave it open.**

In the next lesson, you learn how to share data between different applications.

You can have as many linked or embedded objects in a document as you need; there are no limits. Be advised, though, that the more automatic links in a document, the longer the document takes to load. This can significantly slow down your computer system. If you have a lot of links in a document, you can avoid the system slowdown by setting them for manual updating.

Lesson 6: Sharing Data Across Different Applications

Sometimes you may need to open files that have been created in another application. Likewise, you might want to be able to open a Word file by using a different application. For example, you might use Word 97 at work but have an older version of Word or an application such as WordPerfect at home, or a coworker or client might use a different application or even a Macintosh computer.

Word is able to open and save files in a wide variety of file formats. When you open a file created in a different file format, Word simply converts the data to the Word format so you can easily use all Word commands and options. When you save the file, you have the option of saving it in its original format or in Word 97 format. When you save a file in a different file format, Word converts the file so that you can open it and edit it in the other application. In this lesson, you save the UP Marketing Plan document file in the Rich Text format—a file format that saves text along with most formatting and that can be read by many applications.

To Share Data Across Different Applications

1 **In the UP Marketing Plan document, choose File, Save As.**

The Save As dialog box is displayed. The default file type is Word Document. However, you want to save the file so that you can open it with applications compatible with the Rich Text format.

2 **Click the Save as Type arrow button.**

Word displays a list of file formats that you can use to save the file, as shown in Figure 14.20.

Current folder

Figure 14.20
Word can save a file in a wide variety of formats.

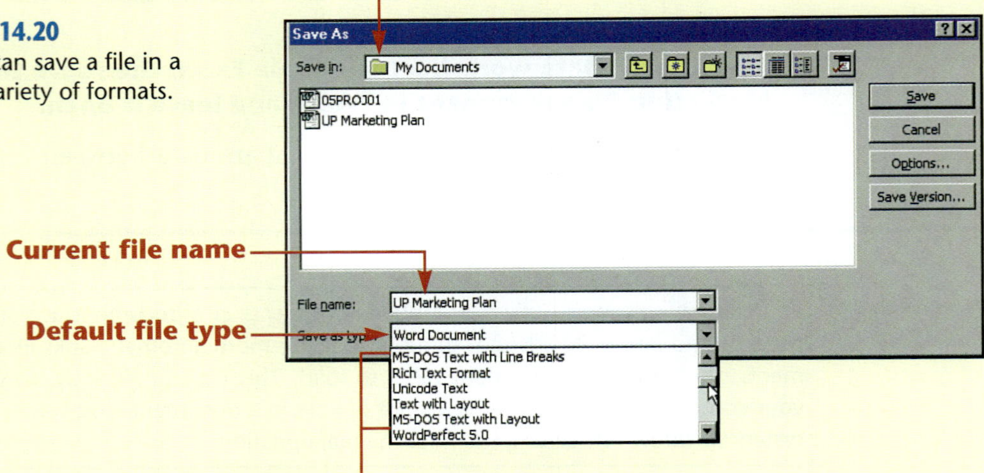

Current file name

Default file type

Select a different file type here

3 **Scroll down the list and select Rich Text Format.**

This step tells Word that you want to save the file in a format that can be read by applications compatible with the Rich Text format.

4 **In the File Name text box, type RTF Marketing Plan.**

This step changes the filename to make it easier to identify which file is the Word 97 file and which is the Rich Text file. If necessary, select the folder or disk where you want to save the file from the Save In drop-down list.

5 **Choose Save.**

Word saves the file in Rich Text format and keeps it open on the screen. The UP Marketing Plan document is saved in its original format and closed. All the data in the RTF Marketing Plan file appears as it did in the Word 97 format file; however, in some cases, when you save a file in a different format, some formatting is lost or changed to conform to the formats of the new application.

If you have problems...

If Word displays a message box asking whether you want to overwrite the file in Word 8 format when you save the file, choose <u>N</u>o to save it in Rich Text format. If Word displays a message box asking whether you want to save the file in Rich Text format when you close the file, choose <u>Y</u>es.

6 Choose <u>F</u>ile, <u>C</u>lose.

Word saves the file in Rich Text format and closes it. Now try opening a file saved in a different file format.

7 In Word, choose <u>F</u>ile, <u>O</u>pen.

The Open dialog box appears. Notice that by default only Word document-formatted files are listed.

8 From the Files of <u>T</u>ype drop-down list, select All Files.

This tells Word to list all files saved in the current folder, no matter what file format they have. The Open dialog box now displays the RTF Marketing Plan filename, as well as the Word and Excel files you have used in this lesson.

9 Select the RTF Marketing Plan file; and choose <u>O</u>pen.

Word opens the file.

10 Close the RTF Marketing Plan file.

You have completed all the lessons in this project. If you have completed your session on the computer, exit all open applications and Windows 95 before turning off the computer. Otherwise, continue with the "Checking Your Skills" and "Applying Your Skills" sections.

Project Summary

To	Do This
Toggle between applications	Press Alt+Tab⇄ or click the appropriate button on the Taskbar.
Copy data between applications	Select the data in the source application. Choose <u>E</u>dit, <u>C</u>opy. Switch to the target application, position the insertion point, and choose <u>E</u>dit, <u>P</u>aste.
Link data between applications	Select the data in the source application. Choose <u>E</u>dit, <u>C</u>opy. Switch to the target application, position the insertion point, and choose <u>E</u>dit, Paste Special. Select the Paste <u>L</u>ink option button, select the data type from the <u>A</u>s list, and click OK.

continues

To	Do This
Edit linked data	Double-click the data in the target file to launch the source application. Edit the data as usual.
Set links for manual updating	In the target file, choose Edit, Links. Select the link. Click the Manual option button. Click OK.
Update links manually	Choose Edit, Links. Select the link. Click the Update Now button.
Embed data	Select the data in the source application. Choose Edit, Copy. Switch to the target application, position the insertion point, and choose Edit, Paste Special. Select the Paste option button and click OK.
Edit embedded data	Double-click the embedded object. Use the source application features to edit the object. Close the source application window.
Save a file in a different format	Choose File, Save As. Select the file format from the Save as Type drop-down list; then choose Save.
Open a file saved in a different format	Choose File, Open. Select the file type from the Files of Type drop-down list, select the file you want to open, and choose Open.

Checking Your Skills

True/False

For each of the following statements, check *T* or *F* to indicate whether the statement is true or false.

__T __F   1. Use the Windows Taskbar to switch among programs but not to open them.

__T __F   2. The only way to permanently sever a link between documents is to delete one of the documents.

__T __F   3. You cannot use the keyboard shortcuts for copying, cutting, and pasting data between applications.

__T __F   4. If your system slows down when you open a program, it could be because you have too many links set to update automatically.

__T __F   5. Use the Edit, Paste Special command to link or embed data between applications.

__T __F **6.** You can copy text but not graphics from one application into another.

__T __F **7.** You can only open two applications at one time.

__T __F **8.** Windows displays a Taskbar button only for the active application.

__T __F **9.** You cannot delete embedded objects.

__T __F **10.** Excel worksheet data is displayed as a table when copied into a Word document.

Multiple Choice

Circle the letter of the correct answer for each of the following questions.

1. Which of the following is an easy way to switch among applications?

   a. Press Ctrl+Del

   b. Press Alt+Ctrl

   c. Click the application's button on the Windows taskbar

   d. Click the application's Start box

2. Which of the following can be passed over a link between applications?

   a. Numbers

   b. Charts

   c. Ranges of cells

   d. All of the above

3. Which operation lets you open one application within another application?

   a. Copying

   b. Linking

   c. Moving

   d. Embedding

4. Which Windows feature includes the operations embedding and linking?

   a. OLE

   b. LEO

   c. ELO

   d. LLE

5. Which operation lets you automatically update data in the destination document when you make a change to the data in the source document?

   a. Linking

   b. Embedding

   c. Copying

   d. Pasting

6. What command do you use when you want to open a document saved in rich text format for use in Word?

   a. Import, File

   b. Open, Type

   c. File, Open

   d. File, Import

7. Which application stores data in a worksheet?

   a. Microsoft Word

   b. Microsoft Excel

   c. Microsoft Access

   d. Microsoft PowerPoint

8. Which Windows feature do you use to cut or copy data from one application to another?

   a. Windows Explorer

   b. My Computer

   c. Windows Clipboard

   d. Windows Start menu

9. What keyboard shortcut do you use to manually update a link?

   a. F7

   b. F9

   c. F5

   d. F3

10. What can you do to temporarily keep a link from being updated?

   a. Remove the link

   b. Block the link

   c. Lock the link

   d. Cut the link

Completion

In the blank provided, write the correct answer for each of the following statements.

1. A link is a _______________-way connection between the source worksheet and the client file.

2. If your system slows when embedding, you may want to consider sharing your data by _______________ instead.

3. The Taskbar displays buttons for all _______________ applications.

4. When pasting data into another program, the data is placed at the _______________ point.

5. The _______________ application is the one in which the original object was created.

6. The _______________ application is the one in which the original object is embedded.

7. Excel data is displayed in a _______ when it is pasted into a Word document.

8. The execution of more than one program or task at a time on a computer system is called _______________.

9. Double-click an _______________ object to open the source application.

10. You can change settings in the _______________ dialog box to control the way in which Word updates linked data.

Matching

In the blank next to each of the following terms or phrases, write the letter of the corresponding term or phrase. (Note that some letters may be used more than once.)

a. OLE

b. Multitasking

c. Save As

d. Integration

e. Taskbar

f. Target

g. Cell

h. Alt + Tab

i. Link

j. Source

________ 1. The execution of more than one program or task at a time on a computer system

________ 2. Using two or more software applications together to create a single document

________ 3. A file where data is created originally

________ 4. A file where data is pasted

________ 5. Key combination used to toggle through open application windows

________ 6. A dynamic connection from an object to the file where it was originally created

________ 7. A Windows feature that lets you create dynamic connections between compatible applications

________ 8. Dialog box used to save Word documents in a different file format

________ 9. Windows element used to switch among open applications

________ 10. One rectangle in an Excel worksheet

Applying Your Skills

Practice

The following exercises enable you to practice the skills you have learned in this project. Take a few minutes to work through these exercises now.

Copying Excel Data into a Word Letter

You have received a request for information about the location of Computer Training Association's field offices. Because you already have a list of sites stored in an Excel worksheet, you simply copy the data into a Word letter document.

To copy Excel data into a Word letter, follow these steps:

1. In Word, open the file Proj1403 from the Project-14 folder on the CD and save it in your `Practices` folder as `CTA Sites`.

2. Start Excel and open the file Proj1404 from the Project-14 folder on the CD and save it in your `Practices` folder as `Site Data`.

3. Click cell A1, hold down the mouse button, and drag over to column B and down to row 9 to select the entire list of offices and locations in the worksheet.

4. Click the Copy button on the Excel Standard toolbar to copy the list of office locations to the Clipboard.

5. Switch to Word, move the insertion point to the end of the Site Letter, and then click the Paste button on Word's Standard toolbar to paste the worksheet data into the document.

6. Click anywhere in the new table and choose T<u>a</u>ble, Table Auto<u>F</u>ormat.

7. Select the Contemporary format and click OK.

8. Save the letter. If requested by your instructor, print it. Close both open documents when you have finished.

Linking Employee Names to a Memo

Link a list of names from an Excel worksheet into a Word memo document. When the address of a new employee is filled in, your memo is updated automatically.

To link employee names to a memo, follow these steps:

1. In Word, open the file Proj1405 from the Project-14 folder on the CD, and save it in the `Practice` folder as `New Hires`.

2. In Excel, open the file Proj1406 from the Project-14 folder on the CD, and save it in the `Practice` folder as `Hire Data`.

3. Click cell A1 in the Excel worksheet and drag over and down to select all of the data; then click the Copy button to copy the data to the Clipboard.

4. Switch to Word, move the insertion point to the end of the document and choose the <u>E</u>dit, Paste <u>S</u>pecial command.

5. Select the Paste <u>l</u>ink option button in the Paste Special dialog box, select Microsoft Excel Worksheet Object, then click OK.

6. Switch back to Excel, click in cell C5, type `1010 East St.`, then save the worksheet.

7. Switch back to Word to see if the link updated. The address should be in the table.

8. Save the memo and the worksheet. If requested by your instructor, print the memo before closing both files.

Embedding Worksheet Data in a Word Document

In this exercise, embed a chart created in Excel showing the savings due to the implementation of new technology into a Word document.

To embed worksheet data in a Word document, follow these steps:

1. In Word, open the file Proj1407 from the Project-14 folder on the CD, and save it in the `Practice` folder as `Technology5`.

2. In Excel, open the file Proj1408 from the Project-14 folder on the CD, and save it in the `Practice` folder as `Tech Data`.

3. Click once on the chart object in the Tech Data worksheet to select it and then click the Copy button on the Excel Standard toolbar.

4. Close Excel.

5. Switch to Word and move the insertion point to the end of the Technology 5 document.

6. Choose Edit, Paste Special.

7. Make sure the Paste option button is selected and that the Excel Chart Object option is selected, then click OK.

8. Save the `Technology5` document. If requested by your instructor, print it. Close the document when you have finished.

Modifying an Excel Chart in a Word Document

In this exercise, enhance and modify the embedded chart object in the Word document. Use the skills you learned in Project 13 for formatting chart objects.

To modify an Excel chart in a Word document, follow these steps:

1. In Word, open the file Proj1409 from the Project-14 folder on the CD, and save it in the `Practice` folder as `Technology6`.

2. Double-click the embedded chart object.

3. Right-click on the value axis and choose Format Axis.

4. Click the Number page tab, choose Currency, and set the Decimal places to 1, then click OK.

5. Drag the lower right sizing handle down and to the right to increase the size of the chart in the Word document.

6. At the bottom of the chart window, click the tab that says `Sheet1`.

7. Use the vertical scroll bar in the chart window to scroll up to the top of the worksheet.

8. Click in the cell that shows the cost of Hardware in Phase 4 as .25.

9. Change the .25 to `.1`, then press `Enter`. Notice that the chart in the chart window changes.

10. At the bottom of the chart window, click the tab that says `Chart1`.

11. Click anywhere in the Word document outside the Chart window.

12. Save the `Technology6` document. If requested by your instructor, print it. Close the document when you have finished.

Import an Excel Worksheet into a Word Document

In this exercise, import an Excel worksheet into a Word document.

To import an Excel worksheet into a Word document, follow these steps:

1. In Word, open the file Proj1410 from the Project-14 folder on the CD and save it in the Practice folder as Café Memo.

2. Press Ctrl+End to move the insertion point to the end of the document.

3. Open the Insert menu and choose File.

4. Locate and open the Excel worksheet file Proj1411 from the Project-14 folder on the CD.

5. In the Open Worksheet dialog box, click the Open document in Workbook drop-down arrow and select Sheet1.

6. Make sure that Entire Worksheet is entered in the Name or Cell Range text box, then click OK.

7. Select the first row in the table inserted into the Café Memo document and choose Table, Merge Cells.

8. Choose Table, Table AutoFormat. Select the Grid 8 format, then click OK.

9. Save the Café Memo document. If requested by your instructor, print it. Close the document when you have finished.

Challenge

The following challenges enable you to use your problem-solving skills. Take time to work through these exercises now.

Creating a Presentation for Potential Investors

You want to include a chart from an Excel worksheet in a report you created in Word. You embed the chart so that you can enhance its appearance in the document using Excel's chart-formatting features.

In Word, open the file Proj1412 from the Project-14 folder on the CD and save it in your Challenges folder as Presentation4. In Excel, open the file Proj1413 from the Project-14 folder on the CD and save it in your Challenges folder as Sales History. In the Sales History worksheet, select the entire chart and copy it to the Clipboard.

Switch to Word and use the Edit, Paste Special command to embed the chart at the end of the Presentation4 document as a Microsoft Excel Chart Object.

From within Word, double-click the chart to start Excel. Using Excel's chart-formatting features, modify the appearance of the chart. For example, change the chart area fill color and move the location of the legend. Increase the size of the Plot Area. Change the colors for each data series. Change the font size used for labels so they are easier to read and fit well in the document. When you are done, close the Excel window in Word.

Save the `Presentation4` document. If requested by your instructor, print each file. Then save and close all open documents.

Incorporating Data from a Different File Format

Open a file saved in an early Word format (Word 3.x-5.x for MS-DOS) and copy the data into a proposal; then save your proposal in Word 3.x-5.x for MS-DOS format.

Open the file Proj1414 from the Project-14 folder on the CD in Word, and save it in your `Challenges` folder as `CTC Sales`. Open the file Proj1415 from the Project-14 folder on the CD, which is in Word for MS-DOS format, and save it in your `Challenges` folder as `DOS Data`. Do not attach a style sheet to the document. Copy the list from the DOS Data file to the end of the CTC Sales file; then close the DOS Data file, still in Word 3.x-5.x for MS-DOS format. Save the `CTC Sales` file, then save a copy of it in your `Challenges` folder in Word 3.x-5.x for MS-DOS format with the name `DOS Sales`. Again, do not attach a style sheet the document. If requested by your instructor, print the document. Close all open documents when you have finished.

Linking Excel Data into a Table in a Word Document

You have a comparison of membership data for the health club saved in an Excel worksheet. You want to link it to a Word memo. That way, as the data changes, the memo remains current.

In Word, open the file Proj1416 from the Project-14 folder on the CD and save it in your `Challenges` folder as `Club Link`. In Excel, open the file Proj1417 from the Project-14 folder on the CD and save it in your `Challenges` folder as `Club Data`.

Copy the range from cell A1 to cell C10 in the Club Data worksheet to the Clipboard. Link the Excel worksheet object into the Club Link document in Word. To make sure the link is working, switch back to Excel and change the number of regular memberships enrolled in 2000 to 130. Save the Excel worksheet and close Excel. Switch back to Word to make sure the table was updated. Save the Club Link document. If requested by your instructor, print it. Close it when you have finished.

Modifying the Linked Table

Practice modifying a linked table by using a version of the `Club Link` document you created in the previous exercise. In Word, open the file Proj1418 from the Project-14 folder on the CD and save it in your `Challenges` folder as `Club Link2`. It contains a table linked to a version of the Club Data worksheet, called `Club Data2`. If Word cannot find the link because the document has been moved to a different folder, use the Edit, Li<u>n</u>ks command to locate and reestablish the link between the two documents.

Start by expanding the size of the table in the document, and centering it on the page. Then double-click it to start Excel and open the source file. Notice that the linked cells are selected. Leave them selected so the changes you make affect only those cells.

On the Excel Formatting toolbar, click the Fill Color drop-down arrow and select a pale yellow. Click the Border drop-down arrow on the Formatting toolbar and select the option to apply borders around the selection and between all cells. Switch to Word to see how the changes affect the table.

Save the `Club Link2` document. Switch back to Excel and change the number of Family memberships in 2000 to `165`. Save the `Club Data2` document. Close Excel. Save the `Club Link2` document. If requested by your instructor, print it. Close all open documents when you have finished.

Importing Excel Worksheet Data in a Word Document

In this exercise, import Excel worksheet data into a Word document; then format the table in Word. Open the file Proj1419 from the Project-14 folder on the CD in Word and save it in your `Challenges` folder as `CTC Sales2`. Import `sheet1` from the Proj1420 Excel worksheet file from the Project-14 folder on the CD into the CTC Sales2 document. Format the table in the Word document by using table formatting commands. When you have finished, save the `CTC Sales 2` document. If requested by your instructor, print it. Close all open documents and applications when you have finished.

You have completed the project and the associated lessons, as well as the "Checking Your Skills" and "Applying Your Skills" sections. Now use the PinPoint software evaluation mode to assess your comprehension of the specific exam tasks you have just learned. You can also use the PinPoint Trainer Mode and the Show Me tutorials to practice these specific exam tasks.

Project 15

Fifteen

Customizing the Word Environment

Customizing Toolbars and New Document Settings

In this Project, you learn how to:

Objectives

Required Activities

- ➤ Work with Word's Toolbars
- ➤ Add and Remove a Button on a Toolbar
- ➤ Create a Custom Keyboard Shortcut
- ➤ Change the Default Font and Font Size
- ➤ Customize Other Options
- ➤ Manage Files

Why Would I Do This?

Default Settings
A setting that the computer uses automatically unless you specify another setting.

Like most Word users, you probably use Word's default settings. That is, you use the toolbars, menus, keyboard shortcuts, fonts, and margins that are automatically in place when you start Word. Most of the time, these default settings serve your word processing needs just fine. As you gain experience with Word, however, you might want to set up the Word environment differently. For example, you might want different toolbars at the top of the screen or different tools displayed on the toolbars. You can create different keyboard shortcuts so that you don't have to take your hands off the keyboard so often. You also can change the default font or the margin settings that Word uses when starting a new document. Word's original settings are called *default settings*.

Word provides a variety of ways to change defaults and customize the Word environment. This project shows you how to customize the toolbars and new document settings so that you can fine-tune Word specifically for your word processing needs.

Lesson 1: Working with Word's Toolbars

By now, you are familiar with Word's default tools, especially the menu and toolbars at the top of the screen. Beneath the row of pull-down menu names, the Standard and Formatting toolbars give you immediate access to Word's most commonly used features (see Figure 15.1). By using the standard tools on these two toolbars, you can instantly manage documents, format text, copy and move data among different documents, and even launch other programs.

Standard toolbar

Figure 15.1
The Standard and Formatting toolbars appear by default when you start Word.

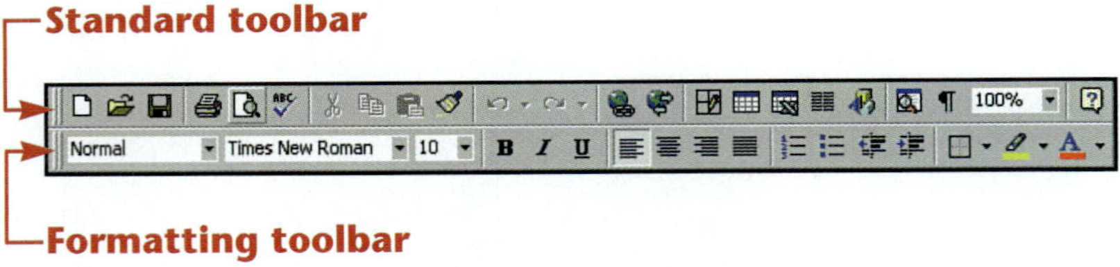

Formatting toolbar

Because you use the tools in the Standard and Formatting toolbars often, you'll probably want to keep them onscreen all the time. Word also provides several other toolbars but hides them from you. Even though these toolbars feature dozens of powerful tools, they are hidden by default because they aren't used as frequently as the Standard and Formatting toolbars and because they take up valuable screen space. Figures 15.2, 15.3, and 15.4 show three toolbars that Word ordinarily hides.

Figure 15.2
The Web toolbar helps you browse the Web.

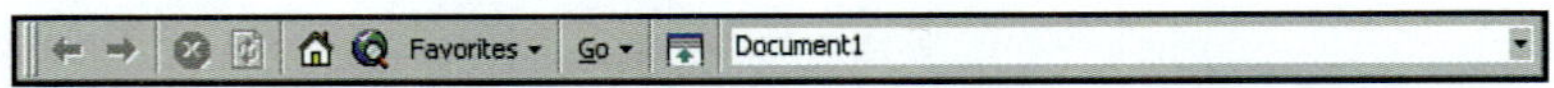

Figure 15.3
The Drawing toolbar helps you draw objects in your document.

Figure 15.4
Use the Tables and Borders toolbar to draw lines in tables or place borders around selected text.

If you create documents in which you frequently use the features in one of Word's hidden toolbars, you can easily "unhide" or display any toolbar so that it's always onscreen. When you no longer need the toolbar, hide it again.

In this lesson, you master different methods for controlling the display of toolbars.

To Work with Word's Toolbars

❶ Right-click either the Standard or Formatting toolbar.

A shortcut menu of available toolbars appears, as shown in Figure 15.5. If a check mark appears next to the name of a toolbar, the toolbar is selected and displayed onscreen. (See Table 15.1 for a description of all toolbars.) By default, the Standard and Formatting toolbars are the only selected toolbars. One additional item is at the bottom of the menu: <u>C</u>ustomize. You learn about this option later in this project.

Figure 15.5
Clicking the right mouse button on a toolbar displays a menu of available toolbars.

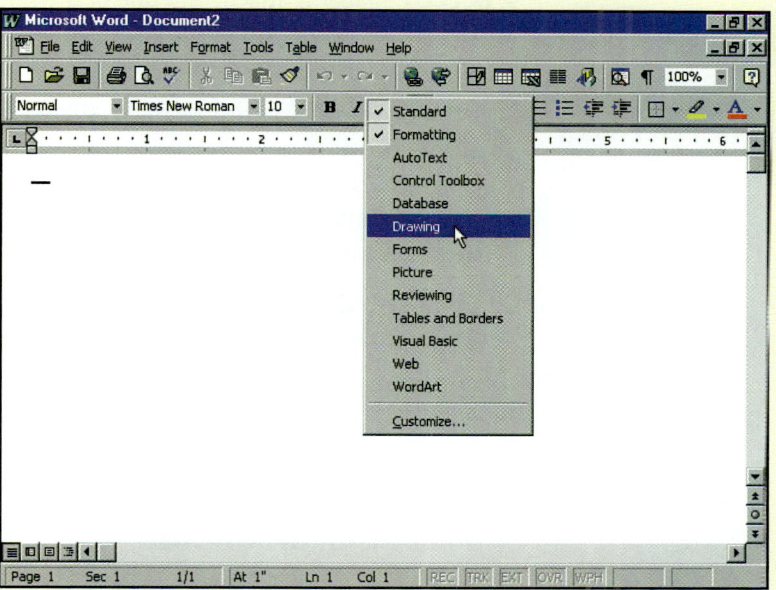

continues

To Work with Word's Toolbars (continued)

2 Select Drawing.

The menu disappears, and Word displays the Drawing toolbar at the bottom of the screen. Now use a different method to add the Borders toolbar to the screen.

3 Choose View, Toolbars, Reviewing.

The Reviewing toolbar appears onscreen. Figure 15.6 shows the screen with four toolbars displayed.

Figure 15.6
This screen displays four toolbars.

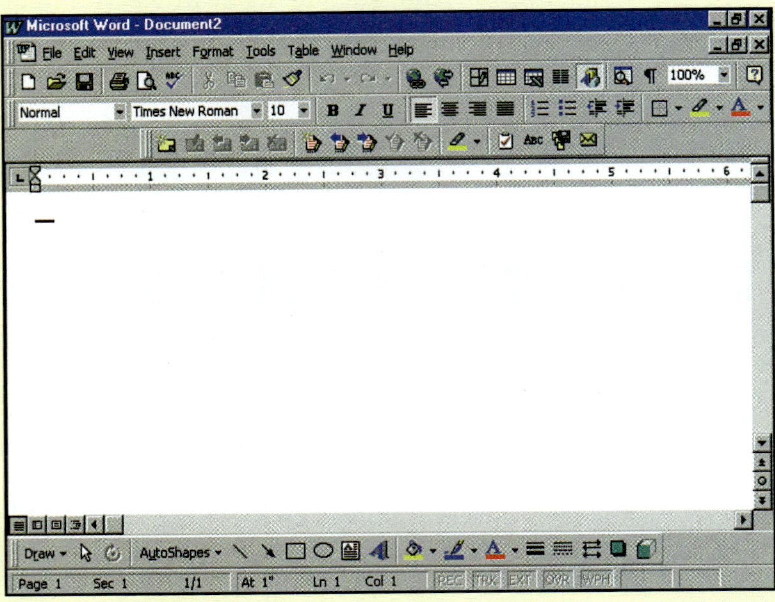

A **docked** toolbar is attached to one of the sides of the screen, usually the top. A **floating** toolbar acts as a palette that you can move and size.

When you add a toolbar to the screen, it might not always line up along the top or bottom of the editing window, as shown in this exercise. Sometimes, a newly opened toolbar "floats" on the screen. You can make any of the toolbars **float** onscreen, or you can **dock** toolbars on any side of the screen.

4 Click the double vertical lines on the left side of the Reviewing toolbar and drag it into your document window.

Your Reviewing toolbar is now floating, as shown in Figure 15.7. You can move a floating toolbar to a new location by double-clicking the toolbar's title bar, or by dragging it to the top.

5 To make the floating toolbar return to the top of the screen, double-click the title bar.

Figure 15.7
You can float toolbars or dock them on any side of your screen.

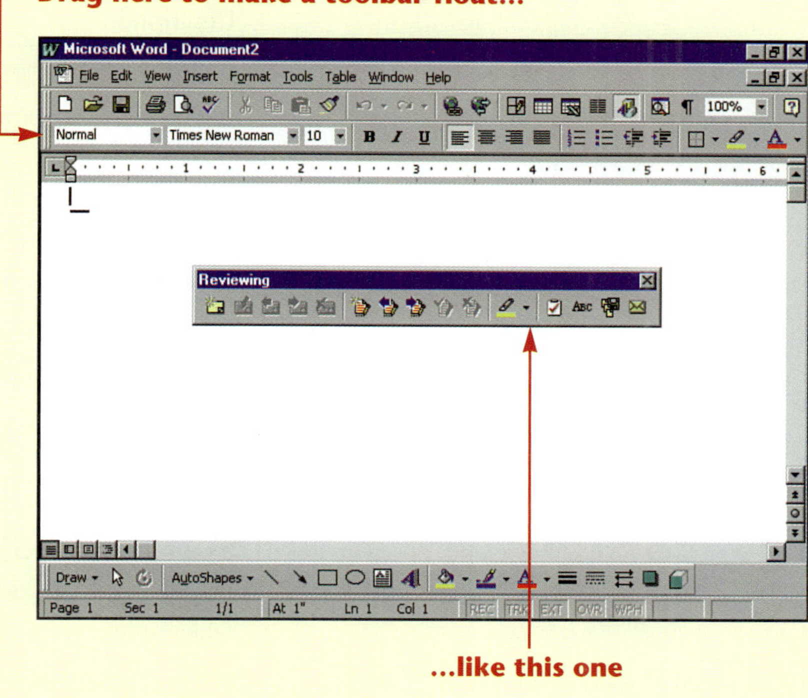

 **Inside Stuff**

You can reshape a floating toolbar by placing the mouse pointer on its edge; when the pointer becomes a double-headed arrow, drag the toolbar border and stretch or shrink the toolbar, changing it from a long rectangle to a square. If you drag a floating toolbar to any edge of the screen and release the mouse button, the toolbar docks on that edge.

These new toolbars are handy, but they take up a lot of screen space. For this reason, you should hide any toolbar that you don't use frequently. Now hide the Drawing and Borders toolbars.

6 Right-click any toolbar, then select the Reviewing toolbar.

7 Right-click any toolbar, then select the Drawing toolbar.

The two toolbars disappear from the screen.

 **Inside Stuff**

For a description of each of the toolbars, see Table 15.1. If you need to do a lot of typing, you probably don't need to use the toolbars—or even the menus, for that matter. You can get rid of all the toolbars by choosing View, Full Screen. You now have the full screen available just for typing. When you need to view the menus and toolbars again, choose Close Full Screen in the Full Screen minitoolbar.

Table 15.1 Toolbars Available in Word 97	
Toolbar	**Description**
Standard	Contains tools to create, print, and edit documents
Formatting	Contains tools to format text, align text, and create lists
AutoText	Gives you easy access to your list of AutoText entries
Control Toolbox	Contains programming tools for building complex macros
Database	Contains tools to help manage a database
Drawing	Contains tools to draw geometric figures in a document
Forms	Contains tools to build forms
Picture	Contains tools to insert and edit graphics
Reviewing	Includes tools for editing and reviewing documents
Tables and Borders	Contains tools to add various borders and lines to tables or selected text
Visual Basic	Makes it easy to play, record, and edit macros
Web	Enables you to browse the World Wide Web
WordArt	Contains tools for shaping text in different forms

Lesson 2: Adding and Removing a Button on a Toolbar

Word enables you to customize all the toolbars by adding or removing buttons. Some people like to add the Double Underline button so that they can format special text. With the Double Underline button on the Formatting toolbar, you can simply click a button (one step) instead of opening the Format menu, choosing Font, selecting Double from the Underline drop-down list, and then choosing OK (four steps).

In this lesson, you add the Double Underline button to the Formatting toolbar and then remove the button to make room for a button that you use more frequently.

To Add and Remove a Button on a Toolbar

❶ Right-click either the Standard or Formatting toolbar, then choose Customize.

The Customize dialog box appears with the Toolbars tab selected, as shown in Figure 15.8.

Figure 15.8
Use the Customize dialog box to modify toolbars and menus and to create keyboard shortcuts.

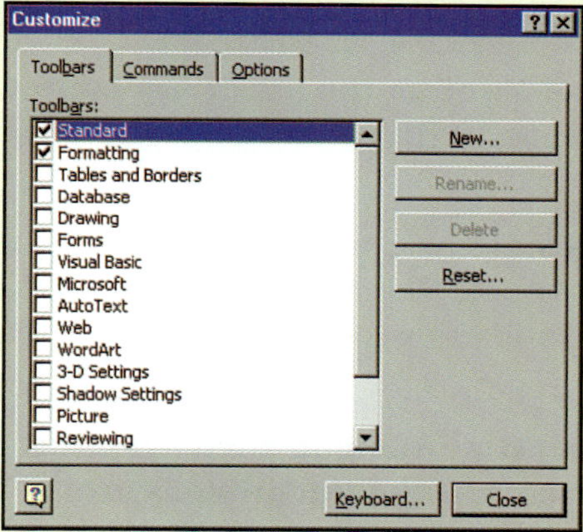

2 **If necessary, click the Toolbars tab, then scroll through the entries in the Toolbars list.**

You find many choices of toolbars in the Toolbars list box, several of which are not listed when you right-click the toolbars. You can select any of these toolbars to display them.

3 **Choose the Commands tab in the Customize dialog box.**

The Commands page displays the commands and buttons that you can add to your toolbar, as shown in Figure 15.9. The Commands list includes a selection of buttons grouped according to the choices in the Categories list. For example, when you select File from the Categories list, the Commands list displays buttons related to file management. When you select a different choice from the Categories list, a different set of buttons appears in the Commands list.

Figure 15.9
The Customize dialog box displays commands available for the File category.

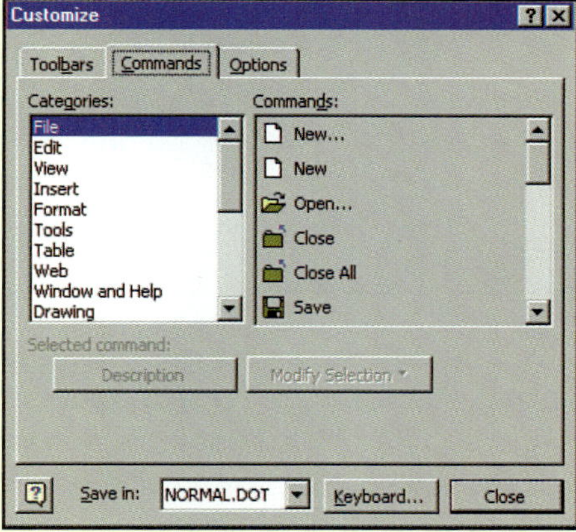

4 **Select Format from the Categories list box.**

A new set of commands appears in the Commands list.

continues

5 **Scroll through the list of available commands in the Format category until you find Double Underline.**

The list includes many different buttons that you can add to the toolbars. If you want to know more about any command, select it and choose Description. Add the Double Underline command to the Formatting toolbar.

6 **Click the Double Underline button once and drag it up to the Formatting toolbar, then drop the button between the Italic button and the Underline button.**

Word adds the Double Underline button to the Formatting toolbar, as shown in Figure 15.10. Depending on your screen resolution, your Formatting toolbar might not have enough room for the new button, in which case the buttons on the Formatting toolbar spill over to a second row.

The Double Underline button being added

Figure 15.10
The Formatting toolbar is about to have a new button.

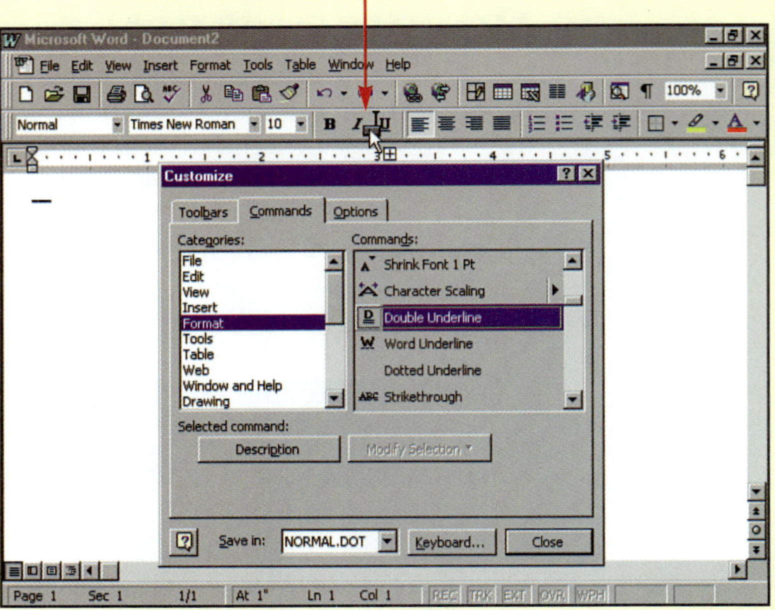

If you have problems...

If you dragged the Double Underline button to the wrong place, just click it again and drag it to the correct place. You can do so because the Customize dialog box is still open. You can add, remove, and rearrange buttons on a toolbar only when the Customize dialog box is open.

7 **Click the Close button in the Customize dialog box.**

Now check whether the new button works by typing some text and clicking the Double Underline button.

8 **Type** Today's Announcement **and press** ⏎Enter **twice.**

9 **Select the text that you just typed and click the Double Underline button.**

The selected text should now be underlined twice.

If you don't use some buttons on the toolbar very often, you might remove them to make room for buttons that you use more frequently. For example, if you don't use Microsoft Excel, you might want to get rid of the Insert Microsoft Excel Worksheet button and replace it with a button that you use more often, such as the Close button or the AutoText button.

Now practice removing buttons from a toolbar by removing the Double Underline button from the Formatting toolbar.

10 **Right-click a toolbar, then choose Customize. Make sure the Commands tab is selected.**

11 **Drag the Double Underline button straight down from the Formatting toolbar, past other toolbars, and into the Customize dialog box; then release the mouse button.**

Make sure not to drag the button onto any other toolbar, or you will add the button to that toolbar. You have removed the Double Underline button from the Formatting toolbar.

12 **Click the Close button in the Customize dialog box.**

The Customize dialog box's Options page enables you to customize toolbars further. If you select the Large Icons check box, the buttons are larger and easier to read, which is great for high-resolution (such as 1,024 x 768) monitors. If you select Show ScreenTips on Toolbars, a description of each button appears onscreen when the mouse pointer touches the button.

While experimenting with toolbars, you can alter them so much that you no longer recall how to return them to their original state. To reset the toolbars, right-click a toolbar and choose Customize. Choose the Toolbars tab, then choose Reset, choose OK, then click Close.

To create your own toolbar, open the Customize dialog box, choose the Toolbars tab, then choose New. After you specify a name for the toolbar, you can then select the Commands tab and add any buttons to this blank toolbar. To delete a custom toolbar, select the toolbar from the Toolbars list in the Customize dialog box and choose Delete. Creating your own toolbar is great for macros and unusual formatting that you use often.

Lesson 3: Creating a Custom Keyboard Shortcut

When you type large amounts of text, you can speed your typing by using *keyboard shortcuts* rather than the mouse to perform certain actions. Word already has many predefined keyboard shortcuts that replace mouse actions. For example, when you open the File menu, you see that the

Keyboard Shortcut
A simple combination of two or three keystrokes that you can press instead of using the mouse to perform certain actions.

shortcuts for <u>N</u>ew, <u>O</u>pen, and <u>S</u>ave are Ctrl+N, Ctrl+O, and Ctrl+S, respectively. You might find, though, that you must frequently use the mouse for an action that has no assigned keyboard shortcut. Word helps you to solve this problem by creating your own keyboard shortcuts.

You also can replace Word's existing shortcuts with shortcuts that better suit your typing preferences. In this lesson, you assign your unique keyboard shortcut to the Double Underline action, replacing Word's default shortcut.

To Create a Custom Keyboard Shortcut

1 **Make sure that a blank document is open onscreen and choose <u>T</u>ools, <u>C</u>ustomize.**

The Customize dialog box—the same one that you used in the previous lesson—appears.

2 **Choose the <u>K</u>eyboard button.**

The Customize Keyboard dialog box appears, as shown in Figure 15.11. This dialog box is similar to the Customize dialog box's Commands page; the entries in the <u>C</u>ategories list match Word's pull-down menu categories. When you select a category, the C<u>o</u>mmands box lists the commands available for that category. When you highlight a command, its keyboard shortcut (if any) appears in the Current Keys box. To assign a new or different shortcut to the command, start in the Press <u>N</u>ew Shortcut Key text box.

Figure 15.11
Use the Customize Keyboard dialog box to create your own keyboard shortcuts.

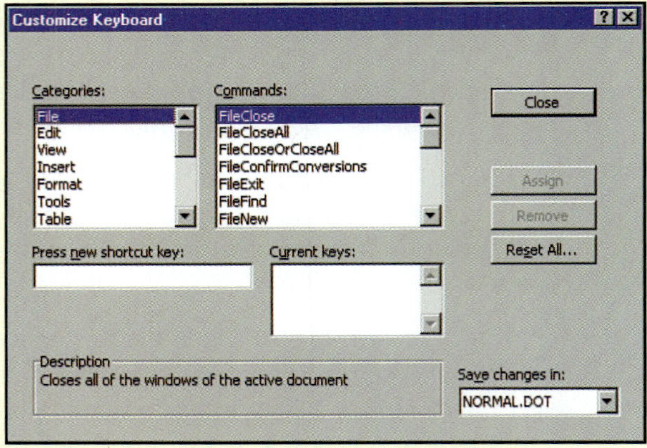

3 **Select Format from the <u>C</u>ategories box.**

A new set of commands appears in the C<u>o</u>mmands box.

4 **Scroll through the list in the C<u>o</u>mmands box until you find DoubleUnderline and click it.**

Your screen should now look like the one in Figure 15.12. The Current Keys box lists the current keyboard shortcuts assigned to Double Underline. When the box lists several keys together, you must press all the keys simultaneously to activate the action. In this case, you press Ctrl, ▲Shift, and D all at the same time to double-underline selected text.

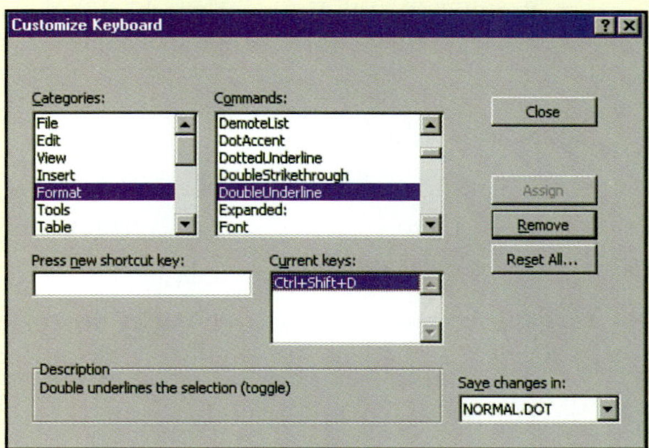

Figure 15.12
Select DoubleUnderline to assign a new shortcut.

Many users find it annoying to press three keys simultaneously to issue a command that they use often. Now assign a different keyboard shortcut to Double Underline, one that requires you to press only two keys—Alt+D—rather than three.

5 **Choose the Press New Shortcut Key text box.**

The insertion point should now be in that text box.

6 **Hold down Alt and press D.**

The screen should now look like Figure 15.13, with Alt+D in the text box. You have made this combination the customized keyboard shortcut for double-underlining text. The text below the box tells you that this keyboard shortcut is unassigned—that is, that no other action is assigned to this combination of keys.

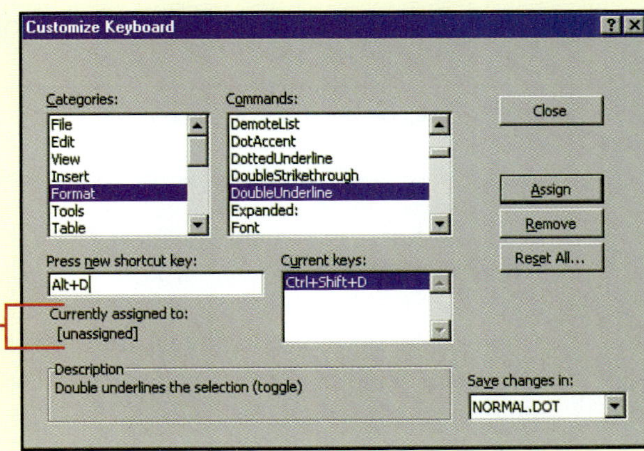

Figure 15.13
To assign a customized keyboard shortcut to Double Underline, choose the Assign button.

Read here to find out whether the keystroke is assigned

continues

To Create a Custom Keyboard Shortcut   (continued)

Be careful to choose only unassigned key combinations. Otherwise, you redefine an existing shortcut already associated with another command. For example, if you assign Ctrl+S to the Superscript command, you can no longer press Ctrl+S to save the document.

7 Choose <u>A</u>ssign.

Word adds the new keyboard shortcut to the C<u>u</u>rrent Keys list. You now have two keyboard shortcuts that add double-underlining to selected text.

8 Click the Close button twice to return to your document.

The dialog box closes. Now check whether the new keyboard shortcut really works by typing some text and then using the Alt+D keystroke to double-underline the text.

9 Type New Division Created and press ↵Enter twice.

10 Select the text that you just typed and press and hold Alt+D.

New Division Created should be double-underlined. Now delete that keyboard shortcut so that the next class can start from scratch with this lesson.

11 Reopen the Customize dialog box and choose <u>K</u>eyboard.

12 Select the Format category from the <u>C</u>ategories list, then select DoubleUnderline from the Co<u>m</u>mands list.

Both the old and new keyboard shortcuts for Double Underline appear in the C<u>u</u>rrent Keys box.

13 Select Alt+D in the C<u>u</u>rrent Keys box, then choose the <u>R</u>emove button.

Word removes Alt+D as a keyboard shortcut for Double Underline.

In this case, be careful not to remove the original shortcut (Ctrl+⬆Shift+D). On your own computer, you can delete that shortcut if you don't plan to use it.

Also, you should not choose the Re<u>s</u>et All button on the Customize Keyboard dialog box. This button resets all keys to default settings and removes all keyboard assignments added since Word was installed on the computer. This action could create havoc in your documents, especially if you share them with other users. Don't let yourself get carried away when you add or remove custom settings of any kind!

14 Click the Close button twice to return to your document.

15 Close the current document without saving the changes.

You can find a list of all the default keyboard shortcuts in <u>H</u>elp. Choose <u>H</u>elp, Microsoft Word Help. When the Assistant appears, type shortcut keys in the box and press ⏎Enter. Select Shortcut Keys from the list of search topics that appear. From the list of keyboard shortcuts categories, click any topic to display a list of shortcut keystrokes. To print this list, choose <u>O</u>ptions, <u>P</u>rint Topic.

Lesson 4: Changing the Default Font and Font Size

The Normal.dot template contains all the default settings that are in place when a Word document opens. The following settings are included with the Normal.dot template:

- Typeface of 10-point Times New Roman
- Margins of 1" at the top and bottom, and 1.25" on the right and left
- Tabs set at every 0.5 inch
- Single line spacing
- No hyphenation
- Left justification
- The status bar, Standard toolbar, and Formatting toolbar displayed

If you find yourself making the same formatting changes for every new document that you create, you might want to change these default settings. For example, if you use 1-inch left and right margins in your documents rather than 1.25-inch margins, or if you prefer a font other than Times New Roman, you should consider making these changes once and for all by editing the Normal.dot template.

You can safeguard against making unwanted changes to the Normal.dot template. To do so, choose <u>T</u>ools, <u>O</u>ptions, then click the Save tab. Select the Prompt to Save Normal Template check box and click OK.

By selecting this check box, you tell Word to display a message each time that you try to exit the program after making changes to your Normal.dot template. The message reminds you that you have made changes that affect the Normal.dot template and also gives you an opportunity to choose not to save the changes. You might want to select this option before you begin the next two lessons.

To Change the Default Font and Font Size

❶ Click the Standard toolbar's New Document button.

This step ensures that a document is open onscreen. Some menus are not available unless a document is open.

continues

Word

To Change the Default Font and Font Size   (continued)

2 Choose Format, Font. Choose the Font tab if the Font page is not already in front.

Your dialog box should look like the one shown in Figure 15.14. The highlighted choices under each box are the defaults. Highlighted selections on your screen might differ from highlighted selections in Figure 15.14 because the defaults might have been changed on your computer. The original default font is Times New Roman, and the original default size is 10.

Figure 15.14
Use the Font dialog box to control all font characteristics.

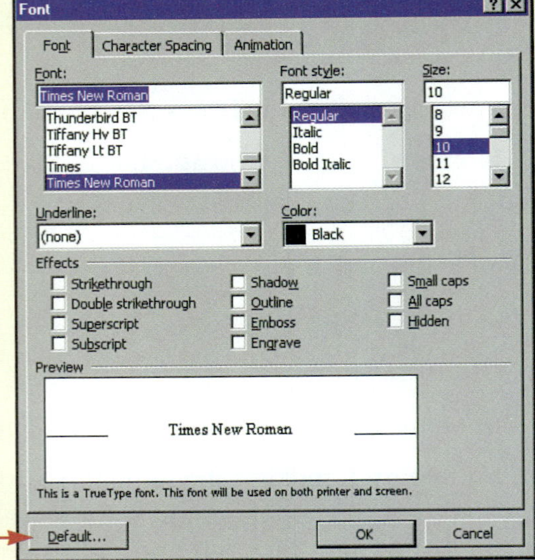

Default button →

3 In the Font list box, scroll up or down until you find Courier New, then select it.

Courier New becomes the new default font.

4 In the Size box, select 8.

This font size becomes the default.

5 Choose the Default button.

An alert box appears, warning you that this change affects all documents that you create with the current template, which is Normal.dot.

6 Click Yes in response to the warning.

The dialog box disappears, and the Formatting toolbar shows that the font for the current document is Courier New and the font size is 8. Any new document that you start will use 8-point Courier New as its default font.

7 Type The sales force has expanded.. **Press** ↵Enter **twice.**

Your text appears in 8-point Courier New. Now see whether a new document starts with 8-point Courier New.

8 **Click the New Document button.**

The Formatting toolbar shows that the font for this document is 8-point Courier New.

9 **Type** `New Sales Personnel will be hired..` **Press** ⏎Enter **twice.**

This text also appears in 8-point Courier New. However, you probably don't want your default font to be 8-point Courier New—it's not widely regarded as an attractive font. Change it back to the way that it was.

10 **Choose F̲ormat, F̲ont. Select Times New Roman from the F̲ont list, select 10 from the S̲ize list, then choose D̲efault.**

Word asks whether you want to change the default font in the Normal template.

11 **Choose Yes to change the default font back to 10-point Times New Roman.**

12 **Close all documents without saving changes.**

A quick way to close all documents is to hold down ⬆Shift and choose F̲ile, C̲lose All. The C̲lose All option appears only when you press ⬆Shift. Word then asks whether you want to make changes to each document that you worked on.

In this lesson, you learned that clicking the D̲efault button in the Font dialog box changes the default font for any document that you create using the Normal.dot template. The Page Setup dialog box also includes a D̲efault button so that you can change default page settings.

For example, if you want to change your default left and right margins from 1.25 inches to 1 inch, choose F̲ile, Page Set̲up. Choose the M̲argins tab if the Margins page is not already in front. After you change the settings, choose D̲efault.

Lesson 5: Customizing Other Options

Word provides an array of options so that you can customize the environment. You can make many changes simply by turning options on and off. You can, for example, customize the look of the Word screen, change certain editing options, and alter the way that the grammar and spell checkers function.

This lesson introduces you to the Options dialog box, a control panel filled with on/off switches for dozens of customizable features in Word.

Word

To Customize Other Options

❶ Open the file Proj1501 from the Project-15 folder of this book's CD, then save it as `Company Meeting`**.**

You need some text onscreen to see the changes that you make in this lesson. Now you're ready to explore the Options dialog box. First, make sure that you're in Normal view.

❷ Choose <u>V</u>iew, <u>N</u>ormal.

The options on the View page of the Options dialog box that you're about to use are different for Normal and Page Layout views.

❸ Choose <u>T</u>ools, <u>O</u>ptions.

The Options dialog box appears. Notice the check boxes; you can use these to turn options on and off. The settings that you now see are your computer's default settings for these options.

❹ Click the View tab if the View page is not already on top.

Your dialog box should resemble what you see Figure 15.15, although the same options might not be selected. Begin by making some minor changes to the document window.

Figure 15.15
With the Options dialog box, you control a variety of Word's default settings.

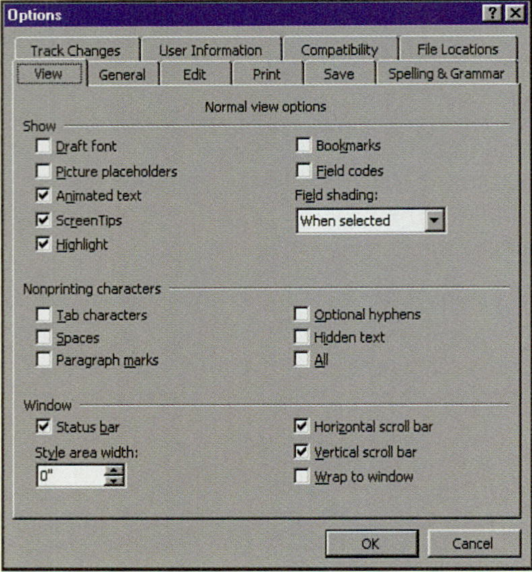

But first, a word of warning. The settings in your dialog box might not match those shown in this lesson. Your instructor or a previous student might have changed them. Before you change any options, write down the current settings. That way, after you see the results of making the changes, you can return the options to their original settings if your instructor wants.

5 **Remove the check from the Horizontal scroll bar check box.**

When you exit the Options dialog box, the horizontal scroll bar on the bottom of the screen is no longer there. By default, Word displays both a horizontal and a vertical scroll bar. Most users seldom need the horizontal scroll bar because the margins of their documents rarely exceed the width of the screen. Now make another quick change.

6 **Clear the All check box in the Nonprinting Characters panel, then select the Spaces check box.**

Word displays or hides all nonprinting characters by default, depending on whether the Show/Hide button on the toolbar is selected. However, instead of accepting this all-or-nothing proposition, you can select which nonprinting characters you want to see. For example, by showing spaces only, you can review the document without the clutter of tab marks and paragraph returns, but still be able to check to be sure that you have the proper number of spaces between words and sentences.

7 **Choose OK.**

The dialog box disappears, and changes take effect. Your screen should look like the one in Figure 15.16.

Figure 15.16
After you make changes to the document window, your screen should look similar to this one.

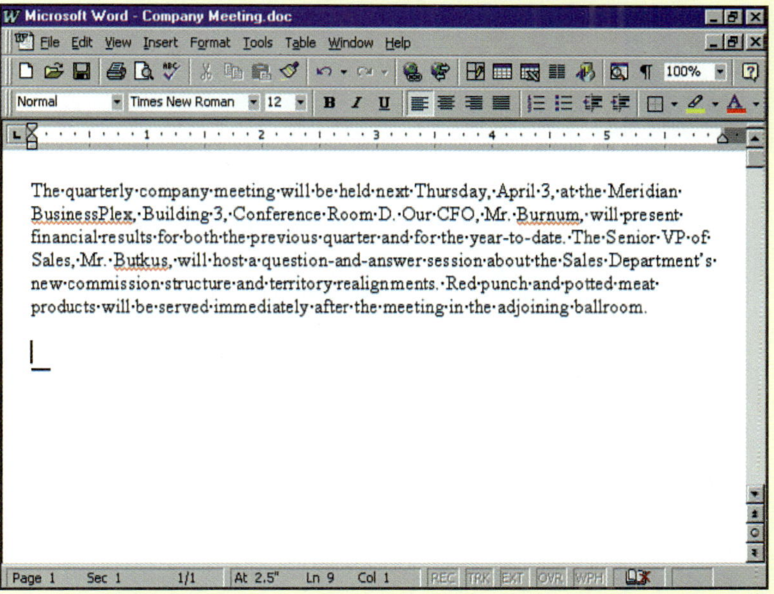

8 **Open the Options dialog box again and click the Spelling & Grammar tab.**

By default, a check mark appears by the Check Spelling as You Type option. When this option is active, Word underscores potentially

continues

To Customize Other Options (continued)

misspelled words. This feature can be useful in preventing embarrassing typing mistakes, but it can also be annoying—it's a matter of preferences.

9 Clear the Check Spelling as You Type check box, then choose OK.

Notice that potentially misspelled words are no longer underscored.

10 Now that you are done experimenting with the Options dialog box, reopen it and restore all settings to the original states.

In the View page, select the Horizontal Scroll Bar and All check boxes, and deselect the Spaces check box. In the Spelling & Grammar page, select the Check Spelling as You Type check box.

11 Click OK to accept the changes and close the document without saving.

As you can see, you can change many options in the Options dialog box. Be careful before you experiment with them, however. Always write down the original settings in case you need to return the options to their defaults. And note that careless changes can cause trouble; without realizing it, you can cause Word to behave in ways that you might not like.

Lesson 6: Managing Files

Some people like to keep all their files in one folder, while others like to keep their files in a group of folders. It helps to know how to manage your files so that you can get organized and not waste valuable time looking all over your hard drive for a missing document.

Word 97 includes a host of features that help you organize your files. One feature that will save you a lot of time is the Favorites folder, which gives you quick access to your most frequently used files and folders. Items placed in the Favorites folder are called shortcuts, items used in Office 97 to jump quickly to a folder, file, or program.

In this lesson, you learn how to create a folder and then add that folder shortcut to the Favorites list. Then you delete the folder and the shortcut.

To Manage Files

1 Open the file Proj1502 from the Project-15 folder of this book's CD, then choose File, Save As.

The Save As dialog box appears, as shown in Figure 15.17. First, locate the My Documents folder.

Figure 15.17
The Save As dialog box enables you to select where you will save the file and in which format.

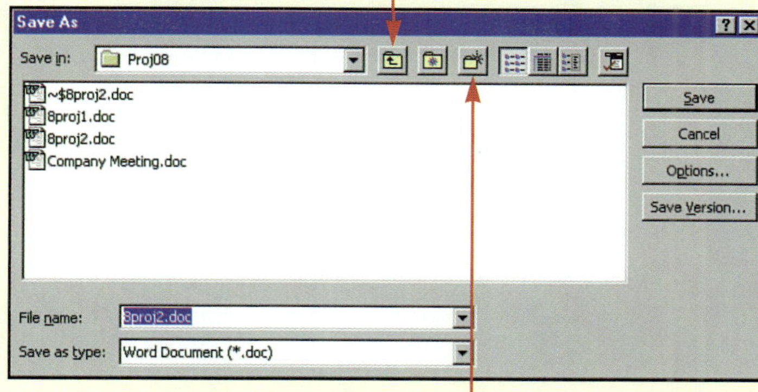

② **Click the Up One Level button until you get to the C: drive, then double-click the My Documents folder.**

The file list displays the files in the My Documents folder. Depending on where you save your files, this folder might be empty, or might have lots of files that you've already saved there. Now create a new folder one level under My Documents.

③ **Click the Create New Folder button.**

The New Folder dialog box appears, as shown in Figure 15.18. Word creates the folder name that you type under the current folder listed in this dialog box, unless you specify a different path name (such as C:\WINDOWS) for the folder.

Figure 15.18
You can create new folders.

④ **Type** `Sample Folder` **in the Name box, then choose OK.**

The folder that you created appears in the list of files and folders. Note that this folder is an Office 97 folder that you can use to store any file, not just Word files. Now open this folder and save the current document there.

⑤ **Double-click the Sample Folder icon that you just created.**

⑥ **Type** `Sample Document` **in the File Name box, then choose Save.**

The Save As dialog box closes and Word saves the document in the folder that you just created. Now close the document and open another.

continues

To Manage Files (continued)

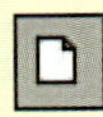

7 Close the current document, then click the Standard toolbar's New button.

Now create a **shortcut** for the Sample Folder located in the Favorites folder. In this folder, you can store the shortcuts of folders and files that you use most frequently.

A **shortcut** is a quick way to open a folder or a document in Office 97. For example, when you click the Start button in Windows, any file, folder, or program that you select is actually a shortcut. You can place shortcuts on the Start menu, on the desktop, or in other folders such as the Favorites folder. Remember, a shortcut folder is not the actual folder—it's a representation of that folder. If you delete a shortcut to a folder, the folder still remains on your hard drive.

8 Choose File, Open, then click the Look in Favorites option.

You should see the My Documents folder in the list of favorites. When you installed Word, the setup program added this shortcut to the Favorites folder. You might have other shortcuts as well, depending on which programs you've installed.

9 Double-click My Documents, then double-click Sample Folder.

The Sample Folder that you created is now open, with Sample Document.doc inside. Now add this folder to your Favorites list.

10 Click the Add to Favorites button, then select Add Sample Folder to Favorites.

Word adds a shortcut to the Favorites folder. Remember, this shortcut is not the actual folder itself, just a marker that takes you to the folder. Now check whether the shortcut works.

11 Click the Up One Level button several times.

12 Click the Look in Favorites button again.

The shortcut items in the Favorites folder appear, as shown in Figure 15.19. Shortcuts have small arrows in the icon to distinguish them from the folder that they represent.

13 Double-click Sample Folder.

The sample document that you saved appears in the list.

You can view a document's contents without actually opening the document. In the Open dialog box, select the file that you want to view, then click the Preview button. When you are finished previewing, click either the List or Details button. Leaving the Preview button on can slow you down when you're opening files.

Figure 15.19
Clicking a shortcut in the Favorites folder jumps you to that folder.

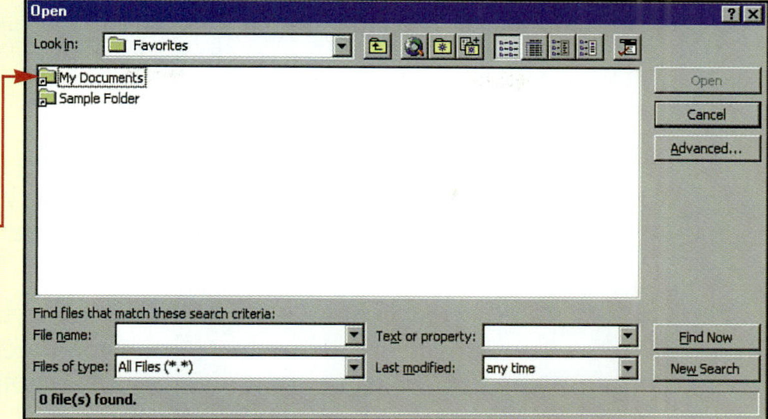

The shortcut folder that you just created

You probably don't want to save the sample folder or sample document on your hard drive. Now delete the sample document, the sample folder, and the Favorites shortcut. When you want to move, copy, or rename a file, right-click it, then select an option from the menu.

14 Right-click Sample Document.doc, then choose Delete from the shortcut menu. When asked to confirm the deletion, choose Yes.

Word deletes the Sample Document.doc file. Make sure that you know what the file contains before you delete it. Even though you can recover deleted files from your Recycle Bin, carelessly deleting them is still a bad idea.

If you have problems...

If you received an error message stating that you cannot delete this file, the file that you want to delete is still open. Close the file, then repeat the steps to delete it.

15 Click the Up One Level button, then delete the Sample Folder folder.

You delete a folder the same way that you delete a file—by right-clicking it and choosing Delete. Even though you deleted the folder, the shortcut to the folder still remains in the Favorites list. Delete the shortcut.

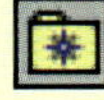

16 Click the Look in Favorites button, then delete the Sample Folder shortcut.

17 Choose Cancel to close the Open dialog box.

Sometimes you can't find the file that you're looking for. Word can help. For example, suppose that you want to find a document named 4Table2.doc. You know it's somewhere on your hard drive, but you can't remember which folder it's in. In fact, you're not even sure of the filename.

To find this file, open the Open dialog box, then select the C: drive from the Look In drop-down list. Type table in the File Name text box. Click the Commands and Settings button, then choose Search Subfolders. Word searches the hard drive for all file names that include table and presents a list.

You have completed all of the lessons in this project. If you have completed your session on the computer, exit Word and Windows 95 before turning off your computer. Otherwise, continue with the "Checking Your Skills" and "Applying Your Skills" sections.

Project Summary

To	Do This
Display a toolbar	Right-click any toolbar, then click the name of the toolbar to display it onscreen. Or choose View, Toolbars and select the toolbar that you want.
Hide a toolbar	Right-click any toolbar, then click the name of the toolbar to be hidden. Or choose View, Toolbars and select the toolbar that you want.
Add a button to a toolbar	Open the Customize dialog box (by right-clicking a toolbar or by choosing View, Toolbars and clicking the Customize button). Choose the Commands tab. Select the category, then drag the button that you want to add to the appropriate toolbar. Close the Customize dialog box.
Remove a button from a toolbar	Open the Customize dialog box. Drag the button from the toolbar. Close the Customize dialog box.
Create a customized keyboard shortcut	Open the Customize dialog box by choosing Tools, Customize. Choose the Keyboard button. Select the command to be assigned to the keyboard shortcut. Click the Press New Shortcut Key check box, then press the combination of keys for the keyboard shortcut. Choose Assign. Close the Customize dialog box.

To	Do This
Remove a customized keyboard shortcut	Open the Customize dialog box by choosing Tools, Customize, Keyboard. Select the command for the keyboard shortcut to be removed from the Current Keys list. Click the keyboard shortcut to remove, then choose the Remove button. Close the Customize dialog box.
Change the font and font size defaults	Choose Format, Font. Select the font and font size that you want, then choose the Default button. Click Yes in the message box.
Change miscellaneous settings	Choose Tools, Options and select or clear the desired options on the appropriate tabs.
Create a new folder	Choose File, Save As, then click the Create New Folder button.
View list of Favorites shortcuts	Choose File, Open, then click the Look in Favorites option.

Checking Your Skills

True/False

For each of the following statements, check *T* or *F* to indicate whether the statement is true or false.

__T __F   **1.** You can display only four toolbars at one time.

__T __F   **2.** When you right-click a toolbar, the shortcut menu displays only the most common available toolbars.

__T __F   **3.** If you assign a keyboard shortcut that has already been assigned to a different command, you can use that keystroke for either command.

__T __F   **4.** When you delete a file in the Open or Save As dialog box, that file remains on your hard drive but no longer appears in Word.

__T __F   **5.** Folders that you create in the Save As dialog box can be used in Word or in any other application.

__T __F   **6.** Only the Standard and Formatting toolbars are displayed by default.

__T __F   **7.** Only the Reviewing toolbar can float on the desktop.

__T __F   **8.** If you are unhappy with customizations you make to a toolbar, you can use the Reset command to revert to the default settings.

__T __F **9.** The default Normal.dot typeface is 10-point Times New Roman.

__T __F **10.** You can hide the horizontal scroll bar if you need more room in the document window.

Multiple Choice

Circle the letter of the correct answer for each of the following questions.

1. In which dialog box can you add and remove toolbar buttons?

a. Options

b. Toolbars

c. Hyphenation

d. Customize

2. Which of the following settings does the Normal.dot template include?

a. A typeface of 12-pt. Arial

b. 1-inch left and right margins

c. Single line spacing

d. All the above

3. Which menu option do you choose to find the Check Spelling as You Type option:

a. Tools, Customize, Options

b. Tools, Spelling and Grammar, Next Sentence

c. Tools, Options, Spelling & Grammar

d. Any of the above

4. In which dialog box can you create a new folder?

a. Save As

b. Open

c. Both a and b

d. Neither a nor b

5. In which dialog box can you add a folder to the Favorites folder?

a. Save As

b. Open

c. Both a and b

d. Neither a nor b

6. Which toolbar has tools for inserting and editing graphics?

a. Formatting

b. Forms

c. Tables and Borders

d. Picture

7. What is the default point size in the Normal.dot template?

a. 14

b. 12

c. 10

d. 8

8. On which page of the Options dialog box do you find options for customizing the way Word is displayed onscreen?

a. Spelling & Grammar

b. View

c. Edit

d. User

9. What is the name of the folder where you can store shortcuts to files, folders, and programs that you use frequently?

    a. My Documents

    b. Windows

    c. Shortcuts

    d. Favorites

10. What element distinguishes a shortcut icon from other icons?

    a. A plus sign

    b. An arrow

    c. A minus sign

    d. A hand with a pointing finger

Completion

In the blank provided, write the correct answer for each of the following statements.

1. When you customize the Word environment, you change the _______________ settings.

2. A toolbar attached to a side of the screen is called a _______________ toolbar.

3. The _______________ template contains all the default settings that are in place when you start Word.

4. To change view settings such as displaying nonprinting characters or displaying scroll bars, choose _______________, _______________, then click the _______________ tab.

5. Use the _______________ folder to store shortcuts that give you quick access to commonly used files and folders.

6. A _______________ toolbar resembles a palette.

7. The _______________ toolbar contains tools for creating, printing, and editing documents.

8. You can assign keyboard _______________ to actions or commands that you use frequently.

9. A _______________ folder is not the actual folder—it's a representation of that folder.

10. _______________-click any toolbar to display a list of available toolbars.

Matching

In the blank next to each of the following terms or phrases, write the letter of the corresponding term or phrase. (Note that some letters may be used more than once.)

a. Shortcut icons

b. Floating toolbar

c. Save As

d. User Information

_______ 1. A setting that the computer uses automatically unless you specify a different setting

_______ 2. A toolbar that is attached to one of the sides of the screen

_______ 3. A toolbar that you can move and size

<table>
<tr><td>

e. 1"

f. Default

g. Control Toolbox

h. Shortcut Key Combination

i. Docked toolbar

j. Formatting tool-bar

</td><td>

_______ **4.** The toolbar that contains buttons for aligning text

_______ **5.** More than one key pressed at the same time to perform a common action or command

_______ **6.** The default top and bottom margin widths

_______ **7.** Options dialog box page on which you can enter your name and address

_______ **8.** Items placed in the Favorites folder

_______ **9.** Dialog box in which you can create a new folder

_______ **10.** Toolbar that contains programming tools for building complex macros

</td></tr>
</table>

Applying Your Skills

Practice

The following exercises enable you to practice the skills you have learned in this project. Take a few minutes to work through these exercises now.

Displaying and Hiding Toolbars

In this exercise, you display and hide several different toolbars.

To display and hide toolbars, follow these steps:

1. Choose View, Toolbars, Tables and Borders.

2. Drag the Formatting toolbar so that it floats in the upper-right corner of the screen.

3. Anchor the Formatting toolbar to the bottom of the screen.

4. Choose View, Toolbars, Tables and Borders to hide the Borders toolbar.

5. Return the Formatting toolbar to its default position.

Customizing Toolbars

In this exercise, you add, move, and remove buttons on the Formatting and Standard toolbars.

To customize toolbars, follow these steps:

1. Choose Tools, Customize to open the Customize dialog box.

2. Click the Commands page tab.

3. Select the Format category and the Small Caps command.

4. Drag the Small Caps button onto the Formatting toolbar, then close the Customize dialog box.

5. Right-click a toolbar, then choose <u>C</u>ustomize. Make sure the <u>C</u>ommands tab is selected.

6. Drag the Small Caps button straight down from the Formatting toolbar, past other toolbars, and into the Customize dialog box; then close the Customize dialog box.

Creating Keyboard Shortcuts

In this exercise, you create and assign keyboard shortcuts to change the zoom to whole page and to page width.

To create keyboard shortcuts, follow these steps:

1. Choose <u>T</u>ools, <u>C</u>ustomize to open the Customize dialog box, then click the Keyboard button.

2. Select the View category and ViewZoomWholePage command.

3. Click in the Press <u>n</u>ew shortcut key text box, then press [Alt]+[W].

4. Click <u>A</u>ssign.

5. Select the ViewZoomPageWidth command.

6. Click in the Press <u>n</u>ew shortcut key text box, then press [Alt]+[Z].

7. Click <u>A</u>ssign, then click Close, then click Close in the Customize dialog box.

8. Test the shortcut keys by opening any document and pressing [Alt]+[W] to change the zoom to whole page, then press [Alt]+[Z] to change the zoom to page width.

Changing Other Options

In this exercise, you change the number of files that Word lists as recently used.

To change other options, follow these steps:

1. Choose <u>T</u>ools, <u>O</u>ptions to open the Options dialog box and select the General tab.

2. Change the number of file names that appear in the <u>R</u>ecently Used Files list from 4 to 2.

3. Click OK.

4. Open the <u>F</u>ile menu to see how many files are listed in the Recently Used Files list.

5. Choose <u>T</u>ools, <u>O</u>ptions to open the Options dialog box and select the General tab again.

6. Change the number of file names that appear in the <u>R</u>ecently Used Files list from 2 back to 4.

Managing Files

In this exercise, you create and delete a folder in your Favorites folder.

To manage files, follow these steps:

1. Choose File, Save As.
2. Click the Look In Favorites button.
3. Click the Create New Folder button.
4. Type the name `New Practices`, then click OK.
5. Select the New Practices folder name in the list.
6. Press Delete.
7. Click OK.

Challenge

The following challenges enable you to use your problem-solving skills. Take time to work through these exercises now

Working with Toolbars

To familiarize yourself with the available toolbars, practice displaying them, rearranging them, and hiding them. See how many toolbars you can display at one time. Dock three toolbars on the left side of the screen. Float and resize two toolbars. Hide all toolbars. Display just the Formatting and Standard toolbars.

Customizing Toolbars

Create a new toolbar called `Challenge`. Add the following buttons to the new Challenge toolbar:

1. From the File menu, add Save, Close, and Page Setup.
2. From the Edit menu, add Go To.
3. From the Format menu, add Strikethrough, Double-space, Change Text direction, and Change Case.
4. Dock the Challenge toolbar along the left side of the screen.
5. Delete the new toolbar.

Customizing Keyboard Shortcuts

Create keyboard shortcuts for the following commands: Strikethrough, Close, and BorderAll. Be sure to use key combinations that have not been assigned to other commands. Create a new document and test your new shortcuts. If requested by your instructor, delete the shortcuts.

Customizing Save and Options

Customize the options on the Save page of the Options dialog box. Set Word so that it saves AutoRecover information every five minutes. Set Word to prompt you to save the Normal.dot templates and to allow fast saves and background saves. On the General page, select the option for displaying documents with a blue background and white text. See how it looks. Change back to a white background with black text.

On the View page, select the option for using the Draft font, then click OK to see how it looks. Go back to the Options View page and deselect that option.

Managing Files

Add your Challenges folder to the Favorites folder. Add your Practices folder to the Favorites folder. Remove your Practices folder from the Favorites folder.

Create a new folder called Skills and add it to the Favorites folder. Remove the Skills folder from the Favorites folder.

You have completed the project and the associated lessons, as well as the "Checking Your Skills" and "Applying Your Skills" sections. Now use the PinPoint software evaluation mode to assess your comprehension of the specific exam tasks you have just learned. You can also use the PinPoint Trainer Mode and the Show Me tutorials to practice these specific exam tasks.

appendix A

Working with Windows 95

Objectives

In this Appendix, you learn how to:

- ➤ Start Windows 95
- ➤ Use the Mouse
- ➤ Understand the Start Menu
- ➤ Identify the Elements of a Window
- ➤ Manipulate Windows
- ➤ Exit the Windows 95 Program

Why Would I Do This?

Microsoft Windows 95 is a powerful operating environment that enables you to access the power of DOS without memorizing DOS commands and syntax. Windows 95 uses a *graphical user interface* (GUI) so that you can easily see onscreen the tools that you need to complete specific file- and program-management tasks.

This appendix, an overview of the Windows 95 environment, is designed to help you learn the basics of Windows 95.

Lesson 1: Starting Windows 95

The first thing you need to know about Windows is how to start the software. In this lesson, you learn how to start Windows; however, before you can start Windows, it must be installed on your computer. If you need to install Windows, refer to your Windows 95 manual or ask your instructor for assistance.

In most cases, Windows starts automatically when you turn on your computer. If your system is set up differently, you must start Windows from the DOS prompt (such as C:\>). Try starting the Windows program now.

To Start Windows 95

1 Turn on your computer and monitor.

Most computers display technical information about the computer and the operating software installed on it.

If Windows starts, you can skip step 2. Otherwise, you will see the DOS prompt C:\>.

2 At the DOS prompt, type win and press ⏎Enter.

When you start the Windows program, a Microsoft Windows 95 banner displays for a few seconds; then the *desktop* appears (see Figure A.1).

Graphical user interface (GUI)
A computer application that uses pictures, graphics, menus, and commands to help users communicate with their computers.

Desktop
The background of the Windows screen, on which windows, icons, and dialog boxes appear.

Icon
A picture that represents an application, a file, or a system resource.

Shortcut
Gives you quick access to frequently used objects so you don't have to look through menus each time you need to use that object.

Taskbar
Contains the Start button, buttons for each open window, and the current time.

Start button
A click of the Start button opens the Start menu.

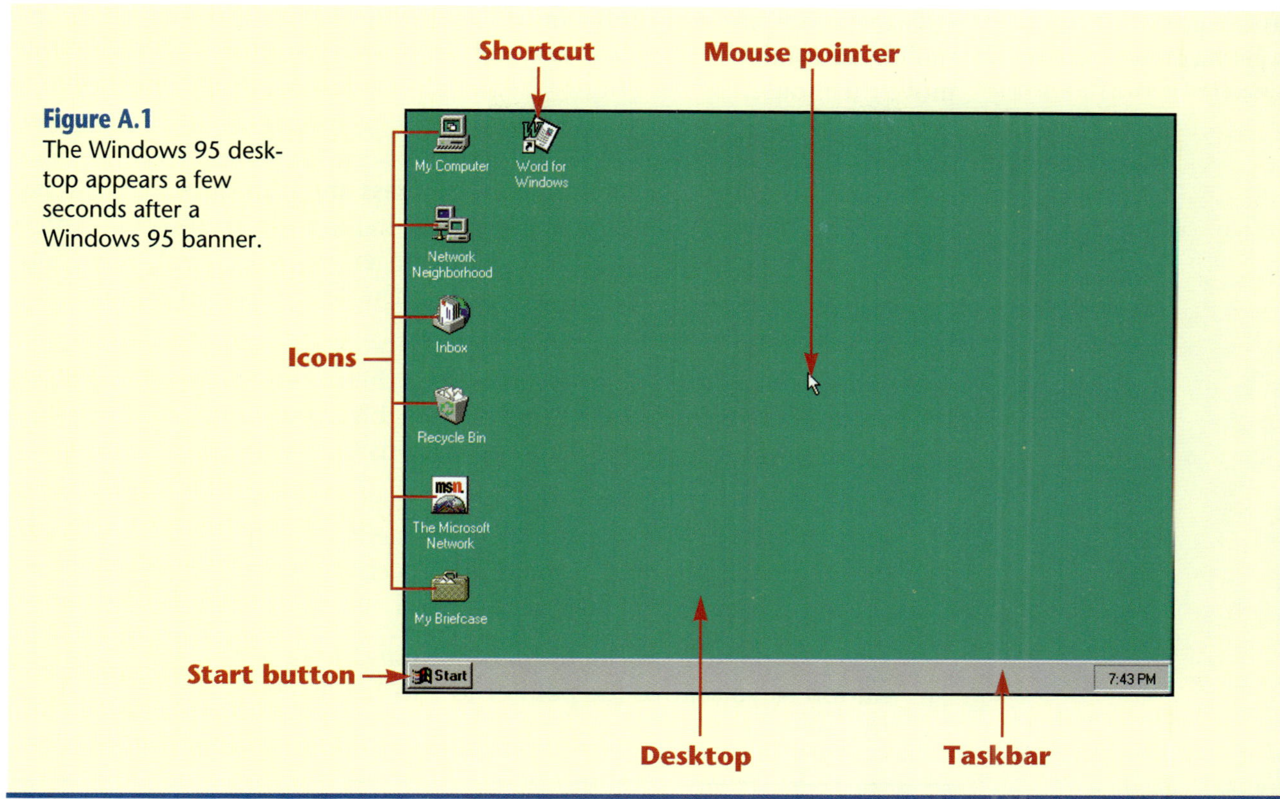

Figure A.1
The Windows 95 desktop appears a few seconds after a Windows 95 banner.

Inside Stuff

Program *icons* that were created during installation (such as My Computer, Recycle Bin, and Network Neighborhood) are displayed on the desktop. Other icons might also appear, depending on how your system is set up. Shortcuts to frequently used objects (such as documents, printers, and network drives) can be placed on the desktop. The *Taskbar* appears along the bottom edge of the desktop. The *Start button* appears at the left end of the Taskbar.

Pull-down menus

Menus that cascade downward into the screen whenever you select a command from the menu bar.

Dialog box

A window that opens onscreen to provide information about the current action or to ask the user to provide additional information to complete the action.

Mouse

A pointing device used in many programs to make choices, select data, and otherwise communicate with the computer.

Mouse pointer

A symbol that appears onscreen to indicate the current location of the mouse.

Lesson 2: Using the Mouse

Windows is designed to be used with a *mouse,* so it's important that you learn how to use a mouse correctly. With a little practice, using a mouse is as easy as pointing to something with your finger. You can use the mouse to select icons, to make selections from *pull-down menus* and *dialog boxes*, and to select objects that you want to move or resize.

In the Windows desktop, you can use a mouse to

- Open windows

- Close windows

- Open menus

- Choose menu commands

- Rearrange onscreen items, such as icons and windows

The position of the mouse is indicated onscreen by a *mouse pointer*. Usually, the mouse pointer is an arrow, but it sometimes changes shape depending on the current action.

Mouse pad
A pad that provides a uniform surface for the mouse to slide on.

Onscreen, the mouse pointer moves according to the movements of the mouse on your desk or on a *mouse pad*. To move the mouse pointer, simply move the mouse.

There are four basic mouse actions:

- *Click.* To point to an item, and then press and quickly release the left mouse button. You click to select an item, such as an option on a menu. To cancel a selection, click an empty area of the desktop. Unless otherwise specified, you use the left mouse button for all mouse actions.

- *Double-click.* To point to an item, and then press and release the left mouse button twice, as quickly as possible. You double-click to open or close windows and to start applications from icons.

- *Right-click.* To point to an item, and then press and release the right mouse button. This opens a Context menu, which gives you a shortcut to frequently used commands. To cancel a Context menu, click the left mouse button outside the menu.

- *Drag.* To point to an item, then press and hold down the left mouse button as you move the pointer to another location, and then release the mouse button. You drag to resize windows, move icons, and scroll.

If you have problems...

If you double-click but nothing happens, you may not be clicking fast enough. Try again.

Lesson 3: Understanding the Start Menu

Program folder
Represented by an icon of a file folder with an application window in front of it, program folders contain shortcut icons and other program folders.

The Start button on the Taskbar gives you access to your applications, settings, recently opened documents, the Find utility, the Run command, the Help system, and the Shut Down command. Clicking the Start button opens the Start menu. Choosing the Programs option at the top of the Start menu displays the Programs submenu, which lists the *program folders* on your system. Program folders are listed first, followed by shortcuts (see Figure A.2).

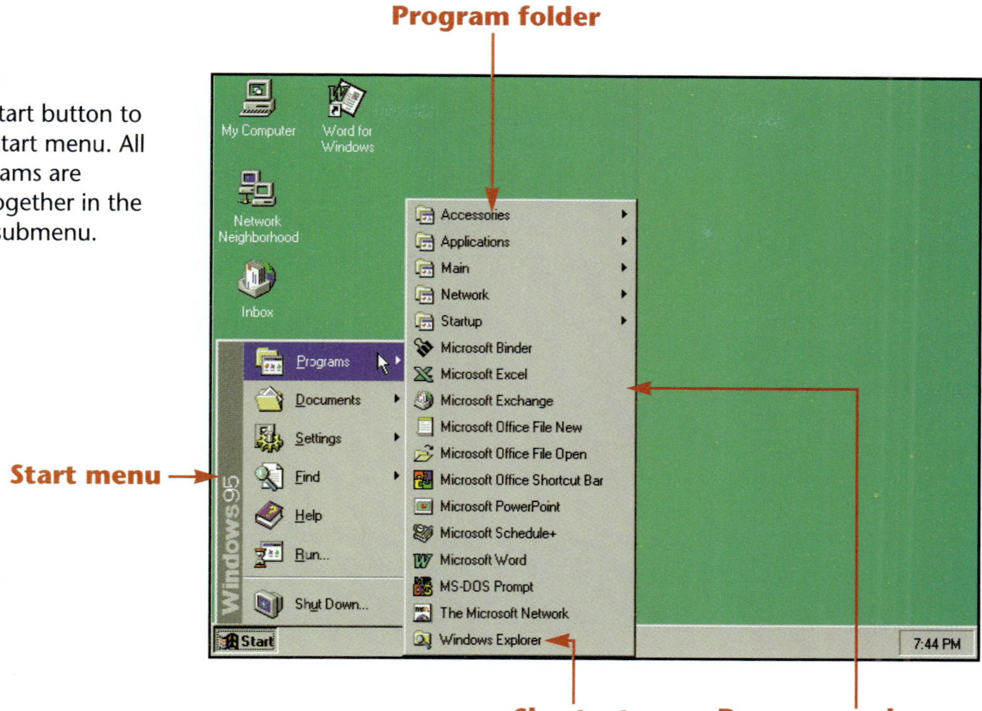

Figure A.2
Click the Start button to open the Start menu. All your programs are grouped together in the Programs submenu.

When the Start menu is open, moving the mouse pointer moves a selection bar through the menu options. When the selection bar highlights a menu command with a right-facing triangle, a submenu opens. Click the shortcut icon to start an application. If a menu command is followed by an ellipsis, clicking that command opens a dialog box.

Lesson 4: Identifying the Elements of a Window

In Windows 95, everything opens in a window. Applications, documents, and dialog boxes all open in windows. For example, double-clicking the My Computer icon opens the My Computer application into a window. Because window elements stay the same for all Windows applications, this section uses the My Computer window for illustration.

Title Bar

Across the top of each window is its title bar. A title bar contains the name of the open window, as well as three buttons to manipulate it. The Minimize button reduces the window to a button on the Taskbar. The Maximize button expands the window to fill the desktop. The Close button closes the window.

Menu Bar

The menu bar gives you access to the application's menus. Menus enable you to select options that perform functions or carry out commands (see Figure A.3). The File menu in My Computer, for example, enables you to open, save, and print files.

Figure A.3
The My Computer window has window elements found in all Windows applications.

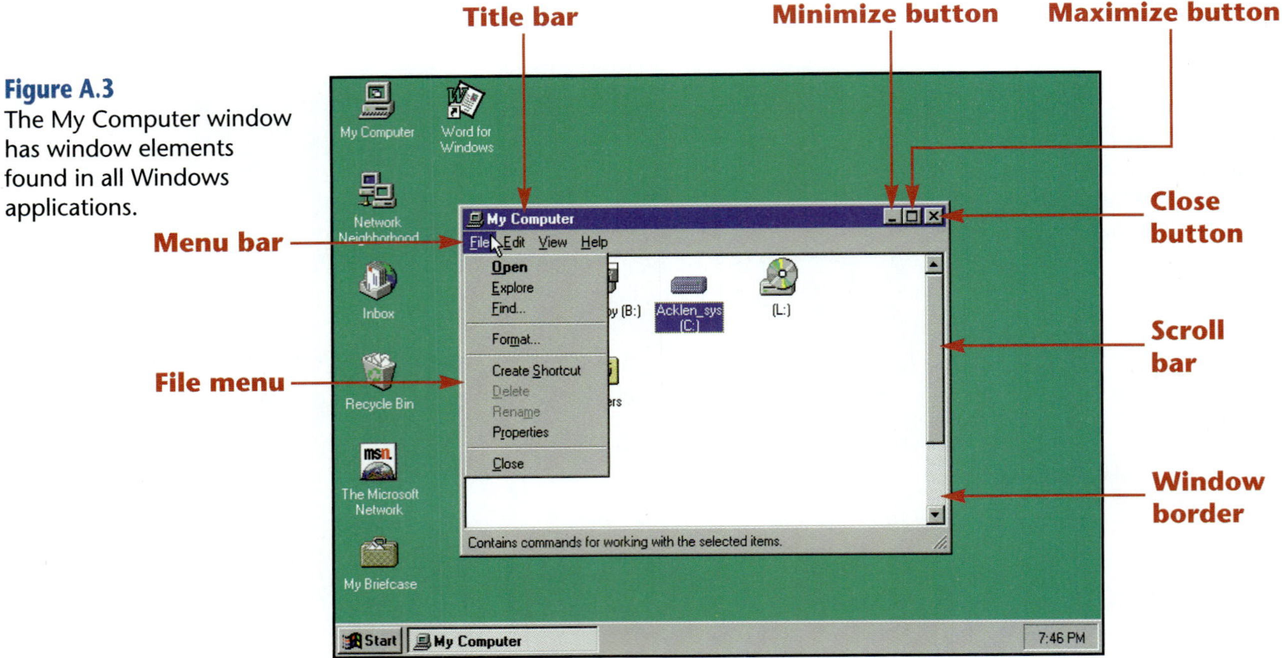

Some menu options require you to enter additional information. When you select one of these options, a dialog box opens (see Figure A.4). You type the additional information, select from a list of options, or select a button. Most dialog boxes have a Cancel button, which closes the dialog box without saving the changes; an OK button, which closes the dialog box and saves the changes; and a Help button, which opens a Help window.

Figure A.4
You can use the options in the Find dialog box to search for a file.

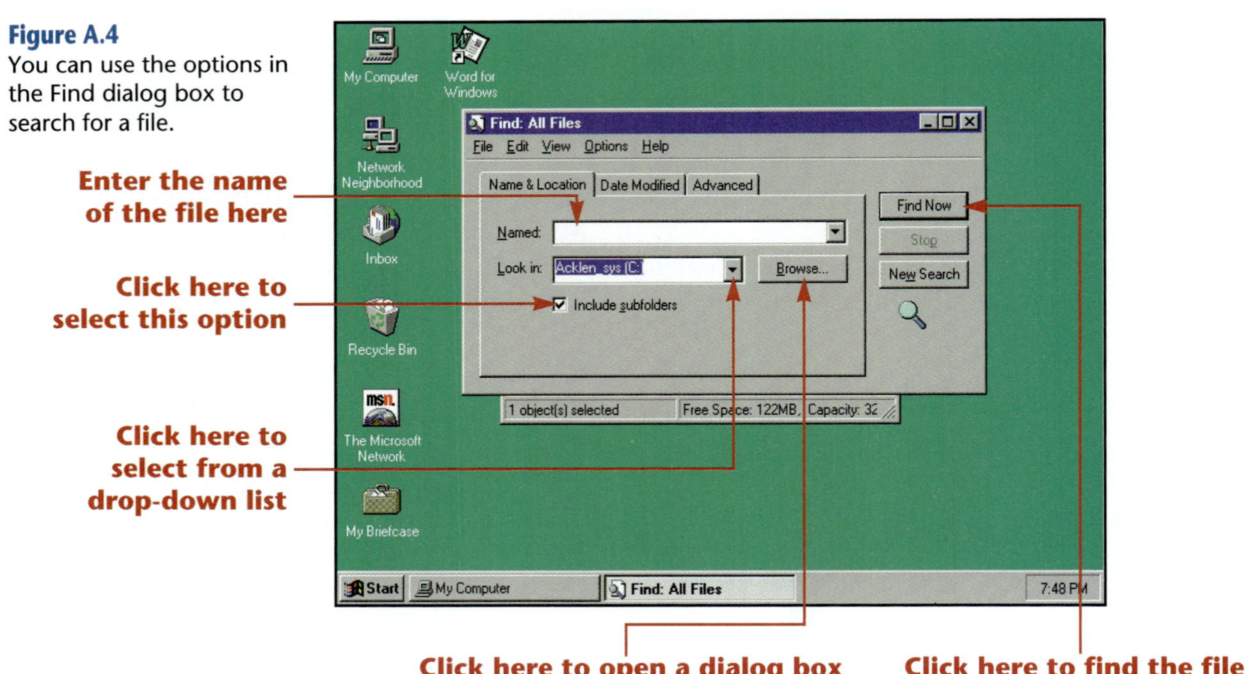

Scroll Bar

Scroll bars appear when you have more information in a window than is currently displayed onscreen. A horizontal scroll bar appears along the bottom of a window, and a vertical scroll bar appears along the right side of a window.

Window Border

The window border identifies the edge of the window. In most windows, it can be used to change the size of a window. The window corner is used to resize a window on two sides at the same time.

Lesson 5: Manipulating Windows

When you work with windows, you need to know how to arrange them. You can shrink the window into an icon or enlarge the window to fill the desktop. You can stack windows together or give them each an equal slice of the desktop.

Maximizing a Window

Maximize

To increase the size of a window so that it fills the entire screen.

You can *maximize* a window so that it fills the desktop. Maximizing a window gives you more space to work in. To maximize a window, click the Maximize button on the title bar.

Minimizing a Window

Minimize

To reduce a window to an icon.

When you *minimize* a window, it shrinks the window to an icon on the Taskbar. Even though you can't see the window anymore, the application stays loaded in the computer's memory. To minimize a window, click the Minimize button on the title bar.

Restoring a Window

When a window is maximized, the Maximize button changes into a Restore button. Clicking the Restore button restores the window back to the original size and position before the window was maximized.

Closing a Window

When you are finished working in a window, you can close the window by clicking the Close button. Closing an application window exits the program, removing it from memory. When you click the Close button, the window (on the desktop) and the window button (on the Taskbar) disappear.

Arranging Windows

Changing the size and position of a window enables you to see more than one application window, which makes copying and pasting data between programs much easier. You can also move a window to any location on the desktop. By moving application windows, you can arrange your work on the Windows desktop just as you arrange papers on your desk.

Use one of the following options to arrange windows:

Tile
To arrange open windows on the desktop so that they do not overlap.

Cascade
To arrange open windows on the desktop so that they overlap, with only the title bar of each window (behind the top window) displayed.

- Right-click the Taskbar and choose Tile <u>H</u>orizontally.

- Right-click the Taskbar and choose Tile <u>V</u>ertically. See Figure A.5 for an example.

- Right-click the Taskbar and choose <u>C</u>ascade. See Figure A.6 for an example.

- Click and drag the window's title bar to move the window around on the desktop.

- Click and drag a window border (or corner) to increase or decrease the size of the window.

Figure A.5
The windows are tiled vertically across the desktop.

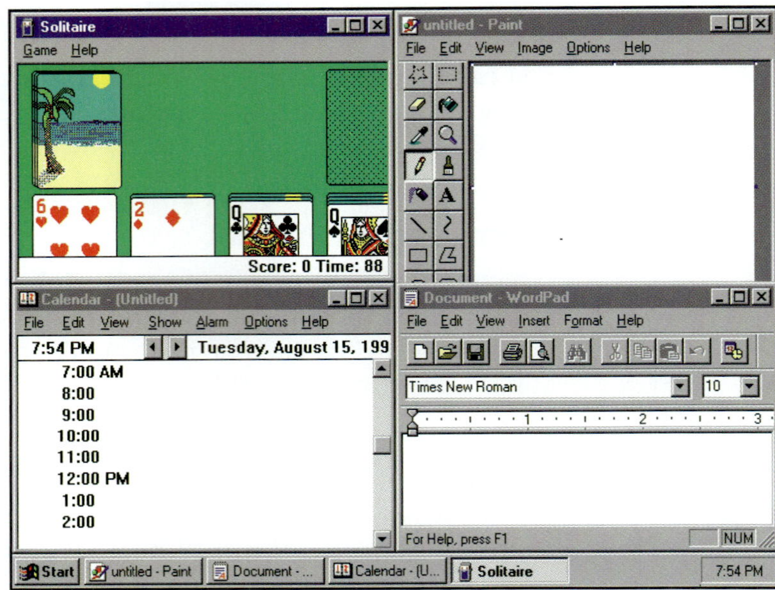

Figure A.6
The windows are cascaded on the desktop.

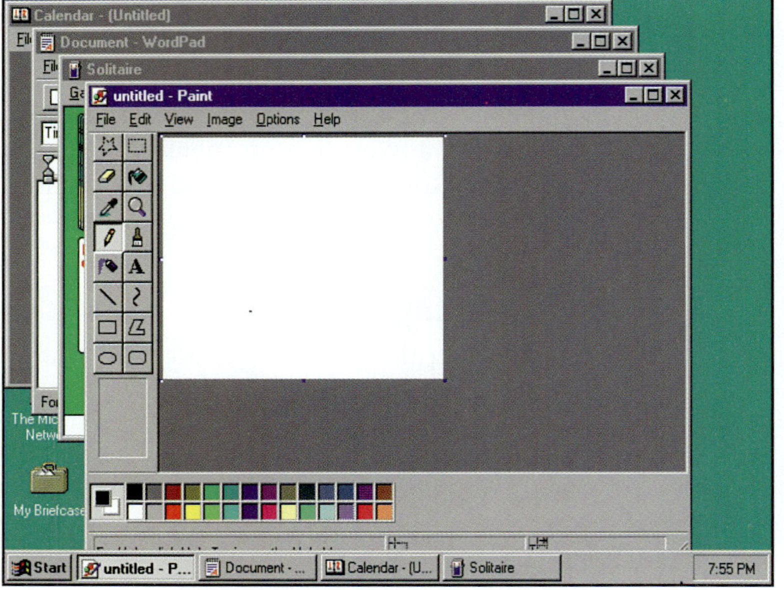

Lesson 6: Exiting the Windows 95 Program

In Windows 95, you use the Shut Down command to exit the Windows 95 program. You should always use this command, which closes all open applications and files, before you turn off the computer. If you haven't saved your work in an application when you choose this command, you'll be prompted to save your changes before Windows shuts down.

To Exit Windows 95

1 **Click the Start button on the Taskbar.**

2 **Choose Shut Down.**

3 **Choose Shut down the computer.**

4 **Choose Yes.**

Windows displays a message asking you to wait while the computer is shutting down. When this process is complete, a message appears telling you that you can safely turn off your computer now.

appendix B

Glossary

Alignment   The arrangement of items on a document, or on the screen in relation to the margins. (See also *Horizontal alignment*, *Indentation*, *Center-aligned*, *Right-aligned,* and *Justified*.)

Antonym   Word with the opposite meaning as the given word.

AutoCorrect   A Word feature that automatically corrects typos—spelling errors and grammar errors—as you type.

AutoFormat   A Word feature that automatically applies styles (such as headings, bullets, and so forth) as you type a document.

AutoRecover   A Word feature that periodically saves a temporary copy of a document while you are working.

AutoShapes   Drawing objects provided by Word and accessed on the Drawing toolbar.

AutoText   A text (name and address) or graphic (logo) entry stored for frequent use. AutoText entries are assigned shortcuts—when you type the shortcut the entire AutoText entry is inserted in your document. In previous versions of Word, AutoText was called "Glossary items."

Boilerplate   This is the text that you want to appear in every document based on the new template.

Bookmark   A location in your document or a selection of text that you name for reference purposes.

Border   The frame of a Microsoft window, table, cell in a table, document, or drawing. Window borders cannot change, but object borders (such as tables, cells and so forth) can have formatting applied that includes colors.

Browser   A program that translates the HTML codes in a Web page to a layout that is viewed by the user.

Callout   A text label identifying an object. Often applied to identify sections of a drawing, picture, or graph.

Caption   A label applied to a table, figure, equation, listing, or graphic to identify it or describe its contents.

Category axis   An axis in a graph. In a graph such as a line, bar, area, or column chart, data is generally plotted in reference to two axes. One contains the values and is called the y-axis or Value axis. The x-axis, or Category axis, shows the different categories into which the data falls, such as months, dates, cities, brand names, and so forth.

Cell   The rectangle created at the intersection of a row and column in a table.

Center-aligned   Paragraph formatting in which all lines of text appear to the left and the right of a center point. The center point is user-defined and may be the center of a document, table, paper, cell, column, and so forth.

Character styles   Attributes assigned to a font. Character styles include such attributes as bold, italic, and underline.

Word

Chart   A graphic representation of data or relationships between data.

Clip Art   Drawings or pictures that you may use in your documents without violating a copyright.

Clipboard   The Clipboard is an area of memory that is accessible to all Windows programs. It is a temporary storage area for items you copy or cut. The contents of the Clipboard remain there and can be pasted again and again. However, each time you copy or cut something, whatever was in the Clipboard disappears. Also, when you exit Windows or shut down your computer, the Clipboard is emptied.

Collapsed   An outline view of text, usually displaying header information. Clicking the headers expands the view and displays additional content.

Column   A layout arrangement that displays information in vertical alignment. Table columns consist of cells; newspaper columns consist of text wrapped within a vertical area defined by margins.

Column break   Word symbol that instructs the program to begin a new column.

Concordance file   A list of words from a document and the context in which they appear in the document, generally used in creating indexes.

Condensed   A font format in which the characters are more narrowly spaced (see also Expanded).

Copy   Duplicate.

Copyright symbol   ©

Cross-reference   Text that refers you to another part of the document or to another document where there is more information on the topic being discussed.

Default   The direction or choice made by a program unless intervention is made by the user. Many program features require values, such as a font size, and defaults are set by the program but can be changed by the user.

Delete   To cut or erase.

Delimited text file   A text file whose contents are set apart by a symbol that separates the values of fields. The symbol used to separate fields is called a delimiter.

Destination file   The receiving file when information is sent to a file from a source file.

Directories   A container (also called folder) that lists filenames and is used to organize files on a computer hard drive. Directories created within directories are called subdirectories. (See also folders).

Document Map   A view in Word that displays an outline view of a document in a separate pane. Documents can be navigated using the Document Map.

Document properties   A listing of an object's characteristics. Document properties include size, author, number of pages, and so forth.

Document summary   Part of document properties that stores information concerning the document contents. Document summary information is indexed and can be searched.

Dot leader   A special tab setting in which the white space that precedes the tab stop is filled with dots. This type of tab setting is frequently used in a table of contents.

Drawing   An object or graphic inserted into a document. Typically used to define user-created objects such as boxes and lines.

Ellipsis   Three dots (…). Commonly found in menus of programs designed to run in Windows and used to indicate that a submenu or dialog box will appear when the user selects the menu choice followed by the ellipsis. Also used in quotations to note that the full text isn't shown.

Em dash   A long dash (—) that is as wide as the uppercase M in the specific font being used. It's often used to express a parenthetical thought.

Embedded object   Data from one document that is placed or *embedded* into another document. After it is embedded, it becomes a part of the other document, but still retains a separate identity for editing.

En dash   A regular dash (–) that is as wide as the uppercase N in the specific font being used. It is often used to separate numbers or dates, to indicate that the numbers or dates are also included (such as "pages 10–25").

Endnotes   Numbered notes appearing at the end of a document that provide information on the source of certain text in a document, or that explain or comment on that text. (See also *footnotes*).

Expanded   A font format in which the characters are more widely spaced (see also *Condensed*). Also, in the Outline view, displaying heading information and the body text accompanying it (see also *Collapsed*).

Export   Save a file in a different file format for use by another application.

Field   A place holder for data.

Field Code   The code that marks where the field information will appear. It's marked by brackets ({}).

Filter Criteria   The information entered in the Field, Comparison, and Compare To boxes is called the *filter criteria* because they filter out any records that don't meet that criteria.

Folder   An organizational unit that specifies a place in your storage memory (hard disk, floppy disk, CD) where a file or group of files is stored.

Footer   Information printed at the bottom of a page. Footer information is determined by the document creator and can contain page numbers, document names, logos, and graphics.

Footnote   Numbered notes appearing at the bottom of a page that provide information on the source of certain text on that page, or that explain or comment on that text (see also *Endnote*).

Footnote separator   A line that separates the body of a document from the footnotes.

Gradient   In the Fill Effects dialog box, gradient is the section in which you can define the background shading of an object in which the background color *gradually* changes from light to dark or from one color to another color.

Graph   A picture of the relationship between two or more variables.

Graphic   A drawing or picture created by a graphics application or scanned and stored in a file.

Gridlines   Optional lines that extend from the tick marks on an axis across the plot area of a chart. Gridlines make it easier to evaluate data values when reading the graph. Also, the non-printing lines used to define cells in a table.

Group objects   Create a single set of objects from two or more individual objects.

Gutter   The area of a page that is lost in the binding of a book.

Hanging indent   Paragraph alignment in which all lines of a paragraph are indented except for the first line.

Hard Page Break   See *Page Break*.

Header   Information printed at the top of a page. Header information is determined by the document creator and can contain page numbers, document names, logos, and graphics.

Heading   A main topic in a document that is followed by body text, for example, outline headings, column headings, headlines, and subheads.

Horizontal alignment   Controls the location of text between the right and left margins of a page.

Hyperlink   A block of text (usually colored and underlined) or a graphic that represents a connection to another place in the document or a separate document. You usually can open the other document or jump to the other place in the currently open document simply by clicking on the text or graphic.

Hypertext Markup Language (HTML)   A collection of instructions or tags that tell a browser program how to display a document—as in when to bold or italicize. HTML tags typically appear embedded within a document, set

Word

apart from the document text by angle brackets. For example, <B> means display the text that follows as boldface; </B> means turn off boldface for the text that follows.

Hyphen   A dash that marks where a word at the end of a line of text has been broken and then continued on the next line. See also *Non-breaking hyphen.*

Import   To insert or copy information from one program into another.

Indentation   The distance between a paragraph's text and the margins for the entire document. For example, if the left margin is set at 1 inch and the paragraph has a 1-inch indentation, the paragraph starts 2 inches from the edge of the paper.

Index   A listing that usually appears at the end of the book. The listing is a set of topics covered in the document along with the pages on which the topics are mentioned. The topics are generally listed in alphabetical order.

Internet   A worldwide conglomeration of computer networks that can talk to each other.

Intranet   A company's computer network working with software that lets it route HTML documents. The documents can be read on the network using a browser.

Justification   Aligning the ends of lines of text so that each end is flush with the left or right margin, or both. See also *Alignment.*

Justified   A paragraph alignment in which the text in the paragraph is even with the right and left margins, except for the last line of the paragraph. The amount of space between words varies to facilitate this balance of text.

Landscape   The orientation in which the text runs parallel to the long edge of the paper.

Leaders   Repeat characters that appear between tab stops (dots, dashes, or underlines).

Left-aligned   Paragraph formatting in which the left ends of lines of text are even distance from the left margins and the right ends are uneven.

Legend   An area on a chart that displays a set of symbols or color boxes that represent each set of series data displayed in the graph. It helps the reader understand what the elements of the chart mean.

Line spacing   The vertical distance between lines of text, usually measured as the number of lines (such as single, one and a half, or double).

Macro   A set of program commands and instructions that are recorded and played back on request. Macros can contain lengthy strings of commands but macros can be played using a single menu command or set of shortcut keystrokes.

Macro recorder   Records the steps involved in a task so they can be played back when you run the macro.

Macro virus   A program that is hidden within a macro. It is designed to destroy files or programs or at least disrupt computer operations. Using a template or document containing such a macro may cause damage to your document files.

Mail merge   An operation that extracts data from a data source and inserts it into fields on a main document to create form letters, envelopes, and labels.

Mail server   In an email system, the server that stores email messages for pickup and sorts incoming messages into the mailboxes for delivery to the correct individuals.

Main Document   The document that contains the information in mail merge that does not change, for example, the return address on an envelope.

Margin(s)   The distances between the text on a document and the edge of the paper.

Master document   A document that acts as a binder for other documents, facilitating the creation of a table of contents, index, headers and footers, and uniform formatting for all documents it binds.

Merged document   The third document that results from a merge of a main document and a data source. (See *Mail merge.*)

Metafile   A file that contains information from which a program can create a desired result. A graphics metafile contains a set of vectors from which a graphics program can draw a picture. In Windows printing, an *enhanced metafile* (EMF) is an intermediate file that the Windows Graphical Device Interface (GDI) creates when you use the Print command in Word. It allows you to more quickly return to working in Word after sending a graphics print job.

Microsoft Graph 97   A Microsoft program used for creating simple charts and graphs.

Mirror margins   In a document that has facing pages, the right margin on the even page is equal to the left margin on the odd page, and the left margin on the even page is equal to the right margin on the odd page.

Multilevel list   An outline.

Newspaper column   A page format in which more than one column appear on a page and text flows down one column, then wraps to the next column and flows down it, and so on, down each column on the page, similar to the way text flows in a newspaper or magazine.

Non-breaking hyphen   A type of hyphen you should use when you want to keep hyphenated words from splitting apart at the end of a line. Word does not insert a line break at a non-breaking hyphen. Use Ctrl+Shift+ Hyphen to insert a non-breaking hyphen.

Non-breaking space   A type of space that you should use when you want to keep two words from splitting apart at the end of a line. Word does not insert a line break at a non-breaking space. Use Ctrl+Shift+Space to insert a non-breaking space.

Normal.dot   The default template that Word bases a document on if you don't tell Word to use a different template. Normal.dot is a *global* template in the sense that its features are always available to all documents, even documents that are primarily based on another template.

Note Reference Mark   A number, character, or combination of characters noting that additional information is contained in a footnote or endnote.

Numeric keypad   A block of keys to the right of the keyboard set up like a calculator used to enter numbers, and has keys for performing mathematical functions.

Object Linking and Embedding (OLE) Allows different applications to share and copy information by either linking two files, or by taking selected data from one file and copying or embedding it in another file. Also known as OLE. Microsoft has released two versions of it; Word 97 supports version 2 of OLE.

Orientation   The direction the lines print on a piece of paper. See also *Portrait* and *Landscape*.

Orphan   When only the first line of a paragraph is at the bottom of one page or column and the rest of the paragraph is continued on the next page or column, that single first line is called an orphan.

Outline view   A view that shows the various levels of a document by using indentations for headings and text.

Page break   A break in the text of a document where a new page is started. *Automatic* or s*oft* page breaks automatically occur when the amount of text reaches a specified maximum. To change the spot where the text breaks, a *hard* page break can be manually inserted.

Paper source   The source where paper is taken from when a document is printed, such as lower tray, upper tray, or manual feed.

Paragraph spacing   The distance between the end of one paragraph and the beginning of another, generally measured in points.

Paragraph style   A predefined set of formats that are stored together under a name. By applying the style to a paragraph, you apply all the formats at once. You apply a style by picking its name from a list of styles.

Password   A word or phrase that must be entered in order to open or edit a protected document. You add a password to give greater security to a document.

Paste   A function that takes data that has been cut or copied from one document and places it into another location.

Pattern   In the Fill Effects dialog box, a panel in which you can choose from a set of background designs for an object.

Plot area   The area in which Microsoft Graph plots your data. This area includes the axes and all markers that represent data points.

Point   A unit of measure used in specifying type size. One inch is equal to 72 points.

Portrait   The orientation in which the text runs parallel to the short edge of the paper.

Print device   A device for making paper copies of documents, or a printer.

Print Preview   A view that shows all the pages of a document in the form in which they will be printed.

Printed form   A form intended to be filled out on paper.

Printer driver   A program that provides the operating system with the language and information necessary to run the printer.

Printer font   A font that resides in a printer but not in the computer. When you use a printer font in your document, Windows must display the document onscreen using some other font because the printer font is not available in the computer for display purposes. Windows would normally substitute a *screen font*.

Properties   The attributes belonging to an item—file, object, picture, text, document, and so forth. See also *document properties*.

Read-only   When a file is read-only, you can open the file and read it but you can't save any changes to the document.

Record   A complete set of data for each field in the data source; in the case of a mailing list it's the mailing information for one person.

Revision mark   An editing mark that shows where changes, such as deletions or substitutions, have been made.

Right-aligned   Paragraph formatting in which the right ends of lines of text are an even distance from the right margins, and the left ends are uneven.

Route documents   A function in email that enables a document to be sent to several people, one after the other, instead of to all of them at once.

Row   Items arranged horizontally in a table or spreadsheet.

Ruler   Bars at the top and side of the document that display measurements, such as inches, and indicate the location of margins, indentation, column width and row height, paper size, and tab settings.

Scalable font   A font that can be changed to allow different character sizes instead of being restricted to a few specific sizes.

Screen font   A font that is used for display on a computer monitor to represent the font as it will be printed.

Search string   A word or phrase that you are trying to find in your document.

Section   Division of a document that allows different formatting to appear in the same document.

Section break   An editing mark used to delineate the end of a section in a document.

Shading   A background color or shade of gray that you can apply to a block of text, a cell, row, or column in a table, or an object (such as a frame or text box) inserted in a document.

Shortcut keystroke   A keystroke or combination of keystrokes that allows a task to be performed more quickly and simply, without using a mouse.

Side-by-side columns   Columns that are parallel to each other on the same page, but whose text flows to the same column on the next page instead of going to the top of the next column on the same page (usually accomplished in Word by using tables).

Sizing handles   Small hollow boxes that appear at the endpoints of lines or arrows, or on the sides and corners of objects. The appearance of these handles means that a line or object is selected. Dragging the handles changes the size of the selected item.

Word

Source document   The document that contains the information that is either linked or embedded into another document.

Source file   The file that contains the information that is either linked or embedded into another file or a document.

Styles   Collections of formatting specifications that have been assigned names and saved. These can then be applied to other paragraphs to give them the same formatting.

Subdocument   A document that is contained within a master document.

Synonyms   Words that have nearly the same meaning as each other.

Table   Organizes information in a row-and-column format.

Table of contents   Lists all the main topics in your document and notes on which page number each topic starts. Listings appear at the beginning of the document and topics are generally listed in page order.

Thesaurus   Provides you with synonyms and antonyms for words in your document.

URL   The Web uses a type of address called a uniform resource locator (URL) to identify specific documents and locations.

Visual Basic Editor   An optionally installed component of Word (or Office) that enables you to do basic programming in Visual Basic, an object-oriented programming language used to create and change programs that use a graphical user interface (GUI). You use the Visual Basic Editor when editing Word macros.

Web   The World Wide Web (or just Web) is a component of the Internet. It's a collection of documents accessible through the Internet.

Web page   One of the documents that make up the World Wide Web.

Widow   When all the lines of the paragraph except the last one are on one page or column, the single line on the next page or column is a widow.

Windows Clipboard   A Windows function that allows data to be cut or copied from one file, stored on the Clipboard, and then transferred to another file.

Wizard   An interactive "mini-program" designed to assist users in a particular feature or function of the software program, such as Word's Letter Wizard.

Word wrap   The automatic break of lines of text by a word processing program to fit text within the boundaries set by the user, such as the margins.

WordArt   A program that creates special effects for text, such as creating shadows, skewing, and stretching.

Workgroup   People who are working together and sharing computer data and resources, often over a company intranet or network.

appendix C

Student Preparation Guide

The purpose of this appendix is to provide you with information you'll need about the certification tests—how to register, what is covered in the tests, how the tests work, and so on.

Studying for the Tests

Although you aren't required to take a training course to pass the Microsoft Office User Specialist exams, you certainly need to be sure you can successfully complete the tasks that are covered by the exams. Although a training class provides guidance, support, and practice, it may not be convenient or necessary for you.

This book provides the tutorial, review questions, and practice to help you complete your exams successfully. It can be used in a classroom situation, or you can work through the projects on your own. You don't have to work through the book from front to back because each project stands on its own. The "Checking Your Skills" and "Applying Your Skills" sections at the end of each project give you a chance to get familiar with the tasks. The Kelly PinPoint CBT trainer located on the accompanying CD has end-of-project computer-based training and evaluation as well as a final practice examination.

Levels of Certification

For the Microsoft Office User Specialist exam for Microsoft Word 97 there are two levels of certification:

- **Microsoft Word Proficient Specialist**   You should be able to handle a wide range of everyday tasks without difficulty.

- **Microsoft Word Expert Specialist**   In addition to the everyday tasks at the Proficient Specialist level, you should be able to handle complex assignments involving advanced formatting and functionality.

Microsoft also has a special Office 97 certification, the Microsoft Office Expert. To attain this level, you must be an Expert User in each of the Microsoft Office applications (Access, Excel, Word, PowerPoint, and FrontPage) and have taken the Office Integration Exam to prove you can integrate these applications.

The specific topics covered at each level are listed in the "Required Tasks" section of this appendix. In this book, these tasks are broken down into projects. At the beginning of each project is a list of which tasks are covered in that project and which subject area they fall under in the tests.

Required Tasks

Each exam involves a list of required tasks that you may be asked to perform. The list of possible tasks is categorized by skill area.

Proficient User

A Proficient User should be able to do the following:

- Basic reports

- Documents for the Internet or intranet

- Envelopes and mailing labels

- Faxes

- Résumés

- Single- and multiple-page letters and memos

- Time sheets

The skill areas covered in the exam and the required tasks for those skill areas are listed in Table C1.

Table C.1 Proficient User Skills	
Skill Set	Required Activity
Process Text	Cut, copy, insert, and move text Add bullets and numbering Use the Undo and Repeat commands Use the Overtype mode
Format characters	Apply font styles (Bold and Italic) Use all underline options Apply character effects (superscript, subscript, strikethrough, small caps, and outline) Select and change fonts and font size (automatically and manually)
Place and align text	Use hyphenation (non-breaking and soft hyphens) Align text (Center, Left, Right and Justified) Set margins Insert page breaks Align text vertically Set line spacing options Insert date and time
Use paragraph formatting and tab setting options	Use TABS command (Center, Decimal, Left and Right) Set tabs with leaders Use indentation options (Left, Right, First Line, and Hanging Indent)
Use page numbers, headers and footers, and sections	Create and modify page numbers Create and modify headers and footers Create sections with formatting that differs from other sections Alternate headers and footers
Use styles and templates	Create and apply styles Edit styles Use templates
Edit text	Find and replace text Find specific text (Go to) Navigate through a document Set AutoCorrect exceptions Create and apply frequently used text
Generate an outline	Create an outline Modify an outline

continues

Table C.1 Proficient User Skills (continued)	
Skill Set	**Required Activity**
Create documents for use on Internet/intranet	Save as HTML Create a hyperlink Browse through files
Use writing tools	Use the Spelling command Use the Grammar command Use the Thesaurus command
Use columns	Key and edit text in columns Revise columns structure
Create tables	Create and format tables Add borders and shading to tables Revise tables Modify table structure (merge cells, change height and width) Rotate text in a table
Manage files	Locate and open an existing document Save a document with the same name Save a document with a different name Create a folder
Use draw	Create and modify lines and objects Create and modify 3D shapes
Print documents and envelopes	Use print preview Print a document Prepare and print envelopes and labels

Expert User

You are not required to pass, or even take, the Proficient User exam before taking the Expert User test. If you feel confident of your skill level, you can take the Expert User exam without taking the Proficient User test and receive the Expert User certification when you pass.

An Expert User should be able to do the following:

- Formal and technical reports

- Forms

- Newsletters, brochures, and manuals

- Personalized form letters, including envelopes and mailing labels

- Proposals and studies

The skill areas covered in the exam and the required tasks for those skill areas are listed in Table C2.

Table C.2 Expert User Skills	
Skill Set	Required Activity
Use advanced formatting	Use text flow options (Widows/Orphans options and keeping lines together) Use non-breaking spaces
Use page numbers, headers and footers	Create watermarks Format first page differently than subsequent pages Use footnotes and endnotes Create footnotes and endnotes Revise footnotes and endnotes
Workgroup editing	Track changes to a document Insert comments Route documents Highlight text in document Create multiple versions of a document Create master documents
Use columns	Balance column length Keep text in columns together
Calculate tabular information	Import worksheets in a table Modify worksheets in a table Perform calculations in a table Create worksheets in a table
Use charts	Create and modify charts Import data into charts
Use forms	Create and modify a form Create catalogs and lists
Apply borders and shading	Create and modify page borders Apply paragraph and section shading
Insert graphics and special characters	Add graphics Delete and position graphics Change page orientation Insert fields Insert special characters
Use macros	Record and run macros Edit macros Copy, rename, and delete macros Use macros to create templates
Generate a mail merge	Merge a document using variable data
Use sort	Sort lists, paragraphs, tables Sort records to be merged
Generate reference documents	Create and modify a table of contents Create and modify an index Create cross-reference Use bookmarks
Manage files	Protect documents Add comments to the file properties

Registering for the Exams

Microsoft Office User Specialist exams are administered by Authorized Testing Centers (ATC). To find out where the nearest ATC center is, call (800) 933-4493. Contact the ATC center to find out what their test policies and schedules are, whether they accept walk-ins or must register the candidates in advance, how the exams are conducted, and what they are charging for the tests. The estimated retail price of each exam is $50.00 in the United States, but that can vary based on the center's sales policies. Payment for the tests must be made in advance. There is no refund for missed exam appointments or failed tests.

Exams are currently available only in English, although Microsoft plans to offer the Office 97 exams in other languages as soon as the courseware in those languages becomes available.

Taking the Tests

Microsoft Office User Specialist exams are not multiple-choice or true-false tests. Instead, they are based on the types of tasks you may encounter in the everyday world. When you take the test you sit at a computer that uses Windows® 95 or Windows NT® Workstation, work with a Microsoft Word 97 document, and use the features of Word to perform the tasks outlined for you.

You can't use notes, manuals, laptops, tape recorders, or other aids during the tests. Word Help is available, but using it may cut down on the time you have available to complete the exam tasks.

Exams are one hour or less (some as short as 30 minutes). Your score is based on the number of tasks you successfully perform in the allotted time. This measures your productivity and efficiency, as well as your skill and knowledge.

Each test has a minimum score. If your score meets or exceeds that minimum, you pass the test. If not, you may take the test as many times as you need to until you pass.

You see your test results as soon as you complete the exam. Successful candidates receive a certificate a week or two after the testing. Test scores are confidential; only you and Microsoft see them.

To keep up to date on the Certified Microsoft Office User exams, check Microsoft's Web sites:

http://www.mous.net
http://www.microsoft.com/office/train_cert/